Crick
Who's Who
2025

Foreword by
RORY BURNS

Editor
BENJ MOOREHEAD

Design
ROB WHITEHOUSE

The
Cricketers'
Who's Who
2025

This edition first published in the UK by Fairfield Books

© Fairfield Books 2025

ISBN:978-1-915237-50-7

Published by Fairfield Books

Editor: *Benj Moorehead;* Research and editorial: *Jo Harman,*
Adam Hopkins, Matt Thacker, Phil Walker, Edwin Burns
Design: *Rob Whitehouse;* Images: *Getty Images;*
Print: *CPI Anthony Rowe*

Acknowledgements
The publishers would like to thank the county clubs and the players for their assistance in helping to put together this book. Additional information has been gathered from espncricinfo.com and cricketarchive.com.

CONTENTS

The
Cricketers'
Who's Who
2025

Openers

FOREWORD

By Rory Burns

I've seen lots of copies of *The Cricketers' Who's Who* over the years. As a kid I used to flick through it, and as an adult I've signed thousands of copies for county fans. No doubt I'll be signing a few more this year, especially as this one has my name on it!

Surrey's third Championship title in a row already seems like a long time ago. Champions three times in three years: it's hard to say which one was sweeter or tougher to win. But what is certain is that, going into the 2025 season, the target is on our backs like never before.

Surrey are in an enviable position, with the resources and squad that we have, and we understand that not everyone wants us to keep winning. Teams are trying to find different ways of combatting our strengths and the focus is on blunting Surrey. Saying that, we've found an efficient way of winning at home, where we know our pitches will suit the seamers. Having spin options in our top order means we can play an extra quick to keep up the intensity when we're in the field.

But you can't just rock up and win the Championship. It's my role as captain, and Gareth Batty's as coach, to drive these players towards more success. Batts has enormous reserves of energy, and when it comes to preparation he'll fill any void that needs filling. I was his vice-captain when he was the skipper before retiring and we dovetail well as two different characters with the same goal.

It's been quite a journey for me. When you are dropped from the Test side it can be tough to come back strong in domestic cricket. It's a child's dream to play for England, so when that's taken away from you there's a tricky mental process to go through. It was very helpful to me that I came back to Surrey as captain, because it meant I wasn't just obsessing over my batting. I had a squad of players to lead and trophies to win.

A lot of our England boys have come through our system and are Surrey through and through. They love playing for the club and that's credit to the team environment we've created.

I've been speaking about some of these things with Johann Myburgh, the coach of the new Surrey women's team who will represent the club for the first time this year. Myburgh wanted to know about club culture and what it means to play for Surrey to help the women transition from being a regional side to making Surrey CCC their home. It will be important to keep that dialogue as an open channel between the men's and women's teams.

If I look at the men's domestic game on a broader level, there is much that is good. The standard in Division One is the strongest I've known. Teams are chasing totals which would have been laughed at when I started out. But, at the risk of sounding like an old man aged 34, I may as well use this space to get a few grumbles off my chest!

Firstly, the growing trend of younger players pursuing the franchise route before honing their skills across the formats. If I could give players coming through one piece of advice it would be that playing four-day cricket will give you the skills to be successful in the white-ball game. I've played with some of the best white-ball players and they tend to have a solid foundation in the longer format to fall back on when power hitting isn't working.

I'm not a fan of the current 50-over competition. With all the top white-ball cricketers playing in The Hundred, there is a noticeable drop in standard. You're certainly not going to pick an England XI from the One-Day Cup.

There is also a question to resolve about the integrity of the County Championship and its fixture list, namely that we currently play some teams once and others twice. In 2023 the title race was between Surrey and Essex, but we only met at Chelmsford. That doesn't seem right.

Lastly, pitches have generally become a bit uniform and lacking in pace. It's good if players are exposed to different conditions according to which part of the country you are in. There aren't enough wickets which wear and tear. We lost our four-day game at Taunton last year, but Somerset prepared a pitch that suited their strengths and it produced a terrific game of cricket.

But no Championship game for Surrey at Taunton this year! That old fixture list…

Rory Burns, Surrey men's captain
March 2025

EDITOR'S NOTES

By Benj Moorehead

Welcome to *The Cricketers' Who's Who*.

Our 46th edition arrives at an intriguing juncture in English cricket. As I write, England Women are subject to the inevitable post-Ashes inquest after the team was liquified in Australia by a scoreline not even Glenn McGrath would have predicted. The men's white-ball sides, previously so dominant but in sharp decline for the last 18 months, also face a reset following Jos Buttler's resignation as captain. Meanwhile, in what promises to be the defining year of the Stokes-McCullum era, the Test team host India this summer followed by the Ashes down under. Bazball is on the line.

There's more. Women's domestic cricket has been revamped, the regional system canned and the teams entrusted to the first-class counties. Surrey's men go for a fourth successive County Championship, something not seen since the 1950s. And if you despaired at the thought of *never* again seeing James Anderson rub a shiny leather ball on his trouser leg at the top of his mark… get yourself to Old Trafford this summer.

And – *and* – we still haven't covered what one reporter described as perhaps the greatest transformation of English cricket in living memory: the sale of The Hundred's eight franchises in February, which is due to recompense the game by close to half a billion pounds. The other implications of the takeovers (four of them by IPL owners) are unclear. How might the schedule change and what will be the impact on the next year's calendar? Will the format switch to Twenty20, as many are suggesting? And if so, what future does the T20 Blast have?

All that to come, but the first 10 weeks of the summer play out to a more familiar rhythm, with eight rounds of the County Championship starting every Friday between April 4 and May 23. With their battery of seamers, Surrey are notoriously strong on fresh, early-season pitches and the challenge for their title rivals – Essex, Somerset and Hampshire – is to be within striking distance come June. Later in the summer, as the pitches dry, their frontline spinners – Simon Harmer, Jack Leach and Liam Dawson – might just give the chasing pack an advantage over the county champions.

Anderson's return is a tasty sub-plot. He has 77 wickets at 13.33 in his last 19 Championship games. Armed with a Dukes ball against Division Two batters… even at 42, it could be some spectacle. At Lancashire he'll line up alongside Rocky Flintoff, son of Andrew – once Anderson's teammate of course – who is breaking records of his own having turned 17 four days into the new season. Jimmy and Rocky, more than 25 years between them, that'll be the snap of the season. Look out, too, for the Denlys at Kent, Joe and Jaydn, uncle and nephew.

James Vince is skipping red-ball cricket this summer for personal reasons, and Alex Hales won't be seen at all, but many will be following the progress of Somerset's Tom Banton, once cast as a white-ball specialist but who last year came of age in the longer format. Interesting to see that Banton's teammate Will Smeed, another self-styled T20 hitter, has announced he too wants to play Championship cricket this season.

Elsewhere, two pugnacious Antipodeans begin their first venture into county cricket as head coaches, with Darren Lehmann and Adam Hollioake taking over at Northants and Kent, two clubs for whom this may be just the shot in the arm that was needed. "Fundamentally a pretty laid-back guy, until I'm not," is how Hollioake described himself pre-season. Essex and Yorkshire have also made coaching changes but have gone the other way, putting faith in iconic figures of their recent history in Chris Silverwood and Anthony McGrath.

Between the opening feast of four-day cricket and September's dash to the finish, the Championship has a mid-summer window of four rounds with the 'no-seam' Kookaburra ball in use. Across these pages we have asked the players what they thought of its use last year. Opinion is split, but there is agreement that nothing is to be gained from using it on the damp, soft early-season pitches, which in 2024 produced such a stack of runs that you'd have fancied Chris Martin to get a few (singer or cricketer). Holding back the Kooka makes sense.

The move from region to county opens another chapter in the women's game. The eight regional sides have transferred across to the eight counties which have been granted Tier One status (see p13), so not all is new, but having the prestige and facilities of a first-class county as a permanent home will be a welcome change to the nomadic life prevalent in the old system. One club, two teams is the new mantra, and a clear responsibility falls on the men to make this transition as smooth as possible. Not everyone likes to share their home.

Until recently this book contained just a score of professional female cricketers but there are now 120. Add in those on rookie deals, plus a scattering of pros among tier two counties, and we're up to 150. They will play more cricket than ever before – over 200 county fixtures spread across the two tiers, 52 of which are T20 double-headers with the men.

Put it all together, and we have not far off 700 games of professional cricket over the next 176 days. So enough number crunching – we had better get started.

Benj Moorehead, editor
March 2025

FIXTURES

CAPTAIN: Ben Stokes (Test), TBC (ODI/T20I)
COACH: Brendon McCullum

ENGLAND MEN'S SUMMER FIXTURES IN 2025

May 22
England vs Zimbabwe
Only Test, Trent Bridge

May 29
England vs West Indies
1st ODI, Edgbaston

June 1
England vs West Indies
2nd ODI, Cardiff

June 3
England vs West Indies
3rd ODI, The Oval

June 6
England vs West Indies
1st T20I, Chester-le-Street

June 8
England vs West Indies
2nd T20I, Bristol

June 10
England vs West Indies
3rd T20I, Southampton

June 20
England vs India
1st Test, Headingley

July 2
England vs India
2nd Test, Edgbaston

July 10
England vs India
3rd Test, Lord's

July 23
England vs India
4th Test, Old Trafford

July 31
England vs India
5th Test, The Oval

September 2
England vs South Africa
1st ODI, Headingley

September 4
England vs South Africa
2nd ODI, Lord's

September 7
England vs South Africa
3rd ODI, Southampton

September 10
England vs South Africa
1st T20I, Cardiff

September 12
England vs South Africa
2nd T20I, Old Trafford

September 14
England vs South Africa
3rd T20I, Trent Bridge

September 17
Ireland vs England
1st ODI, Venue TBC

September 19
Ireland vs England
2nd ODI, Venue TBC

September 21
Ireland vs England
3rd ODI, Venue TBC

The structure of the County Championship remains the same, with a 10-team Division One and an eight-team Division Two. Each county will play 14 four-day games. The bottom two in Division One will be relegated and replaced by the top two in Division Two. T20 Finals Day and the One-Day Cup final take place in September.

Division One: Durham, Essex, Hampshire, Nottinghamshire, Somerset, Surrey, Sussex, Warwickshire, Worcestershire, Yorkshire

Division Two: Derbyshire, Glamorgan, Gloucestershire, Kent, Lancashire, Leicestershire, Middlesex, Northamptonshire

April 4-May 26	First eight rounds of the County Championship
May 29-June 20	First phase of the T20 Blast group stage
June 22-July 2	Rounds 9-10 of the County Championship
July 4-18	Second phase of the T20 Blast group stage
July 22-August 1	Rounds 11-12 of the County Championship
August 5-31	The Hundred (final at Lord's on August 31)
August 5-28	One-Day Cup group stage & quarter-finals
August 31	One-Day Cup semi-finals
September 3-6	T20 Blast quarter-finals
September 8-27	Final three rounds of the County Championship
September 13	T20 Blast Finals Day, Edgbaston
September 20	One-Day Cup final, Trent Bridge

CAPTAIN: Heather Knight
COACH: Jon Lewis

ENGLAND WOMEN'S SUMMER FIXTURES IN 2025

May 21
England vs West Indies
1st T20I, Canterbury

May 23
England vs West Indies
2nd T20I, Hove

May 26
England vs West Indies
3rd T20I, Chelmsford

May 30
England vs West Indies
1st ODI, Derby

June 4
England vs West Indies
2nd ODI, Leicester

June 7
England vs West Indies
3rd ODI, Taunton

June 28
England vs India
1st T20I, Trent Bridge

July 1
England vs India
2nd T20I, Bristol

July 4
England vs India
3rd T20I, The Oval

July 9
England vs India
4th T20I, Old Trafford

July 12
England vs India
5th T20I, Edgbaston

July 16
England vs India
1st ODI, Southampton

July 19
England vs India
2nd ODI, Lord's

July 22
England vs India
3rd ODI, Chester-le-Street

The ECB's overhaul of women's domestic cricket replaces the regional system by allocating a team to each of the 18 first-class counties. These have been divided into two tiers, with the eight fully professional counties in Tier One representing the top division of the women's game. They will compete in League One of the One-Day Cup and the T20 Blast, playing against each other home and away for a total of 14 group games in each competition. The county that finishes first in the T20 Blast group qualifies for the final, with the second- and third-placed teams playing an eliminator on Finals Day to decide the other finalist. The 10 counties in Tier Two will also compete against each other in League Two of the 50-over and T20 competitions.

In addition the T20 County Cup will take place in May and feature 37 teams across the three tiers of the women's domestic structure. The eight Tier One sides will enter in the third round of the competition, which has a knockout format all the way through to Finals Day at Taunton.

League One: Birmingham Bears (Warwickshire), Durham, Essex, Hampshire, Lancashire, Somerset, Surrey, The Blaze (Nottinghamshire)

April 19-May 20	First phase of the One-Day Cup
May 5-26	T20 County Cup (Finals Day at Taunton on May 26)
May 30-July 18	T20 Blast group stage
July 24-30	Two rounds of the One-Day Cup
July 27	T20 Blast Finals Day, The Oval
August 5-31	The Hundred (final at Lord's on August 31)
September 4-13	Final four rounds of the One-Day Cup
September 17	One-Day Cup semi-finals
September 21	One-Day Cup final, Southampton

The ECB's Professional Umpires' Team consists of 42 male and female officials who will share duties for men's and women's domestic cricket in 2025.

Hassan Adnan (Derbyshire, 2003-2007)

Naeem Ashraf (Pakistan, 1995)

Rob Bailey (England, Northamptonshire, Derbyshire, 1982-2001)

Neil Bainton

Paul Baldwin

Grace Bambury

Ian Blackwell (England, Derbyshire, Somerset, Durham, Warwickshire, 1997-2012)

Gabi Brown

Mike Burns (Warwickshire, Somerset, 1991-2005)

Amy Clark

Ben Debenham

Rose Dovey

Michael Gough (Durham, 1998-2003)

Anna Harris

Anthony Harris

Peter Hartley (Warwickshire, Yorkshire, Hampshire, 1982-2000)

Richard Illingworth (England, Worcestershire, Derbyshire, 1982-2001)

Julia Jarvis

Richard Kettleborough (Yorkshire, Middlesex, 1994-1999)

Nigel Llong (Kent, 1989-1999)

Graham Lloyd (England, Lancashire, 1988-2002)

Tom Lungley (Derbyshire, Lancashire, 2000-2010)

Neil Mallender (England, Northamptonshire, Somerset, 1980-1994)

Sophie McLelland

James Middlebrook (Yorkshire, Essex, Northamptonshire, 1998-2015)

David Millns (Nottinghamshire, Leicestershire, 1988-2001)

Jasmine Naeem

Mark Newell (Sussex, Derbyshire, 1996-1999)

Steve O'Shaughnessy (Lancashire, Worcestershire, 1980-1989)

Ben Peverall

Paul Pollard (Nottinghamshire, Worcestershire, 1987-2001)

Neil Pratt

Sue Redfern (England, Derbyshire, Staffordshire, 1995-2008)

Martin Saggers (England, Durham, Kent, Essex, 1996-2009)

Suri Shanmugam

Jack Shantry (Worcestershire, 2009-2017)

James Tredwell (England, Kent, Sussex, 2001-2018)

Russell Warren (Northamptonshire, Nottinghamshire, 1992-2006)

Chris Watts

Alex Wharf (England, Yorkshire, Nottinghamshire, Glamorgan, 1994-2009)

Rob White (Northamptonshire, 2000-2012)

Simon Widdup (Yorkshire, 2000-2001)

Rob Bailey assesses the light
during the Championship
match between Somerset and
Durham at Taunton last year
Photo by Harry Trump

THE PLAYERS

LHB – Left-hand batter
LB – Leg-break bowler
LF – Left-arm fast bowler
LFM – Left-arm fast-medium bowler
LM – Left-arm medium bowler
LMF – Left-arm medium-fast bowler
MCCU – Marylebone Cricket Club University
MVP – Denotes a player's presence in the top 50 places of the 2024 PCA Overall Domestic MVP Rankings (the number next to 'MVP' denotes the player's ranking)
OB – Off-break bowler
R – 1,000 or more first-class runs in an English season (the number next to 'R' denotes how many times the player has achieved this)
RF – Right-arm fast bowler
RFM – Right-arm fast-medium bowler
RHB – Right-hand batter
RM – Right-arm medium bowler
RMF – Right-arm medium-fast bowler
SLA – Slow left-arm orthodox bowler
SLW – Slow left-arm wrist-spin bowler
UCCE – University Centre of Cricketing Excellence
W – 50 or more first-class wickets in an English season (the number next to 'W' denotes how many times the player has achieved this)
WK – Wicketkeeper
* – Not-out innings (e.g. 137*)

THE TEAMS

(s) – A competition has been shared between two or more winners
BWT – Bob Willis Trophy (English domestic first-class competition, 2020-2021)
C&G – Cheltenham & Gloucester Trophy (English domestic 50-over competition, 2001-2006)
CB40 – Clydesdale Bank 40 (English domestic 40-over competition, 2010-2012)
CC1/CC2 – County Championship Division One/Division Two
FP Trophy – Friends Provident Trophy (English domestic 50-over competition, 2007-2009)
Gillette – Gillette Cup (English domestic limited-overs competition, 1963-1980)
NatWest – NatWest Trophy (English domestic limited-overs competition, 1981-2000)
Pro40 – NatWest Pro40 (English domestic 40-over competition, 2005-2009)
REL – A player has been released by the relevant county
RET – A player has retired
ODC – One-Day Cup (English domestic 50-over competition, 2014-2025)
T20 Cup – English domestic T20 competition (2003-2025)
YB40 – Yorkshire Bank 40 (English domestic 40-over competition, 2013)

NOTES: In the men's section, the statistics given for a player's best batting and best bowling performance are for first-class cricket, unless specified. In the women's section, statistics are for List A cricket. A player's T20 stats also include The Hundred. A field within a player's career statistics which is marked with an '-' indicates that a particular statistic is inapplicable – such as a player who has never bowled a ball in first-class cricket – or unavailable. All stats correct as of March 9, 2025.

The
Teams

TEAM PROFILE

FORMED: 1870
HOME GROUND: The County Ground, Derby
ONE-DAY NAME: Derbyshire Falcons
CAPTAIN: Wayne Madsen (CC), Samit Patel (ODC/T20)
2024 RESULTS: CC2: 8/8; ODC: 4/9 Group A; T20: 6/9 North Group
HONOURS: Championship: 1936; Gillette/NatWest/C&G/FP Trophy: 1981; Benson & Hedges Cup: 1993; Sunday League: 1990

THE LOWDOWN

Wayne Madsen danced his way to 1,000 red-ball runs for the seventh time and there was a first home Championship win in nearly five years – but there weren't too many other straws to clutch for Derbyshire, wooden spoonists by some distance in 2024. The batting, bruised by the loss of Shan Masood and Leus du Plooy in successive seasons, had no one who came close to Madsen's consistency. The two Welshmen, David Lloyd and Aneurin Donald, struggled in their first season at Derby, with the former deciding to stand down as red-ball skipper to concentrate on his own form. Madsen will captain the Championship side this summer. Matt Lamb struck a double-ton in May then retired in September due to chronic injury. Australian opener Caleb Jewell has been signed for all formats this summer and will add "real grit" according to Mickey Arthur, Derbyshire's head of cricket. With Kiwi seamer Blair Tickner returning, the club have two overseas committed from April to September. Tickner will be crucial to a seam attack that has lost Sam Conners but boasts an in-form Zak Chappell. Prospects are brightest in white-ball cricket, with batters given a license and 'knuckle' bowler Pat Brown back to his best in the Blast.

IN: Martin Andersson (Mid), Jack Morley (Lan), Caleb Jewell (Aus), Blair Tickner (NZ)
OUT: Sam Conners (Dur)

HEAD OF CRICKET: MICKEY ARTHUR

Arthur took over from David Houghton ahead of the 2022 season and signed a one-year contract extension on the eve of this campaign. The 56-year-old scored over 6,000 first-class runs in South African domestic cricket before moving into coaching, since when he has had spells as head coach with South Africa (2005-10), Australia (2011-13), Pakistan (2016-19) and Sri Lanka (2020-21). Alongside his Derbyshire duties, Arthur has also taken on the role of director of cricket with Northern Superchargers in The Hundred.

Batting

	Mat	Inns	NO	Runs	HS	Ave	100	50	Ct	St
MK Andersson	2	2	0	7	6	3.50	0	0	1	
PR Brown	6	7	6	42	15*	42.00	0	0	2	
HRC Came	8	14	1	336	84	25.84	0	3	2	
ZJ Chappell	12	18	1	345	78	20.29	0	3	0	
S Conners	5	7	2	21	10	4.20	0	0	3	
AK Dal	9	14	1	315	94	24.23	0	2	5	
AHT Donald	13	21	1	502	97	25.10	0	3	14	
DM Dupavillon	6	11	7	67	28	16.75	0	0	0	
BD Guest	13	23	2	638	95	30.38	0	5	26	4
MJ Lamb	4	8	1	345	207	49.28	1	1	0	
DL Lloyd	13	23	0	540	73	23.47	0	4	7	
WL Madsen	13	23	3	1005	138	50.25	3	5	14	
HJ Moore	3	4	1	48	32	16.00	0	0	0	
JP Morley	5	9	0	31	28	3.44	0	0	0	
NJ Potts	1	1	0	10	10	10.00	0	0	0	
LM Reece	13	22	2	588	125	29.40	1	3	7	
AT Thomson	8	13	1	152	46*	12.66	0	0	3	
BM Tickner	5	6	1	70	47	14.00	0	0	0	
MD Wagstaff	3	4	0	48	27	12.00	0	0	0	
RA Whiteley	2	4	0	106	54	26.50	0	2	0	

Bowling

	Balls	Mdns	Runs	Wkts	BB	Ave	5w	10w
MK Andersson	176	4	94	5	3-23	18.80	0	0
PR Brown	528	4	392	5	2-50	78.40	0	0
HRC Came	78	3	32	0				
ZJ Chappell	1567	54	943	31	6-47	30.41	2	0
S Conners	705	15	530	7	2-99	75.71	0	0
AK Dal	1098	21	651	9	2-46	72.33	0	0
DM Dupavillon	815	16	634	15	3-89	42.26	0	0
DL Lloyd	587	10	372	12	3-43	31.00	0	0
WL Madsen	18	1	4	0				
HJ Moore	252	11	143	6	3-55	23.83	0	0
JP Morley	928	19	500	16	3-46	31.25	0	0
NJ Potts	54	1	36	0				
LM Reece	1077	32	660	18	4-74	36.66	0	0
AT Thomson	1612	36	918	24	7-65	38.25	2	1
BM Tickner	824	19	492	8	2-57	61.50	0	0
MD Wagstaff	156	4	78	2	2-24	39.00	0	0
RA Whiteley	36	0	24	1	1-23	24.00	0	0

Catches/Stumpings:
30 Guest (4st), 14 Donald, Madsen, 7 Lloyd, Reece, 5 Dal, 3 Conners, Thomson, 2 Brown, Came, 1 Andersson

Batting

	Mat	Inns	NO	Runs	HS	Ave	100	50	Ct	St
PR Brown	3	2	2	5	5*		250.00	0	0	1
HRC Came	7	7	1	281	113*	46.83	70.25	1	1	3
ZJ Chappell	8	6	2	194	94*	48.50	100.51	0	1	2
S Conners	7	3	1	1	1*	0.50	10.00	0	0	1
AK Dal	4	4	1	168	115	56.00	121.73	1	0	2
AHT Donald	1	1	0	23	23	23.00	100.00	0	0	0
DM Dupavillon	4	3	0	21	16	7.00	67.74	0	0	1
BD Guest	8	8	2	237	85	39.50	80.06	0	1	10
MJ Lamb	6	4	0	28	14	7.00	49.12	0	0	3
DL Lloyd	8	6	0	186	71	31.00	82.66	0	2	4
HJ Moore	7	4	2	83	40	41.50	102.46	0	0	3
MYB Naeem	4	2	0	7	4	3.50	35.00	0	0	2
SR Patel	8	6	1	72	35*	14.40	62.06	0	0	2
LM Reece	8	8	1	274	88	39.14	77.62	0	2	3
MD Wagstaff	3	2	0	2	2	1.00	28.57	0	0	0
RA Whiteley	2	2	0	67	65	33.50	60.90	0	1	1

Bowling

	Balls	Mdns	Runs	Wkts	BB	Ave	5w	10w
PR Brown	138	1	129	6	5-37	21.50	0	1
ZJ Chappell	443	4	364	17	4-39	21.41	1	0
S Conners	294	5	276	4	2-44	69.00	0	0
AK Dal	132	0	110	1	1-49	110.00	0	0
DM Dupavillon	174	0	187	6	3-47	31.16	0	0
DL Lloyd	6	0	11	0			0	0
HJ Moore	354	1	285	10	3-45	28.50	0	0
SR Patel	418	1	339	11	3-30	30.81	0	0
LM Reece	78	1	102	1	1-73	102.00	0	0
MD Wagstaff	102	1	80	2	1-37	40.00	0	0

Catches/Stumpings:
11 Guest (1st), 4 Lloyd, 3 Came, Lamb, Moore, Reece, 2 Chappell, Dal, Naeem, Patel, 1 Brown, Conners, Dupavillon, Whiteley

VITALITY BLAST AVERAGES 2024

Batting

	Mat	Inns	NO	Runs	HS	Ave	100	50	Ct	St
PR Brown	13	2	0	0	0	0.00	0.00	0	0	3
HRC Came	3	3	0	41	26	13.66	107.89	0	0	1
ZJ Chappell	12	8	4	51	18*	12.75	127.50	0	0	1
AK Dal	1	1	0	9	9	9.00	69.23	0	0	0
AHT Donald	10	10	0	315	84	31.50	199.36	0	3	5
DM Dupavillon	7	2	1	5	5*	5.00	71.42	0	0	1
CD Fletcher	5	5	2	88	29	29.33	127.53	0	0	6
BD Guest	12	10	3	188	42	26.85	108.67	0	0	4
DL Lloyd	13	13	1	327	50	27.25	134.56	0	2	2
WL Madsen	12	12	1	336	53	30.54	120.00	0	1	6
Mohammad Aamer	5	2	1	22	13	22.00	122.22	0	0	1
SR Patel	13	13	2	238	67*	21.63	145.12	0	2	4
LM Reece	8	8	0	96	23	12.00	121.51	0	0	6
AT Thomson	8	5	4	73	22*	73.00	123.72	0	0	0
BM Tickner	2	0								2
MD Wagstaff	6	2	2	1	1*		33.33	0	0	4
RA Whiteley	13	11	1	154	46	15.40	141.28	0	0	6

Bowling

	Balls	Mdns	Runs	Wkts	BB	Ave	5w	10w
PR Brown	287	98	400	22	4-23	18.18	1	0
ZJ Chappell	251	76	388	16	3-38	24.25	0	0
DM Dupavillon	131	54	191	9	3-15	21.22	0	0
WL Madsen	24	4	44	0				0
Mohammad Aamer	120	55	145	3	2-23	48.33	0	0
SR Patel	306	96	357	10	2-21	35.70	0	0
LM Reece	42	13	59	1	1-11	59.00	0	0
AT Thomson	168	53	255	4	3-26	63.75	0	0
BM Tickner	48	16	74	0				0
MD Wagstaff	102	22	142	1	1-31	142.00	0	0
RA Whiteley	36	9	47	3	3-23	15.66	0	0

Catches/Stumpings:
6 Fletcher, Guest (2st), Madsen, Reece, Whiteley, 5 Donald, 4 Patel, Wagstaff, 3 Brown, 2 Lloyd, Tickner, 1 Amir, Came, Chappell, Dupavillon

TEAM PROFILE

FORMED: 1882
HOME GROUND: Seat Unique Riverside, Chester-le-Street
CAPTAIN: Alex Lees
2024 RESULTS: CC1: 5/9; ODC: 5/9 Group A; T20: Quarter-finalists
HONOURS: Championship: (3) 2008, 2009, 2013; Gillette/NatWest/C&G/FP Trophy: 2007; Pro40/National League/CB40/YB40/RL50: 2014

THE LOWDOWN

Much hyped after sauntering into the top flight, Durham's momentum was rudely checked hardly had the 2024 season begun. Their opening fixture was abandoned, before Warwickshire racked up 698-3 against them at Edgbaston, with injury forcing Scott Boland to return home 13 overs into a three-month stint. They recovered well, finishing mid-table with four wins and reaching the T20 Blast knockouts. This year they are led across all formats by Alex Lees, who replaces Scott Borthwick as red-ball skipper. Emilio Gay, signed from Northants after scoring 1,000 first-class runs last summer, adds heft to the batting, and experienced allrounder Will Rhodes also joins the fray, while the prolific David Bedingham returns for a sixth summer at Chester-le-Street. With Matthew Potts and Brydon Carse likely to be tied up by England, Ben Raine will need support from new recruit Sam Conners and, in the early season, experienced Aussie seamer Brendan Doggett. Ben McKinney served notice of his burgeoning talent with a maiden first-class ton against Notts, a match in which debutant 6ft 7in seamer Daniel Hogg took 7-66.

IN: Sam Conners (Der), Emilio Gay (Nor), Will Rhodes (War), Brendan Doggett (Aus, CC), Zak Foulkes (NZ, T20)
OUT: Michael Jones (Lan), Jonny Bushnell, Oliver Gibson, Brandon Glover (all REL)

HEAD COACH: RYAN CAMPBELL

A former Australian keeper-batter known for his aggressive style, Campbell made 11 centuries for Western Australia and played two ODIs. The 53-year-old served as Hong Kong's batting coach and played three T20Is for his adopted country. Appointed Netherlands coach in 2017, Campbell suffered a heart attack in April 2022 and spent seven days in an induced coma. The following year he led Durham to the Division Two title in his first season in charge. Scott Borthwick has taken on a player-coach role.

COUNTY CHAMPIONSHIP AVERAGES 2024

Batting

	Mat	Inns	NO	Runs	HS	Ave	100	50	Ct	St
CN Ackermann	11	18	2	743	186	46.43	2	2	12	
DG Bedingham	11	18	1	1331	279	78.29	6	3	3	
SM Boland	1	1	1	0	0*		0	0	0	
SG Borthwick	11	18	0	356	75	19.77	0	2	11	
BA Carse	4	6	2	168	104*	42.00	1	0	1	
G Clark	8	12	1	255	76	23.18	0	2	2	
P Coughlin	4	6	1	57	30	11.40	0	0	2	
BFW de Leede	8	12	1	213	79	19.36	0	1	3	
GS Drissell	1	2	0	41	33	20.50	0	0	2	
EN Gay	2	3	0	100	52	33.33	0	1	0	
DM Hogg	4	5	0	9	6	1.80	0	0	0	
CK Holder	3	3	1	2	2*	1.00	0	0	1	
MA Jones	1	2	0	47	38	23.50	0	0	0	
AZ Lees	13	21	1	924	145	46.20	4	2	9	
BS McKinney	5	7	0	190	121	27.14	1	0	2	
J Minto	2	3	0	40	25	13.33	0	0	2	
CF Parkinson	12	15	3	71	18	5.91	0	0	5	
MJ Potts	8	12	3	333	149*	37.00	1	0	3	
BA Raine	11	14	2	374	93	31.16	0	3	1	
OG Robinson	13	20	2	871	198	48.38	2	5	45	
PM Siddle	4	5	2	45	31*	15.00	0	0	0	
BA Stokes	3	5	0	102	56	20.40	0	1	2	
AJ Turner	2	3	1	138	114*	69.00	1	0	3	
N Wagner	1	0							0	

Bowling

	Balls	Mdns	Runs	Wkts	BB	Ave	5w	10w
CN Ackermann	510	13	268	3	1-12	89.33	0	0
DG Bedingham	6	0	2	0				
SM Boland	78	2	54	0				
SG Borthwick	84	0	55	0				
BA Carse	582	10	424	4	2-100	106.00	0	0
P Coughlin	498	11	311	10	4-45	31.10	0	0
BFW de Leede	837	21	523	11	4-106	47.54	0	0
GS Drissell	162	2	125	2	1-50	62.50	0	0
DM Hogg	453	20	276	12	7-66	23.00	1	0
CK Holder	312	2	192	3	2-56	64.00	0	0
J Minto	166	2	141	2	2-78	70.50	0	0
CF Parkinson	2893	71	1598	30	5-131	53.26	1	0
MJ Potts	1541	45	838	33	9-68	25.39	1	1
BA Raine	1948	74	951	32	5-44	29.71	1	0
OG Robinson	12	0	8	0				
PM Siddle	534	21	233	13	3-27	17.92	0	0
BA Stokes	535	13	339	18	5-98	18.83	1	0
AJ Turner	18	2	6	0				
N Wagner	108	2	68	4	4-68	17.00	0	0

Catches/Stumpings:
45 Robinson, 12 Ackermann, 11 Borthwick, 9 Lees, 5 Parkinson, 3 Bedingham, de Leede, Potts, Turner, 2 Clark, Coughlin, Drissell, McKinney, Minto, Stokes, 1 Carse, Holder, Raine

Batting

	Mat	Inns	NO	Runs	HS	Ave	100	50	Ct	St
CN Ackermann	7	7	0	316	108	45.14	103.60	1	2	4
SG Borthwick	7	6	0	274	104	45.66	83.03	1	0	3
JJ Bushnell	5	4	0	9	4	2.25	56.25	0	0	5
P Coughlin	5	4	1	27	16	9.00	61.36	0	0	2
BFW de Leede	7	7	1	170	72	28.33	100.00	0	1	1
GS Drissell	5	4	0	7	6	1.75	58.33	0	0	1
BD Glover	1	1	1	3	3*		150.00	0	0	0
DM Hogg	2	2	2	3	2*		33.33	0	0	0
MA Jones	7	7	1	102	41*	17.00	75.00	0	0	1
MJ Killeen	2	1	1	20	20*		100.00	0	0	3
AZ Lees	7	7	0	242	111	34.57	84.02	1	1	2
SJC McAlindon	1	0								1
BS McKinney	6	6	0	291	115	48.50	84.34	1	1	2
J Minto	2	1	0	7	7	7.00	50.00	0	0	1
HS Mustard	7	7	1	102	35	17.00	79.68	0	0	11
CF Parkinson	1	1	1	4	4*		400.00	0	0	0
BA Raine	2	1	0	7	7	7.00	53.84	0	0	0
N Wagner	3	3	0	43	33	14.33	97.72	0	0	0

Bowling

	Balls	Mdns	Runs	Wkts	BB	Ave	5w	10w
CN Ackermann	270	0	218	8	3-37	27.25	0	0
SG Borthwick	108	0	111	2	2-42	55.50	0	0
JJ Bushnell	139	0	165	5	2-32	33.00	0	0
P Coughlin	284	0	232	12	3-32	19.33	0	0
BFW de Leede	336	2	276	10	3-33	27.60	0	0
GS Drissell	198	2	147	7	4-38	21.00	1	0
BD Glover	36	0	42	0				
DM Hogg	54	0	32	1	1-13	32.00	0	0
MJ Killeen	64	0	77	1	1-52	77.00	0	0
SJC McAlindon	36	0	45	0				
J Minto	60	0	66	2	2-40	33.00	0	0
CF Parkinson	60	0	42	2	2-42	21.00	0	0
BA Raine	114	1	90	4	4-30	22.50	1	0
N Wagner	150	4	133	4	2-18	33.25	0	0

Catches/Stumpings:
11 Mustard, 5 Bushnell, 4 Ackermann, 3 Borthwick, Killeen, 2 Coughlin, Lees, McKinney, 1 de Leede, Drissell, Jones, McAlindon, Minto

www.durhamcricket.co.uk / tel: 0191 387 1717

VITALITY BLAST AVERAGES 2024

	Mat	Inns	NO	Runs	HS	Ave	100	50	Ct	St
CN Ackermann	9	9	1	219	70	27.37	128.82	0	2	3
DG Bedingham	7	6	0	225	78	37.50	163.04	0	2	0
JJ Bushnell	1	1	0	3	3	3.00	60.00	0	0	0
BA Carse	1	1	0	8	8	8.00	133.33	0	0	1
G Clark	15	15	2	322	87	24.76	121.50	0	2	3
P Coughlin	6	2	0	18	16	9.00	100.00	0	0	4
BFW de Leede	7	6	1	80	28	16.00	126.98	0	0	5
GS Drissell	1	0								1
BJ Dwarshuis	8	5	1	47	24	11.75	120.51	0	0	1
MA Jones	9	9	3	137	39*	22.83	142.70	0	0	2
AZ Lees	15	15	3	301	72*	25.08	115.76	0	2	3
BS McKinney	2	0								1
HS Mustard	2	1	0	9	9	9.00	81.81	0	0	1
CF Parkinson	15	6	5	14	8*	14.00	60.86	0	0	1
MJ Potts	8	4	0	36	15	9.00	97.29	0	0	2
BA Raine	15	10	1	136	33	15.11	136.00	0	0	1
OG Robinson	15	13	3	146	41	14.60	114.96	0	0	9
NA Sowter	15	5	2	11	5*	3.66	78.57	0	0	4
AJ Turner	14	12	3	285	49	31.66	141.08	0	0	10

Batting

	Balls	Mdns	Runs	Wkts	BB	Ave	5w	10w
CN Ackermann	60	24	71	1	1-10	71.00	0	0
JJ Bushnell	6	1	11	0				
BA Carse	24	12	34	2	2-34	17.00	0	0
P Coughlin	96	31	185	5	2-45	37.00	0	0
BFW de Leede	84	37	128	4	2-24	32.00	0	0
GS Drissell	18	3	38	1	1-38	38.00	0	0
BJ Dwarshuis	150	72	183	7	3-35	26.14	0	0
CF Parkinson	293	101	385	18	3-15	21.38	0	0
MJ Potts	150	56	200	6	3-20	33.33	0	0
BA Raine	272	96	354	21	5-21	16.85	0	1
NA Sowter	294	108	318	19	3-23	16.73	0	0
AJ Turner	18	3	31	2	1-13	15.50	0	0

Bowling

Catches/Stumpings:
10 Robinson (1st), Turner, 5 de Leede, 4 Coughlin, Sowter, 3 Ackermann, Clark, Lees, 2 Jones, Potts, 1 Carse, Drissell, Dwarshuis, McKinney, Mustard, Parkinson, Raine

TEAM PROFILE

ESSEX

FORMED: 1876

HOME GROUND: Ambassador Cruise Line Ground, Chelmsford

CAPTAIN: Tom Westley (CC/ODC), Simon Harmer (T20)

2024 RESULTS: CC1: 4/10; ODC: 7/9 Group B; T20: 5/9 South Group

HONOURS: Championship: (8) 1979, 1983, 1984, 1986, 1991, 1992, 2017, 2019; Bob Willis Trophy: 2020; Gillette/NatWest/C&G/FP Trophy: (3) 1985, 1997, 2008; B&H Cup: (2) 1979, 1998; Pro40/National League/CB40/YB40/RL50: (2) 2005, 2006; Sunday League: (3) 1981, 1984, 1985; T20 Cup: 2019

THE LOWDOWN

Strong in every department, Essex are still Surrey's most likely usurpers and the return of Chris Silverwood at the helm could provide the spark needed. It was Silverwood who ushered in a golden spell for the club when he led Essex to the title in 2017, the first of four trophies in as many seasons. The former England seamer has stressed his desire for long-term stability by bringing through the next generation, a reference to the likes of Noah Thain, Charlie Allison, Robin Das, Luc Benkenstein and Jamal Richards, all of whom advanced last year. That Essex have been relatively quiet in the transfer market is no surprise, with Dean Elgar and Jordan Cox stacking up the runs and the pace trio of Porter-Cook-Snater sharing 140 wickets between them in 2024. Michael Pepper earned an England call-up for another outstanding T20 campaign and also chalked up his first two red-ball hundreds last season. Simon Harmer was under par by his own extraordinary standards and will be crucial to Essex's fate in 2025. Indian pacer Shardul Thakur has signed for the club's first seven Championship fixtures.

IN: Shardul Thakur (Ind, CC)
OUT: Ben Allison (Wor), Feroze Khushi (REL), Aaron Beard (RET)

DIRECTOR OF CRICKET: CHRIS SILVERWOOD

The former England seamer returns to the club where he made his name as a coach a decade ago, taking Essex from the depths of Division Two to the Championship title in the space of three seasons before his appointment as England head coach. His successor, Anthony McGrath, now hands back the reins after ending a seven-season spell to take charge at Yorkshire. Silverwood was Sri Lanka's head coach between 2022-24. After three years as CEO, John Stephenson left to take up the same role at Western Australia.

Batting

	Mat	Inns	NO	Runs	HS	Ave	100	50	Ct	St
AP Beard	2	0							2	
LM Benkenstein	2	2	0	8	4	4.00	0	0	2	
E Bosch	2	3	0	17	12	5.66	0	0	2	
NLJ Browne	6	10	0	353	184	35.30	1	1	5	
SJ Cook	11	12	2	178	49	17.80	0	0	5	
JM Cox	11	15	1	918	207	65.57	4	2	5	
MJJ Critchley	14	20	2	662	151*	36.77	2	3	9	
RJ Das	5	6	0	107	46	17.83	0	0	4	
HG Duke	2	3	0	51	25	17.00	0	0	4	
D Elgar	14	21	1	1144	182	57.20	4	5	11	
SR Harmer	14	19	2	275	51	16.17	0	1	25	
FIN Khushi	5	8	0	228	107	28.50	1	1	2	
MS Pepper	10	14	2	523	115	43.58	2	1	32	1
JA Porter	14	15	9	32	7*	5.33	0	0	1	
AM Rossington	2	3	1	71	39*	35.50	0	0	1	
S Snater	14	18	6	407	83*	33.91	0	3	4	
NRM Thain	5	5	0	80	24	16.00	0	0	1	
PI Walter	9	12	0	490	134	40.83	1	4	5	
T Westley	13	20	1	801	135	42.15	2	4	5	

Bowling

	Balls	Mdns	Runs	Wkts	BB	Ave	5w	10w
AP Beard	270	6	140	1	1-68	140.00	0	0
E Bosch	282	6	193	8	3-52	24.12	0	0
SJ Cook	1615	66	744	43	6-14	17.30	2	1
MJJ Critchley	1628	23	1043	34	5-88	30.67	3	0
SR Harmer	2957	103	1492	45	4-16	33.15	0	0
JA Porter	2172	88	1078	56	6-36	19.25	4	0
S Snater	1632	55	907	41	5-13	22.12	1	0
NRM Thain	84	0	104	1	1-27	104.00	0	0
PI Walter	333	7	203	6	2-18	33.83	0	0
T Westley	150	4	51	3	2-25	17.00	0	0

Catches/Stumpings:
33 Pepper (1st), 25 Harmer, 11 Elgar, 9 Critchley, 5 Browne, Cox, Cook, Walter, Westley, 4 Das, Duke, Snater, 2 Beard, Benkenstein, Bosch, Khushi, 1 Porter, Rossington, Thain

ESSEX

Batting

	Mat	Inns	NO	Runs	HS	Ave	100	50	Ct	St
BMJ Allison	7	6	5	140	32*	140.00	104.47	0	0	4
CWJ Allison	3	3	0	134	69	44.66	85.35	0	2	0
AP Beard	5	3	3	51	42*		121.42	0	0	0
LM Benkenstein	8	8	0	287	68	35.87	91.11	0	2	2
NLJ Browne	7	7	2	140	75	28.00	72.91	0	1	2
MJJ Critchley	1	1	0	55	55	55.00	67.90	0	1	2
RJ Das	8	8	1	309	100*	44.14	75.55	1	2	5
SML Fernandes	8	4	1	35	18	11.66	81.39	0	0	13
FIN Khushi	8	7	0	129	31	18.42	75.43	0	0	3
JA Porter	3	1	0	3	3	3.00	33.33	0	0	0
JA Richards	8	6	2	78	27	19.50	83.87	0	0	1
S Snater	6	5	0	39	23	7.80	102.63	0	0	0
NRM Thain	8	8	0	227	83	28.37	79.92	0	2	2
T Westley	8	8	0	289	78	36.12	87.57	0	3	2

Bowling

	Balls	Mdns	Runs	Wkts	BB	Ave	5w	10w
BMJ Allison	393	2	337	7	2-39	48.14	0	0
AP Beard	168	0	210	1	1-48	210.00	0	0
LM Benkenstein	126	0	156	2	1-51	78.00	0	0
MJJ Critchley	60	0	55	3	3-55	18.33	0	0
FIN Khushi	12	0	15	0				
JA Porter	180	1	118	7	4-34	16.85	1	0
JA Richards	403	5	373	15	5-31	24.86	0	1
S Snater	342	5	244	11	3-32	22.18	0	0
NRM Thain	276	1	286	4	1-24	71.50	0	0
T Westley	300	0	275	6	2-38	45.83	0	0

Catches/Stumpings:
13 Fernandes, 5 Das, 4 B Allison, 3 Khushi, 2 Critchley, Benkenstein, Browne, Thain, Westley, 1 Richards

ESSEX

	Mat	Inns	NO	Runs	HS	Ave	100	50	Ct	St	
BMJ Allison	7	3	2	31	17	31.00	114.81	0	0	8	
CWJ Allison	7	5	3	119	69*	59.50	138.37	0	1	6	
AP Beard	8	3	3	16	10*		123.07	0	0	1	
LM Benkenstein	11	6	1	136	54	27.20	158.13	0	1	5	
E Bosch	4	2	2	12	8*		133.33	0	0	1	
SJ Cook	4	0								1	Batting
JM Cox	8	8	2	205	48	34.16	178.26	0	0	2	
MJJ Critchley	13	12	4	122	31*	15.25	111.92	0	0	4	
RJ Das	3	2	0	12	6	6.00	171.42	0	0	1	
D Elgar	13	13	1	331	77	27.58	128.29	0	3	4	
SR Harmer	12	7	2	32	8	6.40	86.48	0	0	5	
MS Pepper	13	13	1	535	120*	44.58	193.84	2	2	3	
AM Rossington	13	13	0	311	78	23.92	149.51	0	1	6	
DR Sams	6	5	1	33	11	8.25	113.79	0	0	2	
S Snater	8	3	2	32	20*	32.00	106.66	0	0	4	
PI Walter	13	12	1	207	53	18.81	141.78	0	1	2	

	Balls	Mdns	Runs	Wkts	BB	Ave	5w	10w	
BMJ Allison	126	39	215	9	3-44	23.88	0	0	
AP Beard	108	44	167	4	2-11	41.75	0	0	
LM Benkenstein	118	31	196	4	2-24	49.00	0	0	Bowling
E Bosch	48	24	79	1	1-25	79.00	0	0	
SJ Cook	96	34	138	2	1-21	69.00	0	0	
MJJ Critchley	234	65	333	14	2-20	23.78	0	0	
SR Harmer	234	67	337	7	3-44	48.14	0	0	
DR Sams	109	45	181	7	3-28	25.85	0	0	
S Snater	108	35	162	8	2-22	20.25	0	0	
PI Walter	246	76	362	17	3-33	21.29	0	0	

Catches/Stumpings:
8 B Allison, Rossington (2st), 6 C Allison, 5 Benkenstein, Harmer, 4 Critchley, Elgar, Snater, 3 Pepper, 2 Cox, Sams, Walter, 1 Beard, Bosch, Cook, Das

TEAM PROFILE

GLAMORGAN

FORMED: 1888
HOME GROUND: Sophia Gardens, Cardiff
CAPTAIN: Sam Northeast (CC), Kiran Carlson (ODC/T20)
2024 RESULTS: CC2: 6/8; ODC: Winners; T20: 6/9 South Group
HONOURS: Championship: (3) 1948, 1969, 1997; Pro40/National League/CB40/YB40/ODC: (4) 2002, 2004, 2021, 2024; Sunday League: 1993

THE LOWDOWN

All had turned out well, a tough year in four-day and T20 cricket rounded off with the 50-over trophy – only for Glamorgan to dismiss head coach Grant Bradburn on grounds of "misconduct" less than a year after appointing him. Thankfully a replacement was on hand, with Richard Dawson taking over the red-ball and T20 sides on an interim basis in between coaching Welsh Fire in The Hundred. Turning Glamorgan into contenders for Championship promotion will be a stern challenge. There were just two wins last year, one of them a contrived result in the last round of games. The bowling still looks light and too reliant on Timm van der Gugten, though there were chinks of light in the form of medium-pacer Andy Gorvin and 21-year-old spinner Ben Kellaway. Asitha Fernando, the spirited Sri Lankan seamer who lit up last summer's Test series, will add some spice up until May. Marnus Labuschagne is gone but another adopted Welshman, Colin Ingram, has signed for two more years on the back of a summer which yielded 1,351 first-class runs at 90.06.

IN: Ned Leonard (Som), Colin Ingram (SA), Asitha Fernando (SL, CC)
OUT: Harry Podmore, Prem Sisodiya (both RET)

HEAD COACH: RICHARD DAWSON

The 44-year-old stepped into the breach at Glamorgan following the club's dismissal of Grant Bradburn last December. Dawson, who has agreed to take on the job until September, will continue his role as assistant coach of Welsh Fire during The Hundred, with a 50-over coach still to be announced. The former England spinner won the One-Day Cup in his first season as Gloucestershire's head coach and had a six-year spell at Bristol before joining the ECB's roster of England pathway coaches.

Batting

	Mat	Inns	NO	Runs	HS	Ave	100	50	Ct	St
TR Bevan	1	2	0	34	22	17.00	0	0	0	
EJ Byrom	6	12	0	325	86	27.08	0	1	3	
KS Carlson	14	25	2	923	148	40.13	1	8	3	
CB Cooke	14	22	3	582	126*	30.63	2	1	36	3
MS Crane	11	18	5	468	61	36.00	0	2	2	
DA Douthwaite	7	10	0	266	50	26.60	0	1	6	
AW Gorvin	7	11	2	90	26	10.00	0	0	3	
JAR Harris	11	14	1	288	61*	22.15	0	1	0	
CA Ingram	11	18	3	1351	257*	90.06	5	6	9	
BI Kellaway	4	6	0	80	36	13.33	0	0	4	
M Labuschagne	4	8	0	468	119	58.50	2	2	5	
EO Leonard	4	5	4	27	15	27.00	0	0	0	
JP McIlroy	5	6	2	14	5	3.50	0	0	1	
Mir Hamza	6	5	3	34	24*	17.00	0	0	1	
BJ Morris	1	2	1	7	7*	7.00	0	0	0	
SA Northeast	14	26	6	1004	335*	50.20	3	2	5	
HW Podmore	1	2	0	2	1	1.00	0	0	1	
WT Root	11	21	1	528	67	26.40	0	2	6	
FW Sheat	2	3	0	62	34	20.66	0	0	0	
WTE Smale	1	1	0	41	41	41.00	0	0	1	
AM Tribe	4	6	0	136	70	22.66	0	2	3	
T van der Gugten	7	10	2	231	46*	28.87	0	0	3	
Zain-ul-Hassan	6	10	1	165	35	18.33	0	0	1	

Bowling

	Balls	Mdns	Runs	Wkts	BB	Ave	5w	10w
TR Bevan	60	0	64	0				
KS Carlson	1104	25	589	10	3-147	58.90	0	0
MS Crane	1826	28	1287	29	5-99	44.37	2	0
DA Douthwaite	756	15	570	15	4-49	38.00	0	0
AW Gorvin	1113	46	575	24	5-40	23.95	1	0
JAR Harris	1859	57	1139	30	5-73	37.96	1	0
CA Ingram	152	0	77	2	2-63	38.50	0	0
BI Kellaway	485	10	270	12	5-142	22.50	1	0
M Labuschagne	168	4	91	1	1-18	91.00	0	0
EO Leonard	548	16	333	5	2-42	66.60	0	0
JP McIlroy	666	18	377	3	2-73	125.66	0	0
CN Miles	156	6	86	2	2-86	43.00	0	0
Mir Hamza	906	35	426	12	4-70	35.50	0	0
BJ Morris	114	0	92	1	1-52	92.00	0	0
HW Podmore	156	3	100	1	1-50	100.00	0	0
FW Sheat	335	8	186	2	2-71	93.00	0	0
AM Tribe	30	1	23	0				
T van der Gugten	1371	50	659	30	5-59	21.96	2	0
BTJ Wheal	142	3	87	1	1-87	87.00	0	0
Zain-ul-Hassan	480	14	236	0				

Catches/Stumpings:
39 Cooke (3st), 9 Ingram, 6 Douthwaite, Root, 5 Labuschagne, Northeast, 4 Kellaway, 3 Byrom, Carlson, Gorvin, Tribe, van der Gugten, 2 Crane, 1 Hamza, McIlroy, Podmore, Smale, Ul-Hassan

GLAMORGAN

Batting

	Mat	Inns	NO	Runs	HS	Ave	100	50	Ct	St
TR Bevan	8	6	0	60	23	10.00	69.76	0	0	5
EJ Byrom	5	5	1	213	123*	53.25	93.42	1	1	0
KS Carlson	10	10	0	139	32	13.90	69.50	0	0	5
DA Douthwaite	10	8	1	176	61	25.14	110.69	0	2	4
AW Gorvin	10	6	2	30	12*	7.50	61.22	0	0	2
HE Hurle	1	0								0
CA Ingram	7	7	2	297	103*	59.40	102.06	1	1	7
BI Kellaway	7	5	1	122	65*	30.50	84.13	0	1	4
JP McIlroy	10	5	5	17	7*		54.83	0	0	2
BJ Morris	1	1	0	0	0	0.00	0.00	0	0	1
SA Northeast	6	6	2	264	89	66.00	106.02	0	3	2
WT Root	10	9	1	296	66	37.00	83.85	0	1	1
WTE Smale	10	10	0	179	42	17.90	76.82	0	0	22
AM Tribe	6	6	1	63	26	12.60	65.62	0	0	3
T van der Gugten	9	6	2	134	34*	33.50	90.54	0	0	2

Bowling

	Balls	Mdns	Runs	Wkts	BB	Ave	5w	10w
TR Bevan	102	0	114	0				
KS Carlson	66	0	45	0				
DA Douthwaite	418	3	391	19	4-25	20.57	2	0
AW Gorvin	410	0	352	19	5-56	18.52	1	1
CA Ingram	24	0	44	0				
BI Kellaway	276	1	256	11	3-33	23.27	0	0
JP McIlroy	416	12	296	14	3-33	21.14	0	0
BJ Morris	60	0	52	3	3-52	17.33	0	0
T van der Gugten	426	16	246	14	5-49	17.57	0	1

Catches/Stumpings:
22 Smale, 7 Ingram, 5 Bevan, Carlson, 4 Douthwaite, Kellaway, 3 Tribe, 2 Gorvin, McIlroy, Northeast, van der Gugten, 1 Morris, Root

www.glamorgancricket.com / tel: 02920 409380

GLAMORGAN

	Mat	Inns	NO	Runs	HS	Ave	100	50	Ct	St
TR Bevan	8	7	0	85	34	12.14	137.09	0	0	3
EJ Byrom	5	5	0	19	10	3.80	67.85	0	0	2
KS Carlson	13	13	0	380	135	29.23	158.33	1	2	6
CB Cooke	13	13	1	204	40*	17.00	146.76	0	0	9
MS Crane	13	6	3	50	19	16.66	116.27	0	0	5
DA Douthwaite	13	12	4	86	21	10.75	94.50	0	0	1
AW Gorvin	8	5	3	33	14*	16.50	122.22	0	0	0
CA Ingram	13	13	0	353	52	27.15	155.50	0	2	1
BI Kellaway	7	7	2	40	11	8.00	102.56	0	0	4
M Labuschagne	13	12	1	228	58	20.72	121.27	0	2	15
JP McIlroy	10	4	3	9	7*	9.00	112.50	0	0	4
SA Northeast	7	7	2	216	67	43.20	130.12	0	2	3
WTE Smale	6	6	0	138	59	23.00	168.29	0	1	4
CB Sole	3	1	1	15	15*		83.33	0	0	0
T van der Gugten	11	9	3	54	17*	9.00	145.94	0	0	0

Batting

	Balls	Mdns	Runs	Wkts	BB	Ave	5w	10w
TR Bevan	12	1	32	1	1-15	32.00	0	0
MS Crane	252	75	358	19	4-25	18.84	1	0
DA Douthwaite	240	85	393	16	4-37	24.56	1	0
AW Gorvin	120	29	165	8	3-26	20.62	0	0
CA Ingram	28	9	35	1	1-10	35.00	0	0
BI Kellaway	42	17	68	1	1-5	68.00	0	0
M Labuschagne	147	53	193	15	5-11	12.86	0	1
JP McIlroy	195	75	313	8	2-35	39.12	0	0
CB Sole	53	18	106	4	2-45	26.50	0	0
T van der Gugten	234	106	334	16	3-20	20.87	0	0

Bowling

Catches/Stumpings:
15 Labuschagne, 12 Cooke (3st), 6 Carlson, 5 Crane, 4 Kellaway, McIlroy, Smale, 3 Bevan, Northeast, 2 Byrom, 1 Douthwaite, Ingram

GLOUCESTERSHIRE

TEAM PROFILE

FORMED: 1871
HOME GROUND: Seat Unique Stadium, Bristol
CAPTAIN: Cameron Bancroft (CC), Jack Taylor (ODC/T20)
2024 RESULTS: CC2: 7/8; ODC: 5/9 Group B; T20: Winners
HONOURS: Gillette/NatWest/C&G/FP Trophy: (5) 1973, 1999, 2000, 2003, 2004; Benson & Hedges Cup: (3) 1977, 1999, 2000; Pro40/National League/CB40/YB40/ODC: (2) 2000, 2015; T20 Cup: 2024

THE LOWDOWN

Some moments transcend the confines of winning or losing, and the sight of James Bracey presenting the T20 trophy to club legend David 'Syd' Lawrence, now stricken with motor neurone disease, resonated deeply with Gloucester supporters and beyond. It was a T20 triumph against the odds, Gloucestershire only sneaking into the knockout stages on net run-rate. For Bracey it capped a sweet summer: 1,000 first-class runs for the first time, as well as that one-handed catch to tie the extraordinary Championship game against Glamorgan at Cheltenham. But the red-ball travails continue, with only Derbyshire above them in Division Two. Graeme van Buuren has handed over to new skipper Cameron Bancroft, who signed a new one-year deal last summer. With Miles Hammond in fine touch and Ben Charlesworth coming of age, the batting looks solid. But the seam attack was fitful last summer, beset by injury and deprived of David Payne (white-ball only). Ajeet Singh Dale and Zaman Akhter show much promise but are raw, so Cameron Green is a valuable addition for the first two months of the season. Zafar Gohar, their frontline spinner, has gone to Middlesex.

IN: Cameron Bancroft (Aus), Cameron Green (Aus, CC)
OUT: Zafar Gohar (Mid)

HEAD COACH: MARK ALLEYNE

The 56-year-old former England allrounder won nine trophies as Gloucestershire captain and returned home to replace Dale Benkenstein ahead of the 2024 season, winning the T20 Blast in his first year back at the club. Alleyne scored well over 20,000 runs and took 810 wickets for Gloucestershire between 1986 and 2005 before a two-year stint as the club's head coach. More recently he had a spell with England's T20 set-up and Welsh Fire in The Hundred, while also taking charge of Glamorgan's white-ball sides in 2023.

Batting

	Mat	Inns	NO	Runs	HS	Ave	100	50	Ct	St
Z Akhter	9	11	2	212	70	23.55	0	1	3	
AG Bailey	2	1	1	0	0*		0	0	0	
CT Bancroft	11	18	1	832	184	48.94	3	2	16	
JR Bracey	13	21	3	1089	207*	60.50	4	3	54	5
BG Charlesworth	11	17	2	723	210	48.20	2	2	7	
LA Charlesworth	1	0							0	
AS Dale	11	12	4	78	32	9.75	0	0	5	
M de Lange	6	5	2	100	46*	33.33	0	0	3	
CDJ Dent	5	7	0	79	61	11.28	0	1	3	
DC Goodman	6	8	1	54	38*	7.71	0	0	3	
MAH Hammond	13	21	0	868	121	41.33	2	4	7	
EWO Middleton	4	6	3	66	24*	22.00	0	0	0	
JP Phillips	2	3	0	85	64	28.33	0	1	0	
OJ Price	13	21	1	616	147	30.80	1	4	7	
TJ Price	6	9	2	172	34*	24.57	0	0	4	
J Shaw	3	3	0	52	44	17.33	0	0	1	
MD Taylor	4	3	0	15	8	5.00	0	0	0	
GL van Buuren	13	20	2	705	187	39.16	2	3	6	
BJ Webster	4	6	2	233	76	58.25	0	2	0	
Zafar Gohar	6	9	1	248	86	31.00	0	3	1	

Bowling

	Balls	Mdns	Runs	Wkts	BB	Ave	5w	10w
Z Akhter	1263	19	862	19	5-89	45.36	1	0
AG Bailey	204	3	181	4	4-30	45.25	0	0
BG Charlesworth	18	1	6	1	1-6	6.00	0	0
LA Charlesworth	108	0	65	0				
AS Dale	1693	40	1073	23	4-70	46.65	0	0
M de Lange	1296	37	808	30	6-49	26.93	2	0
CDJ Dent	6	0	4	0				
DC Goodman	893	26	485	14	3-79	34.64	0	0
MAH Hammond	11	0	10	0				
EWO Middleton	577	17	353	8	3-92	44.12	0	0
OJ Price	1207	22	807	13	2-17	62.07	0	0
TJ Price	572	16	350	9	5-81	38.88	1	0
J Shaw	528	12	354	7	2-56	50.57	0	0
MD Taylor	810	27	448	10	3-62	44.80	0	0
GL van Buuren	425	6	282	6	3-83	47.00	0	0
BJ Webster	685	29	340	16	6-100	21.25	2	0
Zafar Gohar	1037	19	554	19	6-76	29.15	2	0

Catches/Stumpings:
59 Bracey (5st), 16 Bancroft, 7 B Charlesworth, Hammond, O Price, 6 van Buuren, 5 Dale, 4 T Price, 3 Akhter, de Lange, Dent, Goodman, 1 Gohar, Shaw

METRO BANK ONE-DAY CUP AVERAGES 2024

GLOUCESTERSHIRE
COUNTY CRICKET CLUB

Batting

	Mat	Inns	NO	Runs	HS	Ave	100	50	Ct	St
Z Akhter	3	1	0	0	0	0.00	0	0	0	2
CT Bancroft	8	8	1	263	100	37.57	79.69	1	1	7
JR Bracey	8	8	1	179	86	25.57	99.44	0	1	11
C Campher	1	1	0	21	21	21.00	150.00	0	0	0
BG Charlesworth	8	7	1	140	53	23.33	75.67	0	1	3
AS Dale	6	4	2	72	63	36.00	160.00	0	1	2
DC Goodman	7	5	1	18	15	4.50	56.25	0	0	2
MAH Hammond	8	8	0	354	157	44.25	97.52	1	2	4
JP Phillips	1	1	0	10	10	10.00	31.25	0	0	0
OJ Price	7	7	1	222	98	37.00	78.44	0	2	4
J Shaw	5	4	0	6	5	1.50	54.54	0	0	0
TMJ Smith	6	5	2	87	29*	29.00	82.85	0	0	3
JMR Taylor	8	6	1	212	139*	42.40	117.12	1	0	2
MD Taylor	4	3	1	45	19*	22.50	121.62	0	0	0
GL van Buuren	8	6	0	86	23	14.33	82.69	0	0	4

Bowling

	Balls	Mdns	Runs	Wkts	BB	Ave	5w	10w
Z Akhter	132	1	119	5	3-25	23.80	0	0
C Campher	42	0	34	1	1-34	34.00	0	0
BG Charlesworth	12	0	18	0				
AS Dale	312	5	241	13	4-15	18.53	1	0
DC Goodman	354	1	355	12	4-43	29.58	1	0
OJ Price	144	0	138	3	1-27	46.00	0	0
J Shaw	228	2	203	4	2-39	50.75	0	0
TMJ Smith	310	1	246	7	2-30	35.14	0	0
JMR Taylor	35	0	40	1	1-16	40.00	0	0
MD Taylor	215	5	141	8	4-44	17.62	1	0
GL van Buuren	316	1	285	8	3-40	35.62	0	0

Catches/Stumpings:
12 Bracey (1st), 7 Bancroft, 4 Hammond, O Price, van Buuren, 3 B Charlesworth, Smith, 2 Akhter, Dale, Goodman, Taylor

www.gloscricket.co.uk / tel: 0117 910 8000

	Mat	Inns	NO	Runs	HS	Ave	100	50	Ct	St
CT Bancroft	17	17	1	534	87	33.37	127.14	0	2	10
JR Bracey	17	17	2	251	49*	16.73	137.91	0	0	12
BG Charlesworth	17	13	4	221	39	24.55	146.35	0	0	4
AS Dale	4	1	1	0	0*		0.00	0	0	1
M de Lange	10	5	2	22	13*	7.33	115.78	0	0	3
MAH Hammond	17	17	2	487	80	32.46	130.91	0	3	16
DA Payne	17	6	3	35	17*	11.66	145.83	0	0	5
OJ Price	13	11	5	123	43*	20.50	166.21	0	0	8
TJ Price	3	1	0	19	19	19.00	135.71	0	0	1
J Shaw	13	5	2	25	11	8.33	156.25	0	0	2
TMJ Smith	6	1	1	1	1*		100.00	0	0	3
JMR Taylor	17	13	1	333	80*	27.75	157.07	0	3	14
MD Taylor	16	9	2	50	27	7.14	106.38	0	0	6
GL van Buuren	7	6	2	55	22	13.75	98.21	0	0	2
BJ Webster	13	12	1	237	40	21.54	111.79	0	0	6

Batting

	Balls	Mdns	Runs	Wkts	BB	Ave	5w	10w
AS Dale	77	20	143	2	1-25	71.50	0	0
M de Lange	240	67	348	11	2-25	31.63	0	0
DA Payne	401	196	421	33	4-23	12.75	3	0
OJ Price	130	40	200	10	3-32	20.00	0	0
TJ Price	30	13	29	1	1-22	29.00	0	0
J Shaw	271	123	342	19	3-27	18.00	0	0
TMJ Smith	125	30	177	9	3-25	19.66	0	0
MD Taylor	362	144	417	29	4-22	14.37	1	0
GL van Buuren	78	21	109	3	1-29	36.33	0	0
BJ Webster	264	85	340	6	1-13	56.66	0	0

Bowling

Catches/Stumpings:
16 Hammond, 14 J Taylor, 13 Bracey (1st), 10 Bancroft, 8 O Price, 6 M Taylor, Webster, 5 Payne, 4 B Charlesworth, 3 de Lange, Smith, 2 Shaw, van Buuren, 1 Dale, T Price

TEAM PROFILE

Hampshire
Cricket

FORMED: 1863
HOME GROUND: Utilita Bowl, Southampton
CAPTAIN: Ben Brown (CC), Nick Gubbins (ODC), James Vince (T20)
2024 RESULTS: CC1: 2/10; ODC: Quarter-finalists; T20: 7/9 South Group
HONOURS: Championship: (2) 1961, 1973; Gillette/NatWest/C&G/FP Trophy: (3) 1991, 2005, 2009; Benson & Hedges Cup: (2) 1988, 1992; Pro40/National League/CB40/YB40/ODC (2): 2012, 2018; Sunday League: (3) 1975, 1978, 1986; T20 Cup: (3) 2010, 2012, 2022

THE LOWDOWN

Kyle Abbott has signed a new one-year deal to take him into his ninth season on the south coast, and perhaps one last tilt at that elusive four-day trophy, but Mohammad Abbas has moved to Notts and James Vince has hung up his whites after signing a T20-only contract with the club. As the club's leading run-scorer in the previous four Championship campaigns – he has 12,408 first-class runs in all – Vince is virtually irreplaceable. But Hampshire's batting was strong throughout last summer, Liam Dawson reprising his scintillating form of 2023 and Tom Prest, seen as Vince's heir, scoring three hundreds in his best red-ball summer to date. Opener Ali Orr has fully recovered from a broken arm and is likely to contest an opener's slot with Mark Stoneman, brought in on a one-year deal. Jack Edwards, a genuine allrounder who captains New South Wales, is due to be available until May. The experienced Ben Brown leads the side in the Championship, where Hampshire have finished in the top three every year since the Covid pandemic. Expectations will be high in the Blast, especially now skipper Vince is focused solely on that format.

IN: Sonny Baker (Som), Mark Stoneman (Mid), Kyle Abbott (SA), Jack Edwards (Aus, CC), Lhuandre Pretorius (SA, T20)

FIRST-TEAM MANAGER: ADRIAN BIRRELL

The vastly experienced Birrell took over from Craig White in December 2018 and immediately guided Hampshire to the 50-over final before landing the club's first silverware in a decade by winning the T20 Blast in 2022. A former Eastern Province allrounder, Birrell made his name as coach of the Ireland team which enjoyed a famous victory over Pakistan in the 2007 World Cup. In 2010 he was put in charge of England U19 before beginning a four-year stint as South Africa's assistant coach.

COUNTY CHAMPIONSHIP AVERAGES 2024

	Mat	Inns	NO	Runs	HS	Ave	100	50	Ct	St
KJ Abbott	13	15	1	129	26	9.21	0	0	5	
TE Albert	8	12	0	388	124	32.33	2	1	10	
KHD Barker	4	3	0	157	74	52.33	0	1	1	
BC Brown	13	18	2	657	165*	41.06	2	2	35	1
LA Dawson	13	20	4	956	120	59.75	3	5	8	
JK Fuller	13	19	6	383	77*	29.46	0	1	3	
NRT Gubbins	12	18	2	895	201*	55.93	3	3	2	
IG Holland	2	2	0	20	14	10.00	0	0	2	
FS Middleton	13	21	1	604	116	30.20	2	3	9	
Mohammad Abbas	11	11	9	26	13*	13.00	0	0	1	
MG Neser	1	1	0	3	3	3.00	0	0	0	
FS Organ	7	10	2	151	32	18.87	0	0	1	
AGH Orr	5	9	0	196	126	21.77	1	0	1	
TJ Prest	10	13	1	582	156	48.50	3	1	10	
JA Turner	2	2	1	0	0*	0.00	0	0	0	
JM Vince	13	22	2	986	211	49.30	2	5	20	
BTJ Wheal	3	4	1	82	61	27.33	0	1	1	

Batting

	Balls	Mdns	Runs	Wkts	BB	Ave	5w	10w
KJ Abbott	2294	85	1120	55	5-25	20.36	5	0
KHD Barker	814	29	390	16	6-74	24.37	1	0
LA Dawson	3057	90	1358	54	5-47	25.14	5	1
JK Fuller	1423	28	858	12	3-55	71.50	0	0
NRT Gubbins	108	1	96	0				
IG Holland	216	1	144	3	2-66	48.00	0	0
Mohammad Abbas	2113	102	873	36	4-27	24.25	0	0
MG Neser	93	4	55	2	2-39	27.50	0	0
FS Organ	1054	32	504	16	5-104	31.50	1	0
TJ Prest	72	1	41	1	1-7	41.00	0	0
JA Turner	240	6	173	4	3-58	43.25	0	0
JM Vince	6	0	4	0				
BTJ Wheal	384	11	208	6	2-37	34.66	0	0

Bowling

Catches/Stumpings:
36 Brown (1st), 20 Vince, 10 Albert, Prest, 9 Middleton, 8 Dawson, 5 Abbott, 3 Fuller, 2 Gubbins, Holland, 1 Abbas, Barker, Organ, Orr, Wheal

Hampshire Cricket

Batting

	Mat	Inns	NO	Runs	HS	Ave	100	50	Ct	St
KJ Abbott	8	7	4	121	37	40.33	106.14	0	0	1
TE Albert	9	9	2	273	96*	39.00	88.63	0	2	7
BC Brown	9	9	1	286	139*	35.75	85.88	1	0	14
LA Dawson	2	2	0	98	50	49.00	94.23	0	1	0
JR Eckland	4	4	0	50	21	12.50	54.34	0	0	3
NRT Gubbins	9	9	0	285	136	31.66	75.79	1	1	4
EV Jack	5	4	0	46	18	11.50	66.66	0	0	2
DC Kelly	8	7	0	174	45	24.85	81.69	0	0	3
FS Middleton	9	9	0	168	50	18.66	73.36	0	1	4
Mohammad Abbas	4	1	1	0	0*		0.00	0	0	1
FS Organ	9	9	2	219	74*	31.28	88.30	0	2	2
TJ Prest	9	9	0	125	40	13.88	65.78	0	0	3
JA Turner	2	0								0
JJ Weatherley	3	3	0	104	93	34.66	72.72	0	1	1
BTJ Wheal	9	6	4	25	13	12.50	52.08	0	0	2

Bowling

	Balls	Mdns	Runs	Wkts	BB	Ave	5w	10w
KJ Abbott	415	13	299	12	4-48	24.91	1	0
LA Dawson	120	0	109	2	2-51	54.50	0	0
NRT Gubbins	84	1	87	2	1-15	43.50	0	0
EV Jack	263	2	219	10	4-29	21.90	1	0
DC Kelly	252	0	203	10	5-19	20.30	0	1
Mohammad Abbas	156	1	99	3	2-38	33.00	0	0
FS Organ	383	4	305	6	2-31	50.83	0	0
TJ Prest	156	0	119	6	3-41	19.83	0	0
JA Turner	113	1	68	8	4-24	8.50	2	0
BTJ Wheal	423	3	353	13	3-14	27.15	0	0

Catches/Stumpings:
14 Brown, 7 Albert, 4 Gubbins, Middleton, 3 Eckland, Kelly, Prest, 2 Jack, Organ, Wheal, 1 Abbas, Abbott, Weatherley

	Mat	Inns	NO	Runs	HS	Ave	100	50	Ct	St
TE Albert	12	10	2	226	66	28.25	134.52	0	1	2
LA Dawson	11	7	2	84	30	16.80	175.00	0	0	6
JK Fuller	11	9	2	168	39*	24.00	166.33	0	0	6
NRT Gubbins	3	3	0	15	14	5.00	93.75	0	0	0
BAC Howell	12	11	3	169	62*	21.12	160.95	0	1	6
EV Jack	3	1	0	14	14	14.00	107.69	0	0	0
BR McDermott	12	11	0	237	64	21.54	124.73	0	1	10
FS Middleton	2	2	0	34	18	17.00	121.42	0	0	0
MG Neser	7	4	2	39	19	19.50	144.44	0	0	3
FS Organ	1	0								1
AGH Orr	1	1	0	9	9	9.00	90.00	0	0	0
TJ Prest	5	5	0	111	51	22.20	160.86	0	1	3
JA Turner	10	4	4	6	3*		66.66	0	0	2
JM Vince	12	11	0	283	53	25.72	128.63	0	1	12
JJ Weatherley	12	11	2	324	68*	36.00	127.05	0	1	3
BTJ Wheal	7	2	0	4	3	2.00	50.00	0	0	1
CP Wood	11	5	2	41	21	13.66	132.25	0	0	2

Batting

	Balls	Mdns	Runs	Wkts	BB	Ave	5w	10w
LA Dawson	234	66	312	8	2-28	39.00	0	0
JK Fuller	180	60	285	10	2-11	28.50	0	0
BAC Howell	180	45	232	6	2-27	38.66	0	0
EV Jack	60	18	97	2	1-32	48.50	0	0
MG Neser	143	50	211	11	3-32	19.18	0	0
JA Turner	206	80	334	15	4-23	22.26	1	0
BTJ Wheal	144	49	244	9	4-35	27.11	1	0
CP Wood	224	82	290	12	2-13	24.16	0	0

Bowling

Catches/Stumpings:
12 Vince, 11 McDermott (1st), 6 Dawson, Fuller, Howell, 3 Neser, Prest, Weatherley, 2 Albert, Turner, Wood, 1 Organ, Wheal

TEAM PROFILE

FORMED: 1870
HOME GROUND: The Spitfire Ground, St Lawrence, Canterbury
ONE-DAY NAME: Kent Spitfires
CAPTAIN: Daniel Bell-Drummond (CC), Jack Leaning (ODC), Sam Billings (T20)
2024 RESULTS: CC1: 10/10; ODC: 7/9 Group A; T20: 9/9 South Group
HONOURS: Championship: (7) 1906, 1909, 1910, 1913, 1970, 1977(s), 1978; Gillette/NatWest/C&G/FP Trophy: (2) 1967, 1974; Pro40/National League/CB40/ODC: (2) 2001, 2022; Benson & Hedges Cup: (3) 1973, 1976, 1978; Sunday League: (4) 1972, 1973, 1976, 1995; T20 Cup: (2) 2007, 2021

THE LOWDOWN

Matt Walker's resignation as coach came as no surprise after a crushing season in which Kent lost eight Championship games and 15 of 22 in white-ball cricket. After a narrow escape in 2023, relegation was emphatic last summer: bottom of Division One by some 56 points. In Adam Hollioake, Kent have found an energetic coach who will bring much-needed freshness and passion. An inability to take 20 wickets was the chronic problem last year, due to a mix of form, fitness and an unsettled bowling attack: 14 bowlers sent down 40 or more overs in the Championship. Matt Parkinson bowled more than anyone else (2,481 balls in all), taking 36 wickets with his leg-spin but paying 47.5 runs for each of them, though finishing as Kent's leading wicket-taker in each format wasn't a bad return in his first full season at Canterbury. Overseas contributions were bitty, with Aussie quick Wes Agar going home halfway through a four-month deal. Agar returns for an April-July stint this summer. The batting lacked consistency and nobody topped the 853 run-tally of skipper Daniel Bell-Drummond.

IN: Chris Benjamin (War), Wes Agar (Aus, CC/T20), Tom Rogers (Aus, T20)
OUT: Arafat Bhuiyan, Hamidullah Qadri (both REL)

HEAD COACH: ADAM HOLLIOAKE

This is Hollioake's first high-profile coaching role. The former England allrounder captained the Surrey side which won seven trophies either side of the turn of the century and led the national team to a famous ODI trophy at Sharjah. Hollioake fled cricket after retirement, briefly resurfacing as a cage fighter before returning as head coach of Boost Defenders in Afghanistan. He has served as batting coach for Pakistan and England Lions, and was on the backroom staff at Surrey last summer.

COUNTY CHAMPIONSHIP AVERAGES 2024

	Mat	Inns	NO	Runs	HS	Ave	100	50	Ct	St
WA Agar	5	6	0	35	13	5.83	0	0	0	
Arafat Bhuiyan	2	4	3	23	22*	23.00	0	0	1	
DJ Bell-Drummond	13	26	2	853	135	35.54	2	5	6	
BG Compton	13	26	0	833	165	32.03	1	5	3	
Z Crawley	5	10	0	322	238	32.20	1	0	6	
JK Denly	2	3	1	53	41*	26.50	0	0	2	
JL Denly	10	19	1	620	110	34.44	1	4	5	
JDM Evison	13	23	3	753	85	37.65	0	6	4	
HZ Finch	14	26	2	656	85	27.33	0	4	24	5
GA Garrett	9	16	9	120	48	17.14	0	0	2	
NN Gilchrist	8	11	3	106	41	13.25	0	0	1	
A Jordan	2	4	1	82	32	27.33	0	0	1	
FIN Khushi	1	2	0	57	53	28.50	0	1	1	
JA Leaning	11	20	1	728	179*	38.31	3	1	13	
TS Muyeye	9	17	0	572	211	33.64	1	3	7	
ARJ Ogborne	2	4	1	27	12	9.00	0	0	2	
MK O'Riordan	4	7	0	86	30	12.28	0	0	4	
MW Parkinson	13	21	1	241	48	12.05	0	0	3	
J Singh	4	7	3	43	18	10.75	0	0	2	
G Stewart	7	12	1	241	45	21.90	0	0	1	
CH Stobo	4	8	0	159	64	19.87	0	1	2	
B Swanepoel	3	5	0	112	54	22.40	0	1	1	

Batting

	Balls	Mdns	Runs	Wkts	BB	Ave	5w	10w
WA Agar	648	13	411	12	4-35	34.25	0	0
Arafat Bhuiyan	276	10	190	2	2-114	95.00	0	0
JK Denly	72	0	63	1	1-52	63.00	0	0
JL Denly	174	2	156	0				
JDM Evison	1223	24	721	19	4-83	37.94	0	0
GA Garrett	1102	26	732	21	3-75	34.85	0	0
NN Gilchrist	1087	25	811	19	6-24	42.68	1	0
A Jordan	314	10	237	8	5-97	29.62	1	0
JA Leaning	504	5	361	3	1-21	120.33	0	0
ARJ Ogborne	254	3	222	4	2-87	55.50	0	0
MK O'Riordan	382	7	290	3	1-36	96.66	0	0
MW Parkinson	2481	25	1708	36	6-109	47.44	2	0
J Singh	336	1	295	1	1-61	295.00	0	0
G Stewart	1046	27	638	7	3-78	91.14	0	0
CH Stobo	585	19	338	6	2-73	56.33	0	0
B Swanepoel	462	10	267	5	2-61	53.40	0	0

Bowling

Catches/Stumpings:
29 Finch (5st), 13 Leaning, 7 Muyeye, 6 Crawley, Bell-Drummond, 5 JL Denly, 4 Evison, O'Riordan, 3 Compton, Parkinson, 2 JK Denly, Garrett, Ogbourne, Singh, Stobo, 1 Bhuiyan, Gilchrist, Jordan, Khushi, Swanepoel

METRO BANK ONE-DAY CUP AVERAGES 2024

Batting

	Mat	Inns	NO	Runs	HS	Ave	100	50	Ct	St
JK Denly	8	8	0	154	32	19.25	62.85	0	0	2
JDM Evison	8	8	0	176	55	22.00	71.25	0	1	5
HZ Finch	8	8	1	260	104	37.14	74.49	1	1	8
GA Garrett	4	3	2	13	6*	13.00	43.33	0	0	0
NN Gilchrist	7	6	2	26	10	6.50	52.00	0	0	2
Hamidullah Qadri	3	3	0	70	43	23.33	98.59	0	0	0
JA Leaning	8	8	1	262	81*	37.42	69.12	0	2	3
MK O'Riordan	6	6	0	83	58	13.83	91.20	0	1	3
MW Parkinson	8	7	4	65	19	21.66	45.13	0	0	0
E Singh	5	5	0	54	16	10.80	43.20	0	0	0
J Singh	1	0								1
G Stewart	8	7	0	200	78	28.57	112.35	0	2	4
CH Stobo	7	7	1	153	72	25.50	84.06	0	1	5
B Swanepoel	7	7	0	70	30	10.00	86.41	0	0	4

Bowling

	Balls	Mdns	Runs	Wkts	BB	Ave	5w	10w
JK Denly	54	0	52	4	3-15	13.00	0	0
JDM Evison	48	0	47	0				
GA Garrett	120	2	106	2	2-47	53.00	0	0
NN Gilchrist	210	1	194	4	2-44	48.50	0	0
Hamidullah Qadri	48	0	57	0				
JA Leaning	102	1	90	0				
MK O'Riordan	43	0	36	3	3-36	12.00	0	0
MW Parkinson	358	1	320	12	4-30	26.66	1	0
J Singh	42	0	52	0				
G Stewart	308	1	269	11	3-73	24.45	0	0
CH Stobo	332	5	255	8	2-21	31.87	0	0
B Swanepoel	288	4	201	10	3-26	20.10	0	0

Catches/Stumpings:
9 Finch (1st), 5 Evison, Stobo, 4 Stewart, Swanepoel, 3 Leaning, O'Riordan, 2 JK Denly, Gilchrist, 1 Singh

www.kentcricket.co.uk / tel: 01227 456 886

Batting

	Mat	Inns	NO	Runs	HS	Ave	100	50	Ct	St
XC Bartlett	8	6	5	31	12*	31.00	88.57	0	0	5
DJ Bell-Drummond	14	14	0	373	76	26.64	134.65	0	3	5
SW Billings	14	14	1	411	106	31.61	157.47	1	1	6
Z Crawley	8	8	0	82	26	10.25	124.24	0	0	10
JL Denly	6	6	1	162	56	32.40	140.86	0	1	1
JDM Evison	14	13	6	173	34*	24.71	120.97	0	0	1
HZ Finch	5	3	2	46	24*	46.00	106.97	0	0	4
NN Gilchrist	9	3	0	3	2	1.00	25.00	0	0	2
FIN Khushi	3	3	0	57	35	19.00	123.91	0	0	0
JA Leaning	6	5	1	67	33*	16.75	115.51	0	0	5
TS Muyeye	14	13	0	298	73	22.92	149.00	0	2	5
MK O'Riordan	14	13	0	153	33	11.76	140.36	0	0	3
MW Parkinson	13	4	2	7	6*	3.50	77.77	0	0	2
TS Rogers	6	5	3	47	31*	23.50	188.00	0	0	6
J Singh	3	1	0	1	1	1.00	50.00	0	0	0
G Stewart	10	7	4	37	21	12.33	115.62	0	0	2
CH Stobo	1	0								0
B Swanepoel	6	5	0	17	8	3.40	80.95	0	0	0

Bowling

	Balls	Mdns	Runs	Wkts	BB	Ave	5w	10w
XC Bartlett	157	57	236	9	3-34	26.22	0	0
JL Denly	24	10	34	1	1-21	34.00	0	0
JDM Evison	108	29	172	6	3-31	28.66	0	0
NN Gilchrist	132	45	222	14	3-46	15.85	0	0
JA Leaning	30	6	41	2	2-28	20.50	0	0
MK O'Riordan	142	36	217	7	2-28	31.00	0	0
MW Parkinson	218	63	293	16	4-25	18.31	1	0
TS Rogers	102	38	143	1	1-36	143.00	0	0
J Singh	54	23	93	5	3-27	18.60	0	0
G Stewart	149	40	267	7	2-22	38.14	0	0
CH Stobo	6	3	12	1	1-12	12.00	0	0
B Swanepoel	132	55	213	5	1-11	42.60	0	0

Catches/Stumpings:
10 Crawley, 7 Billings (1st), 6 Rogers, 5 Bartlett, Bell-Drummond, Leaning, Muyeye, 4 Finch, 3 O'Riordan, 2 Gilchrist, Parkinson, Stewart, 1 JL Denly, Evison

TEAM PROFILE

Lancashire County Cricket Club
™

FORMED: 1864
HOME GROUND: Emirates Old Trafford, Manchester
ONE-DAY NAME: Lancashire Lightning
CAPTAIN: Keaton Jennings
2024 RESULTS: CC1 9/10; ODC: 9/9 Group A; T20: Quarter-finalists
HONOURS: Championship: (9) 1897, 1904, 1926, 1927, 1928, 1930, 1934, 1950(s), 2011; Gillette/NatWest/C&G/FP Trophy: (7) 1970, 1971, 1972, 1985, 1990, 1996, 1998; Benson & Hedges Cup: (4) 1984, 1990, 1995, 1996; Pro40/National League/CB40/YB40/ODC: 1999; Sunday League: (4) 1969, 1970, 1989, 1998; T20 Cup: 2015

THE LOWDOWN

Head coach Dale Benkenstein cited his players' lack of experience in trying to explain a chastening summer in which Lancashire were relegated from Division One and finished bottom of their 50-over group. No wonder the club have agreed a one-year deal with 42-year-old James Anderson, fit as a fiddle, oozing experience, and available all season (Championship and the Blast) for the first time since 2005. Aussie Test opener Marcus Harris will also be on hand from April through September. These additions, and the overall strength of the squad, put Lancashire in pole position for an immediate return to the top flight. But they will need better returns from some of their established first-teamers. Only Keaton Jennings could be relied upon for runs in 2024, while seamers Tom Bailey and Will Williams were both under par. Batter-keeper Matty Hurst, who debuted for England Lions over the winter, leads a cast of young talents which includes 17-year-old Rocky Flintoff. Trinidadian quick Anderson Phillip returns for an 11-game red-ball stint until July. Steven Croft has hung up his boots after nearly two decades of service.

IN: Michael Jones (Dur), Marcus Harris (Aus, CC/ODC), Anderson Phillip (WI, CC/T20), Ashton Turner (Aus, CC/T20), Chris Green (Aus, T20)
OUT: Jack Morley (Der), George Lavelle (REL), Steven Croft (RET)

HEAD COACH: DALE BENKENSTEIN

Benkenstein enjoyed a long career at Durham, winning three Championships. The South African batter coached Hampshire between 2014-16 and had a brief spell as Lancashire's batting consultant, before taking over at Gloucestershire. After a difficult time at Bristol, Benkenstein replaced Glen Chapple as Lancashire head coach in December 2023. The retired Steven Croft has joined the backroom staff on a full-time basis.

L

	Mat	Inns	NO	Runs	HS	Ave	100	50	Ct	St
JM Anderson	1	1	1	0	0*		0	0	0	
TH Aspinwall	6	10	4	76	26*	12.66	0	0	0	
TE Bailey	12	18	2	210	31*	13.12	0	0	0	
GP Balderson	14	22	0	454	48	20.63	0	0	2	
GJ Bell	12	20	0	428	99	21.40	0	2	16	
JM Blatherwick	3	4	0	48	18	12.00	0	0	1	
JJ Bohannon	14	23	0	803	205	34.91	1	3	4	
JA Boyden	1	2	0	5	5	2.50	0	0	0	
TC Bruce	7	12	1	271	73	24.63	0	1	7	
R Flintoff	4	7	0	87	32	12.42	0	0	0	
CJ Green	1	1	0	9	9	9.00	0	0	0	
TW Hartley	6	11	1	162	50	16.20	0	1	1	
MF Hurst	14	23	2	677	104	32.23	1	5	41	1
VR Iyer	3	6	0	116	35	19.33	0	0	1	
KK Jennings	14	23	1	1006	187*	45.72	4	3	18	
GID Lavelle	1	1	0	0	0	0.00	0	0	1	
NM Lyon	8	9	5	38	12	9.50	0	0	1	
S Mahmood	2	4	2	64	46	32.00	0	0	0	
JP Morley	1	1	0	0	0	0.00	0	0	0	
A Phillip	3	5	1	77	41	19.25	0	0	2	
HPN Singh	2	3	0	42	31	14.00	0	0	2	
LWP Wells	14	23	0	674	150	29.30	2	2	6	
WSA Williams	11	17	5	101	32*	8.41	0	0	4	

Batting

	Balls	Mdns	Runs	Wkts	BB	Ave	5w	10w
JM Anderson	186	7	64	8	7-35	8.00	1	0
TH Aspinwall	562	6	446	14	5-41	31.85	1	0
TE Bailey	1893	53	923	27	4-36	34.18	0	0
GP Balderson	1852	54	1080	36	4-50	30.00	0	0
GJ Bell	24	0	21	0				
JM Blatherwick	247	4	198	1	1-70	198.00	0	0
JJ Bohannon	36	0	29	0				
JA Boyden	108	2	81	0				
CJ Green	90	5	20	1	1-20	20.00	0	0
TW Hartley	756	10	409	5	2-46	81.80	0	0
VR Iyer	30	0	20	0				
NM Lyon	1849	52	790	26	4-59	30.38	0	0
S Mahmood	276	3	173	2	1-22	86.50	0	0
JP Morley	119	1	60	3	2-34	20.00	0	0
A Phillip	470	6	359	15	5-65	23.93	1	0
HPN Singh	12	0	13	0				
LWP Wells	880	15	545	24	4-36	22.70	0	0
WSA Williams	1323	42	606	16	3-26	37.87	0	0

Bowling

Catches/Stumpings:
42 Hurst (1st), 18 Jennings, 16 Bell, 7 Bruce, 6 Wells, 4 Bohannon, Williams, 2 Balderson, Phillip, Singh, 1 Blatherwick, Hartley, Iyer, Lavelle, Lyon

Batting

	Mat	Inns	NO	Runs	HS	Ave	100	50	Ct	St
TH Aspinwall	3	3	0	4	4	1.33	40.00	0	0	0
TE Bailey	5	5	1	50	30	12.50	64.10	0	0	0
GP Balderson	8	8	0	192	53	24.00	75.59	0	2	1
CM Barnard	7	7	2	25	9	5.00	39.06	0	0	3
GJ Bell	8	8	0	142	56	17.75	63.39	0	1	7
JM Blatherwick	4	4	0	39	25	9.75	61.90	0	0	1
JJ Bohannon	8	8	0	274	147	34.25	84.56	1	1	1
JA Boyden	3	3	2	47	44*	47.00	111.90	0	0	0
TC Bruce	1	1	0	16	16	16.00	123.07	0	0	0
R Flintoff	7	7	0	167	88	23.85	60.72	0	1	0
DK Fonseka	3	3	0	42	42	14.00	72.41	0	0	0
CJ Green	6	6	0	216	100	36.00	99.53	1	1	5
VR Iyer	5	5	0	68	25	13.60	80.00	0	0	0
KK Jennings	2	2	1	151	107*	151.00	82.51	1	0	1
GID Lavelle	3	3	0	2	2	0.66	14.28	0	0	4
JP Morley	2	1	1	10	10*		76.92	0	0	0
HPN Singh	7	7	0	87	25	12.42	64.44	0	0	2
MT Stanley	1	1	0	0	0	0.00	0.00	0	0	0
OW Sutton	1	1	0	0	0	0.00	0.00	0	0	0
WSA Williams	4	4	2	21	10	10.50	37.50	0	0	3

Bowling

	Balls	Mdns	Runs	Wkts	BB	Ave	5w	10w
TH Aspinwall	84	0	95	1	1-70	95.00	0	0
TE Bailey	258	2	206	2	2-45	103.00	0	0
GP Balderson	372	5	254	3	1-20	84.66	0	0
CM Barnard	318	2	246	8	3-47	30.75	0	0
JM Blatherwick	149	0	160	3	1-36	53.33	0	0
JJ Bohannon	33	1	24	0				
JA Boyden	120	0	110	6	2-26	18.33	0	0
CJ Green	291	1	230	5	3-38	46.00	0	0
VR Iyer	108	0	110	3	2-38	36.66	0	0
JP Morley	118	3	89	5	3-45	17.80	0	0
HPN Singh	36	0	32	2	1-10	16.00	0	0
MT Stanley	30	0	37	0				
OW Sutton	3	0	1	1	1-1	1.00	0	0
WSA Williams	210	2	167	5	2-41	33.40	0	0

Catches/Stumpings:
10 Bell (3st), 5 Green, 4 Lavelle, 3 Barnard, Williams, 2 Singh, 1 Balderson, Blatherwick, Bohannon, Jennings

	Mat	Inns	NO	Runs	HS	Ave	100	50	Ct	St
TH Aspinwall	5	3	1	9	5	4.50	128.57	0	0	1
GP Balderson	3	3	1	76	37*	38.00	146.15	0	0	1
GJ Bell	2	2	1	22	22*	22.00	104.76	0	0	0
JM Blatherwick	8	4	3	36	17*	36.00	180.00	0	0	6
JJ Bohannon	8	8	0	87	39	10.87	133.84	0	0	2
TC Bruce	8	7	1	139	50*	23.16	116.80	0	1	4
SJ Croft	12	10	2	205	52*	25.62	119.18	0	1	7
GH Dockrell	3	2	0	46	45	23.00	153.33	0	0	2
CJ Green	11	8	2	155	38	25.83	161.45	0	0	7
TW Hartley	4	3	0	20	18	6.66	166.66	0	0	0
MF Hurst	12	10	1	228	45	25.33	128.81	0	0	5
KK Jennings	10	10	1	278	64	30.88	158.85	0	1	1
GID Lavelle	2	2	0	35	20	17.50	184.21	0	0	1
LS Livingstone	3	3	1	133	54*	66.50	138.54	0	1	3
S Mahmood	9	3	1	6	3	3.00	50.00	0	0	0
JP Morley	1	0								0
PD Salt	3	3	0	79	70	26.33	154.90	0	1	1
MT Stanley	4	0								0
LWP Wells	12	12	1	233	66	21.18	154.30	0	1	7
L Wood	12	8	5	51	15*	17.00	204.00	0	0	3

Batting

	Balls	Mdns	Runs	Wkts	BB	Ave	5w	10w
TH Aspinwall	81	30	113	5	4-18	22.60	1	0
GP Balderson	42	8	63	3	2-15	21.00	0	0
JM Blatherwick	108	33	174	8	3-14	21.75	0	0
SJ Croft	18	4	30	1	1-22	30.00	0	0
GH Dockrell	6	3	13	1	1-13	13.00	0	0
CJ Green	238	75	294	14	4-12	21.00	1	0
TW Hartley	30	7	39	1	1-10	39.00	0	0
LS Livingstone	58	14	80	4	2-41	20.00	0	0
S Mahmood	210	90	314	12	3-41	26.16	0	0
JP Morley	12	3	19	0				
MT Stanley	48	17	78	3	1-11	26.00	0	0
LWP Wells	241	62	285	11	2-23	25.90	0	0
L Wood	255	108	318	10	3-23	31.80	0	0

Bowling

Catches/Stumpings:
7 Croft, Green, Wells, 6 Blatherwick, 5 Hurst, 4 Bruce, 3 Livingstone, Wood, 2 Bohannon, 1 Aspinwall, Balderson, Jennings, Lavelle, Salt

TEAM PROFILE

LEICESTERSHIRE
COUNTY CRICKET CLUB
ESTABLISHED 1879

FORMED: 1879
HOME GROUND: Uptonsteel County Ground, Leicester
ONE-DAY NAME: Leicestershire Foxes
CAPTAIN: Peter Handscomb
2024 RESULTS: CC2: 5/8; ODC: Semi-finalists; T20: 5/9 North Group
HONOURS: Championship: (3) 1975, 1996, 1998; Benson & Hedges Cup: (3) 1972, 1975, 1985; Pro40/National League/CB40/YB40/ODC: 2023; Sunday League: (2) 1974, 1977; T20 Cup: (3) 2004, 2006, 2011

THE LOWDOWN

Genuine contenders in white-ball cricket, stubborn if uninspired in the Championship, Leicestershire held their own in 2024. The club put up a spirited defence of the One-Day Cup, nearly toppling Somerset in the semi-finals, and were a point from making the T20 knockouts. In Division Two there were just three defeats but only one victory with 10 draws, a record which spoke of three things: rain, the resistance of the batters throughout the order, and a seam-bowling attack short of the quality needed to win matches. What's more, Scott Currie – the best of the quicks – has now returned to Hampshire after a successful loan spell. England pace bowler Josh Hull is still a work in progress, but Dutch seamer Logan van Beek will bring some experience to the attack. Chris Wright has put a drug scandal behind him but turns 40 in July. Peter Handscomb is back after a superb 2024 in which he stacked up well over 1,600 runs across all formats. The Australian takes over as captain from Lewis Hill, who resigned at the end of last summer after making just two half-centuries in 21 red-ball innings.

IN: Logan van Beek (Net, CC/T20), Ben Green (Som, loan)
OUT: Sam Evans (REL)

HEAD COACH: ALFONSO THOMAS

The former Somerset fast bowler was promoted from assistant to joint interim head coach – sharing the role with James Taylor – after Paul Nixon was put on gardening leave in June 2024. The pair immediately guided Leicestershire to the One-Day Cup, the club's first trophy in 12 years, before Thomas was announced as head coach and Taylor as his assistant. Thomas, 49, played one T20I for South Africa and took 558 wickets for Somerset. He has previously had coaching roles for West Indies, Hampshire, Kent and Surrey.

COUNTY CHAMPIONSHIP AVERAGES 2024

	Mat	Inns	NO	Runs	HS	Ave	100	50	Ct	St
R Ahmed	8	13	0	432	85	33.23	0	4	0	
SG Budinger	3	5	0	174	87	34.80	0	2	1	
OB Cox	12	17	3	478	69	34.14	0	2	19	
SW Currie	11	14	4	353	120	35.30	1	1	12	
LP Goldsworthy	2	4	0	131	75	32.75	0	1	3	
AM Green	1	1	0	0	0	0.00	0	0	0	
BGF Green	6	7	1	143	77	23.83	0	1	2	
PSP Handscomb	10	14	2	894	139*	74.50	3	6	8	1
MS Harris	7	10	1	388	214	43.11	1	1	2	
LJ Hill	14	21	0	431	92	20.52	0	2	2	
IG Holland	7	12	0	324	104	27.00	1	1	1	
JO Hull	3	4	2	4	4*	2.00	0	0	1	
LPJ Kimber	13	21	2	629	243	33.10	1	1	9	
BWM Mike	9	12	2	290	90	29.00	0	1	0	
PWA Mulder	1	2	0	74	53	37.00	0	1	0	
RK Patel	13	22	2	719	117	35.95	1	3	6	
AM Rahane	3	6	0	202	102	33.66	1	0	3	
MET Salisbury	5	5	3	10	7	5.00	0	0	0	
TAR Scriven	12	14	4	385	60	38.50	0	3	0	
HJ Swindells	2	3	0	45	22	15.00	0	0	0	
L Trevaskis	7	10	3	299	82	42.71	0	3	4	
SB Wood	3	4	1	94	57*	31.33	0	1	0	
CJC Wright	2	3	1	41	15	20.50	0	0	0	

Batting

	Balls	Mdns	Runs	Wkts	BB	Ave	5w	10w
R Ahmed	1030	15	789	13	3-60	60.69	0	0
SG Budinger	57	0	40	1	1-13	40.00	0	0
SW Currie	1491	38	904	29	5-64	31.17	1	0
LP Goldsworthy	132	2	91	2	1-32	45.50	0	0
AM Green	48	1	41	0			0	0
BGF Green	738	28	429	11	4-28	39.00	0	0
MS Harris	3	0	1	0				
LJ Hill	6	0	6	0				
IG Holland	1008	35	505	14	4-53	36.07	0	0
JO Hull	408	5	365	2	1-58	182.50	0	0
LPJ Kimber	485	6	367	4	1-21	91.75	0	0
BWM Mike	1203	25	910	26	5-22	35.00	1	0
PWA Mulder	198	2	131	3	2-84	43.66	0	0
MET Salisbury	729	24	440	10	3-77	44.00	0	0
TAR Scriven	1452	33	883	15	4-103	58.86	0	0
L Trevaskis	612	7	420	4	1-15	105.00	0	0
SB Wood	272	4	164	2	1-32	82.00	0	0
CJC Wright	306	7	160	2	2-75	80.00	0	0

Bowling

Catches/Stumpings:
19 Cox, 12 Currie, 9 Handscomb (1st), Kimber, 6 Patel, 4 Trevaskis, 3 Goldsworthy, Rahane, 2 Green, Harris, Hill, 1 Budinger, Holland, Hull

Batting

	Mat	Inns	NO	Runs	HS	Ave	100	50	Ct	St
SG Budinger	10	10	0	458	120	45.80	100.21	1	3	4
OB Cox	10	9	0	235	49	26.11	94.00	0	0	4
AM Green	3	0								1
PSP Handscomb	10	9	1	539	119	67.37	117.94	3	2	7
LJ Hill	10	10	1	246	81	27.33	99.59	0	2	1
IG Holland	6	6	0	160	65	26.66	91.95	0	1	5
LPJ Kimber	4	4	0	32	28	8.00	91.42	0	0	2
BWM Mike	4	4	3	50	21	50.00	116.27	0	0	4
AM Rahane	10	10	1	378	71	42.00	89.15	0	4	3
MET Salisbury	4	1	1	0	0*		0.00	0	0	1
TAR Scriven	10	7	5	124	55	62.00	116.98	0	1	2
HJ Swindells	3	3	0	61	35	20.33	57.54	0	0	0
L Trevaskis	10	9	3	140	60*	23.33	74.86	0	1	4
RI Walker	6	4	1	42	16	14.00	110.52	0	0	3
SB Wood	1	1	0	22	22	22.00	62.85	0	0	0
CJC Wright	9	3	2	2	1*	2.00	25.00	0	0	2

Bowling

	Balls	Mdns	Runs	Wkts	BB	Ave	5w	10w
SG Budinger	14	0	20	0				
AM Green	126	0	123	4	2-39	30.75	0	0
IG Holland	342	5	264	8	2-39	33.00	0	0
LPJ Kimber	66	0	68	1	1-29	68.00	0	0
BWM Mike	156	0	193	6	3-63	32.16	0	0
MET Salisbury	150	0	161	4	2-58	40.25	0	0
TAR Scriven	504	2	470	18	3-20	26.11	0	0
L Trevaskis	354	0	348	10	4-54	34.80	1	0
RI Walker	334	1	321	9	3-40	35.66	0	0
SB Wood	30	0	34	1	1-34	34.00	0	0
CJC Wright	420	5	378	6	2-17	63.00	0	0

Catches/Stumpings:
7 Handscomb, 5 Holland, 4 Budinger, Cox, Mike, Trevaskis, 3 Rahane, Walker, 2 Kimber, Scriven, Wright, 1 Green, Hill, Salisbury

	Mat	Inns	NO	Runs	HS	Ave	100	50	Ct	St	
R Ahmed	11	10	1	119	36*	13.22	103.47	0	0	2	
SG Budinger	12	11	0	172	50	15.63	152.21	0	1	2	
OB Cox	14	11	2	250	61*	27.77	147.05	0	3	6	
SW Currie	12	6	4	47	20	23.50	134.28	0	0	10	
LP Goldsworthy	11	10	3	179	67	25.57	140.94	0	1	7	
PSP Handscomb	12	12	2	229	75*	22.90	108.53	0	1	3	
IG Holland	4	2	2	10	9*		142.85	0	0	0	Batting
JO Hull	14	4	2	24	12*	12.00	114.28	0	0	4	
LPJ Kimber	14	13	1	205	53	17.08	150.73	0	1	7	
BWM Mike	14	11	4	102	28	14.57	130.76	0	0	5	
PWA Mulder	8	8	1	115	28*	16.42	129.21	0	0	2	
JDS Neesham	6	5	1	135	67	33.75	158.82	0	1	3	
RK Patel	14	13	0	414	104	31.84	144.75	1	1	2	
TAR Scriven	1	0								1	
PR Stirling	2	1	0	2	2	2.00	50.00	0	0	0	
HJ Swindells	2	2	0	26	22	13.00	123.80	0	0	1	
RI Walker	1	0								0	
SB Wood	2	0								0	

	Balls	Mdns	Runs	Wkts	BB	Ave	5w	10w	
R Ahmed	240	59	304	7	2-27	43.42	0	0	
SW Currie	275	91	379	20	4-25	18.95	1	0	
LP Goldsworthy	192	55	257	14	3-20	18.35	0	0	
IG Holland	54	20	78	2	1-14	39.00	0	0	
JO Hull	309	135	434	18	3-28	24.11	0	0	Bowling
LPJ Kimber	54	20	81	1	1-23	81.00	0	0	
BWM Mike	258	87	401	14	3-17	28.64	0	0	
PWA Mulder	99	35	137	4	2-19	34.25	0	0	
JDS Neesham	84	25	166	3	1-15	55.33	0	0	
TAR Scriven	24	11	38	1	1-38	38.00	0	0	
PR Stirling	12	4	15	0					
RI Walker	12	5	27	0					
SB Wood	30	8	38	1	1-25	38.00	0	0	

Catches/Stumpings:
10 Currie, 8 Cox (2st), 7 Goldsworthy, Kimber, 5 Mike, 4 Hull, 3 Handscomb, Neesham, 2 Ahmed, Budinger, Mulder, Patel, 1 Scriven, Swindells

MIDDLESEX CRICKET

FORMED: 1864
HOME GROUND: Lord's Cricket Ground, London
CAPTAIN: Toby Roland-Jones (CC), Stevie Eskinazi (ODC/T20)
2024 RESULTS: CC2: 3/8; ODC: 6/9 Group A; T20: 8/9 South Group
HONOURS: Championship: (13) 1903, 1920, 1921, 1947, 1949(s), 1976, 1977(s), 1980, 1982, 1985, 1990, 1993, 2016; Gillette/NatWest/C&G/FP Trophy: (4) 1977, 1980, 1984, 1998; Benson & Hedges Cup: (2) 1983, 1986; Sunday League: 1992; T20 Cup: 2008

THE LOWDOWN

In the end there was huge disappointment for Middlesex after late-summer defeats stalled an immediate return to Division One last year. But set against a 2023 campaign among the worst the club have known, alongside ECB-imposed financial restrictions which left no budget for overseas players – not to mention a payments scandal involving a former CEO – then for supporters it was some consolation to see the side look something like themselves again. Though wobbly at times, the batting emerged from the depths of 2023, with Sam Robson and Max Holden back in the groove and Leus du Plooy enjoying a fine first season at Lord's. But standing head and shoulders above the rest – again – was allrounder Ryan Higgins: 1,133 runs at 70 and 30 wickets at 28. Red-ball skipper Toby Roland-Jones was back to his best with ball in hand, and the signing of Dane Paterson for the first seven games strengthens a seam attack that has lost Ethan Bamber. Middlesex have also acquired potential match-winning spinner Zafar Gohar, Ireland left-armer Josh Little and – for the second half of the summer – Kane Williamson.

IN: Ben Geddes (Sur), Zafar Gohar (Glo), Josh Little (Ire), Dane Paterson (SA, CC), Kane Williamson (NZ, CC/T20)
OUT: Martin Andersson (Der), Ethan Bamber (War), Mark Stoneman (Ham), Thilan Walallawita (REL), Robbie White (RET)

FIRST-TEAM COACH: RICHARD JOHNSON

Johnson replaced Stuart Law in January 2022, returning to the county he was first connected with at the age of 10. The former England seamer represented the club on more than 200 occasions between 1992 and 2000 and was Middlesex bowling coach for seven years from 2011, helping the club win the Championship in 2016. After working as a spin-bowling consultant last year, Ian Salisbury has taken on the role on a full-time basis.

 www.middlesexccc.com / tel: 0207 289 1300

	Mat	Inns	NO	Runs	HS	Ave	100	50	Ct	St
ER Bamber	12	12	7	86	21*	17.20	0	0	4	
HJH Brookes	9	12	4	87	52*	10.87	0	1	0	
NB Cornwell	2	2	1	2	2*	2.00	0	0	0	
JLB Davies	14	18	2	425	91	26.56	0	4	25	
JM de Caires	8	10	0	324	80	32.40	0	3	4	
JL du Plooy	14	21	2	955	196*	50.26	2	5	16	
SS Eskinazi	5	6	2	123	65*	30.75	0	1	2	
NS Fernandes	8	12	0	354	103	29.50	1	1	4	
TG Helm	10	12	6	157	64	26.16	0	1	8	
RF Higgins	13	18	2	1133	221	70.81	5	2	16	
MDE Holden	14	21	1	981	211*	49.05	2	5	2	
LBK Hollman	8	12	0	208	39	17.33	0	0	2	
SD Robson	11	16	1	872	162	58.13	4	4	12	
TS Roland-Jones	12	15	0	274	59	18.26	0	2	5	
MD Stoneman	14	21	0	698	129	33.23	2	2	6	

Batting

	Balls	Mdns	Runs	Wkts	BB	Ave	5w	10w
ER Bamber	2095	68	1111	30	4-68	37.03	0	0
HJH Brookes	1212	19	769	22	3-29	34.95	0	0
NB Cornwell	160	3	133	1	1-4	133.00	0	0
JLB Davies	9	0	12	0				
JM de Caires	851	9	536	6	3-45	89.33	0	0
JL du Plooy	288	3	229	3	1-9	76.33	0	0
NS Fernandes	216	2	142	2	1-17	71.00	0	0
TG Helm	1623	49	945	23	4-44	41.08	0	0
RF Higgins	1645	63	858	30	4-31	28.60	0	0
LBK Hollman	1290	24	748	20	4-194	37.40	0	0
SD Robson	84	0	75	0				
TS Roland-Jones	2118	74	1173	52	6-58	22.55	7	2
MD Stoneman	42	0	42	0				

Bowling

Catches/Stumpings:
25 Davies, 16 du Plooy, Higgins, 12 Robson, 8 Helm, 6 Stoneman, 5 Roland-Jones, 4 Bamber, De Caires, Fernandes, 2 Eskinazi, Holden, Hollman

MIDDLESEX CRICKET

Batting

	Mat	Inns	NO	Runs	HS	Ave	100	50	Ct	St
MK Andersson	5	5	1	143	46	35.75	91.66	0	0	0
ER Bamber	6	4	1	32	13	10.66	72.72	0	0	1
HJH Brookes	6	3	1	45	29*	22.50	100.00	0	0	0
NB Cornwell	4	2	0	12	10	6.00	120.00	0	0	2
JB Cracknell	7	7	0	306	98	43.71	83.83	0	3	3
BC Cullen	2	2	1	15	8	15.00	55.55	0	0	0
JLB Davies	7	7	1	144	46	24.00	98.63	0	0	3
JM de Caires	6	4	0	55	23	13.75	93.22	0	0	7
NS Fernandes	7	7	0	152	83	21.71	68.77	0	1	3
RF Higgins	1	1	0	0	0	0.00	0.00	0	0	1
LBK Hollman	7	6	3	134	38*	44.66	75.70	0	0	3
I Kaushal	2	0								1
SD Robson	7	7	1	146	87*	24.33	69.85	0	1	3
TS Roland-Jones	2	2	0	6	6	3.00	50.00	0	0	0
MD Stoneman	7	7	1	266	83	44.33	117.18	0	3	0
RG White	1	1	0	50	50	50.00	106.38	0	1	0

Bowling

	Balls	Mdns	Runs	Wkts	BB	Ave	5w	10w
MK Andersson	48	0	46	0				
ER Bamber	306	5	244	5	2-31	48.80	0	0
HJH Brookes	286	4	271	10	4-43	27.10	1	0
NB Cornwell	168	1	195	2	2-54	97.50	0	0
BC Cullen	66	0	113	0				
JM de Caires	174	0	133	5	2-25	26.60	0	0
NS Fernandes	252	0	252	4	2-31	63.00	0	0
LBK Hollman	408	1	348	12	4-62	29.00	1	0
I Kaushal	66	0	87	2	1-26	43.50	0	0
TS Roland-Jones	90	0	74	0				

Catches/Stumpings:
7 Davies (4st), De Caires, 3 Cracknell, Fernandes, Hollman, Robson, 2 Cornwell, 1 Bamber, Higgins, Kaushal

**MIDDLESEX
CRICKET**

	Mat	Inns	NO	Runs	HS	Ave	100	50	Ct	St	
MK Andersson	11	11	1	282	57	28.20	134.28	0	2	7	
HJH Brookes	7	5	2	7	5	2.33	53.84	0	0	0	
NB Cornwell	11	4	4	25	15*		113.63	0	0	2	
JB Cracknell	9	8	1	77	24	11.00	130.50	0	0	7	
BC Cullen	10	5	2	24	11	8.00	114.28	0	0	1	
JLB Davies	12	11	0	214	53	19.45	128.14	0	2	2	Batting
JM de Caires	9	8	2	64	31*	10.66	120.75	0	0	3	
JL du Plooy	7	7	1	148	73*	24.66	132.14	0	1	2	
SS Eskinazi	9	9	0	164	48	18.22	129.13	0	0	4	
TG Helm	11	8	4	59	26*	14.75	105.35	0	0	7	
RF Higgins	12	12	0	166	44	13.83	110.66	0	0	6	
MDE Holden	10	10	2	188	85*	23.50	160.68	0	1	0	
LBK Hollman	12	11	2	126	28	14.00	116.66	0	0	5	
MD Stoneman	2	1	0	6	6	6.00	85.71	0	0	1	

	Balls	Mdns	Runs	Wkts	BB	Ave	5w	10w	
MK Andersson	6	1	5	0					
HJH Brookes	108	28	204	5	3-31	40.80	0	0	
NB Cornwell	170	68	251	8	2-25	31.37	0	0	Bowling
BC Cullen	197	70	319	11	3-47	29.00	0	0	
JM de Caires	62	13	112	4	1-9	28.00	0	0	
JL du Plooy	6	1	12	0					
TG Helm	206	84	282	9	2-24	31.33	0	0	
RF Higgins	147	34	220	9	2-25	24.44	0	0	
LBK Hollman	222	81	289	23	5-16	12.56	1	1	

Catches/Stumpings:
7 Andersson, Cracknell, Helm, 6 Higgins, 5 Davies (3st), Hollman, 4 Eskinazi, 3 De Caires, 2 Cornwell, du Plooy, 1 Cullen, Stoneman

NORTHAMPTONSHIRE

TEAM PROFILE

FORMED: 1878
HOME GROUND: County Ground, Northampton
ONE-DAY NAME: Northamptonshire Steelbacks
CAPTAIN: Luke Procter (CC), Lewis McManus (ODC), David Willey (T20)
2024 RESULTS: CC2: 4/8; ODC: 8/9 Group A; T20: Quarter-finalists
HONOURS: Gillette/NatWest/C&G/FP Trophy: (2) 1976, 1992; Benson & Hedges Cup: 1980; T20 Cup: (2) 2013, 2016

THE LOWDOWN

A new era dawns under Darren Lehmann, the pugnacious Australian who is Northants' first head coach chosen from outside the club's coaching staff in over two decades. Lehmann's appointment was a welcome tonic for supporters who endured a tough year back in Division Two, John Sadler resigning before the season was out with the club winless in 11 matches. They won their next two largely down to Indian leggie Yuzvendra Chahal, highlighting a long-standing problem: the lack of a match-winning spinner. Ben Sanderson continues to lead the seam attack superbly but needs greater support after the loss of Jack White to Yorkshire. George Scrimshaw has recovered from a back injury that ruined his first season at the club. The batting looks solid, although Emilio Gay's defection to Durham is a blow. Skipper Luke Procter signed a new two-year deal after a fine season with bat and ball, while 22-year-old James Sales scored his first two red-ball hundreds. The T20 side, revived under David Willey, welcomes back Ravi Bopara, Ashton Agar and Matt Breetzke, with the South African batter also due for the first eight Championship matches.

IN: Dom Leech (Yor), Liam Guthrie (Aus), Matt Breetzke (SA, CC/T20), Ashton Agar (Aus, T20), Ravi Bopara (T20)
OUT: Emilio Gay (Dur), Jack White (Yor), Alex Russell, George Gowler, George Weldon (all REL)

HEAD COACH: DARREN LEHMANN

A gifted Australian left-hander who in another era would have played many more than his 27 Tests, Lehmann made a big impact at Yorkshire, scoring nearly 15,000 runs and playing a starring role in 2001 when the club won the Championship. The South Australian, 55, had domestic coaching success both at home and in the IPL before masterminding two Ashes victories as head coach of Australia, eventually stepping down in the wake of the ball-tampering scandal in South Africa.

	Mat	Inns	NO	Runs	HS	Ave	100	50	Ct	St
GA Bartlett	10	16	4	491	126*	40.91	1	3	2	
MP Breetzke	1	2	0	16	12	8.00	0	0	2	
J Broad	11	17	1	284	75	17.75	0	1	8	
YS Chahal	4	5	4	5	5*	5.00	0	0	1	
MGA Finan	2	3	0	15	14	5.00	0	0	1	
EN Gay	10	17	1	919	261	57.43	2	4	13	
S Kaul	3	5	1	15	6*	3.75	0	0	0	
RI Keogh	10	16	1	439	102	29.26	1	2	0	
DJ Leech	3	4	0	20	8	5.00	0	0	0	
LD McManus	13	19	8	484	168*	44.00	1	1	33	7
AH Miller	5	8	0	162	42	20.25	0	0	0	
KK Nair	7	11	1	487	202*	48.70	1	3	6	
K Patel	1	2	0	35	26	17.50	0	0	0	
LA Patterson-White	3	6	1	102	30	20.40	0	0	1	
LA Procter	14	22	3	923	116*	48.57	1	7	8	
AK Russell	1	1	1	4	4*		0	0	0	
JJG Sales	7	8	2	364	135	60.66	2	0	7	
BW Sanderson	12	15	0	149	40	9.93	0	0	1	
GLS Scrimshaw	2	2	0	10	7	5.00	0	0	1	
PP Shaw	5	9	0	164	37	18.22	0	0	2	
F Singh	1	1	0	4	4	4.00	0	0	0	
CP Tremain	4	3	2	59	37	59.00	0	0	1	
RS Vasconcelos	9	15	2	708	182	54.46	2	2	13	
RA Weatherall	4	4	1	15	13	5.00	0	0	1	
C White	4	5	2	21	21	7.00	0	0	0	
SA Zaib	8	11	0	399	100	36.27	1	2	1	

Batting

	Balls	Mdns	Runs	Wkts	BB	Ave	5w	10w
J Broad	855	19	577	19	7-33	30.36	1	0
YS Chahal	717	18	401	19	5-45	21.10	2	0
MGA Finan	138	0	144	0				
S Kaul	574	12	388	13	5-76	29.84	1	0
RI Keogh	1083	27	615	23	5-44	26.73	2	0
DJ Leech	136	5	93	1	1-35	93.00	0	0
AH Miller	174	4	160	0				
LA Patterson-White	931	30	498	13	3-58	38.30	0	0
LA Procter	1302	39	723	21	4-45	34.42	0	0
AK Russell	113	1	82	3	2-51	27.33	0	0
JJG Sales	90	0	89	0				
BW Sanderson	2247	87	1096	41	6-64	26.73	3	0
GLS Scrimshaw	222	3	216	4	2-85	54.00	0	0
F Singh	240	0	193	3	3-193	64.33	0	0
CP Tremain	588	14	360	2	1-63	180.00	0	0
RA Weatherall	426	8	320	6	2-55	53.33	0	0
C White	509	24	227	9	4-23	25.22	0	0
SA Zaib	689	13	492	9	4-84	54.66	0	0

Bowling

Catches/Stumpings:
40 McManus (7st), 13 Gay, Vasconcelos, 8 Broad, Procter, 7 Sales, 6 Nair, 2 Bartlett, Breetzke, Shaw, 1 Chahal, Finan, Patterson-White, Sanderson, Scrimshaw, Tremain, Weatherall, Zaib

METRO BANK ONE-DAY CUP AVERAGES 2024

NORTHAMPTONSHIRE STEELBACKS

Batting

	Mat	Inns	NO	Runs	HS	Ave	100	50	Ct	St
GA Bartlett	8	8	1	253	60	36.14	77.13	0	2	1
J Broad	6	5	3	128	63	64.00	82.58	0	1	1
YS Chahal	1	0								0
MGA Finan	3	3	0	18	15	6.00	58.06	0	0	1
EN Gay	3	3	0	94	59	31.33	73.43	0	1	3
FJ Heldreich	5	2	0	1	1	0.50	12.50	0	0	1
RI Keogh	3	3	0	36	19	12.00	49.31	0	0	0
LD McManus	8	7	0	140	45	20.00	80.45	0	0	9
AH Miller	8	7	1	192	73	32.00	90.99	0	1	4
LA Procter	1	0								0
JJG Sales	5	5	1	51	33*	12.75	67.10	0	0	1
BW Sanderson	5	4	2	10	4	5.00	47.61	0	0	1
PP Shaw	8	8	0	343	97	42.87	117.86	0	3	8
RS Vasconcelos	7	7	0	153	68	21.85	61.20	0	1	3
RA Weatherall	5	4	4	15	12*		71.42	0	0	2
C White	4	3	0	5	4	1.66	45.45	0	0	1
SA Zaib	8	7	0	234	58	33.42	82.97	0	2	2

Bowling

	Balls	Mdns	Runs	Wkts	BB	Ave	5w	10w
GA Bartlett	48	0	52	0				
J Broad	253	5	212	13	3-16	16.30	0	0
YS Chahal	60	5	14	5	5-14	2.80	0	1
MGA Finan	114	0	115	0				
EN Gay	24	0	25	1	1-25	25.00	0	0
FJ Heldreich	141	0	135	2	1-25	67.50	0	0
RI Keogh	132	0	128	2	1-35	64.00	0	0
AH Miller	204	2	202	3	1-19	67.33	0	0
LA Procter	60	2	25	2	2-25	12.50	0	0
JJG Sales	54	1	48	1	1-16	48.00	0	0
BW Sanderson	226	4	149	6	2-28	24.83	0	0
RA Weatherall	187	0	218	6	4-50	36.33	1	0
C White	186	6	90	6	3-6	15.00	0	0
SA Zaib	372	3	292	12	3-44	24.33	0	0

Catches/Stumpings:
10 McManus (1st), 8 Shaw, 4 Miller, 3 Gay, Vasconcelos, 2 Weatherall, Zaib, 1 Bartlett, Broad, Finan, Heldreich, Sales, Sanderson, White

STEELBACKS

	Mat	Inns	NO	Runs	HS	Ave	100	50	Ct	St
AC Agar	6	6	4	92	31	46.00	191.66	0	0	2
GA Bartlett	9	5	0	13	7	2.60	59.09	0	0	4
RS Bopara	13	13	2	340	61	30.90	128.30	0	2	3
MP Breetzke	13	13	1	460	94	38.33	153.84	0	4	5
J Broad	4	3	1	48	29	24.00	154.83	0	0	1
FJ Heldreich	14	1	1	21	21*		77.77	0	0	0
LD McManus	14	12	7	129	26	25.80	155.42	0	0	15
AH Miller	6	3	2	16	8*	16.00	177.77	0	0	2
BW Sanderson	12	3	1	11	10*	5.50	68.75	0	0	4
GLS Scrimshaw	3	1	1	6	6*		100.00	0	0	0
Sikandar Raza	8	7	2	206	43	41.20	152.59	0	0	9
RS Vasconcelos	11	11	0	259	42	23.54	126.96	0	0	7
RA Weatherall	9	1	1	21	21*		100.00	0	0	2
C White	4	0								2
DJ Willey	14	14	0	313	79	22.35	133.76	0	3	8
SA Zaib	14	13	3	275	86	27.50	167.68	0	2	6

Batting

	Balls	Mdns	Runs	Wkts	BB	Ave	5w	10w
AC Agar	126	46	193	4	2-39	48.25	0	0
RS Bopara	204	55	258	13	4-34	19.84	1	0
J Broad	6	2	14	0				
FJ Heldreich	162	39	284	11	3-23	25.81	0	0
AH Miller	6	1	12	0				
BW Sanderson	252	101	375	15	4-15	25.00	1	0
GLS Scrimshaw	56	20	90	6	3-16	15.00	0	0
Sikandar Raza	120	32	174	2	1-23	87.00	0	0
RA Weatherall	127	49	243	11	4-50	22.09	1	0
C White	72	36	99	5	3-16	19.80	0	0
DJ Willey	288	112	423	16	2-17	26.43	0	0
SA Zaib	126	43	162	8	3-12	20.25	0	0

Bowling

Catches/Stumpings:
17 McManus (2st), 9 Raza, 8 Willey, 7 Vasconcelos, 6 Zaib, 5 Breetzke, 4 Bartlett, Sanderson, 3 Bopara, 2 Agar, Miller, Weatherall, White, 1 Broad

NOTTINGHAMSHIRE

TEAM PROFILE

FORMED: 1841
HOME GROUND: Trent Bridge, Nottingham
ONE-DAY NAME: Notts Outlaws
CAPTAIN: Haseeb Hameed (CC/ODC), Joe Clarke (T20)
2024 RESULTS: CC1: 8/10; ODC: 4/9 Group B; T20: 9/9 North Group
HONOURS: County Championship: (6) 1907, 1929, 1981, 1987, 2005, 2010; Gillette/NatWest/C&G/FP Trophy: 1987; Pro40/National League/CB40/YB40/ODC: (2) 2013, 2017; Benson & Hedges Cup: 1989; Sunday League: 1991; T20 Cup: (2) 2017, 2020

THE LOWDOWN

It's five years since Notts last won a trophy and they looked no nearer to silverware last summer. Eighth in Division One, the Outlaws also endured one of their worst T20 campaigns after losing their first five group games. It was a tough baptism for new four-day captain Haseeb Hameed, who topped 1,000 runs but was handicapped by an injury-cursed seam attack that is in transition. Dillon Pennington was outstanding until tearing a hamstring in The Hundred, while Josh Tongue – also brought in from neighbours Worcestershire – was never seen, though both returned for England Lions over the winter. Dane Paterson has left for Middlesex, but Mohammad Abbas will feature across two stints in May and September. South Africa's Kyle Verreynne returns for 12 Championship fixtures after averaging 248 in four innings last year. Alex Hales has opted out of the T20 Blast, ending his time at the club, but Daniel Sams and Moises Henriques make for a strong overseas pair. The club have released Luke Fletcher, who leaves with a tally of 643 wickets and many more friends after 17 seasons at Trent Bridge.

IN: Conor McKerr (Sur), Mohammad Abbas (Pak, CC), Fergus O'Neill (Aus, CC), Kyle Verreynne (SA, CC), Moises Henriques, Daniel Sams (both Aus, T20)
OUT: Fateh Singh (Wor), Alex Hales, Luke Fletcher (both REL), Tom Loten, Steven Mullaney, Toby Pettman (all RET)

HEAD COACH: PETER MOORES

The former Sussex keeper had two short spells as England head coach and won the Championship with his former club in 2003 and Lancashire in 2011. Moores, 62, joined Notts in 2016 and immediately led the club to the cup double as well as Championship promotion. Assistant coach Paul Franks will look after the 50-over side. Former club captain Steven Mullaney has become a full-time coach after confirming his retirement.

Batting

	Mat	Inns	NO	Runs	HS	Ave	100	50	Ct	St
F Ahmed	4	5	1	18	10	4.50	0	0	1	
JM Clarke	14	21	3	917	213*	50.94	4	4	17	
BM Duckett	3	6	0	323	218	53.83	1	1	2	
JA Duffy	2	2	1	31	29	31.00	0	0	0	
LJ Fletcher	6	8	2	35	22	5.83	0	0	0	
H Hameed	14	26	5	1091	247*	51.95	3	4	9	
CG Harrison	10	13	1	216	52	18.00	0	1	19	
JA Haynes	14	19	0	622	77	32.73	0	7	3	
BA Hutton	5	7	0	64	29	9.14	0	0	1	
LW James	14	19	5	502	106*	35.85	1	2	4	
R Lord	4	5	0	63	31	12.60	0	0	2	
FW McCann	5	7	0	358	154	51.14	2	1	7	
M Montgomery	4	7	0	119	48	17.00	0	0	3	
TJ Moores	4	4	0	23	17	5.75	0	0	10	
D Paterson	8	9	3	67	19	11.16	0	0	0	
LA Patterson-White	4	6	1	23	10	4.60	0	0	2	
DY Pennington	8	9	2	70	29*	10.00	0	0	2	
DJ Schadendorf	1	1	0	29	29	29.00	0	0	6	
BT Slater	14	26	5	949	168*	45.19	2	5	3	
OP Stone	6	9	0	315	90	35.00	0	3	3	
K Verreynne	3	4	3	248	148*	248.00	1	1	5	1
WA Young	7	12	3	377	174*	41.88	1	1	8	

Bowling

	Balls	Mdns	Runs	Wkts	BB	Ave	5w	10w
F Ahmed	1045	19	511	22	7-140	23.22	1	1
JA Duffy	288	5	194	6	4-60	32.33	0	0
LJ Fletcher	602	23	346	9	3-18	38.44	0	0
H Hameed	6	0	3	0				
CG Harrison	1247	19	780	20	5-128	39.00	1	0
BA Hutton	712	25	364	6	3-73	60.66	0	0
LW James	1401	33	933	27	4-61	34.55	0	0
R Lord	397	9	278	10	3-42	27.80	0	0
FW McCann	300	5	206	2	1-6	103.00	0	0
M Montgomery	36	0	30	1	1-4	30.00	0	0
D Paterson	1176	42	572	20	5-49	28.60	1	0
LA Patterson-White	777	10	436	8	5-96	54.50	1	0
DY Pennington	1347	47	738	31	5-96	23.80	1	0
BT Slater	42	0	24	0				
OP Stone	916	25	579	11	4-62	52.63	0	0

Catches/Stumpings:
19 Harrison, 17 Clarke, 10 Moores, 9 Hameed, 7 McCann, Young, 6 Schadendorf, Verreynne,
4 Haynes, James, 3 Montgomery, Slater, Stone, 2 Duckett, Lord, Patterson-White,
Pennington, 1 Ahmed, Hutton

Batting

	Mat	Inns	NO	Runs	HS	Ave	100	50	Ct	St
F Ahmed	1	0								0
LJ Fletcher	6	3	1	8	4	4.00	57.14	0	0	0
H Hameed	8	7	1	345	105	57.50	82.14	2	1	4
CG Harrison	2	2	0	1	1	0.50	6.25	0	0	0
JPH Hayes	1	0								0
JA Haynes	8	8	1	171	86	24.42	76.68	0	2	1
BA Hutton	4	3	0	23	13	7.66	71.87	0	0	0
LW James	7	6	0	148	76	24.66	91.35	0	2	3
SIM King	1	1	0	2	2	2.00	33.33	0	0	1
R Lord	5	3	2	26	12*	26.00	100.00	0	0	2
TW Loten	1	1	1	14	14*		155.55	0	0	0
FW McCann	8	8	0	168	48	21.00	75.33	0	0	8
M Montgomery	7	6	0	111	52	18.50	74.49	0	1	1
TJ Moores	8	7	3	210	40	52.50	107.69	0	0	9
LA Patterson-White	8	6	2	127	38*	31.75	123.30	0	0	3
THS Pettman	5	2	1	9	9*	9.00	75.00	0	0	1
BT Slater	8	8	1	398	164	56.85	101.27	2	0	0

Bowling

	Balls	Mdns	Runs	Wkts	BB	Ave	5w	10w
F Ahmed	54	0	69	1	1-69	69.00	0	0
LJ Fletcher	265	4	213	6	3-35	35.50	0	0
CG Harrison	114	0	107	2	1-33	53.50	0	0
JPH Hayes	36	1	28	1	1-28	28.00	0	0
BA Hutton	180	3	135	7	6-38	19.28	0	1
LW James	252	0	300	8	3-105	37.50	0	0
R Lord	261	1	249	11	5-45	22.63	0	0
TW Loten	48	1	36	0				
FW McCann	196	1	188	1	1-48	188.00	0	0
M Montgomery	84	1	75	2	2-38	37.50	0	0
LA Patterson-White	432	2	369	9	3-26	41.00	0	0
THS Pettman	192	3	162	3	3-44	54.00	0	0
BT Slater	6	0	17	0				

Catches/Stumpings:
9 Moores, 8 McCann, 4 Hameed, 3 James, Patterson-White, 2 Lord, 1 Haynes, King, Montgomery, Pettman

	Mat	Inns	NO	Runs	HS	Ave	100	50	Ct	St
JM Clarke	14	13	0	306	79	23.53	151.48	0	1		4
BM Duckett	1	1	0	39	39	39.00	185.71	0	0	0	0
Fazal Haque	6	3	3	20	16*		142.85	0	0	0	0
LJ Fletcher	3	3	2	5	5*	5.00	62.50	0	0	0	0
AD Hales	8	7	1	138	50*	23.00	110.40	0	1		2
CG Harrison	14	9	2	76	19	10.85	92.68	0	0	6	
JA Haynes	14	13	0	229	51	17.61	121.80	0	2	4	
LW James	14	11	2	149	51	16.55	102.75	0	1		5
SIM King	1	1	0	44	44	44.00	176.00	0	0	1	
BG Lister	8	3	1	1	1*	0.50	16.66	0	0	1	
FW McCann	1	1	0	48	48	48.00	150.00	0	0	1	
BJR Martindale	7	6	0	78	44	13.00	90.69	0	0	3	
M Montgomery	13	11	2	156	33	17.33	106.12	0	0	7	
TJ Moores	14	13	2	173	31	15.72	108.12	0	0	4	
LA Patterson-White	10	7	2	121	44*	24.20	142.35	0	0	2	
DY Pennington	3	2	0	5	5	2.50	100.00	0	0	1	
BT Slater	3	3	1	20	20	10.00	133.33	0	0	0	0
OP Stone	14	8	4	57	16*	14.25	98.27	0	0	3	
WA Young	6	6	0	56	25	9.33	77.77	0	0	3	

Batting

	Balls	Mdns	Runs	Wkts	BB	Ave	5w	10w
Fazal Haque	111	39	149	5	1-24	29.80	0	0
LJ Fletcher	66	20	101	4	2-19	25.25	0	0
CG Harrison	242	75	309	8	2-19	38.62	0	0
LW James	138	32	205	9	3-31	22.77	0	0
BG Lister	162	69	211	8	2-20	26.37	0	0
M Montgomery	122	34	185	3	1-10	61.66	0	0
LA Patterson-White	120	39	142	7	2-9	20.28	0	0
DY Pennington	66	25	106	2	1-37	53.00	0	0
OP Stone	264	104	418	15	3-30	27.86	0	0

Bowling

Catches/Stumpings:
7 Montgomery, 6 Harrison, 5 James, 4 Clarke, Haynes, Moores, 3 Martindale, Stone, Young,
2 Hales, Patterson-White, 1 King, Lister, McCann, Pennington

TEAM PROFILE

SOMERSET CCC

FORMED: 1875
HOME GROUND: The Cooper Associates County Ground, Taunton
CAPTAIN: Lewis Gregory (CC/T20), TBC (ODC)
2024 RESULTS: CC1: 3/10; ODC: Runners-up; T20: Runners-up
HONOURS: Gillette/NatWest/C&G/FP Trophy: (3) 1979, 1983, 2001; Pro40/National League/CB40/YB40/ODC: 2019; Benson & Hedges Cup: (2) 1981, 1982; Sunday League: 1979; T20 Cup: (2) 2005, 2023

THE LOWDOWN

It was mid-September, a rookie part-timer called Archie Vaughan was running amok, and Surrey, the county champions, were in a spin at Ciderabad. At that moment all seemed possible, yet within days the dream was shattered: the pennant went back to The Oval, while both white-ball campaigns ended with runners-up medals. But not many are as good at dusting themselves down as the Cidermen. They go again in 2025 with every reason to believe this is the year they will win their maiden Championship title, not least given the return of Matt Henry for the first seven red-ball fixtures. The Kiwi seamer shone across formats at Taunton in 2023 as Somerset were crowned T20 champions and joins a strong pace attack featuring the returning Migael Pretorius. Australia's Riley Meredith, genuinely fast, is also back for another T20 stint. There is much excitement around Tom Banton – known as a short-format specialist, he hit 891 runs at nearly 50 in the Championship last year. Two club stalwarts have retired in Jack Brooks and Steven Davies, while another, Roelof van der Merwe, has been let go.

IN: Migael Pretorius (SA), Matt Henry (NZ, CC/T20), Riley Meredith (Aus, T20)
OUT: Sonny Baker (Ham), Ned Leonard (Gla), George Thomas, Roelof van der Merwe (both REL), Jack Brooks, Steven Davies (both RET)

HEAD COACH: JASON KERR

The former Somerset allrounder has been on the coaching staff since 2005. Kerr was promoted from bowling coach to head coach in 2017 and works alongside director of cricket Andy Hurry. Somerset were Championship runners-up in Kerr's first two seasons in charge and won the One-Day Cup in 2019. He has led the club to T20 Finals Day in each of the last four seasons, winning the Blast in 2023. Jamie Cox, the former Tasmania and Somerset batter, is the club's chief executive.

Batting

	Mat	Inns	NO	Runs	HS	Ave	100	50	Ct	St
TB Abell	8	15	2	658	152*	50.61	3	2	8	
KL Aldridge	10	14	0	306	84	21.85	0	2	8	
JT Ball	6	7	3	43	29	10.75	0	0	0	
T Banton	12	19	1	891	133	49.50	2	5	11	
S Bashir	4	6	2	14	10*	3.50	0	0	1	
JH Davey	7	8	2	116	45	19.33	0	0	1	
SR Dickson	6	10	0	173	72	17.30	0	1	2	
LP Goldsworthy	5	8	0	191	58	23.87	0	1	4	
L Gregory	11	17	2	385	80	25.66	0	4	13	
T Kohler-Cadmore	5	9	0	233	63	25.88	0	1	2	
TA Lammonby	14	25	1	941	100	39.20	1	5	12	
MJ Leach	9	13	6	146	37	20.85	0	0	2	
EO Leonard	1	1	0	1	1	1.00	0	0	1	
ARJ Ogborne	1	2	1	2	1*	2.00	0	0	0	
C Overton	11	16	5	356	95*	32.36	0	2	13	
M Pretorius	8	11	1	324	95*	32.40	0	3	1	
BG Randell	2	4	0	13	9	3.25	0	0	0	
MT Renshaw	7	12	1	414	87	37.63	0	3	2	
JEK Rew	14	23	3	726	114	36.30	2	3	43	2
ARI Umeed	10	19	1	410	73*	22.77	0	2	7	
AM Vaughan	4	8	1	236	68	33.71	0	1	1	

Bowling

	Balls	Mdns	Runs	Wkts	BB	Ave	5w	10w
KL Aldridge	1201	19	851	24	5-64	35.45	2	0
JT Ball	851	24	498	15	5-62	33.20	1	0
T Banton	30	1	16	0				
S Bashir	678	22	377	4	2-97	94.25	0	0
JH Davey	948	29	496	16	4-80	31.00	0	0
LP Goldsworthy	270	4	203	5	2-73	40.60	0	0
L Gregory	1227	38	771	31	4-50	24.87	0	0
TA Lammonby	156	3	81	0				
MJ Leach	2372	102	1025	45	7-50	22.77	5	1
EO Leonard	120	2	92	1	1-47	92.00	0	0
ARJ Ogborne	84	6	32	1	1-12	32.00	0	0
C Overton	2125	77	1067	32	4-32	33.34	0	0
M Pretorius	1420	31	907	23	5-104	39.43	1	0
BG Randell	249	9	136	3	3-71	45.33	0	0
MT Renshaw	204	6	135	2	1-40	67.50	0	0
JEK Rew	6	0	1	0				
ARI Umeed	181	4	123	1	1-3	123.00	0	0
AM Vaughan	766	37	302	15	6-102	20.13	2	1

Catches/Stumpings:
45 Rew (2st), 13 Gregory, Overton, 12 Lammonby, 11 Banton, 8 Abell, Aldridge, 7 Umeed, 4 Goldsworthy, 2 Dickson, Kohler-Cadmore, Leach, Renshaw, 1 Bashir, Davey, Leonard, Pretorius, Vaughan

**SOMERSET
CCC**

Batting

	Mat	Inns	NO	Runs	HS	Ave	100	50	Ct	St
KL Aldridge	9	5	2	54	24	18.00	83.07	0	0	4
S Bashir	1	0								1
CAA Cassell	3	0								0
JH Davey	6	1	0	20	20	20.00	117.64	0	0	0
SR Dickson	10	8	1	238	86	34.00	133.70	0	1	4
LP Goldsworthy	10	10	2	427	115*	53.37	86.61	1	2	4
BGF Green	4	3	2	43	23*	43.00	134.37	0	0	2
JP Heywood	1	1	1	0	0*		0.00	0	0	0
MJ Leach	10	3	2	23	11	23.00	74.19	0	0	8
EO Leonard	4	1	0	28	28	28.00	175.00	0	0	2
RP Meredith	3	0								0
ARJ Ogborne	7	2	0	8	7	4.00	114.28	0	0	5
JEK Rew	10	10	3	464	88	66.28	101.08	0	6	14
GW Thomas	9	9	1	277	106*	34.62	73.08	1	0	4
JF Thomas	6	4	1	97	54*	32.33	93.26	0	1	0
ARI Umeed	10	10	1	492	114*	54.66	84.68	1	4	6
AM Vaughan	7	4	2	72	32*	36.00	116.12	0	0	1

Bowling

	Balls	Mdns	Runs	Wkts	BB	Ave	5w	10w
KL Aldridge	325	1	347	13	6-33	26.69	0	1
S Bashir	42	0	45	0				
CAA Cassell	84	1	90	0				
JH Davey	246	2	205	9	3-46	22.77	0	0
LP Goldsworthy	243	3	213	11	4-44	19.36	1	0
BGF Green	162	3	160	8	3-58	20.00	0	0
JP Heywood	6	0	20	0				
MJ Leach	489	5	333	15	6-26	22.20	0	1
EO Leonard	162	0	142	2	1-36	71.00	0	0
RP Meredith	150	1	128	6	4-27	21.33	1	0
ARJ Ogborne	291	5	259	10	3-58	25.90	0	0
GW Thomas	174	1	141	7	3-41	20.14	0	0
JF Thomas	30	0	23	0				
ARI Umeed	12	0	6	1	1-6	6.00	0	0
AM Vaughan	90	0	63	3	1-7	21.00	0	0

Catches/Stumpings:
14 Rew, 8 Leach, 6 Umeed, 5 Ogbourne, 4 Aldridge, Dickson, Goldsworthy, Thomas, 2 Green, Leonard, 1 Bashir, Vaughan

SOMERSET CCC

	Mat	Inns	NO	Runs	HS	Ave	100	50	Ct	St
TB Abell	16	13	2	352	96*	32.00	138.58	0	2	11
S Baker	1	0								1
JT Ball	13	3	0	8	8	2.66	66.66	0	0	5
T Banton	14	14	3	515	79*	46.81	151.02	0	4	5
JH Davey	8	1	1	4	4*		50.00	0	0	3
SR Dickson	16	14	4	333	78	33.30	152.75	0	2	13
BGF Green	16	9	3	74	47	12.33	125.42	0	0	3
L Gregory	15	13	5	216	53	27.00	168.75	0	1	6
T Kohler-Cadmore	16	16	2	386	63	27.57	140.87	0	2	4
TA Lammonby	1	1	0	19	19	19.00	100.00	0	0	3
MJ Leach	5	1	0	0	0	0.00	0.00	0	0	2
RP Meredith	12	3	2	6	6*	6.00	150.00	0	0	0
C Overton	12	6	3	60	42	20.00	136.36	0	0	8
M Pretorius	1	0								0
JEK Rew	2	2	1	68	62*	68.00	130.76	0	1	0
WCF Smeed	12	12	0	260	86	21.66	175.67	0	2	5
GW Thomas	4	4	0	127	42	31.75	135.10	0	0	1
RE van der Merwe	12	4	2	28	21*	14.00	116.66	0	0	6

Batting

	Balls	Mdns	Runs	Wkts	BB	Ave	5w	10w
S Baker	24	6	44	1	1-44	44.00	0	0
JT Ball	264	84	395	15	2-9	26.33	0	0
JH Davey	141	59	184	8	3-34	23.00	0	0
BGF Green	252	60	456	21	5-29	21.71	2	1
L Gregory	270	96	359	19	3-11	18.89	0	0
MJ Leach	90	27	126	6	2-23	21.00	0	0
RP Meredith	252	117	319	14	4-12	22.78	1	0
C Overton	258	114	350	9	2-21	38.88	0	0
M Pretorius	18	8	22	2	2-22	11.00	0	0
RE van der Merwe	148	42	238	6	2-0	39.66	0	0

Bowling

Catches/Stumpings:
13 Dickson, 11 Abell, 8 Overton, 6 Banton (1st), Gregory, van der Merwe, 5 Ball, Smeed, 4 Kohler-Cadmore, 3 Davey, Green, Lammonby, 2 Leach, 1 Baker, Thomas

TEAM PROFILE

SURREY
COUNTY CRICKET CLUB

FORMED: 1845
GROUND: The Kia Oval, London
CAPTAIN: Rory Burns (CC/ODC), Chris Jordan (T20)
2024 RESULTS: CC1: Winners; ODC: 8/9 Group B; T20: Semi-finalists
HONOURS: Championship: (23) 1890, 1891, 1892, 1894, 1895, 1899, 1914, 1950, 1952, 1953, 1954, 1955, 1956, 1957, 1958, 1971, 1999, 2000, 2002, 2018, 2022, 2023, 2024; Gillette/NatWest/C&G/FP Trophy: 1982; Benson & Hedges Cup: (3) 1974, 1997, 2001; Pro40/National League/CB40/YB40/ODC: (2) 2003, 2011; Sunday League: 1996; T20 Cup: 2003

THE LOWDOWN

Win the Championship for a fourth year running and even the grey-haired members will have to concede comparisons with the great Surrey side of the 1950s. Each year the Brown Hatters are the team everyone wants to beat, but few manage it. Somerset trumped them at Taunton last year to revive the title race, only for Surrey to progress serenely to the trophy thereafter. The international pedigree at The Oval is well-known, with the likes of Rory Burns, Dom Sibley and Dan Lawrence channelling their disappointment at losing their England status into a ruthless pursuit of domestic supremacy. But bowlers win matches and Surrey have a wicket machine in Aussie seamer Dan Worrall (52 at 16.15 last summer). Now 33, Worrall becomes eligible for England in April. Jordan Clark (38 scalps and 467 runs in 2024) continues to fly under the radar but, with Gus Atkinson on England's books, Surrey have boosted their bowling stocks with the additions of Matthew Fisher and Nathan Smith. Mitchell Santner has signed up as Surrey try for that elusive second T20 title following two consecutive Finals Day flops.

IN: Matthew Fisher (Yor), Nathan Smith (NZ, CC/T20), Mitchell Santner (NZ, T20)
OUT: Ben Geddes (Mid), Conor McKerr (Not), Amar Virdi (REL)

HEAD COACH: GARETH BATTY

Initially appointed on a short-term basis after Vikram Solanki left for the IPL ahead of the 2022 season, Batty has led Surrey to a hat-trick of Championship titles in his first three seasons as head coach, as well as two Finals Day appearances. The former England off-spinner retired in 2021 after a 24-year career. Alec Stewart has stepped down as director of cricket – the club do not intend to appoint a replacement – but has taken on a high-performance advisor role on a part-time basis.

COUNTY CHAMPIONSHIP AVERAGES 2024

	Mat	Inns	NO	Runs	HS	Ave	100	50	Ct	St
SA Abbott	4	6	1	118	50*	23.60	0	1	1	
AAP Atkinson	5	8	1	47	15	6.71	0	0	3	
JW Blake	1	1	1	38	38*		0	0	1	
RJ Burns	14	22	2	1073	227	53.65	3	5	3	
J Clark	13	17	3	467	106*	33.35	1	2	1	
SM Curran	2	2	0	16	8	8.00	0	0	0	
TK Curran	2	3	0	113	86	37.66	0	1	1	
BT Foakes	12	16	1	404	82	26.93	0	4	49	3
BBA Geddes	2	3	0	53	50	17.66	0	1	1	
WG Jacks	2	3	0	92	59	30.66	0	1	1	
TE Lawes	7	8	2	122	58	20.33	0	1	5	
DW Lawrence	11	14	1	617	175	47.46	2	3	8	
C McKerr	3	4	0	49	32	12.25	0	0	3	
Y Majid	1	1	0	5	5	5.00	0	0	0	
J Overton	2	2	0	38	35	19.00	0	0	7	
RS Patel	8	11	0	519	134	47.18	2	2	4	
OJD Pope	7	10	1	206	63	22.88	0	1	12	
KAJ Roach	8	7	3	37	19	9.25	0	0	3	
B Sai Sudharsan	3	5	0	165	105	33.00	1	0	2	
Shakib Al Hasan	1	2	0	12	12	6.00	0	0	0	
DP Sibley	14	22	3	832	150	43.78	3	3	13	
JL Smith	9	12	0	677	155	56.41	2	5	12	
CT Steel	8	10	2	138	43*	17.25	0	0	0	
OFM Sykes	1	1	0	0	0	0.00	0	0	0	
JPA Taylor	3	3	0	36	19	12.00	0	0	1	
DJ Worrall	11	14	8	93	48	15.50	0	0	2	

	Balls	Mdns	Runs	Wkts	BB	Ave	5w	10w
SA Abbott	612	22	317	10	2-50	31.70	0	0
AAP Atkinson	816	26	417	14	3-40	29.78	0	0
J Clark	1974	56	987	38	5-65	25.97	1	0
SM Curran	304	9	113	6	4-23	18.83	0	0
TK Curran	234	9	96	4	2-33	24.00	0	0
WG Jacks	389	6	188	7	7-129	26.85	1	0
TE Lawes	832	18	520	14	4-26	37.14	0	0
DW Lawrence	1028	17	609	15	4-91	40.60	0	0
C McKerr	228	4	128	6	4-27	21.33	0	0
Y Majid	180	0	128	2	2-128	64.00	0	0
J Overton	180	6	103	0				
RS Patel	72	1	41	3	3-41	13.66	0	0
KAJ Roach	1112	42	590	20	6-46	29.50	1	0
Shakib Al Hasan	380	8	193	9	5-96	21.44	1	0
CT Steel	1047	18	674	23	5-25	29.30	2	0
JPA Taylor	372	8	280	7	3-19	40.00	0	0
DJ Worrall	1987	77	840	52	6-22	16.15	2	1

Catches/Stumpings:
52 Foakes (3st), 13 Sibley, 12 Pope, Smith, 8 Lawrence, 7 Overton, 5 Lawes, 4 Patel, 3 Atkinson, Burns, McKerr, Roach, 2 Sudharsan, Worrall, 1 Abbott, Blake, Clark, T Curran, Geddes, Jacks, Taylor

SURREY
COUNTY CRICKET CLUB

Batting

	Mat	Inns	NO	Runs	HS	Ave	100	50	Ct	St
NA Barnwell	6	4	2	56	17	28.00	86.15	0	0	1
JW Blake	8	8	1	268	100*	38.28	98.16	1	2	10
RJ Burns	6	6	0	42	16	7.00	60.00	0	0	6
MP Dunn	2	2	1	13	13*	13.00	118.18	0	0	2
BT Foakes	5	5	0	131	44	26.20	71.58	0	0	4
BBA Geddes	8	8	0	269	81	33.62	92.75	0	3	3
C McKerr	8	7	1	179	71	29.83	122.60	0	1	2
Y Majid	8	6	1	17	7	3.40	41.46	0	0	2
RS Patel	8	8	0	363	87	45.37	81.94	0	3	4
DP Sibley	8	8	0	350	149	43.75	90.20	2	1	2
CT Steel	8	8	1	74	37	10.57	74.74	0	0	5
SH Stuart-Reckling	1	1	0	0	0	0.00	0.00	0	0	0
OFM Sykes	3	3	1	115	87*	57.50	125.00	0	1	0
JPA Taylor	7	5	4	25	10*	25.00	73.52	0	0	1
ARG Thomas	2	1	0	1	1	1.00	16.66	0	0	0

Bowling

	Balls	Mdns	Runs	Wkts	BB	Ave	5w	10w
NA Barnwell	243	0	279	2	1-23	139.50	0	0
MP Dunn	60	0	81	2	1-40	40.50	0	0
BBA Geddes	54	0	50	1	1-30	50.00	0	0
C McKerr	391	2	414	15	4-32	27.60	1	0
Y Majid	384	1	337	6	1-26	56.16	0	0
RS Patel	156	1	156	3	1-17	52.00	0	0
CT Steel	366	1	371	17	4-50	21.82	2	0
SH Stuart-Reckling	48	0	53	1	1-53	53.00	0	0
JPA Taylor	337	3	311	10	3-43	31.10	0	0

Catches/Stumpings:
14 Blake (4st), 6 Burns, 5 Steel, 4 Foakes, Patel, 3 Geddes, 2 Dunn, Majid, McKerr, Sibley, 1 Barnwell, Taylor

VITALITY BLAST AVERAGES 2024

SURREY
COUNTY CRICKET CLUB

Batting

	Mat	Inns	NO	Runs	HS	Ave	100	50	Ct	St
SA Abbott	8	6	1	45	24*	9.00	132.35	0	0	3
AAP Atkinson	8	5	4	14	10*	14.00	87.50	0	0	0
RJ Burns	10	9	1	150	62	18.75	122.95	0	1	4
J Clark	14	10	2	93	23	11.62	109.41	0	0	5
SM Curran	5	5	1	237	102*	59.25	153.89	1	2	1
TK Curran	9	9	2	140	48	20.00	157.30	0	0	0
MP Dunn	2	1	0	6	6	6.00	150.00	0	0	1
LJ Evans	15	15	1	279	41	19.92	146.07	0	0	4
BBA Geddes	1	1	1	7	7*		233.33	0	0	1
WG Jacks	5	5	0	129	86	25.80	167.53	0	1	1
SH Johnson	8	2	1	6	4*	6.00	100.00	0	0	5
CJ Jordan	7	6	2	35	14	8.75	92.10	0	0	3
TE Lawes	4	2	0	17	12	8.50	130.76	0	0	2
DW Lawrence	10	10	0	125	32	12.50	121.35	0	0	5
J Overton	5	5	2	71	30*	23.66	169.04	0	0	5
RS Patel	1	1	0	5	5	5.00	100.00	0	0	0
OJD Pope	9	8	1	224	99*	32.00	131.76	0	1	5
JJ Roy	5	5	0	122	55	24.40	119.60	0	1	5
DP Sibley	11	11	1	269	67	26.90	133.83	0	1	5
JL Smith	9	8	0	285	87	35.62	203.57	0	2	8
CT Steel	10	6	5	45	14*	45.00	125.00	0	0	5
DJ Worrall	6	2	2	2	1*		50.00	0	0	1

Bowling

	Balls	Mdns	Runs	Wkts	BB	Ave	5w	10w
SA Abbott	180	77	238	15	5-18	15.86	0	1
AAP Atkinson	175	73	248	10	3-19	24.80	0	0
J Clark	182	68	232	12	3-24	19.33	0	0
SM Curran	72	23	104	2	1-24	52.00	0	0
TK Curran	174	72	219	16	3-16	13.68	0	0
MP Dunn	36	12	61	4	2-21	15.25	0	0
WG Jacks	42	10	59	1	1-19	59.00	0	0
SH Johnson	174	85	189	9	2-15	21.00	0	0
CJ Jordan	143	38	245	4	3-34	61.25	0	0
TE Lawes	60	14	135	2	1-21	67.50	0	0
DW Lawrence	156	55	176	10	2-20	17.60	0	0
CT Steel	144	38	226	6	2-29	37.66	0	0
RJW Topley	36	20	47	4	2-20	11.75	0	0
DJ Worrall	102	56	124	5	2-14	24.80	0	0

Catches/Stumpings:
8 Smith, 5 Clark, Johnson, Lawrence, Overton, Pope, Roy, Sibley, Steel, 4 Evans, 3 Abbott,
Burns, Jordan, 2 Lawes, 1 Burns, S Curran, Dunn, Geddes, Jacks, Worrall

TEAM PROFILE

FORMED: 1839

HOME GROUND: The 1st Central County Ground, Hove

ONE-DAY NAME: Sussex Sharks

CAPTAIN: John Simpson (CC/ODC), Tymal Mills (T20)

2024 RESULTS: CC2: Winners; ODC: 9/9 Group B; T20: Semi-finalists

HONOURS: Championship: (3) 2003, 2006, 2007; Gillette/NatWest/C&G/FP Trophy: (5) 1963, 1964, 1978, 1986, 2006; Pro40/National League/CB40/YB40/ODC: (2) 2008, 2009; Sunday League: 1982; T20 Cup: 2009

THE LOWDOWN

The Sussex rebuild continues apace under head coach Paul Farbrace and – after a stellar year in which they reached Finals Day and topped Division Two – the challenge for the Sharks is to swim with the big fish of the Championship's elite. Brought to Hove a year ago after 15 summers at Middlesex, John Simpson was an inspired choice as four-day skipper, leading the way with 1,197 runs, the highest season's tally of his career. At the other end of the age spectrum, there were notable contributions from the club's Academy graduates, including another impressive all-round season for 20-year-old James Coles. Off-spinner Jack Carson took 50 wickets at 22.46. Sussex welcome back four of their overseas players who did so well for the club in 2024, with Jayden Seales and Jaydev Unadkat bookending the season, Nathan McAndrew returning for a mid-summer stint, and Daniel Hughes locked in from April to September. They can also count on the class of Ollie Robinson, who reacted to being dropped by England with 39 wickets in the Championship as well as unexpectedly strong showings in the Blast.

IN: Daniel Hughes, Nathan McAndrew, Gurinder Sandhu (all Aus, CC/T20), Jayden Seales (WI, CC), Jaydev Unadkat (Ind, CC)

OUT: (none)

HEAD COACH: PAUL FARBRACE

The 57-year-old made his name as a coach following a career as a keeper for Middlesex and Kent between 1987 and 1995. He has twice worked as assistant coach to Trevor Bayliss, first with Sri Lanka (2007-09) and then England (2015-19). Farbrace was also head coach of the Sri Lanka team which won the T20 World Cup in 2014. At domestic level he had a two-year spell in charge of Kent and won the Championship as Warwickshire's director of cricket.

COUNTY CHAMPIONSHIP AVERAGES 2024

	Mat	Inns	NO	Runs	HS	Ave	100	50	Ct	St
TP Alsop	14	20	2	799	86*	44.38	0	8	15	
JJ Carson	14	18	0	458	97	25.44	0	3	10	
OJ Carter	5	7	0	205	96	29.28	0	1	5	
TGR Clark	12	16	1	366	112*	24.40	1	1	12	
JM Coles	14	20	2	707	132*	39.27	1	3	15	
HT Crocombe	4	2	0	64	54	32.00	0	1	2	
AM Foreman	1	1	0	2	2	2.00	0	0	0	
TJ Haines	14	20	0	819	133	40.95	3	2	16	
FJ Hudson-Prentice	13	18	0	401	73	22.27	0	2	6	
DP Hughes	4	6	0	340	144	56.66	1	2	4	
SF Hunt	4	8	4	74	65	18.50	0	1	1	
A Karvelas	2	3	1	109	55	54.50	0	1	0	
DJ Lamb	8	11	1	375	134	37.50	1	1	2	
NJ McAndrew	2	3	0	77	53	25.66	0	1	0	
CA Pujara	6	9	1	501	129	62.62	2	1	0	
OE Robinson	12	14	6	158	32*	19.75	0	0	2	
JNT Seales	6	5	2	33	17	11.00	0	0	0	
JA Simpson	14	20	4	1197	205*	74.81	5	4	42	2
JD Unadkat	5	4	0	4	4	1.00	0	0	1	

	Balls	Mdns	Runs	Wkts	BB	Ave	5w	10w
TP Alsop	24	0	22	0				
JJ Carson	2113	73	1123	50	6-67	22.46	3	1
TGR Clark	304	6	183	9	3-17	20.33	0	0
JM Coles	996	21	642	18	4-61	35.66	0	0
HT Crocombe	389	10	255	11	4-22	23.18	0	0
AM Foreman	72	1	36	0				
TJ Haines	198	4	109	1	1-16	109.00	0	0
FJ Hudson-Prentice	1241	42	702	18	5-50	39.00	1	0
SF Hunt	441	10	325	13	4-64	25.00	0	0
A Karvelas	221	3	194	3	1-33	64.66	0	0
DJ Lamb	912	24	519	13	3-69	39.92	0	0
NJ McAndrew	306	8	187	11	5-73	17.00	1	0
OE Robinson	2060	97	996	39	4-42	25.53	0	0
JNT Seales	1012	30	582	24	5-29	24.25	2	0
JD Unadkat	708	34	317	22	4-32	14.40	0	0

Catches/Stumpings:
44 Simpson (2st), 16 Haines, 15 Alsop, Coles, 12 Clark, 10 Carson, 6 Hudson-Prentice, 5 Carter, 4 Hughes, 2 Crocombe, Lamb, Robinson, 1 Hunt, Unadkat

SUSSEX SHARKS

Batting

	Mat	Inns	NO	Runs	HS	Ave	100	50	Ct	St
TP Alsop	2	2	1	112	108*	112.00	79.43	1	0	0
JOI Campbell	4	4	3	11	5*	11.00	73.33	0	0	0
JJ Carson	3	2	0	18	11	9.00	94.73	0	0	1
OJ Carter	7	7	0	99	43	14.14	65.56	0	0	1
TGR Clark	8	8	0	227	72	28.37	81.36	0	2	1
HT Crocombe	6	4	3	56	43*	56.00	88.88	0	0	4
AM Foreman	5	5	0	127	48	25.40	60.76	0	0	1
TJ Haines	7	7	0	326	129	46.57	83.37	1	1	4
FJ Hudson-Prentice	3	3	0	101	90	33.66	78.29	0	1	0
SF Hunt	2	2	1	16	8*	16.00	57.14	0	0	0
DK Ibrahim	7	6	0	60	30	10.00	59.40	0	0	3
A Karvelas	5	5	0	25	9	5.00	73.52	0	0	0
AD Lenham	7	6	1	71	31	14.20	62.28	0	0	1
ZB Lion-Cachet	5	5	0	58	27	11.60	50.43	0	0	2
OE Robinson	1	0								1
HP Rogers	6	6	1	75	35	15.00	63.55	0	0	1
JA Simpson	5	5	1	171	85	42.75	111.76	0	2	6
CJ Tear	5	5	0	76	43	15.20	61.29	0	0	5

Bowling

	Balls	Mdns	Runs	Wkts	BB	Ave	5w	10w
JOI Campbell	177	1	173	3	1-33	57.66	0	0
JJ Carson	157	2	138	4	2-49	34.50	0	0
TGR Clark	114	2	119	1	1-17	119.00	0	0
HT Crocombe	298	2	250	10	4-47	25.00	1	0
AM Foreman	198	4	146	2	1-31	73.00	0	0
TJ Haines	60	1	50	1	1-22	50.00	0	0
FJ Hudson-Prentice	144	1	110	4	3-34	27.50	0	0
SF Hunt	78	0	82	2	2-32	41.00	0	0
DK Ibrahim	234	0	168	4	3-34	42.00	0	0
A Karvelas	228	2	236	6	2-43	39.33	0	0
AD Lenham	316	1	243	8	3-29	30.37	0	0
ZB Lion-Cachet	32	0	27	1	1-10	27.00	0	0
OE Robinson	46	1	40	3	3-40	13.33	0	0

Catches/Stumpings:
6 Simpson, 5 Tear, 4 Crocombe, Haines, 3 Ibrahim, 2 Lion-Catchet, 1 Carson, Carter, Clark, Foreman, Lenham, Robinson, Rogers

SUSSEX
SHARKS

	Mat	Inns	NO	Runs	HS	Ave	100	50	Ct	St
TP Alsop	16	13	3	337	87*	33.70	164.39	0	2	8
JC Archer	1	0								1
JJ Carson	12	5	2	68	26	22.66	117.24	0	0	5
OJ Carter	4	4	0	39	33	9.75	84.78	0	0	3
TGR Clark	8	8	3	179	72*	35.80	123.44	0	1	10
JM Coles	16	14	3	354	69*	32.18	142.74	0	2	5
BJ Currie	5	1	1	1	1*		12.50	0	0	1
FJ Hudson-Prentice	10	9	1	125	47	15.62	113.63	0	0	10
DP Hughes	16	16	1	596	96*	39.73	167.88	0	5	8
A Karvelas	1	1	1	4	4*		200.00	0	0	0
DJ Lamb	12	8	0	147	40	18.37	123.52	0	0	4
AD Lenham	3	0								0
NJ McAndrew	13	10	6	157	32*	39.25	201.28	0	0	5
TS Mills	15	4	3	2	1*	2.00	100.00	0	0	0
OE Robinson	15	6	2	71	20	17.75	131.48	0	0	4
JA Simpson	16	12	2	204	53*	20.40	125.92	0	1	6
HD Ward	13	13	0	350	68	26.92	157.65	0	3	2

Batting

	Balls	Mdns	Runs	Wkts	BB	Ave	5w	10w
JC Archer	21	13	20	2	2-20	10.00	0	0
JJ Carson	108	29	176	10	2-10	17.60	0	0
JM Coles	312	102	414	20	4-12	20.70	2	0
BJ Currie	90	38	118	6	2-16	19.66	0	0
FJ Hudson-Prentice	60	16	101	2	2-28	50.50	0	0
A Karvelas	18	3	46	0				
DJ Lamb	207	46	374	8	3-36	46.75	0	0
AD Lenham	42	10	70	1	1-35	70.00	0	0
NJ McAndrew	263	88	432	14	3-32	30.85	0	0
TS Mills	348	126	468	24	4-25	19.50	3	0
OE Robinson	336	157	390	18	3-27	21.66	0	0

Bowling

Catches/Stumpings:
10 Clark, Hudson-Prentice, 8 Alsop, Hughes, 7 Simpson (1st), 5 Carson, Coles, McAndrew, 4
Lamb, Robinson, 3 Carter, 2 Ward, 1 Archer, Currie

TEAM PROFILE

FORMED: 1882

HOME GROUND: Edgbaston Stadium, Birmingham

T20 NAME: Birmingham Bears

CAPTAIN: Alex Davies (CC), Ed Barnard (ODC),
Moeen Ali (T20)

2024 RESULTS: CC1: 7/10; ODC: Semi-finalists; T20:
Quarter-finalists

HONOURS: Championship: (8) 1911, 1951, 1972, 1994,
1995, 2004, 2012, 2021; Bob Willis Trophy: 2021; Gillette/
NatWest/C&G/FP Trophy: (5) 1966, 1968, 1989, 1993,
1995; Benson & Hedges Cup: (2) 1994, 2002; Pro40/
National League/CB40/YB40/ODC: (2) 2010, 2016;
Sunday League: (3) 1980, 1994, 1997; T20 Cup: 2014

THE LOWDOWN

Following a dismal four-day campaign tinged with white-ball disappointment, and much grumbling among members, the pressure finally told on Mark Robinson in February when the club promoted his assistant, Ian Westwood, to replace him as head coach. It wasn't the ideal start for Alex Davies, the Championship skipper who nevertheless handsomely passed 1,000 runs in his first season at the helm. There's plenty of talent in the batting – featuring the likes of Jacob Bethell, Rob Yates and Dan Mousley, with Tom Latham signed for the whole season – but the bowling came up short last summer. The exception, as ever, was Oliver Hannon-Dalby, who took 50 Championship wickets but lacked support from the other end, with Chris Rushworth and Hasan Ali both waylaid by injury. Hasan returns this summer to make amends and proven pacer Ethan Bamber has joined from Middlesex, while Beau Webster is available in the heart of the summer. The departures of Will Rhodes and keeper Michael Burgess leave big shoes to fill. Moeen Ali retires after this summer's Blast – can the Bears get over their quarter-final curse and send him off in style?

IN: Ethan Bamber (Mid), Hasan Ali (Pak), Tom Latham (NZ), Vishwa Fernando (SL, CC), Beau Webster (CC/T20)

OUT: Chris Benjamin (Ken), Will Rhodes (Dur), Michael Burgess, Liam Norwell (both RET)

FIRST-TEAM COACH: IAN WESTWOOD

The 42-year-old former Bears captain replaces Mark Robinson, who he had been working alongside as assistant coach. Westwood's appointment was part of a broader backroom reshuffle, with Matt Walker joining as batting coach after leaving Kent and Tony Frost becoming head of cricket operations. James Thomas, director of performance services for Manchester City, has taken over the role of performance director from Gavin Larsen, who has returned to his native New Zealand after two years in the job.

Batting

	Mat	Inns	NO	Runs	HS	Ave	100	50	Ct	St
Aamer Jamal	2	3	0	67	40	22.33	0	0	0	
EG Barnard	14	22	1	840	165	40.00	2	5	6	
CG Benjamin	1	1	0	2	2	2.00	0	0	0	
JG Bethell	11	16	1	466	93	31.06	0	4	10	
MG Booth	4	4	1	49	31	16.33	0	0	1	
DR Briggs	8	9	0	160	51	17.77	0	1	4	
MGK Burgess	14	19	2	745	147	43.82	2	3	37	3
AL Davies	14	23	1	1115	256	50.68	4	3	10	
SR Hain	8	13	2	430	153*	39.09	2	0	5	
OJ Hannon-Dalby	14	17	10	35	8*	5.00	0	0	5	
Hasan Ali	3	3	0	38	29	12.66	0	0	2	
JB Lintott	1	1	0	9	9	9.00	0	0	1	
CN Miles	6	6	1	55	29	11.00	0	0	3	
DR Mousley	11	18	2	402	62	25.12	0	3	3	
MD Rae	5	7	0	56	28	8.00	0	0	0	
WMH Rhodes	14	23	2	1020	201	48.57	3	3	11	
C Rushworth	6	7	4	17	14	5.66	0	0	0	
H Shaikh	3	6	1	81	33*	16.20	0	0	1	
CB Simmons	1	2	0	25	17	12.50	0	0	1	
CR Woakes	2	4	0	47	39	11.75	0	0	0	
RM Yates	13	21	1	738	191	36.90	1	5	28	

Bowling

	Balls	Mdns	Runs	Wkts	BB	Ave	5w	10w
Aamer Jamal	198	2	142	1	1-79	142.00	0	0
EG Barnard	1534	39	910	25	5-54	36.40	1	0
JG Bethell	792	14	486	7	4-20	69.42	0	0
MG Booth	458	1	387	11	3-13	35.18	0	0
DR Briggs	1156	26	698	8	3-73	87.25	0	0
MGK Burgess	6	0	5	0				
OJ Hannon-Dalby	2283	88	1114	50	6-43	22.28	3	0
Hasan Ali	306	5	165	3	2-65	55.00	0	0
JB Lintott	41	1	18	3	3-10	6.00	0	0
CN Miles	627	7	445	14	5-43	31.78	1	0
DR Mousley	140	3	109	5	2-33	21.80	0	0
MD Rae	666	14	424	14	3-39	30.28	0	0
WMH Rhodes	840	27	473	10	2-36	47.30	0	0
C Rushworth	684	24	410	13	3-42	31.53	0	0
CB Simmons	122	3	71	5	3-12	14.20	0	0
CR Woakes	426	14	220	1	1-36	220.00	0	0
RM Yates	1092	22	620	16	4-37	38.75	0	0

Catches/Stumpings:
40 Burgess (3st), 28 Yates, 11 Rhodes, 10 Bethell, Davies, 6 Barnard, 5 Hain, Hannon-Dalby, 4 Briggs, 3 Miles, Mousley, 2 Ali, 1 Booth, Lintott, Shaikh, Simmons

	Mat	Inns	NO	Runs	HS	Ave	100	50	Ct	St
TC Ali	7	4	2	41	16*	20.50	56.94	0	0	4
EG Barnard	10	9	2	433	173*	61.85	100.93	2	0	1
CG Benjamin	10	7	1	210	75	35.00	90.51	0	1	6
MG Booth	9	5	0	60	35	12.00	90.90	0	0	0
MGK Burgess	10	8	1	264	85	37.71	91.66	0	3	8
OJ Hannon-Dalby	8	3	3	10	7*		83.33	0	0	3
JB Lintott	10	6	3	92	27	30.66	59.35	0	0	3
ZA Malik	2	2	0	2	1	1.00	22.22	0	0	1
CN Miles	3	0								2
MD Rae	3	2	0	8	8	4.00	114.28	0	0	0
WMH Rhodes	10	9	1	309	75	38.62	66.73	0	2	8
H Shaikh	8	7	1	131	39	21.83	69.68	0	0	2
K Smith	9	6	1	248	130*	49.60	114.28	1	0	3
TO Wylie	4	3	0	16	11	5.33	55.17	0	0	2
RM Yates	7	6	0	176	72	29.33	76.19	0	1	9

Batting

	Balls	Mdns	Runs	Wkts	BB	Ave	5w	10w
TC Ali	186	0	202	7	3-53	28.85	0	0
EG Barnard	417	7	298	19	4-21	15.68	2	0
MG Booth	400	0	372	13	3-16	28.61	0	0
OJ Hannon-Dalby	402	2	366	13	3-69	28.15	0	0
JB Lintott	433	1	409	10	3-38	40.90	0	0
CN Miles	118	0	132	4	3-16	33.00	0	0
MD Rae	156	0	104	5	3-54	20.80	0	0
WMH Rhodes	174	1	153	2	1-13	76.50	0	0
RM Yates	120	0	126	1	1-36	126.00	0	0

Bowling

Catches/Stumpings:
8 Burgess, Rhodes, Yates, 6 Benjamin, 4 Ali, 3 Hannon-Dalby, Lintott, Smith, 2 Barnard, Miles, Shaikh, Wylie, 1 Malik

www.edgbaston.com / tel: 0121 369 1994

BIRMINGHAM BEARS

	Mat	Inns	NO	Runs	HS	Ave	100	50	Ct	St
Aamer Jamal	1	1	0	0	0	0.00	0.00	0	0	0
MM Ali	6	5	0	205	103	41.00	161.41	1	1	3
EG Barnard	5	5	1	69	48	17.25	168.29	0	0	4
CG Benjamin	15	13	3	114	33	11.40	117.52	0	0	12
JG Bethell	15	12	2	361	71*	36.10	153.61	0	4	10
MG Booth	1	0								0
DR Briggs	15	6	5	34	13	34.00	130.76	0	0	8
AL Davies	14	14	0	240	47	17.14	137.14	0	0	7
ZG Foulkes	7	3	0	7	6	2.33	140.00	0	0	0
GHS Garton	14	9	4	105	29*	21.00	141.89	0	0	3
RJ Gleeson	7	2	2	0	0*		0.00	0	0	1
SR Hain	14	13	4	569	98*	63.22	137.43	0	6	10
Hasan Ali	5	3	1	23	17*	11.50	135.29	0	0	0
JB Lintott	15	4	0	5	3	1.25	50.00	0	0	9
CN Miles	6	0								6
DR Mousley	15	15	3	385	68	32.08	136.52	0	3	10
CR Woakes	2	1	0	6	6	6.00	50.00	0	0	2
RM Yates	8	8	1	143	68	20.42	133.64	0	1	8

Batting

	Balls	Mdns	Runs	Wkts	BB	Ave	5w	10w
Aamer Jamal	6	1	25	0				
MM Ali	44	12	62	5	2-2	12.40	0	0
EG Barnard	5	2	11	0				
JG Bethell	76	31	86	6	2-5	14.33	0	0
MG Booth	6	4	11	1	1-11	11.00	0	0
DR Briggs	348	132	370	29	3-24	12.75	0	0
ZG Foulkes	120	46	185	8	3-22	23.12	0	0
GHS Garton	186	87	280	13	3-41	21.53	0	0
RJ Gleeson	144	71	116	9	2-2	12.88	0	0
Hasan Ali	97	39	153	10	3-20	15.30	0	0
JB Lintott	282	80	372	18	3-15	20.66	0	0
CN Miles	80	31	124	7	2-12	17.71	0	0
DR Mousley	292	102	330	15	3-22	22.00	0	0
CR Woakes	36	12	57	1	1-21	57.00	0	0

Bowling

Catches/Stumpings:
13 Davies (6st), Mousley, 10 Benjamin, Bethell, Hain, 9 Lintott, 8 Briggs, Yates, 6 Miles, 4 Barnard, Garton, 3 M Ali, 2 Woakes, 1 Gleeson

TEAM PROFILE

FORMED: 1865
HOME GROUND: Visit Worcestershire New Road, Worcester
ONE-DAY NAME: Worcestershire Rapids
CAPTAIN: Brett D'Oliveira (CC/T20), Jake Libby (ODC)
2024 RESULTS: CC1: 6/10; ODC: Quarter-finalists; T20: 8/9 North Group
HONOURS: Championship: (5) 1964, 1965, 1974, 1988, 1989; Gillette/NatWest/C&G/FP Trophy: 1994; Benson & Hedges Cup: 1991; Pro40/National League/CB40/YB40/ODC: 2007; Sunday League: (3) 1971, 1987, 1988; T20 Cup: 2018

THE LOWDOWN

Avoiding relegation on their return to Division One last summer was an impressive achievement for Worcestershire, especially as their neighbours had just poached three of their brightest talents – Dillon Pennington, Josh Tongue and Jack Haynes. And they made the 50-over knockouts too (only to lose to those Bears!). But it was all overshadowed by the announcement that one of their own, Josh Baker, a left-arm spinner, had died of a heart condition on May 2 aged 20. The players wore his number, 33, on their backs for the rest of the season. Baker will still be in everybody's thoughts as Worcestershire look to defy the odds and stay up once more. Kashif Ali, a graduate from the South Asian Cricket Academy, was the bright spot of the batting last year, although it was a concern that no one topped his 767 runs. With Joe Leach retired – 469 wickets at 27.16 for the Pears – the pace attack is full of new faces with plenty to prove. Jacob Duffy, the experienced Kiwi seamer, is on board for the first three months of the season.

IN: Ben Allison (Ess), Fateh Singh (Not), Jacob Duffy (NZ, CC/T20), Ben Dwarshuis (Aus, T20)
OUT: Josh Cobb (REL), Joe Leach (RET)

FIRST-TEAM COACH: ALAN RICHARDSON

The former Staffordshire seamer was appointed to replace Alex Gidman in November 2022. Richardson had successful spells for Middlesex and Warwickshire but his greatest days were at New Road when he was well into his 30s, taking 254 wickets in four seasons for the Pears before retiring in 2013. He spent four years as Warwickshire's bowling coach before taking up the same role at Worcestershire in 2018 and has also worked in the England set-up. Ashley Giles was appointed chief executive in 2023.

www.wccc.co.uk / tel: 01905 748474

Batting

	Mat	Inns	NO	Runs	HS	Ave	100	50	Ct	St
BMJ Allison	2	3	0	28	21	9.33	0	0	0	
JO Baker	2	3	0	19	9	6.33	0	0	2	
S Bashir	1	2	1	8	8	8.00	0	0	2	
EA Brookes	7	12	1	345	132	31.36	1	1	6	
BL D'Oliveira	12	17	1	518	97	32.37	0	6	3	
AW Finch	7	9	2	121	43	17.28	0	0	0	
BJ Gibbon	4	3	1	80	75	40.00	0	1	2	
JW Hartshorn	1	1	1	12	12*		0	0	0	
JO Holder	5	6	1	186	123*	37.20	1	0	7	
JE Home	2	3	2	45	29	45.00	0	0	1	
AJ Hose	14	22	1	526	90	25.04	0	4	11	
RP Jones	13	22	1	456	90	21.71	0	1	17	
Kashif Ali	12	20	2	767	133	42.61	2	5	2	
J Leach	11	16	4	169	48*	14.08	0	0	1	
JD Libby	14	23	1	710	101*	32.27	1	6	3	
EJ Pollock	1	1	0	1	1	1.00	0	0	0	
GH Roderick	14	23	0	695	122	30.21	2	4	46	
NG Smith	7	8	1	214	60	30.57	0	3	3	
TAI Taylor	6	9	3	141	62*	23.50	0	1	0	
LV van Beek	4	7	1	144	48	24.00	0	0	1	
GS Virdi	4	6	2	63	42	15.75	0	0	2	
MJ Waite	10	14	1	433	100*	33.30	1	3	3	
Yadvinder Singh	1	2	1	14	14*	14.00	0	0	0	

Bowling

	Balls	Mdns	Runs	Wkts	BB	Ave	5w	10w
BMJ Allison	302	12	142	7	3-57	20.28	0	0
JO Baker	414	10	222	4	2-55	55.50	0	0
S Bashir	228	2	162	2	2-162	81.00	0	0
EA Brookes	528	23	250	8	3-34	31.25	0	0
BL D'Oliveira	516	10	235	4	1-15	58.75	0	0
AW Finch	875	19	621	17	3-37	36.52	0	0
BJ Gibbon	613	16	347	8	3-102	43.37	0	0
JW Hartshorn	180	9	89	3	2-71	29.66	0	0
JO Holder	727	28	399	9	3-47	44.33	0	0
JE Home	102	1	78	1	1-25	78.00	0	0
RP Jones	6	0	1	0				
Kashif Ali	206	1	145	2	2-13	72.50	0	0
J Leach	1744	61	903	27	6-52	33.44	1	0
JD Libby	108	1	39	0				
NG Smith	1071	36	571	27	4-29	21.14	0	0
TAI Taylor	966	20	580	27	6-28	21.48	1	0
LV van Beek	546	7	374	13	4-26	28.76	0	0
GS Virdi	820	14	469	14	5-133	33.50	1	0
MJ Waite	1266	46	618	19	3-19	32.52	0	0
Yadvinder Singh	165	1	146	4	4-103	36.50	0	0

Catches/Stumpings:
46 Roderick, 17 Jones, 11 Hose, 7 Holder, 6 Brookes, 3 D'Oliveira, Libby, Smith, Waite, 2 Ali, Baker, Bashir, Gibbon, Virdi, 1 Home, Leach, van Beek

Batting

	Mat	Inns	NO	Runs	HS	Ave	100	50	Ct	St
EA Brookes	9	7	0	113	33	16.14	71.97	0	0	4
JJ Cobb	1	1	0	8	8	8.00	40.00	0	0	0
HC Darley	7	5	3	9	8	4.50	21.95	0	0	1
RM Edavalath	7	4	0	22	15	5.50	57.89	0	0	1
TI Hinley	9	6	1	96	32	19.20	154.83	0	0	7
JE Home	5	1	1	5	5*		166.66	0	0	0
AJ Hose	1	1	0	13	13	13.00	56.52	0	0	0
RP Jones	9	9	2	177	57	25.28	59.00	0	1	6
HM Khan	6	3	2	18	15*	18.00	81.81	0	0	3
JD Libby	9	9	4	526	112	105.20	85.38	1	5	3
EJ Pollock	9	9	0	387	180	43.00	109.63	1	2	3
GH Roderick	9	9	1	405	152*	50.62	82.31	2	0	19
F Singh	8	6	0	131	60	21.83	125.96	0	1	1
TG Sturgess	5	2	0	9	8	4.50	75.00	0	0	0
TAI Taylor	5	5	0	224	73	44.80	99.55	0	2	2

Bowling

	Balls	Mdns	Runs	Wkts	BB	Ave	5w	10w
EA Brookes	400	1	241	6	2-15	40.16	0	0
HC Darley	258	3	270	6	3-45	45.00	0	0
TI Hinley	411	1	373	13	5-56	28.69	0	1
JE Home	226	1	231	16	6-51	14.43	0	1
HM Khan	225	0	233	4	2-44	58.25	0	0
JD Libby	9	0	19	1	1-9	19.00	0	0
F Singh	438	2	362	15	4-52	24.13	1	0
TG Sturgess	154	1	135	5	3-37	27.00	0	0
TAI Taylor	264	3	209	8	3-14	26.12	0	0

Catches/Stumpings:
23 Roderick (4st), 7 Hinley, 6 Jones, 4 Brookes, 3 Khan, Libby, Pollock, 2 Taylor, 1 Darley, Edavalath, Singh

www.wccc.co.uk / tel: 01905 748474

	Mat	Inns	NO	Runs	HS	Ave	100	50	Ct	St
S Bashir	2	1	1	0	0*		0.00	0	0	0
EA Brookes	14	14	2	315	44	26.25	145.83	0	0	5
JJ Cobb	12	12	0	271	74	22.58	130.28	0	1	4
HJ Cullen	1	1	0	0	0	0.00	0.00	0	0	1
HC Darley	4	0								0
BL D'Oliveira	11	11	0	225	61	20.45	114.21	0	1	2
AW Finch	9	3	2	11	6*	11.00	68.75	0	0	2
JE Home	1	1	1	1	1*		100.00	0	0	0
AJ Hose	12	12	1	290	63	26.36	130.04	0	1	5
RP Jones	6	5	2	79	35*	26.33	105.33	0	0	4
Kashif Ali	5	5	0	156	46	31.20	157.57	0	0	0
JD Libby	2	2	1	17	16	17.00	130.76	0	0	1
EJ Pollock	14	13	4	184	67	20.44	135.29	0	1	3
GH Roderick	14	11	1	181	39	18.10	143.65	0	0	9
NG Smith	9	8	2	144	51*	24.00	132.11	0	1	5
TAI Taylor	14	11	5	96	21*	16.00	104.34	0	0	11
MJ Waite	11	9	1	149	40	18.62	139.25	0	0	0
HR Walsh	13	6	2	31	12*	7.75	134.78	0	0	1

Batting

	Balls	Mdns	Runs	Wkts	BB	Ave	5w	10w
S Bashir	36	10	52	2	2-38	26.00	0	0
EA Brookes	174	47	238	11	4-41	21.63	1	0
JJ Cobb	114	31	158	2	1-19	79.00	0	0
HC Darley	66	19	98	4	2-11	24.50	0	0
BL D'Oliveira	150	30	220	6	2-24	36.66	0	0
AW Finch	192	69	267	9	3-43	29.66	0	0
JE Home	24	10	33	1	1-33	33.00	0	0
NG Smith	174	66	242	8	3-39	30.25	0	0
TAI Taylor	286	98	433	17	3-31	25.47	0	0
MJ Waite	90	40	130	12	5-21	10.83	1	1
HR Walsh	248	67	302	6	2-16	50.33	0	0

Bowling

Catches/Stumpings:
11 Taylor, 10 Roderick (1st), 5 Brookes, Hose, Smith, 4 Cobb, Jones, 3 Pollock, 2 D'Oliveira, Finch, 1 Cullen, Libby, Walsh

THE YORKSHIRE
COUNTY CRICKET CLUB

FORMED: 1863

HOME GROUND: Headingley Stadium, Leeds

ONE-DAY NAME: Yorkshire Vikings

CAPTAIN: TBC

2024 RESULTS: CC2: 2/8; ODC: 6/9 Group B; T20: 7/9 North Group

HONOURS: County Championship: (33) 1893, 1896, 1898, 1900, 1901, 1902, 1905, 1908, 1912, 1919, 1922, 1923, 1924, 1925, 1931, 1932, 1933, 1935, 1937, 1938, 1939, 1946, 1949, 1959, 1960, 1962, 1963, 1966, 1967, 1968, 2001, 2014, 2015; Gillette/NatWest/C&G/FP Trophy: (3) 1965, 1969, 2002; Benson & Hedges Cup: 1987; Sunday League: 1983

THE LOWDOWN

Back in Division One, and able to smirk at relegated Lancashire on their way up, but there has been quite a shake-up east of the Pennines. Ottis Gibson left after three years as head coach in which he navigated the club through exceptionally choppy waters, replaced by a homegrown stalwart, Anthony McGrath, who returns to Headingley as part of a revamped coaching team. By early March there was still no confirmation if skipper Shan Masood would be coming back. Last summer Masood managed eight Championship outings between his international commitments but the batting standout was the old master Adam Lyth, who notched 1,215 runs to take him within touching distance of 15,000 for the club. James Wharton confirmed his talent with two centuries, including 285 against Northants in late September, while George Hill looked the real deal as an allrounder with 600 runs and 27 wickets. Ben Coad leads a pace attack which has lost Matthew Fisher to Surrey but gained Jack White from Northants, with Aussie quick Jordan Buckingham signed for four matches in May and compatriot Will Sutherland combining formats in mid-season.

IN: Jack White (Nor), Jordan Buckingham (Aus, CC), Will Sutherland (Aus, CC/T20), Will O'Rourke (NZ, T20)
OUT: Matthew Fisher (Sur), Dom Leech (Nor), Micky Edwards (RET)

HEAD COACH: ANTHONY MCGRATH

McGrath scored more than 23,000 runs and took 240 wickets for Yorkshire, also appearing in four Tests and 14 ODIs. He was assistant coach to Chris Silverwood at Essex when they won the Championship in 2017 and went on to win four trophies in seven seasons as the club's head coach. Bowling coach Mick Lewis has also joined from Chelmsford, with John Sadler appointed batting coach after leaving Northants. Gavin Hamilton, the former allrounder, has rejoined the club as general manager.

	Mat	Inns	NO	Runs	HS	Ave	100	50	Ct	St	
JM Bairstow	5	7	0	321	160	45.85	1	2	11		
FJ Bean	14	22	0	746	173	33.90	2	2	22		
DM Bess	6	7	2	203	60*	40.60	0	2	5		
HC Brook	5	7	2	388	126*	77.60	2	2	5		
BO Coad	12	10	2	119	38	14.87	0	0	1		
MW Edwards	1	2	2	6	6*		0	0	0		
MVT Fernando	3	3	3	4	4*		0	0	0		
MD Fisher	7	4	0	133	88	33.25	0	1	2		
GCH Hill	13	18	2	608	169*	38.00	1	4	13		Batting
DJ Leech	2	4	2	0	0	0.00	0	0	1		
WA Luxton	6	9	2	195	59	27.85	0	1	1		
A Lyth	14	22	1	1215	147	57.85	5	5	21		
C McKerr	1	1	0	17	17	17.00	0	0	0		
ME Milnes	2	3	2	65	51	65.00	0	1	1		
DT Moriarty	8	8	3	56	17	11.20	0	0	0		
ML Revis	7	8	3	96	34	19.20	0	0	3		
JE Root	5	8	0	442	156	55.25	2	2	4		
Shan Masood	8	12	1	520	140	47.27	2	1	3		
JA Tattersall	14	20	4	643	126	40.18	2	2	28	1	
JA Thompson	12	14	2	277	56*	23.08	0	2	5		
JH Wharton	9	14	1	833	285	64.07	2	2	7		

	Balls	Mdns	Runs	Wkts	BB	Ave	5w	10w	
DM Bess	862	28	377	14	7-179	26.92	1	0	
HC Brook	22	0	22	0					
BO Coad	2007	79	885	56	6-30	15.80	3	0	
MW Edwards	84	0	71	1	1-61	71.00	0	0	
MVT Fernando	443	18	227	17	5-30	13.35	1	0	
MD Fisher	1107	50	601	27	4-55	22.25	0	0	
GCH Hill	1312	57	631	27	6-59	23.37	1	0	Bowling
DJ Leech	174	2	136	3	1-12	45.33	0	0	
A Lyth	326	5	188	8	4-56	23.50	0	0	
C McKerr	175	7	76	5	3-48	15.20	0	0	
ME Milnes	231	9	148	6	4-73	24.66	0	0	
DT Moriarty	1596	48	769	12	4-74	64.08	0	0	
ML Revis	767	21	445	11	3-30	40.45	0	0	
JE Root	490	22	243	5	3-78	48.60	0	0	
JA Thompson	1589	46	985	32	5-80	30.78	1	0	
JH Wharton	12	0	14	0					

Catches/Stumpings:
29 Tattersall (1st), 22 Bean, 21 Lyth, 13 Hill, 11 Bairstow, 7 Wharton, 5 Bess, Brook, Thompson, 4 Root, 3 Masood, Revis, 2 Fisher, 1 Coad, Leech, Luxton, Milnes

Batting

	Mat	Inns	NO	Runs	HS	Ave	100	50	Ct	St
FJ Bean	7	7	0	78	37	11.14	67.82	0	0	4
DM Bess	8	7	1	176	60	29.33	99.43	0	2	3
BM Cliff	6	3	2	3	2	3.00	30.00	0	0	1
BO Coad	6	4	1	68	31	22.66	103.03	0	0	1
HG Duke	8	8	1	114	60	16.28	61.95	0	1	7
GCH Hill	8	7	0	79	51	11.28	74.52	0	1	3
NM Kelly	1	1	0	3	3	3.00	15.78	0	0	1
DJ Leech	4	3	1	32	21	16.00	54.23	0	0	0
WA Luxton	8	8	1	247	105*	35.28	78.16	1	1	5
DT Moriarty	8	4	2	40	16*	20.00	55.55	0	0	1
ML Revis	8	8	3	232	55*	46.40	92.06	0	2	3
Shan Masood	6	6	0	235	76	39.16	91.79	0	3	1
JA Tattersall	2	2	0	60	51	30.00	72.28	0	1	3
YV Vagadia	2	2	0	22	21	11.00	62.85	0	0	1
JH Wharton	6	6	0	231	71	38.50	70.00	0	2	7

Bowling

	Balls	Mdns	Runs	Wkts	BB	Ave	5w	10w
DM Bess	264	0	229	7	3-26	32.71	0	0
BM Cliff	238	2	231	8	3-37	28.87	0	0
BO Coad	342	7	174	12	4-14	14.50	1	0
GCH Hill	388	4	300	17	6-28	17.64	0	1
DJ Leech	150	1	161	6	3-48	26.83	0	0
DT Moriarty	384	3	325	9	3-47	36.11	0	0
ML Revis	288	0	290	6	2-40	48.33	0	0

Catches/Stumpings:
7 Duke, Wharton, 5 Luxton, 4 Bean, 3 Bess, Hill, Revis, Tattersall, 1 Cliff, Coad, Kelly, Masood, Moriarty, Vagadia

	Mat	Inns	NO	Runs	HS	Ave	100	50	Ct	St
DM Bess	13	8	2	68	28	11.33	101.49	0	0	6
JA Chohan	10	4	1	19	15*	6.33	118.75	0	0	1
BM Cliff	5	1	1	2	2*		100.00	0	0	0
HG Duke	1	0								0
D Ferreira	12	11	1	257	66	25.70	158.64	0	1	6
GCH Hill	6	4	1	49	15*	16.33	119.51	0	0	1
DJ Leech	3	0								0
WA Luxton	2	2	0	45	33	22.50	195.65	0	0	2
A Lyth	12	12	1	302	84	27.45	125.31	0	3	5
C McKerr	5	4	3	17	10	17.00	100.00	0	0	1
DJ Malan	12	12	2	420	93*	42.00	135.04	0	3	3
DT Moriarty	13	3	3	12	8*		85.71	0	0	2
ML Revis	9	5	0	50	30	10.00	84.74	0	0	5
JE Root	8	8	2	197	43	32.83	127.09	0	0	4
Shan Masood	12	11	3	211	61	26.37	140.66	0	1	8
JA Thompson	13	10	4	196	50*	32.66	161.98	0	1	6
JH Wharton	7	6	0	132	52	22.00	129.41	0	1	3

	Balls	Mdns	Runs	Wkts	BB	Ave	5w	10w
DM Bess	280	80	357	12	2-10	29.75	0	0
JA Chohan	203	65	264	17	5-14	15.52	1	1
BM Cliff	96	41	149	8	4-31	18.62	1	0
GCH Hill	48	10	84	0				
DJ Leech	43	21	51	2	2-10	25.50	0	0
C McKerr	78	28	152	4	2-55	38.00	0	0
DT Moriarty	306	93	412	14	4-25	29.42	1	0
ML Revis	78	26	157	6	2-10	26.16	0	0
JE Root	48	17	58	3	2-20	19.33	0	0
JA Thompson	257	77	393	20	4-31	19.65	1	0

Catches/Stumpings:
11 Ferreira (5st), 8 Masood, 6 Bess, Thompson, 5 Lyth, Revis, 4 Root, 3 Malan, Wharton, 2 Luxton, Moriarty, 1 Chohan, Hill, McKerr

Men's Players

MOHAMMAD ABBAS · RHB / RMF / R0 / W3

FULL NAME: Mohammad Abbas
BORN: March 10, 1990, Sialkot, Punjab
SQUAD NO: TBC
TEAMS: Pakistan, Nottinghamshire, Hampshire, Islamabad, Khan Research Laboratories, Lahore Blues, Leicestershire, Multan Sultans, Pakistan Television, Rawalpindi, Sialkot, Southern Punjab, State Bank of Pakistan, Sui Northern Gas Pipelines Limited
ROLE: Bowler
DEBUT: Test: 2017; ODI: 2019; First-class: 2009; List A: 2009; T20: 2013

BEST BATTING: 40 Khan Research Laboratories vs Karachi Whites, Karachi, 2016
BEST BOWLING: 8-46 Khan Research Laboratories vs Karachi Whites, Karachi, 2016
COUNTY CAP: 2018 (Leicestershire); 2022 (Hampshire)

NOTES: Abbas has been a key member of Hampshire's stellar pace attack for the past four seasons but, following James Vince's decision to opt out of red-ball cricket this summer, the county released Abbas in order to "rebalance the squad", with Nottinghamshire sweeping in to secure the services of the 35-year-old veteran. Abbas is scheduled to feature in May – following Fergus O'Neill's short spell at the beginning of the season – and then again in September. In total he is set to play six Championship games for Notts, whom he had signed to play for in 2020 only for Covid to force a cancellation. "Players of Mo's experience and track record don't come around all that often, so we're really excited about what he can bring to us this summer," said Nottinghamshire head coach Peter Moores. "His control and his ability to find a way of getting wickets on any sort of surface make him extremely valuable; he's certainly been a tough opponent for us to face over the years"

Batting	Mat	Inns	NO	Runs	HS	Ave	SR	100	50	Ct	St
Tests	27	40	19	120	29	5.71	17.44	0	0	8	-
ODIs	3	0	-	-	-	-	-	-	-	0	-
First-class	192	259	113	925	40	6.33	26.66	0	0	47	-
List A	63	33	15	140	15*	7.77	52.63	0	0	15	-
T20s	38	13	9	34	15*	8.50	141.66	0	0	7	-

Bowling	Mat	Balls	Mdns	Runs	Wkts	BB	Ave	4wI	5wI	SR	Econ
Tests	27	5554	272	2318	100	6-54	23.18	-	5	55.54	2.50
ODIs	3	162	0	153	1	1-44	153.00	0	0	162.00	5.66
First-class	192	36594	1682	15981	775	8-46	20.62	-	47	47.21	2.62
List A	63	3065	31	2515	84	4-31	29.94	4	0	36.48	4.92
T20s	38	798	1	1137	32	3-22	35.53	0	0	24.93	8.54

KYLE ABBOTT   RHB / RFM / R0 / W5 / MVP42

FULL NAME: Kyle John Abbott
BORN: June 18, 1987, Empangeni, KwaZulu-Natal, South Africa
SQUAD NO: 11
HEIGHT: 6ft 2in
NICKNAME: Jimmy
TEAMS: South Africa, Hampshire, Boland, Dolphins, Durban Heat, Jafna Stallions, Kings XI Punjab, KwaZulu-Natal, Lahore Qalandars, Middlesex, Titans, Worcestershire
ROLE: Bowler
DEBUT: Test: 2013; ODI: 2013; T20I: 2013; First-class: 2009; List A: 2009; T20: 2011

BEST BATTING: 97* Hampshire vs Lancashire, Old Trafford, 2017
BEST BOWLING: 9-40 Hampshire vs Somerset, Southampton, 2019
COUNTY CAP: 2017 (Hampshire)

WHICH TEAMMATE HAS HAD THE BIGGEST IMPACT ON YOUR GAME? Keith Barker – he's always blunt and honest with me
WHAT PART OF THE SEASON DO YOU MOST ENJOY? The four-day stuff
WHO IS THE MOST TALENTED U19 TEENAGER IN THE COUNTY GAME? Eddie Jack (Ham)
IF YOU COULD PINCH A PLAYER FROM ANOTHER COUNTY, WHO WOULD IT BE? Simon Harmer
WHAT KEEPS YOU AWAKE AT NIGHT? My new-born
WHAT'S THE SILLIEST OUTFIT YOU'VE EVER WORN? An Incredible Hulk costume
CHOOSE A FANTASY SLIP CORDON TO SPEND A DAY IN THE FIELD WITH: Adam Gilchrist (wk), Graeme Smith, Jacques Kallis, Steve Smith, AB de Villiers

Batting	Mat	Inns	NO	Runs	HS	Ave	SR	100	50	Ct	St
Tests	11	14	0	95	17	6.78	28.10	0	0	4	-
ODIs	28	13	4	76	23	8.44	60.31	0	0	7	-
T20Is	21	6	4	23	9*	11.50	115.00	0	0	7	-
First-class	168	225	42	3257	97*	17.79	48.38	0	12	30	-
List A	120	62	26	657	56	18.25	84.99	0	1	30	-
T20s	156	53	29	324	30	13.50	118.68	0	0	33	-

Bowling	Mat	Balls	Mdns	Runs	Wkts	BB	Ave	4wI	5wI	SR	Econ
Tests	11	2081	95	886	39	7-29	22.71	-	3	53.35	2.55
ODIs	28	1303	13	1051	34	4-21	30.91	2	0	38.32	4.83
T20Is	21	436	0	579	26	3-20	22.26	0	0	16.76	7.96
First-class	168	28927	1210	13719	652	9-40	21.04	-	42	44.36	2.84
List A	120	5488	69	4713	161	5-43	29.27	7	1	34.08	5.15
T20s	156	3252	7	4484	157	5-14	28.56	1	1	20.71	8.27

TOM ABELL

RHB / RM / R1 / W0

FULL NAME: Thomas Benjamin Abell
BORN: March 5, 1994, Taunton
SQUAD NO: 28
HEIGHT: 5ft 11in
NICKNAME: Sid
EDUCATION: Taunton School; University of Exeter
TEAMS: Somerset, Welsh Fire, Birmingham Phoenix, Brisbane Heat, Dambulla Aura, England Lions, Lahore Qalandars, Rangpur Rangers, Sunrisers Eastern Cape
ROLE: Batter
DEBUT: First-class: 2014; List A: 2015; T20: 2016

BEST BATTING: 152* Somerset vs Warwickshire, Taunton, 2024
BEST BOWLING: 4-39 Somerset vs Warwickshire, Edgbaston, 2019
COUNTY CAP: 2018

FIRST CRICKET CLUB? Taunton CC, Somerset
WHICH TEAMMATE HAS HAD THE BIGGEST IMPACT ON YOUR GAME? Tom Lammonby – we spend a fair bit of time working together but also away from cricket
WHICH AWAY GROUND DO YOU MOST ENJOY VISITING? Edgbaston
IF YOU COULD PINCH A PLAYER FROM ANOTHER COUNTY, WHO WOULD IT BE? Sam Cook
HOW IS BAZBALL AFFECTING CHAMPIONSHIP CRICKET? It's affecting how people play and how teams are looking to win
WHAT DO YOU THINK OF THE CURRENT 50-OVER COMPETITION? It's good, but I'd like to see it return to being an integral format of domestic cricket
WHO IS THE TOUGHEST BOWLER TO FACE? Dan Worrall
WHAT KEEPS YOU AWAKE AT NIGHT? My front pad
CHOOSE A FANTASY SLIP CORDON TO SPEND A DAY IN THE FIELD WITH: Ricky Gervais (wk), David Beckham, Jimmy Carr, Michael Jordan

Batting	Mat	Inns	NO	Runs	HS	Ave	SR	100	50	Ct	St
First-class	130	230	21	7318	152*	35.01	49.64	17	36	102	-
List A	27	22	1	649	106	30.90	79.33	1	1	8	-
T20s	152	136	27	3277	101*	30.06	133.75	1	16	85	-

Bowling	Mat	Balls	Mdns	Runs	Wkts	BB	Ave	4wl	5wl	SR	Econ
First-class	130	3431	122	2024	64	4-39	31.62	-	0	53.60	3.53
List A	27	49	1	28	2	2-19	14.00	0	0	24.50	3.42
T20s	152	60	0	100	2	1-11	50.00	0	0	30.00	10.00

COLIN ACKERMANN   RHB / OB / R0 / W0 / MVP37

FULL NAME: Colin Niel Ackermann
BORN: April 4, 1991, Cape Province, SA
SQUAD NO: 48
HEIGHT: 6ft 1in
EDUCATION: Grey High School, Port Elizabeth; University of South Africa
TEAMS: Netherlands, Durham, Eastern Province, Leicestershire, Manchester Originals, Pretoria Capitals, SA U19, Southern Brave, Warriors
ROLE: Allrounder
DEBUT: ODI: 2021; T20I: 2019; First-class: 2010; List A: 2010; T20: 2011

DURHAM

BEST BATTING: 277* Leicestershire vs Sussex, Hove, 2022
BEST BOWLING: 5-69 Leicestershire vs Sussex, Hove, 2019
COUNTY CAP: 2019 (Leicestershire)

FIRST CRICKET CLUB? Kibworth CC, Leicestershire
BIGGEST INFLUENCE ON YOUR DEVELOPMENT AS A CRICKETER (EXCLUDING PARENTS)?
Attending Grey High School, Port Elizabeth
GREATEST PERFORMANCE YOU HAVE WITNESSED? Sam Northeast's 410 not out against Leicestershire in 2022
FAVOURITE FORMAT? The T20 Blast
HOBBIES? Fishing

Batting	Mat	Inns	NO	Runs	HS	Ave	SR	100	50	Ct	St
ODIs	20	18	0	451	81	25.05	77.75	0	3	9	-
T20Is	25	25	4	515	62	24.52	114.69	0	1	7	-
First-class	177	309	34	11404	277*	41.46	50.40	26	65	192	-
List A	118	109	17	3333	152*	36.22	82.25	4	22	76	-
T20s	201	193	29	4311	90*	26.28	122.29	0	25	91	-

Bowling	Mat	Balls	Mdns	Runs	Wkts	BB	Ave	4wI	5wI	SR	Econ
ODIs	20	680	9	520	15	4-22	34.66	1	0	45.33	4.58
T20Is	25	282	1	284	11	3-15	25.81	0	0	25.63	6.04
First-class	177	7538	212	4133	87	5-69	47.50	-	1	86.64	3.28
List A	118	3291	16	2641	70	4-22	37.72	2	0	47.01	4.81
T20s	201	2145	4	2590	93	7-18	27.84	0	1	23.06	7.24

ASHTON AGAR

NORTHAMPTONSHIRE

FULL NAME: Ashton Charles Agar
BORN: October 14, 1993, Melbourne, Australia
SQUAD NO: 46
EDUCATION: De La Salle College, Melbourne
TEAMS: Australia, Northamptonshire, Middlesex, Perth Scorchers, Warwickshire, Western Australia
ROLE: Bowler
DEBUT: Test: 2013; ODI: 2015; T20I: 2016; First-class: 2013; List A: 2013; T20: 2013

BEST BATTING: 68 Perth Scorchers vs Sydney Thunder, Sydney, 2016 (T20)
BEST BOWLING: 6-30 Australia vs New Zealand, Wellington, 2021 (T20)

NOTES: The Australian left-arm spinner and lower-order hitter is back for his second stint at Northants and his fourth season overall in the T20 Blast after previously appearing for Middlesex and Warwickshire. He is slated to appear in the full group stage this term, having made six appearances last time out, during which he made his mark predominantly with the bat, striking at 190. Agar is primarily viewed, however, as a naggingly accurate spinner, whose T20I economy rate of 6.50 is the lowest of any Australian bowler to have taken at least 10 wickets in the format's history. And while he has registered only two fifties in his T20 career at a modest strike-rate of 118, he does possess the remarkable record of having made the highest-ever score by a No.11 in Test cricket, compiled on debut in the first Ashes Test of the 2013 series

Batting	Mat	Inns	NO	Runs	HS	Ave	SR	100	50	Ct	St
Tests	5	7	1	195	98	32.50	55.55	0	1	0	-
ODIs	22	18	5	322	48*	24.76	82.98	0	0	10	-
T20Is	49	29	5	279	29	11.62	100.35	0	0	32	-
First-class	66	95	12	2347	114*	28.27	52.50	3	13	23	-
List A	77	59	14	1047	64	23.26	90.02	0	2	34	-
T20s	174	122	38	1406	68	16.73	118.35	0	2	91	-
Bowling	Mat	Balls	Mdns	Runs	Wkts	BB	Ave	4wI	5wI	SR	Econ
Tests	5	1006	36	468	9	3-46	52.00	-	0	111.77	2.79
ODIs	22	1098	4	958	21	2-31	45.61	0	0	52.28	5.23
T20Is	49	1042	2	1129	49	6-30	23.04	0	2	21.26	6.50
First-class	66	13281	460	6688	161	6-110	41.54	-	6	82.49	3.02
List A	77	3709	14	3169	93	5-39	34.07	0	2	39.88	5.12
T20s	174	3378	5	4055	137	6-30	29.59	0	2	24.65	7.20

WES AGAR — RHB / RFM / R0 / W0

FULL NAME: Wesley Austin Agar
BORN: February 5, 1997, Malvern, Victoria, Australia
SQUAD NO: 8
TEAMS: Australia, Kent, Adelaide Strikers, South Australia, Sydney Thunder, Victoria
ROLE: Bowler
DEBUT: ODI: 2021; First-class: 2019; List A: 2016; T20: 2017

KENT

BEST BATTING: 57 South Australia vs New South Wales, Wollongong, 2022
BEST BOWLING: 6-42 South Australia vs Western Australia, Adelaide, 2023

NOTES: The Australian seamer returns to Canterbury after injury forced him to cut short his stay last year. Agar was restricted to five Championship games in 2024, taking a further 12 wickets to go with his 21 in six appereances during the previous summer. He is avaliable for all formats and is scheduled to be with the club until the end of July. "Wes is a talented multi-format cricketer and a very popular member of our dressing room – we're extremely pleased that he will be joining us again," said Simon Cook, Kent's director of cricket. "His ethos and work ethic is great to have around the place, and we're looking forward to him being an important part of our attack at the front end of our 2025 season. We know that he will come back with the same enthusiasm to perform at his best in a Kent shirt." The 27-year-old, younger brother of Australian spinner Ashton Agar, played two ODIs in 2021 but hasn't appeared for his country since. Down under he plays for his home state, South Australia

Batting	Mat	Inns	NO	Runs	HS	Ave	SR	100	50	Ct	St
ODIs	2	2	0	50	41	25.00	119.04	0	0	0	-
First-class	44	64	11	632	57	11.92	58.35	0	2	11	-
List A	37	26	10	205	41	12.81	95.79	0	0	15	-
T20s	69	21	8	89	15	6.84	105.95	0	0	14	-

Bowling	Mat	Balls	Mdns	Runs	Wkts	BB	Ave	4wi	5wi	SR	Econ
ODIs	2	66	1	39	0	0-15	-	-	-	-	3.54
First-class	44	8186	288	4467	141	6-42	31.68	-	5	58.05	3.27
List A	37	1850	20	1851	47	5-40	39.38	0	2	39.36	6.00
T20s	69	1385	1	2089	87	4-6	24.01	4	0	15.91	9.04

FARHAN AHMED

RHB / OB / RO / WO

FULL NAME: Farhan Ahmed
BORN: February 22, 2008, Nottingham
SQUAD NO: 97
HEIGHT: 5ft 9in
NICKNAME: Frankie
EDUCATION: Bluecoat Wollaton Academy, Nottingham
TEAMS: Nottinghamshire, England Lions
ROLE: Bowler
DEBUT: First-class: 2024; List A: 2024

BEST BATTING: 13 England Lions vs Sri Lankans, Worcester, 2024
BEST BOWLING: 7-140 Nottinghamshire vs Surrey, Trent Bridge, 2024

FIRST CRICKET CLUB? Cavaliers & Carrington CC, Nottingham
EARLIEST CRICKETING MEMORY? Getting two wickets for Notts U10 against Yorkshire U10
WHAT'S THE BIGGEST PRIZE IN DOMESTIC CRICKET? The County Championship
THE KOOKABURRA BALL: YES OR NO? Yes – it's good to change the conditions and good for the professional players to be adaptable
OPPONENT YOU MOST LOOK FORWARD TO PLAYING AGAINST? Either Surrey (the best) or Derbyshire (local rivals)
HOW MANY HOURS DO YOU SPEND ON YOUR PHONE A DAY? Four hours on a good day
ONE THING YOU WANT TO DO BEFORE YOU DIE: Become a World Cup winner
HOBBY YOU WOULD LIKE TO LEARN: Padel
WHICH PUBLIC FIGURE INSPIRES YOU (EXCLUDING SPORTSPEOPLE)?
Khabib Nurmagomedov
SURPRISING FACT ABOUT YOU: I'm simple really

Batting	Mat	Inns	NO	Runs	HS	Ave	SR	100	50	Ct	St
First-class	5	6	1	31	13	6.20	22.79	0	0	2	-
List A	1	0	-	-	-	-	-	-	-	0	-

Bowling	Mat	Balls	Mdns	Runs	Wkts	BB	Ave	4wI	5wI	SR	Econ
First-class	5	1219	25	598	25	7-140	23.92	-	1	48.76	2.94
List A	1	54	0	69	1	1-69	69.00	0	0	54.00	7.66

REHAN AHMED

RHB / LB / RO / WO

FULL NAME: Rehan Ahmed
BORN: August 13, 2004, Nottingham
SQUAD NO: 16
HEIGHT: 5ft 8in
NICKNAME: Ray
EDUCATION: Bluecoat School, Nottingham
TEAMS: England, Leicestershire, Southern Brave
ROLE: Allrounder
DEBUT: Test: 2022; ODI: 2023; T20I: 2023; First-class: 2022; List A: 2021; T20: 2022

BEST BATTING: 122 Leicestershire vs Derbyshire, Derby, 2022
BEST BOWLING: 5-48 England vs Pakistan, Karachi, 2022

FIRST CRICKET CLUB? Thoresby Colliery CC, Mansfield, Nottinghamshire
WHAT WOULD YOU CHANGE ABOUT THE STRUCTURE OF THE COUNTY SEASON? Play more red-ball cricket in the middle of the summer
WHO WOULD YOU MOST AND LEAST LIKE TO HAVE A NET WITH? Most – Sachin Tendulkar. Least Shoaib Akhtar (scariest bowler alive)
HOBBIES? Boxing

Batting	Mat	Inns	NO	Runs	HS	Ave	SR	100	50	Ct	St
Tests	5	10	0	103	28	10.30	56.59	0	0	3	-
ODIs	6	4	0	35	15	8.75	76.08	0	0	1	-
T20Is	10	6	2	38	11	9.50	131.03	0	0	2	-
First-class	25	45	1	1259	122	28.61	73.79	1	8	7	-
List A	13	10	4	124	40*	20.66	68.88	0	0	1	-
T20s	65	46	12	450	49	13.23	115.97	0	0	14	-

Bowling	Mat	Balls	Mdns	Runs	Wkts	BB	Ave	4wI	5wI	SR	Econ
Tests	5	1038	19	687	22	5-48	31.22	-	1	47.18	3.97
ODIs	6	282	2	233	10	4-54	23.30	1	0	28.20	4.95
T20Is	10	186	0	300	12	3-39	25.00	0	0	15.50	9.67
First-class	25	3354	47	2276	52	5-48	43.76	-	2	64.50	4.07
List A	13	614	4	551	15	4-54	36.73	1	0	40.93	5.38
T20s	65	1300	1	1753	59	4-22	29.71	1	0	22.03	8.09

DERBYSHIRE

BEN AITCHISON

RHB / RFM / R0 / W0

FULL NAME: Benjamin William Aitchison
BORN: July 6, 1999, Southport, Lancashire
SQUAD NO: 11
HEIGHT: 6ft 4in
NICKNAME: Biggen
EDUCATION: Merchant Taylors' School,
Crosby, Merseyside
TEAMS: Derbyshire
ROLE: Bowler
DEBUT: First-class: 2020; List A: 2021; T20: 2022

BEST BATTING: 50 Derbyshire vs Nottinghamshire, Derby, 2021
BEST BOWLING: 6-28 Derbyshire vs Durham, Derby, 2021

FIRST CRICKET CLUB? Formby CC, Liverpool
WHICH TEAMMATE HAS HAD THE BIGGEST IMPACT ON YOUR GAME? Sam Conners – a great
mate and someone you can rely on
WHICH AWAY GROUND DO YOU MOST ENJOY VISITING? Worcester – a lovely ground
where I enjoy bowling
WHO IS THE MOST TALENTED U19 TEENAGER IN THE COUNTY GAME? Harry Moore (Der)
HOW IS BAZBALL AFFECTING CHAMPIONSHIP CRICKET? Unfortunately it's making
pitches flatter
WHAT DO YOU THINK OF THE CURRENT 50-OVER COMPETITION? Love it
WHAT KEEPS YOU AWAKE AT NIGHT? Mark Wood running in

Batting	Mat	Inns	NO	Runs	HS	Ave	SR	100	50	Ct	St
First-class	27	37	6	383	50	12.35	43.92	0	1	20	-
List A	13	9	2	60	19	8.57	63.15	0	0	2	-
T20s	3	2	1	2	2	2.00	200.00	0	0	2	-

Bowling	Mat	Balls	Mdns	Runs	Wkts	BB	Ave	4wI	5wI	SR	Econ
First-class	27	3966	129	2083	68	6-28	30.63	-	1	58.32	3.15
List A	13	543	4	435	15	4-39	29.00	1	0	36.20	4.80
T20s	3	60	0	126	4	2-30	31.50	0	0	15.00	12.60

ZAMAN AKHTER — RHB / RFM / RO / WO

FULL NAME: Zaman Akhter
BORN: March 12, 1999, Cambridge
SQUAD NO: 17
EDUCATION: Perse School, Cambridge;
Oxford University
TEAMS: Gloucestershire, England Lions
ROLE: Bowler
DEBUT: First-class: 2019; List A: 2023; T20: 2023

BEST BATTING: 70 Gloucestershire vs Yorkshire, Scarborough, 2024
BEST BOWLING: 5-32 England Lions vs Sri Lanka, Worcester, 2024

NOTES: The 26-year-old fast bowler signed a contract extension at Gloucestershire in August that ties him to Bristol until the end of the 2025 season. Having been identified as a talent by the South Asian Cricket Academy (SACA) and invited for trials at Gloucestershire, Akhter made his professional debut for the club in the Championship game against Durham in 2023, going on to claim 19 wickets in seven first-class matches. He continued to impress last summer, registering his first five-fer and first half-century in the format. Akhter then took 5-32 on his England Lions debut in August against the touring Sri Lankans. "It's excellent news that Zaman has extended his stay at Gloucestershire," said Mark Alleyne, the club's head coach. "He arrived with good potential and has excelled ever since with some important spells in Championship cricket. Zaman will be integral to the team as he looks to extend this contribution across all formats. He is truly a multi-skilled cricketer with exciting pace, a great athlete in the field and also an emerging batter with good ability"

Batting	Mat	Inns	NO	Runs	HS	Ave	SR	100	50	Ct	St
First-class	18	26	9	366	70	21.52	60.29	0	1	6	-
List A	6	2	1	27	27*	27.00	84.37	0	0	4	-
T20s	3	3	2	24	11*	24.00	85.71	0	0	0	-

Bowling	Mat	Balls	Mdns	Runs	Wkts	BB	Ave	4wI	5wI	SR	Econ
First-class	18	2666	40	1850	45	5-32	41.11	-	2	59.24	4.16
List A	6	288	2	273	10	3-25	27.30	0	0	28.80	5.68
T20s	3	66	0	93	3	2-36	31.00	0	0	22.00	8.45

TOBY ALBERT

RHB / WK / R0 / W0

FULL NAME: Toby Edward Albert
BORN: November 12, 2001, Basingstoke, Hampshire
SQUAD NO: 15
HEIGHT: 6ft 1in
EDUCATION: Park House School, Newbury, Berkshire
TEAMS: Hampshire, Kent
ROLE: Batter
DEBUT: First-class: 2022; List A: 2022; T20: 2021

BEST BATTING: 124 Hampshire vs Essex, Southampton, 2024

WHICH TEAMMATE HAS HAD THE BIGGEST IMPACT ON YOUR GAME? Joe Weatherley – he's very easy to chat to about my game
WHAT PART OF THE SEASON DO YOU MOST ENJOY? June and July
WHICH AWAY GROUND DO YOU MOST ENJOY VISITING? The Oval
WHO IS THE MOST TALENTED U19 TEENAGER IN THE COUNTY GAME? Eddie Jack (Ham)
IF YOU COULD PINCH A PLAYER FROM ANOTHER COUNTY, WHO WOULD IT BE? Will Jacks
HOW IS BAZBALL AFFECTING CHAMPIONSHIP CRICKET? I wouldn't say it is affecting our team but others are adapting their approach
WHO IS THE TOUGHEST BOWLER TO FACE? Simon Harmer
WHAT'S THE SILLIEST OUTFIT YOU'VE EVER WORN? A pimp costume

Batting	Mat	Inns	NO	Runs	HS	Ave	SR	100	50	Ct	St
First-class	13	21	1	611	124	30.55	40.86	2	2	14	-
List A	22	21	4	676	96*	39.76	94.54	0	4	13	-
T20s	39	32	8	531	66	22.12	124.35	0	1	8	-

Bowling	Mat	Balls	Mdns	Runs	Wkts	BB	Ave	4wI	5wI	SR	Econ
First-class	13	-	-	-	-	-	-	-	-	-	-
List A	22	-	-	-	-	-	-	-	-	-	-
T20s	39	-	-	-	-	-	-	-	-	-	-

KASEY ALDRIDGE

RHB / RFM / R0 / W0

FULL NAME: Kasey Luke Aldridge
BORN: December 24, 2000, Bristol
SQUAD NO: 5
HEIGHT: 6ft 4in
NICKNAME: Fred
EDUCATION: Millfield School, Somerset
TEAMS: Somerset, England Lions
ROLE: Allrounder
DEBUT: First-class: 2021; List A: 2021; T20: 2022

BEST BATTING: 101* Somerset vs Lancashire, Old Trafford, 2023
BEST BOWLING: 6-110 Somerset vs Kent, Canterbury, 2022

FIRST CRICKET CLUB? Brislington CC, Bristol
BIGGEST INFLUENCE ON YOUR DEVELOPMENT AS A CRICKETER (EXCLUDING PARENTS)? My prep-school coach Dave Beal
WHO WOULD YOU MOST AND LEAST LIKE TO HAVE A NET WITH? Most – Andrew Flintoff. Least – Brett Lee
MAKE ONE PREDICTION FOR THE FUTURE OF CRICKET: Lewis Goldsworthy will play for England
CHILDHOOD SPORTING HERO? Andrew Flintoff
HOBBIES? Trying to hit the golf ball miles

Batting	Mat	Inns	NO	Runs	HS	Ave	SR	100	50	Ct	St
First-class	28	40	4	963	101*	26.75	51.08	1	6	19	-
List A	23	13	3	92	24	9.20	68.14	0	0	10	-
T20s	5	3	3	43	32*	-	130.30	0	0	2	-

Bowling	Mat	Balls	Mdns	Runs	Wkts	BB	Ave	4wl	5wl	SR	Econ
First-class	28	3561	75	2481	64	6-110	38.76	-	3	55.64	4.18
List A	23	883	4	937	32	6-33	29.28	0	2	27.59	6.36
T20s	5	30	0	58	0	0-13	-	-	-	-	11.60

HASAN ALI

RHB / RFM / R0 / W0

WARWICKSHIRE

FULL NAME: Hasan Ali
BORN: July 2, 1994, Mandi Bahauddin, Pakistan
SQUAD NO: 32
TEAMS: Pakistan, Warwickshire, Central Punjab, Comilla Victorians, Dambulla Aura, Islamabad, Karachi Kings, Lancashire, St Kitts & Nevis Patriots, Peshawar Zalmi, Sialkot, Southern Punjab
ROLE: Bowler
DEBUT: Test: 2017; ODI: 2016; T20I: 2016; First-class: 2013; List A: 2013; T20: 2014

BEST BATTING: 106* Central Punjab vs Khyber Pakhtunkhwa, Karachi, 2021
BEST BOWLING: 8-107 Sialkot Stallions vs State Bank of Pakistan, Sialkot, 2014
COUNTY CAP: 2022 (Lancashire)

NOTES: The seasoned Pakistani quick has re-signed for Warwickshire for the third year running after injury and an unexpected recall to the national side cut his stay in Birmingham last summer to just three Championship games and five Blast fixtures. Ali is scheduled to arrive on May 29, in time for the start of the T20 campaign, and to be available across all three formats for the rest of the summer. He enjoyed a successful three-month stint with the Bears in 2023 when he took 24 Championship wickets and endeared himself to the faithful with a string of wholehearted performances. He said: "I love playing for Warwickshire, playing for the Bears fans. Being awarded my White Bear Cap in 2023 was among the proudest moments in my career and I want to make lots more special memories with the Bears"

Batting	Mat	Inns	NO	Runs	HS	Ave	SR	100	50	Ct	St
Tests	24	38	6	382	30	11.93	72.48	0	0	6	-
ODIs	66	38	11	383	59	14.18	117.12	0	2	13	-
T20Is	51	19	10	129	23	14.33	186.95	0	0	12	-
First-class	83	120	24	1550	106*	16.14	77.92	1	7	25	-
List A	97	61	16	733	59	16.28	122.57	0	3	35	-
T20s	189	88	34	616	45	11.40	145.62	0	0	47	-

Bowling	Mat	Balls	Mdns	Runs	Wkts	BB	Ave	4wI	5wI	SR	Econ
Tests	24	4295	164	2185	80	5-27	27.31	-	6	53.68	3.05
ODIs	66	3188	16	3084	100	5-34	30.84	2	4	31.88	5.80
T20Is	51	1033	5	1456	60	4-18	24.26	1	0	17.21	8.45
First-class	83	14734	476	8047	318	8-107	25.30	-	18	46.33	3.27
List A	97	4674	26	4357	152	5-34	28.66	6	4	30.75	5.59
T20s	189	4116	7	5493	251	5-20	21.88	7	1	16.39	8.00

KASHIF ALI
RHB / LB / R0 / W0

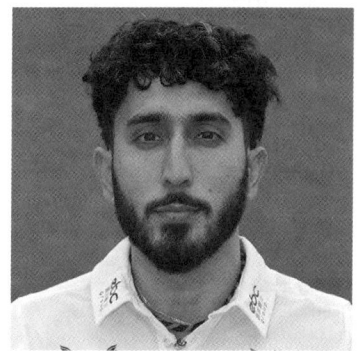

FULL NAME: Kashif Ali
BORN: February 7, 1998, Kashmir, Pakistan
SQUAD NO: 27
HEIGHT: 5ft 9in
NICKNAME: Kash
EDUCATION: Dunstable College, Bedfordshire
TEAMS: Worcestershire, Ghani Glass
ROLE: Batter
DEBUT: First-class: 2022; List A: 2022; T20: 2018

BEST BATTING: 133 Ghani Glass vs Pakistan Television, Karachi, 2025
BEST BOWLING: 2-13 Worcestershire vs Kent, Canterbury, 2024

FIRST CRICKET CLUB? Dunstable Town CC, Bedfordshire
WHICH TEAMMATE HAS HAD THE BIGGEST IMPACT ON YOUR GAME? Jake Libby for his calmness, confidence and trust in my ability
WHICH AWAY GROUND DO YOU MOST ENJOY VISITING? Headingley
WHO IS THE MOST TALENTED U19 TEENAGER IN THE COUNTY GAME? Harry Darley (Wor)
IF YOU COULD PINCH A PLAYER FROM ANOTHER COUNTY, WHO WOULD IT BE? Tom Kohler-Cadmore
WHO IS THE TOUGHEST BOWLER TO FACE? Liam Dawson – smart bowler
CHOOSE A FANTASY SLIP CORDON TO SPEND A DAY IN THE FIELD WITH: Ben Cox (wk), Jake Libby, Matthew Waite, Rehaan Edavalath
SURPRISING FACT ABOUT YOU: I write poetry in my free time

Batting	Mat	Inns	NO	Runs	HS	Ave	SR	100	50	Ct	St
First-class	26	46	3	1452	133	33.76	60.90	3	8	7	-
List A	13	13	2	559	114	50.81	119.18	1	4	4	-
T20s	29	26	4	534	69	24.27	128.05	0	1	8	-

Bowling	Mat	Balls	Mdns	Runs	Wkts	BB	Ave	4wl	5wl	SR	Econ
First-class	26	314	1	276	3	2-13	92.00	-	0	104.66	5.27
List A	13	-	-	-	-	-	-	-	-	-	-
T20s	29	6	0	14	0	0-14	-	-	-	-	14.00

MOEEN ALI

LHB / OB / R2 / W0

WARWICKSHIRE

FULL NAME: Moeen Munir Ali
BORN: June 18, 1987, Birmingham
SQUAD NO: 1
HEIGHT: 6ft
NICKNAME: Brother Mo
EDUCATION: Moseley School, Birmingham
TEAMS: England, Warwickshire, Birmingham Phoenix, Cape Town Blitz, Chennai SK, Joburg Super Kings, Matabeleland Tuskers, Multan Sultans, RCB, Worcestershire
ROLE: Allrounder
DEBUT: Test: 2014; ODI: 2014; T20I: 2014; First-class: 2005; List A: 2006; T20: 2007

BEST BATTING: 250 Worcestershire vs Glamorgan, Worcester, 2013
BEST BOWLING: 6-29 Worcestershire vs Lancashire, Old Trafford, 2012
COUNTY CAP: 2007 (Worcestershire)

FIRST CRICKET CLUB? Moseley Ashfield CC, Birmingham
FAMILY TIES? My cousin Kabir played for England and my brother Kadeer played for Worcestershire, Gloucestershire and Leicestershire
CHILDHOOD SPORTING HERO? Saeed Anwar
NOTES: Moeen has opted out of The Hundred and intends to retire from all cricket after this summer's T20 Blast competition. "I still have passion for the game and I love being in a team environment, " he said after making the announcement. "I also enjoy talking to players about cricket, the tactics, and I think that'll help me move smoothly into coaching after my playing days are over. I came back to Warwickshire with an aim of trying to help them win the Blast and I still want to play a role this year"

Batting	Mat	Inns	NO	Runs	HS	Ave	SR	100	50	Ct	St
Tests	68	118	8	3094	155*	28.12	51.79	5	15	40	-
ODIs	138	112	15	2355	128	24.27	98.16	3	6	48	-
T20Is	92	75	17	1229	72*	21.18	142.41	0	7	22	-
First-class	202	346	27	11514	250	36.09	55.16	20	70	119	-
List A	255	223	17	5650	158	27.42	100.30	11	21	81	-
T20s	373	334	40	7135	121*	24.26	138.65	3	35	115	-

Bowling	Mat	Balls	Mdns	Runs	Wkts	BB	Ave	4wI	5wl	SR	Econ
Tests	68	12610	293	7612	204	6-53	37.31	-	5	61.81	3.62
ODIs	138	5988	13	5311	111	4-46	47.84	2	0	53.94	5.32
T20Is	92	999	1	1384	51	3-24	27.13	0	0	19.58	8.31
First-class	202	25340	606	14953	391	6-29	38.24	-	12	64.80	3.54
List A	255	9099	23	8194	186	4-33	44.05	3	0	48.91	5.40
T20s	373	4748	4	6024	243	5-34	24.79	3	1	19.53	7.61

BEN ALLISON   RHB / RFM / R0 / W0

FULL NAME: Benjamin Michael John Allison
BORN: December 18, 1999, Colchester, Essex
SQUAD NO: 65
HEIGHT: 6ft 6in
NICKNAME: Pooey
EDUCATION: New Hall School, Chelmsford; Chelmsford College
TEAMS: Worcestershire, England U19, Essex, Gloucestershire
ROLE: Bowler
DEBUT: First-class: 2019; List A: 2021; T20: 2020

WORCESTERSHIRE

BEST BATTING: 75 Worcestershire vs Yorkshire, Headingley, 2023
BEST BOWLING: 5-32 Essex vs Northamptonshire, Northampton, 2022

BIGGEST INFLUENCE ON YOUR DEVELOPMENT AS A CRICKETER (EXCLUDING PARENTS)?
My brothers
MOST EXCITING DAY AS A CRICKETER? Winning the T20 Blast in 2019, even though I wasn't playing
CHILDHOOD SPORTING HERO? Stuart Broad

Batting	Mat	Inns	NO	Runs	HS	Ave	SR	100	50	Ct	St
First-class	14	20	4	427	75	26.68	43.48	0	4	4	-
List A	21	13	8	200	32*	40.00	92.59	0	0	9	-
T20s	25	9	5	48	17	12.00	100.00	0	0	17	-

Bowling	Mat	Balls	Mdns	Runs	Wkts	BB	Ave	4wl	5wl	SR	Econ
First-class	14	1701	61	868	30	5-32	28.93	-	1	56.70	3.06
List A	21	994	5	948	17	2-33	55.76	0	0	58.47	5.72
T20s	25	404	0	689	23	3-33	29.95	0	0	17.56	10.23

CHARLIE ALLISON — RHB / OB / R0 / W0

ESSEX

FULL NAME: Charles William James Allison
BORN: 6ft
SQUAD NO: 56
HEIGHT: 6ft
NICKNAME: Chaz
EDUCATION: Royal Hospital School, Ipswich
TEAMS: Essex, England U19
ROLE: Batter
DEBUT: List A: 2023; T20: 2024

FIRST CRICKET CLUB? Colchester CC, Essex
EARLIEST CRICKETING MEMORY? Corridor cricket with my brothers
WHAT'S THE BIGGEST PRIZE IN DOMESTIC CRICKET? The County Championship
THE KOOKABURRA BALL: YES OR NO? No – the ball gets too soft
OPPONENT YOU MOST LOOK FORWARD TO PLAYING AGAINST? My brother Ben Allison
FAVOURITE WARM-UP SONG? Freelove Freeway by David Brent
HOW MANY HOURS DO YOU SPEND ON YOUR PHONE A DAY? Three
SPECIALITY SUBJECT IN A PUB QUIZ (EXCLUDING SPORT)? Maths
ONE THING YOU WANT TO DO BEFORE YOU DIE: Perform in a band
WHICH PUBLIC FIGURE INSPIRES YOU (EXCLUDING SPORTSPEOPLE)? Daniel Craig
SURPRISING FACT ABOUT YOU: I take part in baseball training
FILM YOU CAN WATCH OVER AND OVER: Casino Royale

Batting	Mat	Inns	NO	Runs	HS	Ave	SR	100	50	Ct	St
List A	11	10	0	388	85	38.80	85.27	0	4	0	-
T20s	7	5	3	119	69*	59.50	138.37	0	1	6	-
Bowling	Mat	Balls	Mdns	Runs	Wkts	BB	Ave	4wI	5wI	SR	Econ
List A	11	-	-	-	-	-	-	-	-	-	-
T20s	7	-	-	-	-	-	-	-	-	-	-

TOM ALSOP — LHB / SLA / WK / R0 / W0 / MVP44

FULL NAME: Thomas Philip Alsop
BORN: November 27, 1995, High Wycombe, Buckinghamshire
SQUAD NO: 45
HEIGHT: 5ft 11in
NICKNAME: Lance
EDUCATION: Lavington School; The John Bentley School, Wiltshire
TEAMS: Sussex, Trent Rockets, Brisbane Heat, England Lions, Hampshire
ROLE: Batter/wicketkeeper
DEBUT: First-class: 2014; List A: 2014; T20: 2016

BEST BATTING: 182* Sussex vs Leicestershire, Leicester, 2023
BEST BOWLING: 2-59 Hampshire vs Yorkshire, Headingley, 2016

FIRST CRICKET CLUB? Bishop Canning CC, Wiltshire
WHICH TEAMMATE HAS HAD THE BIGGEST IMPACT ON YOUR GAME? Cheteshwar Pujara
BEST PLAYER IN COUNTY CRICKET (EXCLUDING TEAMMATES)? Sam Cook
BEST DELIVERY YOU HAVE EVER BOWLED OR FACED? My 'straight-break' into the slot that had Jonny Bairstow caught at long-on
GREATEST PERFORMANCE YOU HAVE WITNESSED? Ali Orr's double hundred at Taunton in the 50-over competition in 2022
FAVOURITE FORMAT? T20 – it's fun!
WHAT DO YOU THINK OF THE CURRENT 50-OVER COMPETITION? It's lacking an identity
HOBBIES? Ice hockey – I follow the Toronto Maple Leafs
WHICH PERSON INSPIRES YOU MOST? Matthew McConaughey
CHOOSE A FANTASY SLIP CORDON TO SPEND A DAY IN THE FIELD WITH: David Brent (wk), Bobby Lee, Theo Von, Andrew Santino
SURPRISING FACT ABOUT YOU: I used to play field hockey for England

Batting	Mat	Inns	NO	Runs	HS	Ave	SR	100	50	Ct	St
First-class	104	172	12	5112	182*	31.95	46.49	10	30	124	-
List A	72	71	5	2383	189*	36.10	81.16	6	12	46	6
T20s	87	82	13	1950	87*	28.26	129.31	0	11	32	4

Bowling	Mat	Balls	Mdns	Runs	Wkts	BB	Ave	4wI	5wI	SR	Econ
First-class	104	167	2	134	3	2-59	44.66	-	0	55.66	4.81
List A	72	-	-	-	-	-	-	-	-	-	-
T20s	87	-	-	-	-	-	-	-	-	-	-

JAMES ANDERSON LHB / RFM / R0 / W3

FULL NAME: James Michael Anderson
BORN: July 30, 1982, Burnley, Lancashire
SQUAD NO: 9
HEIGHT: 6ft 2in
NICKNAME: Jimmy
EDUCATION: St Theodore's Roman Catholic High School, Burnley
TEAMS: England, Lancashire, Auckland
ROLE: Bowler
DEBUT: Test: 2003; ODI: 2002; T20I: 2007; First-class: 2002; List A: 2000; T20: 2004

BEST BATTING: 81 England vs India, Trent Bridge, 2014
BEST BOWLING: 7-19 Lancashire vs Kent, Old Trafford, 2021
COUNTY CAP: 2003; **BENEFIT:** 2012

FIRST CRICKET CLUB? Burnley CC
FAMILY TIES? My dad and uncle played for Burnley CC
CHILDHOOD SPORTING HERO? Peter Martin
SURPRISING FACT ABOUT YOU: I'm allergic to mushrooms

Batting	Mat	Inns	NO	Runs	HS	Ave	SR	100	50	Ct	St
Tests	188	265	114	1353	81	8.96	39.42	0	1	107	-
ODIs	194	79	43	275	28	7.63	49.01	0	0	53	-
T20Is	19	4	3	1	1*	1.00	50.00	0	0	3	-
First-class	298	381	161	2039	81	9.26	-	0	1	165	-
List A	261	105	63	378	28	9.00	-	0	0	68	-
T20s	44	10	6	23	16	5.75	88.46	0	0	8	-

Bowling	Mat	Balls	Mdns	Runs	Wkts	BB	Ave	4wl	5wl	SR	Econ
Tests	188	40037	1730	18627	704	7-42	26.45	-	32	56.87	2.79
ODIs	194	9584	125	7861	269	5-23	29.22	11	2	35.62	4.92
T20Is	19	422	1	552	18	3-23	30.66	0	0	23.44	7.84
First-class	298	59223	2567	27610	1126	7-19	24.52	-	55	52.59	2.79
List A	261	12730	169	10230	358	5-23	28.57	11	2	35.55	4.82
T20s	44	933	1	1318	41	3-23	32.14	0	0	22.75	8.47

MARTIN ANDERSSON

RHB / RM / RO / WO

FULL NAME: Martin Kristoffer Andersson
BORN: September 6, 1996, Reading
SQUAD NO: 2
HEIGHT: 6ft 2in
NICKNAME: Pasty
EDUCATION: Reading Blue Coat School;
University of Leeds
TEAMS: Derbyshire, Middlesex
ROLE: Allrounder
DEBUT: First-class: 2017; List A: 2021; T20: 2018

BEST BATTING: 92 Middlesex vs Hampshire, Radlett, 2020
BEST BOWLING: 4-25 Derbyshire vs Glamorgan, Derby, 2018

FIRST CRICKET CLUB? Reading CC, Berkshire
EARLIEST CRICKETING MEMORY? Watching the 2005 Ashes
WHAT'S THE BIGGEST PRIZE IN DOMESTIC CRICKET? The County Championship
THE KOOKABURRA BALL: YES OR NO? Yes – it provides a different challenge
OPPONENT YOU MOST LOOK FORWARD TO PLAYING AGAINST? Ethan Bamber
FAVOURITE WARM-UP SONG? Intro by The XX
HOW MANY HOURS DO YOU SPEND ON YOUR PHONE A DAY? Two
SPECIALITY SUBJECT IN A PUB QUIZ (EXCLUDING SPORT)? Geography
WHICH PUBLIC FIGURE INSPIRES YOU (EXCLUDING SPORTSPEOPLE)? Brian Cox
SURPRISING FACT ABOUT YOU: I am half Swedish
FILM YOU CAN WATCH OVER AND OVER: Any of the Lord of the Rings trilogy

Batting	Mat	Inns	NO	Runs	HS	Ave	SR	100	50	Ct	St
First-class	34	57	4	1103	92	20.81	57.09	0	7	18	-
List A	24	22	10	616	100	51.33	109.60	1	0	12	-
T20s	46	41	9	547	57	17.09	122.09	0	2	29	-

Bowling	Mat	Balls	Mdns	Runs	Wkts	BB	Ave	4wI	5wI	SR	Econ
First-class	34	3472	75	2168	72	4-25	30.11	-	0	48.22	3.74
List A	24	828	3	977	15	3-55	65.13	0	0	55.20	7.07
T20s	46	472	0	855	28	3-32	30.53	0	0	16.85	10.86

JOFRA ARCHER

RHB / RF / RO / W1

SUSSEX

FULL NAME: Jofra Chioke Archer
BORN: April 1, 1995, Bridgetown, Barbados
SQUAD NO: 22
HEIGHT: 6ft 2in
NICKNAME: Jof
EDUCATION: Christ Church Foundation
School, Bridgetown, Barbados
TEAMS: England, Sussex, Southern Brave, Hobart
Hurricanes, MI Cape Town, Mumbai Indians,
Quetta Gladiators, Rajasthan Royals, WI U19
ROLE: Bowler
DEBUT: Test: 2019; ODI: 2019; T20I: 2019;
First-class: 2016; List A: 2016; T20: 2016

BEST BATTING: 81* Sussex vs Northamptonshire, Northampton, 2017
BEST BOWLING: 7-67 Sussex vs Kent, Hove, 2017
COUNTY CAP: 2017

FIRST CRICKET CLUB? Pickwick CC, Bridgetown, Barbados

Batting	Mat	Inns	NO	Runs	HS	Ave	SR	100	50	Ct	St
Tests	13	20	0	155	30	7.75	50.65	0	0	2	-
ODIs	31	18	9	162	38*	18.00	108.00	0	0	9	-
T20Is	34	12	5	82	21	11.71	132.25	0	0	10	-
First-class	43	63	10	1201	81*	22.66	66.94	0	6	21	-
List A	45	29	12	354	45	20.82	114.93	0	0	13	-
T20s	163	81	38	645	36	15.00	141.13	0	0	48	-
Bowling	Mat	Balls	Mdns	Runs	Wkts	BB	Ave	4wI	5wI	SR	Econ
Tests	13	2609	95	1304	42	6-45	31.04	-	3	62.11	2.99
ODIs	31	1631	18	1421	54	6-40	26.31	0	1	30.20	5.22
T20Is	34	754	2	1002	41	4-33	24.43	1	0	18.39	7.97
First-class	43	8856	316	4510	181	7-67	24.91	-	8	48.92	3.05
List A	45	2362	26	2066	75	6-40	27.54	0	2	31.49	5.24
T20s	163	3611	6	4694	203	4-18	23.12	2	0	17.78	7.79

GUS ATKINSON

RHB / RFM / R0 / W0

FULL NAME: Angus Alexander Patrick Atkinson
BORN: January 19, 1998, Chelsea, Middlesex
SQUAD NO: 37
HEIGHT: 6ft 2in
NICKNAME: G-bus
EDUCATION: Northcote Lodge, London; Bradfield College, Berkshire
TEAMS: England, Surrey, Oval Invincibles
ROLE: Bowler
DEBUT: Test: 2024; ODI: 2023; T20I: 2023; First-class: 2020; List A: 2021; T20: 2020

BEST BATTING: 118 England vs Sri Lanka, Lord's, 2024
BEST BOWLING: 7-45 England vs West Indies, Lord's, 2024

FIRST CRICKET CLUB? Spencer CC, London
BIGGEST INFLUENCE ON YOUR DEVELOPMENT AS A CRICKETER (EXCLUDING PARENTS)?
Julian Wood, my school coach who believed in my ability before I did
GREATEST PERFORMANCE YOU HAVE WITNESSED? Aaron Finch's 117 not out from 52 balls against Middlesex at The Oval in the 2018 T20 Blast. Never seen anything like it
CHILDHOOD SPORTING HERO? Andrew Flintoff
HOBBIES? Call of Duty (video game)
SURPRISING FACT ABOUT YOU: I had a rugby trial for Harlequins aged 13

Batting	Mat	Inns	NO	Runs	HS	Ave	SR	100	50	Ct	St
Tests	11	16	1	352	118	23.46	79.10	1	0	5	-
ODIs	11	8	2	104	38	17.33	136.84	0	0	1	-
T20Is	4	2	1	10	8*	10.00	43.47	0	0	1	-
First-class	30	42	6	793	118	22.02	65.16	1	3	10	-
List A	13	9	2	119	38	17.00	146.91	0	0	2	-
T20s	56	26	15	98	14	8.90	94.23	0	0	16	-

Bowling	Mat	Balls	Mdns	Runs	Wkts	BB	Ave	4wI	5wI	SR	Econ
Tests	11	1852	52	1152	52	7-45	22.15	-	3	35.61	3.73
ODIs	11	472	0	527	13	2-28	40.53	0	0	36.30	6.69
T20Is	4	65	0	122	6	4-20	20.33	1	0	10.83	11.26
First-class	30	4703	124	2768	111	7-45	24.93	-	4	42.36	3.53
List A	13	568	1	640	18	4-43	35.55	1	0	31.55	6.76
T20s	56	1029	1	1531	72	4-20	21.26	3	0	14.29	8.92

TOM BAILEY

RHB / RFM / R0 / W4

FULL NAME: Thomas Ernest Bailey
BORN: April 21, 1991, Preston, Lancashire
SQUAD NO: 8
HEIGHT: 6ft 4in
NICKNAME: Big Poppa
EDUCATION: Myerscough College, Lancashire
TEAMS: Lancashire, England Lions
ROLE: Bowler
DEBUT: First-class: 2012; List A: 2014; T20: 2015

BEST BATTING: 78 Lancashire vs Kent, Canterbury, 2023
BEST BOWLING: 7-37 Lancashire vs Hampshire, Liverpool, 2021
COUNTY CAP: 2018

FIRST CRICKET CLUB? Vernon Carus CC, Lancashire
WHAT'S THE BIGGEST PRIZE IN DOMESTIC CRICKET? The County Championship
THE KOOKABURRA BALL: YES OR NO? No, not suitable on flat English wickets
FAVOURITE WARM-UP SONG? Baby Shark
SPECIALITY SUBJECT IN A PUB QUIZ (EXCLUDING SPORT)? History, in particular the period 1636-1701
HOBBY YOU WOULD LIKE TO LEARN: Laser tag
WHICH PUBLIC FIGURE INSPIRES YOU (EXCLUDING SPORTSPEOPLE)? Donald Trump
FILM YOU CAN WATCH OVER AND OVER: WALL E

Batting	Mat	Inns	NO	Runs	HS	Ave	SR	100	50	Ct	St
First-class	111	148	21	2390	78	18.81	54.64	0	11	20	-
List A	39	26	9	325	60	19.11	87.13	0	1	5	-
T20s	35	9	3	27	10	4.50	93.10	0	0	10	-

Bowling	Mat	Balls	Mdns	Runs	Wkts	BB	Ave	4wl	5wl	SR	Econ
First-class	111	19943	816	9342	386	7-37	24.20	-	15	51.66	2.81
List A	39	1925	18	1624	49	3-22	33.14	0	0	39.28	5.06
T20s	35	528	0	811	31	5-17	26.16	0	1	17.03	9.21

JONNY BAIRSTOW

RHB / WK / R3 / W0

FULL NAME: Jonathan Marc Bairstow
BORN: September 26, 1989, Bradford
SQUAD NO: 21
NICKNAME: Bluey
EDUCATION: St Peter's School, York; Leeds Metropolitan University
TEAMS: England, Yorkshire, Welsh Fire, Joburg Super Kings, Peshawar Zalmi, Punjab Kings, Sunrisers Hyderabad
ROLE: Batter/wicketkeeper
DEBUT: Test: 2012; ODI: 2011; T20I: 2011; First-class: 2009; List A: 2009; T20: 2010

YORKSHIRE

BEST BATTING: 246 Yorkshire vs Hampshire, Headingley, 2016

COUNTY CAP: 2011; **BENEFIT:** 2023

FAMILY TIES? My father David played for Yorkshire and England
CHILDHOOD SPORTING HERO? Sachin Tendulkar
SURPRISING FACT ABOUT YOU: I played football for the Leeds United Academy for seven years

Batting	Mat	Inns	NO	Runs	HS	Ave	SR	100	50	Ct	St
Tests	100	178	12	6042	167*	36.39	59.07	12	26	242	14
ODIs	107	98	8	3868	141*	42.97	102.95	11	17	55	3
T20Is	80	72	16	1671	90	29.83	137.53	0	10	46	1
First-class	220	368	39	14094	246	42.83	-	31	70	552	25
List A	175	160	14	5790	174	39.65	102.64	14	27	106	9
T20s	227	210	34	5385	114	30.59	137.44	4	29	120	17

Bowling	Mat	Balls	Mdns	Runs	Wkts	BB	Ave	4wI	5wI	SR	Econ
Tests	100	-	-	-	-	-	-	-	-	-	-
ODIs	107	-	-	-	-	-	-	-	-	-	-
T20Is	80	-	-	-	-	-	-	-	-	-	-
First-class	220	6	0	1	0	0-1	-	-	-	-	1.00
List A	175	-	-	-	-	-	-	-	-	-	-
T20s	227	-	-	-	-	-	-	-	-	-	-

SONNY BAKER

RHB / RFM / R0 / W0

HAMPSHIRE

FULL NAME: Sonny Baker
BORN: March 13, 2003, Torbay, Devon
SQUAD NO: 95
HEIGHT: 6ft
NICKNAME: Bakes
EDUCATION: Torquay Boys' Grammar School; King's College, Taunton
TEAMS: Hampshire, England Lions, Somerset, Southern Brave
ROLE: Bowler
DEBUT: First-class: 2025; List A: 2021; T20: 2022

BEST BATTING: 5 England Lions vs Australia A, Sydney, 2025
BEST BOWLING: 3-60 England Lions vs Australia A, Sydney, 2025

FIRST CRICKET CLUB? Torquay CC, Devon
WHICH TEAMMATE HAS HAD THE BIGGEST IMPACT ON YOUR GAME? Steve Davies at Somerset – he's a wise man
IF YOU COULD PINCH A PLAYER FROM ANOTHER COUNTY, WHO WOULD IT BE? Simon Harmer
HOW IS BAZBALL AFFECTING CHAMPIONSHIP CRICKET? Bowlers seem to set more aggressive fields, batters try to change momentum rather than nominally counting runs
WHAT DO YOU THINK OF THE CURRENT 50-OVER COMPETITION? It gives game time to young players in front of decent crowds, although there is a drop-off in standard compared to the other competitions. But I think the trade-off is worth it
WHO IS THE TOUGHEST BOWLER TO FACE? Kyle Abbott – based on what I've heard about some of his bowling spells
CHOOSE A FANTASY SLIP CORDON TO SPEND A DAY IN THE FIELD WITH: Jack Russell (wk), Will Ferrell, Patrick Bet-David, Sacha Baron Cohen

Batting	Mat	Inns	NO	Runs	HS	Ave	SR	100	50	Ct	St
First-class	1	2	0	8	5	4.00	11.11	0	0	0	-
List A	11	4	2	12	7*	6.00	27.90	0	0	3	-
T20s	8	3	1	0	0*	0.00	0.00	0	0	2	-

Bowling	Mat	Balls	Mdns	Runs	Wkts	BB	Ave	4wI	5wI	SR	Econ
First-class	1	108	6	60	3	3-60	20.00	-	0	36.00	3.33
List A	11	455	2	483	19	6-46	25.42	0	1	23.94	6.36
T20s	8	141	0	222	7	2-28	31.71	0	0	20.14	9.44

GEORGE BALDERSON

LHB / RM / R0 / W0

FULL NAME: George Philip Balderson
BORN: October 11, 2000, Manchester
SQUAD NO: 10
HEIGHT: 5ft 10in
NICKNAME: Baldy
EDUCATION: Cheadle Hulme High School, Greater Manchester
TEAMS: Lancashire, England U19
ROLE: Allrounder
DEBUT: First-class: 2020; List A: 2021; T20: 2024

BEST BATTING: 116* Lancashire vs Warwickshire, Edgbaston, 2023
BEST BOWLING: 5-14 Lancashire vs Essex, Chelmsford, 2022

FIRST CRICKET CLUB? Cheadle Hulme CC, Greater Manchester. I'd watch my dad play there every Saturday
EARLIEST CRICKETING MEMORY? Watching my dad play at Cheadle Hulme
WHAT'S THE BIGGEST PRIZE IN DOMESTIC CRICKET? The County Championship
THE KOOKABURRA BALL: YES OR NO? Yes, because it brings new skill sets into the game
WHO IS THE TOUGHEST BOWLER TO FACE? Mohammad Abbas
WHICH TEAMMATE HAS HAD THE BIGGEST IMPACT ON YOUR GAME? Dane Vilas – he was the captain who gave me my first chance
HOW MANY HOURS DO YOU SPEND ON YOUR PHONE A DAY? Three
SPECIALITY SUBJECT IN A PUB QUIZ (EXCLUDING SPORT)? Maths

Batting	Mat	Inns	NO	Runs	HS	Ave	SR	100	50	Ct	St
First-class	47	70	8	1776	116*	28.64	44.46	2	8	6	-
List A	29	25	4	655	106*	31.19	80.96	1	3	5	-
T20s	3	3	1	76	37*	38.00	146.15	0	0	1	-

Bowling	Mat	Balls	Mdns	Runs	Wkts	BB	Ave	4wI	5wI	SR	Econ
First-class	47	6161	202	3324	102	5-14	32.58	-	1	60.40	3.23
List A	29	1134	6	902	26	3-25	34.69	0	0	43.61	4.77
T20s	3	42	0	63	3	2-15	21.00	0	0	14.00	9.00

JAKE BALL

RHB / RFM / R0 / W1

SOMERSET

FULL NAME: Jacob Timothy Ball
BORN: March 14, 1991, Mansfield, Nottinghamshire
SQUAD NO: 14
HEIGHT: 6ft 3in
NICKNAME: Yak
EDUCATION: Meden School, Mansfield
TEAMS: England, Somerset, Nottinghamshire, Sydney Sixers, Welsh Fire
ROLE: Bowler
DEBUT: Test: 2016; ODI: 2016; T20I: 2018; First-class: 2011; List A: 2009; T20: 2011

BEST BATTING: 49* Nottinghamshire vs Warwickshire, Trent Bridge, 2015
BEST BOWLING: 6-49 Nottinghamshire vs Sussex, Trent Bridge, 2015
COUNTY CAP: 2016 (Nottinghamshire)

FIRST CRICKET CLUB? Welbeck Colliery CC, Nottinghamshire
FAMILY TIES? My uncle Bruce French played for England
BEST PERFORMANCE AS A PRO? Taking 5-51 on my England ODI debut at Mirpur in 2016
FAVOURITE FORMAT? T20
THE KOOKABURRA BALL: YES OR NO? Definitely no!
DESCRIBE YOURSELF IN THREE WORDS: Tall fast bowler
WHICH PUBLIC FIGURE INSPIRES YOU (EXCLUDING SPORTSPEOPLE)? Ricky Gervais
SURPRISING FACT ABOUT YOU: I don't like swimming in the sea – I don't trust it
FILM YOU CAN WATCH OVER AND OVER: Moneyball

Batting	Mat	Inns	NO	Runs	HS	Ave	SR	100	50	Ct	St
Tests	4	8	0	67	31	8.37	53.60	0	0	1	-
ODIs	18	6	2	38	28	9.50	77.55	0	0	5	-
T20Is	2	0	-	-	-	-	-	-	-	1	-
First-class	78	117	29	1120	49*	12.72	69.65	0	0	15	-
List A	95	38	15	198	28	8.60	99.00	0	0	19	-
T20s	134	24	14	63	18*	6.30	78.75	0	0	34	-

Bowling	Mat	Balls	Mdns	Runs	Wkts	BB	Ave	4wI	5wI	SR	Econ
Tests	4	612	23	343	3	1-47	114.33	-	0	204.00	3.36
ODIs	18	947	5	980	21	5-51	46.66	0	1	45.09	6.20
T20Is	2	42	0	83	2	1-39	41.50	0	0	21.00	11.85
First-class	78	11696	386	6757	228	6-49	29.63	-	7	51.29	3.46
List A	95	4036	16	3955	118	5-51	33.51	4	1	34.20	5.87
T20s	134	2661	3	3968	177	4-11	22.41	4	0	15.03	8.94

ETHAN BAMBER

RHB / RFM / R0 / W1

FULL NAME: Ethan Read Bamber
BORN: December 17, 1998, Westminster
SQUAD NO: TBC
HEIGHT: 5ft 11in
NICKNAME: Sorry
EDUCATION: Mill Hill School, London;
University of Exeter
TEAMS: Warwickshire, England U19,
Gloucestershire, Middlesex
ROLE: Bowler
DEBUT: First-class: 2018; List A: 2021; T20: 2019

BEST BATTING: 46* Middlesex vs Surrey, Lord's, 2023
BEST BOWLING: 5-20 Middlesex vs Warwickshire, Edgbaston, 2023
COUNTY CAP: 2022 (Middlesex)

FIRST CRICKET CLUB? North Middlesex CC, London
WHICH AWAY GROUND DO YOU MOST ENJOY VISITING? Old Trafford – a great ground and
my family is from Manchester
WHO IS THE MOST TALENTED U19 TEENAGER IN THE COUNTY GAME? Seb Morgan (Mid)
HOW IS BAZBALL AFFECTING CHAMPIONSHIP CRICKET? Batters run at me and hit me for six
WHAT DO YOU THINK OF THE CURRENT 50-OVER COMPETITION? A good mix of developing
youngsters and some really high-quality players
WHAT'S THE SILLIEST OUTFIT YOU'VE EVER WORN? A deckchair from The Titanic

Batting	Mat	Inns	NO	Runs	HS	Ave	SR	100	50	Ct	St
First-class	61	88	30	652	46*	11.24	36.73	0	0	16	-
List A	22	14	3	117	21	10.63	82.97	0	0	4	-
T20s	7	2	2	5	3*	-	100.00	0	0	2	-

Bowling	Mat	Balls	Mdns	Runs	Wkts	BB	Ave	4wI	5wI	SR	Econ
First-class	61	11391	435	5438	196	5-20	27.74	-	3	58.11	2.86
List A	22	1126	14	935	32	3-27	29.21	0	0	35.18	4.98
T20s	7	95	0	167	4	3-29	41.75	0	0	23.75	10.54

CAMERON BANCROFT RHB / WK / R0 / W0 / MVP23

GLOUCESTERSHIRE

FULL NAME: Cameron Timothy Bancroft
BORN: November 19, 1992, Perth, Australia
SQUAD NO: 4
HEIGHT: 6ft 1in
NICKNAME: Bangers
EDUCATION: Aquinas College, Perth
TEAMS: Australia, Gloucestershire, Durham, Perth Scorchers, Somerset, Sydney Thunder, Western Australia
ROLE: Batter/wicketkeeper
DEBUT: Test: 2017; T20I: 2016; First-class: 2013; List A: 2011; T20: 2014

BEST BATTING: 228* Western Australia vs South Australia, Perth, 2017
BEST BOWLING: 1-10 Western Australia vs Queensland, Brisbane, 2019
COUNTY CAP: 2016 (Gloucestershire)

NOTES: The experienced Australian batter returns for his fourth season at Bristol following a glorious 2024 in which he was a key member of the Gloucestershire side which won the club's first T20 title. Bancroft, 33, also contributed 832 runs at 48.94 in the County Championship and now inherits the four-day captaincy after Graeme van Buuren stepped down. "I love his dedication to preparation and his subsequent transference of that in the middle," said Mark Alleyne, Gloucestershire's head coach. "His experience of playing Test match cricket and winning four-day titles gives him a broad base of experience which our players can feed off." Bancroft, who has also had spells with Durham and Somerset, was previously suspended for nine months by Cricket Australia for his role in the ball-tampering scandal at Cape Town. He returned to the Test side for the 2019 Ashes but hasn't appeared for Australia since then

Batting	Mat	Inns	NO	Runs	HS	Ave	SR	100	50	Ct	St
Tests	10	18	1	446	82*	26.23	42.80	0	3	16	-
T20Is	1	1	1	0	0*	-	0.00	0	0	1	-
First-class	169	305	24	10861	228*	38.65	43.14	30	38	259	1
List A	101	96	15	3267	176	40.33	83.08	5	22	83	2
T20s	121	113	21	2918	95*	31.71	123.90	0	19	54	6

Bowling	Mat	Balls	Mdns	Runs	Wkts	BB	Ave	4wI	5wI	SR	Econ
Tests	10	-	-	-	-	-	-	-	-	-	-
T20Is	1	-	-	-	-	-	-	-	-	-	-
First-class	169	66	1	77	2	1-10	38.50	-	0	33.00	7.00
List A	101	-	-	-	-	-	-	-	-	-	-
T20s	121	-	-	-	-	-	-	-	-	-	-

TOM BANTON RHB / WK / R0 / W0 / MVP10

FULL NAME: Thomas Banton
BORN: November 11, 1998, Chiltern, Bucks
SQUAD NO: 18
HEIGHT: 6ft 2in
EDUCATION: Bromsgrove School, Worcestershire; King's College, Taunton
TEAMS: England, Somerset, Trent Rockets, Brisbane Heat, Colombo Stars, Fortune Barisal, Kolkata Knight Riders, Northern Superchargers, Welsh Fire
ROLE: Batter/wicketkeeper
DEBUT: ODI: 2020; T20I: 2019; First-class: 2018; List A: 2018; T20: 2017

SOMERSET

BEST BATTING: 133 Somerset vs Kent, Taunton, 2024

FIRST CRICKET CLUB? Sutton Coldfield CC, Birmingham
GREATEST PERFORMANCE YOU HAVE WITNESSED? Johann Myburgh smashing 103 off 44 balls against Essex in the 2018 T20 Blast. I was batting at the other end as we chased down 136 without losing a wicket
BIGGEST CRICKETING REGRET? Not playing for Somerset at the age of 10
WHO WOULD YOU MOST LIKE TO HAVE A NET WITH? AB de Villiers
HOBBIES? Hockey
MOST BEAUTIFUL THING YOU HAVE EVER SEEN? Mountains in Switzerland

Batting	Mat	Inns	NO	Runs	HS	Ave	SR	100	50	Ct	St
ODIs	7	6	0	172	58	28.66	92.47	0	1	3	-
T20Is	14	14	0	327	73	23.35	147.96	0	2	9	-
First-class	42	67	2	2089	133	32.13	61.09	3	13	26	-
List A	25	23	0	696	112	30.26	87.76	2	4	17	1
T20s	164	162	9	4232	107*	27.66	144.28	4	24	90	10

Bowling	Mat	Balls	Mdns	Runs	Wkts	BB	Ave	4wl	5wl	SR	Econ
ODIs	7	-	-	-	-	-	-	-	-	-	-
T20Is	14	-	-	-	-	-	-	-	-	-	-
First-class	42	42	3	16	0	0-0	-	-	-	-	2.28
List A	25	-	-	-	-	-	-	-	-	-	-
T20s	164	-	-	-	-	-	-	-	-	-	-

KEITH BARKER

LHB / LFM / RO / W4

FULL NAME: Keith Hubert Douglas Barker
BORN: October 21, 1986, Manchester
SQUAD NO: 13
HEIGHT: 6ft 3in
NICKNAME: Barks
EDUCATION: Moorhead High School,
Accrington; Preston College
TEAMS: Hampshire, Warwickshire
ROLE: Allrounder
DEBUT: First-class: 2009; List A: 2009; T20: 2009

BEST BATTING: 125 Warwickshire vs Surrey, Guildford, 2013
BEST BOWLING: 7-46 Hampshire vs Nottinghamshire, Southampton, 2021
COUNTY CAP: 2013 (Warwickshire)

FIRST CRICKET CLUB? Enfield CC, Lancashire
WHICH TEAMMATE HAS HAD THE BIGGEST IMPACT ON YOUR GAME? There's two: Chris
Wright when we were at Warwickshire together, and Kyle Abbott at Hampshire
WHAT PART OF THE SEASON DO YOU MOST ENJOY? The end
WHICH AWAY GROUND DO YOU MOST ENJOY VISITING? Edgbaston, home of my old club
IF YOU COULD PINCH A PLAYER FROM ANOTHER COUNTY, WHO WOULD IT BE?
Chris Wright
WHAT KEEPS YOU AWAKE AT NIGHT? My kids
CHOOSE A FANTASY SLIP CORDON TO SPEND A DAY IN THE FIELD WITH: Tim Ambrose (wk),
Joe Rogan, Joey Diaz, Dave Chappelle
SURPRISING FACT ABOUT YOU: I never scored a hundred for the Enfield first team

Batting	Mat	Inns	NO	Runs	HS	Ave	SR	100	50	Ct	St
First-class	167	226	35	5450	125	28.53	57.92	6	26	40	-
List A	72	47	13	639	56	18.79	95.08	0	1	15	-
T20s	65	35	7	383	46	13.67	111.01	0	0	17	-

Bowling	Mat	Balls	Mdns	Runs	Wkts	BB	Ave	4wI	5wI	SR	Econ
First-class	167	27828	1104	13376	533	7-46	25.09	-	23	52.21	2.88
List A	72	2870	14	2681	86	4-33	31.17	1	0	33.37	5.60
T20s	65	1206	0	1588	69	4-19	23.01	2	0	17.47	7.90

CHARLIE BARNARD RHB / SLA / RO / WO

FULL NAME: Charlie Mark Barnard
BORN: November 5, 2004, Ashton-under-Lyne, Lancashire
SQUAD NO: 5
HEIGHT: 5ft 9in
NICKNAME: Barny
EDUCATION: Hyde High School; Ashton Sixth Form College
TEAMS: Lancashire, England U19
ROLE: Bowler
DEBUT: List A: 2024

LANCASHIRE

FIRST CRICKET CLUB? Newton CC, Cheshire
EARLIEST CRICKETING MEMORY? Playing with my dad in the garden
WHAT'S THE BIGGEST PRIZE IN DOMESTIC CRICKET? Division One of the County Championship
THE KOOKABURRA BALL: YES OR NO? Yes – it's better for spinners like me
OPPONENT YOU MOST LOOK FORWARD TO PLAYING AGAINST? Any of the England U19 lads that I have played with over the last few years
FAVOURITE WARM-UP SONG? Are You in Love With A Notion? by The Courteeners
HOW MANY HOURS DO YOU SPEND ON YOUR PHONE A DAY? Six
SPECIALITY SUBJECT IN A PUB QUIZ (EXCLUDING SPORT)? Only Fools and Horses
HOBBY YOU WOULD LIKE TO LEARN: The piano
WHICH PUBLIC FIGURE INSPIRES YOU (EXCLUDING SPORTSPEOPLE)? Noel Gallagher
SURPRISING FACT ABOUT YOU: I follow my local football team Hyde United home and away
FILM YOU CAN WATCH OVER AND OVER: Four Lions

Batting	Mat	Inns	NO	Runs	HS	Ave	SR	100	50	Ct	St
List A	7	7	2	25	9	5.00	39.06	0	0	3	-
Bowling	Mat	Balls	Mdns	Runs	Wkts	BB	Ave	4wI	5wI	SR	Econ
List A	7	318	2	246	8	3-47	30.75	0	0	39.75	4.64

ED BARNARD RHB / RMF / R0 / W0 / MVP3

WARWICKSHIRE

FULL NAME: Edward George Barnard
BORN: November 20, 1995, Shrewsbury
SQUAD NO: 30
HEIGHT: 6ft
NICKNAME: Barndoor
EDUCATION: Meole Brace School, Shrewsbury; Shrewsbury School
TEAMS: Warwickshire, England Lions, Worcestershire
ROLE: Bowler
DEBUT: First-class: 2015; List A: 2015; T20: 2015

BEST BATTING: 165 Warwickshire vs Essex, Chelmsford, 2024
BEST BOWLING: 6-37 Worcestershire vs Somerset, Taunton, 2018

FIRST CRICKET CLUB? Shrewsbury CC, Shropshire. We were the National Knockout champions in 1983 and 2011

WHICH TEAMMATE HAS HAD THE BIGGEST IMPACT ON YOUR GAME? Daryl Mitchell at Worcestershire – helped me learn about keeping level through the ups and downs

WHAT PART OF THE SEASON DO YOU MOST ENJOY? Championship cricket at the height of summer in good weather with decent crowds

WHICH AWAY GROUND DO YOU MOST ENJOY VISITING? Lord's for four-day cricket, Trent Bridge for T20

HOW IS BAZBALL AFFECTING CHAMPIONSHIP CRICKET? The increase in batting bonus points has put up the run-rates and batters are generally more positive, especially against spin

WHAT DO YOU THINK OF THE CURRENT 50-OVER COMPETITION? Still a great competition – I love the chance to play at different outgrounds in front of good crowds

Batting	Mat	Inns	NO	Runs	HS	Ave	SR	100	50	Ct	St
First-class	120	174	27	5075	165	34.52	54.35	7	27	70	-
List A	78	65	19	1970	173*	42.82	96.56	4	8	32	-
T20s	117	81	22	901	48	15.27	130.95	0	0	57	-

Bowling	Mat	Balls	Mdns	Runs	Wkts	BB	Ave	4wl	5wl	SR	Econ
First-class	120	17659	630	9518	315	6-37	30.21	-	7	56.06	3.23
List A	78	3243	22	2993	95	4-21	31.50	2	0	34.13	5.53
T20s	117	1599	0	2403	61	3-29	39.39	0	0	26.21	9.01

NATHAN BARNWELL RHB / RFM / RO / WO

FULL NAME: Nathan André Barnwell
BORN: February 3, 2003, Ashford, Kent
SQUAD NO: 29
EDUCATION: Caterham School
TEAMS: Surrey, England U19
ROLE: Bowler
DEBUT: First-class: 2022; List A: 2022

SURREY

BEST BATTING: 22 Surrey vs Sri Lanka Development XI, Guildford, 2022
BEST BOWLING: 1-68 Surrey vs Sri Lanka Development XI, Guildford, 2022

NOTES: Barnwell was a regular throughout Surrey age-group cricket, having started at U9 level. He made his debut for England U19 in 2021 against West Indies, taking 3 for 30 in the third Youth ODI, and was in the squad for the 2022 U19 World Cup in the Caribbean. He made five Championship appearances for Surrey's Second XI in the 2022 season, when he was also the side's leading wicket-taker in the T20 competition. Barnwell is capable of bowling at high pace and is developing as a lower-order finisher with the bat in white-ball fixtures. He made his List A debut in August 2022 in the One-Day Cup and played the majority of Surrey's Second XI T20s in 2023 before injury cut his season short in June. On getting into cricket, he says: "My dad used to play at school in the Caribbean and we played a bit of backyard cricket with my brother and sister. I used to be a wicketkeeper at my first club, but at the first game the kit we got was way too big! I grew up looking up to Chris Jordan, so it's crazy how he's in the same changing room as me now"

Batting	Mat	Inns	NO	Runs	HS	Ave	SR	100	50	Ct	St
First-class	1	1	0	22	22	22.00	122.22	0	0	0	-
List A	8	6	2	88	31	22.00	87.12	0	0	1	-

Bowling	Mat	Balls	Mdns	Runs	Wkts	BB	Ave	4wI	5wI	SR	Econ
First-class	1	138	1	100	1	1-68	100.00	-	0	138.00	4.34
List A	8	255	0	296	2	1-23	148.00	0	0	127.50	6.96

GEORGE BARTLETT

RHB / OB / R0 / W0

NORTHAMPTONSHIRE

FULL NAME: George Anthony Bartlett
BORN: March 14, 1998, Frimley, Surrey
SQUAD NO: 14
HEIGHT: 6ft 1in
NICKNAME: GB
EDUCATION: Millfield School, Somerset
TEAMS: Northamptonshire, England U19, Somerset
ROLE: Batter
DEBUT: First-class: 2017; List A: 2019; T20: 2020

BEST BATTING: 137 Somerset vs Surrey, Guildford, 2019

FIRST CRICKET CLUB? Westlands CC, Yeovil, Somerset
WHAT PART OF THE SEASON DO YOU MOST ENJOY? The T20 block
WHICH AWAY GROUND DO YOU MOST ENJOY VISITING? Old Trafford
IF YOU COULD PINCH A PLAYER FROM ANOTHER COUNTY, WHO WOULD IT BE? Ben Green
HOW IS BAZBALL AFFECTING CHAMPIONSHIP CRICKET? In a good way – players are expressing themselves more and there's no one way to play
WHO IS THE TOUGHEST BOWLER TO FACE? R Ashwin – so many variations

Batting	Mat	Inns	NO	Runs	HS	Ave	SR	100	50	Ct	St
First-class	65	108	9	3053	137	30.83	54.79	9	11	14	-
List A	39	38	7	985	108	31.77	88.97	1	5	15	-
T20s	17	13	1	161	82*	13.41	135.29	0	1	6	-

Bowling	Mat	Balls	Mdns	Runs	Wkts	BB	Ave	4wI	5wI	SR	Econ
First-class	65	32	0	40	0	0-13	-	-	-	-	7.50
List A	39	48	0	52	0	0-8	-	-	-	-	6.50
T20s	17	-	-	-	-	-	-	-	-	-	-

SHOAIB BASHIR RHB / OB / R0 / W0

FULL NAME: Shoaib Bashir
BORN: October 13, 2003, Chertsey, Surrey
SQUAD NO: 13
HEIGHT: 6ft 4in
NICKNAME: Bash
EDUCATION: Fulbrook School, Surrey;
Woking College
TEAMS: England, Somerset, Worcestershire
ROLE: Bowler
DEBUT: Test: 2024; First-class: 2023; List A:
2023; T20: 2023

BEST BATTING: 44* Somerset vs Hampshire, Taunton, 2023
BEST BOWLING: 5-41 England vs West Indies, Trent Bridge, 2024

WHICH COUNTY PLAYER WOULD YOU MOST LIKE TO GO FOR A DRINK WITH? Jack Leach –
to talk about the way he goes about his bowling in different situations
GREATEST PERFORMANCE YOU HAVE WITNESSED? Kevin Pietersen's double-hundred for
Surrey against Leicestershire at Guildford in 2012
FAVOURITE FORMAT? The longer form – because it's a test of character
DESCRIBE YOURSELF IN THREE WORDS: Relaxed, dedicated, cultured
HOBBIES? Spending time with family and friends
FAVOURITE TOY AS A KID? Match Attax trading football cards
WHAT WOULD BE YOUR PERFECT BREAKFAST? A Full English
WHICH PERSON INSPIRES YOU MOST? My uncle Saj
SURPRISING FACT ABOUT YOU: I was once hit in the face by a cricket ball and all my front
teeth were smashed

Batting	Mat	Inns	NO	Runs	HS	Ave	SR	100	50	Ct	St
Tests	15	23	12	76	13	6.90	36.71	0	0	4	-
First-class	27	42	19	178	44*	7.73	35.60	0	0	9	-
List A	8	4	2	10	7	5.00	43.47	0	0	7	-
T20s	7	1	1	0	0*	-	0.00	0	0	1	-

Bowling	Mat	Balls	Mdns	Runs	Wkts	BB	Ave	4wl	5wl	SR	Econ
Tests	15	3147	37	1968	49	5-41	40.16	-	3	64.22	3.75
First-class	27	5385	112	3251	66	5-41	49.25	-	3	81.59	3.62
List A	8	319	1	344	3	1-46	114.66	0	0	106.33	6.47
T20s	7	102	0	146	6	3-26	24.33	0	0	17.00	8.58

FINLAY BEAN

LHB / RO / WO

YORKSHIRE

FULL NAME: Finlay Joseph Bean
BORN: April 16, 2002, Harrogate, Yorkshire
SQUAD NO: 33
HEIGHT: 6ft 2in
NICKNAME: Flickma
EDUCATION: Queen Ethelburga's College, York; Ripon Grammar School
TEAMS: Yorkshire, England U19
ROLE: Batter
DEBUT: First-class: 2022; List A: 2022

BEST BATTING: 173 Yorkshire vs Glamorgan, Headingley, 2024

FIRST CRICKET CLUB? Studley Royal CC, Ripon, North Yorkshire
EARLIEST CRICKETING MEMORY? Backgarden cricket with my brother
THE KOOKABURRA BALL: YES OR NO? Yes, as a batter it gives you a break from the nipping Dukes!
SPECIALITY SUBJECT IN A PUB QUIZ (EXCLUDING SPORT)? Politics
ONE THING YOU WANT TO DO BEFORE YOU DIE: Drive the Nürburgring in Germany
HOBBY YOU WOULD LIKE TO LEARN: Play the guitar
SURPRISING FACT ABOUT YOU: I was an assistant mechanic at C&C Services
FILM YOU CAN WATCH OVER AND OVER: The Hangover

Batting	Mat	Inns	NO	Runs	HS	Ave	SR	100	50	Ct	St
First-class	30	49	0	1867	173	38.10	57.64	5	5	37	-
List A	16	16	0	242	61	15.12	73.33	0	1	8	-

Bowling	Mat	Balls	Mdns	Runs	Wkts	BB	Ave	4wI	5wI	SR	Econ
First-class	30	66	0	105	0	0-4	-	-	-	-	9.54
List A	16	-	-	-	-	-	-	-	-	-	-

DAVID BEDINGHAM   RHB / OB / R3 / W0 / MVP16

FULL NAME: David Guy Bedingham
BORN: April 22, 1994, George, Western Cape, South Africa
SQUAD NO: 5
HEIGHT: 6ft
EDUCATION: Wynberg Boys' High School, Cape Town; Stellenbosch University
TEAMS: South Africa, Durham, Birmingham Phoenix, Boland, Cape Cobras, Sunrisers Eastern Cape, Western Province
ROLE: Batter
DEBUT: Test: 2023; First-class: 2013; List A: 2013; T20: 2015

BEST BATTING: 257 Durham vs Derbyshire, Chester-le-Street, 2021

FIRST CRICKET CLUB? Milnerton CC, Cape Town, South Africa
BEST PLAYER IN COUNTY CRICKET (EXCLUDING TEAMMATES)? Simon Harmer
BEST PERFORMANCE AS A PRO? 180 not out at Trent Bridge in the 2021
County Championship
GREATEST PERFORMANCE YOU HAVE WITNESSED? Joe Clarke's T20 hundred against us at the Riverside in 2020
FAVOURITE FORMAT? T20 because of the fans that come to watch
DESCRIBE YOURSELF IN THREE WORDS: Ambitious, selfless, quiet
HOBBIES? Walking my dog
FAVOURITE TOY AS A KID? Action Man
WHAT WOULD BE YOUR PERFECT BREAKFAST? Cheese and bacon toastie
SURPRISING FACT ABOUT YOU: I like rugby more than cricket!

Batting	Mat	Inns	NO	Runs	HS	Ave	SR	100	50	Ct	St
Tests	12	21	2	645	110	33.94	69.72	1	3	15	-
First-class	110	177	18	8014	279	50.40	67.07	25	28	92	-
List A	49	48	5	1868	188*	43.44	108.22	6	10	14	-
T20s	83	77	1	1624	78	21.36	132.03	0	8	18	1

Bowling	Mat	Balls	Mdns	Runs	Wkts	BB	Ave	4wI	5wI	SR	Econ
Tests	12	-	-	-	-	-	-	-	-	-	-
First-class	110	30	0	27	0	0-2	-	-	-	-	5.40
List A	49	39	0	25	0	0-25	-	-	-	-	3.84
T20s	83	-	-	-	-	-	-	-	-	-	-

GEORGE BELL

RHB / WK / R0 / W0

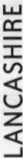

LANCASHIRE

FULL NAME: George Joseph Bell
BORN: September 25, 2002, Manchester
SQUAD NO: 17
HEIGHT: 5ft 8in
NICKNAME: Belly
EDUCATION: Manchester Grammar School
TEAMS: Lancashire, England U19
ROLE: Wicketkeeper/batter
DEBUT: First-class: 2022; List A: 2022; T20: 2022

BEST BATTING: 99 Lancashire vs Hampshire, Southampton, 2024
BEST BOWLING: 1-28 Lancashire vs Hampshire, Southport, 2023

FIRST CRICKET CLUB? Urmston CC, Trafford, Cheshire
WHAT'S THE BIGGEST PRIZE IN DOMESTIC CRICKET? The County Championship
THE KOOKABURRA BALL: YES OR NO? Yes
OPPONENT YOU MOST LOOK FORWARD TO PLAYING AGAINST? My former teammate Jack Morley – I want to hit him out of Derbyshire!
FAVOURITE WARM-UP SONG? Tell Me What You Want by Oden & Fatzo
HOW MANY HOURS DO YOU SPEND ON YOUR PHONE A DAY? Six
ONE THING YOU WANT TO DO BEFORE YOU DIE: Play football at Old Trafford
HOBBY YOU WOULD LIKE TO LEARN: Darts
WHICH PUBLIC FIGURE INSPIRES YOU (EXCLUDING SPORTSPEOPLE)? Bill Gates
SURPRISING FACT ABOUT YOU: I played for Manchester City's Academy when I was 11
FILM YOU CAN WATCH OVER AND OVER: Ted

Batting	Mat	Inns	NO	Runs	HS	Ave	SR	100	50	Ct	St
First-class	26	39	0	917	99	23.51	49.24	0	5	42	2
List A	17	17	1	414	78*	25.87	74.06	0	3	9	3
T20s	9	6	2	87	31	21.75	116.00	0	0	4	-

Bowling	Mat	Balls	Mdns	Runs	Wkts	BB	Ave	4wI	5wI	SR	Econ
First-class	26	132	0	85	1	1-28	85.00	-	0	132.00	3.86
List A	17	18	0	20	1	1-20	20.00	0	0	18.00	6.66
T20s	9	-	-	-	-	-	-	-	-	-	-

DANIEL BELL-DRUMMOND RHB / RM / R1 / W0 / MVP40

FULL NAME: Daniel James Bell-Drummond
BORN: August 4, 1993, Lewisham, London
SQUAD NO: 23
HEIGHT: 5ft 11in
NICKNAME: DBD
EDUCATION: Millfield School, Somerset; Anglia Ruskin University
TEAMS: Kent, Auckland, Birmingham Phoenix, Colombo Kings, England Lions, London Spirit, Rajshahi Kings
ROLE: Batter
DEBUT: First-class: 2011; List A: 2011; T20: 2011

BEST BATTING: 300* Kent vs Northamptonshire, Northampton, 2023
BEST BOWLING: 3-37 Kent vs Essex, Canterbury, 2022
COUNTY CAP: 2015

FIRST CRICKET CLUB? Catford Wanderers CC, London
EARLIEST CRICKETING MEMORY? Following my dad around on the weekends
THE KOOKABURRA BALL: YES OR NO? Yes, because it brings in different styles of play so players have to adapt
HOW MANY HOURS DO YOU SPEND ON YOUR PHONE A DAY? Five or more!
SPECIALITY SUBJECT IN A PUB QUIZ (EXCLUDING SPORT)? Geography
ONE THING YOU WANT TO DO BEFORE YOU DIE: Travel the world (beyond the cricketing countries)
HOBBY YOU WOULD LIKE TO LEARN: Re-learn an instrument
WHICH PUBLIC FIGURE INSPIRES YOU (EXCLUDING SPORTSPEOPLE)? Denzel Washington
SURPRISING FACT ABOUT YOU: I loved the drums before I got into cricket
FILM YOU CAN WATCH OVER AND OVER: The Equaliser

Batting	Mat	Inns	NO	Runs	HS	Ave	SR	100	50	Ct	St
First-class	163	284	26	8771	300*	33.99	51.48	18	42	67	-
List A	94	93	8	3771	171*	44.36	82.58	7	25	33	-
T20s	166	164	11	4722	112*	30.86	136.63	2	37	53	-

Bowling	Mat	Balls	Mdns	Runs	Wkts	BB	Ave	4wI	5wI	SR	Econ
First-class	163	1352	33	745	25	3-37	29.80	-	0	54.08	3.30
List A	94	155	2	121	5	2-22	24.20	0	0	31.00	4.68
T20s	166	111	0	191	5	2-19	38.20	0	0	22.20	10.32

CHRIS BENJAMIN

RHB / WK / R0 / W0

FULL NAME: Christopher Gavin Benjamin
BORN: April 29, 1999, Johannesburg, South Africa
SQUAD NO: 12
HEIGHT: 6ft 2in
NICKNAME: Benji
EDUCATION: St Andrew's College, Johannesburg; Durham University
TEAMS: Kent, Birmingham Phoenix, Durham, MI Cape Town, Warwickshire
ROLE: Wicketkeeper/batter
DEBUT: First-class: 2019; List A: 2021; T20: 2021

BEST BATTING: 127 Warwickshire vs Lancashire, Old Trafford, 2021

BEST DELIVERY YOU HAVE EVER FACED? It was more of a spell of bowling to be honest: Hasan Ali reverse-swinging it against my former club Warwickshire at Old Trafford in 2022
BEST PERFORMANCE AS A PRO? Either my hundred on my Championship debut in 2021 or my match-winning knock for Birmingham Phoenix on my Hundred debut in the same year
GREATEST PERFORMANCE YOU HAVE WITNESSED? Liam Norwell taking nine wickets on the final day of the 2022 season to keep Warwickshire in Division One
FAVOURITE FORMAT? Four-day cricket
DESCRIBE YOURSELF IN THREE WORDS: Passionate, caring, motivated
FAVOURITE TOY AS A KID? Any bit of sporting equipment
SURPRISING FACT ABOUT YOU: I have lived in Uganda and Tanzania

Batting	Mat	Inns	NO	Runs	HS	Ave	SR	100	50	Ct	St
First-class	14	24	2	539	127	24.50	49.31	1	1	12	-
List A	11	8	1	260	75	37.14	89.96	0	2	6	-
T20s	70	62	15	962	68*	20.46	138.02	0	3	34	1

Bowling	Mat	Balls	Mdns	Runs	Wkts	BB	Ave	4wI	5wI	SR	Econ
First-class	14	-	-	-	-	-	-	-	-	-	-
List A	11	-	-	-	-	-	-	-	-	-	-
T20s	70	-	-	-	-	-	-	-	-	-	-

LUC BENKENSTEIN

RHB / LB / RO / WO

FULL NAME: Luc Martin Benkenstein
BORN: November 2, 2004, Durban, South Africa
SQUAD NO: 99
HEIGHT: 6ft
NICKNAME: Benki
EDUCATION: Hilton College; Seaford College
TEAMS: Essex, England U19
ROLE: Allrounder
DEBUT: First-class: 2024; List A: 2021; T20: 2024

BEST BATTING: 4 Essex vs Nottinghamshire, Chelmsford, 2024

WHICH TEAMMATE HAS HAD THE BIGGEST IMPACT ON YOUR GAME? Matt Critchley – he has helped me with the hardships of being a young leg-spinner
WHAT PART OF THE SEASON DO YOU MOST ENJOY? Around June when the ball starts to turn
WHICH AWAY GROUND DO YOU MOST ENJOY VISITING? Old Trafford – a great atmosphere and big boundaries
IF YOU COULD PINCH A PLAYER FROM ANOTHER COUNTY, WHO WOULD IT BE?
John Turner
WHAT DO YOU THINK OF THE CURRENT 50-OVER COMPETITION? It's great for youngsters to play alongside senior players
WHO IS THE TOUGHEST BOWLER TO FACE? Adil Rashid
WHAT KEEPS YOU AWAKE AT NIGHT? Mosquitos
CHOOSE A FANTASY SLIP CORDON TO SPEND A DAY IN THE FIELD WITH: David Goggins (wk), Kobe Bryant, Shane Warne, Dale Benkenstein

Batting	Mat	Inns	NO	Runs	HS	Ave	SR	100	50	Ct	St
First-class	2	2	0	8	4	4.00	50.00	0	0	2	-
List A	19	18	0	451	68	25.05	88.08	0	3	4	-
T20s	11	6	1	136	54	27.20	158.13	0	1	5	-

Bowling	Mat	Balls	Mdns	Runs	Wkts	BB	Ave	4wI	5wI	SR	Econ
First-class	2	-	-	-	-	-	-	-	-	-	-
List A	19	348	0	353	13	6-42	27.15	0	1	26.76	6.08
T20s	11	118	0	196	4	2-24	49.00	0	0	29.50	9.96

DOM BESS

RHB / OB / R0 / W0

FULL NAME: Dominic Mark Bess
BORN: July 22, 1997, Exeter, Devon
SQUAD NO: 47
HEIGHT: 5ft 11in
NICKNAME: Moonhead
EDUCATION: Blundell's School, Tiverton, Devon
TEAMS: England, Yorkshire, Somerset, Southern Rocks, Warwickshire
ROLE: Bowler
DEBUT: Test: 2018; First-class: 2016; List A: 2018; T20: 2016

BEST BATTING: 107 MCC vs Essex, Barbados, 2018
BEST BOWLING: 7-43 Yorkshire vs Northamptonshire, Northampton, 2021
COUNTY CAP: 2021 (Yorkshire)

FIRST CRICKET CLUB? Sidmouth CC, Devon. A beautiful coastal cricket club with a thatched roof
GREATEST PERFORMANCE YOU HAVE WITNESSED? James Hildreth scoring a hundred on one leg against Nottinghamshire in 2016
CHILDHOOD SPORTING HERO? Graeme Swann

Batting	Mat	Inns	NO	Runs	HS	Ave	SR	100	50	Ct	St
Tests	14	19	5	319	57	22.78	44.92	0	1	3	-
First-class	100	150	23	3348	107	26.36	53.82	1	20	46	-
List A	42	35	6	553	60	19.06	82.66	0	3	22	-
T20s	58	27	12	187	42*	12.46	111.97	0	0	14	-

Bowling	Mat	Balls	Mdns	Runs	Wkts	BB	Ave	4wl	5wl	SR	Econ
Tests	14	2502	82	1223	36	5-30	33.97	-	2	69.50	2.93
First-class	100	18138	666	9068	270	7-43	33.58	-	16	67.17	2.99
List A	42	1822	9	1725	37	5-37	46.62	0	1	49.24	5.68
T20s	58	1030	0	1308	43	3-15	30.41	0	0	23.95	7.61

JACOB BETHELL — LHB / SLA / R0 / W0 / MVP31

WARWICKSHIRE

FULL NAME: Jacob Graham Bethell
BORN: October 23, 2003, Barbados
SQUAD NO: 2
HEIGHT: 5ft 10in
NICKNAME: Beth
EDUCATION: Harrison College, Barbados; Rugby School, Warwickshire
TEAMS: England, Warwickshire, Birmingham Phoenix, Gloucestershire, Melbourne Renegades, Welsh Fire
ROLE: Batter
DEBUT: Test: 2024; ODI: 2024; T20I: 2024; First-class: 2021; List A: 2021; T20: 2021

BEST BATTING: 96 England vs New Zealand, Wellington, 2024
BEST BOWLING: 4-20 Warwickshire vs Lancashire, Old Trafford, 2024

WHICH TEAMMATE HAS HAD THE BIGGEST IMPACT ON YOUR GAME? Oliver Hannon-Dalby – I can chat with him about anything and he has great perspective from all his experience
WHAT PART OF THE SEASON DO YOU MOST ENJOY? The T20 block
WHO IS THE MOST TALENTED U19 TEENAGER IN THE COUNTY GAME? Hamza Shaikh
WHAT DO YOU THINK OF THE CURRENT 50-OVER COMPETITION? It's allowing young players to perform under pressure. I love the 50-over format because it has so many different phases
WHO IS THE TOUGHEST BOWLER TO FACE? Simon Harmer
WHAT'S THE SILLIEST OUTFIT YOU'VE EVER WORN? A netball skirt
CHOOSE A FANTASY SLIP CORDON TO SPEND A DAY IN THE FIELD WITH: Tiger Woods (wk), Matthew McConaughey, Shane Warne, Julia Roberts

Batting	Mat	Inns	NO	Runs	HS	Ave	SR	100	50	Ct	St
Tests	3	6	1	260	96	52.00	75.14	0	3	4	-
ODIs	9	8	1	218	55	31.14	80.14	0	2	2	-
T20Is	10	9	3	196	62*	32.66	147.36	0	2	4	-
First-class	23	36	2	998	96	29.35	53.19	0	8	20	-
List A	25	23	2	557	66	26.52	84.52	0	5	7	-
T20s	63	57	11	1127	87	24.50	136.77	0	7	33	-

Bowling	Mat	Balls	Mdns	Runs	Wkts	BB	Ave	4wI	5wI	SR	Econ
Tests	3	92	0	77	3	3-72	25.66	-	0	30.66	5.02
ODIs	9	138	1	162	5	2-33	32.40	0	0	27.60	7.04
T20Is	10	18	0	28	0	0-28	-	-	-	-	9.33
First-class	23	1154	19	750	10	4-20	75.00	-	0	115.40	3.89
List A	25	630	2	589	20	4-36	29.45	1	0	31.50	5.60
T20s	63	232	0	296	11	2-5	26.90	0	0	21.09	7.65

TOM BEVAN

RHB / OB / R0 / W0

GLAMORGAN

FULL NAME: Thomas Rhys Bevan
BORN: September 9, 1999, Cardiff, Wales
SQUAD NO: 13
HEIGHT: 6ft 2in
NICKNAME: Bevs
EDUCATION: Millfield School, Somerset;
Cardiff Metropolitan University
TEAMS: Glamorgan
ROLE: Batter
DEBUT: First-class: 2022; List A: 2022; T20: 2022

BEST BATTING: 48 Glamorgan vs Derbyshire, Cardiff, 2022

FIRST CRICKET CLUB? Cardiff CC
EARLIEST CRICKETING MEMORY? The 2009 Ashes
WHAT'S THE BIGGEST PRIZE IN DOMESTIC CRICKET? The T20 Blast
THE KOOKABURRA BALL: YES OR NO? As a batter: yes!
OPPONENT YOU MOST LOOK FORWARD TO PLAYING AGAINST? Harry Came
FAVOURITE WARM-UP SONG? Charlie Brown by The Coasters
HOW MANY HOURS DO YOU SPEND ON YOUR PHONE A DAY? Six
SPECIALITY SUBJECT IN A PUB QUIZ (EXCLUDING SPORT)? Egyptian history
ONE THING YOU WANT TO DO BEFORE YOU DIE: Live
HOBBY YOU WOULD LIKE TO LEARN: Speak French
WHICH PUBLIC FIGURE INSPIRES YOU (EXCLUDING SPORTSPEOPLE)? Nelson Mandela
SURPRISING FACT ABOUT YOU: I can speak Welsh
FILM YOU CAN WATCH OVER AND OVER: Casino Royale

Batting	Mat	Inns	NO	Runs	HS	Ave	SR	100	50	Ct	St
First-class	3	5	0	97	48	19.40	39.11	0	0	2	-
List A	16	14	0	278	134	19.85	87.97	1	0	8	-
T20s	12	10	0	127	34	12.70	124.50	0	0	6	-
Bowling	Mat	Balls	Mdns	Runs	Wkts	BB	Ave	4wI	5wI	SR	Econ
First-class	3	72	0	70	0	0-6	-	-	-	-	5.83
List A	16	102	0	114	0	0-17	-	-	-	-	6.70
T20s	12	24	0	56	1	1-15	56.00	0	0	24.00	14.00

SAM BILLINGS

RHB / WK / R0 / W0

FULL NAME: Samuel William Billings
BORN: June 15, 1991, Pembury, Kent
SQUAD NO: 7
HEIGHT: 6ft
NICKNAME: Bilbo
EDUCATION: Haileybury & Imperial College, Herts; Loughborough University
TEAMS: England, Kent, Oval Invincibles, Brisbane Heat, CSK, Delhi Capitals, KKR, Sydney Thunder
ROLE: Batter/wicketkeeper
DEBUT: Test: 2022; ODI: 2015; T20I: 2015; First-class: 2011; List A: 2011; T20: 2011

BEST BATTING: 106 Kent vs Somerset, Canterbiry, 2024 (T20)

COUNTY CAP: 2015

FIRST CRICKET CLUB? Hartley Country Club, Dartford, Kent
WHO WOULD YOU MOST LIKE TO HAVE A NET WITH? Ricky Ponting – best cricket eye I've ever come across
HOBBIES? Padel tennis
NOTES: Billings resigned as Kent's club captain in 2023 and is now concentrating on the short formats after signing a white-ball contract which runs until the end of the 2025 season. He is scheduled to continue as Kent's T20 skipper for this summer's Blast

Batting	Mat	Inns	NO	Runs	HS	Ave	SR	100	50	Ct	St
Tests	3	3	0	66	36	22.00	57.89	0	0	8	-
ODIs	28	23	2	702	118	33.42	91.05	1	5	19	1
T20Is	36	32	5	474	87	17.55	130.93	0	2	17	2
First-class	88	128	12	3628	171	31.27	58.39	6	15	219	12
List A	103	90	15	3125	175	41.66	103.27	7	21	88	9
T20s	351	330	47	6836	106	24.15	132.73	1	34	217	31

Bowling	Mat	Balls	Mdns	Runs	Wkts	BB	Ave	4wI	5wI	SR	Econ
Tests	3	-	-	-	-	-	-	-	-	-	-
ODIs	28	-	-	-	-	-	-	-	-	-	-
T20Is	36	-	-	-	-	-	-	-	-	-	-
First-class	88	1	0	4	0	0-4	-	-	-	-	24.00
List A	103	-	-	-	-	-	-	-	-	-	-
T20s	351	-	-	-	-	-	-	-	-	-	-

JOSH BLAKE

LHB / WK / R0 / W0

SURREY

FULL NAME: Joshua William Blake
BORN: September 18, 1998, Carshalton, Surrey
SQUAD NO: 18
EDUCATION: Trinity School, Croydon
TEAMS: Surrey
ROLE: Wicketkeeper/batter
DEBUT: First-class: 2024; List A: 2022; T20: 2023

BEST BATTING: 38* Surrey vs Essex, Chelmsford, 2024

NOTES: The 26-year-old wicketkeeper signed his first professional contract with Surrey in July 2022 after making an impression in the Second XI. Blake had represented the county from U9 to U15 but could not immediately make the step-up to the next level, instead honing his skills with Sutton CC and in Sydney during the off season. In 2018 he started working at the Surrey Cricket Foundation, working as a part-time coach on their Chance to Shine programme. Blake became a full-time community coach, delivering 578 hours of Chance to Shine coaching to primary-school children last year. He was a regular in the club's One-Day Cup side in 2022 and made his T20 and first-class debuts in 2023 and 2024 respectively

Batting	Mat	Inns	NO	Runs	HS	Ave	SR	100	50	Ct	St
First-class	1	1	1	38	38*	-	30.15	0	0	1	-
List A	20	19	1	546	100*	30.33	83.35	1	2	19	7
T20s	2	0	-	-	-	-	-	-	-	4	-

Bowling	Mat	Balls	Mdns	Runs	Wkts	BB	Ave	4wI	5wI	SR	Econ
First-class	1	-	-	-	-	-	-	-	-	-	-
List A	20	-	-	-	-	-	-	-	-	-	-
T20s	2	-	-	-	-	-	-	-	-	-	-

JACK BLATHERWICK

RHB / RFM / R0 / W0

FULL NAME: Jack Morgan Blatherwick
BORN: June 4, 1998, Nottingham
SQUAD NO: 4
HEIGHT: 6ft 3in
NICKNAME: The Milkman
EDUCATION: Holgate Academy, Hucknall;
Central College, Nottingham
TEAMS: Lancashire, England U19,
Northamptonshire, Nottinghamshire
ROLE: Bowler
DEBUT: First-class: 2019; List A: 2018; T20: 2023

BEST BATTING: 35 Lancashire vs Surrey, The Oval, 2023
BEST BOWLING: 4-28 Lancashire vs Somerset, Taunton, 2021

FIRST CRICKET CLUB? Kimberley Institute CC, Nottingham
FAMILY TIES? My uncle is the former Nottingham Forest defender Steve Blatherwick
EARLIEST CRICKETING MEMORY? Watching my old man and uncle play in the Notts premier
league against West Indian Cavaliers
THE KOOKABURRA BALL: YES OR NO? Yes – I enjoy the challenge. It encourages you to bowl
fast as there's less lateral movement. However, I don't think it works in early season as the
ball collects a lot of moisture and goes very soft early
OPPONENT YOU MOST LOOK FORWARD TO PLAYING AGAINST? Any of the overseas players
– good to test your game against the best
HOW MANY HOURS DO YOU SPEND ON YOUR PHONE A DAY? Six
SPECIALITY SUBJECT IN A PUB QUIZ (EXCLUDING SPORT)? Music
WHICH PUBLIC FIGURE INSPIRES YOU (EXCLUDING SPORTSPEOPLE)? Sylvester Stallone
FILM YOU CAN WATCH OVER AND OVER: Rocky

Batting	Mat	Inns	NO	Runs	HS	Ave	SR	100	50	Ct	St
First-class	15	20	6	163	35	11.64	47.94	0	0	4	-
List A	15	10	4	75	25	12.50	60.97	0	0	6	-
T20s	13	5	3	43	17*	21.50	179.16	0	0	9	-

Bowling	Mat	Balls	Mdns	Runs	Wkts	BB	Ave	4wI	5wI	SR	Econ
First-class	15	1377	32	1019	20	4-28	50.95	-	0	68.85	4.44
List A	15	563	0	618	19	4-52	32.52	1	0	29.63	6.58
T20s	13	196	0	319	13	3-14	24.53	0	0	15.07	9.76

JOSH BOHANNON
RHB / RMF / R1 / W0

LANCASHIRE

FULL NAME: Joshua James Bohannon
BORN: April 9, 1997, Bolton, Lancashire
SQUAD NO: 20
HEIGHT: 5ft 9in
NICKNAME: Bosh
EDUCATION: Harper Green High School, Bolton
TEAMS: Lancashire, England Lions
ROLE: Batter
DEBUT: First-class: 2018; List A: 2018; T20: 2018

BEST BATTING: 231 Lancashire vs Gloucestershire, Old Trafford, 2022
BEST BOWLING: 3-46 Lancashire vs Hampshire, Southampton, 2018
COUNTY CAP: 2021

FIRST CRICKET CLUB? Farnworth CC, Greater Manchester
WHICH AWAY GROUND DO YOU MOST ENJOY VISITING? Durham – a good wicket and a great city
IF YOU COULD PINCH A PLAYER FROM ANOTHER COUNTY, WHO WOULD IT BE? Brydon Carse – a genuine allrounder and a good guy on and off the field
CHOOSE A FANTASY SLIP CORDON TO SPEND A DAY IN THE FIELD WITH: Kumar Sangakkara (wk), Ricky Ponting, Jacques Kallis, Graeme Swann
SURPRISING FACT ABOUT YOU: I'm studying accountancy

Batting	Mat	Inns	NO	Runs	HS	Ave	SR	100	50	Ct	St
First-class	84	125	8	5190	231	44.35	52.55	12	23	36	-
List A	45	39	4	1162	147	33.20	80.13	2	6	6	-
T20s	34	26	5	217	39	10.33	105.85	0	0	14	-

Bowling	Mat	Balls	Mdns	Runs	Wkts	BB	Ave	4wI	5wI	SR	Econ
First-class	84	1043	28	591	13	3-46	45.46	-	0	80.23	3.39
List A	45	183	1	232	1	1-33	232.00	0	0	183.00	7.60
T20s	34	-	-	-	-	-	-	-	-	-	-

RAVI BOPARA

RHB / RM / R1 / W0

FULL NAME: Ravinder Singh Bopara
BORN: May 4, 1985, Forest Gate, London
SQUAD NO: 25
HEIGHT: 5ft 10in
NICKNAME: Puppy
EDUCATION: Brampton Manor, London
TEAMS: England, Northamptonshire, Auckland, Essex, Gloucestershire, Kings XI Punjab, London Spirit, Sunrisers Hyderabad, Sussex, Sydney Sixers
ROLE: Allrounder
DEBUT: Test: 2007; ODI: 2007; T20I: 2008; First-class: 2002; List A: 2002; T20: 2003

BEST BATTING: 108 Sussex vs Kent, Canterbury, 2023 (T20)
BEST BOWLING: 6-16 Karachi Kings vs Lahore Qalandars, Sharjah, 2016 (T20)
COUNTY CAP: 2005 (Essex); **BENEFIT:** 2015 (Essex)

BIGGEST INFLUENCE ON YOUR DEVELOPMENT AS A CRICKETER (EXCLUDING PARENTS)?
Graham Gooch and Sachin Tendulkar
MOST EXCITING DAY AS A CRICKETER? Playing against Sachin Tendulkar
WHAT WOULD YOU DO IF YOU WERE IN CHARGE OF COUNTY CRICKET? Introduce a 10-over competition
SURPRISING FACT ABOUT YOU: I have a fast-food business

Batting	Mat	Inns	NO	Runs	HS	Ave	SR	100	50	Ct	St
Tests	13	19	1	575	143	31.94	52.89	3	0	6	-
ODIs	120	109	21	2695	101*	30.62	77.84	1	14	35	-
T20Is	38	35	10	711	65*	28.44	118.69	0	3	7	-
First-class	221	357	40	12821	229	40.44	51.54	31	55	118	-
List A	323	301	56	9845	201*	40.18	-	15	60	104	-
T20s	478	437	94	9486	108	27.65	122.47	2	48	155	-

Bowling	Mat	Balls	Mdns	Runs	Wkts	BB	Ave	4wI	5wI	SR	Econ
Tests	13	434	10	290	1	1-39	290.00	-	0	434.00	4.00
ODIs	120	1860	11	1523	40	4-38	38.07	1	0	46.50	4.91
T20Is	38	322	1	387	16	4-10	24.18	1	0	20.12	7.21
First-class	221	15462	401	9381	257	5-49	36.50	-	3	60.16	3.64
List A	323	8097	30	7197	248	5-63	29.02	6	1	32.64	5.33
T20s	478	5858	1	7353	291	6-16	25.26	6	1	20.13	7.53

SCOTT BORTHWICK

LHB / LB / R3 / W0

DURHAM

FULL NAME: Scott George Borthwick
BORN: April 19, 1990, Sunderland, County Durham
SQUAD NO: 16
HEIGHT: 5ft 10in
NICKNAME: Badger
EDUCATION: Farringdon Community Sports College, Sunderland
TEAMS: England, Durham, Chilaw Marians, Surrey, Wellington
ROLE: Batter
DEBUT: Test: 2014; ODI: 2011; T20I: 2011; First-class 2009; List A: 2009; T20: 2008

BEST BATTING: 216 Durham vs Middlesex, Chester-le-Street, 2014
BEST BOWLING: 6-70 Durham vs Surrey, The Oval, 2013
COUNTY CAP: 2018 (Surrey)

FIRST CRICKET CLUB? Eppleton CC, Sunderland. I made my first-team debut aged 13 and got a 44-ball duck (on a poor pitch)
BIGGEST INFLUENCE ON YOUR DEVELOPMENT AS A CRICKETER (EXCLUDING PARENTS)? Geoff Cook – he was Academy director when I joined the Durham Academy, and he was head coach when I made my first-team debut
MOST EXCITING DAY AS A CRICKETER? Making my England debut
CHILDHOOD SPORTING HERO? Shane Warne
HOBBIES? Eating Galaxy chocolate while playing Football Manager

Batting	Mat	Inns	NO	Runs	HS	Ave	SR	100	50	Ct	St
Tests	1	2	0	5	4	2.50	26.31	0	0	2	-
ODIs	2	2	0	18	15	9.00	112.50	0	0	0	-
T20Is	1	1	0	14	14	14.00	87.50	0	0	1	-
First-class	222	369	31	11678	216	34.55	52.95	22	66	275	-
List A	127	97	12	2203	104	25.91	79.50	1	12	50	-
T20s	116	61	20	729	62	17.78	100.96	0	1	55	-

Bowling	Mat	Balls	Mdns	Runs	Wkts	BB	Ave	4wI	5wI	SR	Econ
Tests	1	78	0	82	4	3-33	20.50	-	0	19.50	6.30
ODIs	2	54	0	72	0	0-13	-	-	-	-	8.00
T20Is	1	24	0	15	1	1-15	15.00	0	0	24.00	3.75
First-class	222	13998	269	9175	229	6-70	40.06	-	3	61.12	3.93
List A	127	3663	2	3720	84	5-38	44.28	1	1	43.60	6.09
T20s	116	1538	0	2107	82	4-18	25.69	1	0	18.75	8.21

JOSH BOYDEN

LHB / LMF / R0 / W0

FULL NAME: Joshua Ashton Boyden
BORN: April 16, 2004, Chorley, Lancashire
SQUAD NO: 27
NICKNAME: Boyds
EDUCATION: Parklands High School, Chorley; Runshaw College
TEAMS: Lancashire, England U19
ROLE: Bowler
DEBUT: First-class: 2024; List A: 2024

BEST BATTING: 5 Lancashire vs Surrey, The Oval, 2024

FIRST CRICKET CLUB? Euxton CC, Chorley, Lancashire
EARLIEST CRICKETING MEMORY? Playing U9 cricket when I was six and had no kit (somone got injured so I had to play)
WHAT'S THE BIGGEST PRIZE IN DOMESTIC CRICKET? Winning the County Championship
THE KOOKABURRA BALL: YES OR NO? Yes, it's something different and provides more attritional cricket, though often the pitches are too flat for the Kookaburra
OPPONENT YOU MOST LOOK FORWARD TO PLAYING AGAINST? Will Luxton (Yorkshire) – it's always a good contest playing against him
FAVOURITE WARM-UP SONG? Money For Nothing by Dire Straits
HOW MANY HOURS DO YOU SPEND ON YOUR PHONE A DAY? Four
SPECIALITY SUBJECT IN A PUB QUIZ (EXCLUDING SPORT)? Films
ONE THING YOU WANT TO DO BEFORE YOU DIE: Hold a koala
HOBBY YOU WOULD LIKE TO LEARN: The guitar
WHICH PUBLIC FIGURE INSPIRES YOU (EXCLUDING SPORTSPEOPLE)? James Acaster
SURPRISING FACT ABOUT YOU: My toes aren't straight
FILM YOU CAN WATCH OVER AND OVER: Deadpool

Batting	Mat	Inns	NO	Runs	HS	Ave	SR	100	50	Ct	St
First-class	1	2	0	5	5	2.50	25.00	0	0	0	-
List A	3	3	2	47	44*	47.00	111.90	0	0	0	-

Bowling	Mat	Balls	Mdns	Runs	Wkts	BB	Ave	4wI	5wI	SR	Econ
First-class	1	108	2	81	0	0-81	-	-	-	-	4.50
List A	3	120	0	110	6	2-26	18.33	0	0	20.00	5.50

JAMES BRACEY — LHB / WK / R1 / W0 / MVP13

GLOUCESTERSHIRE

FULL NAME: James Robert Bracey
BORN: May 3, 1997, Bristol
SQUAD NO: 25
HEIGHT: 6ft 1in
NICKNAME: Sony
EDUCATION: The Ridings High School, Bristol; SGS Filton College; Loughborough University
TEAMS: England, Gloucestershire
ROLE: Batter/wicketkeeper
DEBUT: Test: 2021; First-class: 2016; List A: 2019; T20: 2019

BEST BATTING: 207* Gloucestershire vs Leicestershire, Bristol, 2024

COUNTY CAP: 2016

FIRST CRICKET CLUB? Winterbourne CC, Bristol
WHICH TEAMMATE HAS HAD THE BIGGEST IMPACT ON YOUR GAME? Tom Smith – he's got a great cricket mind and is an excellent coach as well as player
WHAT DO YOU THINK OF THE CURRENT 50-OVER COMPETITION? It's my favourite format
WHO IS THE TOUGHEST BOWLER TO FACE? Mohammad Abbas
WHAT KEEPS YOU AWAKE AT NIGHT? Bristol Rovers losing
CHOOSE A FANTASY SLIP CORDON TO SPEND A DAY IN THE FIELD WITH: Me (wk), Andrew Flintoff, Paul Rudd, Shane Lowry
SURPRISING FACT ABOUT YOU: I'm scared of Ketchup

Batting	Mat	Inns	NO	Runs	HS	Ave	SR	100	50	Ct	St
Tests	2	3	0	8	8	2.66	29.62	0	0	6	-
First-class	93	163	13	5211	207*	34.74	51.36	13	23	218	14
List A	40	40	4	1553	224*	43.13	106.58	3	8	39	5
T20s	68	61	6	1060	70	19.27	126.79	0	3	37	13

Bowling	Mat	Balls	Mdns	Runs	Wkts	BB	Ave	4wl	5wl	SR	Econ
Tests	2	-	-	-	-	-	-	-	-	-	-
First-class	93	60	0	35	0	0-5	-	-	-	-	3.50
List A	40	18	0	23	1	1-23	23.00	0	0	18.00	7.66
T20s	68	-	-	-	-	-	-	-	-	-	-

MATTHEW BREETZKE

RHB / WK / R0 / W0

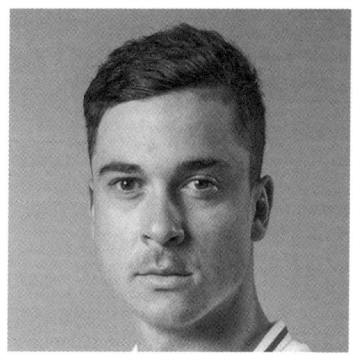

FULL NAME: Matthew Paul Breetzke
BORN: November 3, 1998, Port Elizabeth, South Africa
SQUAD NO: 3
EDUCATION: Grey High School, Port Elizabeth
TEAMS: South Africa, Northamptonshire, Durban's Super Giants, Eastern Province, Nelson Mandela Bay Giants, Warriors
ROLE: Batter
DEBUT: Test: 2024; ODI: 2025; T20I: 2023; First-class: 2017; List A: 2017: T20: 2017

BEST BATTING: 188 Eastern Province vs KwaZulu-Natal Inland, Pietermaritzburg, 2024
BEST BOWLING: 1-13 Eastern Province vs Gauteng, Johannesburg, 2023

NOTES: After an impressive first season at Wantage Road in which he played 13 games in the T20 Blast, striking at over 150 and guiding Northants to a home quarter-final with an ice-cold knock against Lancashire, the South African top-order star re-joins the Steelbacks for the first eight Championship fixtures and the full Blast group stage. The club are buoyed to have secured a player whose versatility has already seen him debut for South Africa across all three formats. Long considered potential leadership material for his country, Breetzke smashed 150 on his ODI debut against New Zealand in February, a new record for a player on his international 50-over debut

Batting	Mat	Inns	NO	Runs	HS	Ave	SR	100	50	Ct	St
Tests	1	1	0	0	0	0.00	0.00	0	0	0	-
ODIs	2	2	0	233	150	116.50	100.43	1	1	0	-
T20Is	10	10	1	151	51	16.77	122.76	0	1	6	-
First-class	57	102	9	3417	188	36.74	47.83	8	16	37	-
List A	65	65	6	2053	150	34.79	82.61	2	13	32	-
T20s	112	106	10	2783	94	28.98	132.27	0	19	39	1

Bowling	Mat	Balls	Mdns	Runs	Wkts	BB	Ave	4wI	5wI	SR	Econ
Tests	1	-	-	-	-	-	-	-	-	-	-
ODIs	2	-	-	-	-	-	-	-	-	-	-
T20Is	10	-	-	-	-	-	-	-	-	-	-
First-class	57	297	9	176	2	1-13	88.00	-	0	148.50	3.55
List A	65	54	0	44	1	1-20	44.00	0	0	54.00	4.88
T20s	112	-	-	-	-	-	-	-	-	-	-

DANNY BRIGGS

RHB / SLA / R0 / W0

WARWICKSHIRE

FULL NAME: Danny Richard Briggs
BORN: April 30, 1991, Newport, Isle of Wight
SQUAD NO: 14
HEIGHT: 6ft 2in
NICKNAME: Briggsy
EDUCATION: Carisbrooke High School, Isle of Wight
TEAMS: England, Warwickshire, Southern Brave, Adelaide Strikers, Hampshire, Oval Invincibles, Sussex
ROLE: Bowler
DEBUT: ODI: 2012; T20I: 2012; First-class: 2009; List A: 2009; T20: 2010

BEST BATTING: 120* Sussex vs South Africa A, Arundel, 2017
BEST BOWLING: 6-45 England Lions vs Windward Islands, Roseau, 2011
COUNTY CAP: 2012 (Hampshire); 2021 (Warwickshire)

FIRST CRICKET CLUB? Ventnor CC, Isle of Wight
BIGGEST INFLUENCE ON YOUR DEVELOPMENT AS A CRICKETER (EXCLUDING PARENTS)?
Sam Garaway – my first coach who made me fall in love with the game
MOST EXCITING DAY AS A CRICKETER? It's a toss-up between my England debut, playing in T20 Finals Day, and winning the Championship
CHILDHOOD SPORTING HERO? Shane Warne

Batting	Mat	Inns	NO	Runs	HS	Ave	SR	100	50	Ct	St
ODIs	1	0	-	-	-	-	-	-	-	0	-
T20Is	7	1	1	0	0*	-	0.00	0	0	1	-
First-class	150	197	45	2877	120*	18.92	-	1	7	52	-
List A	110	58	25	421	37*	12.75	94.60	0	0	35	-
T20s	256	72	46	291	35*	11.19	119.75	0	0	48	-

Bowling	Mat	Balls	Mdns	Runs	Wkts	BB	Ave	4wI	5wI	SR	Econ
ODIs	1	60	0	39	2	2-39	19.50	0	0	30.00	3.90
T20Is	7	108	0	199	5	2-25	39.80	0	0	21.60	11.05
First-class	150	24918	860	12475	351	6-45	35.54	-	8	70.99	3.00
List A	110	5048	22	4288	114	4-32	37.61	1	0	44.28	5.09
T20s	256	5138	3	6200	290	5-19	21.37	5	1	17.71	7.24

JUSTIN BROAD
RHB / RMF / R0 / W0

FULL NAME: Justin Broad
BORN: June 30, 2000, Cape Town, South Africa
SQUAD NO: 75
HEIGHT: 6ft 2in
EDUCATION: Rondesbosch Boy's High School
TEAMS: Germany, Northamptonshire
ROLE: Allrounder
DEBUT: T20I: 2022; First-class: 2023; List A: 2023; T20: 2022

BEST BATTING: 75 Northamptonshire vs Derbyshire, Derby, 2024
BEST BOWLING: 7-33 Northamptonshire vs Gloucestershire, Bristol, 2024

FIRST CRICKET CLUB? Bury St Edmunds CC, Suffolk
EARLIEST CRICKETING MEMORY? Playing garden cricket with my dad and friends from the age of five
WHAT'S THE BIGGEST PRIZE IN DOMESTIC CRICKET? Winning the County Championship
THE KOOKABURRA BALL: YES OR NO? No, I feel it's not suited to English conditions and the ball doesn't stay in good nick for long enough
OPPONENT YOU MOST LOOK FORWARD TO PLAYING AGAINST? James Anderson – the best to ever do it!
ONE THING YOU WANT TO DO BEFORE YOU DIE: Play golf in America
WHICH PUBLIC FIGURE INSPIRES YOU (EXCLUDING SPORTSPEOPLE)? Nelson Mandela
SURPRISING FACT ABOUT YOU: I played cricket for Germany
FILM YOU CAN WATCH OVER AND OVER: Good Will Hunting

Batting	Mat	Inns	NO	Runs	HS	Ave	SR	100	50	Ct	St
T20Is	9	9	2	288	62	41.14	119.50	0	3	4	-
First-class	17	27	3	439	75	18.29	48.34	0	2	12	-
List A	12	11	5	167	63	27.83	81.46	0	1	3	-
T20s	19	18	5	466	62	35.84	125.60	0	3	5	-

Bowling	Mat	Balls	Mdns	Runs	Wkts	BB	Ave	4wI	5wI	SR	Econ
T20Is	9	69	0	93	1	1-9	93.00	0	0	69.00	8.08
First-class	17	1017	20	694	21	7-33	33.04	-	1	48.42	4.09
List A	12	325	5	305	13	3-16	23.46	0	0	25.00	5.63
T20s	19	105	0	148	4	2-11	37.00	0	0	26.25	8.45

HARRY BROOK RHB / RM / RO / WO

YORKSHIRE

FULL NAME: Harry Cherrington Brook
BORN: February 22, 1999, Keighley, Yorkshire
SQUAD NO: 88
HEIGHT: 6ft
EDUCATION: Sedbergh School, Cumbria
TEAMS: England, Yorkshire, Northern Superchargers, Delhi Capitals, Hobart Hurricanes, Lahore Qalandars, Sunrisers Hyderabad
ROLE: Batter
DEBUT: Test: 2022; ODI: 2023; T20I: 2022; First-class: 2016; List A: 2017; T20: 2018

BEST BATTING: 317 England vs Pakistan, Multan, 2024
BEST BOWLING: 3-15 Yorkshire vs Glamorgan, Cardiff, 2021
COUNTY CAP: 2021

CHILDHOOD SPORTING HERO? Jacques Kallis
NOTES: The star England batter, seen as the greatest of his generation, made a withering 317 from 322 balls against Pakistan at Multan at the end of last year – the highest first-class score of his career – as England pulled off a stunning Test victory after their opponents had racked up 556 in the first innings

Batting	Mat	Inns	NO	Runs	HS	Ave	SR	100	50	Ct	St
Tests	24	40	1	2281	317	58.48	88.37	8	10	27	-
ODIs	26	26	2	816	110*	34.00	100.74	1	5	3	-
T20Is	44	37	9	798	81*	28.50	146.15	0	4	29	-
First-class	85	137	8	5736	317	44.46	74.24	17	29	76	-
List A	41	38	3	1159	110*	33.11	100.34	2	6	7	-
T20s	149	137	32	3449	105*	32.84	149.95	3	14	90	-

Bowling	Mat	Balls	Mdns	Runs	Wkts	BB	Ave	4wI	5wI	SR	Econ
Tests	24	96	2	50	1	1-25	50.00	-	0	96.00	3.12
ODIs	26	-	-	-	-	-	-	-	-	-	-
T20Is	44	-	-	-	-	-	-	-	-	-	-
First-class	85	1111	33	514	9	3-15	57.11	-	0	123.44	2.77
List A	41	18	0	19	0	0-19	-	-	-	-	6.33
T20s	149	12	0	26	1	1-13	26.00	0	0	12.00	13.00

ETHAN BROOKES
RHB / RMF / RO / WO

FULL NAME: Ethan Alexander Brookes
BORN: May 23, 2001, Solihull, Warwickshire
SQUAD NO: 77
HEIGHT: 6ft 2in
NICKNAME: Eth
EDUCATION: Solihull School
TEAMS: Worcestershire, Warwickshire
ROLE: Bowler
DEBUT: First-class: 2019; List A: 2021; T20: 2024

WORCESTERSHIRE

BEST BATTING: 132 Worcestershire vs Hampshire, Southampton, 2024
BEST BOWLING: 3-34 Worcestershire vs Essex, Chelmsford, 2024

FIRST CRICKET CLUB? Olton & West Warwicks CC, Solihull
BIGGEST INFLUENCE ON YOUR DEVELOPMENT AS A CRICKETER (EXCLUDING PARENTS)?
Dave Cowper – my very first coach who helped me with the fundamentals
MOST EXCITING DAY AS A CRICKETER? Playing at Lord's for the English Schools Cricket
Association and winning the County Championship with Warwickshire in 2021
WHAT WOULD YOU DO IF YOU WERE IN CHARGE OF COUNTY CRICKET? Introduce the
Decision Review System
CHILDHOOD SPORTING HERO? Andrew Flintoff
HOBBIES? Call of Duty (video game)

Batting	Mat	Inns	NO	Runs	HS	Ave	SR	100	50	Ct	St
First-class	10	15	2	366	132	28.15	55.37	1	1	6	-
List A	34	27	3	469	63	19.54	85.42	0	2	23	-
T20s	14	14	2	315	44	26.25	145.83	0	0	5	-

Bowling	Mat	Balls	Mdns	Runs	Wkts	BB	Ave	4wl	5wl	SR	Econ
First-class	10	660	28	326	8	3-34	40.75	-	0	82.50	2.96
List A	34	662	1	561	15	3-15	37.40	0	0	44.13	5.08
T20s	14	174	0	238	11	4-41	21.63	1	0	15.81	8.20

HENRY BROOKES

RHB / RMF / RO / WO

MIDDLESEX

FULL NAME: Henry James Hamilton Brookes
BORN: August 21, 1999, Solihull, Warwickshire
SQUAD NO: 8
HEIGHT: 6ft 4in
EDUCATION: Tudor Grange Academy, Solihull
TEAMS: Middlesex, Birmingham Phoenix, Derbyshire, England Lions, Rhinos, Warwickshire
ROLE: Bowler
DEBUT: First-class: 2017; List A: 2018; T20: 2018

BEST BATTING: 84 Warwickshire vs Kent, Edgbaston, 2019
BEST BOWLING: 6-20 Derbyshire vs Leicestershire, Derby, 2023

FIRST CRICKET CLUB? Olton & West Warwicks CC, Solihull
FAMILY TIES? My younger brother Ethan played with me at Warwickshire before we both left the club at the end of last season. My older brother Ben has played age-group cricket for Warwickshire
GREATEST PERFORMANCE YOU HAVE WITNESSED? Liam Norwell's nine-fer to keep the Bears up at the end of the 2022 season
FAVOURITE FORMAT? The Championship – proper wins
DESCRIBE YOURSELF IN THREE WORDS: Tall, bowler, stylish
FAVOURITE TOY AS A KID? PlayStation
WHICH PERSON INSPIRES YOU MOST? Steve Rouse (former Warwickshire groundsman)

Batting	Mat	Inns	NO	Runs	HS	Ave	SR	100	50	Ct	St
First-class	45	63	12	949	84	18.60	50.31	0	6	13	-
List A	26	13	5	87	29*	10.87	89.69	0	0	2	-
T20s	56	31	14	195	31*	11.47	124.20	0	0	14	-

Bowling	Mat	Balls	Mdns	Runs	Wkts	BB	Ave	4wI	5wI	SR	Econ
First-class	45	6661	157	4245	114	6-20	37.23	-	1	58.42	3.82
List A	26	1149	6	1180	36	4-43	32.77	1	0	31.91	6.16
T20s	56	1085	2	1707	63	5-25	27.09	1	1	17.22	9.43

BEN BROWN

RHB / WK / R1 / W0

FULL NAME: Ben Christopher Brown
BORN: November 23, 1988, Crawley, Sussex
SQUAD NO: 10
HEIGHT: 5ft 8in
NICKNAME: Goblin
EDUCATION: Ardingly College, West Sussex;
Manchester Metropolitan University
TEAMS: Hampshire, England U19, Sussex
ROLE: Batter/wicketkeeper
DEBUT: First-class: 2007; List A: 2007; T20: 2008

BEST BATTING: 165* Hampshire vs Surrey, Southampton, 2024
BEST BOWLING: 1-48 Sussex vs Essex, Colchester, 2016
COUNTY CAP: 2014 (Sussex)

FIRST CRICKET CLUB? Balcombe CC, West Sussex
EARLIEST CRICKETING MEMORY? Riding my bike across the square at Balcombe and being shouted at by the seniors!
WHAT'S THE BIGGEST PRIZE IN DOMESTIC CRICKET? The County Championship
THE KOOKABURRA BALL: YES OR NO? Yes, because it demands different skills from the bowlers and brings spinners in to play. But it must be used at the right time of the year (the drier months). Last year in April and May the Kookaburra went too soft in the wet and produce boring run fests
FAVOURITE WARM-UP SONG? Mustang Sally by Wilson Pickett
SPECIALITY SUBJECT IN A PUB QUIZ (EXCLUDING SPORT)? The Office (UK version)
HOBBY YOU WOULD LIKE TO LEARN: Padel (keep improving)
SURPRISING FACT ABOUT YOU: I hate any type of cheese
FILM YOU CAN WATCH OVER AND OVER: Love Actually

Batting	Mat	Inns	NO	Runs	HS	Ave	SR	100	50	Ct	St
First-class	197	310	41	10503	165*	39.04	59.86	25	53	562	28
List A	108	90	14	2113	139*	27.80	85.37	2	13	115	12
T20s	82	65	9	840	68	15.00	112.00	0	1	41	7

Bowling	Mat	Balls	Mdns	Runs	Wkts	BB	Ave	4wl	5wl	SR	Econ
First-class	197	120	3	109	1	1-48	109.00	-	0	120.00	5.45
List A	108	-	-	-	-	-	-	-	-	-	-
T20s	82	-	-	-	-	-	-	-	-	-	-

PAT BROWN · RHB / RMF / R0 / W0

DERBYSHIRE

FULL NAME: Patrick Rhys Brown
BORN: August 23, 1998, Peterborough, Cambridgeshire
SQUAD NO: 36
HEIGHT: 6ft 2in
EDUCATION: Bourne Grammar School, Lincolnshire; University of Worcester
TEAMS: England, Derbyshire, Northern Superchargers, Birmingham Phoenix, Oval Invincibles, Peshawar Zalmi, Worcestershire
ROLE: Bowler
DEBUT: T20I: 2019; First-class: 2017; List A: 2018; T20: 2017

BEST BATTING: 15* Derbyshire vs Glamorgan, Derby, 2024
BEST BOWLING: 2-15 Worcestershire vs Gloucestershire, Worcester, 2017

FIRST CRICKET CLUB? Market Deeping CC, Lincolnshire
WHAT'S THE BIGGEST PRIZE IN DOMESTIC CRICKET? The T20 Blast
THE KOOKABURRA BALL: YES OR NO? No – it goes too soft and produces boring cricket
OPPONENT YOU MOST LOOK FORWARD TO PLAYING AGAINST? Adam Finch – so I can hook him for six
WHICH TEAMMATE HAS HAD THE BIGGEST IMPACT ON YOUR GAME? Wayne Parnell
WHICH AWAY GROUND DO YOU MOST ENJOY VISITING? Trent Bridge
IF YOU COULD PINCH A PLAYER FROM ANOTHER COUNTY, WHO WOULD IT BE? Sam Hain
GREATEST PERFORMANCE YOU HAVE WITNESSED? Martin Guptill's 35-ball hundred at Northampton in 2018
ONE THING YOU WANT TO DO BEFORE YOU DIE: See Sunderland win a trophy
FILM YOU CAN WATCH OVER AND OVER: Step Brothers

Batting	Mat	Inns	NO	Runs	HS	Ave	SR	100	50	Ct	St
T20Is	4	1	1	4	4*	-	44.44	0	0	2	-
First-class	14	14	10	56	15*	14.00	36.12	0	0	5	-
List A	17	5	4	10	5*	10.00	76.92	0	0	8	-
T20s	100	22	14	64	10*	8.00	70.32	0	0	32	-

Bowling	Mat	Balls	Mdns	Runs	Wkts	BB	Ave	4wI	5wI	SR	Econ
T20Is	4	78	0	128	3	1-29	42.66	0	0	26.00	9.84
First-class	14	1165	13	848	15	2-15	56.53	-	0	77.66	4.36
List A	17	754	3	778	27	5-37	28.81	1	1	27.92	6.19
T20s	100	1942	2	3033	127	4-21	23.88	3	0	15.29	9.37

NICK BROWNE

LHB / LB / R3 / W0

FULL NAME: Nicholas Laurence Joseph Browne
BORN: March 24, 1991, Leytonstone, Essex
SQUAD NO: 10
HEIGHT: 6ft 3in
NICKNAME: Orse
EDUCATION: Trinity Catholic High School, London
TEAMS: Essex
ROLE: Batter
DEBUT: First-class: 2013; List A: 2015; T20: 2015

BEST BATTING: 255 Essex vs Derbyshire, Chelmsford, 2016

COUNTY CAP: 2015; BENEFIT: 2025

FIRST CRICKET CLUB? South Woodford CC, London. My parents met each other at the club
BIGGEST INFLUENCE ON YOUR DEVELOPMENT AS A CRICKETER (EXCLUDING PARENTS)? My two older brothers, both of whom I played club cricket with
MOST EXCITING DAY AS A CRICKETER? Winning the County Championship on the last day at Taunton in 2019
WHAT WOULD YOU DO IF YOU WERE IN CHARGE OF COUNTY CRICKET? Keep an elite first division with eight teams, with two overseas players per county
CHILDHOOD SPORTING HERO? Marcus Trescothick

Batting	Mat	Inns	NO	Runs	HS	Ave	SR	100	50	Ct	St
First-class	144	238	17	7922	255	35.84	46.95	20	32	107	-
List A	33	30	2	764	99	27.28	82.41	0	4	12	1
T20s	14	12	2	165	38	16.50	114.58	0	0	6	-

Bowling	Mat	Balls	Mdns	Runs	Wkts	BB	Ave	4wl	5wl	SR	Econ
First-class	144	278	9	189	0	0-0	-	-	-	-	4.07
List A	33	-	-	-	-	-	-	-	-	-	-
T20s	14	-	-	-	-	-	-	-	-	-	-

JORDAN BUCKINGHAM

RHB / RFM / R0 / W0

YORKSHIRE

FULL NAME: Jordan Steven Dermott Buckingham
BORN: March 17, 2000, Bundoora, Victoria, Australia
SQUAD NO: TBC
TEAMS: Yorkshire, Adelaide Strikers, Northamptonshire, South Australia
ROLE: Bowler
DEBUT: First-class: 2022; List A: 2023; T20: 2025

BEST BATTING: 17 South Australia vs Victoria, Melbourne, 2023
BEST BOWLING: 7-71 South Australia vs Tasmania, Adelaide, 2023

NOTES: The South Australian quick joins Yorkshire for four Championship fixtures between April 29 and May 29 to bolster the White Rose bowling ranks as they return to Division One. Part of the South Australia squad that won the 2024/25 One-Day Cup, Buckingham also featured for Australia A versus England Lions over the winter. "There is no bigger county than Yorkshire so I'm incredibly excited to get started in April," Buckingham said upon signing. "There are some key fixtures in that period and I'm looking forward to helping the guys out. Head coach Anthony McGrath added: "It's great to have Jordan sign for us for this period of the season. With four really key fixtures before we hit the white-ball games, I know he will impact our squad in a really positive manner"

Batting	Mat	Inns	NO	Runs	HS	Ave	SR	100	50	Ct	St
First-class	24	35	17	72	17	4.00	20.99	0	0	13	-
List A	5	2	1	11	8	11.00	100.00	0	0	1	-
T20s	3	1	1	0	0*	-	0.00	0	0	1	-

Bowling	Mat	Balls	Mdns	Runs	Wkts	BB	Ave	4wl	5wl	SR	Econ
First-class	24	4180	124	2357	90	7-71	26.18	-	4	46.44	3.38
List A	5	225	3	204	10	6-41	20.40	0	1	22.50	5.44
T20s	3	60	0	96	2	1-23	48.00	0	0	30.00	9.60

SOL BUDINGER

LHB / OB / R0 / W0

FULL NAME: Soloman George Budinger
BORN: August 21, 1999, Colchester, Essex
SQUAD NO: 1
HEIGHT: 6ft
NICKNAME: Lord
EDUCATION: The Southport School, Queensland, Australia
TEAMS: Leicestershire, Birmingham Phoenix, Nottinghamshire
ROLE: Batter
DEBUT: First-class: 2022; List A: 2021; T20: 2021

BEST BATTING: 87 Leicestershire vs Derbyshire, Leicester, 2024
BEST BOWLING: 1-13 Leicestershie vs Northamptonshire, Northampton, 2024

FIRST CRICKET CLUB? Coomera Hope Island CC, Queensland, Australia
EARLIEST CRICKETING MEMORY? The 2005 Ashes
WHAT'S THE BIGGEST PRIZE IN DOMESTIC CRICKET? The T20 Blast
THE KOOKABURRA BALL: YES OR NO? No
FAVOURITE WARM-UP SONG? The Fox (What Does The Fox Say?) by Hlvis
SPECIALITY SUBJECT IN A PUB QUIZ (EXCLUDING SPORT)? National flags
ONE THING YOU WANT TO DO BEFORE YOU DIE: Jump out of a plane
HOBBY YOU WOULD LIKE TO LEARN: To speak Spanish
WHICH PUBLIC FIGURE INSPIRES YOU (EXCLUDING SPORTSPEOPLE)? Don McLean
SURPRISING FACT ABOUT YOU: I can speak four languages
FILM YOU CAN WATCH OVER AND OVER: Star Wars

Batting	Mat	Inns	NO	Runs	HS	Ave	SR	100	50	Ct	St
First-class	17	31	0	693	87	22.35	79.20	0	5	8	-
List A	37	37	1	1379	120	38.30	120.33	2	10	9	-
T20s	26	24	1	303	50	13.17	134.07	0	1	7	-

Bowling	Mat	Balls	Mdns	Runs	Wkts	BB	Ave	4wI	5wI	SR	Econ
First-class	17	87	0	67	1	1-13	67.00	-	0	87.00	4.62
List A	37	20	0	37	0	0-4	-	-	-	-	11.10
T20s	26	24	0	21	2	2-21	10.50	0	0	12.00	5.25

RORY BURNS

LHB / RM / R7 / W0

FULL NAME: Rory Joseph Burns
BORN: August 26, 1990, Epsom, Surrey
SQUAD NO: 17
HEIGHT: 5ft 10in
NICKNAME: Fong
EDUCATION: Whitgift School, Croydon, London; City of London Freemen's; Cardiff Metropolitan University
TEAMS: England, Surrey
ROLE: Batter
DEBUT: Test: 2018; First-class: 2011; List A: 2012; T20: 2012

BEST BATTING: 227 Surrey vs Lancashire, The Oval, 2024
BEST BOWLING: 1-18 Surrey vs Middlesex, Lord's, 2013
COUNTY CAP: 2014; BENEFIT: 2025

FIRST CRICKET CLUB? Banstead CC, Surrey
HOBBIES? Golf
WHO WOULD YOU MOST LIKE TO HAVE A NET WITH? Brian Lara
MOST BEAUTIFUL THING YOU HAVE EVER SEEN? My wife and daughter
SURPRISING FACT ABOUT YOU: I have a strong whisky collection at home

Batting	Mat	Inns	NO	Runs	HS	Ave	SR	100	50	Ct	St
Tests	32	59	0	1789	133	30.32	43.80	3	11	24	-
First-class	201	349	23	13337	227	40.91	49.15	27	74	143	-
List A	69	67	6	1871	95	30.67	82.56	0	12	36	-
T20s	78	67	11	976	62	17.42	119.31	0	3	32	2

Bowling	Mat	Balls	Mdns	Runs	Wkts	BB	Ave	4wI	5wI	SR	Econ
Tests	32	-	-	-	-	-	-	-	-	-	-
First-class	201	302	6	176	2	1-18	88.00	-	0	151.00	3.49
List A	69	-	-	-	-	-	-	-	-	-	-
T20s	78	-	-	-	-	-	-	-	-	-	-

JOS BUTTLER   RHB / WK / R0 / W0

FULL NAME: Joseph Charles Buttler
BORN: September 8, 1990, Taunton
SQUAD NO: 6
NICKNAME: Jose
EDUCATION: King's College, Taunton
TEAMS: England, Lancashire, Manchester Originals, Comilla Victorians, Melbourne Renegades, Mumbai Indians, Paarl Royals, Rajasthan Royals, Somerset, Sydney Thunder
ROLE: Batter/wicketkeeper
DEBUT: Test: 2014; ODI: 2012; T20I: 2011; First-class: 2009; List A: 2009; T20: 2009

BEST BATTING: 152 England vs Pakistan, Southampton, 2020

COUNTY CAP: 2013 (Somerset), 2018 (Lancashire)

NOTES: The 34-year-old keeper-batter resigned as England's white-ball captain after his side were knocked out of the Champions Trophy at the end of February. Although the last 18 months have proved difficult, with underwhelming performances in both the 50-over and T20 World Cups, Buttler is destined to be remembered as one of English cricket's most ferocious hitters and a World Cup-winning captain after leading England to T20 glory down under in November 2022. He was also the man who broke the stumps to seal a famous victory in the 2019 World Cup final. Buttler's immediate future as a cricketer for England or Lancashire wasn't clear in the wake of his resignation, with his county contract due to expire at the end of the upcoming season, but he was retained by Manchester Originals ahead of this summer's Hundred. The most recent of his 57 Test appearances came in the 2021/22 Ashes and he hasn't played any four-day cricket in seven years

Batting	Mat	Inns	NO	Runs	HS	Ave	SR	100	50	Ct	St
Tests	57	100	9	2907	152	31.94	54.18	2	18	153	1
ODIs	187	160	27	5196	162*	39.06	115.31	11	27	225	37
T20Is	134	123	23	3535	101*	35.35	146.61	1	26	77	13
First-class	122	199	16	5888	152	32.17	57.20	7	33	274	3
List A	257	219	47	7361	162*	42.79	116.98	13	43	275	42
T20s	434	409	62	12113	124	34.90	145.15	8	84	257	43

Bowling	Mat	Balls	Mdns	Runs	Wkts	BB	Ave	4wI	5wI	SR	Econ
Tests	57	-	-	-	-	-	-	-	-	-	-
ODIs	187	-	-	-	-	-	-	-	-	-	-
T20Is	134	-	-	-	-	-	-	-	-	-	-
First-class	122	12	0	11	0	0-11	-	-	-	-	5.50
List A	257	-	-	-	-	-	-	-	-	-	-
T20s	434	-	-	-	-	-	-	-	-	-	-

EDDIE BYROM

LHB / OB / R0 / W0

GLAMORGAN

FULL NAME: Edward James Byrom
BORN: June 17, 1997, Harare, Zimbabwe
SQUAD NO: 97
HEIGHT: 6ft
NICKNAME: Muta
EDUCATION: King's College, Taunton
TEAMS: Glamorgan, Rhinos, Rising Stars, Somerset, Southern Rocks
ROLE: Batter
DEBUT: First-class: 2017; List A: 2021; T20: 2019

BEST BATTING: 176 Glamorgan vs Sussex, Cardiff, 2022
BEST BOWLING: 2-64 Glamorgan vs Surrey, The Oval, 2021

FIRST CRICKET CLUB? Taunton St Andrews CC, Somerset
WHICH TEAMMATE HAS HAD THE BIGGEST IMPACT ON YOUR GAME? Kiran Carlson – we spent a winter away training together in Zimbabwe
WHAT PART OF THE SEASON DO YOU MOST ENJOY? Pre-season or the T20 phase
WHICH AWAY GROUND DO YOU MOST ENJOY VISITING? Taunton – for the atmosphere and to see old teammates
WHO IS THE MOST TALENTED U19 TEENAGER IN THE COUNTY GAME? Ben Kellaway (Gla)
IF YOU COULD PINCH A PLAYER FROM ANOTHER COUNTY, WHO WOULD IT BE?
Matt Parkinson
WHAT DO YOU THINK OF THE CURRENT 50-OVER COMPETITION? A better option would be a 40-over format using just one ball rather than the current two
WHO IS THE TOUGHEST BOWLER TO FACE? Sam Cook – accurate, tests both edges
CHOOSE A FANTASY SLIP CORDON TO SPEND A DAY IN THE FIELD WITH: Chris Cooke (wk), Simon Harmer, Rikki Clarke, AB de Villiers

Batting	Mat	Inns	NO	Runs	HS	Ave	SR	100	50	Ct	St
First-class	65	116	6	3526	176	32.05	50.85	7	16	37	-
List A	22	21	3	693	123*	38.50	85.66	2	5	8	-
T20s	50	45	3	777	78*	18.50	132.82	0	3	14	-

Bowling	Mat	Balls	Mdns	Runs	Wkts	BB	Ave	4wI	5wI	SR	Econ
First-class	65	247	4	173	3	2-64	57.66	-	0	82.33	4.20
List A	22	-	-	-	-	-	-	-	-	-	-
T20s	50	-	-	-	-	-	-	-	-	-	-

HARRY CAME

RHB / OB / R0 / W0

FULL NAME: Harry Robert Charles Came
BORN: August 27, 1998, Hampshire
SQUAD NO: 4
HEIGHT: 5ft 8in
NICKNAME: Hazza, Cameo
EDUCATION: Bradfield College, Berkshire
TEAMS: Derbyshire, Hampshire
ROLE: Batter
DEBUT: First-class: 2019; List A: 2021; T20: 2021

DERBYSHIRE

BEST BATTING: 141* Derbyshire vs Glamorgan, Derby, 2023

FIRST CRICKET CLUB? Odiham & Greywell CC, Hampshire
FAMILY TIES? My great grandfather Walter Robins captained England at cricket and played football for Nottingham Forest
WHICH TEAMMATE HAS HAD THE BIGGEST IMPACT ON YOUR GAME? Wayne Madsen for his knowledge of the game and batting
WHAT PART OF THE SEASON DO YOU MOST ENJOY? The T20 Blast
IF YOU COULD PINCH A PLAYER FROM ANOTHER COUNTY, WHO WOULD IT BE?
Harry Brook
HOW IS BAZBALL AFFECTING CHAMPIONSHIP CRICKET? Less chance of a draw
WHAT KEEPS YOU AWAKE AT NIGHT? TikTok
WHAT'S THE SILLIEST OUTFIT YOU'VE EVER WORN? Dressing up as a hotdog

Batting	Mat	Inns	NO	Runs	HS	Ave	SR	100	50	Ct	St
First-class	32	52	4	1471	141*	30.64	40.40	2	10	11	-
List A	29	28	2	884	113*	34.00	80.00	1	4	7	-
T20s	26	25	0	567	56	22.68	132.16	0	2	8	-

Bowling	Mat	Balls	Mdns	Runs	Wkts	BB	Ave	4wI	5wI	SR	Econ
First-class	32	126	4	69	0	0-7	-	-	-	-	3.28
List A	29	-	-	-	-	-	-	-	-	-	-
T20s	26	-	-	-	-	-	-	-	-	-	-

KIRAN CARLSON

RHB / OB / R1 / W0 / MVP12

GLAMORGAN

FULL NAME: Kiran Shah Carlson
BORN: May 16, 1998, Cardiff
SQUAD NO: 5
HEIGHT: 5ft 11in
NICKNAME: Dink
EDUCATION: Whitchurch High School, Cardiff; Cardiff University
TEAMS: Glamorgan, Rhinos
ROLE: Batter
DEBUT: First-class: 2016; List A: 2016; T20: 2017

BEST BATTING: 192 Glamorgan vs Sussex, Hove, 2023
BEST BOWLING: 5-28 Glamorgan vs Northamptonshire, Northampton, 2016
COUNTY CAP: 2021

FIRST CRICKET CLUB? Cardiff CC
WHAT'S THE BIGGEST PRIZE IN DOMESTIC CRICKET? The County Championship
THE KOOKABURRA BALL: YES OR NO? Yes – it provides a different challenge between bat and ball
OPPONENT YOU MOST LOOK FORWARD TO PLAYING AGAINST? He's not a county opponent, but Mike Bubbins (Welsh comedian). He's got a great slower ball
FAVOURITE WARM-UP SONG? TOO COOL TO BE CARELESS by PAWSA
SPECIALITY SUBJECT IN A PUB QUIZ (EXCLUDING SPORT)? Lord of the Rings
ONE THING YOU WANT TO DO BEFORE YOU DIE: Hike up one of the tallest mountains in the world
HOBBY YOU WOULD LIKE TO LEARN: Barista-style coffee
WHICH PUBLIC FIGURE INSPIRES YOU (EXCLUDING SPORTSPEOPLE)? Joaquin Phoenix
SURPRISING FACT ABOUT YOU: I'm half-Indian

Batting	Mat	Inns	NO	Runs	HS	Ave	SR	100	50	Ct	St
First-class	94	162	10	5290	192	34.80	61.67	12	28	40	-
List A	56	54	3	1320	82	25.88	93.41	0	10	22	-
T20s	73	67	3	1398	135	21.84	142.94	1	5	26	-
Bowling	Mat	Balls	Mdns	Runs	Wkts	BB	Ave	4wI	5wI	SR	Econ
First-class	94	3249	60	2005	37	5-28	54.18	-	1	87.81	3.70
List A	56	635	5	595	18	4-41	33.05	2	0	35.27	5.62
T20s	73	33	0	61	2	2-13	30.50	0	0	16.50	11.09

BRYDON CARSE

RHB / RFM / R0 / W0

DURHAM

FULL NAME: Brydon Alexander Carse
BORN: July 31, 1995, Port Elizabeth, South Africa
SQUAD NO: 99
HEIGHT: 6ft 2in
NICKNAME: Cheesy
EDUCATION: Pearson High School, Port Elizabeth
TEAMS: England, Durham, Eastern Province, Northern Superchargers, Sunrisers Eastern Cape
ROLE: Bowler
DEBUT: Test: 2024; ODI: 2021; T20I: 2023; First-class: 2016; List A: 2019; T20: 2014

BEST BATTING: 108* Durham vs Derbyshire, Chester-le-Street, 2023
BEST BOWLING: 6-26 Durham vs Middlesex, Lord's, 2019

FIRST CRICKET CLUB? Union CC, South Africa
FAMILY TIES? My dad James played for Northamptonshire, Rhodesia, Eastern Province, Border and Western Province
BIGGEST INFLUENCE ON YOUR DEVELOPMENT AS A CRICKETER (EXCLUDING PARENTS)? Geoff Cook (former Durham head coach)
WHAT WOULD YOU DO IF YOU WERE IN CHARGE OF COUNTY CRICKET? Allow a free hit for no-balls in four-day cricket
CHILDHOOD SPORTING HERO? Mark Boucher

Batting	Mat	Inns	NO	Runs	HS	Ave	SR	100	50	Ct	St
Tests	5	7	2	94	33*	18.80	78.99	0	0	6	-
ODIs	21	14	4	210	32	21.00	81.08	0	0	6	-
T20Is	8	6	1	37	31	7.40	127.58	0	0	5	-
First-class	53	72	17	1667	108*	30.30	56.85	2	5	17	-
List A	30	17	4	229	32	17.61	80.63	0	0	8	-
T20s	82	62	16	783	58	17.02	139.57	0	2	33	-

Bowling	Mat	Balls	Mdns	Runs	Wkts	BB	Ave	4wl	5wl	SR	Econ
Tests	5	937	22	536	27	6-42	19.85	-	1	34.70	3.43
ODIs	21	874	0	947	24	5-61	39.45	0	1	36.41	6.50
T20Is	8	168	0	226	15	3-23	15.06	0	0	11.20	8.07
First-class	53	7545	173	4827	154	6-26	31.34	-	6	48.99	3.83
List A	30	1185	5	1245	34	5-61	36.61	0	1	34.85	6.30
T20s	82	1257	1	1872	53	3-23	35.32	0	0	23.71	8.93

JACK CARSON RHB / OB / R0 / W1 / MVP34

SUSSEX

FULL NAME: Jack Joshua Carson
BORN: December 3, 2000, Craigavon, County Armagh, Northern Ireland
SQUAD NO: 16
HEIGHT: 6ft 2in
NICKNAME: Carse
EDUCATION: Bainbridge Academy, County Down, Northern Ireland; Hurstpierpoint College, West Sussex
TEAMS: Sussex, England Lions
ROLE: Bowler
DEBUT: First-class: 2020; List A: 2023; T20: 2024

BEST BATTING: 97 Sussex vs Derbyshire, Hove, 2024
BEST BOWLING: 6-67 Sussex vs Derbyshire, Hove, 2024
COUNTY CAP: 2024

FIRST CRICKET CLUB? Waringstown CC, Craigavon, Northern Ireland
WHICH TEAMMATE HAS HAD THE BIGGEST IMPACT ON YOUR GAME? Mitchell Claydon – he helped keep things in perspective
WHAT PART OF THE SEASON DO YOU MOST ENJOY? Championship cricket in the middle of the summer
WHO IS THE MOST TALENTED U19 TEENAGER IN THE COUNTY GAME? Henry Rogers (Sus)
IF YOU COULD PINCH A PLAYER FROM ANOTHER COUNTY, WHO WOULD IT BE? Sam Cook
HOW IS BAZBALL AFFECTING CHAMPIONSHIP CRICKET? I've started to get smaked around a bit more
WHO IS THE TOUGHEST BOWLER TO FACE? Ben Raine – he just doesn't miss
CHOOSE A FANTASY SLIP CORDON TO SPEND A DAY IN THE FIELD WITH: Allan McGregor (wk), George Best, Mick Jagger, Paul Gascoigne

Batting	Mat	Inns	NO	Runs	HS	Ave	SR	100	50	Ct	St
First-class	50	78	11	1514	97	22.59	56.42	0	11	26	-
List A	9	8	2	101	20*	16.83	132.89	0	0	3	-
T20s	12	5	2	68	26	22.66	117.24	0	0	5	-

Bowling	Mat	Balls	Mdns	Runs	Wkts	BB	Ave	4wI	5wI	SR	Econ
First-class	50	8555	227	4849	150	6-67	32.32	-	6	57.03	3.40
List A	9	467	3	495	16	4-83	30.93	1	0	29.18	6.35
T20s	12	108	0	176	10	2-10	17.60	0	0	10.80	9.77

OLI CARTER

RHB / WK / RO / WO

FULL NAME: Oliver James Carter
BORN: November 2, 2001, Eastbourne, Sussex
SQUAD NO: 11
HEIGHT: 5ft 8in
NICKNAME: Tiger
EDUCATION: Eastbourne College
TEAMS: Sussex
ROLE: Wicketkeeper/batter
DEBUT: First-class: 2021; List A: 2021; T20: 2021

BEST BATTING: 185 Sussex vs Glamorgan, Cardiff, 2022

FIRST CRICKET CLUB? Barcombe CC, East Sussex
BEST PLAYER IN COUNTY CRICKET (EXCLUDING TEAMMATES)? Simon Harmer
GREATEST PERFORMANCE YOU HAVE WITNESSED? Cheteshwar Pujara and Tom Alsop putting on 200-plus runs in the heat at Lord's in 2022
FAVOURITE FORMAT? Four-day cricket because it's the closest to Test cricket
DESCRIBE YOURSELF IN THREE WORDS: Relaxed, interesting, boring
HOBBIES? Having a punt
FAVOURITE TOY AS A KID? The Xbox
WHAT WOULD BE YOUR PERFECT BREAKFAST? Two sausages, poached eggs, ketchup, yoghurt with honey
SURPRISING FACT ABOUT YOU: I'm a big Newcastle fan

Batting	Mat	Inns	NO	Runs	HS	Ave	SR	100	50	Ct	St
First-class	34	57	4	1848	185	34.86	48.56	1	14	82	2
List A	22	22	3	366	59	19.26	89.70	0	2	17	3
T20s	15	14	1	172	64	13.23	119.44	0	1	5	1

Bowling	Mat	Balls	Mdns	Runs	Wkts	BB	Ave	4wI	5wI	SR	Econ
First-class	34	-	-	-	-	-	-	-	-	-	-
List A	22	-	-	-	-	-	-	-	-	-	-
T20s	15	-	-	-	-	-	-	-	-	-	-

ZAK CHAPPELL

RHB / RFM / R0 / W0

FULL NAME: Zachariah John Chappell
BORN: August 21, 1996, Grantham, Lincolnshire
SQUAD NO: 32
HEIGHT: 6ft 5in
NICKNAME: Jonny Sins
EDUCATION: Stamford School, Lincolnshire
TEAMS: Derbyshire, England Lions, Gloucestershire, Leicestershire, Nottinghamshire, Oval Invincibles, Rangpur Riders
ROLE: Bowler
DEBUT: First-class: 2015; List A: 2015; T20: 2015

BEST BATTING: 96 Leicestershire vs Derbyshire, Derby, 2015
BEST BOWLING: 6-44 Leicestershire vs Northamptonshire, Northampton, 2018
COUNTY CAP: 2024 (Derbyshire)

FIRST CRICKET CLUB? Stamford Town CC, Lincolnshire
WHAT'S THE BIGGEST PRIZE IN DOMESTIC CRICKET? The Hundred
THE KOOKABURRA BALL: YES OR NO? No – it just knocks in bats
WHICH AWAY GROUND DO YOU MOST ENJOY VISITING? Hove – love the seaside
WHAT WOULD YOU CHANGE ABOUT THE STRUCTURE OF THE COUNTY SEASON? Have fewer games in the County Championship
ONE THING YOU WANT TO DO BEFORE YOU DIE: Nail a yorker
WHICH PUBLIC FIGURE INSPIRES YOU (EXCLUDING SPORTSPEOPLE)? Reece Wabara
SURPRISING FACT ABOUT YOU: I love otter-watching

Batting	Mat	Inns	NO	Runs	HS	Ave	SR	100	50	Ct	St
First-class	52	76	11	1275	96	19.61	57.04	0	5	7	-
List A	31	25	11	403	94*	28.78	84.84	0	2	6	-
T20s	59	30	14	165	18*	10.31	118.70	0	0	14	-

Bowling	Mat	Balls	Mdns	Runs	Wkts	BB	Ave	4wi	5wi	SR	Econ
First-class	52	7091	210	4258	123	6-44	34.61	-	4	57.65	3.60
List A	31	1466	8	1447	47	4-39	30.78	1	0	31.19	5.92
T20s	59	1094	0	1689	81	5-23	20.85	2	1	13.50	9.26

BEN CHARLESWORTH

LHB / RMF / R0 / W0

FULL NAME: Ben Geoffrey Charlesworth
BORN: November 19, 2000, Oxford
SQUAD NO: 64
HEIGHT: 6ft 3in
NICKNAME: Charlie
EDUCATION: St Edward's School, Oxford
TEAMS: Gloucestershire, England U19
ROLE: Batter
DEBUT: First-class: 2018; List A: 2019; T20: 2023

BEST BATTING: 210 Gloucestershire vs Leicestershire, Bristol, 2024
BEST BOWLING: 3-25 Gloucestershire vs Middlesex, Bristol, 2018
COUNTY CAP: 2018

FIRST CRICKET CLUB? Abingdon Vale CC, Oxfordshire. It was 10 minutes down the road from my house. I played and trained there from the age of five to 16
FAMILY TIES? My brother Luke Charlesworth is on a rookie contract at Gloucestershire
WHAT WOULD YOU DO IF YOU WERE IN CHARGE OF COUNTY CRICKET? Introduce free hits in red-ball cricket to bring more excitement into the longer format – and to punish bowlers for no-balls
BIGGEST CRICKETING REGRET? Not speaking to Eoin Morgan in 2018 when I played against Middlesex. I could have learned a thing or two by having a chat with him
CHILDHOOD SPORTING HERO? Kumar Sangakkara

Batting	Mat	Inns	NO	Runs	HS	Ave	SR	100	50	Ct	St
First-class	43	69	4	1840	210	28.30	43.07	2	10	25	-
List A	19	18	2	598	99*	37.37	79.31	0	4	9	-
T20s	30	26	5	520	56	24.76	149.85	0	2	7	-

Bowling	Mat	Balls	Mdns	Runs	Wkts	BB	Ave	4wl	5wl	SR	Econ
First-class	43	711	19	493	14	3-25	35.21	-	0	50.78	4.16
List A	19	24	0	31	0	0-13	-	-	-	-	7.75
T20s	30	45	0	93	1	1-32	93.00	0	0	45.00	12.40

JAFER CHOHAN — RHB / LB / R0 / W0

FULL NAME: Jafer Ali Chohan
BORN: July 11, 2002, Camden, London
SQUAD NO: 5
EDUCATION: Harrow School; Loughborough University
TEAMS: Yorkshire, Sydney Sixers
ROLE: Bowler
DEBUT: T20: 2023

NOTES: The promising leg-spinner made a big splash last summer after taking 17 wickets in his first full T20 Blast campaign and being called up to the England party for the white-ball series in the Caribbean which followed the English season. Chohan, the first graduate from the South Asian Cricket Academy (SACA) to be named in an England squad, did not get a chance to make his international debut but has had a busy winter with Sydney Sixers in Australia's Big Bash alongside working with England Lions. After initially impressing for SACA, as well as catching the eye of Joe Root in the nets at Loughborough, Chohan earned a trial at Yorkshire which in turn saw him win a rookie contract for the 2023 season before signing a full-time professional deal with Yorkshire for the 2024 summer

Batting	Mat	Inns	NO	Runs	HS	Ave	SR	100	50	Ct	St
T20s	27	9	4	74	37	14.80	139.62	0	0	4	-

Bowling	Mat	Balls	Mdns	Runs	Wkts	BB	Ave	4wI	5wI	SR	Econ
T20s	27	461	0	590	25	5-14	23.60	1	1	18.44	7.67

JORDAN CLARK RHB / RM / R0 / W0 / MVP41

FULL NAME: Jordan Clark
BORN: October 14, 1990, Whitehaven, Cumbria
SQUAD NO: 8
HEIGHT: 6ft 4in
EDUCATION: Sedbergh School, Cumbria
TEAMS: Surrey, Hobart Hurricanes, Lancashire, Northern Superchargers, Oval Invincibles
ROLE: Allrounder
DEBUT: First-class: 2015; List A: 2010; T20: 2011

BEST BATTING: 140 Lancashire vs Surrey, The Oval, 2017
BEST BOWLING: 6-21 Surrey vs Hampshire, The Oval, 2021
COUNTY CAP: 2022 (Surrey)

FIRST CRICKET CLUB? Cleator CC – based in a little village in north-west Cumbria. They won the Village Cup at Lord's a few summers back
FAMILY TIES? My younger brother Graham plays for Durham. My older brother Darren has played Minor Counties with Cumberland and together with my dad won the National Village Cup with Cleator CC in 2013
GREATEST PERFORMANCE YOU HAVE WITNESSED? Ashwell Prince's hundred for my old club Lancashire at Colwyn Bay in 2015. He was playing one-handed reverse-sweeps
MOST EXCITING DAY AS A CRICKETER? Taking a hat-trick against Yorkshire in the Championship match at Old Trafford in 2018

Batting	Mat	Inns	NO	Runs	HS	Ave	SR	100	50	Ct	St
First-class	102	141	19	3475	140	28.48	57.08	4	20	14	-
List A	53	41	8	1028	79*	31.15	100.09	0	6	9	-
T20s	130	91	31	1211	60	20.18	127.60	0	1	44	-

Bowling	Mat	Balls	Mdns	Runs	Wkts	BB	Ave	4wI	5wI	SR	Econ
First-class	102	13496	362	7368	247	6-21	29.82	-	6	54.63	3.27
List A	53	1530	4	1640	36	4-34	45.55	1	0	42.50	6.43
T20s	130	1465	1	2176	75	4-22	29.01	1	0	19.53	8.91

TOM CLARK

LHB / RM / R0 / W0

FULL NAME: Thomas Geoffrey Reeves Clark
BORN: July 2, 2001, Haywards Heath, Sussex
SQUAD NO: 27
HEIGHT: 6ft 2in
EDUCATION: Ardingly College, West Sussex
TEAMS: Sussex, England U19
ROLE: Batter
DEBUT: First-class: 2019; List A: 2021; T20: 2023

BEST BATTING: 138 Sussex vs Leicestershire, Leicester, 2022
BEST BOWLING: 3-17 Sussex vs Gloucestershire, Bristol, 2024

FIRST CRICKET CLUB? Horsham CC, West Sussex
WHICH TEAMMATE HAS HAD THE BIGGEST IMPACT ON YOUR GAME? Cheteshwar Pujara
BEST PERFORMANCE AS A PRO? My maiden first-class century against Nottinghamshire at Hove in 2022
GREATEST PERFORMANCE YOU HAVE WITNESSED? Ollie Robinson's nine-fer at Cardiff in 2021
WHO IS THE MOST TALENTED U19 TEENAGER IN THE COUNTY GAME? Henry Rogers (Sus)
FAVOURITE FORMAT? Four-day cricket is the most rewarding form of the game
WHICH PERSON INSPIRES YOU MOST? David Brent
CHOOSE A FANTASY SLIP CORDON TO SPEND A DAY IN THE FIELD WITH: Oli Carter (wk), David Brent, Alan Partridge, Ruby Walsh

Batting	Mat	Inns	NO	Runs	HS	Ave	SR	100	50	Ct	St
First-class	49	84	5	2139	138	27.07	45.56	3	13	47	-
List A	25	25	1	663	104	27.62	82.87	1	3	9	-
T20s	22	22	3	473	72*	24.89	135.53	0	1	15	-

Bowling	Mat	Balls	Mdns	Runs	Wkts	BB	Ave	4wI	5wI	SR	Econ
First-class	49	994	25	535	16	3-17	33.43	-	0	62.12	3.22
List A	25	132	2	136	1	1-17	136.00	0	0	132.00	6.18
T20s	22	-	-	-	-	-	-	-	-	-	-

JOE CLARKE

RHB / WK / R2 / W0 / MVP26

FULL NAME: Joseph Michael Clarke
BORN: May 26, 1996, Shrewsbury, Shropshire
SQUAD NO: 33
HEIGHT: 6ft
EDUCATION: Llanfyllin High School, Powys
TEAMS: Nottinghamshire, England Lions, Karachi Kings, Manchester Originals, Melbourne Renegades, Melbourne Stars, Perth Scorchers, Victoria, Welsh Fire, Worcestershire
ROLE: Batter
DEBUT: First-class: 2015; List A: 2015; T20: 2015

NOTTINGHAMSHIRE

BEST BATTING: 229* Nottinghamshire vs Warwickshire, Trent Bridge, 2023

COUNTY CAP: 2021 (Nottinghamshire)

FIRST CRICKET CLUB? Oswestry CC, Shropshire
GREATEST PERFORMANCE YOU HAVE WITNESSED? Callum Ferguson's 192 for Worcestershire against Leicestershire in the 2018 One-Day Cup. Pure skill, and so good to watch from the other end
BIGGEST CRICKETING REGRET? Being not out overnight before Bank Holiday Monday
CHILDHOOD SPORTING HERO? Adam Gilchrist
SURPRISING FACT ABOUT YOU: I can speak (some) Welsh

Batting	Mat	Inns	NO	Runs	HS	Ave	SR	100	50	Ct	St
First-class	135	227	20	8261	229*	39.90	59.10	24	39	95	-
List A	62	59	5	1846	139	34.18	92.85	4	9	22	2
T20s	222	216	13	5269	136	25.95	142.67	4	29	84	6

Bowling	Mat	Balls	Mdns	Runs	Wkts	BB	Ave	4wI	5wI	SR	Econ
First-class	135	48	0	48	0	0-22	-	-	-	-	6.00
List A	62	-	-	-	-	-	-	-	-	-	-
T20s	222	-	-	-	-	-	-	-	-	-	-

BEN COAD   RHB / RFM / R0 / W2

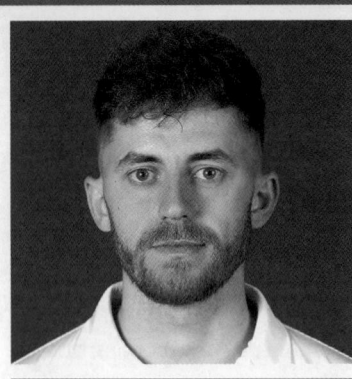

FULL NAME: Benjamin Oliver Coad
BORN: January 10, 1994, Harrogate, Yorkshire
SQUAD NO: 10
HEIGHT: 6ft 3in
NICKNAME: Hench
EDUCATION: Thirsk School & Sixth Form College, North Yorkshire
TEAMS: Yorkshire
ROLE: Bowler
DEBUT: First-class: 2016; List A: 2013; T20: 2015

BEST BATTING: 69 Yorkshire vs Essex, Headingley, 2022
BEST BOWLING: 6-25 Yorkshire vs Lancashire, Headingley, 2017
COUNTY CAP: 2018

FIRST CRICKET CLUB? Studley Royal CC, Ripon, North Yorkshire
FAMILY TIES? My brothers played representative cricket at junior levels. My dad played Minor Counties for Suffolk
MOST EXCITING DAY AS A CRICKETER? My second T20 game in 2015, playing against Warwickshire at home in front of a very good crowd and managing to take two wickets and winning the game against the defending champions
SURPRISING FACT ABOUT YOU: I'm a Newcastle United fan

Batting	Mat	Inns	NO	Runs	HS	Ave	SR	100	50	Ct	St
First-class	76	94	29	987	69	15.18	69.45	0	1	5	-
List A	44	21	10	210	45	19.09	79.24	0	0	10	-
T20s	12	4	1	14	7	4.66	56.00	0	0	6	-

Bowling	Mat	Balls	Mdns	Runs	Wkts	BB	Ave	4wI	5wI	SR	Econ
First-class	76	13090	607	5868	302	6-25	19.43	-	14	43.34	2.68
List A	44	2152	31	1646	53	4-14	31.05	2	0	40.60	4.58
T20s	12	217	0	323	13	3-40	24.84	0	0	16.69	8.93

MICHAEL COHEN

LHB / LFM / R0 / W0

FULL NAME: Michael Alexander Robert Cohen
BORN: August 4, 1998, Cape Town, South Africa
SQUAD NO: 45
HEIGHT: 5ft 10in
NICKNAME: Uncoh
EDUCATION: Reddam House Constantia, Cape Town; University of South Africa
TEAMS: Kent, Cape Cobras, Derbyshire, South Africa U19, Western Province
ROLE: Bowler
DEBUT: First-class: 2017; List A: 2018; T20: 2017

BEST BATTING: 30* Derbyshire vs Nottinghamshire, Trent Bridge, 2020
BEST BOWLING: 5-40 Western Province vs South Western Districts, Rondesbosch, 2018

FIRST CRICKET CLUB? Western Province CC, Cape Town
WHAT WOULD YOU CHANGE ABOUT THE STRUCTURE OF THE COUNTY SEASON? Have more county cricket played in August to allow for more breathing room between fixtures and a greater chance for fans to watch during the peak of summer
MOST UNDERRATED PLAYER IN COUNTY CRICKET? Fynn Hudson-Prentice
HOBBIES? Playing the guitar, which serves as a welcome change from trying to evade balls launched at me
WHO WOULD YOU MOST AND LEAST LIKE TO HAVE A NET WITH? Most – Wasim Akram (my boyhood hero). Least – Shaun Tait
MAKE ONE PREDICTION FOR THE FUTURE OF CRICKET: The emergence of ambidextrous batters

Batting	Mat	Inns	NO	Runs	HS	Ave	SR	100	50	Ct	St
First-class	22	28	15	172	30*	13.23	30.71	0	0	2	-
List A	4	1	0	16	16	16.00	123.07	0	0	1	-
T20s	12	5	4	22	7*	22.00	115.78	0	0	0	-

Bowling	Mat	Balls	Mdns	Runs	Wkts	BB	Ave	4wI	5wI	SR	Econ
First-class	22	2828	68	1777	68	5-40	26.13	-	3	41.58	3.77
List A	4	192	2	160	3	1-17	53.33	0	0	64.00	5.00
T20s	12	202	1	289	9	2-17	32.11	0	0	22.44	8.58

JAMES COLES — RHB / SLA / R0 / W0 / MVP32

SUSSEX

FULL NAME: James Matthew Coles
BORN: April 2, 2004, Aylesbury, Buckinghamshire
SQUAD NO: 30
HEIGHT: 6ft 1in
NICKNAME: Roller
EDUCATION: Magdalen College School, Oxford
TEAMS: Sussex, Southern Brave, England Lions
ROLE: Allrounder
DEBUT: First-class: 2020; List A: 2021; T20: 2023

BEST BATTING: 180 Sussex vs Derbyshire, Hove, 2023
BEST BOWLING: 4-61 Sussex vs Middlesex, Hove, 2024
COUNTY CAP: 2024

FIRST CRICKET CLUB? Aston Rowant CC, Chinnor, Oxfordshire
EARLIEST CRICKETING MEMORY? Playing 'save the boundary' with my brother
WHICH TEAMMATE HAS HAD THE BIGGEST IMPACT ON YOUR GAME? Steven Finn – he's helped me understand about all the ups and downs and how you just have to ride them out
THE KOOKABURRA BALL: YES OR NO? Yes, it's a nice change
FAVOURITE WARM-UP SONG? Sweet Disposition by The Temper Trap
HOW MANY HOURS DO YOU SPEND ON YOUR PHONE A DAY? Six
SPECIALITY SUBJECT IN A PUB QUIZ (EXCLUDING SPORT)? Types of river fish
ONE THING YOU WANT TO DO BEFORE YOU DIE: Catch a tuna
WHICH PUBLIC FIGURE INSPIRES YOU (EXCLUDING SPORTSPEOPLE)? Winston Churchill
SURPRISING FACT ABOUT YOU: I have type 1 diabetes
FILM YOU CAN WATCH OVER AND OVER: The Imitation Game

Batting	Mat	Inns	NO	Runs	HS	Ave	SR	100	50	Ct	St
First-class	36	58	4	1888	180	34.96	58.11	4	8	29	-
List A	20	17	3	320	59	22.85	86.72	0	1	7	-
T20s	35	29	8	520	69*	24.76	138.29	0	2	18	-

Bowling	Mat	Balls	Mdns	Runs	Wkts	BB	Ave	4wI	5wI	SR	Econ
First-class	36	2997	47	1992	37	4-61	53.83	-	0	81.00	3.98
List A	20	760	1	753	21	3-27	35.85	0	0	36.19	5.94
T20s	35	406	1	555	22	4-12	25.22	2	0	18.45	8.20

BEN COMPTON

LHB / OB / R1 / W0

FULL NAME: Benjamin Garnet Compton
BORN: March 29, 1994, Durban, South Africa
SQUAD NO: 2
HEIGHT: 6ft 1in
NICKNAME: Compo
EDUCATION: Clifton College, Durban; The Open University
TEAMS: Kent, KwaZulu-Natal Inland, Mountaineers, Nottinghamshire
ROLE: Batter
DEBUT: First-class: 2019; List A: 2021

KENT

BEST BATTING: 217 Mountaineers vs Southern Rocks, Harare, 2022

FIRST CRICKET CLUB? Wimbledon CC, London
WHAT PART OF THE SEASON DO YOU MOST ENJOY? Every time I'm batting
IF YOU COULD PINCH A PLAYER FROM ANOTHER COUNTY, WHO WOULD IT BE?
Jamie Porter
HOW IS BAZBALL AFFECTING CHAMPIONSHIP CRICKET? It's delusional
WHAT DO YOU THINK OF THE CURRENT 50-OVER COMPETITION? It's good – I hope 50-over cricket has a resurgence
WHO IS THE TOUGHEST BOWLER TO FACE? Tom Bailey – he's got me in his pocket
WHAT KEEPS YOU AWAKE AT NIGHT? Loud frogs
WHAT'S THE SILLIEST OUTFIT YOU'VE EVER WORN? Dressing up as Woody from Toy Story
CHOOSE A FANTASY SLIP CORDON TO SPEND A DAY IN THE FIELD WITH: Eric Cantona (wk), Jacques Kallis, Herschelle Gibbs

Batting	Mat	Inns	NO	Runs	HS	Ave	SR	100	50	Ct	St
First-class	66	121	10	4875	217	43.91	44.33	13	24	46	-
List A	26	25	0	1143	110	45.72	74.65	3	10	8	-
Bowling	Mat	Balls	Mdns	Runs	Wkts	BB	Ave	4wI	5wI	SR	Econ
First-class	66	48	0	34	0	0-2	-	-	-	-	4.25
List A	26	-	-	-	-	-	-	-	-	-	-

DURHAM

SAM CONNERS · RHB / RFM / R0 / W1

FULL NAME: Samuel Conners
BORN: February 13, 1999, Nottingham
SQUAD NO: 59
HEIGHT: 6ft
NICKNAME: Sammy
EDUCATION: George Spencer Academy, Nottingham
TEAMS: Durham, Derbyshire, England Lions
ROLE: Bowler
DEBUT: First-class: 2019; List A: 2019; T20: 2020

BEST BATTING: 39 Derbyshire vs Kent, Derby, 2021
BEST BOWLING: 5-51 Derbyshire vs Leicestershire, Derby, 2022
COUNTY CAP: 2022 (Derbyshire)

FIRST CRICKET CLUB? Attenborough CC, Nottingham
WHICH TEAMMATE HAS HAD THE BIGGEST IMPACT ON YOUR GAME? Tony Palladino – a man who spoke sense about cricket
WHAT PART OF THE SEASON DO YOU MOST ENJOY? The early season
WHICH AWAY GROUND DO YOU MOST ENJOY VISITING? Cardiff – a great night out
WHO IS THE MOST TALENTED U19 TEENAGER IN THE COUNTY GAME? Harry Moore (Der)
HOW IS BAZBALL AFFECTING CHAMPIONSHIP CRICKET? Pitches are flatter and batters are whacking it
WHO IS THE TOUGHEST BOWLER TO FACE? Mark Wood or Alzarri Joseph – the ball comes so fast I can't see it
CHOOSE A FANTASY SLIP CORDON TO SPEND A DAY IN THE FIELD WITH: Tiger Woods (wk), Ben Aitchison, Harry Came, Me

Batting	Mat	Inns	NO	Runs	HS	Ave	SR	100	50	Ct	St
First-class	48	57	14	404	39	9.39	36.26	0	0	13	-
List A	24	14	5	70	36*	7.77	59.82	0	0	3	-
T20s	18	5	2	7	2*	2.33	70.00	0	0	5	-

Bowling	Mat	Balls	Mdns	Runs	Wkts	BB	Ave	4wI	5wI	SR	Econ
First-class	48	7479	197	4727	124	5-51	38.12	-	4	60.31	3.79
List A	24	1158	13	1086	30	5-28	36.20	0	1	38.60	5.62
T20s	18	218	0	407	13	3-25	31.30	0	0	16.76	11.20

SAM COOK

RHB / RFM / R0 / W2

FULL NAME: Samuel James Cook
BORN: August 4, 1997, Chelmsford, Essex
SQUAD NO: 16
HEIGHT: 6ft 2in
NICKNAME: Little Chef
EDUCATION: Great Baddow High School, Chelmsford; Loughborough University
TEAMS: Essex, Trent Rockets, England Lions, Joburg Super Kings
ROLE: Bowler
DEBUT: First-class: 2016; List A: 2018; T20: 2018

BEST BATTING: 49 Essex vs Lancashire, Chelmsford, 2024
BEST BOWLING: 7-23 Essex vs Kent, Canterbury, 2019
COUNTY CAP: 2020

FIRST CRICKET CLUB? Writtle CC, Essex
BIGGEST INFLUENCE ON YOUR DEVELOPMENT AS A CRICKETER (EXCLUDING PARENTS)? Ryan ten Doeschate and Anthony McGrath
WHAT WOULD YOU DO IF YOU WERE IN CHARGE OF COUNTY CRICKET? Introduce pyrotechnics at Championship games
CHILDHOOD SPORTING HERO? Cristiano Ronaldo

Batting	Mat	Inns	NO	Runs	HS	Ave	SR	100	50	Ct	St
First-class	86	102	32	771	49	11.01	43.29	0	0	19	-
List A	15	6	3	17	6	5.66	77.27	0	0	1	-
T20s	84	23	15	47	18	5.87	100.00	0	0	23	-

Bowling	Mat	Balls	Mdns	Runs	Wkts	BB	Ave	4wl	5wl	SR	Econ
First-class	86	13847	625	6088	311	7-23	19.57	-	14	44.52	2.63
List A	15	750	8	599	17	3-37	35.23	0	0	44.11	4.79
T20s	84	1639	2	2375	92	4-15	25.81	5	0	17.81	8.69

CHRIS COOKE

RHB / WK / R0 / W0

GLAMORGAN

FULL NAME: Christopher Barry Cooke
BORN: May 30, 1986, Johannesburg, South Africa
SQUAD NO: 46
HEIGHT: 5ft 11in
NICKNAME: Jelly
EDUCATION: Bishops School, Cape Town; University of Cape Town
TEAMS: Glamorgan, Birmingham Phoenix, Western Province
ROLE: Batter/wicketkeeper
DEBUT: First-class: 2009; List A: 2009; T20: 2011

BEST BATTING: 205* Glamorgan vs Surrey, The Oval, 2021

COUNTY CAP: 2016; **BENEFIT:** 2024

FIRST CRICKET CLUB? Cape Town CC, South Africa
MOST EXCITING DAY AS A CRICKETER? Playing in the one-day final at Lord's in 2013
WHAT WOULD YOU DO IF YOU WERE IN CHARGE OF COUNTY CRICKET? Bring back the 40-over format and push for T20 cricket to be an Olympic sport
CHILDHOOD SPORTING HERO? Jonty Rhodes

Batting	Mat	Inns	NO	Runs	HS	Ave	SR	100	50	Ct	St
First-class	144	238	40	7743	205*	39.10	54.67	14	41	322	17
List A	92	84	9	2616	161	34.88	97.10	3	14	58	5
T20s	165	147	28	2797	113*	23.50	140.27	1	7	98	17

Bowling	Mat	Balls	Mdns	Runs	Wkts	BB	Ave	4wI	5wI	SR	Econ
First-class	144	45	0	38	0	0-4	-	-	-	-	5.06
List A	92	-	-	-	-	-	-	-	-	-	-
T20s	165	-	-	-	-	-	-	-	-	-	-

PAUL COUGHLIN   RHB / RFM / R0 / W0

FULL NAME: Paul Coughlin
BORN: October 23, 1992, Sunderland
SQUAD NO: 23
HEIGHT: 6ft 2in
NICKNAME: Coggers
EDUCATION: St Robert of Newminster Catholic School, Sunderland
TEAMS: Durham, England Lions, Nottinghamshire
ROLE: Allrounder
DEBUT: First-class: 2012; List A: 2012; T20: 2014

BEST BATTING: 100* Durham vs Worcestershire, Chester-le-Street, 2022
BEST BOWLING: 5-49 Durham vs Northamptonshire, Chester-le-Street, 2017

FAMILY TIES? My younger brother Josh has played for Durham. My uncle Tommy Harland played for the club when it was a Minor County. A different uncle had a homemade net in his back garden when I was a kid, and that's how I got into cricket
MOST EXCITING DAY AS A CRICKETER? Winning the One-Day Cup at Lord's in 2014
CHILDHOOD SPORTING HERO? Andrew Flintoff
SURPRISING FACT ABOUT YOU: I started out aiming to be a wicketkeeper. Then I tried myself as a batter. But I ended up being more of a bowler

Batting	Mat	Inns	NO	Runs	HS	Ave	SR	100	50	Ct	St
First-class	62	90	13	1950	100*	25.32	57.00	1	10	33	-
List A	42	32	5	402	77	14.88	100.00	0	1	14	-
T20s	71	49	11	825	53	21.71	136.58	0	1	24	-

Bowling	Mat	Balls	Mdns	Runs	Wkts	BB	Ave	4wI	5wI	SR	Econ
First-class	62	7900	255	4556	138	5-49	33.01	-	3	57.24	3.46
List A	42	1476	5	1380	35	3-32	39.42	0	0	42.17	5.60
T20s	71	1093	2	1752	70	5-42	25.02	2	1	15.61	9.61

BEN COX

RHB / WK / R0 / W0

FULL NAME: Oliver Benjamin Cox
BORN: February 2, 1992, Wordsley, Stourbridge, Worcestershire
SQUAD NO: 7
HEIGHT: 5ft 10in
NICKNAME: Cocko
EDUCATION: Bromsgrove School, Worcestershire
TEAMS: Leicestershire, Boost Defenders, Otago, Worcestershire
ROLE: Wicketkeeper
DEBUT: First-class: 2009; List A: 2010; T20: 2010

BEST BATTING: 124 Worcestershire vs Gloucestershire, Cheltenham, 2017

COUNTY CAP: BENEFIT: 2023 (Worcestershire)

FIRST CRICKET CLUB? Belbroughton CC, Worcestershire – a tiny village club which I had to leave because I couldn't get in the first team as a wicketkeeper
THE KOOKABURRA BALL: YES OR NO? Yes, why not? It should keep the Dukes manufacturers on their toes after two poor years in terms of standards of the ball (going out of shape etc)
OPPONENT YOU MOST LOOK FORWARD TO PLAYING AGAINST? All the Notts boys, lots of friends and old housemates in their side
FAVOURITE WARM-UP SONG? Give Me Love by Ed Sheeran
HOW MANY HOURS DO YOU SPEND ON YOUR PHONE A DAY? Three
HOBBY YOU WOULD LIKE TO LEARN: Play an instrument
SURPRISING FACT ABOUT YOU: I had an England U18 trial as a fly half and my two other competitors were Owen Farrell and George Ford
FILM YOU CAN WATCH OVER AND OVER: The Greatest Showman

Batting	Mat	Inns	NO	Runs	HS	Ave	SR	100	50	Ct	St
First-class	159	251	37	5977	124	27.92	58.54	4	33	428	17
List A	100	80	14	2038	122*	30.87	99.41	1	10	102	10
T20s	170	148	48	2609	61*	26.09	126.95	0	8	80	36

Bowling	Mat	Balls	Mdns	Runs	Wkts	BB	Ave	4wI	5wI	SR	Econ
First-class	159	-	-	-	-	-	-	-	-	-	-
List A	100	-	-	-	-	-	-	-	-	-	-
T20s	170	-	-	-	-	-	-	-	-	-	-

JORDAN COX

RHB / WK / R0 / W0 / MVP17

ESSEX

FULL NAME: Jordan Matthew Cox
BORN: October 21, 2000, Portsmouth
SQUAD NO: 77
HEIGHT: 5ft 11in
NICKNAME: Chief
EDUCATION: Felsted School, Essex
TEAMS: England, Essex, Oval Invincibles, Dambulla Aura, Kent, Hobart Hurricanes, Islamabad United, Melbourne Renegades, Sunrisers Eastern Cape
ROLE: Batter/wicketkeeper
DEBUT: ODI: 2024; T20I: 2024; First-class: 2019; List A: 2019; T20: 2019

BEST BATTING: 238* Kent vs Sussex, Canterbury, 2020

FIRST CRICKET CLUB? Sandwich Town CC, Dover, Kent
WHICH COUNTY PLAYER WOULD YOU MOST LIKE TO GO FOR A DRINK WITH?
Adam Rossington
BEST DELIVERY YOU HAVE EVER FACED? Mohammad Abbas sending my off stump flying
GREATEST PERFORMANCE YOU HAVE WITNESSED? Darren Stevens hitting 237 off 225 balls at Headingley in 2019
FAVOURITE FORMAT? T20 because it's fast and we wear pyjamas
WHAT WOULD BE YOUR PERFECT BREAKFAST? Kellogg's Krave
WHICH PERSON INSPIRES YOU MOST? Barack Obama

Batting	Mat	Inns	NO	Runs	HS	Ave	SR	100	50	Ct	St
ODIs	3	3	0	22	17	7.33	39.28	0	0	1	-
T20Is	2	2	0	17	17	8.50	121.42	0	0	1	-
First-class	53	85	5	3194	238*	39.92	52.92	8	12	48	-
List A	7	7	0	120	46	17.14	67.41	0	0	4	-
T20s	135	125	26	2801	94	28.29	136.76	0	13	89	7

Bowling	Mat	Balls	Mdns	Runs	Wkts	BB	Ave	4wI	5wI	SR	Econ
ODIs	3	-	-	-	-	-	-	-	-	-	-
T20Is	2	-	-	-	-	-	-	-	-	-	-
First-class	53	6	0	3	0	0-3	-	-	-	-	3.00
List A	7	-	-	-	-	-	-	-	-	-	-
T20s	135	-	-	-	-	-	-	-	-	-	-

JOE CRACKNELL

RHB / WK / R0 / W0

MIDDLESEX

FULL NAME: Joseph Benjamin Cracknell
BORN: March 16, 2000, Enfield, London
SQUAD NO: 48
HEIGHT: 5ft 11in
NICKNAME: Crackers
EDUCATION: London Oratory School;
Durham University
TEAMS: Middlesex, London Spirit
ROLE: Batter/wicketkeeper
DEBUT: First-class: 2021; List A: 2021; T20: 2020

BEST BATTING: 33 Middlesex vs Lancashire, Old Trafford, 2023

FIRST CRICKET CLUB? North Middlesex CC, London
OPPONENT YOU MOST LOOK FORWARD TO PLAYING AGAINST? Ethan Bamber, my former
Middlesex teammate. I grew up playing with him
FAVOURITE WARM-UP SONG? The Gambler by Kenny Rogers
HOW MANY HOURS DO YOU SPEND ON YOUR PHONE A DAY? Three
SPECIALITY SUBJECT IN A PUB QUIZ (EXCLUDING SPORT)? PDC Darts 2019-present
ONE THING YOU WANT TO DO BEFORE YOU DIE: Play a season for Hornsey CC
SURPRISING FACT ABOUT YOU: I've hit more 180s than I have played cricket games
FILM YOU CAN WATCH OVER AND OVER: I'm more of a TV series person

Batting	Mat	Inns	NO	Runs	HS	Ave	SR	100	50	Ct	St
First-class	4	8	0	110	33	13.75	49.32	0	0	3	-
List A	23	21	0	754	98	35.90	90.73	0	6	17	2
T20s	55	54	3	1148	77	22.50	132.87	0	5	25	-

Bowling	Mat	Balls	Mdns	Runs	Wkts	BB	Ave	4wI	5wI	SR	Econ
First-class	4	-	-	-	-	-	-	-	-	-	-
List A	23	-	-	-	-	-	-	-	-	-	-
T20s	55	-	-	-	-	-	-	-	-	-	-

MASON CRANE
RHB / LB / RO / WO

FULL NAME: Mason Sidney Crane
BORN: February 18, 1997, Shoreham-by-Sea, Sussex
SQUAD NO: 3
HEIGHT: 5ft 10in
NICKNAME: Mase
EDUCATION: Lancing College, West Sussex
TEAMS: England, Glamorgan, Welsh Fire, Hampshire, London Spirit, New South Wales, Sunrisers Eastern Cape, Sussex
ROLE: Bowler
DEBUT: Test: 2018; T20I: 2017; First-class: 2015; List A: 2015; T20: 2015

BEST BATTING: 61 Glamorgan vs Northamptonshire, Northampton, 2024
BEST BOWLING: 5-35 Hampshire vs Warwickshire, Southampton, 2015

FIRST CRICKET CLUB? Worthing CC, West Sussex
EARLIEST CRICKETING MEMORY? The 2005 Ashes
WHAT'S THE BIGGEST PRIZE IN DOMESTIC CRICKET? The County Championship
THE KOOKABURRA BALL: YES OR NO? Yes, but at the right time of year
OPPONENT YOU MOST LOOK FORWARD TO PLAYING AGAINST? Joe Weatherley, my old teammate, because I will go crazy if I get him out
FAVOURITE WARM-UP SONG? Yma o Hyd by Dafydd Iwan
SPECIALITY SUBJECT IN A PUB QUIZ (EXCLUDING SPORT)? Squad numbers in county cricket
FILM YOU CAN WATCH OVER AND OVER: Groundhog Day

Batting	Mat	Inns	NO	Runs	HS	Ave	SR	100	50	Ct	St
Tests	1	2	0	6	4	3.00	54.54	0	0	0	-
T20Is	2	0	-	-	-	-	-	-	-	0	-
First-class	64	88	25	1044	61	16.57	38.29	0	2	15	-
List A	47	22	14	168	31	21.00	75.00	0	0	15	-
T20s	106	31	24	153	19	21.85	94.44	0	0	29	-
Bowling	Mat	Balls	Mdns	Runs	Wkts	BB	Ave	4wI	5wI	SR	Econ
Tests	1	288	3	193	1	1-193	193.00	-	0	288.00	4.02
T20Is	2	48	0	62	1	1-38	62.00	0	0	48.00	7.75
First-class	64	10227	203	6658	154	5-35	43.23	-	5	66.40	3.90
List A	47	2374	5	2359	79	4-30	29.86	4	0	30.05	5.96
T20s	106	2055	0	2765	118	4-24	23.43	2	0	17.41	8.07

ZAK CRAWLEY

RHB / RM / R1 / W0

KENT

FULL NAME: Zak Crawley
BORN: February 3, 1998, Bromley, Kent
SQUAD NO: 16
HEIGHT: 6ft 5in
EDUCATION: Tonbridge School, Kent
TEAMS: England, Kent, Hobart Hurricanes, London Spirit, Perth Scorchers, Sunrisers Eastern Cape
ROLE: Batter
DEBUT: Test: 2019; ODI: 2021; First-class: 2017; List A: 2017; T20: 2018

BEST BATTING: 267 England vs Pakistan, Southampton, 2020

COUNTY CAP: 2019

FIRST CRICKET CLUB? Holmesdale CC, Sevenoaks, Kent
BIGGEST INFLUENCE ON YOUR DEVELOPMENT AS A CRICKETER (EXCLUDING PARENTS)? Rob Key
WHAT WOULD YOU DO IF YOU WERE IN CHARGE OF COUNTY CRICKET? Ban the second new ball, make compulsory the use of the heavy roller
CHILDHOOD SPORTING HERO? Tiger Woods

Batting	Mat	Inns	NO	Runs	HS	Ave	SR	100	50	Ct	St
Tests	53	97	2	2899	267	30.51	65.72	4	16	60	-
ODIs	8	8	1	199	58*	28.42	97.07	0	2	8	-
First-class	124	223	5	6931	267	31.79	62.72	11	39	120	-
List A	31	30	2	942	120	33.64	76.83	1	6	20	-
T20s	84	80	4	1859	108*	24.46	133.35	1	8	39	-

Bowling	Mat	Balls	Mdns	Runs	Wkts	BB	Ave	4wl	5wl	SR	Econ
Tests	53	-	-	-	-	-	-	-	-	-	-
ODIs	8	-	-	-	-	-	-	-	-	-	-
First-class	124	66	2	33	0	0-33	-	-	-	-	3.00
List A	31	12	0	17	0	0-17	-	-	-	-	8.50
T20s	84	-	-	-	-	-	-	-	-	-	-

MATT CRITCHLEY

RHB / LB / R1 / W0 / MVP11

FULL NAME: Matthew James John Critchley
BORN: August 13, 1996, Preston, Lancashire
SQUAD NO: 20
HEIGHT: 6ft 2in
NICKNAME: Critch
EDUCATION: St Michael's CE High School, Chorley; Cardinal Newman College, Preston; University of Derby
TEAMS: Essex, London Spirit, Derbyshire, England Lions, Melbourne Renegades, Welsh Fire
ROLE: Allrounder
DEBUT: First-class: 2015; List A: 2015; T20: 2016

ESSEX

BEST BATTING: 151* Essex vs Kent, Chelmsford, 2024
BEST BOWLING: 6-73 Derbyshire vs Leicestershire, Leicester, 2020
COUNTY CAP: 2019 (Derbyshire); 2023 (Essex)

FIRST CRICKET CLUB? Chorley CC, Lancashire
EARLIEST CRICKETING MEMORY? Watching my dad play club cricket and the 2005 Ashes
WHAT'S THE BIGGEST PRIZE IN DOMESTIC CRICKET? The County Championship
THE KOOKABURRA BALL: YES OR NO? Yes – it brings in all skill-sets
OPPONENT YOU MOST LOOK FORWARD TO PLAYING AGAINST? My former teammate Ben Slater – he's a very tough competitor
FAVOURITE WARM-UP SONG? Chase the Sun by Planet Funk
HOW MANY HOURS DO YOU SPEND ON YOUR PHONE A DAY? Half an hour
SPECIALITY SUBJECT IN A PUB QUIZ (EXCLUDING SPORT)? Plants
ONE THING YOU WANT TO DO BEFORE YOU DIE: Go back to Ally Pally for the darts
HOBBY YOU WOULD LIKE TO LEARN: Become a darts pro
WHICH PUBLIC FIGURE INSPIRES YOU (EXCLUDING SPORTSPEOPLE)? SAS rougue heroes
FILM YOU CAN WATCH OVER AND OVER: Any in the Harry Potter series

Batting	Mat	Inns	NO	Runs	HS	Ave	SR	100	50	Ct	St
First-class	108	180	16	5352	151*	32.63	57.56	9	29	71	-
List A	46	37	10	749	64*	27.74	99.46	0	3	8	-
T20s	141	120	28	1973	80*	21.44	122.16	0	5	43	-

Bowling	Mat	Balls	Mdns	Runs	Wkts	BB	Ave	4wI	5wI	SR	Econ
First-class	108	10923	170	7169	190	6-73	37.73	-	6	57.48	3.93
List A	46	1620	2	1768	34	4-48	52.00	1	0	47.64	6.54
T20s	141	2210	0	2968	120	5-28	24.73	1	1	18.41	8.05

HENRY CROCOMBE

RHB / RFM / RO / WO

SUSSEX

FULL NAME: Henry Thomas Crocombe
BORN: September 20, 2001, Eastbourne, Sussex
SQUAD NO: 14
HEIGHT: 6ft 2in
NICKNAME: Crocs
EDUCATION: Bede's Senior School, Hailsham, East Sussex
TEAMS: Sussex, England Lions
ROLE: Allrounder
DEBUT: First-class: 2020; List A: 2021; T20: 2021

BEST BATTING: 54 Sussex vs Glamorgan, Hove, 2024
BEST BOWLING: 4-22 Sussex vs Gloucestershire, Bristol, 2024

FIRST CRICKET CLUB? Hellingly CC, Hailsham, East Sussex
EARLIEST CRICKETING MEMORY? Playing an U21 game when I was seven
WHAT'S THE BIGGEST PRIZE IN DOMESTIC CRICKET? Winning Division One of the County Championship
THE KOOKABURRA BALL: YES OR NO? Yes, it helps prepare you for playing Test cricket abroad
OPPONENT YOU MOST LOOK FORWARD TO PLAYING AGAINST? My former Sussex teammate Ali Orr
FAVOURITE WARM-UP SONG? Big City Life by Mattafix
HOW MANY HOURS DO YOU SPEND ON YOUR PHONE A DAY? Five
ONE THING YOU WANT TO DO BEFORE YOU DIE: Go to space
WHICH PUBLIC FIGURE INSPIRES YOU (EXCLUDING SPORTSPEOPLE)? Elon Musk
FILM YOU CAN WATCH OVER AND OVER: Interstellar

Batting	Mat	Inns	NO	Runs	HS	Ave	SR	100	50	Ct	St
First-class	36	52	13	427	54	10.94	39.94	0	1	11	-
List A	24	15	8	149	47	21.28	93.71	0	0	8	-
T20s	17	8	7	21	12*	21.00	100.00	0	0	5	-

Bowling	Mat	Balls	Mdns	Runs	Wkts	BB	Ave	4wI	5wI	SR	Econ
First-class	36	4408	104	2778	69	4-22	40.26	-	0	63.88	3.78
List A	24	1090	3	1103	32	4-47	34.46	2	0	34.06	6.07
T20s	17	258	0	464	14	3-31	33.14	0	0	18.42	10.79

BLAKE CULLEN

RHB / RFM / R0 / W0

FULL NAME: Blake Carlton Cullen
BORN: February 19, 2002, Isleworth, Middlesex
SQUAD NO: 19
HEIGHT: 6ft 3in
NICKNAME: The Professor
EDUCATION: Hampton School, London
TEAMS: Middlesex, England U19, London Spirit
ROLE: Bowler
DEBUT: First-class: 2020; List A: 2023; T20: 2021

MIDDLESEX

BEST BATTING: 34 Middlesex vs Sussex, Radlett, 2020
BEST BOWLING: 3-30 Middlesex vs Surrey, The Oval, 2021

FIRST CRICKET CLUB? Wycombe House CC, London
WHICH TEAMMATE HAS HAD THE BIGGEST IMPACT ON YOUR GAME? Toby Roland-Jones
WHICH AWAY GROUND DO YOU MOST ENJOY VISITING? Hove – good facilities and a lovely town
WHO IS THE MOST TALENTED U19 TEENAGER IN THE COUNTY GAME? Seb Morgan (Mid)
IF YOU COULD PINCH A PLAYER FROM ANOTHER COUNTY, WHO WOULD IT BE? Sam Cook
WHAT KEEPS YOU AWAKE AT NIGHT? Wondering if I've locked my car (my kit bag was stolen last summer)
CHOOSE A FANTASY SLIP CORDON TO SPEND A DAY IN THE FIELD WITH: Matt Hancock (wk), Robbie White, Mark Stoneman, Rishi Sunak

Batting	Mat	Inns	NO	Runs	HS	Ave	SR	100	50	Ct	St
First-class	7	9	0	105	34	11.66	30.17	0	0	2	-
List A	4	2	1	15	8	15.00	55.55	0	0	0	-
T20s	41	18	8	96	20*	9.60	111.62	0	0	8	-

Bowling	Mat	Balls	Mdns	Runs	Wkts	BB	Ave	4wI	5wI	SR	Econ
First-class	7	1004	27	648	14	3-30	46.28	-	0	71.71	3.87
List A	4	133	1	170	2	2-32	85.00	0	0	66.50	7.66
T20s	41	782	0	1226	53	4-32	23.13	2	0	14.75	9.40

SAM CURRAN

LHB / LMF / R0 / W0

SURREY

FULL NAME: Samuel Matthew Curran
BORN: June 3, 1998, Northampton
SQUAD NO: 58
HEIGHT: 5ft 9in
NICKNAME: Junior
EDUCATION: Wellington College, Berkshire
TEAMS: England, Surrey, Oval Invincibles, Auckland, Chennai Super Kings, Kings XI Punjab, MI Cape Town, Punjab Kings
ROLE: Allrounder
DEBUT: Test: 2018; ODI: 2018; T20I: 2019; First-class: 2015; List A: 2015; T20: 2015

BEST BATTING: 126 Surrey vs Kent, The Oval, 2022
BEST BOWLING: 7-58 Surrey vs Durham, Chester-le-Street, 2016
COUNTY CAP: 2018

FAMILY TIES? My father Kevin played for Zimbabwe, and my brother Tom plays with me at Surrey. Ben, my other brother, has played for Northants and represents Zimbabwe in international cricket. We have always been a competitive family
CHILDHOOD SPORTING HERO? Brian Lara

Batting	Mat	Inns	NO	Runs	HS	Ave	SR	100	50	Ct	St
Tests	24	38	5	815	78	24.69	64.12	0	3	5	-
ODIs	35	27	3	597	95*	24.87	91.98	0	2	9	-
T20Is	58	34	9	356	50	14.24	124.47	0	1	22	-
First-class	82	124	14	3266	126	29.69	63.18	1	23	26	-
List A	84	59	8	1177	95*	23.07	88.56	0	3	29	-
T20s	268	215	44	4071	102*	23.80	135.15	1	24	102	-

Bowling	Mat	Balls	Mdns	Runs	Wkts	BB	Ave	4wI	5wI	SR	Econ
Tests	24	3091	96	1669	47	4-58	35.51	-	0	65.76	3.23
ODIs	35	1325	10	1376	33	5-48	41.69	1	1	40.15	6.23
T20Is	58	1043	2	1462	54	5-10	27.07	0	1	19.31	8.41
First-class	82	11502	360	6335	212	7-58	29.88	-	7	54.25	3.30
List A	84	3545	21	3415	99	5-48	34.49	2	1	35.80	5.77
T20s	268	4970	7	7297	254	5-10	28.72	4	4	19.56	8.80

TOM CURRAN

RHB / RFM / R0 / W1

FULL NAME: Thomas Kevin Curran
BORN: March 12, 1995, Cape Town, SA
SQUAD NO: 59
HEIGHT: 6ft
EDUCATION: Wellington College, Berkshire
TEAMS: England, Surrey, Oval Invincibles,
Delhi Capitals, Islamabad United, Kolkata
Knight Riders, Melbourne Rengades,
Rajasthan Royals, Sydney Sixers, Trinbago
Knight Riders
ROLE: Bowler
DEBUT: Test: 2017; ODI: 2017; T20I: 2017;
First-class: 2014; List A: 2013; T20: 2014

SURREY

BEST BATTING: 67* Oval Invincibles vs Manchester Originals (T20/Hundred)
BEST BOWLING: 4-22 Sydney Sixers vs Adelaide Strikers, Adelaide, 2020 (T20)
COUNTY CAP: 2016

FAMILY TIES? My father Kevin played for Northamptonshire and Zimbabwe, my brother Sam
also plays for Surrey, and my other younger brother Ben made his Test debut for Zimbabwe
in 2024
CHILDHOOD SPORTING HERO? Hamilton Masakadza
SURPRISING FACT ABOUT YOU: I have a degree in Law

Batting	Mat	Inns	NO	Runs	HS	Ave	SR	100	50	Ct	St
Tests	2	3	1	66	39	33.00	55.00	0	0	0	-
ODIs	28	17	9	303	47*	37.87	94.39	0	0	5	-
T20Is	30	13	7	64	14*	10.66	114.28	0	0	8	-
First-class	63	87	11	1480	115	19.47	53.81	1	6	24	-
List A	86	56	21	739	47*	21.11	93.54	0	0	26	-
T20s	222	146	48	2144	67*	21.87	142.74	0	6	62	-

Bowling	Mat	Balls	Mdns	Runs	Wkts	BB	Ave	4wI	5wI	SR	Econ
Tests	2	396	14	200	2	1-65	100.00	-	0	198.00	3.03
ODIs	28	1308	8	1290	34	5-35	37.94	2	1	38.47	5.91
T20Is	30	588	1	907	29	4-36	31.27	1	0	20.27	9.25
First-class	63	10743	375	5805	199	7-20	29.17	-	7	53.98	3.24
List A	86	3909	27	3633	126	5-16	28.83	6	3	31.02	5.57
T20s	222	4068	5	5959	235	4-22	25.35	4	0	17.31	8.78

BRADLEY CURRIE

RHB / LFM / R0 / W0

SUSSEX

FULL NAME: Bradley James Currie
BORN: November 8, 1998, Poole, Dorset
SQUAD NO: 12
HEIGHT: 6ft 1in
NICKNAME: Ruby Murray
EDUCATION: Poole Grammar School;
Millfield School; Bournemouth University
TEAMS: Scotland, Sussex
ROLE: Bowler
DEBUT: ODI: 2024; T20I: 2023; First-class: 2022;
List A: 2022; T20: 2023

BEST BATTING: 7 Sussex vs Worcestershire, Hove, 2022
BEST BOWLING: 6-93 Sussex vs Middlesex, Lord's, 2022

WHICH AWAY GROUND DO YOU MOST ENJOY VISITING? Taunton – the atmosphere is electric
IF YOU COULD PINCH A PLAYER FROM ANOTHER COUNTY, WHO WOULD IT BE? Scott Currie
HOW IS BAZBALL AFFECTING CHAMPIONSHIP CRICKET? I have to ask the keeper to stand up at the stumps when I'm bowling!
CHOOSE A FANTASY SLIP CORDON TO SPEND A DAY IN THE FIELD WITH: Michael Phelps, Michael Scofield, Walter White, Cristiano Ronaldo
SURPRISING FACT ABOUT YOU: I nearly gave up cricket aged 13 to pursue my swimming career

Batting	Mat	Inns	NO	Runs	HS	Ave	SR	100	50	Ct	St
ODIs	9	2	2	9	8*	-	45.00	0	0	2	-
T20Is	15	4	3	15	8*	15.00	62.50	0	0	9	-
First-class	6	9	5	17	7	4.25	20.23	0	0	1	-
List A	21	6	4	31	18*	15.50	62.00	0	0	5	-
T20s	26	6	5	16	8*	16.00	48.48	0	0	14	-

Bowling	Mat	Balls	Mdns	Runs	Wkts	BB	Ave	4wI	5wI	SR	Econ
ODIs	9	396	8	242	16	4-32	15.12	1	0	24.75	3.66
T20Is	15	300	3	266	26	5-13	10.23	0	1	11.53	5.32
First-class	6	964	29	630	24	6-93	26.25	-	1	40.16	3.92
List A	21	930	11	730	31	4-32	23.54	1	0	30.00	4.70
T20s	26	480	3	497	37	5-13	13.43	0	1	12.97	6.21

SCOTT CURRIE — RHB / RMF / R0 / W0 / MVP48

FULL NAME: Scott William Currie
BORN: May 2, 2001, Poole, Dorset
SQUAD NO: 44
HEIGHT: 6ft 5in
NICKNAME: Ruby
EDUCATION: St Edward's RC & COFE School, Poole
TEAMS: Scotland, Hampshire, Manchester Originals, England U19, Leicestershire
ROLE: Bowler
DEBUT: ODI: 2024; First-class: 2020; List A: 2021; T20: 2020

HAMPSHIRE

BEST BATTING: 120 Leicestershire vs Northamptonshire, Northampton, 2024
BEST BOWLING: 5-64 Leicestershire vs Glamorgan, Leicester, 2024

FIRST CRICKET CLUB? Poole Town CC, Dorset
EARLIEST CRICKETING MEMORY? Glenn McGrath's five-fer at Lord's in the 2005 Ashes
OPPONENT YOU MOST LOOK FORWARD TO PLAYING AGAINST? My brother Bradley Currie
– it will be the first time we come up against each other in professional cricket
FAVOURITE WARM-UP SONG? Enter Sandman by Metallica
HOW MANY HOURS DO YOU SPEND ON YOUR PHONE A DAY? Not enough
SPECIALITY SUBJECT IN A PUB QUIZ (EXCLUDING SPORT)? Gavin & Stacey
ONE THING YOU WANT TO DO BEFORE YOU DIE: Manage AFC Bournemouth
SURPRISING FACT ABOUT YOU: I was born on the same day as David Beckham, Brian Lara and Dwayne 'The Rock' Johnson
FILM YOU CAN WATCH OVER AND OVER: Legend

Batting	Mat	Inns	NO	Runs	HS	Ave	SR	100	50	Ct	St
ODIs	3	2	0	10	5	5.00	55.55	0	0	0	-
First-class	15	21	5	407	120	25.43	45.37	1	1	16	-
List A	25	18	7	191	43*	17.36	86.42	0	0	19	-
T20s	41	17	11	82	26*	13.66	105.12	0	0	17	-

Bowling	Mat	Balls	Mdns	Runs	Wkts	BB	Ave	4wI	5wI	SR	Econ
ODIs	3	120	3	86	3	2-16	28.66	0	0	40.00	4.30
First-class	15	2036	48	1268	41	5-64	30.92	-	1	49.65	3.73
List A	25	1065	8	1013	41	3-25	24.70	0	0	25.97	5.70
T20s	41	778	1	1111	55	4-24	20.20	3	0	14.14	8.56

BRETT D'OLIVEIRA

RHB / LB / R0 / W0

WORCESTERSHIRE

FULL NAME: Brett Louis D'Oliveira
BORN: February 28, 1992, Worcester
SQUAD NO: 15
HEIGHT: 5ft 9in
NICKNAME: Dolly
EDUCATION: Blessed Edward Oldcorne Catholic College, Worcester; Worcester Sixth Form College
TEAMS: Worcestershire, Birmingham Phoenix, England Lions
ROLE: Allrounder
DEBUT: First-class: 2012; List A: 2011; T20: 2012

BEST BATTING: 202* Worcestershire vs Glamorgan, Cardiff, 2016
BEST BOWLING: 7-92 Worcestershire vs Glamorgan, Cardiff, 2019
COUNTY CAP: 2012

FIRST CRICKET CLUB? Worcester Dominies & Guild CC
FAMILY TIES? My grandad Basil played for England and Worcestershire and also went on to coach Worcestershire. My dad Damian played for Worcestershire and went on to be assistant coach and Academy director
WHICH TEAMMATE HAS HAD THE BIGGEST IMPACT ON YOUR GAME? Vikram Solanki – he showed me how to be a professional on and off the field
GREATEST PERFORMANCE YOU HAVE WITNESSED? Moeen Ali's 121 off 60 balls at Hove to take us to Finals Day in 2019
WHO IS THE TOUGHEST BOWLER TO FACE? Saeed Ajmal in the nets – he was always one step ahead, sometimes two
WHAT KEEPS YOU AWAKE AT NIGHT? A crying baby
CHOOSE A FANTASY SLIP CORDON TO SPEND A DAY IN THE FIELD WITH: Michael Jordan (wk), Shane Warne, Denzel Washington, Elon Musk
SURPRISING FACT ABOUT YOU: I'm a Level 1 basketball coach

Batting	Mat	Inns	NO	Runs	HS	Ave	SR	100	50	Ct	St
First-class	115	186	15	5587	202*	32.67	53.20	12	23	47	-
List A	76	66	11	1389	123	25.25	89.15	1	7	31	-
T20s	147	121	22	2375	71	23.98	128.51	0	13	43	-

Bowling	Mat	Balls	Mdns	Runs	Wkts	BB	Ave	4wl	5wl	SR	Econ
First-class	115	7796	147	4420	82	7-92	53.90	-	2	95.07	3.40
List A	76	2869	6	2529	65	3-8	38.90	0	0	44.13	5.28
T20s	147	1906	0	2471	83	4-11	29.77	3	0	22.96	7.77

ANUJ DAL RHB / RM / RO / WO

FULL NAME: Anuj Kailash Dal
BORN: July 8, 1996, Newcastle-under-Lyme, Staffordshire
SQUAD NO: 65
HEIGHT: 5ft 9in
NICKNAME: Nuj
EDUCATION: Nottingham High School
TEAMS: Derbyshire
ROLE: Allrounder
DEBUT: First-class: 2018; List A: 2019; T20: 2018

BEST BATTING: 146* Derbyshire vs Sussex, Hove, 2022
BEST BOWLING: 6-69 Derbyshire vs Gloucestershire, Bristol, 2023
COUNTY CAP: 2022

FIRST CRICKET CLUB? Kimberley Institute CC, Nottinghamshire
EARLIEST CRICKETING MEMORY? Corridor cricket with my brother
WHAT'S THE BIGGEST PRIZE IN DOMESTIC CRICKET? The County Championship
THE KOOKABURRA BALL: YES OR NO? No – it's pointless in English conditions
OPPONENT YOU MOST LOOK FORWARD TO PLAYING AGAINST? Leus du Plooy – my old teammate and always a challenge to bowl to
FAVOURITE WARM-UP SONG? DtMF by Bad Bunny
HOW MANY HOURS DO YOU SPEND ON YOUR PHONE A DAY? My phone tells me… five
SPECIALITY SUBJECT IN A PUB QUIZ (EXCLUDING SPORT)? Finance
WHICH PUBLIC FIGURE INSPIRES YOU (EXCLUDING SPORTSPEOPLE)? David Ryley of Ryley Wealth Management
SURPRISING FACT ABOUT YOU: I speak fluent spanish
FILM YOU CAN WATCH OVER AND OVER: Any James Bond film

Batting	Mat	Inns	NO	Runs	HS	Ave	SR	100	50	Ct	St
First-class	59	89	15	2410	146*	32.56	49.83	5	11	38	-
List A	29	24	3	579	115	27.57	100.69	2	1	11	-
T20s	26	21	6	201	35	13.40	112.92	0	0	11	-

Bowling	Mat	Balls	Mdns	Runs	Wkts	BB	Ave	4wI	5wI	SR	Econ
First-class	59	5649	159	2950	85	6-69	34.70	-	4	66.45	3.13
List A	29	468	1	406	4	1-16	101.50	0	0	117.00	5.20
T20s	26	6	0	8	0	0-8	-	-	-	-	8.00

AJEET DALE

RHB / RFM / RO / WO

GLOUCESTERSHIRE

FULL NAME: Ajeet Singh Dale
BORN: July 3, 2000, Slough, Berkshire
SQUAD NO: 39
HEIGHT: 6ft 1in
NICKNAME: AJ
EDUCATION: Hall Grove School, Bagshot, Surrey; Wellington College, Berkshire
TEAMS: Gloucestershire, England Lions, Hampshire
ROLE: Bowler
DEBUT: First-class: 2020; List A: 2022; T20: 2022

BEST BATTING: 52 Gloucestershire vs Leicestershire, Bristol, 2023
BEST BOWLING: 6-41 Gloucestershire vs Worcestershire, Worcester, 2023

FIRST CRICKET CLUB? Slough CC, Berkshire
EARLIEST CRICKETING MEMORY? Waking up in the middle of the night to watch India vs Pakistan
WHAT'S THE BIGGEST PRIZE IN DOMESTIC CRICKET? Division One of the County Championship
THE KOOKABURRA BALL: YES OR NO? Yes, as long as the pitches are hard
OPPONENT YOU MOST LOOK FORWARD TO PLAYING AGAINST? Zafar Gohar, so he can take me out for dinner after I remove his off peg
FAVOURITE WARM-UP SONG? Grown Simba by J.Cole
HOW MANY HOURS DO YOU SPEND ON YOUR PHONE A DAY? One hour max
SPECIALITY SUBJECT IN A PUB QUIZ (EXCLUDING SPORT)? American hip-hop
ONE THING YOU WANT TO DO BEFORE YOU DIE: Win the cricket World Cup
HOBBY YOU WOULD LIKE TO LEARN: How to deejay
SURPRISING FACT ABOUT YOU: I jumped off the wrong foot when bowling until I was 11 or 12
FILM YOU CAN WATCH OVER AND OVER: The Bourne films

Batting	Mat	Inns	NO	Runs	HS	Ave	SR	100	50	Ct	St
First-class	28	39	14	270	52	10.80	49.63	0	1	6	-
List A	11	6	2	83	63	20.75	123.88	0	1	3	-
T20s	7	2	1	0	0*	0.00	0.00	0	0	1	-

Bowling	Mat	Balls	Mdns	Runs	Wkts	BB	Ave	4wl	5wl	SR	Econ
First-class	28	3725	91	2314	61	6-41	37.93	-	1	61.06	3.72
List A	11	528	7	431	19	4-15	22.68	2	0	27.78	4.89
T20s	7	143	0	260	6	2-36	43.33	0	0	23.83	10.90

ROBIN DAS

RHB / RO / W0

FULL NAME: Robin James Das
BORN: February 27, 2002, Leytonstone, Essex
SQUAD NO: 47
HEIGHT: 5ft 10in
NICKNAME: Ticklar
EDUCATION: Brentwood School, Essex; London School of Economics and Political Science
TEAMS: Essex, Dhaka Dominators
ROLE: Batter
DEBUT: First-class: 2023; List A: 2022; T20: 2020

BEST BATTING: 132 Essex vs Ireland, Chelmsford, 2023

BEST PLAYER IN COUNTY CRICKET (EXCLUDING TEAMMATES)? James Vince
BEST DELIVERY YOU HAVE EVER FACED? A lethal double-bouncing yorker from Luc Benkenstein in the nets
GREATEST PERFORMANCE YOU HAVE WITNESSED? Feroze Khushi's hundred at Northampton in the 2022 One-Day Cup
FAVOURITE FORMAT? There's nothing in the world better than Friday night T20 at Chelmsford
HOBBIES? Surfing
FAVOURITE TOY AS A KID? I preferred books to toys
WHAT WOULD BE YOUR PERFECT BREAKFAST? Pancakes, bacon, maple syrup
WHICH PERSON INSPIRES YOU MOST? Pete Davidson
SURPRISING FACT ABOUT YOU: I'm an eighth Swedish

Batting	Mat	Inns	NO	Runs	HS	Ave	SR	100	50	Ct	St
First-class	7	9	0	275	132	30.55	67.90	1	0	5	-
List A	21	21	1	593	100*	29.65	87.59	1	3	8	-
T20s	22	20	2	323	72	17.94	150.23	0	2	8	-
Bowling	Mat	Balls	Mdns	Runs	Wkts	BB	Ave	4wl	5wl	SR	Econ
First-class	7	-	-	-	-	-	-	-	-	-	-
List A	21	-	-	-	-	-	-	-	-	-	-
T20s	22	-	-	-	-	-	-	-	-	-	-

JOSH DAVEY

RHB / RFM / R0 / W0

SOMERSET

FULL NAME: Joshua Henry Davey
BORN: August 3, 1990, Aberdeen, Scotland
SQUAD NO: 38
HEIGHT: 6ft
NICKNAME: JD
EDUCATION: Culford School, Bury St
Edmunds; Oxford Brookes University
TEAMS: Scotland, Somerset, Hampshire,
Leicestershire, Middlesex
ROLE: Bowler
DEBUT: ODI: 2010; T20I: 2012; First-class: 2010;
List A: 2010; T20: 2010

BEST BATTING: 75* Somerset vs Leicestershire, Taunton, 2021
BEST BOWLING: 5-21 Somerset vs Yorkshire, Taunton, 2019
COUNTY CAP: 2021 (Somerset)

FIRST CRICKET CLUB? Bury St Edmunds CC, Suffolk
GREATEST PERFORMANCE YOU HAVE WITNESSED? Chris Gayle's 151 not out against Kent at
Taunton in 2015
MOST EXCITING DAY AS A CRICKETER? Beating Hampshire in the One-Day Cup final at
Lord's in 2019

Batting	Mat	Inns	NO	Runs	HS	Ave	SR	100	50	Ct	St
ODIs	31	28	6	497	64	22.59	66.98	0	2	10	-
T20Is	31	16	8	115	24	14.37	130.68	0	0	15	-
First-class	73	107	28	1599	75*	20.24	45.34	0	5	21	-
List A	99	73	17	1300	91	23.21	68.34	0	6	27	-
T20s	95	44	28	342	24	21.37	130.03	0	0	42	-

Bowling	Mat	Balls	Mdns	Runs	Wkts	BB	Ave	4wI	5wI	SR	Econ
ODIs	31	1301	18	1082	49	6-28	22.08	1	2	26.55	4.99
T20Is	31	653	0	887	37	4-18	23.97	2	0	17.64	8.15
First-class	73	9498	384	4595	198	5-21	23.20	-	4	47.96	2.90
List A	99	3716	37	3276	126	6-28	26.00	3	2	29.49	5.28
T20s	95	1687	2	2454	115	4-18	21.33	4	0	14.66	8.72

ALEX DAVIES

RHB / WK / R2 / W0 / MVP6

FULL NAME: Alexander Luke Davies
BORN: August 23, 1994, Darwen, Lancashire
SQUAD NO: 71
HEIGHT: 5ft 8in
NICKNAME: Davo
EDUCATION: Queen Elizabeth's Grammar School, Blackburn
TEAMS: Warwickshire, England Lions, Lancashire, Southern Brave
ROLE: Batter/wicketkeeper
DEBUT: First-class: 2012; List A: 2011; T20: 2014

WARWICKSHIRE

BEST BATTING: 256 Warwickshire vs Durham, Edgbaston, 2024

COUNTY CAP: 2017 (Lancashire); 2023 (Warwickshire)

FIRST CRICKET CLUB? Darwen CC, Lancashire
MOST EXCITING DAY AS A CRICKETER? T20 Finals Day in 2015
CHILDHOOD SPORTING HERO? Sachin Tendulkar
NOTES: Following his best season in four-day cricket – 1,115 runs at 50.68 – the Warwickshire captain signed a one-year extension to his contract last November. "I was relatively happy with my red-ball form last season, but I'm hungry for more," said Davies. "I don't feel I quite matched that or showed 100 per cent of my ability in the Vitality Blast so the goal for me is to nail that consistency of runs for the Bears across all formats. I'm hopefully at an age and experience now where I can do that and let the youngsters flourish around me"

Batting	Mat	Inns	NO	Runs	HS	Ave	SR	100	50	Ct	St
First-class	134	209	10	7002	256	35.18	57.37	11	41	211	19
List A	51	48	3	1390	147	30.88	90.31	1	7	49	11
T20s	150	143	15	3042	94*	23.76	130.72	0	16	88	28

Bowling	Mat	Balls	Mdns	Runs	Wkts	BB	Ave	4wl	5wl	SR	Econ
First-class	134	12	0	7	0	0-1	-	-	-	-	3.50
List A	51	-	-	-	-	-	-	-	-	-	-
T20s	150	-	-	-	-	-	-	-	-	-	-

JACK DAVIES

LHB / WK / R0 / W0

MIDDLESEX

FULL NAME: Jack Leo Benjamin Davies
BORN: March 30, 2000, Reading
SQUAD NO: 23
HEIGHT: 5ft 8in
NICKNAME: Davo
EDUCATION: Wellington College, Berkshire
TEAMS: Middlesex, England U19
ROLE: Wicketkeeper
DEBUT: First-class: 2020; List A: 2021; T20: 2020

BEST BATTING: 91 Middlesex vs Gloucestershire, Lord's, 2024

FIRST CRICKET CLUB? Henley CC, Oxfordshire
WHAT'S THE BIGGEST PRIZE IN DOMESTIC CRICKET? Winning Division One of the County Championship
THE KOOKABURRA BALL: YES OR NO? Yes, if the pitch is dicey
OPPONENT YOU MOST LOOK FORWARD TO PLAYING AGAINST? James Anderson
FAVOURITE WARM-UP SONG? Anything that Ryan Higgins has on the list
HOW MANY HOURS DO YOU SPEND ON YOUR PHONE A DAY? Four (more if it rains)
SPECIALITY SUBJECT IN A PUB QUIZ (EXCLUDING SPORT)? Sharks
ONE THING YOU WANT TO DO BEFORE YOU DIE: Find a way to enjoy the taste of whisky
HOBBY YOU WOULD LIKE TO LEARN: Painting
WHICH PUBLIC FIGURE INSPIRES YOU (EXCLUDING SPORTSPEOPLE)? Werner Bronkhorst
SURPRISING FACT ABOUT YOU: I have a serious skincare routine
FILM YOU CAN WATCH OVER AND OVER: Wedding Crashers

Batting	Mat	Inns	NO	Runs	HS	Ave	SR	100	50	Ct	St
First-class	25	37	4	661	91	20.03	42.18	0	5	32	-
List A	19	19	1	405	70	22.50	96.19	0	2	8	4
T20s	37	35	4	640	53	20.64	122.84	0	2	7	5

Bowling	Mat	Balls	Mdns	Runs	Wkts	BB	Ave	4wI	5wI	SR	Econ
First-class	25	9	0	12	0	0-12	-	-	-	-	8.00
List A	19	-	-	-	-	-	-	-	-	-	-
T20s	37	-	-	-	-	-	-	-	-	-	-

LIAM DAWSON

RHB / SLA / R1 / W1 / MVP1

FULL NAME: Liam Andrew Dawson
BORN: March 1, 1990, Swindon
SQUAD NO: 8
HEIGHT: 5ft 8in
NICKNAME: Lemmy
EDUCATION: The John Bentley School, Wilts
TEAMS: England, Hampshire, London Spirit, Essex, Islamabad United, Lahore Qalandars, Melbourne Stars, Mountaineers, Southern Brave, Sunrisers Eastern Cape
ROLE: Allrounder
DEBUT: Test: 2016; ODI: 2016; T20I: 2016; First-class: 2007; List A: 2007; T20: 2008

HAMPSHIRE

BEST BATTING: 171 Hampshire vs Kent, Canterbury, 2022
BEST BOWLING: 7-51 Mountaineers vs Mashonaland Eagles, Mutare Sports Club, 2011
COUNTY CAP: 2013 (Hampshire)

FIRST CRICKET CLUB? Goatacre CC, Wiltshire
FAMILY TIES? I got into the game watching my dad play for Goatacre CC in Wiltshire. My brother Brad has played Minor Counties for Wiltshire
WHO IS THE MOST TALENTED U19 TEENAGER IN THE COUNTY GAME? Eddie Jack (Ham)

Batting	Mat	Inns	NO	Runs	HS	Ave	SR	100	50	Ct	St
Tests	3	6	2	84	66*	21.00	42.63	0	1	2	-
ODIs	6	5	0	63	20	12.60	85.13	0	0	2	-
T20Is	11	5	1	57	34	14.25	158.33	0	0	2	-
First-class	203	327	35	10195	171	34.91	51.68	17	54	205	-
List A	167	136	23	3722	113*	32.93	94.73	3	20	77	-
T20s	296	210	53	2817	82	17.94	119.41	0	6	115	-

Bowling	Mat	Balls	Mdns	Runs	Wkts	BB	Ave	4wI	5wI	SR	Econ
Tests	3	526	12	298	7	2-34	42.57	-	0	75.14	3.39
ODIs	6	264	0	284	5	2-70	56.80	0	0	52.80	6.45
T20Is	11	204	0	242	6	3-27	40.33	0	0	34.00	7.11
First-class	203	22605	774	10862	350	7-51	31.03	-	14	64.58	2.88
List A	167	6607	29	5244	174	7-15	30.13	7	2	37.97	4.76
T20s	296	5006	7	6152	237	5-17	25.95	3	1	21.12	7.37

JOSH DE CAIRES

RHB / OB / RO / WO

FULL NAME: Joshua Michael De Caires
BORN: April 25, 2002, Paddington, London
SQUAD NO: 99
HEIGHT: 6ft
EDUCATION: St Albans School, Hertfordshire; University of Leeds
TEAMS: Middlesex
ROLE: Allrounder
DEBUT: First-class: 2021; List A: 2021; T20: 2021

BEST BATTING: 80 Middlesex vs Derbyshire, Lord's, 2022
BEST BOWLING: 8-106 Middlesex vs Essex, Chelmsford, 2023

FIRST CRICKET CLUB? Radlett CC, Hertfordshire
EARLIEST CRICKETING MEMORY? Corridor cricket
WHAT'S THE BIGGEST PRIZE IN DOMESTIC CRICKET? The Middlesex darts trophy of course
THE KOOKABURRA BALL: YES OR NO? Not sure – good to bat against, bad to bowl with
OPPONENT YOU MOST LOOK FORWARD TO PLAYING AGAINST? My former Middlesex teammate Martin Andersson
HOW MANY HOURS DO YOU SPEND ON YOUR PHONE A DAY? Too much
SPECIALITY SUBJECT IN A PUB QUIZ (EXCLUDING SPORT)? Geography
SURPRISING FACT ABOUT YOU: I'm not bad at chess
FILM YOU CAN WATCH OVER AND OVER: Remember the Titans

Batting	Mat	Inns	NO	Runs	HS	Ave	SR	100	50	Ct	St
First-class	21	34	3	770	80	24.83	51.99	0	4	7	-
List A	16	13	0	171	43	13.15	93.95	0	0	11	-
T20s	20	15	2	169	31*	13.00	119.85	0	0	8	-

Bowling	Mat	Balls	Mdns	Runs	Wkts	BB	Ave	4wI	5wI	SR	Econ
First-class	21	2408	43	1387	34	8-106	40.79	-	2	70.82	3.45
List A	16	492	1	432	11	3-52	39.27	0	0	44.72	5.26
T20s	20	224	0	359	12	2-34	29.91	0	0	18.66	9.61

MARCHANT DE LANGE

RHB / RF / RO / WO

FULL NAME: Marchant de Lange
BORN: October 13, 1990, Tzaneen, Transvaal,
South Africa
SQUAD NO: 90
HEIGHT: 6ft 7in
TEAMS: South Africa, Gloucestershire,
Dambulla Giants, Durban Heat, Easterns, Free
State, Glamorgan, Islamabad United, Knights,
Kolkata Knight Riders, Mumbai Indians,
Somerset, Titans, Trent Rockets
ROLE: Bowler
DEBUT: Test: 2011; ODI: 2012; T20I: 2012;
First-class: 2010; List A: 2010; T20: 2011

GLOUCESTERSHIRE

BEST BATTING: 113 Glamorgan vs Northamptonshire, Northampton, 2020
BEST BOWLING: 7-23 Knights vs Titans, Centurion, 2016

FIRST CRICKET CLUB? Tzaneen CC, Limpopo, South Africa
MOST EXCITING DAY AS A CRICKETER? Making my international debut for South Africa
CHILDHOOD SPORTING HERO? Brett Lee
SURPRISING FACT ABOUT YOU: I love art

Batting	Mat	Inns	NO	Runs	HS	Ave	SR	100	50	Ct	St
Tests	2	2	0	9	9	4.50	47.36	0	0	1	-
ODIs	4	0	-	-	-	-	-	-	-	0	-
T20Is	6	0	-	-	-	-	-	-	-	1	-
First-class	108	141	20	2033	113	16.80	81.22	1	5	45	-
List A	98	69	19	776	58*	15.52	108.22	0	2	25	-
T20s	151	64	26	420	28*	11.05	132.07	0	0	40	-

Bowling	Mat	Balls	Mdns	Runs	Wkts	BB	Ave	4wI	5wI	SR	Econ
Tests	2	448	10	277	9	7-81	30.77	-	1	49.77	3.70
ODIs	4	209	1	198	10	4-46	19.80	1	0	20.90	5.68
T20Is	6	140	0	228	7	2-26	32.57	0	0	20.00	9.77
First-class	108	19217	609	11356	375	7-23	30.28	-	13	51.24	3.54
List A	98	4792	50	4426	170	5-49	26.03	8	4	28.18	5.54
T20s	151	2963	6	4318	166	5-20	26.01	4	1	17.84	8.74

BAS DE LEEDE

RHB / RMF / R0 / W0

DURHAM

FULL NAME: Bastiaan Franciscus Wilhelmus de Leede
BORN: November 15, 1999, Nootdorp, Netherlands
SQUAD NO: 27
EDUCATION: St Maartens College, Maastricht, Netherlands
TEAMS: Netherlands, Durham
ROLE: Allrounder
DEBUT: ODI: 2018; T20I: 2018; First-class: 2017; List A: 2017; T20: 2018

BEST BATTING: 103 Durham vs Sussex, Chester-le-Street, 2023
BEST BOWLING: 4-76 Durham vs Glamorgan, Chester-le-Street, 2023

NOTES: Durham signed de Leede in February 2023 to play across all formats and the Netherlands seam-bowling allrounder impressed in his first season at the Riverside, scoring his maiden first-class hundred along with two half-centuries in six Championship appereances. He also collected 17 wickets at 29.05 and was a regular in Durham's T20 side. Described as "arguably the most exciting allrounder in Associate cricket" by Marcus North, Durham's director of cricket, de Leede was an important part of the side which impressed at the 2022 T20 World Cup, where Netherlands produced a shock win against South Africa. Durham head coach Ryan Campbell worked closely with the player during his spell in charge of Netherlands

Batting	Mat	Inns	NO	Runs	HS	Ave	SR	100	50	Ct	St
ODIs	49	46	2	1111	123	25.25	66.44	1	5	25	-
T20Is	41	39	11	724	91*	25.85	102.25	0	4	20	-
First-class	16	21	4	568	103	33.41	57.48	1	4	7	-
List A	63	60	3	1386	123	24.31	66.50	1	6	28	-
T20s	65	58	15	1127	91*	26.20	112.47	0	6	29	-

Bowling	Mat	Balls	Mdns	Runs	Wkts	BB	Ave	4wI	5wI	SR	Econ
ODIs	49	1410	3	1412	44	5-52	32.09	1	1	32.04	6.00
T20Is	41	491	1	681	33	3-19	20.63	0	0	14.87	8.32
First-class	16	1599	44	1044	30	4-76	34.80	-	0	53.30	3.91
List A	63	1872	5	1845	57	5-52	32.36	1	1	32.84	5.91
T20s	65	771	3	1125	47	3-19	23.93	0	0	16.40	8.75

JAYDN DENLY

LHB / SLA / RO / WO

FULL NAME: Jaydn Kennick Denly
BORN: January 5, 2006, Margate, England
SQUAD NO: 42
EDUCATION: Canterbury Academy
TEAMS: Kent, England U19
ROLE: Allrounder
DEBUT: First-class: 2024; List A: 2023

BEST BATTING: 41* Kent vs Essex, Chelmsford, 2024
BEST BOWLING: 1-52 Kent vs Essex, Chelmsford, 2024

NOTES: The 19-year-old left-hander, nephew of Joe, signed a two-year deal at Kent last October. A graduate from the club's Academy, Denly made his county debut in August 2023, hitting his first ball for four against Surrey in the One-Day Cup and then bowling a wicket maiden with his left-arm spin. He made a defiant 41 not out on his first-class debut against Essex at Chelmsford last summer, sharing a 51-run stand with his uncle to secure Kent a draw against a strong bowling attack. Denly junior was also a regular presence in the 50-over side in 2024. "Jaydn is a top prospect and by making the step up to the first team, he has shown that he already has the skill to make an impact for us in the near future," said Simon Cook, Kent's director of cricket. "I know our members and supporters value the work we are doing in improving our talent pathway, and to get us back to a stage where a Kent team is a majority of homegrown talent. There are more exciting prospects coming down the line for us, and Jaydn can now show these players that there is a clear path to getting into the first team through hard work"

Batting	Mat	Inns	NO	Runs	HS	Ave	SR	100	50	Ct	St
First-class	2	3	1	53	41*	26.50	31.92	0	0	2	-
List A	13	13	2	232	37	21.09	68.63	0	0	0	-

Bowling	Mat	Balls	Mdns	Runs	Wkts	BB	Ave	4wI	5wI	SR	Econ
First-class	2	72	0	63	1	1-52	63.00	-	0	72.00	5.25
List A	13	207	1	187	8	3-15	23.37	0	0	25.87	5.42

JOE DENLY

RHB / LB / R4 / W0

KENT

FULL NAME: Joseph Liam Denly
BORN: March 16, 1986, Canterbury, Kent
SQUAD NO: 6
HEIGHT: 6ft
EDUCATION: Chaucer Technology School, Canterbury
TEAMS: England, Kent, Barisal Burners, Brisbane Heat, Kolkata Knight Riders, Lahore Qalandars, London Spirit, Middlesex, Sydney Sixers
ROLE: Allrounder
DEBUT: Test: 2019; ODI: 2009; T20I: 2009; First-class: 2004; List A: 2004; T20: 2004

BEST BATTING: 227 Kent vs Worcestershire, Worcester, 2017
BEST BOWLING: 4-36 Kent vs Derbyshire, Derby, 2018
COUNTY CAP: 2008 (Kent); 2012 (Middlesex); **BENEFIT:** 2019 (Kent)

FIRST CRICKET CLUB? Whitstable CC, Kent
EARLIEST CRICKETING MEMORY? Watching my dad down at Whitstable
WHAT'S THE BIGGEST PRIZE IN DOMESTIC CRICKET? From a team perspective, winning Division One of the County Championship. For a player, it's the MVP
THE KOOKABURRA BALL: YES OR NO? Yes, bowlers will benefit in the long run, especially for the Ashes in Australia
ONE THING YOU WANT TO DO BEFORE YOU DIE: See all my grandchildren
HOBBY YOU WOULD LIKE TO LEARN: Padel
SURPRISING FACT ABOUT YOU: I love cold-water therapy

Batting	Mat	Inns	NO	Runs	HS	Ave	SR	100	50	Ct	St
Tests	15	28	0	827	94	29.53	39.64	0	6	7	-
ODIs	16	13	0	446	87	34.30	70.90	0	4	7	-
T20Is	13	12	2	125	30	12.50	105.93	0	0	4	-
First-class	247	425	27	14157	227	35.57	54.89	32	72	97	-
List A	168	159	16	5220	150*	36.50	77.81	8	29	59	-
T20s	285	277	24	6795	127	26.85	122.76	5	35	108	-

Bowling	Mat	Balls	Mdns	Runs	Wkts	BB	Ave	4wl	5wl	SR	Econ
Tests	15	390	11	219	2	2-42	109.50	-	0	195.00	3.36
ODIs	16	102	0	101	1	1-24	101.00	0	0	102.00	5.94
T20Is	13	72	0	93	7	4-19	13.28	1	0	10.28	7.75
First-class	247	6683	161	3692	83	4-36	44.48	-	0	80.51	3.31
List A	168	1688	16	1440	55	4-35	26.18	3	0	30.69	5.11
T20s	285	975	1	1299	50	4-19	25.98	1	0	19.50	7.99

CHRIS DENT

LHB / SLA / WK / R4 / W0

FULL NAME: Christopher David James Dent
BORN: January 20, 1991, Bristol
SQUAD NO: 15
HEIGHT: 5ft 9in
NICKNAME: Denty
EDUCATION: Backwell School, North Somerset; SGS Filton College, Bristol
TEAMS: Gloucestershire, England U19
ROLE: Batter
DEBUT: First-class: 2010; List A: 2009; T20: 2010

BEST BATTING: 268 Gloucestershire vs Glamorgan, Bristol, 2015
BEST BOWLING: 2-21 Gloucestershire vs Sussex, Hove, 2016
COUNTY CAP: 2010; BENEFIT: 2024

FIRST CRICKET CLUB? Cleeve CC, Somerset
BEST DELIVERY YOU HAVE EVER FACED? From David Wainwright against Derbyshire in the 2014 One-Day Cup – best delivery ever bowled
BEST PERFORMANCE AS A PRO? 151 not out in a 40-over game at Cardiff in 2013
GREATEST PERFORMANCE YOU HAVE WITNESSED? Any of Michael Klinger's seven T20 hundreds for Gloucestershire
FAVOURITE FORMAT? Four-day cricket – the hardest format
DESCRIBE YOURSELF IN THREE WORDS: A big kid
WHAT WOULD BE YOUR PERFECT BREAKFAST? Eggs and avocado on sourdough
WHICH PERSON INSPIRES YOU MOST? Michael Jordan
SURPRISING FACT ABOUT YOU: I can do a 3×3 and a 4×4 Rubik's cube

Batting	Mat	Inns	NO	Runs	HS	Ave	SR	100	50	Ct	St
First-class	187	335	26	11198	268	36.23	50.90	21	67	185	-
List A	90	85	6	2446	151*	30.96	94.73	5	7	31	-
T20s	78	71	7	1543	87	24.10	134.05	0	8	28	-

Bowling	Mat	Balls	Mdns	Runs	Wkts	BB	Ave	4wI	5wI	SR	Econ
First-class	187	1283	27	846	10	2-21	84.60	-	0	128.30	3.95
List A	90	444	0	420	12	4-43	35.00	1	0	37.00	5.67
T20s	78	120	0	168	5	1-4	33.60	0	0	24.00	8.40

SEAN DICKSON — RHB / RM / R0 / W0

SOMERSET

FULL NAME: Sean Robert Dickson
BORN: September 2, 1991, Johannesburg, South Africa
SQUAD NO: 58
HEIGHT: 5ft 11in
NICKNAME: Dicko
EDUCATION: King Edward VII School, Johannesburg; University of Pretoria
TEAMS: Somerset, Durham, Kent, Northerns
ROLE: Batter
DEBUT: First-class: 2013; List A: 2013; T20: 2014

BEST BATTING: 318 Kent vs Northamptonshire, Beckenham, 2017
BEST BOWLING: 1-15 Northerns vs Griqualand West, Centurion, 2015

FIRST CRICKET CLUB? Old Park Sports Club, Johannesburg
WHICH TEAMMATE HAS HAD THE BIGGEST IMPACT ON YOUR GAME? Daniel Bell-Drummond – an example of how to remain humble and enjoy the process
WHAT PART OF THE SEASON DO YOU MOST ENJOY? The T20 Blast
WHICH AWAY GROUND DO YOU MOST ENJOY VISITING? Beckenham – it's the home of runs
WHO IS THE MOST TALENTED U19 TEENAGER IN THE COUNTY GAME? James Langridge (Som)
IF YOU COULD PINCH A PLAYER FROM ANOTHER COUNTY, WHO WOULD IT BE? Simon Harmer
WHAT DO YOU THINK OF THE CURRENT 50-OVER COMPETITION? It should not be played at the same time as The Hundred to improve the standard
WHAT KEEPS YOU AWAKE AT NIGHT? My children
WHAT'S THE SILLIEST OUTFIT YOU'VE EVER WORN? An Oompa Loompa costume

Batting	Mat	Inns	NO	Runs	HS	Ave	SR	100	50	Ct	St
First-class	104	177	12	5353	318	32.44	51.56	14	21	76	-
List A	75	68	7	1900	103*	31.14	90.13	1	12	26	-
T20s	59	50	13	1164	78	31.45	136.45	0	6	39	-

Bowling	Mat	Balls	Mdns	Runs	Wkts	BB	Ave	4wl	5wl	SR	Econ
First-class	104	99	3	54	2	1-15	27.00	-	0	49.50	3.27
List A	75	12	0	20	0	0-20	-	-	-	-	10.00
T20s	59	6	0	9	1	1-9	9.00	0	0	6.00	9.00

BRENDAN DOGGETT

RHB / RMF / R0 / W0

FULL NAME: Brendan James Doggett
BORN: May 3, 1994, Rockhampton, Australia
SQUAD NO: TBC
TEAMS: Durham, Adelaide Strikers, Australia A, Brisbane Heat, Queensland, South Australia, Sydney Thunder
ROLE: Bowler
DEBUT: First-class: 2017; List A: 2016; T20: 2017

BEST BATTING: 49 South Australia vs New South Wales, Wollongong, 2022
BEST BOWLING: 6-15 Australia A vs India A, Mackay, 2024

NOTES: South Australia's Queensland-born opening bowler joins Durham for the early weeks of their Championship campaign on a short-term visa to give the club extra pace-bowling support. The 30-year-old is in the best form of his career, spearheading Australia A against their Indian counterparts – against whom he claimed 6-15 in a Test win last October – and latterly England Lions. As a seamer who relies on lateral movement, he will enjoy conditions in the North-East, and Marcus North, director of cricket, is delighted to have secured his capture: "It is great to have recruited an experienced red-ball player in Brendan to Durham for the opening part of the season. Whilst we can only secure his services on a short-term basis due to visa restrictions, Brendan has been in outstanding form for South Australia in the Sheffield Shield and for Australia A. He is the perfect fit for us to further strengthen our strong seam attack in the first few months of the County Championship"

Batting	Mat	Inns	NO	Runs	HS	Ave	SR	100	50	Ct	St
First-class	44	58	18	362	49	9.05	41.37	0	0	17	-
List A	16	7	3	27	11	6.75	49.09	0	0	7	-
T20s	48	16	8	87	47*	10.87	102.35	0	0	15	-

Bowling	Mat	Balls	Mdns	Runs	Wkts	BB	Ave	4wI	5wI	SR	Econ
First-class	44	8111	286	4396	157	6-15	28.00	-	5	51.66	3.25
List A	16	775	7	864	24	4-75	36.00	1	0	32.29	6.68
T20s	48	890	0	1236	43	5-35	28.74	2	1	20.69	8.33

ANEURIN DONALD

RHB / OB / R1 / W0

DERBYSHIRE

FULL NAME: Aneurin Henry Thomas Donald
BORN: December 20, 1996, Swansea
SQUAD NO: 12
HEIGHT: 6ft 3in
NICKNAME: Don
EDUCATION: Pontarddulais Comprehensive School, Swansea; Gower College Swansea
TEAMS: Derbyshire, Birmingham Phoenix, England U19, Glamorgan, Hampshire
ROLE: Batter
DEBUT: First-class: 2014; List A: 2015; T20: 2015

BEST BATTING: 234 Glamorgan vs Derbyshire, Colwyn Bay, 2016

FAMILY TIES? My grand-uncle Bernard Hedges scored Glamorgan's first one-day century
WHICH TEAMMATE HAS HAD THE BIGGEST IMPACT ON YOUR GAME? Jacques Rudolph – he taught me how to cope with the pressure of being a pro cricketer
HOW IS BAZBALL AFFECTING CHAMPIONSHIP CRICKET? Run-rates are up and there's more entertainment
WHAT DO YOU THINK OF THE CURRENT 50-OVER COMPETITION? Important for blooding youngsters
WHO IS THE TOUGHEST BOWLER TO FACE? Rashid Khan – mystery spin bowled at pace
WHAT KEEPS YOU AWAKE AT NIGHT? The nip-backer
CHOOSE A FANTASY SLIP CORDON TO SPEND A DAY IN THE FIELD WITH: Leigh Halfpenny (wk), Tiger Woods, Tom Brady, Alun Wyn Jones

Batting	Mat	Inns	NO	Runs	HS	Ave	SR	100	50	Ct	St
First-class	71	122	6	3526	234	30.39	74.68	3	21	69	-
List A	50	46	2	1023	115	23.25	97.89	2	4	24	-
T20s	78	73	5	1340	84	19.70	144.70	0	8	42	-

Bowling	Mat	Balls	Mdns	Runs	Wkts	BB	Ave	4wl	5wl	SR	Econ
First-class	71	-	-	-	-	-	-	-	-	-	-
List A	50	-	-	-	-	-	-	-	-	-	-
T20s	78	-	-	-	-	-	-	-	-	-	-

DAN DOUTHWAITE — RHB / RMF / R0 / W0

FULL NAME: Daniel Alexander Douthwaite
BORN: February 8, 1997, Kingston-upon-Thames, Surrey
SQUAD NO: 88
HEIGHT: 6ft 1in
NICKNAME: Jugs
EDUCATION: Reed's School, Cobham, Surrey; Cardiff Metropolitan University
TEAMS: Glamorgan, Manchester Originals, Warwickshire
ROLE: Allrounder
DEBUT: First-class: 2019; List A: 2018; T20: 2018

BEST BATTING: 100* Cardiff MCCU vs Sussex, Hove, 2019
BEST BOWLING: 4-48 Glamorgan vs Derbyshire, Derby, 2019

FIRST CRICKET CLUB? Stoke d'Abernon CC, Cobham, Surrey
BIGGEST INFLUENCE ON YOUR DEVELOPMENT AS A CRICKETER (EXCLUDING PARENTS)?
Keith Medlycott at Surrey
WHO WOULD YOU MOST AND LEAST LIKE TO HAVE A NET WITH? Most – Andrew Flintoff (idolised him as a kid). Least – Brett Lee (just too quick)
MAKE ONE PREDICTION FOR THE FUTURE OF CRICKET: There will be more day/night matches in four-day cricket

Batting	Mat	Inns	NO	Runs	HS	Ave	SR	100	50	Ct	St
First-class	38	57	5	1429	100*	27.48	50.38	1	7	13	-
List A	22	17	4	327	61	25.15	105.82	0	3	8	-
T20s	62	51	14	630	53	17.02	135.19	0	2	13	-

Bowling	Mat	Balls	Mdns	Runs	Wkts	BB	Ave	4wI	5wI	SR	Econ
First-class	38	4040	71	2930	71	4-48	41.26	-	0	56.90	4.35
List A	22	881	7	840	32	4-25	26.25	2	0	27.53	5.72
T20s	62	982	0	1524	57	4-23	26.73	2	0	17.22	9.31

GEORGE DRISSELL — RHB / OB / R0 / W0

DURHAM

FULL NAME: George Samuel Drissell
BORN: January 20, 1999, Bristol
SQUAD NO: 8
HEIGHT: 6ft 2in
NICKNAME: Dris, Lemon, Lethal
EDUCATION: Bedminster Down Secondary School, Bristol; SGS Filton College, Bristol
TEAMS: Durham, Gloucestershire, Somerset
ROLE: Bowler
DEBUT: First-class: 2017; List A: 2018; T20: 2022

BEST BATTING: 33 Durham vs Somerset, Taunton, 2024
BEST BOWLING: 4-83 Gloucestershire vs Glamorgan, Newport, 2019
COUNTY CAP: 2017 (Gloucestershire)

FIRST CRICKET CLUB? Bedminster CC, Bristol
WHAT'S THE BIGGEST PRIZE IN DOMESTIC CRICKET? The County Championship
THE KOOKABURRA BALL: YES OR NO? Yes, I think it's good to experiment with it but the pitches may have to help the bowler a little more
FAVOURITE WARM-UP SONG? Angels by Robbie Williams
HOW MANY HOURS DO YOU SPEND ON YOUR PHONE A DAY? Three to four – too long!
SPECIALITY SUBJECT IN A PUB QUIZ (EXCLUDING SPORT)? Geography
ONE THING YOU WANT TO DO BEFORE YOU DIE: Fly a fighter jet
HOBBY YOU WOULD LIKE TO LEARN: Play the trumpet
WHICH PUBLIC FIGURE INSPIRES YOU (EXCLUDING SPORTSPEOPLE)? Peter Kay
SURPRISING FACT ABOUT YOU: I am the scorer of a last-minute goal (with my weak foot) to see Cheddar Grove Primary School to their only Coronation Cup success. Still spoken about on the streets of Bemmi Down
FILM YOU CAN WATCH OVER AND OVER: Step Brothers

Batting	Mat	Inns	NO	Runs	HS	Ave	SR	100	50	Ct	St
First-class	12	19	2	176	33	10.35	35.12	0	0	3	-
List A	22	19	5	196	37*	14.00	80.65	0	0	11	-
T20s	6	1	0	0	0	0.00	0.00	0	0	3	-

Bowling	Mat	Balls	Mdns	Runs	Wkts	BB	Ave	4wI	5wI	SR	Econ
First-class	12	1489	24	934	11	4-83	84.90	-	0	135.36	3.76
List A	22	858	4	806	20	4-38	40.30	1	0	42.90	5.63
T20s	6	73	0	101	2	1-20	50.50	0	0	36.50	8.30

LEUS DU PLOOY

LHB / SLA / R1 / W0

FULL NAME: Jacobus Leus du Plooy
BORN: January 12, 1995, Pretoria, South Africa
SQUAD NO: 76
HEIGHT: 5ft 11in
NICKNAME: Duppa
EDUCATION: University of South Africa
TEAMS: Middlesex, Southern Brave, Boland, Derbyshire, Free State, Joburg Super Kings, Knights, Northerns, South Western Districts, Titans, Welsh Fire
ROLE: Batter
DEBUT: First-class: 2015; List A: 2014; T20: 2014

BEST BATTING: 238* Derbyshire vs Worcestershire, Worcester, 2023
BEST BOWLING: 3-76 Northerns vs Western Province, Pretoria, 2019
COUNTY CAP: 2022 (Derbyshire)

FIRST CRICKET CLUB? Tuks CC, Pretoria, South Africa
EARLIEST CRICKETING MEMORY? Batting on a tennis court at the age of six with a men's-size bat
WHAT'S THE BIGGEST PRIZE IN DOMESTIC CRICKET? Receiving national honours
THE KOOKABURRA BALL: YES OR NO? Yes, because it provides a different challenge to the bowlers. The pitches though have been too soft to have the impact it should. You either need reverse swing to come in to play or for it to spin heavily on days three and four
OPPONENT YOU MOST LOOK FORWARD TO PLAYING AGAINST? Cameron Green
HOW MANY HOURS DO YOU SPEND ON YOUR PHONE A DAY? Four
ONE THING YOU WANT TO DO BEFORE YOU DIE: Win the Ashes down under
HOBBY YOU WOULD LIKE TO LEARN: How to become a barista
WHICH PUBLIC FIGURE INSPIRES YOU (EXCLUDING SPORTSPEOPLE)? Matthew McConaughey
SURPRISING FACT ABOUT YOU: I toured the UK at school, not for cricket, but for choir, competing in the Eisteddfod at Llangollen
FILM YOU CAN WATCH OVER AND OVER: White Chicks

Batting	Mat	Inns	NO	Runs	HS	Ave	SR	100	50	Ct	St
First-class	116	185	26	7579	238*	47.66	53.41	21	38	86	-
List A	50	47	10	2002	155	54.10	87.23	5	11	24	-
T20s	170	158	36	3609	92	29.58	133.37	0	20	71	-

Bowling	Mat	Balls	Mdns	Runs	Wkts	BB	Ave	4wI	5wI	SR	Econ
First-class	116	2477	32	1746	30	3-76	58.20	-	0	82.56	4.22
List A	50	417	0	420	11	3-19	38.18	0	0	37.90	6.04
T20s	170	217	0	302	14	4-15	21.57	1	0	15.50	8.35

BEN DUCKETT

LHB / OB / WK / R3 / W0

NOTTINGHAMSHIRE

FULL NAME: Ben Matthew Duckett
BORN: October 17, 1994, Farnborough, Kent
SQUAD NO: 17
HEIGHT: 5ft 9in
EDUCATION: Millfield School, Somerset;
Winchester House School; Stowe School
TEAMS: England, Notts, Birmingham Phoenix,
Brisbane Heat, Melbourne Stars, Northants,
Quetta Gladiators, Welsh Fire
ROLE: Batter
DEBUT: Test: 2016; ODI: 2016; T20I: 2019;
First-class: 2013; List A: 2013; T20: 2012

BEST BATTING: 282* Northamptonshire vs Sussex, Northampton, 2016
BEST BOWLING: 1-15 Northamptonshire vs Middlesex, Trent Bridge, 2022
COUNTY CAP: 2016 (Northamptonshire); 2018 (Nottinghamshire)

FIRST CRICKET CLUB? Glastonbury CC, Somerset
WHICH TEAMMATE HAS HAD THE BIGGEST IMPACT ON YOUR GAME? Harry Brook
WHAT PART OF THE SEASON DO YOU MOST ENJOY? The Test matches
HOW IS BAZBALL AFFECTING CHAMPIONSHIP CRICKET? It's making it a lot more fun!
WHO IS THE TOUGHEST BOWLER TO FACE? Sam Cook – a very skillful bowler
WHAT KEEPS YOU AWAKE AT NIGHT? Not getting my pads on quickly enough and being timed out
WHAT'S THE SILLIEST OUTFIT YOU'VE EVER WORN? Dressing up as a jockey

Batting	Mat	Inns	NO	Runs	HS	Ave	SR	100	50	Ct	St
Tests	32	60	3	2270	182	39.82	85.88	4	13	27	-
ODIs	22	22	1	1058	165	50.38	103.92	3	6	6	-
T20Is	17	17	2	412	70*	27.46	149.81	0	2	7	-
First-class	154	267	13	10741	282*	42.28	75.08	28	50	135	3
List A	93	88	8	3320	220*	41.50	101.93	6	20	45	3
T20s	205	198	31	5159	96	30.89	140.38	0	33	98	2

Bowling	Mat	Balls	Mdns	Runs	Wkts	BB	Ave	4wI	5wI	SR	Econ
Tests	32	-	-	-	-	-	-	-	-	-	-
ODIs	22	-	-	-	-	-	-	-	-	-	-
T20Is	17	-	-	-	-	-	-	-	-	-	-
First-class	154	149	0	99	2	1-15	49.50	-	0	74.50	3.98
List A	93	-	-	-	-	-	-	-	-	-	-
T20s	205	-	-	-	-	-	-	-	-	-	-

JACOB DUFFY

RHB / RFM / R0 / W0

FULL NAME: Jacob Andrew Duffy
BORN: August 2, 1994, Lumsden, Southland, New Zealand
SQUAD NO: TBC
TEAMS: New Zealand, Worcestershire, Kent, Otago
ROLE: Bowler
DEBUT: ODI: 2022; T20I: 2020; First-class: 2012; List A: 2013; T20: 2012

WORCESTERSHIRE

BEST BATTING: 71 Otago vs Auckland, Dunedin, 2019
BEST BOWLING: 7-89 Otago vs Wellington, Wellington, 2019

NOTES: The New Zealand pace bowler is scheduled to be at New Road from early April until the end of June. He'll play in both the County Championship and the T20 Blast and comes to Worcestershire off the back of being awarded his first New Zealand central contract over the winter. A white-ball international, Duffy is Otago's all-time leading wicket-taker across all formats and has previously had county spells at Kent and more recently Nottinghamshire. "With there being no Joe [Leach], it was important to see how we try and fill that gap in different ways," said Alan Richardson, the club's head coach. "Jacob bowls a heavy ball, bowls with good pace, gets it to bounce, gets it to move. He ticks a lot of boxes for people who are going to be successful over here and is someone who gives us something in both formats as well"

Batting	Mat	Inns	NO	Runs	HS	Ave	SR	100	50	Ct	St
ODIs	11	5	4	9	4*	9.00	56.25	0	0	1	-
T20Is	18	4	2	17	8*	8.50	89.47	0	0	8	-
First-class	103	145	39	1417	71	13.36	51.24	0	3	40	-
List A	96	53	22	371	39	11.96	91.83	0	0	33	-
T20s	121	48	26	188	18	8.54	130.55	0	0	36	-

Bowling	Mat	Balls	Mdns	Runs	Wkts	BB	Ave	4wI	5wI	SR	Econ
ODIs	11	490	2	515	19	3-41	27.10	0	0	25.78	6.30
T20Is	18	336	0	407	19	4-15	21.42	2	0	17.68	7.26
First-class	103	18894	723	9886	299	7-89	33.06		12	63.19	3.13
List A	96	4548	36	4132	162	6-35	25.50	4	5	28.07	5.45
T20s	121	2424	4	3422	126	5-18	27.15	4	2	19.23	8.47

HARRY DUKE

RHB / WK / R0 / W0

FULL NAME: Harry George Duke
BORN: September 6, 2001, Wakefield, Yorkshire
SQUAD NO: 22
HEIGHT: 5ft 9in
EDUCATION: Queen Elizabeth Grammar School, Wakefield
TEAMS: Yorkshire, England U19, Essex
ROLE: Wicketkeeper/batter
DEBUT: First-class: 2021; List A: 2021; T20: 2021

BEST BATTING: 54 Yorkshire vs Sussex, Headingley, 2021

FIRST CRICKET CLUB? Wakefield Thornes CC, Wakefield
EARLIEST CRICKETING MEMORY? Watching my dad and grandad on a Saturday
WHAT'S THE BIGGEST PRIZE IN DOMESTIC CRICKET? Winning the County Championship
THE KOOKABURRA BALL: YES OR NO? No, it's not as good as the Dukes
FAVOURITE WARM-UP SONG? The Path by Concept Neuf
HOW MANY HOURS DO YOU SPEND ON YOUR PHONE A DAY? Two
SPECIALITY SUBJECT IN A PUB QUIZ (EXCLUDING SPORT)? History
ONE THING YOU WANT TO DO BEFORE YOU DIE: Visit Central and South America
WHICH PUBLIC FIGURE INSPIRES YOU (EXCLUDING SPORTSPEOPLE)? Anthony Bourdain
FILM YOU CAN WATCH OVER AND OVER: There Will Be Blood

Batting	Mat	Inns	NO	Runs	HS	Ave	SR	100	50	Ct	St
First-class	19	28	2	487	54	18.73	36.42	0	2	54	1
List A	31	29	2	851	125	31.51	73.93	2	4	27	3
T20s	5	0	-	-	-	-	-	-	-	3	-

Bowling	Mat	Balls	Mdns	Runs	Wkts	BB	Ave	4wl	5wl	SR	Econ
First-class	19	4	0	1	0	0-1	-	-	-	-	1.50
List A	31	-	-	-	-	-	-	-	-	-	-
T20s	5	-	-	-	-	-	-	-	-	-	-

MATT DUNN

LHB / RFM / R0 / W0

FULL NAME: Matthew Peter Dunn
BORN: May 5, 1992, Egham, Surrey
SQUAD NO: 4
HEIGHT: 6ft 1in
NICKNAME: Dunny
EDUCATION: Bishopsgate School; Bearwood College, Wokingham
TEAMS: Surrey, England U19
ROLE: Bowler
DEBUT: First-class: 2010; List A: 2011; T20: 2013

SURREY

BEST BATTING: 31* Surrey vs Kent, Guildford, 2014
BEST BOWLING: 5-43 Surrey vs Somerset, Guildford, 2019

FIRST CRICKET CLUB? Egham CC, Surrey
MOST EXCITING DAY AS A CRICKETER? Taking five wickets on debut for Surrey in 2011
BIGGEST CRICKETING REGRET? Not working on my batting from a younger age
GREATEST PERFORMANCE YOU HAVE WITNESSED? Aaron Finch's hundred against Middlesex at The Oval in the 2018 T20 Blast
WHO WOULD YOU LEAST LIKE TO HAVE A NET WITH? Fidel Edwards – he once broke my rib
CHILDHOOD SPORTING HERO? Brett Lee
HOBBIES? Breakdancing
SURPRISING FACT ABOUT YOU: I lived in Norway when I was younger

Batting	Mat	Inns	NO	Runs	HS	Ave	SR	100	50	Ct	St
First-class	43	50	22	197	31*	7.03	21.62	0	0	10	-
List A	23	12	6	80	34	13.33	86.02	0	0	6	-
T20s	25	5	2	10	6	3.33	83.33	0	0	6	-

Bowling	Mat	Balls	Mdns	Runs	Wkts	BB	Ave	4wI	5wI	SR	Econ
First-class	43	6511	180	4237	117	5-43	36.21	-	4	55.64	3.90
List A	23	866	3	928	23	2-32	40.34	0	0	37.65	6.42
T20s	25	441	0	679	31	3-8	21.90	0	0	14.22	9.23

BEN DWARSHUIS

LHB / LFM

WORCESTERSHIRE

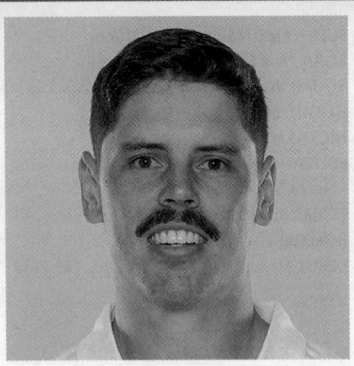

FULL NAME: Benjamin James Dwarshuis
BORN: June 23, 1994, Kareela, New South Wales, Australia
SQUAD NO: TBC
TEAMS: Australia, Worcestershire, Northern Superchargers, Birmingham Phoenix, Durham, New South Wales, Sydney Sixers
ROLE: Bowler
DEBUT: ODI: 2024; T20I: 2022; First-class: 2022; List A: 2016; T20: 2014

BEST BATTING: 66 Sydney Sixers vs Perth Scorchers, Melbourne, 2022 (T20)
BEST BOWLING: 5-21 Sydney Sixers vs Brisbane Heat, Carrara, 2024 (T20)

NOTES: The Australian international has signed for Worcestershire for the entire T20 Blast campaign. A skillful left-arm seamer and powerful lower-order hitter, Dwarshuis returns to New Road for the first time since a spell there in 2021 that saw him pick up 15 Blast wickets. As a veteran of four Big Bash finals with the Sydney Sixers and a member of Australia's squad at the recent ICC Champions Trophy, he is the Rapids' second overseas signing available for the competition, joining Kiwi quick Jacob Duffy. Head coach Alan Richardson said: "Ben has been part of us before and we really enjoyed having him here. He was probably at the start of his journey then, when he was less experienced. Ben is someone who fits the skill sets we need, someone who can bowl at the top and bottom of the innings and someone who has become quite destructive with the bat as well"

Batting	Mat	Inns	NO	Runs	HS	Ave	SR	100	50	Ct	St
ODIs	5	2	0	28	19	14.00	70.00	0	0	1	-
T20Is	3	3	1	1	1	0.50	20.00	0	0	1	-
First-class	9	15	4	270	60*	24.54	48.91	0	2	2	-
List A	26	17	5	243	44	20.25	101.67	0	0	8	-
T20s	144	82	39	762	66	17.72	139.56	0	1	33	-

Bowling	Mat	Balls	Mdns	Runs	Wkts	BB	Ave	4wI	5wI	SR	Econ
ODIs	5	240	1	217	9	3-47	24.11	0	0	26.66	5.42
T20Is	3	66	0	112	5	3-40	22.40	0	0	13.20	10.18
First-class	9	1446	38	914	24	4-48	38.08	-	0	60.25	3.79
List A	26	1198	5	1071	42	4-39	25.50	3	0	28.52	5.36
T20s	144	3012	4	4121	179	5-21	23.02	4	2	16.82	8.20

TOMMY EALHAM

LHB / OB / R0 / W0

FULL NAME: Thomas Mark Ealham
BORN: March 26, 2004, Guildford, Surrey
SQUAD NO: 5
HEIGHT: 5ft 10in
NICKNAME: Ealy
EDUCATION: Cranleigh School
TEAMS: Surrey
ROLE: Bowler
DEBUT: List A: 2023

FIRST CRICKET CLUB? Cranleigh CC, Surrey
EARLIEST CRICKETING MEMORY? Playing cricket in the garden with my brother
WHAT'S THE BIGGEST PRIZE IN DOMESTIC CRICKET? The County Championship
THE KOOKABURRA BALL: YES OR NO? Yes – it brings different skills and tactics into the game at different points in the season
OPPONENT YOU MOST LOOK FORWARD TO PLAYING AGAINST? Ben Geddes – we played at Surrey together and I've bowled plenty of overs against him in the nets, so I'd love to have a crack against him out in the middle!
FAVOURITE WARM-UP SONG? Can't Stop by Red Hot Chilli Peppers
HOW MANY HOURS DO YOU SPEND ON YOUR PHONE A DAY? Five
SPECIALITY SUBJECT IN A PUB QUIZ (EXCLUDING SPORT)? Movies
ONE THING YOU WANT TO DO BEFORE YOU DIE: Skydive
HOBBY YOU WOULD LIKE TO LEARN: Padel
WHICH PUBLIC FIGURE INSPIRES YOU (EXCLUDING SPORTSPEOPLE)? Nick Vujicic
SURPRISING FACT ABOUT YOU: I grew up in a village called Elham, which is pronounced the same as Ealham
FILM YOU CAN WATCH OVER AND OVER: 22 Jump Street

Batting	Mat	Inns	NO	Runs	HS	Ave	SR	100	50	Ct	St
List A	2	2	0	9	5	4.50	29.03	0	0	0	-
Bowling	Mat	Balls	Mdns	Runs	Wkts	BB	Ave	4wl	5wl	SR	Econ
List A	2	36	0	29	0	0-29	-	-	-	-	4.83

JACK EDWARDS

RHB / RMF / R0 / W0

HAMPSHIRE

FULL NAME: Jack Richard Edwards
BORN: April 19, 2000, Allambie Heights, New South Wales, Australia
SQUAD NO: TBC
TEAMS: Hampshire, Australia U19, New South Wales, Sydney Sixers
ROLE: Allrounder
DEBUT: First-class: 2018; List A: 2018; T20: 2018

BEST BATTING: 139 New South Wales vs South Australia, Adelaide, 2023
BEST BOWLING: 6-36 New South Wales vs Queensland, Sydney, 2023

NOTES: The Australian allrounder, who turns 25 in April, has signed for Hampshire to play in the County Championship during the first two months of the season. Edwards, who captains New South Wales in the Sheffield Shield, is a genuine allrounder whose pace bowling will help fill the void left by Mohammad Abbas, while his qualities as a batter can provide balance to the side following James Vince's decision to opt out of red-ball cricket this summer. He and Vince have been teammates for the Sydney Sixers in Australia's Big Bash. Edwards said: "I've played alongside James Vince for the last few years and have gotten to know him pretty well, so it's great to know I'll be playing under the Rose and Crown. Watching from afar, the club has been really close to winning titles across formats the last few years, so hopefully I can help the team go one step further in 2025"

Batting	Mat	Inns	NO	Runs	HS	Ave	SR	100	50	Ct	St
First-class	40	67	6	1800	138	29.50	53.06	3	4	48	-
List A	31	29	1	792	116	28.28	88.29	2	4	22	-
T20s	51	39	1	563	47	14.81	112.60	0	0	25	-

Bowling	Mat	Balls	Mdns	Runs	Wkts	BB	Ave	4wl	5wl	SR	Econ
First-class	40	4069	148	1879	71	6-36	26.46	-	3	57.30	2.77
List A	31	684	12	532	19	4-38	28.00	1	0	36.00	4.66
T20s	51	414	2	559	19	3-24	29.42	0	0	21.78	8.10

DEAN ELGAR — LHB / SLA / R1 / W0 / MVP30

FULL NAME: Dean Elgar
BORN: June 11, 1987, Welkom, Orange Free State, South Africa
SQUAD NO: 64
TEAMS: South Africa, Essex, Eagles, Free State, Knights, Northerns, Somerset, Surrey, Titans, Tshwane Spartans
ROLE: Batter
DEBUT: Test: 2012; ODI: 2012; First-class: 2006; List A: 2006; T20: 2008

ESSEX

BEST BATTING: 268 South Africa A vs Australia A, Pretoria, 2013
BEST BOWLING: 4-22 South Africa vs India, Mohali, 2015
COUNTY CAP: 2017 (Somerset)

NOTES: Ex-South Africa skipper Dean Elgar joined the Eagles on a three-year deal in January 2024 and lived up to his billing in his first season at Chelmsford, scoring 1,144 runs in Division One as well as contributing 331 runs in the T20 Blast. After retiring from international cricket at the beginning of last year, the left-handed opener arrived at Essex to fill the role vacated by Alastair Cook, who called time on his career at the end of 2023. Elgar, who hit a brilliant 185 against India in his final Test series to boost his average in home Tests to 47 from 48 Tests, has also appeared for Surrey and Somerset in the past

Batting	Mat	Inns	NO	Runs	HS	Ave	SR	100	50	Ct	St
Tests	86	152	11	5347	199	37.92	47.78	14	23	92	-
ODIs	8	7	1	104	42	17.33	58.75	0	0	4	-
First-class	259	451	32	17820	268	42.52	50.39	52	73	217	-
List A	178	171	27	6264	137	43.50	81.49	10	45	54	-
T20s	95	91	19	2359	88*	32.76	113.19	0	14	39	-

Bowling	Mat	Balls	Mdns	Runs	Wkts	BB	Ave	4wI	5wI	SR	Econ
Tests	86	1036	12	673	15	4-22	44.86	-	0	69.06	3.89
ODIs	8	96	1	67	2	1-11	33.50	0	0	48.00	4.18
First-class	259	4165	51	2798	56	4-22	49.96	-	0	74.37	4.03
List A	178	3109	6	2843	57	4-37	49.87	1	0	54.54	5.48
T20s	95	627	0	723	29	4-23	24.93	1	0	21.62	6.91

STEVIE ESKINAZI

RHB / WK / R0 / W0

MIDDLESEX

FULL NAME: Stephen Sean Eskinazi
BORN: March 28, 1994, Johannesburg, South Africa
SQUAD NO: 28
HEIGHT: 6ft 2in
NICKNAME: Eski
EDUCATION: Christ Church Grammar School, Perth; University of Western Australia; University of Hertfordshire
TEAMS: Middlesex, Welsh Fire, Dhaka Capitals, Perth Scorchers
ROLE: Batter
DEBUT: First-class: 2015; List A: 2018; T20: 2016

BEST BATTING: 179 Middlesex vs Warwickshire, Edgbaston, 2017

COUNTY CAP: 2018

FIRST CRICKET CLUB? Fair Oak CC, Hampshire
EARLIEST CRICKETING MEMORY? Getting knocked over for a golden duck for Hampshire U10 and crying the whole walk off. Not much has changed to be fair
THE KOOKABURRA BALL: YES OR NO? Definitely yes (runs!)
OPPONENT YOU MOST LOOK FORWARD TO PLAYING AGAINST? Cameron steel – he is very funny and often has a nice moustache
FAVOURITE WARM-UP SONG? Whatever It Takes by Imagine Dragons
SPECIALITY SUBJECT IN A PUB QUIZ (EXCLUDING SPORT)? Coffee
ONE THING YOU WANT TO DO BEFORE YOU DIE: Take a wicket
WHICH PUBLIC FIGURE INSPIRES YOU (EXCLUDING SPORTSPEOPLE)? Sabrina Carpenter
SURPRISING FACT ABOUT YOU: I am a trained barista. And I could potentially hold four passports
FILM YOU CAN WATCH OVER AND OVER: Remember the Titans

Batting	Mat	Inns	NO	Runs	HS	Ave	SR	100	50	Ct	St
First-class	88	152	12	4321	179	30.86	51.33	9	17	85	-
List A	30	29	3	1434	182	55.15	103.68	6	3	12	-
T20s	114	111	10	3173	102*	31.41	138.68	1	21	49	-
Bowling	Mat	Balls	Mdns	Runs	Wkts	BB	Ave	4wl	5wl	SR	Econ
First-class	88	18	1	4	0	0-0	-	-	-	-	1.33
List A	30	-	-	-	-	-	-	-	-	-	-
T20s	114	-	-	-	-	-	-	-	-	-	-

LAURIE EVANS — RHB / RM / R0 / W0

FULL NAME: Laurie John Evans
BORN: October 12, 1987, Lambeth, London
SQUAD NO: 10
HEIGHT: 6ft
EDUCATION: Whitgift School; The John Fisher School, Purley; Durham University
TEAMS: Surrey, Southern Brave, Barbados Royals, Colombo Kings, England Lions, Manchester Originals, Melbourne Renegades, Multan Sultans, Northants, Oval Invincibles, Perth Scorchers, Sussex, Warwickshire
ROLE: Batter
DEBUT: First-class: 2007; List A: 2009; T20: 2009

SURREY

BEST BATTING: 118* Surrey vs Glamorgan, Cardiff, 2023 (T20)
BEST BOWLING: 1-5 Warwickshire vs Gloucestershire, Cheltenham, 2013 (T20)

MOST EXCITING DAY AS A CRICKETER? Winning the T20 Blast with Warwickshire in 2014
WHAT WOULD YOU DO IF YOU WERE IN CHARGE OF COUNTY CRICKET? Reduce the amount of games, use DRS for TV games, offer free entry for kids
CHILDHOOD SPORTING HERO? Jonny Wilkinson
NOTES: Evans signed a white-ball-only contract with Surrey in March 2022

Batting	Mat	Inns	NO	Runs	HS	Ave	SR	100	50	Ct	St
First-class	73	125	6	3495	213*	29.36	46.43	6	18	58	-
List A	63	57	11	1735	134*	37.71	96.98	3	5	25	-
T20s	320	293	61	6961	118*	30.00	137.95	3	42	138	1

Bowling	Mat	Balls	Mdns	Runs	Wkts	BB	Ave	4wI	5wI	SR	Econ
First-class	73	366	3	270	2	1-29	135.00	-	0	183.00	4.42
List A	63	54	0	82	1	1-29	82.00	0	0	54.00	9.11
T20s	320	22	0	35	1	1-5	35.00	0	0	22.00	9.54

JOEY EVISON
RHB / RM / R0 / W0

KENT

FULL NAME: Joseph David Michael Evison
BORN: November 14, 2001, Peterborough, Cambridgeshire
SQUAD NO: 33
HEIGHT: 6ft 2in
NICKNAME: Evo
EDUCATION: Stamford School, Lincolnshire
TEAMS: Kent, England U19, Leicestershire, Nottinghamshire
ROLE: Allrounder
DEBUT: First-class: 2019; List A: 2021; T20: 2022

BEST BATTING: 109* Nottinghamshire vs Sussex, Hove, 2022
BEST BOWLING: 5-21 Nottinghamshire vs Durham, Chester-le-Street, 2021

FIRST CRICKET CLUB? Bourne CC, Lincolnshire
WHICH COUNTY PLAYER WOULD YOU MOST LIKE TO GO FOR A DRINK WITH? Ben Stokes
BEST PERFORMANCE AS A PRO? My maiden first-class hundred for Nottinghamshire at Hove in 2022
GREATEST PERFORMANCE YOU HAVE WITNESSED? Dom Sibley hitting a double-hundred and then a hundred in the same match at Trent Bridge in 2019
FAVOURITE FORMAT? Red-ball cricket – young players want to play Test cricket, the history of it is inspiring
DESCRIBE YOURSELF IN THREE WORDS: Calm, passionate, hard-working
WHICH PERSON INSPIRES YOU MOST? Michael Jordan

Batting	Mat	Inns	NO	Runs	HS	Ave	SR	100	50	Ct	St
First-class	39	64	7	1813	109*	31.80	50.17	1	11	9	-
List A	26	24	1	744	136	32.34	87.52	2	4	11	-
T20s	24	16	7	235	46	26.11	125.66	0	0	6	-

Bowling	Mat	Balls	Mdns	Runs	Wkts	BB	Ave	4wl	5wl	SR	Econ
First-class	39	3899	83	2405	60	5-21	40.08	-	1	64.98	3.70
List A	26	472	2	529	11	3-62	48.09	0	0	42.90	6.72
T20s	24	246	0	394	10	3-25	39.40	0	0	24.60	9.49

NATHAN FERNANDES — LHB / SLA / RO / WO

FULL NAME: Nathan Shane Fernandes
BORN: April 26, 2004, Goa, India
SQUAD NO: 18
HEIGHT: 5ft 10in
NICKNAME: Bruno
EDUCATION: St Gregory's Catholic Science College, Harrow, London; Royal Holloway, University of London
TEAMS: Middlesex
ROLE: Batter
DEBUT: First-class: 2024; List A: 2024; T20: 2023

MIDDLESEX

BEST BATTING: 103 Middlesex vs Northamptonshire, Northampton, 2024
BEST BOWLING: 1-17 Middlesex vs Leicestershire, Lord's, 2024

FIRST CRICKET CLUB? South Hampstead CC, London
WHAT'S THE BIGGEST PRIZE IN DOMESTIC CRICKET? Winning Division One of the County Championship
THE KOOKABURRA BALL: YES OR NO? Yes, being a batter and having faced both types of balls. The Kookaburra does significantly less than the Dukes
OPPONENT YOU MOST LOOK FORWARD TO PLAYING AGAINST? James Anderson
FAVOURITE WARM-UP SONG? Blinding Lights by The Weekend
HOW MANY HOURS DO YOU SPEND ON YOUR PHONE A DAY? Three to four
ONE THING YOU WANT TO DO BEFORE YOU DIE: Have a family of my own
HOBBY YOU WOULD LIKE TO LEARN: The piano
WHICH PUBLIC FIGURE INSPIRES YOU (EXCLUDING SPORTSPEOPLE)? Jesus Christ
SURPRISING FACT ABOUT YOU: I am ambidextrous – I bowl and bat left-handed but I throw right-handed
FILM YOU CAN WATCH OVER AND OVER: The Lion King

Batting	Mat	Inns	NO	Runs	HS	Ave	SR	100	50	Ct	St
First-class	8	12	0	354	103	29.50	46.45	1	1	4	-
List A	7	7	0	152	83	21.71	68.77	0	1	3	-
T20s	7	4	0	11	8	2.75	73.33	0	0	1	-

Bowling	Mat	Balls	Mdns	Runs	Wkts	BB	Ave	4wl	5wl	SR	Econ
First-class	8	216	2	142	2	1-17	71.00	-	0	108.00	3.94
List A	7	252	0	252	4	2-31	63.00	0	0	63.00	6.00
T20s	7	78	0	140	4	1-6	35.00	0	0	19.50	10.76

F

ASITHA FERNANDO

RHB / RMF / R0 / W0

FULL NAME: Asitha Madusanka Fernando
BORN: July 31, 1997, Katuneriya, Sri Lanka
SQUAD NO: TBC
TEAMS: Sri Lanka, Glamorgan, Chilaw Marians, Colombo, Galle Gladiatiors, Jaffna Kings, Nondescripts, Nottinghamshire
ROLE: Bowler
DEBUT: Test: 2021; ODI: 2017; T20I: 2022; First-class: 2016; List A: 2017; T20: 2018

BEST BATTING: 30 Sri Lanka A vs England Lions, Pallekele, 2017
BEST BOWLING: 7-139 Chilaw Marians vs Badureliya, Katunayake, 2020

NOTES: Glamorgan have secured the services of Fernando for the first seven County Championship games of the season, adding some much-needed venom to their pace attack. The Sri Lankan had a brief spell at Nottinghamshire in 2023 and impressed during his country's Test tour of England last summer, taking 17 wickets across three matches at an average of 24.64. Fernando had previously become only the second Sri Lankan pace bowler to take 10 wickets in a Test match, returning figures of 10-144 in a 10-wicket win over Bangladesh at Mirpur in May 2022. "Asitha has good experience of conditions in the UK having played county cricket previously and also while performing very well in Sri Lanka's series with England here last summer," said Mark Wallace, Glamorgan's director of cricket. "We look forward to Asitha taking the field for Glamorgan as the first Sri Lankan player to represent the club"

Batting	Mat	Inns	NO	Runs	HS	Ave	SR	100	50	Ct	St
Tests	22	32	16	54	11	3.37	25.71	0	0	6	-
ODIs	20	5	2	3	2	1.00	15.78	0	0	4	-
T20Is	7	3	3	11	10*	-	220.00	0	0	2	-
First-class	82	103	46	276	30	4.84	39.26	0	0	20	-
List A	89	31	15	67	11	4.18	52.75	0	0	15	-
T20s	54	13	8	44	10*	8.80	112.82	0	0	7	-

Bowling	Mat	Balls	Mdns	Runs	Wkts	BB	Ave	4wI	5wI	SR	Econ
Tests	22	3339	74	1997	72	6-51	27.73	-	2	46.37	3.58
ODIs	20	720	3	687	22	3-23	31.22	0	0	32.72	5.72
T20Is	7	120	0	208	4	1-11	52.00	0	0	30.00	10.40
First-class	82	10425	256	6103	254	7-139	24.02	-	10	41.04	3.51
List A	89	3705	22	3168	136	5-32	23.29	6	3	27.24	5.13
T20s	54	1068	4	1531	60	6-8	25.51	2	1	17.80	8.60

VISHWA FERNANDO

RHB / LFM / R0 / W0

FULL NAME: Muthuthanthrige Vishwa Thilina Fernando
BORN: September 18, 1991, Colombo, Sri Lanka
SQUAD NO: TBC
TEAMS: Sri Lanka, Warwickshire, Bloomfield Cricket & Athletic, Colombo, Durham, Galle Titans, Kandy Tuskers, Yorkshire
ROLE: Bowler
DEBUT: Test: 2016; ODI: 2017; T20I: 2017; First-class: 2012; List A: 2012; T20: 2012

WARWICKSHIRE

BEST BATTING: 41 Colombo vs Moor Sports, Colombo, 2020
BEST BOWLING: 5-14 Dambulla District vs Jaffna District, Colombo, 2023

NOTES: The Sri Lankan left-arm quick is set to turn out for Warwickshire in three County Championship matches in April – against Sussex, his former side Durham, and Nottinghamshire. Fernando took 17 wickets in three red-ball appearances for Yorkshire last summer, including nine in the match against Derbyshire, and will bolster the Bears' seam-bowling ranks, which have also been strengthened by the acquisition of Ethan Bamber from Middlesex. "I am thrilled to be joining Warwickshire for the early stages of the season," Fernando said. "Playing county cricket has been hugely enjoyable for me over the last two years. The county have some very good cricketers and I am looking forward to playing with Alex Davies, Ed Barnard and all the boys"

Batting	Mat	Inns	NO	Runs	HS	Ave	SR	100	50	Ct	St
Tests	27	39	16	159	38	6.91	26.32	0	0	7	-
ODIs	8	8	6	30	7*	15.00	49.18	0	0	0	-
T20Is	1	1	0	2	2	2.00	100.00	0	0	0	-
First-class	128	150	67	771	41	9.28	34.55	0	0	40	-
List A	60	34	23	135	18*	12.27	36.58	0	0	8	-
T20s	29	5	1	11	7	2.75	57.89	0	0	4	-

Bowling	Mat	Balls	Mdns	Runs	Wkts	BB	Ave	4wI	5wI	SR	Econ
Tests	27	4272	94	2534	79	5-101	32.07	-	1	54.07	3.55
ODIs	8	297	4	337	5	1-35	67.40	0	0	59.40	6.80
T20Is	1	12	0	16	0	0-16	-	-	-	-	8.00
First-class	128	16467	400	10120	348	5-14	29.08	-	11	47.31	3.68
List A	60	2443	25	2321	76	4-61	30.53	1	0	32.14	5.70
T20s	29	423	0	551	26	3-22	21.19	0	0	16.26	7.81

ADAM FINCH

RHB / RFM / R0 / W0

WORCESTERSHIRE

FULL NAME: Adam William Finch
BORN: May 28, 2000, Wordsley, Stourbridge, Worcestershire
SQUAD NO: 61
HEIGHT: 6ft 4in
EDUCATION: Kingswinford School, West Midlands; Oldswinford Hospital Sixth Form College, Stourbridge
TEAMS: Worcestershire, England U19, Surrey
ROLE: Bowler
DEBUT: First-class: 2019; List A: 2021; T20: 2020

BEST BATTING: 43 Worcestershire vs Kent, Worcester, 2024
BEST BOWLING: 5-74 Worcestershire vs Glamorgan, Cardiff, 2023

FIRST CRICKET CLUB? Himley CC, Staffordshire
WHICH TEAMMATE HAS HAD THE BIGGEST IMPACT ON YOUR GAME? Joe Leach
BIGGEST INFLUENCE ON YOUR DEVELOPMENT AS A CRICKETER (EXCLUDING PARENTS)?
Paul Pridgeon, former Worcestershire seamer who worked with the Academy to help bring through young players
BEST PLAYER IN COUNTY CRICKET (EXCLUDING TEAMMATES)? Simon Harmer
GREATEST PERFORMANCE YOU HAVE WITNESSED? Ben Cox's match-winning performances on T20 Finals Day in 2018
WHICH PERSON INSPIRES YOU MOST? Glenn McGrath
MOST BEAUTIFUL THING YOU HAVE EVER SEEN? Queenstown in New Zealand
CHOOSE A FANTASY SLIP CORDON TO SPEND A DAY IN THE FIELD WITH: Muhammad Ali, Professor Brian Cox, David Beckham, Jeff Bezos

Batting	Mat	Inns	NO	Runs	HS	Ave	SR	100	50	Ct	St
First-class	31	43	17	458	43	17.61	32.45	0	0	4	-
List A	14	7	2	71	24	14.20	131.48	0	0	1	-
T20s	25	11	6	61	30*	12.20	98.38	0	0	4	-

Bowling	Mat	Balls	Mdns	Runs	Wkts	BB	Ave	4wI	5wI	SR	Econ
First-class	31	4310	101	2831	78	5-74	36.29	-	2	55.25	3.94
List A	14	591	1	608	14	3-54	43.42	0	0	42.21	6.17
T20s	25	518	0	807	23	3-38	35.08	0	0	22.52	9.34

HARRY FINCH

RHB / RM / R0 / W0

FULL NAME: Harry Zacariah Finch
BORN: February 10, 1995, Hastings, Sussex
SQUAD NO: 72
HEIGHT: 5ft 9in
NICKNAME: Chozza
EDUCATION: St Richard's Catholic College, Bexhill; Eastbourne College, East Sussex
TEAMS: Kent, England U19, Sussex
ROLE: Batter/wicketkeeper
DEBUT: First-class: 2013; List A: 2013; T20: 2014

BEST BATTING: 135* Sussex vs Leeds/Bradford MCCU, Hove, 2016
BEST BOWLING: 1-9 Sussex vs Leeds/Bradford MCCU, Hove, 2016

FIRST CRICKET CLUB? Hastings & St Leonards Priory CC, East Sussex
BEST DELIVERY YOU HAVE EVER BOWLED? I once bowled a jaffa to Younis Khan and he nearly nicked it
BEST PERFORMANCE AS A PRO? Either 92 not out off 58 balls in my first List A innings in 2014 or 115 not out on my Kent debut against Sussex in 2021
GREATEST PERFORMANCE YOU HAVE WITNESSED? Luke Wright's 153 at Chelmsford in the 2014 T20 Blast
FAVOURITE FORMAT? Four-day cricket – it's the hardest to win at
HOBBIES? Puzzles
FAVOURITE TOY AS A KID? My train set
WHICH PERSON INSPIRES YOU MOST? Harry Kane
SURPRISING FACT ABOUT YOU: I'm good at impressions

Batting	Mat	Inns	NO	Runs	HS	Ave	SR	100	50	Ct	St
First-class	75	129	8	3375	135*	27.89	50.05	5	19	107	7
List A	66	63	7	1867	108	33.33	78.74	2	13	27	3
T20s	32	25	7	356	47	19.77	106.58	0	0	14	-

Bowling	Mat	Balls	Mdns	Runs	Wkts	BB	Ave	4wI	5wI	SR	Econ
First-class	75	168	1	118	2	1-9	59.00	-	0	84.00	4.21
List A	66	16	0	24	0	0-2	-	-	-	-	9.00
T20s	32	-	-	-	-	-	-	-	-	-	-

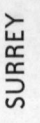

MATTHEW FISHER

RHB / RFM / R0 / W0

SURREY

FULL NAME: Matthew David Fisher
BORN: November 9, 1997, York
SQUAD NO: 15
HEIGHT: 6ft 2in
NICKNAME: Nemo
EDUCATION: Easingwold School, North Yorkshire
TEAMS: England, Surrey, Northern Superchargers, Southern Brave, Yorkshire
ROLE: Bowler
DEBUT: Test: 2022; First-class: 2015; List A: 2013; T20: 2015

BEST BATTING: 88 Yorkshire vs Leicestershire, Leicester, 2024
BEST BOWLING: 5-30 Yorkshire vs Derbyshire, Chesterfield, 2023
COUNTY CAP: 2022 (Yorkshire)

BIGGEST INFLUENCE ON YOUR DEVELOPMENT AS A CRICKETER (EXCLUDING PARENTS)?
Tony Pickersgill, the former age-group bowling coach at Yorkshire. He helped make my bowling technically sound and adapted to a high level at a young age
WHAT WOULD YOU DO IF YOU WERE IN CHARGE OF COUNTY CRICKET? Make boundaries bigger, have six stumps in T20 cricket, blindfold the batters (it's a batters' game)
SURPRISING FACT ABOUT YOU: I'm deaf in one ear

Batting	Mat	Inns	NO	Runs	HS	Ave	SR	100	50	Ct	St
Tests	1	1	1	0	0*	-	0.00	0	0	1	-
First-class	44	57	16	738	88	18.00	42.36	0	2	15	-
List A	35	19	10	236	36*	26.22	98.74	0	0	11	-
T20s	45	12	5	61	19	8.71	129.78	0	0	12	-

Bowling	Mat	Balls	Mdns	Runs	Wkts	BB	Ave	4wI	5wI	SR	Econ
Tests	1	162	6	71	1	1-67	71.00	-	0	162.00	2.62
First-class	44	7003	262	3828	144	5-30	26.58	-	4	48.63	3.27
List A	35	1414	6	1402	32	3-32	43.81	0	0	44.18	5.94
T20s	45	828	0	1247	46	5-22	27.10	0	1	18.00	9.03

ROCKY FLINTOFF

RHB / RM / RO / WO

FULL NAME: Rocky Flintoff
BORN: April 7, 2008, Manchester
SQUAD NO: 11
EDUCATION: Manchester Grammar School
TEAMS: Lancashire, England Lions
ROLE: Batter
DEBUT: First-class: 2024; List A: 2024

BEST BATTING: 32 Lancashire vs Surrey, The Oval, 2024

NOTES: It's been quite a year for Andrew's younger son, who's brother, Corey, is also on Lancashire's books. Rocky, a middle-order batter, was handed his first professional contract last June after a series of eye-catching performances for the club's Second XI, which included scoring his first hundred in only his third game for the twos. On signing the deal, he said: "I've been with the club since I was eight years old, so to have the opportunity to keep representing the Red Rose is a big honour. I have loved playing for the Second XI so far this season and I'm looking forward to continuing to work hard on all aspects of my game." It was only the start. After becoming Lancashire's youngest-ever player – 16 years and 113 days old – when making his senior debut against Kent in the One-Day Cup, Flintoff went on to score his maiden List A half-century and play four times in the Championship. Selected for last summer's U19 series against Sri Lanka, he beat Ian Bell's record for the youngest player to score a hundred for England U19. By the winter he was with England Lions – who are coached by Andrew – first in South Africa and then Australia, where he made 108 against a Cricket Australia XI in Brisbane

Batting	Mat	Inns	NO	Runs	HS	Ave	SR	100	50	Ct	St
First-class	5	9	0	137	32	15.22	37.74	0	0	0	-
List A	7	7	0	167	88	23.85	60.72	0	1	0	-
Bowling	Mat	Balls	Mdns	Runs	Wkts	BB	Ave	4wI	5wI	SR	Econ
First-class	5	-	-	-	-	-	-	-	-	-	-
List A	7	-	-	-	-	-	-	-	-	-	-

BEN FOAKES

RHB / WK / R0 / W0

FULL NAME: Benjamin Thomas Foakes
BORN: February 15, 1993, Colchester, Essex
SQUAD NO: 7
HEIGHT: 6ft 2in
EDUCATION: Tendring Technology College, Essex
TEAMS: England, Surrey, Essex
ROLE: Wicketkeeper/batter
DEBUT: Test: 2018; ODI: 2019; T20I: 2019; First-class: 2011; List A: 2013; T20: 2014

BEST BATTING: 141* Surrey vs Hampshire, Southampton, 2016

COUNTY CAP: 2016 (Surrey)

FIRST CRICKET CLUB? Frinton-on-Sea CC, Essex
WHAT WOULD YOU CHANGE ABOUT THE STRUCTURE OF THE COUNTY SEASON? Not have Championship matches randomly scheduled in the middle of the T20 competition
MOST BEAUTIFUL THING YOU HAVE EVER SEEN? Exuma, Bahamas
WHO WOULD YOU MOST LIKE TO HAVE A NET WITH? Kumar Sangakkara
SURPRISING FACT ABOUT YOU? I once had a tooth glued back together after being involved in a car crash. Later, while I was batting, it came unstuck and was dangling, so I tore it out at lunch and batted with no front teeth

Batting	Mat	Inns	NO	Runs	HS	Ave	SR	100	50	Ct	St
Tests	25	46	7	1139	113*	29.20	47.24	2	4	69	10
ODIs	1	1	1	61	61*	-	80.26	0	1	2	1
T20Is	1	0	-	-	-	-	-	-	-	1	
First-class	174	271	42	8649	141*	37.76	49.79	16	45	457	39
List A	82	72	11	2278	106	37.34	85.92	1	19	92	12
T20s	78	53	12	859	75*	20.95	123.41	0	4	38	10
Bowling	Mat	Balls	Mdns	Runs	Wkts	BB	Ave	4wI	5wI	SR	Econ
Tests	25	-	-	-	-	-	-	-	-	-	-
ODIs	1	-	-	-	-	-	-	-	-	-	-
T20Is	1	-	-	-	-	-	-	-	-	-	-
First-class	174	6	0	6	0	0-6	-	-	-	-	6.00
List A	82	-	-	-	-	-	-	-	-	-	-
T20s	78	-	-	-	-	-	-	-	-	-	-

KESH FONSEKA — RHB / OB / RO / WO

FULL NAME: Dineth Keshana Fonseka
BORN: December 1, 2005, Colombo, Sri Lanka
SQUAD NO: 26
HEIGHT: 5ft 5in
EDUCATION: Bolton School
TEAMS: Lancashire, England U19
ROLE: Batter
DEBUT: List A: 2024

LANCASHIRE

FIRST CRICKET CLUB? Little Hulton CC, Salford, Manchester
EARLIEST CRICKETING MEMORY? Playing cricket with my dad in the living room
WHAT'S THE BIGGEST PRIZE IN DOMESTIC CRICKET? The County Championship
THE KOOKABURRA BALL: YES OR NO? Yes – it's easier for batters and they use it more in other countries
FAVOURITE WARM-UP SONG? Treasure by Bruno Mars
HOW MANY HOURS DO YOU SPEND ON YOUR PHONE A DAY? Five to six
SPECIALITY SUBJECT IN A PUB QUIZ (EXCLUDING SPORT)? Science
ONE THING YOU WANT TO DO BEFORE YOU DIE: Go on safari in Kruger Park, South Africa
HOBBY YOU WOULD LIKE TO LEARN: Mountain climbing
WHICH PUBLIC FIGURE INSPIRES YOU (EXCLUDING SPORTSPEOPLE)? Any doctor
SURPRISING FACT ABOUT YOU: I can play the guitar and ukulele
FILM YOU CAN WATCH OVER AND OVER: How to Train Your Dragon

Batting	Mat	Inns	NO	Runs	HS	Ave	SR	100	50	Ct	St
List A	3	3	0	42	42	14.00	72.41	0	0	0	-

Bowling	Mat	Balls	Mdns	Runs	Wkts	BB	Ave	4wI	5wI	SR	Econ
List A	3	-	-	-	-	-	-	-	-	-	-

BERTIE FOREMAN

LHB / OB / RO / W0

SUSSEX

FULL NAME: Albert Michael Foreman
BORN: May 13, 2004, Worthing, Sussex
SQUAD NO: 13
HEIGHT: 5ft 9in
EDUCATION: Hurstpierpoint College, West Sussex
TEAMS: Sussex, England U19
ROLE: Bowler
DEBUT: First-class: 2024; List A: 2023

BEST BATTING: 2 Sussex vs Gloucestershire, Bristol, 2024

FIRST CRICKET CLUB? St James Montifiore CC, East Sussex
EARLIEST CRICKETING MEMORY? Playing in the back garden with my older brothers and dad
WHAT'S THE BIGGEST PRIZE IN DOMESTIC CRICKET? Division One of the County Championship
THE KOOKABURRA BALL: YES OR NO? Yes, because it's much easier to grip as a spinner
FAVOURITE WARM-UP SONG? Champion Sound by Crystal Fighters
HOW MANY HOURS DO YOU SPEND ON YOUR PHONE A DAY? Three to four
SPECIALITY SUBJECT IN A PUB QUIZ (EXCLUDING SPORT)? Capital cities
ONE THING YOU WANT TO DO BEFORE YOU DIE: Grow to 6ft tall
FILM YOU CAN WATCH OVER AND OVER: The Waterboy

Batting	Mat	Inns	NO	Runs	HS	Ave	SR	100	50	Ct	St
First-class	1	1	0	2	2	2.00	40.00	0	0	0	-
List A	7	7	1	190	48	31.66	70.11	0	0	3	-

Bowling	Mat	Balls	Mdns	Runs	Wkts	BB	Ave	4wI	5wI	SR	Econ
First-class	1	72	1	36	0	0-1	-	-	-	-	3.00
List A	7	258	4	228	4	1-31	57.00	0	0	64.50	5.30

ZAK FOULKES

RHB / RMF

FULL NAME: Zakary Glen Foulkes
BORN: June 5, 2002, Christchurch, New Zealand
SQUAD NO: TBC
TEAMS: New Zealand, Durham, Canterbury, Warwickshire
ROLE: Bowler
DEBUT: ODI: 2024; T20I: 2024; First-class: 2022; List A: 2022; T20: 2023

DURHAM

BEST BATTING: 32 Canterbury vs Wellington, Wellington, 2023 (T20)
BEST BOWLING: 4-23 Canterbury vs Northern Districts, Christchurch, 2023 (T20)

NOTES: The tall, versatile New Zealand international seamer has signed up with Durham for the duration of the T20 Blast group stages. He played for Birmingham Bears last summer and has taken nine T20 wickets to date for the national team, with a best of 3-20 against Sri Lanka in his most recent outing. "We are very pleased to have recruited Zak for our T20 Blast season," said Marcus North, Durham's director of cricket. "It was important we brought in a player who will provide us with a clear point of difference within our bowling attack and that is exactly what Zak brings. At only 22, Zak has already shown across the international and domestic game how much of a dynamic and well-rounded player he is in the T20 format. We look forward to welcoming him to Durham this summer"

Batting	Mat	Inns	NO	Runs	HS	Ave	SR	100	50	Ct	St
ODIs	1	0	-	-	-	-	-	-	-	0	-
T20Is	7	5	2	55	27*	18.33	148.64	0	0	0	-
First-class	17	27	2	487	75*	19.48	46.29	0	3	13	-
List A	26	17	3	272	49*	19.42	75.76	0	0	6	-
T20s	43	24	7	231	32	13.58	131.25	0	0	5	-

Bowling	Mat	Balls	Mdns	Runs	Wkts	BB	Ave	4wI	5wI	SR	Econ
ODIs	1	-	-	-	-	-	-	-	-	-	-
T20Is	7	157	0	237	9	3-20	26.33	0	0	17.44	9.05
First-class	17	2430	75	1302	50	5-38	26.04	-	2	48.60	3.21
List A	26	1079	9	883	37	3-15	23.86	0	0	29.16	4.91
T20s	43	837	0	1109	56	4-23	19.80	1	0	14.94	7.94

JAMES FULLER

RHB / RFM / RO / WO

FULL NAME: James Kerr Fuller
BORN: January 24, 1990, Cape Town, SA
SQUAD NO: 26
HEIGHT: 6ft 2in
NICKNAME: Foz
EDUCATION: Westlake Boys High School, Auckland; University of Otago
TEAMS: Hampshire, Birmingham Phoenix, Auckland, England Lions, Gloucestershire, Karachi Kings, Middlesex, Otago, Southern Brave, Sunrisers Eastern Cape
ROLE: Bowler
DEBUT: First-class: 2010; List A: 2011; T20: 2011

BEST BATTING: 93 Middlesex vs Somerset, Taunton, 2016
BEST BOWLING: 6-24 Otago vs Wellington, Dunedin, 2013
COUNTY CAP: 2022 (Hampshire); 2011 (Gloucestershire)

FIRST CRICKET CLUB? North Shore CC, Auckland, New Zealand
EARLIEST CRICKETING MEMORY? Watching the Black Caps beat Australia
WHAT'S THE BIGGEST PRIZE IN DOMESTIC CRICKET? The County Championship
THE KOOKABURRA BALL: YES OR NO? Yes, it adds greater variety to the county game and promotes spin
OPPONENT YOU MOST LOOK FORWARD TO PLAYING AGAINST? Adam Rossington
FAVOURITE WARM-UP SONG? Back in Black by AC/DC
HOW MANY HOURS DO YOU SPEND ON YOUR PHONE A DAY? Two
SPECIALITY SUBJECT IN A PUB QUIZ (EXCLUDING SPORT)? Biology
WHICH PUBLIC FIGURE INSPIRES YOU (EXCLUDING SPORTSPEOPLE)? David Goggins
SURPRISING FACT ABOUT YOU: I'm the best underwater swimmer at Hampshire
FILM YOU CAN WATCH OVER AND OVER: Home Alone

Batting	Mat	Inns	NO	Runs	HS	Ave	SR	100	50	Ct	St
First-class	96	135	22	2628	93	23.25	70.28	0	11	32	-
List A	69	55	17	884	55*	23.26	103.63	0	2	23	-
T20s	198	135	41	1893	57	20.13	141.79	0	3	81	-

Bowling	Mat	Balls	Mdns	Runs	Wkts	BB	Ave	4wI	5wI	SR	Econ
First-class	96	12488	314	7581	226	6-24	33.54	-	7	55.25	3.64
List A	69	2641	16	2610	79	6-35	33.03	2	1	33.43	5.92
T20s	198	3059	4	4471	173	6-28	25.84	4	1	17.68	8.76

GEORGE GARRETT

RHB / RMF / R0 / W0

FULL NAME: George Anthony Garrett
BORN: March 4, 2000, Harpenden, Hertfordshire
SQUAD NO: 44
HEIGHT: 6ft 4in
NICKNAME: Gazza
EDUCATION: Shrewsbury School; University of Birmingham
TEAMS: Kent, Warwickshire
ROLE: Bowler
DEBUT: First-class: 2019; List A: 2021; T20: 2019

BEST BATTING: 48 Kent vs Surrey, Canterbury, 2024
BEST BOWLING: 3-75 Kent vs Warwickshire, Edgbaston, 2024

FIRST CRICKET CLUB? Harpenden CC, Hertfordshire
WHAT WOULD YOU CHANGE ABOUT THE STRUCTURE OF THE COUNTY SEASON? Set up an FA-Cup-style one-day competition which includes Minor Counties
HOBBIES? Reading
WHO WOULD YOU MOST LIKE TO HAVE A NET WITH? Glenn McGrath
MOST BEAUTIFUL THING YOU HAVE EVER SEEN? Lord's when the sun is out

Batting	Mat	Inns	NO	Runs	HS	Ave	SR	100	50	Ct	St
First-class	13	22	12	162	48	16.20	37.67	0	0	3	-
List A	15	8	3	52	18	10.40	60.46	0	0	1	-
T20s	2	0	-	-	-	-	-	-	-	0	-

Bowling	Mat	Balls	Mdns	Runs	Wkts	BB	Ave	4wI	5wI	SR	Econ
First-class	13	1737	50	1112	30	3-75	37.06	-	0	57.90	3.84
List A	15	629	3	610	16	3-50	38.12	0	0	39.31	5.81
T20s	2	24	0	39	1	1-19	39.00	0	0	24.00	9.75

GEORGE GARTON

LHB / LF / RO / WO

WARWICKSHIRE

FULL NAME: George Henry Simmons Garton
BORN: April 15, 1997, Brighton
SQUAD NO: 7
HEIGHT: 6ft 1in
EDUCATION: Hurstpierpoint College, West
Sussex
TEAMS: England, Warwickshire, Adelaide
Strikers, Joburg Super Kings, Royal
Challengers Bangalore, Southern Brave,
Sydney Thunder, Sussex
ROLE: Bowler
DEBUT: T20I: 2022; First-class: 2016; List A:
2016; T20: 2016

BEST BATTING: 97 Sussex vs Glamorgan, Cardiff, 2021
BEST BOWLING: 5-26 Sussex vs Essex, Hove, 2020

FIRST CRICKET CLUB? Preston Nomads CC, West Sussex
WHICH COUNTY PLAYER WOULD YOU MOST LIKE TO GO FOR A DRINK WITH? My former
Sussex teammate Phil Salt
BEST INNINGS YOU'VE SEEN? Phil Salt's Championship hundred against Derbyshire at Hove
in 2018 – that was some serious ball-striking
WHAT WOULD YOU DO IF YOU WERE IN CHARGE OF COUNTY CRICKET? Remove the limit
on bouncers
FAVOURITE TOY AS A KID? A tennis ball
WHAT WOULD BE YOUR PERFECT BREAKFAST? A breakfast burrito and a cappuccino

Batting	Mat	Inns	NO	Runs	HS	Ave	SR	100	50	Ct	St
T20Is	1	1	0	2	2	2.00	50.00	0	0	0	-
First-class	26	36	6	650	97	21.66	57.42	0	5	14	-
List A	24	11	2	103	38	11.44	86.55	0	0	11	-
T20s	101	64	20	675	46	15.34	133.92	0	0	24	-

Bowling	Mat	Balls	Mdns	Runs	Wkts	BB	Ave	4wI	5wI	SR	Econ
T20Is	1	24	0	57	1	1-57	57.00	0	0	24.00	14.25
First-class	26	2990	47	2049	55	5-26	37.25	-	1	54.36	4.11
List A	24	942	2	993	29	4-43	34.24	1	0	32.48	6.32
T20s	101	1529	7	2301	88	4-16	26.14	3	0	17.37	9.02

EMILIO GAY

LHB / RM / R1 / W0

FULL NAME: Emilio Nico Gay
BORN: April 14, 2000, Bedford
SQUAD NO: 24
HEIGHT: 6ft 2in
NICKNAME: Nico
EDUCATION: Rushmoor School, Bedford; Bedford School
TEAMS: Durham, Northamptonshire
ROLE: Batter
DEBUT: First-class: 2019; List A: 2021; T20: 2021

BEST BATTING: 261 Northamptonshire vs Middlesex, Northampton, 2024
BEST BOWLING: 1-8 Northamptonshire vs Kent, Northampton, 2021

FIRST CRICKET CLUB? Bedford CC, Bedfordshire
IF YOU COULD PINCH A PLAYER FROM ANOTHER COUNTY, WHO WOULD IT BE?
Keith Barker
HOW IS BAZBALL AFFECTING CHAMPIONSHIP CRICKET? Perhaps it's affected one or two individuals, but overall I don't think it's had much of an impact given the different conditions in county cricket
WHAT DO YOU THINK OF THE CURRENT 50-OVER COMPETITION? Good for players that don't normally play in the first team, but there is a drop in standard
CHOOSE A FANTASY SLIP CORDON TO SPEND A DAY IN THE FIELD WITH: My uncle Gladstone (wk), Brian Lara, Sachin Tendulkar, Viv Richards
SURPRISING FACT ABOUT YOU: I speak Spanish

Batting	Mat	Inns	NO	Runs	HS	Ave	SR	100	50	Ct	St
First-class	50	86	3	2945	261	35.48	53.79	6	14	54	-
List A	30	30	5	958	131	38.32	93.46	1	7	20	-
T20s	13	12	0	290	53	24.16	133.64	0	1	3	-

Bowling	Mat	Balls	Mdns	Runs	Wkts	BB	Ave	4wI	5wI	SR	Econ
First-class	50	156	0	95	2	1-8	47.50	-	0	78.00	3.65
List A	30	42	0	44	1	1-25	44.00	0	0	42.00	6.28
T20s	13	6	0	8	0	0-8	-	-	-	-	8.00

BEN GEDDES

RHB / RM / R0 / W0

FULL NAME: Benedict Brodie Albert Geddes
BORN: July 31, 2001, Epsom, Surrey
SQUAD NO: 14
HEIGHT: 6ft 2in
NICKNAME: Geddo
EDUCATION: St John's School, Leatherhead
TEAMS: Middlesex, Kent, Surrey
ROLE: Batter
DEBUT: First-class: 2021; List A: 2021; T20: 2021

BEST BATTING: 124 Surrey vs Kent, The Oval, 2022

FIRST CRICKET CLUB? Ashtead CC, Surrey
EARLIEST CRICKETING MEMORY? New Zealand vs England, Lord's, 2008
THE KOOKABURRA BALL: YES OR NO? No, Dukes balls are better suited to English wickets
OPPONENT YOU MOST LOOK FORWARD TO PLAYING AGAINST? James Anderson
FAVOURITE WARM-UP SONG? Heartbreaker by Crazy P
SPECIALITY SUBJECT IN A PUB QUIZ (EXCLUDING SPORT)? National flags
ONE THING YOU WANT TO DO BEFORE YOU DIE: Watch Arsenal win the Champions League
FILM YOU CAN WATCH OVER AND OVER: Shutter Island

Batting	Mat	Inns	NO	Runs	HS	Ave	SR	100	50	Ct	St
First-class	8	12	0	389	124	32.41	38.90	2	1	4	-
List A	27	27	1	777	92	29.88	90.66	0	7	10	-
T20s	7	7	1	51	28	8.50	98.07	0	0	1	-

Bowling	Mat	Balls	Mdns	Runs	Wkts	BB	Ave	4wl	5wl	SR	Econ
First-class	8	12	0	12	0	0-12	-	-	-	-	6.00
List A	27	70	0	58	1	1-30	58.00	0	0	70.00	4.97
T20s	7	-	-	-	-	-	-	-	-	-	-

BEN GIBBON

RHB / LFM / R0 / W0

FULL NAME: Benjamin James Gibbon
BORN: June 9, 2000, Chester, Cheshire
SQUAD NO: 21
HEIGHT: 6ft 3in
EDUCATION: Ellesmere College, Shropshire;
Myerscough College, Lancashire
TEAMS: Worcestershire
ROLE: Bowler
DEBUT: First-class: 2022; List A: 2022

BEST BATTING: 75 Worcestershire vs Surrey, The Oval, 2024
BEST BOWLING: 4-87 Worcestershire vs Glamorgan, Cardiff, 2022

FIRST CRICKET CLUB? Tattenhall CC, Cheshire
BEST PLAYER IN COUNTY CRICKET (EXCLUDING TEAMMATES)? Ben Duckett
WHICH COUNTY PLAYER WOULD YOU MOST LIKE TO GO FOR A DRINK WITH?
Darren Stevens
BEST PERFORMANCE AS A PRO? Taking 12 wickets in a Second XI match against Somerset
in 2023
GREATEST PERFORMANCE YOU HAVE WITNESSED? Ben Stokes at New Road in 2022
FAVOURITE FORMAT? Four-day cricket
DESCRIBE YOURSELF IN THREE WORDS: Hard-working, determined, easy-going
FAVOURITE TOY AS A KID? A bat and ball
WHAT WOULD BE YOUR PERFECT BREAKFAST? Full English
SURPRISING FACT ABOUT YOU: I've completed the National Three Peaks Challenge (Ben
Nevis, Scafell Pike, Snowdon)

Batting	Mat	Inns	NO	Runs	HS	Ave	SR	100	50	Ct	St
First-class	19	18	7	233	75	21.18	47.35	0	1	10	-
List A	9	4	1	29	13*	9.66	103.57	0	0	5	-

Bowling	Mat	Balls	Mdns	Runs	Wkts	BB	Ave	4wI	5wI	SR	Econ
First-class	19	2920	74	1921	48	4-87	40.02	-	0	60.83	3.94
List A	9	408	1	423	13	3-58	32.53	0	0	31.38	6.22

NATHAN GILCHRIST

RHB / RFM / R0 / W0

KENT

FULL NAME: Nathan Nicholas Gilchrist
BORN: June 11, 2000, Harare, Zimbabwe
SQUAD NO: 17
HEIGHT: 6ft 5in
NICKNAME: Gilly
EDUCATION: St Stithians School, Johannesburg; King's College, Taunton
TEAMS: Kent
ROLE: Bowler
DEBUT: First-class: 2020; List A: 2021; T20: 2024

BEST BATTING: 41 Kent vs Essex, Chelmsford, 2024
BEST BOWLING: 6-61 Kent vs Somerset, Canterbury, 2022

FIRST CRICKET CLUB? Staplegrove CC, Somerset. The cricket field was right next to a herd of cows
WHAT PART OF THE SEASON DO YOU MOST ENJOY? The end, when the pressure is on to finish well
WHICH AWAY GROUND DO YOU MOST ENJOY VISITING? The Oval – a great stadium where I made my first-class debut
WHO IS THE MOST TALENTED U19 TEENAGER IN THE COUNTY GAME? Jaydn Denly (Kent)
IF YOU COULD PINCH A PLAYER FROM ANOTHER COUNTY, WHO WOULD IT BE?
Lewis Gregory
HOW IS BAZBALL AFFECTING CHAMPIONSHIP CRICKET? Bowlers are getting smacked!
WHAT DO YOU THINK OF THE CURRENT 50-OVER COMPETITION? Great for young players, but the standard has dropped
WHO IS THE TOUGHEST BOWLER TO FACE? Dan Worrall
WHAT KEEPS YOU AWAKE AT NIGHT? Forgetting to pay a parking fine
SURPRISING FACT ABOUT YOU: When I was younger I wanted to be a pro fisherman

Batting	Mat	Inns	NO	Runs	HS	Ave	SR	100	50	Ct	St
First-class	29	36	4	255	41	7.96	34.69	0	0	8	-
List A	27	17	5	91	33	7.58	68.42	0	0	8	-
T20s	9	3	0	3	2	1.00	25.00	0	0	2	-

Bowling	Mat	Balls	Mdns	Runs	Wkts	BB	Ave	4wI	5wI	SR	Econ
First-class	29	4025	90	2776	84	6-24	33.04	-	3	47.91	4.13
List A	27	910	2	1023	28	5-45	36.53	0	1	32.50	6.74
T20s	9	132	0	222	14	3-46	15.85	0	0	9.42	10.09

RICHARD GLEESON

RHB / RFM

FULL NAME: Richard James Gleeson
BORN: December 2, 1987, Blackpool
SQUAD NO: 33
HEIGHT: 6ft 4in
EDUCATION: Baines High School,
Lancashire; University of Cumbria
TEAMS: England, Warwickshire, London Spirit,
CSK, Durban's Super Giants, Lancashire,
Manchester Originals, Melbourne Renegades,
Northants, Sunrisers Eastern Cape
ROLE: Bowler
DEBUT: T20I: 2022; First-class: 2015; List A:
2016; T20: 2016

BEST BATTING: 8 Manchester Originals vs Trent Rockets, Lord's, 2022 (T20)
BEST BOWLING: 5-33 Lancashire vs Worcestershire, Old Trafford, 2022 (T20)

FIRST CRICKET CLUB? Blackpool CC, Lancashire
FAMILY TIES? My father ran the bar at our local cricket club, my sister ran the kitchen, and
my brother-in-law was the first XI captain
HOBBIES? Fishing
SURPRISING FACT ABOUT YOU? I am a published poet
NOTES: Warwickshire have confirmed that the 37-year-old fast bowler will return for a
second T20 Blast campaign with the Bears this summer. "I'm really happy to be heading
back to Edgbaston and being a Bear again," he said. "I was very happy with the way I
performed in the group games [last year]. Losing that quarter-final [against Gloucestershire]
really hurt. We know collectively we should have made Finals Day. But it makes us all
doubly determined to get there [this] season"

Batting	Mat	Inns	NO	Runs	HS	Ave	SR	100	50	Ct	St
T20Is	6	2	0	2	2	1.00	50.00	0	0	4	-
First-class	34	39	16	259	31	11.26	34.07	0	0	8	-
List A	21	13	5	53	13	6.62	42.06	0	0	3	-
T20s	115	29	18	57	8	5.18	74.02	0	0	21	-

Bowling	Mat	Balls	Mdns	Runs	Wkts	BB	Ave	4wI	5wI	SR	Econ
T20Is	6	126	1	187	9	3-15	20.77	0	0	14.00	8.90
First-class	34	5526	196	3053	143	6-43	21.34	-	10	38.64	3.31
List A	21	841	5	816	28	5-47	29.14	1	1	30.03	5.82
T20s	115	2291	2	3066	129	5-33	23.76	1	1	17.75	8.02

ZAFAR GOHAR

LHB / SLA / R0 / W0

MIDDLESEX

FULL NAME: Zafar Gohar Khan
BORN: 1st February 1995, Lahore, Punjab, Pakistan
SQUAD NO: 77
HEIGHT: 5ft 9in
TEAMS: Pakistan, Middlesex, Central Punjab, Gloucestershire, Islamabad United, Lahore Blues, Lahore Qalandars, State Bank of Pakistan, Sui Southern Gas Corporation, Zarai Taraqiati Bank Limited
ROLE: Bowler
DEBUT: Test: 2021; ODI: 2015; First-class: 2013; List A: 2013; T20: 2013

BEST BATTING: 100* Central Punjab vs Baluchistan, Quetta, 2019
BEST BOWLING: 7-79 Central Punjab vs Northern, Faisalabad, 2019

FIRST CRICKET CLUB? Shafqat Rana CC, Punjab, Pakistan
EARLIEST CRICKETING MEMORY? Tennis-ball cricket with my brother
THE KOOKABURRA BALL: YES OR NO? Yes, because it provides opportunities for everyone
OPPONENT YOU MOST LOOK FORWARD TO PLAYING AGAINST? Joe Root (I'd love to get him out!)
FAVOURITE WARM-UP SONG? Ginger by Burna Boy
HOW MANY HOURS DO YOU SPEND ON YOUR PHONE A DAY? Three
ONE THING YOU WANT TO DO BEFORE YOU DIE: Build a school in my home village
WHICH PUBLIC FIGURE INSPIRES YOU (EXCLUDING SPORTSPEOPLE)? Thomas Shelby (Peaky Blinders)
SURPRISING FACT ABOUT YOU: I often forget things
FILM YOU CAN WATCH OVER AND OVER: The Punisher

Batting	Mat	Inns	NO	Runs	HS	Ave	SR	100	50	Ct	St
Tests	1	2	0	71	37	35.50	56.34	0	0	0	-
ODIs	1	1	0	15	15	15.00	100.00	0	0	0	-
First-class	84	127	14	2538	100*	22.46	49.32	1	13	33	-
List A	90	72	13	1071	62	18.15	85.20	0	5	16	-
T20s	70	38	14	352	37*	14.66	116.55	0	0	21	-

Bowling	Mat	Balls	Mdns	Runs	Wkts	BB	Ave	4wl	5wl	SR	Econ
Tests	1	192	0	159	0	0-159	-	-	-	-	4.96
ODIs	1	60	0	54	2	2-54	27.00	0	0	30.00	5.40
First-class	84	18254	557	9457	300	7-79	31.52	-	20	60.84	3.10
List A	90	4658	32	3716	125	5-56	29.72	3	1	37.26	4.78
T20s	70	1378	0	1766	74	4-14	23.86	3	0	18.62	7.68

LEWIS GOLDSWORTHY RHB / SLA / R0 / W0 / MVP25

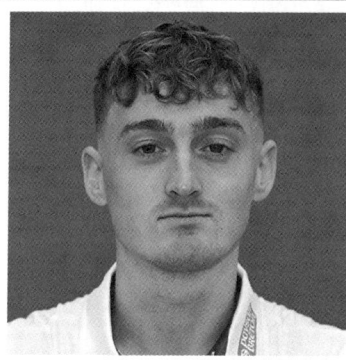

FULL NAME: Lewis Peter Goldsworthy
BORN: January 8, 2001, Cornwall
SQUAD NO: 44
HEIGHT: 5ft 7in
NICKNAME: Golders
EDUCATION: Cambourne Science & International Academy, Cornwall; Millfield School, Street, Somerset
TEAMS: Somerset, England U19, Leicestershire
ROLE: Allrounder
DEBUT: First-class: 2021; List A: 2021; T20: 2020

SOMERSET

BEST BATTING: 130 Somerset vs Lancashire, Southport, 2022
BEST BOWLING: 2-73 Somerset vs Kent, Canterbury, 2024

FIRST CRICKET CLUB? Troon CC, Cornwall
WHO WOULD YOU MOST LIKE TO HAVE A NET WITH? Monty Panesar
MOST BEAUTIFUL THING YOU HAVE EVER SEEN? St Ives, Cornwall

Batting	Mat	Inns	NO	Runs	HS	Ave	SR	100	50	Ct	St
First-class	29	47	3	1308	130	29.72	44.20	2	5	12	-
List A	31	30	4	1309	115*	50.34	80.40	2	8	9	-
T20s	36	26	6	436	67	21.80	125.64	0	1	13	-

Bowling	Mat	Balls	Mdns	Runs	Wkts	BB	Ave	4wI	5wI	SR	Econ
First-class	29	636	15	397	7	2-73	56.71	-	0	90.85	3.74
List A	31	987	3	902	22	4-44	41.00	1	0	44.86	5.48
T20s	36	564	0	751	37	3-14	20.29	0	0	15.24	7.98

DOMINIC GOODMAN

RHB / RFM / R0 / W0

GLOUCESTERSHIRE

FULL NAME: Dominic Charles Goodman
BORN: October 23, 2000, Ashford, Kent
SQUAD NO: 83
HEIGHT: 6ft 5in
NICKNAME: Len
EDUCATION: Dr Challenor's Grammar School, Amersham, Buckinghamshire; University of Exeter
TEAMS: Gloucestershire
ROLE: Bowler
DEBUT: First-class: 2021; List A: 2022

BEST BATTING: 38* Gloucestershire vs Yorkshire, Scarborough, 2024
BEST BOWLING: 4-73 Gloucestershire vs Durham, Chester-le-Street, 2023

WHICH TEAMMATE HAS HAD THE BIGGEST IMPACT ON YOUR GAME? Tom Price – we've grown up together and he has helped a lot with my bowling. His brother Ollie has helped with my batting – it's useful living together!
WHICH AWAY GROUND DO YOU MOST ENJOY VISITING? Taunton – always enjoy the chance to turn over our local rivals
WHO IS THE MOST TALENTED U19 TEENAGER IN THE COUNTY GAME? Archie Bailey (Glo)
IF YOU COULD PINCH A PLAYER FROM ANOTHER COUNTY, WHO WOULD IT BE? John Turner
WHO IS THE TOUGHEST BOWLER TO FACE? Matt Taylor from around the wicket – as a batter you can't win from that angle
WHAT KEEPS YOU AWAKE AT NIGHT? A Tom Price nip-backer
WHAT'S THE SILLIEST OUTFIT YOU'VE EVER WORN? Dressing up as SpongeBob SquarePants
CHOOSE A FANTASY SLIP CORDON TO SPEND A DAY IN THE FIELD WITH: Matthew McConaughey (wk), Dan Carter, Sam Fender, Gerry Cinnamon
SURPRISING FACT ABOUT YOU: I spent some of my childhood living just outside Glasgow, which is why I love Glaswegian singer Gerry Cinnamon

Batting	Mat	Inns	NO	Runs	HS	Ave	SR	100	50	Ct	St
First-class	15	20	6	116	38*	8.28	29.21	0	0	7	-
List A	9	5	1	18	15	4.50	56.25	0	0	2	-

Bowling	Mat	Balls	Mdns	Runs	Wkts	BB	Ave	4wI	5wI	SR	Econ
First-class	15	2067	63	1121	28	4-73	40.03	-	0	73.82	3.25
List A	9	390	1	390	12	4-43	32.50	1	0	32.50	6.00

ANDY GORVIN
RHB / RMF / R0 / W0

FULL NAME: Andrew William Gorvin
BORN: May 10, 1997, Winchester, Hampshire
SQUAD NO: 11
HEIGHT: 5ft 9in
NICKNAME: Gorv
EDUCATION: Portsmouth High School;
Cardiff Metropolitan University
TEAMS: Glamorgan
ROLE: Bowler
DEBUT: First-class: 2022; List A: 2021; T20: 2023

GLAMORGAN

BEST BATTING: 47 Glamorgan vs Yorkshire, Cardiff, 2023
BEST BOWLING: 5-40 Glamorgan vs Sussex, Cardiff, 2024

FIRST CRICKET CLUB? Hayling Island CC, Hampshire
WHAT PART OF THE SEASON DO YOU MOST ENJOY? The T20 Blast
THE KOOKABURRA BALL: YES OR NO? Yes, it's great for improving skills and reverse swing
at the right time of the year
WHICH AWAY GROUND DO YOU MOST ENJOY VISITING? Hove – so close to the sea
WHO IS THE MOST TALENTED U19 TEENAGER IN THE COUNTY GAME? Tazeem Ali (War)
WHAT DO YOU THINK OF THE CURRENT 50-OVER COMPETITION? It's a great opportunity
for younger players to test their skills in a first-team environment
CHOOSE A FANTASY SLIP CORDON TO SPEND A DAY IN THE FIELD WITH: Tiger Woods (wk),
Roger Federer, The Queen, Ed Sheeran
SURPRISING FACT ABOUT YOU: My family home is on a small island off the south coast and I
took the ferry to school every morning

Batting	Mat	Inns	NO	Runs	HS	Ave	SR	100	50	Ct	St
First-class	15	21	4	203	47	11.94	35.24	0	0	5	-
List A	22	11	5	66	12*	11.00	54.54	0	0	7	-
T20s	13	9	3	74	14*	12.33	113.84	0	0	1	-

Bowling	Mat	Balls	Mdns	Runs	Wkts	BB	Ave	4wI	5wI	SR	Econ
First-class	15	2089	85	1080	36	5-40	30.00	-	1	58.02	3.10
List A	22	923	0	816	29	5-56	28.13	1	1	31.82	5.30
T20s	13	217	0	315	11	3-26	28.63	0	0	19.72	8.70

BEN GREEN

RHB / RFM / R0 / W0

LEICESTERSHIRE

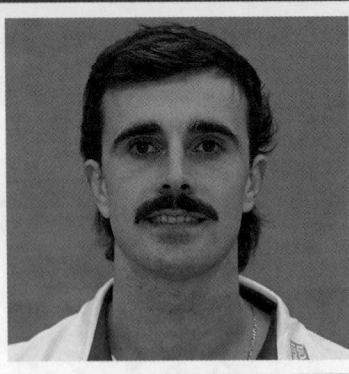

FULL NAME: Benjamin George Frederick Green
BORN: September 28, 1997, Exeter, Devon
SQUAD NO: 54
HEIGHT: 6ft 2in
NICKNAME: Neil
EDUCATION: St Peter's Preparatory School, Lympstone, Devon; Exeter School
TEAMS: Leicestershire, England U19, Somerset, Welsh Fire
ROLE: Allrounder
DEBUT: First-class: 2018; List A: 2018; T20: 2016

BEST BATTING: 77 Leicestershire vs Middlesex, Leicester, 2024
BEST BOWLING: 4-28 Leicestershire vs Middlesex, Leicester, 2024

FIRST CRICKET CLUB? Clyst St George CC, East Devon
EARLIEST CRICKETING MEMORY? Walloping Dad around the garden with my plastic Hunts County bat
WHAT'S THE BIGGEST PRIZE IN DOMESTIC CRICKET? The County Championship
THE KOOKABURRA BALL: YES OR NO? Yes, but with pitches that are still conducive to a result. Otherwise absolutely not!
OPPONENT YOU MOST LOOK FORWARD TO PLAYING AGAINST? George Bartlett – we've grown up playing together
FAVOURITE WARM-UP SONG? Nuvole Bianche by Ludovico Einaudi
SPECIALITY SUBJECT IN A PUB QUIZ (EXCLUDING SPORT)? Archeology
WHICH PUBLIC FIGURE INSPIRES YOU (EXCLUDING SPORTSPEOPLE)? David Attenborough
SURPRISING FACT ABOUT YOU: I've played international age group water polo
FILM YOU CAN WATCH OVER AND OVER: Top Gun: Maverick
NOTES: Green has been loaned out to the Foxes for the duration of the season but remains a Somerset player

Batting	Mat	Inns	NO	Runs	HS	Ave	SR	100	50	Ct	St
First-class	21	36	3	611	77	18.51	44.05	0	2	11	-
List A	17	14	6	399	157	49.87	121.27	1	1	3	-
T20s	73	48	15	630	47	19.09	136.36	0	0	26	-

Bowling	Mat	Balls	Mdns	Runs	Wkts	BB	Ave	4wI	5wI	SR	Econ
First-class	21	1500	60	795	21	4-28	37.85	-	0	71.42	3.18
List A	17	633	6	611	20	3-58	30.55	0	0	31.65	5.79
T20s	73	1117	1	1753	85	5-29	20.62	5	2	13.14	9.41

CAMERON GREEN

RHB / RFM / R0 / W0

FULL NAME: Cameron Donald Green
BORN: June 3, 1999, Subiaco, Western Australia, Australia
SQUAD NO: TBC
TEAMS: Australia, Gloucestershire, Mumbai Indians, Perth Scorchers, Royal Challengers Bangalore, Western Australia
ROLE: Allrounder
DEBUT: Test: 2020; ODI: 2020; T20I: 2022; First-class: 2017; List A: 2017; T20: 2019

BEST BATTING: 251 Western Australia vs Queensland, Brisbane, 2021
BEST BOWLING: 6-30 Western Australia vs Tasmania, Perth, 2018

NOTES: Gloucestershire have signed the big Australian allrounder for five Championship fixtures during the first two months of the season. A regular in all formats for Australia, Green has been sidelined with a lower back injury since last September but was expected to make a return to cricket ahead of the English season. Following his stint at Bristol, the 25-year-old is due to join up with the Australian Test squad to prepare for the World Test Championship final against South Africa at Lord's on June 11. This will be his first taste of county cricket. "Cameron Green's ability is unquestionable, and he is clearly first-class," said Mark Alleyne, Gloucestershire's head coach. "He usually operates in a key position for the best Test team in the world at the moment and having that pedigree in our camp is amazing for the players alongside him"

Batting	Mat	Inns	NO	Runs	HS	Ave	SR	100	50	Ct	St
Tests	28	43	5	1377	174*	36.23	48.57		6	31	-
ODIs	28	24	8	626	89*	39.12	82.80	0	2	13	-
T20Is	13	12	2	263	62*	26.30	152.90	0	3	6	-
First-class	61	96	15	3872	251	47.80	52.55	11	13	45	-
List A	48	43	12	1225	144	39.51	88.38	2	4	23	-
T20s	55	49	15	1076	100*	31.64	147.39	1	5	20	-

Bowling	Mat	Balls	Mdns	Runs	Wkts	BB	Ave	4wI	5wI	SR	Econ
Tests	28	2190	63	1236	35	5-27	35.31		1	62.57	3.38
ODIs	28	814	0	784	20	5-33	39.20	0	1	40.70	5.77
T20Is	13	188	0	279	12	3-35	23.25	0	0	15.66	8.90
First-class	61	4706	151	2582	77	6-30	33.53	-	3	61.11	3.29
List A	48	1376	4	1321	30	5-33	44.03	0	1	45.86	5.76
T20s	55	639	0	964	28	3-35	34.42	0	0	22.82	9.05

CHRIS GREEN RHB / OB

LANCASHIRE

FULL NAME: Christopher James Green
BORN: October 1, 1993, Durban, South Africa
SQUAD NO: 93
EDUCATION: Knox Grammar School, Wahroonga, New South Wales
TEAMS: Australia, Lancashire, Antigua & Barbuda Falcons, Guyana Amazon Warriors, Jamaica Tallawahs, Kolkata Knight Riders, Middlesex, Multan Sultans, New South Wales, Sydney Thunder, Trent Rockets
ROLE: Allrounder
DEBUT: T20I: 2023; First-class: 2022; List A: 2014; T20: 2015

BEST BATTING: 50 Sydney Thunder vs Sydney Sixers, Sydney, 2022 (T20)
BEST BOWLING: 5-32 Middlesex vs Kent, Canterbury, 2021 (T20)
COUNTY CAP: 2024 (Lancashire)

NOTES: Leading wicket-taker for Lancashire in last year's Blast, the Australian spin-bowling allrounder has signed a two-year deal for the club covering 2025 and 2026. Primarily a T20 contract, it also includes provision for Green to play in the County Championship and One-Day Cup, subject to availability. Green, who made a solitary T20I appearance for Australia in 2023, played 11 Blast fixtures last summer, taking 14 wickets, and also represented Lancs in the 50-over competition, notching a maiden List-A hundred – a 95-ball knock against Hampshire at Southampton. He also turned out for Trent Rockets in The Hundred. Lancashire's director of cricket performance, Mark Chilton, said: "One of our key priorities heading into the winter was to secure Chris' services. He made a huge impact for us on the field and had a number of options and offers to play around the world, but we are delighted that he has committed to being here"

Batting	Mat	Inns	NO	Runs	HS	Ave	SR	100	50	Ct	St
T20Is	1	1	1	2	2*	-	66.66	0	0	2	-
First-class	20	30	11	734	63*	38.63	51.14	0	6	12	-
List A	31	26	5	494	100	23.52	92.85	1	2	18	-
T20s	236	156	53	1673	50	16.24	134.81	0	1	134	-
Bowling	Mat	Balls	Mdns	Runs	Wkts	BB	Ave	4wI	5wI	SR	Econ
T20Is	1	24	0	36	0	0-36	-	-	-	-	9.00
First-class	20	3841	126	1633	45	6-83	36.28	-	2	85.35	2.55
List A	31	1346	8	1125	32	5-53	35.15	1	1	42.06	5.01
T20s	236	4695	7	5512	203	5-32	27.15	5	1	23.12	7.04

LEWIS GREGORY — RHB / RFM / R0 / W1 / MVP4

FULL NAME: Lewis Gregory
BORN: May 24, 1992, Plymouth, Devon
SQUAD NO: 24
HEIGHT: 6ft
NICKNAME: Mowgli
EDUCATION: Hele's School, Plymouth
TEAMS: England, Somerset, Brisbane Heat, Islamabad United, Joburg Super Kings, Karachi Kings, Peshawar Zalmi, Rangpur Rangers, Trent Rockets
ROLE: Allrounder
DEBUT: ODI: 2021; T20I: 2019; First-class: 2011; List A: 2010; T20: 2011

BEST BATTING: 137 Somerset vs Middlesex, Lord's, 2017
BEST BOWLING: 7-84 Somerset vs Nottinghamshire, Trent Bridge, 2023
COUNTY CAP: 2015

MOST EXCITING DAY AS A CRICKETER? Taking my maiden first-class five-wicket haul at Lord's and scoring my maiden first-class hundred at the same ground
CHILDHOOD SPORTING HERO? Tiger Woods
SURPRISING FACT ABOUT YOU: I'm a black belt in taekwondo

Batting	Mat	Inns	NO	Runs	HS	Ave	SR	100	50	Ct	St
ODIs	3	2	0	117	77	58.50	100.86	0	1	0	-
T20Is	9	7	1	45	15	7.50	109.75	0	0	0	-
First-class	129	189	21	4218	137	25.10	58.45	4	19	85	-
List A	79	59	6	1323	105*	24.96	100.83	1	8	27	-
T20s	236	186	50	2762	76*	20.30	137.75	0	8	102	-

Bowling	Mat	Balls	Mdns	Runs	Wkts	BB	Ave	4wI	5wI	SR	Econ
ODIs	3	114	1	97	4	3-44	24.25	0	0	28.50	5.10
T20Is	9	78	0	117	2	1-10	58.50	0	0	39.00	9.00
First-class	129	18164	655	10045	383	7-84	26.22	-	16	47.42	3.31
List A	79	3068	16	3043	110	4-23	27.66	6	0	27.89	5.95
T20s	236	3415	2	4995	197	5-24	25.35	5	1	17.33	8.77

NICK GUBBINS

LHB / LB / R1 / W0

HAMPSHIRE

FULL NAME: Nicholas Richard Trail Gubbins
BORN: December 31, 1993, Richmond, Surrey
SQUAD NO: 31
HEIGHT: 6ft
NICKNAME: Cathy
EDUCATION: Radley College, Oxfordshire;
University of Leeds
TEAMS: Hampshire, England Lions,
Middlesex, Southern Rocks, Tuskers
ROLE: Batter
DEBUT: First-class: 2013; List A: 2014; T20: 2015

BEST BATTING: 201* Middlesex vs Lancashire, Lord's, 2016
BEST BOWLING: 4-41 Tuskers vs Eagles, Harare, 2022
COUNTY CAP: 2022 (Hampshire); 2016 (Middlesex)

FIRST CRICKET CLUB? Stirlands CC, Chichester, West Sussex
EARLIEST CRICKETING MEMORY? Playing with my brother on the boundary while watching my dad play club cricket
THE KOOKABURRA BALL: YES OR NO? Yes. It brings in other skills and ways to take 20 wickets. You need to be inventive in the field and score big runs with the bat. And 70mph blokes can't just run up and lob it on a length
FAVOURITE WARM-UP SONG? Back to Bedlam by James Blunt (the whole album)
HOW MANY HOURS DO YOU SPEND ON YOUR PHONE A DAY? One
SPECIALITY SUBJECT IN A PUB QUIZ (EXCLUDING SPORT)? Harry Potter
ONE THING YOU WANT TO DO BEFORE YOU DIE: A skydive
SURPRISING FACT ABOUT YOU: I grew up in Singapore. And I'm highly allergic to Brazil nuts
FILM YOU CAN WATCH OVER AND OVER: The Shawshank Redemption

Batting	Mat	Inns	NO	Runs	HS	Ave	SR	100	50	Ct	St
First-class	134	233	12	8167	201*	36.95	48.70	19	41	48	-
List A	90	89	3	3460	141	40.23	88.78	9	19	31	-
T20s	49	44	1	641	57*	14.90	118.92	0	2	17	-
Bowling	Mat	Balls	Mdns	Runs	Wkts	BB	Ave	4wI	5wI	SR	Econ
First-class	134	407	10	243	6	4-41	40.50	-	0	67.83	3.58
List A	90	570	2	542	12	4-38	45.16	1	0	47.50	5.70
T20s	49	162	0	212	10	3-27	21.20	0	0	16.20	7.85

BROOKE GUEST

RHB / WK / R0 / W0

FULL NAME: Brooke David Guest
BORN: May 14, 1997, Whitworth Park, Manchester
SQUAD NO: 29
HEIGHT: 5ft 11in
NICKNAME: Guesty
EDUCATION: Kent Street Senior High School, Perth; Murdoch University, Perth
TEAMS: Derbyshire, Australia U19, Comilla Victorians, Lancashire
ROLE: Batter/wicketkeeper
DEBUT: First-class: 2018; List A: 2019; T20: 2020

BEST BATTING: 197 Derbyshire vs Durham, Derby, 2023

COUNTY CAP: 2022 (Derbyshire)

FIRST CRICKET CLUB? South Perth CC, Australia
EARLIEST CRICKETING MEMORY? Playing with my brother and dad in the garden
WHAT'S THE BIGGEST PRIZE IN DOMESTIC CRICKET? The County Championship
WHICH TEAMMATE HAS HAD THE BIGGEST IMPACT ON YOUR GAME? Wayne Madsen – so much experience to learn from
WHICH AWAY GROUND DO YOU MOST ENJOY VISITING? Chesterfield
WHAT DO YOU THINK OF THE CURRENT 50-OVER COMPETITION? It's providing an opportunity for younger players
FAVOURITE WARM-UP SONG? Greenlight by Pitbull
ONE THING YOU WANT TO DO BEFORE YOU DIE: Run a marathon
FILM YOU CAN WATCH OVER AND OVER: Any of the Harry Potter films

Batting	Mat	Inns	NO	Runs	HS	Ave	SR	100	50	Ct	St
First-class	56	92	3	2827	197	31.76	47.06	7	10	146	8
List A	32	29	2	911	88	33.74	80.90	0	6	30	3
T20s	58	53	23	852	54	28.40	127.35	0	1	33	7

Bowling	Mat	Balls	Mdns	Runs	Wkts	BB	Ave	4wI	5wI	SR	Econ
First-class	56	-	-	-	-	-	-	-	-	-	-
List A	32	-	-	-	-	-	-	-	-	-	-
T20s	58	-	-	-	-	-	-	-	-	-	-

LIAM GUTHRIE

LHB / LFM / R0 / W0

FULL NAME: Liam Christopher James Guthrie
BORN: April 9, 1997, Subiaco, Western Australia, Australia
SQUAD NO: TBC
TEAMS: Northamptonshire, Australia U19, Brisbane Heat, Queenland, Hobart Hurricanes
ROLE: Bowler
DEBUT: First-class: 2018; List A: 2021; T20: 2021

BEST BATTING: 19 Western Australia vs New South Wales, Sydney, 2019
BEST BOWLING: 6-60 Queensland vs Victoria, Melbourne, 2023

NOTES: The Australian left-armer, who holds a UK passport, joins Northants as a local player on a three-year contract. Guthrie made his Sheffield Shield debut aged 20 for Western Australia and played 12 first-class games before a switch to Queensland in 2022. The following year he took career-best first-class bowling figures for Queensland against Victoria, finishing with 6-60 at the MCG. During his time at Queensland and Brisbane Heat, Guthrie worked with Darren Lehmann, Northants' new head coach, who said: "We're really excited about Liam joining us as a local player for the next three years. He brings left-arm swing, genuine pace and having worked with him at Brisbane Heat and Queensland, his attitude is excellent and he has real wicket-taking abilities"

Batting	Mat	Inns	NO	Runs	HS	Ave	SR	100	50	Ct	St
First-class	18	27	7	164	19	8.20	35.57	0	0	11	-
List A	19	14	5	73	21	8.11	97.33	0	0	9	-
T20s	7	3	1	17	11*	8.50	141.66	0	0	3	-

Bowling	Mat	Balls	Mdns	Runs	Wkts	BB	Ave	4wI	5wI	SR	Econ
First-class	18	2935	81	1891	50	6-60	37.82	-	1	58.70	3.86
List A	19	807	4	746	27	4-15	27.62	1	0	29.88	5.54
T20s	7	132	0	204	6	2-32	34.00	0	0	22.00	9.27

SAM HAIN

RHB / RM / R1 / W0

FULL NAME: Samuel Robert Hain
BORN: July 16, 1995, Hong Kong
SQUAD NO: 16
HEIGHT: 6ft
EDUCATION: The Southport School, Queensland, Australia
TEAMS: England, Warwickshire, Trent Rockets, Australia U19, Brisbane Heat, Hobart Hurricanes, Manchester Originals, Paarl Royals, Welsh Fire
ROLE: Batter
DEBUT: ODI: 2023; First-class: 2014; List A: 2013; T20: 2016

WARWICKSHIRE

BEST BATTING: 208 Warwickshire vs Northamptonshire, Edgbaston, 2014

COUNTY CAP: 2018

NOTES: Hain has matured into one of the most consistent batters in the country in recent seasons, plundering runs in all formats and overtaking Ian Bell as the Bears' leading run-scorer in T20 cricket. He has played for three different teams in The Hundred as well as for Brisbane Heat and Hobart Hurricanes in Australia's Big Bash. Hain's form earned him an ODI debut against Ireland at Trent Bridge in 2023, where he grabbed his chance with both hands by scoring 89 in an England victory. He played in the next match against Ireland but since then has been curiously overlooked. Born and raised in Australia, the 28-year-old found a route into the county game after he was spotted by former Bears captain Michael Powell while on an exchange programme at a school in Edinburgh

Batting	Mat	Inns	NO	Runs	HS	Ave	SR	100	50	Ct	St
ODIs	2	2	0	106	89	53.00	106.00	0	1	0	-
First-class	126	201	20	7197	208	39.76	44.68	19	36	116	-
List A	64	62	10	3004	161*	57.76	86.77	10	17	23	-
T20s	160	154	36	4576	112*	38.77	132.75	1	34	79	-

Bowling	Mat	Balls	Mdns	Runs	Wkts	BB	Ave	4wI	5wI	SR	Econ
ODIs	2	-	-	-	-	-	-	-	-	-	-
First-class	126	43	0	35	0	0-4	-	-	-	-	4.88
List A	64	-	-	-	-	-	-	-	-	-	-
T20s	160	-	-	-	-	-	-	-	-	-	-

TOM HAINES

LHB / RM / R1 / W0

SUSSEX

FULL NAME: Thomas Jacob Haines
BORN: October 28, 1998, Crawley, West Sussex
SQUAD NO: 20
HEIGHT: 5ft 11in
NICKNAME: Hainus
EDUCATION: Tanbridge House School, Horsham; Hurstpierpoint College, West Sussex
TEAMS: Sussex, England Lions
ROLE: Batter
DEBUT: First-class: 2016; List A: 2021; T20: 2022

BEST BATTING: 243 Sussex vs Derbyshire, Derby, 2022
BEST BOWLING: 3-50 Sussex vs Worcestershire, Worcester, 2022
COUNTY CAP: 2021

FIRST CRICKET CLUB? Brockham Green CC, Surrey
BIGGEST INFLUENCE ON YOUR DEVELOPMENT AS A CRICKETER (EXCLUDING PARENTS)?
Former Sussex batter Jeremy Heath. He coached me from the age of 10 and I still speak to him now
FAVOURITE FORMAT? Four-day cricket
BIGGEST CRICKETING REGRET? Not bowling leggies
WHO WOULD YOU MOST LIKE TO HAVE A NET WITH? Brian Lara
HOBBIES? Tottenham Hotspur
MOST BEAUTIFUL THING YOU HAVE EVER SEEN? Lucas Moura's hat-trick for Spurs against Ajax in the 2019 Champions League semi-final

Batting	Mat	Inns	NO	Runs	HS	Ave	SR	100	50	Ct	St
First-class	73	125	3	4588	243	37.60	59.05	12	19	33	-
List A	23	23	0	945	129	41.08	83.70	2	5	10	-
T20s	4	4	0	52	27	13.00	118.18	0	0	0	-

Bowling	Mat	Balls	Mdns	Runs	Wkts	BB	Ave	4wI	5wI	SR	Econ
First-class	73	2732	88	1298	26	3-50	49.92	-	0	105.07	2.85
List A	23	120	1	122	1	1-22	122.00	0	0	120.00	6.10
T20s	4	-	-	-	-	-	-	-	-	-	-

HASEEB HAMEED — RHB / LB / R3 / W0 / MVP47

FULL NAME: Haseeb Hameed
BORN: January 17, 1997, Bolton, Lancashire
SQUAD NO: 99
HEIGHT: 6ft
NICKNAME: Has
EDUCATION: Bolton School
TEAMS: England, Nottinghamshire, Lancashire
ROLE: Batter
DEBUT: Test: 2016; First-class: 2015; List A: 2017; T20: 2023

NOTTINGHAMSHIRE

BEST BATTING: 247* Nottinghamshire vs Lancashire, Trent Bridge, 2024
BEST BOWLING: 1-0 Nottinghamshire vs Kent, Trent Bridge, 2023
COUNTY CAP: 2016 (Lancashire); 2020 (Nottinghamshire)

FIRST CRICKET CLUB? Tonge CC, Bolton
BIGGEST INFLUENCE ON YOUR DEVELOPMENT AS A CRICKETER (EXCLUDING PARENTS)?
John Stanworth, Academy director at Lancashire
WHICH TEAMMATE HAS HAD THE BIGGEST IMPACT ON YOUR GAME? Luke Fletcher
WHICH AWAY GROUND DO YOU MOST ENJOY VISITING? The Oval
WHO IS THE MOST TALENTED U19 TEENAGER IN THE COUNTY GAME? Farhan Ahmed (Not)
WHO IS THE TOUGHEST BOWLER TO FACE? Brett Hutton
CHOOSE A FANTASY SLIP CORDON TO SPEND A DAY IN THE FIELD WITH: Muhammad Ali (wk), Khabib Nurmagomedov, Cristiano Ronaldo

Batting	Mat	Inns	NO	Runs	HS	Ave	SR	100	50	Ct	St
Tests	10	19	1	439	82	24.38	32.02	0	4	7	-
First-class	131	226	22	7350	247*	36.02	43.93	15	40	80	-
List A	45	43	6	1414	114	38.21	81.97	4	7	15	-
T20s	2	2	0	41	23	20.50	110.81	0	0	2	-

Bowling	Mat	Balls	Mdns	Runs	Wkts	BB	Ave	4wI	5wI	SR	Econ
Tests	10	-	-	-	-	-	-	-	-	-	-
First-class	131	123	3	63	1	1-0	63.00	-	0	123.00	3.07
List A	45	-	-	-	-	-	-	-	-	-	-
T20s	2	-	-	-	-	-	-	-	-	-	-

MILES HAMMOND   LHB / OB / R0 / W0 / MVP14

GLOUCESTERSHIRE

FULL NAME: Miles Arthur Halhead Hammond
BORN: January 11, 1996, Cheltenham, Gloucestershire
SQUAD NO: 88
HEIGHT: 6ft 1in
NICKNAME: Hammer
EDUCATION: St Edward's School, Oxford; University of the Arts London
TEAMS: Gloucestershire, Birmingham Phoenix, England U19
ROLE: Batter
DEBUT: First-class: 2013; List A: 2013; T20: 2013

BEST BATTING: 169 Gloucestershire vs Hampshire, Cheltenham, 2022
BEST BOWLING: 2-37 Gloucestershire vs Leicestershire, Leicester, 2021
COUNTY CAP: 2013

FIRST CRICKET CLUB? Cumnor CC, Oxford
FAVOURITE FORMAT? Four-day cricket – it's the most satisfying form of the game
DESCRIBE YOURSELF IN THREE WORDS: Work in progress
HOBBIES? Doodling
FAVOURITE TOY AS A KID? A cricket bat
WHAT WOULD BE YOUR PERFECT BREAKFAST? Two croissants with some strawberry jam
SURPRISING FACT ABOUT YOU? I wear my house key around my neck

Batting	Mat	Inns	NO	Runs	HS	Ave	SR	100	50	Ct	St
First-class	76	134	8	4077	169	32.35	50.81	5	27	58	-
List A	20	18	1	669	157	39.35	91.64	2	3	8	-
T20s	111	104	6	2193	80	22.37	134.04	0	8	58	-

Bowling	Mat	Balls	Mdns	Runs	Wkts	BB	Ave	4wl	5wl	SR	Econ
First-class	76	921	12	712	6	2-37	118.66	-	0	153.50	4.63
List A	20	114	0	97	5	2-18	19.40	0	0	22.80	5.10
T20s	111	12	0	17	0	0-17	-	-	-	-	8.50

PETER HANDSCOMB   RHB / WK / R0 / W0 / MVP46

FULL NAME: Peter Stephen Patrick Handscomb
BORN: April 26, 1991, Melbourne, Australia
SQUAD NO: 29
HEIGHT: 6ft 4in
TEAMS: Australia, Leicestershire, Durham, Gloucestershire, Hobart Hurricanes, Melbourne Renegades, Melbourne Stars, Middlesex, Rising Pune Supergiants, Victoria, Yorkshire
ROLE: Batter/wicketkeeper
DEBUT: Test: 2016; ODI: 2017; T20I: 2019; First-class: 2011; List A: 2011; T20: 2012

LEICESTERSHIRE

BEST BATTING: 281* Victoria vs Western Australia, Melbourne, 2022

COUNTY CAP: 2015 (Gloucestershire)

NOTES: The Australian batter-wicketkeeper was outstanding for the Foxes last summer and has been appointed club captain as he returns to complete a two-year contract signed at the end of the 2023 season. Subject to availability, Handscomb, who turns 34 in April, is due to lead in all formats. Last year he was in scintillating form, the Foxes's leading run-scorer in four-day and 50-over cricket, with 894 Championship runs at an average of 74.50 alongside 539 at 67.37 in the One-Day Cup. Handscomb, who has also played for three other counties, was a key member of the Leicestershire side which won the 50-over trophy in 2023. This will be his third consecutive year at Grace Road. He has represented Australia in all three formats but hasn't played for his country since the most recent of his 20 Tests in March 2023

Batting	Mat	Inns	NO	Runs	HS	Ave	SR	100	50	Ct	St
Tests	20	35	6	1079	110	37.20	48.29	2	5	30	-
ODIs	22	20	1	632	117	33.26	97.38	1	4	14	-
T20Is	2	2	1	33	20*	33.00	100.00	0	0	0	-
First-class	189	320	25	11876	281*	40.25	53.05	26	70	321	9
List A	162	151	19	5249	140	39.76	91.78	8	33	149	7
T20s	136	120	26	2120	103*	22.55	117.12	1	7	65	15

Bowling	Mat	Balls	Mdns	Runs	Wkts	BB	Ave	4wI	5wI	SR	Econ
Tests	20	-	-	-	-	-	-	-	-	-	-
ODIs	22	-	-	-	-	-	-	-	-	-	-
T20Is	2	-	-	-	-	-	-	-	-	-	-
First-class	189	66	0	79	0	0-21	-	-	-	-	7.18
List A	162	-	-	-	-	-	-	-	-	-	-
T20s	136	-	-	-	-	-	-	-	-	-	-

OLIVER HANNON-DALBY   LHB / RMF / R0 / W3

FULL NAME: Oliver James Hannon-Dalby
BORN: June 20, 1989, Halifax, Yorkshire
SQUAD NO: 20
HEIGHT: 6ft 8in
NICKNAME: Owl Face
EDUCATION: Brooksbank School, West Yorkshire; Leeds Metropolitan University
TEAMS: Warwickshire, Yorkshire
ROLE: Bowler
DEBUT: First-class: 2008; List A: 2011; T20: 2012

BEST BATTING: 40 Warwickshire vs Somerset, Taunton, 2014
BEST BOWLING: 7-46 Warwickshire vs Northamptonshire, Edgbaston, 2023
COUNTY CAP: 2019 (Warwickshire); BENEFIT: 2024 (Warwickshire)

FIRST CRICKET CLUB? Copley CC, West Yorkshire
EARLIEST CRICKETING MEMORY? Playing on the boundary at Sowerby Bridge CC
WHAT'S THE BIGGEST PRIZE IN DOMESTIC CRICKET? The County Championship
THE KOOKABURRA BALL: YES OR NO? Yes, it's a good challenge and if it helps bridge the gap to international cricket then why not? I would still like the majority of games to use the Dukes though
OPPONENT YOU MOST LOOK FORWARD TO PLAYING AGAINST? Dom Sibley. He's my favourite run-out candidate
FAVOURITE WARM-UP SONG? Live Is Life by Opus (love that Maradona warm-up)
WHICH PUBLIC FIGURE INSPIRES YOU (EXCLUDING SPORTSPEOPLE)? Tobias, my chocolate Labrador
SURPRISING FACT ABOUT YOU: I am the reigning Warwickshire CCC karaoke champion
FILM YOU CAN WATCH OVER AND OVER: Any of the Lord of the Rings trilogy

Batting	Mat	Inns	NO	Runs	HS	Ave	SR	100	50	Ct	St
First-class	124	151	64	673	40	7.73	26.16	0	0	19	-
List A	68	23	14	130	21*	14.44	87.83	0	0	19	-
T20s	63	13	7	55	14*	9.16	88.70	0	0	13	-
Bowling	Mat	Balls	Mdns	Runs	Wkts	BB	Ave	4wI	5wI	SR	Econ
First-class	124	20568	805	10205	381	7-46	26.78	-	16	53.98	2.97
List A	68	3268	26	3202	118	5-27	27.13	4	2	27.69	5.87
T20s	63	1305	0	1919	75	4-20	25.58	2	0	17.40	8.82

SIMON HARMER

RHB / OB / R0 / W6

FULL NAME: Simon Ross Harmer
BORN: February 10, 1989, Pretoria, SA
SQUAD NO: 11
HEIGHT: 6ft 2in
NICKNAME: Big Red
EDUCATION: Pretoria Boys High School;
Nelson Mandela Metropolitan University
TEAMS: South Africa, Essex, Border, Eastern
Province, Jozi Stars, Northern, Sunrisers
Eastern Cape, Titans, Warriors
ROLE: Bowler
DEBUT: Test: 2015; First-class: 2009; List A: 2010;
T20: 2011

BEST BATTING: 102* Essex vs Surrey, The Oval, 2018
BEST BOWLING: 9-80 Essex vs Derbyshire, Chelmsford, 2021
COUNTY CAP: 2018

FIRST CRICKET CLUB? Pretoria High School Old Boys CC, South Africa
MOST EXCITING DAY AS A CRICKETER? Making my international debut for South Africa
at Newlands
CHILDHOOD SPORTING HERO? Jacques Kallis
WHAT WOULD YOU DO IF YOU WERE IN CHARGE OF COUNTY CRICKET? Create a revenue-
share model, like the one Cricket Australia implements, to commercialise the image rights
of county players; make it mandatory that every county has a director of cricket to bridge
the gap between the changeroom and the boardroom; allow overseas players who sign
multi-year deals the choice of a tier-two or tier-five visa so they can have similar rights to
their colleagues

Batting	Mat	Inns	NO	Runs	HS	Ave	SR	100	50	Ct	St
Tests	10	14	2	221	47	18.41	35.41	0	0	4	-
First-class	219	320	61	6200	102*	23.93	47.37	2	32	234	-
List A	98	83	25	1223	68	21.08	97.99	0	1	64	-
T20s	198	116	39	1145	43	14.87	125.00	0	0	110	-

Bowling	Mat	Balls	Mdns	Runs	Wkts	BB	Ave	4wI	5wI	SR	Econ
Tests	10	2105	68	1075	39	4-61	27.56	-	0	53.97	3.06
First-class	219	52091	2024	24921	947	9-80	26.31	-	57	55.00	2.87
List A	98	4734	29	3858	100	4-42	38.58	1	0	47.34	4.88
T20s	198	3696	2	4727	167	4-18	28.30	5	0	22.13	7.67

JAMES HARRIS
RHB / RMF / R0 / W3

GLAMORGAN

FULL NAME: James Alexander Russell Harris
BORN: May 16, 1990, Morriston, Swansea
SQUAD NO: 9
HEIGHT: 6ft 1in
NICKNAME: Bones
EDUCATION: Pontarddulais Comprehensive School, Swansea; Gorseinon College, Swansea
TEAMS: Glamorgan, England Lions, Kent, Middlesex
ROLE: Bowler
DEBUT: First-class: 2007; List A: 2007; T20: 2008

BEST BATTING: 87* Glamorgan vs Nottinghamshire, Swansea, 2007
BEST BOWLING: 9-34 Middlesex vs Durham, Lord's, 2015
COUNTY CAP: 2010 (Glamorgan); 2015 (Middlesex)

FIRST CRICKET CLUB? Pontarddulais CC, South Wales
WHICH TEAMMATE HAS HAD THE BIGGEST IMPACT ON YOUR GAME? Three of them: Tim Murtagh, Steven Finn and Toby Roland-Jones. Spending nine years bowling with them made me a far better bowler and person
WHICH AWAY GROUND DO YOU MOST ENJOY VISITING? Lord's – no place like it. I'm very lucky for how much I've played there
IF YOU COULD PINCH A PLAYER FROM ANOTHER COUNTY, WHO WOULD IT BE? Any high-class spinner
HOW IS BAZBALL AFFECTING CHAMPIONSHIP CRICKET? Making everyone think more about how to push games forward. Players are definitely playing more expansively when conditions and match situations suit
WHAT DO YOU THINK OF THE CURRENT 50-OVER COMPETITION? Not sure any of the schedule is sustainable, but the One-Day Cup needs to find a better slot during the summer

Batting	Mat	Inns	NO	Runs	HS	Ave	SR	100	50	Ct	St
First-class	186	263	57	4561	87*	22.14	-	0	19	47	-
List A	72	44	9	469	117	13.40	73.05	1	0	15	-
T20s	60	30	14	168	18	10.50	101.81	0	0	8	-

Bowling	Mat	Balls	Mdns	Runs	Wkts	BB	Ave	4wI	5wI	SR	Econ
First-class	186	31774	973	18092	601	9-34	30.10	-	17	52.86	3.41
List A	72	3105	18	3052	96	4-38	31.79	3	0	32.34	5.89
T20s	60	1060	2	1652	48	4-23	34.41	1	0	22.08	9.35

MARCUS HARRIS

LHB / OB / R0 / W0

FULL NAME: Marcus Sinclair Harris
BORN: July 21, 1992, Perth, Australia
SQUAD NO: TBC
TEAMS: Australia, Lancashire, Gloucestershire, Leicestershire, Melbourne Renegades, Perth Scorchers, Victoria, Western Australia
ROLE: Batter
DEBUT: Test: 2018; First-class: 2011; List A: 2011; T20: 2014

BEST BATTING: 250* Victoria vs New South Wales, Melbourne, 2018

NOTES: The Australian opener has signed for Lancashire for the duration of the 2025 season and will be available in both the red-ball and 50-over formats. This will be Harris's third county, having previously represented Leicestershire and Gloucestershire. In two seasons with the Foxes, in 2021 and last year, the 32-year-old scored over 1,000 Championship runs at an average just below 50. His record for Gloucestershire is just as impressive, with 1,183 runs across two summers at Bristol. He has made nine Championship hundreds to date. Harris first made waves in 2011 when aged 18 he scored 157 for Western Australia in his third first-class match, but it was only after his move to Victoria five years later that he began to fulfil his talent. He scored a career-best 250 not out against New South Wales in the 2018/19 Sheffield Shield and made his Test debut that season. He said: "I am really excited by the opportunity to join Lancashire for the English summer and will give my all to help this great club win promotion back to Division One of the County Championship"

Batting	Mat	Inns	NO	Runs	HS	Ave	SR	100	50	Ct	St
Tests	14	26	2	607	79	25.29	45.91	0	3	8	-
First-class	175	315	19	11583	250*	39.13	52.78	29	49	91	-
List A	81	80	5	2614	142*	34.85	85.31	3	15	23	-
T20s	54	53	1	1012	85	19.46	118.64	0	4	20	-

Bowling	Mat	Balls	Mdns	Runs	Wkts	BB	Ave	4wl	5wl	SR	Econ
Tests	14	-	-	-	-	-	-	-	-	-	-
First-class	175	99	2	68	0	0-0	-	-	-	-	4.12
List A	81	-	-	-	-	-	-	-	-	-	-
T20s	54	-	-	-	-	-	-	-	-	-	-

CALVIN HARRISON

RHB / LB / R0 / W0

NOTTINGHAMSHIRE

FULL NAME: Calvin Grant Harrison
BORN: April 29, 1998, Durban, South Africa
SQUAD NO: 31
HEIGHT: 6ft 3in
EDUCATION: King's College, Taunton; Oxford Brookes University
TEAMS: Nottinghamshire, Trent Rockets, Hampshire, Manchester Originals
ROLE: Bowler
DEBUT: First-class: 2019; List A: 2023; T20: 2020

BEST BATTING: 52 Nottinghamshire vs Worcestershire, Trent Bridge, 2024
BEST BOWLING: 5-128 Nottinghamshire vs Worcestershire, Trent Bridge, 2024

FIRST CRICKET CLUB? Onslow CC, Wellington, New Zealand
WHICH AWAY GROUND DO YOU MOST ENJOY VISITING? The dust bowl at Old Trafford
WHO IS THE MOST TALENTED U19 TEENAGER IN THE COUNTY GAME? Farhan Ahmed (Not)

Batting	Mat	Inns	NO	Runs	HS	Ave	SR	100	50	Ct	St
First-class	20	27	4	489	52	21.26	39.08	0	1	34	-
List A	8	8	1	94	41	13.42	71.21	0	0	7	-
T20s	61	36	14	227	23	10.31	106.57	0	0	29	-

Bowling	Mat	Balls	Mdns	Runs	Wkts	BB	Ave	4wl	5wl	SR	Econ
First-class	20	2429	37	1505	40	5-128	37.62	-	1	60.72	3.71
List A	8	337	0	312	5	1-0	62.40	0	0	67.40	5.55
T20s	61	932	1	1190	53	5-11	22.45	2	1	17.58	7.66

TOM HARTLEY
LHB / SLA / R0 / W0

FULL NAME: Tom William Hartley
BORN: May 3, 1998, Ormskirk, Lancashire
SQUAD NO: 2
HEIGHT: 6ft 4in
NICKNAME: TDF
EDUCATION: Merchant Taylors' School, Crosby, Merseyside
TEAMS: England, Lancashire, Manchester Originals
ROLE: Bowler
DEBUT: Test: 2024; ODI: 2023; First-class: 2020; List A: 2023; T20: 2020

BEST BATTING: 73* Lancashire vs Essex, Chelmsford, 2023
BEST BOWLING: 7-62 England vs India, Hyderabad, 2024
COUNTY CAP: 2024

FIRST CRICKET CLUB? Ormskirk CC, Lancashire
BIGGEST INFLUENCE ON YOUR DEVELOPMENT AS A CRICKETER (EXCLUDING PARENTS)? My captain at Ormskirk CC – for giving me plenty of overs in my younger years
BEST PLAYER IN COUNTY CRICKET (EXCLUDING TEAMMATES)? Simon Harmer
WHICH COUNTY PLAYER WOULD YOU MOST LIKE TO GO FOR A DRINK WITH? Matt Parkinson – a great man with great stories to tell
DESCRIBE YOURSELF IN THREE WORDS: Tall, lanky, funny
HOBBIES? Gardening

Batting	Mat	Inns	NO	Runs	HS	Ave	SR	100	50	Ct	St
Tests	5	10	0	185	36	18.50	65.14	0	0	2	-
ODIs	2	1	1	12	12*	-	133.33	0	0	0	-
First-class	31	46	8	869	73*	22.86	53.21	0	3	16	-
List A	5	4	2	60	23	30.00	109.09	0	0	0	-
T20s	92	43	19	273	39	11.37	122.97	0	0	35	-

Bowling	Mat	Balls	Mdns	Runs	Wkts	BB	Ave	4wI	5wI	SR	Econ
Tests	5	1504	30	795	22	7-62	36.13	-	1	68.36	3.17
ODIs	2	60	0	48	0	0-48	-	-	-	-	4.80
First-class	31	5633	199	2667	67	7-62	39.80	-	2	84.07	2.84
List A	5	223	0	215	1	1-46	215.00	0	0	223.00	5.78
T20s	92	1460	1	1928	73	4-16	26.41	2	0	20.00	7.92

JAMES HAYES

RHB / RFM / RO / WO

NOTTINGHAMSHIRE

FULL NAME: James Philip Henry Hayes
BORN: June 27, 2001, Haywards Heath, Sussex
SQUAD NO: 35
HEIGHT: 6ft 3in
EDUCATION: King's College, Taunton; Richard Huish College
TEAMS: Nottinghamshire
ROLE: Bowler
DEBUT: List A: 2022

FIRST CRICKET CLUB? Cuckfield CC, West Sussex
WHICH TEAMMATE HAS HAD THE BIGGEST IMPACT ON YOUR GAME? Steven Mullaney – he helped develop my wobble seam and also linked me up with a club in Australia where I've been playing over the winter
WHAT PART OF THE SEASON DO YOU MOST ENJOY? The final red-ball block – when everyone's tired and winning means more
WHICH AWAY GROUND DO YOU MOST ENJOY VISITING? Durham – the hotel is lovely and so is the town in summer
IF YOU COULD PINCH A PLAYER FROM ANOTHER COUNTY, WHO WOULD IT BE? Ali Orr
HOW IS BAZBALL AFFECTING CHAMPIONSHIP CRICKET? It may be causing players to question their game and take a more aggressive approach
WHAT KEEPS YOU AWAKE AT NIGHT? Eating sugar too close to bedtime
WHAT'S THE SILLIEST OUTFIT YOU'VE EVER WORN? A morph suit
CHOOSE A FANTASY SLIP CORDON TO SPEND A DAY IN THE FIELD WITH: David Attenborough (wk), Warren Buffett, Tom Brady, Ryan Reynolds
SURPRISING FACT ABOUT YOU: I love the NFL

Batting	Mat	Inns	NO	Runs	HS	Ave	SR	100	50	Ct	St
List A	3	1	1	1	1*	-	100.00	0	0	0	-

Bowling	Mat	Balls	Mdns	Runs	Wkts	BB	Ave	4wI	5wI	SR	Econ
List A	3	120	1	118	3	2-58	39.33	0	0	40.00	5.90

JACK HAYNES

RHB / OB / R0 / W0

FULL NAME: Jack Alexander Haynes
BORN: January 30, 2001, Worcester
SQUAD NO: 30
HEIGHT: 6ft 1in
NICKNAME: Clunesy
EDUCATION: Malvern College
TEAMS: Nottinghamshire, England Lions, Oval Invincibles, Worcestershire
ROLE: Batter
DEBUT: First-class: 2019; List A: 2018; T20: 2020

BEST BATTING: 134* Worcestershire vs Durham, Chester-le-Street, 2023

FIRST CRICKET CLUB? Ombersley CC, Worcestershire
FAMILY TIES? My father Gavin played more than 200 matches for Worcestershire in the 1990s and my older brother Josh plays for Leeds/Bradford MCCU
BEST DELIVERY YOU HAVE EVER FACED? Joe Leach every ball in the nets
GREATEST PERFORMANCE YOU HAVE WITNESSED? Ben Stokes smashing 161 at New Road in the Championship in 2022
FAVOURITE FORMAT? Championship cricket
WHO WOULD YOU MOST LIKE TO HAVE A NET WITH? Graeme Hick
HOBBIES? Horse racing
FAVOURITE TOY AS A KID? A cricket bat

Batting	Mat	Inns	NO	Runs	HS	Ave	SR	100	50	Ct	St
First-class	59	92	7	2960	134*	34.82	52.03	5	15	43	-
List A	19	19	1	640	153	35.55	87.43	1	4	8	-
T20s	48	47	1	990	63	21.52	137.69	0	5	13	-

Bowling	Mat	Balls	Mdns	Runs	Wkts	BB	Ave	4wI	5wI	SR	Econ
First-class	59	-	-	-	-	-	-	-	-	-	-
List A	19	-	-	-	-	-	-	-	-	-	-
T20s	48	-	-	-	-	-	-	-	-	-	-

FREDDIE HELDREICH

LHB / SLW / RO / WO

FULL NAME: Frederick James Heldreich
BORN: September 12, 2001, Ipswich
SQUAD NO: 80
HEIGHT: 6ft 2in
EDUCATION: Framlingham College, Suffolk;
Loughborough University
TEAMS: Northamptonshire
ROLE: Bowler
DEBUT: List A: 2021; T20: 2021

WHICH TEAMMATE HAS HAD THE BIGGEST IMPACT ON YOUR GAME? Josh Cobb – he always backed me during my first two seasons playing in the T20 Blast. We spent a lot of time discussing plans and skills to improve my game

WHAT PART OF THE SEASON DO YOU MOST ENJOY? The T20 Blast

WHICH AWAY GROUND DO YOU MOST ENJOY VISITING? Edgbaston

IF YOU COULD PINCH A PLAYER FROM ANOTHER COUNTY, WHO WOULD IT BE? Sam Hain

HOW IS BAZBALL AFFECTING CHAMPIONSHIP CRICKET? It's allowing players to play their natural game

WHAT DO YOU THINK OF THE CURRENT 50-OVER COMPETITION? Good experience for the younger players coming through

WHAT KEEPS YOU AWAKE AT NIGHT? The fear of failure

WHAT'S THE SILLIEST OUTFIT YOU'VE EVER WORN? A ballerina costume

Batting	Mat	Inns	NO	Runs	HS	Ave	SR	100	50	Ct	St
List A	11	5	2	8	5	2.66	36.36	0	0	4	-
T20s	44	5	2	34	21*	11.33	62.96	0	0	6	-

Bowling	Mat	Balls	Mdns	Runs	Wkts	BB	Ave	4wI	5wI	SR	Econ
List A	11	363	0	405	6	2-69	67.50	0	0	60.50	6.69
T20s	44	741	0	1130	49	4-27	23.06	1	0	15.12	9.14

TOM HELM RHB / RFM / R0 / W0

FULL NAME: Thomas George Helm
BORN: May 7, 1994, Aylesbury, Buckinghamshire
SQUAD NO: 7
HEIGHT: 6ft 4in
NICKNAME: Cheddy
EDUCATION: The Misbourne School, Buckinghamshire
TEAMS: Middlesex, Birmingham Phoenix, England Lions, Glamorgan
ROLE: Bowler
DEBUT: First-class: 2013; List A: 2013; T20: 2016

BEST BATTING: 64 Middlesex vs Glamorgan, Lord's, 2024
BEST BOWLING: 6-110 Middlesex vs Surrey, Lord's, 2023
COUNTY CAP: 2019 (Middlesex)

FIRST CRICKET CLUB? Chesham CC, Buckinghamshire
WHAT'S THE BIGGEST PRIZE IN DOMESTIC CRICKET? Winning the County Championship
THE KOOKABURRA BALL: YES OR NO? Yes, when played on good wickets that offer some reverse swing for the bowlers
OPPONENT YOU MOST LOOK FORWARD TO PLAYING AGAINST? Miles Hammond, always a fun joust
FAVOURITE WARM-UP SONG? Here Comes The Hot Stepper by Ini Kamoze
HOW MANY HOURS DO YOU SPEND ON YOUR PHONE A DAY? Less than one
ONE THING YOU WANT TO DO BEFORE YOU DIE: Visit Hawaii
HOBBY YOU WOULD LIKE TO LEARN: Surfing
WHICH PUBLIC FIGURE INSPIRES YOU (EXCLUDING SPORTSPEOPLE)? Big Zuu
SURPRISING FACT ABOUT YOU: I'm losing my hair
FILM YOU CAN WATCH OVER AND OVER: Top Gun

Batting	Mat	Inns	NO	Runs	HS	Ave	SR	100	50	Ct	St
First-class	60	83	23	1085	64	18.08	49.20	0	4	23	-
List A	40	24	8	206	30	12.87	71.28	0	0	15	-
T20s	101	49	26	275	28*	11.95	101.47	0	0	22	-

Bowling	Mat	Balls	Mdns	Runs	Wkts	BB	Ave	4wI	5wI	SR	Econ
First-class	60	9632	290	5241	167	6-110	31.38	-	5	57.67	3.26
List A	40	1816	11	1742	56	5-33	31.10	2	2	32.42	5.75
T20s	101	1945	0	2943	109	5-11	27.00	1	1	17.84	9.07

MOISES HENRIQUES RHB / RMF

NOTTINGHAMSHIRE

FULL NAME: Moises Constantino Henriques
BORN: February 1, 1987, Funchal, Portugal
SQUAD NO: TBC
HEIGHT: 6ft 1in
NICKNAME: Moey
TEAMS: Australia, Nottinghamshire, Delhi
Daredevils, Glamorgan, Kolkata Knight
Riders, New South Wales, Punjab Kings, Royal
Challengers Bangalore, Sunrisers, Surrey,
Sydney Sixers
ROLE: Allrounder
DEBUT: Test: 2013; ODI: 2009; T20I: 2009;
First-class: 2006; List A: 2006; T20: 2006

BEST BATTING: 77 Sydney Sixers vs Perth Scorchers, Canberra, 2015 (T20)
BEST BOWLING: 3-11 New South Wales vs Victoria, Delhi, 2009 (T20)

NOTES: Nottinghamshire will be desperate to improve upon last place in the North Group in the 2024 Blast and signing veteran Aussie Moises Henriques is a step in the right direction. The short-format specialist, capped 44 times by his country, has previously played for both Glamorgan and Surrey and has experience of franchise cricket all round the world, including in the IPL. Henriques, now 38, has been with the Sydney Sixers for 14 years and captained them to two Big Bash titles. He will join up with fellow Aussie Daniel Sams as the Outlaws attempt to revive their form in a competition in which traditionally they are strong contenders. "Moises's experience and quality as a player will add a huge amount to our squad, while he'll also be another leader in the group," said Peter Moores, Notts' head coach. "His ability to negotiate a run chase or set a score with the bat has been well proven over the years, providing experience and stability in a new-look batting line-up"

Batting	Mat	Inns	NO	Runs	HS	Ave	SR	100	50	Ct	St
Tests	4	8	1	164	81*	23.42	47.39	0	2	1	-
ODIs	16	15	2	117	22	9.00	60.93	0	0	6	-
T20Is	24	21	4	355	62*	20.88	124.56	0	2	6	-
First-class	131	219	23	6830	265	34.84	54.39	13	31	58	-
List A	136	126	20	3672	164*	34.64	86.84	4	17	51	-
T20s	282	255	57	5396	77	27.25	127.38	0	26	127	-

Bowling	Mat	Balls	Mdns	Runs	Wkts	BB	Ave	4wI	5wI	SR	Econ
Tests	4	330	12	164	2	1-48	82.00	-	0	165.00	2.98
ODIs	16	402	1	347	8	3-32	43.37	0	0	50.25	5.17
T20Is	24	138	0	194	7	3-22	27.71	0	0	19.71	8.43
First-class	131	7629	252	3906	127	5-17	30.75	-	2	60.07	3.07
List A	136	3729	21	3266	86	4-17	37.97	2	0	43.36	5.25
T20s	282	2534	0	3458	119	3-11	29.05	0	0	21.29	8.18

MATT HENRY

RHB / RFM / RO / W1

FULL NAME: Matthew James Henry
BORN: December 14, 1991, Christchurch, New Zealand
SQUAD NO: 21
HEIGHT: 6ft 2in
EDUCATION: St Bede's College, Christchurch
TEAMS: New Zealand, Somerset, Welsh Fire, Derbyshire, Canterbury, Kent, Kings XI Punjab, Lucknow Super Giants, Worcestershire
ROLE: Bowler
DEBUT: Test: 2015; ODI: 2014; T20I: 2014; First-class: 2011; List A: 2011; T20: 2011

BEST BATTING: 81 Kent vs Derbyshire, Derby, 2018
BEST BOWLING: 7-23 New Zealand vs South Africa, Christchurch, 2022
COUNTY CAP: 2018 (Kent)

NOTES: The veteran Kiwi seamer returns to Taunton between April 7 and June 25 and will be available for seven Championship and eight T20 fixtures. A key member of their T20 Blast title-winning side in 2023, Henry took 31 wickets in the competition that season, including 4-24 against Essex in the final. He returns to the southwest after being named in Wisden's World Test Championship XI for 2023-25 and brings with him bags of international experience. Somerset's director of cricket, Andy Hurry, said: "Matt is a world-class bowler, and we are delighted to be able to welcome back a player of his ability. He understands what it means to represent Somerset County Cricket Club and there is no doubt that the squad as a whole will benefit from his quality and experience"

Batting	Mat	Inns	NO	Runs	HS	Ave	SR	100	50	Ct	St
Tests	30	42	6	649	72	18.02	77.81	0	4	13	-
ODIs	91	38	12	270	48*	10.38	93.10	0	0	31	-
T20Is	21	7	3	24	12	6.00	88.88	0	0	4	-
First-class	106	145	21	2368	81	19.09	79.86	0	9	45	-
List A	174	90	24	770	48*	11.66	107.24	0	0	66	-
T20s	152	77	31	587	44	12.76	149.36	0	0	62	-

Bowling	Mat	Balls	Mdns	Runs	Wkts	BB	Ave	4wI	5wI	SR	Econ
Tests	30	6750	230	3581	120	7-23	29.84		4	56.25	3.18
ODIs	91	4734	57	4094	165	5-30	24.81	12	3	28.69	5.18
T20Is	21	462	1	639	27	3-32	23.66	0	0	17.11	8.29
First-class	106	22498	861	11260	488	7-23	23.07	-	25	46.10	3.00
List A	174	8775	110	7532	290	6-45	25.97	15	5	30.25	5.15
T20s	152	3050	7	4219	178	5-18	23.70	3	1	17.13	8.29

RYAN HIGGINS RHB / RMF / R1 / W2 / MVP28

FULL NAME: Ryan Francis Higgins
BORN: January 6, 1995, Harare, Zimbabwe
SQUAD NO: 29
HEIGHT: 5ft 11in
NICKNAME: Fizzer
EDUCATION: Peterhouse School, Marondera, Zimbabwe; Bradfield College, Reading
TEAMS: Middlesex, Boost Defenders, England U19, Gloucestershire, London Spirit, Southern Rocks, Welsh Fire
ROLE: Allrounder
DEBUT: First-class: 2017; List A: 2014; T20: 2014

BEST BATTING: 221 Middlesex vs Glamorgan, Lord's, 2024
BEST BOWLING: 7-42 Gloucestershire vs Warwickshire, Bristol, 2020
COUNTY CAP: 2018 (Gloucestershire); 2023 (Middlesex)

FIRST CRICKET CLUB? Falkland CC, Berkshire
THE KOOKABURRA BALL: YES OR NO? Yes, if the Test team use it in England as well
OPPONENT YOU MOST LOOK FORWARD TO PLAYING AGAINST? James Anderson
FAVOURITE WARM-UP SONG? Blah Blah Blah by Armin van Buuren
HOW MANY HOURS DO YOU SPEND ON YOUR PHONE A DAY? None at a cricket game obviously. Three hours when I'm chilling at home
SPECIALITY SUBJECT IN A PUB QUIZ (EXCLUDING SPORT)? Countries
WHICH PUBLIC FIGURE INSPIRES YOU (EXCLUDING SPORTSPEOPLE)? Winston Churchill
FILM YOU CAN WATCH OVER AND OVER: Both Top Gun films

Batting	Mat	Inns	NO	Runs	HS	Ave	SR	100	50	Ct	St
First-class	96	152	16	5098	221	37.48	62.44	12	22	46	-
List A	44	40	5	1174	89	33.54	100.77	0	8	7	-
T20s	128	115	29	2095	77*	24.36	133.43	0	6	39	-

Bowling	Mat	Balls	Mdns	Runs	Wkts	BB	Ave	4wl	5wl	SR	Econ
First-class	96	15473	639	7158	281	7-42	25.47	-	7	55.06	2.77
List A	44	1449	4	1285	36	4-33	35.69	3	0	40.25	5.32
T20s	128	1553	0	2394	93	5-13	25.74	1	1	16.69	9.24

GEORGE HILL

RHB / RMF / RO / WO

FULL NAME: George Christopher Hindley Hill
BORN: January 24, 2001, Keighley, Yorkshire
SQUAD NO: 18
HEIGHT: 6ft 3in
EDUCATION: Sedbergh School, Cumbria
TEAMS: Yorkshire, England U19
ROLE: Allrounder
DEBUT: First-class: 2020; List A: 2021; T20: 2020

BEST BATTING: 169* Yorkshire vs Middlesex, Headingley, 2024
BEST BOWLING: 6-26 Yorkshire vs Lancashire, Old Trafford, 2022

FIRST CRICKET CLUB? Olicanians CC, Ilkley, West Yorkshire
EARLIEST CRICKETING MEMORY? Playing in the back garden with my grandad and dad
WHAT'S THE BIGGEST PRIZE IN DOMESTIC CRICKET? Winning Division One of the County Championship
OPPONENT YOU MOST LOOK FORWARD TO PLAYING AGAINST? Dom Leech, a former Yorkshire teammate and a best mate. Really hope he doesn't hit me on the shins!
FAVOURITE WARM-UP SONG? Lovely Day by Bill Withers
SPECIALITY SUBJECT IN A PUB QUIZ (EXCLUDING SPORT)? The Cold War
ONE THING YOU WANT TO DO BEFORE YOU DIE: Go to the Amazon rainforest
WHICH PUBLIC FIGURE INSPIRES YOU (EXCLUDING SPORTSPEOPLE)? Bill Withers
SURPRISING FACT ABOUT YOU: I'm starting to go grey
FILM YOU CAN WATCH OVER AND OVER: Dead Poets Society

Batting	Mat	Inns	NO	Runs	HS	Ave	SR	100	50	Ct	St
First-class	49	76	6	2327	169*	33.24	53.35	4	13	31	-
List A	30	27	3	552	130	23.00	83.25	1	3	6	-
T20s	20	12	3	121	19*	13.44	99.18	0	0	7	-

Bowling	Mat	Balls	Mdns	Runs	Wkts	BB	Ave	4wI	5wI	SR	Econ
First-class	49	3883	151	1916	74	6-26	25.89	-	2	52.47	2.96
List A	30	868	8	691	32	6-28	21.59	0	1	27.12	4.77
T20s	20	111	0	169	2	1-9	84.50	0	0	55.50	9.13

LEWIS HILL

RHB / WK / RO / WO

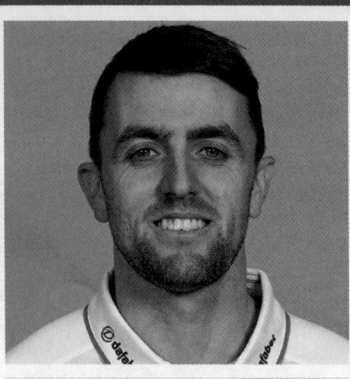

FULL NAME: Lewis John Hill
BORN: October 5, 1990, Leicester
SQUAD NO: 23
HEIGHT: 5ft 8in
NICKNAME: Hilly
EDUCATION: Hastings High School, Hinckley; John Cleveland College, Hinckley
TEAMS: Leicestershire
ROLE: Batter
DEBUT: First-class: 2015; List A: 2012; T20: 2015

BEST BATTING: 162* Leicestershire vs Derbyshire, Leicester, 2023

COUNTY CAP: 2021

FIRST CRICKET CLUB? Lutterworth CC, Leicestershire
WHICH TEAMMATE HAS HAD THE BIGGEST IMPACT ON YOUR GAME? Harry Swindells with his match-winning hundred in the 2023 One-Day Cup final
WHAT PART OF THE SEASON DO YOU MOST ENJOY? The Championship phases
IF YOU COULD PINCH A PLAYER FROM ANOTHER COUNTY, WHO WOULD IT BE? Tom Abell
HOW IS BAZBALL AFFECTING CHAMPIONSHIP CRICKET? Batting strike-rates are going up
WHO IS THE TOUGHEST BOWLER TO FACE? James Pattinson – fast and skilful
SURPRISING FACT ABOUT YOU? I was targeted by armed robbers twice while working at my local newsagents

Batting	Mat	Inns	NO	Runs	HS	Ave	SR	100	50	Ct	St
First-class	90	151	12	4217	162*	30.33	53.76	7	21	108	3
List A	77	72	3	1755	118	25.43	92.31	3	8	33	2
T20s	85	70	12	1097	59	18.91	125.08	0	4	34	3

Bowling	Mat	Balls	Mdns	Runs	Wkts	BB	Ave	4wI	5wI	SR	Econ
First-class	90	54	0	47	0	0-4	-	-	-	-	5.22
List A	77	-	-	-	-	-	-	-	-	-	-
T20s	85	-	-	-	-	-	-	-	-	-	-

DANIEL HOGG

RHB / RMF / RO / WO

FULL NAME: Daniel Maxwell Hogg
BORN: December 19, 2004, Manchester
SQUAD NO: TBC
HEIGHT: 6ft 7in
NICKNAME: Hoggy
EDUCATION: St Joseph's Primary School, Stanley; Durham Cathedral School
TEAMS: Durham, England U19
ROLE: Bowler
DEBUT: First-class: 2024; List A: 2024

DURHAM

BEST BATTING: 6 Durham vs Surrey, The Oval, 2024
BEST BOWLING: 7-66 Durham vs Nottinghamshire, Chester-le-Street, 2024

FIRST CRICKET CLUB? Beamish & East Stanley CC, Stanley, County Durham
EARLIEST CRICKETING MEMORY? Kwik Cricket during PE lessons at school
WHAT'S THE BIGGEST PRIZE IN DOMESTIC CRICKET? The County Championship
THE KOOKABURRA BALL: YES OR NO? No, it gets too scuffed up in England
OPPONENT YOU MOST LOOK FORWARD TO PLAYING AGAINST? Rory Burns – we had a good battle last year and I look forward to the next time
FAVOURITE WARM-UP SONG? We Are the People by Empire of the Sun
HOW MANY HOURS DO YOU SPEND ON YOUR PHONE A DAY? Three to four
SPECIALITY SUBJECT IN A PUB QUIZ (EXCLUDING SPORT)? National flags
HOBBY YOU WOULD LIKE TO LEARN: To play the piano better
SURPRISING FACT ABOUT YOU: I've never drunk coffee
FILM YOU CAN WATCH OVER AND OVER: Cars

Batting	Mat	Inns	NO	Runs	HS	Ave	SR	100	50	Ct	St
First-class	4	5	0	9	6	1.80	15.00	0	0	0	-
List A	2	2	2	3	2*	-	33.33	0	0	0	-

Bowling	Mat	Balls	Mdns	Runs	Wkts	BB	Ave	4wI	5wI	SR	Econ
First-class	4	453	20	276	12	7-66	23.00	-	1	37.75	3.65
List A	2	54	0	32	1	1-13	32.00	0	0	54.00	3.55

MAX HOLDEN

LHB / OB / R0 / W0

FULL NAME: Max David Edward Holden
BORN: December 18, 1997, Cambridge
SQUAD NO: 4
HEIGHT: 6ft 1in
NICKNAME: Pepsi
EDUCATION: Sawston Village College, Cambridge; Hills Road Sixth Form College, Cambridge
TEAMS: Middlesex, England Lions, Manchester Originals, Northamptonshire
ROLE: Batter
DEBUT: First-class: 2017; List A: 2017; T20: 2018

BEST BATTING: 211* Middlesex vs Northamptonshire, Northampton, 2024
BEST BOWLING: 2-59 Northamptonshire vs Kent, Beckenham, 2017
COUNTY CAP: 2023 (Middlesex)

FIRST CRICKET CLUB? Cambridge St Giles CC, Cambridgeshire
THE KOOKABURRA BALL: YES OR NO? Yes, it's about time that batters had it their way
OPPONENT YOU MOST LOOK FORWARD TO PLAYING AGAINST? None of them
FAVOURITE WARM-UP SONG? Delliah (pull me out of this) by Fred Again
SPECIALITY SUBJECT IN A PUB QUIZ (EXCLUDING SPORT)? Harry Potter
ONE THING YOU WANT TO DO BEFORE YOU DIE: Climb a mountain
SURPRISING FACT ABOUT YOU: My grandma is from Singapore
FILM YOU CAN WATCH OVER AND OVER: The Dark Knight

Batting	Mat	Inns	NO	Runs	HS	Ave	SR	100	50	Ct	St
First-class	94	162	8	4523	211*	29.37	48.33	5	22	32	-
List A	24	22	2	845	166	42.25	95.05	1	5	7	-
T20s	87	86	10	2029	121*	26.69	143.08	2	9	29	-

Bowling	Mat	Balls	Mdns	Runs	Wkts	BB	Ave	4wI	5wI	SR	Econ
First-class	94	642	7	460	5	2-59	92.00	-	0	128.40	4.29
List A	24	126	1	104	1	1-29	104.00	0	0	126.00	4.95
T20s	87	6	0	12	0	0-12	-	-	-	-	12.00

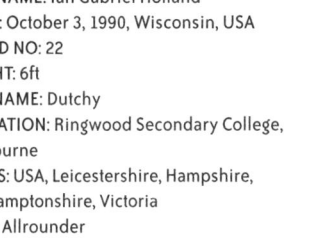

IAN HOLLAND

RHB / RMF / RO / WO

FULL NAME: Ian Gabriel Holland
BORN: October 3, 1990, Wisconsin, USA
SQUAD NO: 22
HEIGHT: 6ft
NICKNAME: Dutchy
EDUCATION: Ringwood Secondary College, Melbourne
TEAMS: USA, Leicestershire, Hampshire, Northamptonshire, Victoria
ROLE: Allrounder
DEBUT: ODI: 2019; T20I: 2021; First-class: 2016; List A: 2017; T20: 2017

LEICESTERSHIRE

BEST BATTING: 146* Hampshire vs Middlesex, Southampton, 2021
BEST BOWLING: 6-60 Hampshire vs Surrey, Arundel, 2020

FIRST CRICKET CLUB? Ringwood CC, Victoria, Australia
EARLIEST CRICKETING MEMORY? Backyard cricket with my brother
WHAT'S THE BIGGEST PRIZE IN DOMESTIC CRICKET? The County Championship
THE KOOKABURRA BALL: YES OR NO? Yes, we love the bird
OPPONENT YOU MOST LOOK FORWARD TO PLAYING AGAINST? My old Hampshire teammate Kyle Abbott
FAVOURITE WARM-UP SONG? Born in the U.S.A. by Bruce Springsteen
HOW MANY HOURS DO YOU SPEND ON YOUR PHONE A DAY? One
SPECIALITY SUBJECT IN A PUB QUIZ (EXCLUDING SPORT)? NFL fantasy knowledge
ONE THING YOU WANT TO DO BEFORE YOU DIE: Watch the Green Bay Packers at Lambou Field
SURPRISING FACT ABOUT YOU: I have three passports
FILM YOU CAN WATCH OVER AND OVER? Shrek

Batting	Mat	Inns	NO	Runs	HS	Ave	SR	100	50	Ct	St
ODIs	15	14	0	368	75	26.28	77.47	0	2	6	-
T20Is	6	3	1	47	39*	23.50	90.38	0	0	1	-
First-class	77	124	11	2928	146*	25.91	43.67	5	13	38	-
List A	57	52	13	926	75	23.74	86.62	0	5	23	-
T20s	32	20	11	248	65	27.55	115.88	0	1	10	-

Bowling	Mat	Balls	Mdns	Runs	Wkts	BB	Ave	4wl	5wl	SR	Econ
ODIs	15	628	6	466	19	3-11	24.52	0	0	33.05	4.45
T20Is	6	138	3	89	10	2-3	8.90	0	0	13.80	3.86
First-class	77	7276	301	3390	110	6-60	30.81	-	1	66.14	2.79
List A	57	2498	22	1966	71	5-35	27.69	1	1	35.18	4.72
T20s	32	427	3	491	19	2-3	25.84	0	0	22.47	6.89

LUKE HOLLMAN

LHB / LB / RO / WO

FULL NAME: Luke Barnaby Kurt Hollman
BORN: September 16, 2000, Islington, London
SQUAD NO: 56
HEIGHT: 6ft 3in
NICKNAME: Donny
EDUCATION: Acland Burghley School, Camden, London
TEAMS: Middlesex, England U19
ROLE: Allrounder
DEBUT: First-class: 2021; List A: 2021; T20: 2020

BEST BATTING: 82 Middlesex vs Sussex, Hove, 2022
BEST BOWLING: 5-65 Middlesex vs Sussex, Hove, 2021

FIRST CRICKET CLUB? North Middlesex CC, London
EARLIEST CRICKETING MEMORY? Hitting tennis balls in the back garden with my parents when I was four
THE KOOKABURRA BALL: YES OR NO? Yes. But it has to be used in the middle of summer to allow more spin to be bowled and reverse swing to come into play
OPPONENT YOU MOST LOOK FORWARD TO PLAYING AGAINST? Tom Lammonby – he's a good friend
FAVOURITE WARM-UP SONG? Chihiro by Gravagerz
HOW MANY HOURS DO YOU SPEND ON YOUR PHONE A DAY? Three
ONE THING YOU WANT TO DO BEFORE YOU DIE: Visit Machu Picchu
HOBBY YOU WOULD LIKE TO LEARN: Water ski
SURPRISING FACT ABOUT YOU: My third cousin is Jack Lynch, the former prime minister of Ireland
FILM YOU CAN WATCH OVER AND OVER: The Covenant

Batting	Mat	Inns	NO	Runs	HS	Ave	SR	100	50	Ct	St
First-class	34	51	2	1146	82	23.38	49.22	0	5	19	-
List A	26	22	5	371	38*	21.82	88.12	0	0	11	-
T20s	59	53	11	749	51	17.83	130.26	0	1	29	-

Bowling	Mat	Balls	Mdns	Runs	Wkts	BB	Ave	4wI	5wI	SR	Econ
First-class	34	3916	73	2506	57	5-65	43.96	-	2	68.70	3.83
List A	26	1374	4	1220	43	4-34	28.37	4	0	31.95	5.32
T20s	59	944	0	1324	61	5-16	21.70	1	1	15.47	8.41

JACK HOME

RHB / RFM / R0 / W0

FULL NAME: Jack Edward Home
BORN: May 2, 2006, Shrewsbury, Shropshire
SQUAD NO: 24
HEIGHT: 6ft
NICKNAME: Homey
EDUCATION: Shrewsbury School; Prestfelde School, Shrewsbury
TEAMS: Worcestershire, England U19
ROLE: Bowler
DEBUT: First-class: 2024; List A: 2024; T20: 2024

WORCESTERSHIRE

BEST BATTING: 29 Worcestershire vs Warwickshire, Worcester, 2024
BEST BOWLING: 1-25 Worcestershire vs Lancashire, Worcester, 2024

FIRST CRICKET CLUB? Shifnal CC, Shropshire
EARLIEST CRICKETING MEMORY? Playing upstairs in my corridor at home
THE KOOKABURRA BALL: YES OR NO? Yes, but only for the first four games when pitches could potentially be more seamer-friendly
OPPONENT YOU MOST LOOK FORWARD TO PLAYING AGAINST? Joe Root – would love to see how he bats
FAVOURITE WARM-UP SONG? Cry by Take That
HOW MANY HOURS DO YOU SPEND ON YOUR PHONE A DAY? Three
SPECIALITY SUBJECT IN A PUB QUIZ (EXCLUDING SPORT)? WW1 and WW2
HOBBY YOU WOULD LIKE TO LEARN: Coding
WHICH PUBLIC FIGURE INSPIRES YOU (EXCLUDING SPORTSPEOPLE)? David Attenborough
SURPRISING FACT ABOUT YOU: I used to be a male model
FILM YOU CAN WATCH OVER AND OVER: War Dogs

Batting	Mat	Inns	NO	Runs	HS	Ave	SR	100	50	Ct	St
First-class	2	3	2	45	29	45.00	42.85	0	0	1	-
List A	5	1	1	5	5*	-	166.66	0	0	0	-
T20s	1	1	1	1	1*	-	100.00	0	0	0	-

Bowling	Mat	Balls	Mdns	Runs	Wkts	BB	Ave	4wI	5wI	SR	Econ
First-class	2	102	1	78	1	1-25	78.00	-	0	102.00	4.58
List A	5	226	1	231	16	6-51	14.43	0	1	14.12	6.13
T20s	1	24	0	33	1	1-33	33.00	0	0	24.00	8.25

ALEX HORTON

GLAMORGAN

FULL NAME: Alex Jack Horton
BORN: January 7, 2004, Newport, Monmouthshire
SQUAD NO: 12
HEIGHT: 5ft 10in
NICKNAME: Horts
EDUCATION: St Edward's School, Oxford
TEAMS: Glamorgan, England U19
ROLE: Wicketkeeper
DEBUT: List A: 2023; T20: 2022

FIRST CRICKET CLUB? Newbridge CC, Monmouthshire, Wales
WHICH TEAMMATE HAS HAD THE BIGGEST IMPACT ON YOUR GAME? Colin Ingram
WHAT PART OF THE SEASON DO YOU MOST ENJOY? The T20 phase
WHICH AWAY GROUND DO YOU MOST ENJOY VISITING? Hove – a great place for a four-day trip
IF YOU COULD PINCH A PLAYER FROM ANOTHER COUNTY, WHO WOULD IT BE? Leus du Plooy
WHAT DO YOU THINK OF THE CURRENT 50-OVER COMPETITION? An excellent competition which should be given more emphasis in the county game
WHO IS THE TOUGHEST BOWLER TO FACE? Zafar Gohar – for his accuracy and ability to read batters
WHAT'S THE SILLIEST OUTFIT YOU'VE EVER WORN? The Manchester United kit when I was a boy
CHOOSE A FANTASY SLIP CORDON TO SPEND A DAY IN THE FIELD WITH: Jeremy Clarkson (wk), Viv Richards, Jennifer Aniston, Drake

Batting	Mat	Inns	NO	Runs	HS	Ave	SR	100	50	Ct	St
List A	7	6	1	81	44*	16.20	97.59	0	0	1	2
T20s	4	2	1	1	1*	1.00	16.66	0	0	0	1

Bowling	Mat	Balls	Mdns	Runs	Wkts	BB	Ave	4wl	5wl	SR	Econ
List A	7	-	-	-	-	-	-	-	-	-	-
T20s	4	-	-	-	-	-	-	-	-	-	-

ADAM HOSE

RHB / RM / R0 / W0

FULL NAME: Adam John Hose
BORN: October 25, 1992, Newport, Isle of Wight
SQUAD NO: 54
HEIGHT: 6ft 5in
NICKNAME: Pipe
EDUCATION: Carisbrooke School, Newport
TEAMS: Worcestershire, Adelaide Strikers, Northern Superchargers, Somerset, St Lucia Kings, Warwickshire, Wellington
ROLE: Batter
DEBUT: First-class: 2016; List A: 2015; T20: 2015

WORCESTERSHIRE

BEST BATTING: 111 Warwickshire vs Nottinghamshire, Edgbaston, 2019

FIRST CRICKET CLUB? Ventnor CC, Isle of Wight
WHICH COUNTY PLAYER WOULD YOU MOST LIKE TO GO FOR A DRINK WITH? Oliver Hannon-Dalby – an all-round top fella
MOST EXCITING DAY AS A CRICKETER? T20 Finals Day with Birmingham Bears in 2017
GREATEST PERFORMANCE YOU HAVE WITNESSED? Roelof van der Merwe's 165 not out to beat Surrey in the 2017 One-Day Cup. We were chasing 291 and it wasn't looking good at 22-5…
WHAT WOULD BE YOUR PERFECT BREAKFAST? Poached eggs and smashed avocado

Batting	Mat	Inns	NO	Runs	HS	Ave	SR	100	50	Ct	St
First-class	44	76	3	1838	111	25.17	50.48	1	11	24	-
List A	31	26	1	778	101*	31.12	88.50	1	4	17	-
T20s	172	163	27	3916	119	28.79	140.66	2	19	79	-

Bowling	Mat	Balls	Mdns	Runs	Wkts	BB	Ave	4wI	5wI	SR	Econ
First-class	44	-	-	-	-	-	-	-	-	-	-
List A	31	-	-	-	-	-	-	-	-	-	-
T20s	172	-	-	-	-	-	-	-	-	-	-

BENNY HOWELL

RHB / RM

HAMPSHIRE

FULL NAME: Benny Alexander Cameron Howell
BORN: October 5, 1988, Bordeaux, France
SQUAD NO: 7
HEIGHT: 5ft 11in
NICKNAME: Novak
EDUCATION: The Oratory School, Reading
TEAMS: Hampshire, Birminham Phoenix, Colombo Stars, Gloucestershire, Melbourne Renegades, Peshawar Zalmi, St Kitts & Nevis Patriots, Sylhet Strikers
ROLE: Allrounder
DEBUT: First-class: 2011; List A: 2010; T20: 2011

BEST BATTING: 62* Sylhet Strikers vs Comilla Victorians, Chittagong, 2024 (T20)
BEST BOWLING: 5-18 Gloucestershire vs Glamorgan, Cheltenham, 2019 (T20)
COUNTY CAP: 2012 (Gloucestershire)

FIRST CRICKET CLUB? Stoke Row CC, Oxfordshire
WHICH TEAMMATE HAS HAD THE BIGGEST IMPACT ON YOUR GAME? Michael Klinger, my former captain at Gloucestershire. He allowed me the freedom to bowl what I want and more generally fed belief into that team
WHAT PART OF THE SEASON DO YOU MOST ENJOY? The Hundred
WHICH AWAY GROUND DO YOU MOST ENJOY VISITING? Bristol – five minutes from home
WHO IS THE TOUGHEST BOWLER TO FACE? Sunil Narine – can't pick him
WHAT KEEPS YOU AWAKE AT NIGHT? My kids
WHAT'S THE SILLIEST OUTFIT YOU'VE EVER WORN? When I dressed up as Hamish Marshall in cricket whites for end-of-season celebrations
CHOOSE A FANTASY SLIP CORDON TO SPEND A DAY IN THE FIELD WITH: Dalai Lama (wk), Ricky Gervais, JFK, Prince Harry
NOTES: Howell signed a three-year white-ball contract with Hampshire in August 2022

Batting	Mat	Inns	NO	Runs	HS	Ave	SR	100	50	Ct	St
First-class	86	136	13	3378	163	27.46	54.35	2	18	52	-
List A	87	73	14	2090	122	35.42	91.14	1	13	29	-
T20s	241	195	60	3070	62*	22.74	135.78	0	9	96	-
Bowling	Mat	Balls	Mdns	Runs	Wkts	BB	Ave	4wI	5wI	SR	Econ
First-class	86	6455	237	3222	96	5-57	33.56	-	1	67.23	2.99
List A	87	3103	8	2698	79	3-37	34.15	0	0	39.27	5.21
T20s	241	4361	2	5315	231	5-18	23.00	3	1	18.87	7.31

FYNN HUDSON-PRENTICE RHB / RMF / RO / WO

FULL NAME: Fynn Jake Hudson-Prentice
BORN: January 12, 1996, Haywards Heath, Sussex
SQUAD NO: 33
HEIGHT: 6ft
NICKNAME: Jack Sparrow
EDUCATION: Warden Park School, Cuckfield, West Sussex; Bede's Senior School, Hailsham, East Sussex
TEAMS: Sussex, Derbyshire
ROLE: Allrounder
DEBUT: First-class: 2015; List A: 2014; T20: 2019

BEST BATTING: 99 Derbyshire vs Middlesex, Derby, 2019
BEST BOWLING: 5-50 Sussex vs Leicestershire, Leicester, 2024
COUNTY CAP: 2023 (Sussex)

FIRST CRICKET CLUB? St Andrews CC, Burgess Hill, West Sussex
EARLIEST CRICKETING MEMORY? The 2005 Ashes
BIGGEST INFLUENCE ON YOUR DEVELOPMENT AS A CRICKETER (EXCLUDING PARENTS)?
Steve Kirby – he has been a great friend, mentor and coach over the last four years of my career, helping me to where I am now
THE KOOKABURRA BALL: YES OR NO? Yes, at the right time of year, because it improves your skills as a bowler
OPPONENT YOU MOST LOOK FORWARD TO PLAYING AGAINST? Nathan Smith
HOBBIES? Listening to The High Performance Podcast
MOST BEAUTIFUL THING YOU HAVE EVER SEEN? The views from the Southern Alps in New Zealand
FILM YOU CAN WATCH OVER AND OVER: Inception

Batting	Mat	Inns	NO	Runs	HS	Ave	SR	100	50	Ct	St
First-class	57	91	11	2286	99	28.57	66.64	0	16	18	-
List A	22	19	2	665	93	39.11	107.77	0	6	4	-
T20s	51	41	8	548	49*	16.60	119.65	0	0	23	-

Bowling	Mat	Balls	Mdns	Runs	Wkts	BB	Ave	4wI	5wI	SR	Econ
First-class	57	5521	193	3114	85	5-50	36.63	-	2	64.95	3.38
List A	22	802	5	786	22	3-34	35.72	0	0	36.45	5.88
T20s	51	621	1	1030	33	3-36	31.21	0	0	18.81	9.95

DANIEL HUGHES

LHB / R0 / W0

SUSSEX

FULL NAME: Daniel Peter Hughes
BORN: February 16, 1989, Bathurst, New South Wales, Australia
SQUAD NO: 89
HEIGHT: 6ft 2in
EDUCATION: Cowra High School, New South Wales; TAFE NSW Ryde
TEAMS: Sussex, New South Wales, Southern Brave, Sydney Sixers, Sydney Thunder
ROLE: Batter
DEBUT: First-class: 2013; List A: 2013; T20: 2012

BEST BATTING: 178 New South Wales vs Tasmania, Sydney, 2023

COUNTY CAP: 2024

FIRST CRICKET CLUB? Cowra Junior CC, New South Wales, Australia
EARLIEST CRICKETING MEMORY? Being fully padded-up in the backyard and Dad throwing me balls
WHAT'S THE BIGGEST PRIZE IN DOMESTIC CRICKET? Winning Division One of the County Championship
THE KOOKABURRA BALL: YES OR NO? Yes, it's something different in English conditions and a good way to learn new skills
OPPONENT YOU MOST LOOK FORWARD TO PLAYING AGAINST? Daniel Worrall – to see where I'm at against one of the best bowlers
FAVOURITE WARM-UP SONG? Candy Shop by 50 Cent
HOW MANY HOURS DO YOU SPEND ON YOUR PHONE A DAY? Two to three
SPECIALITY SUBJECT IN A PUB QUIZ (EXCLUDING SPORT)? Friends (the TV series)
WHICH PUBLIC FIGURE INSPIRES YOU (EXCLUDING SPORTSPEOPLE)? Russell Crowe
SURPRISING FACT ABOUT YOU: I am a qualified greenkeeper
FILM YOU CAN WATCH OVER AND OVER: Any Denzel Washington movie

Batting	Mat	Inns	NO	Runs	HS	Ave	SR	100	50	Ct	St
First-class	81	150	15	5097	178	37.75	47.91	10	30	55	-
List A	48	47	3	2547	152	57.88	86.78	11	11	21	-
T20s	123	116	15	3006	96*	29.76	129.12	0	20	37	-
Bowling	Mat	Balls	Mdns	Runs	Wkts	BB	Ave	4wI	5wI	SR	Econ
First-class	81	-	-	-	-	-	-	-	-	-	-
List A	48	-	-	-	-	-	-	-	-	-	-
T20s	123	-	-	-	-	-	-	-	-	-	-

JOSH HULL

LHB / LFM / R0 / W0

FULL NAME: Joshua Owen Hull
BORN: August 20, 2004, Huntingdon, Cambridgeshire
SQUAD NO: 20
HEIGHT: 6ft 7in
EDUCATION: Stamford School, Lincolnshire
TEAMS: England, Leicestershire, Manchester Originals
ROLE: Bowler
DEBUT: Test: 2024; First-class: 2023; List A: 2023; T20: 2023

LEICESTERSHIRE

BEST BATTING: 15 Leicestershire vs Yorkshire, Headingley, 2023
BEST BOWLING: 3-30 England Lions vs Sri Lankans, Worcester, 2024

WHICH TEAMMATE HAS HAD THE BIGGEST IMPACT ON YOUR GAME? Lewis Hill for his leadership and advice
WHICH AWAY GROUND DO YOU MOST ENJOY VISITING? The Oval
IF YOU COULD PINCH A PLAYER FROM ANOTHER COUNTY, WHO WOULD IT BE? James Anderson
WHAT DO YOU THINK OF THE CURRENT 50-OVER COMPETITION? I learnt a lot playing a full part in it when we won the competition in 2023 – including the final! It has really helped with my development
CHOOSE A FANTASY SLIP CORDON TO SPEND A DAY IN THE FIELD WITH: Adam Gilchrist (wk), Andrew Flintoff, Ricky Ponting, Jacques Kallis

Batting	Mat	Inns	NO	Runs	HS	Ave	SR	100	50	Ct	St
Tests	1	2	1	9	7*	9.00	56.25	0	0	0	-
First-class	11	15	6	39	15	4.33	24.37	0	0	4	-
List A	9	1	1	3	3*	-	75.00	0	0	6	-
T20s	21	5	3	26	12*	13.00	108.33	0	0	4	-

Bowling	Mat	Balls	Mdns	Runs	Wkts	BB	Ave	4wI	5wI	SR	Econ
Tests	1	102	0	91	3	3-53	30.33	-	0	34.00	5.35
First-class	11	1327	16	1095	19	3-30	57.63	-	0	69.84	4.95
List A	9	430	1	412	17	4-43	24.23	2	0	25.29	5.74
T20s	21	436	1	649	24	3-28	27.04	0	0	18.16	8.93

SEAN HUNT

RHB / LFM / R0 / W0

SUSSEX

FULL NAME: Sean Frank Hunt
BORN: December 7, 2001, Guildford, Surrey
SQUAD NO: 21
HEIGHT: 6ft 5in
NICKNAME: Hunty
EDUCATION: Howard of Effingham School, Surrey
TEAMS: Sussex
ROLE: Bowler
DEBUT: First-class: 2021; List A: 2022

BEST BATTING: 65 Sussex vs Leicestershire, Hove, 2024
BEST BOWLING: 4-64 Sussex vs Yorkshire, Hove, 2024

FIRST CRICKET CLUB? Horsley & Send CC, West Horsley, Surrey
GREATEST PERFORMANCE YOU HAVE WITNESSED? Tom Haines and Ali Orr putting on 328 for the first wicket against Glamorgan at Hove in 2022
WHICH TEAMMATE HAS HAD THE BIGGEST IMPACT ON YOUR GAME? Steven Finn
WHICH AWAY GROUND DO YOU MOST ENJOY VISITING? Worcester
FAVOURITE FORMAT? The County Championship – the feeling of winning after four days can't be topped
FAVOURITE TOY AS A KID? The Xbox
WHAT WOULD BE YOUR PERFECT BREAKFAST? A Full English with plenty of hash browns
WHICH PERSON INSPIRES YOU MOST? Chris Bumstead
CHOOSE A FANTASY SLIP CORDON TO SPEND A DAY IN THE FIELD WITH: Tom Holland (wk), Patrick Mahomes, Stephen Curry, Giannis Antetokounmpo

Batting	Mat	Inns	NO	Runs	HS	Ave	SR	100	50	Ct	St
First-class	23	35	16	172	65	9.05	30.60	0	1	2	-
List A	9	7	4	35	13	11.66	64.81	0	0	1	-

Bowling	Mat	Balls	Mdns	Runs	Wkts	BB	Ave	4wI	5wI	SR	Econ
First-class	23	3192	80	2032	58	4-64	35.03	-	0	55.03	3.81
List A	9	390	3	394	8	2-32	49.25	0	0	48.75	6.06

MATTY HURST

RHB / WK / R0 / W0

FULL NAME: Matthew Frederick Hurst
BORN: December 10, 2003, Billinge, Wigan
SQUAD NO: 21
HEIGHT: 5ft 8in
EDUCATION: Byrchall High School, Wigan;
Winstanley College
TEAMS: Lancashire, Manchester Originals,
England Lions, Perth Scorchers
ROLE: Wicketkeeper/batter
DEBUT: First-class: 2023; List A: 2023; T20: 2024

LANCASHIRE

BEST BATTING: 104 Lancashire vs Nottinghamshire, Trent Bridge, 2024

WHICH TEAMMATE HAS HAD THE BIGGEST IMPACT ON YOUR GAME? Josh Bohannon – he
has advised me about facing different bowlers and my batting technique is very similar
to his
WHO IS THE MOST TALENTED U19 TEENAGER IN THE COUNTY GAME? Ben McKinney (Dur)
HOW IS BAZBALL AFFECTING CHAMPIONSHIP CRICKET? There is generally less fear
of failure
WHAT DO YOU THINK OF THE CURRENT 50-OVER COMPETITION? As a new pro, I really
enjoyed it when I played in the One-Day Cup in 2023. It gave me the chance to perform in
the first team and learn from some of the senior pros about how they train
CHOOSE A FANTASY SLIP CORDON TO SPEND A DAY IN THE FIELD WITH: Ian Healy (wk),
Tiger Woods, Conor McGregor, Sachin Tendulkar

Batting	Mat	Inns	NO	Runs	HS	Ave	SR	100	50	Ct	St
First-class	17	28	4	875	104	36.45	49.37	1	7	43	1
List A	8	6	2	108	66	27.00	128.57	0	1	6	-
T20s	23	21	1	441	78	22.05	130.08	0	2	11	1
Bowling	Mat	Balls	Mdns	Runs	Wkts	BB	Ave	4wl	5wl	SR	Econ
First-class	17	-	-	-	-	-	-	-	-	-	-
List A	8	-	-	-	-	-	-	-	-	-	-
T20s	23	-	-	-	-	-	-	-	-	-	-

BRETT HUTTON

RHB / RMF / RO / W1

NOTTINGHAMSHIRE

FULL NAME: Brett Alan Hutton
BORN: February 6, 1993, Doncaster, Yorkshire
SQUAD NO: 16
HEIGHT: 6ft 3in
NICKNAME: Bert
EDUCATION: Worksop College, Nottinghamshire
TEAMS: Nottinghamshire, England U19, Northamptonshire, Surrey
ROLE: Bowler
DEBUT: First-class: 2011; List A: 2011; T20: 2016

BEST BATTING: 84 Nottinghamshire vs Kent, Canterbury, 2023
BEST BOWLING: 8-57 Northamptonshire vs Gloucestershire, Northampton, 2018
COUNTY CAP: 2021 (Nottinghamshire)

FIRST CRICKET CLUB? Worksop CC, Nottinghamshire
BIGGEST INFLUENCE ON YOUR DEVELOPMENT AS A CRICKETER (EXCLUDING PARENTS)?
Paul Franks, Nottinghamshire's assistant coach – I played cricket with him from a young age, watching him and learning
WHAT WOULD YOU CHANGE ABOUT THE STRUCTURE OF THE COUNTY SEASON? More red-ball cricket in the middle of the summer
WHO WOULD YOU MOST AND LEAST LIKE TO HAVE A NET WITH? Brett Lee – both the most and least I'd like to have a net with. It would be great to have faced him even though he bowls too fast to bat against
CHILDHOOD SPORTING HERO? Tiger Woods
SURPRISING FACT ABOUT YOU: I like country music
MOST BEAUTIFUL THING YOU HAVE EVER SEEN? Barbados

Batting	Mat	Inns	NO	Runs	HS	Ave	SR	100	50	Ct	St
First-class	91	134	16	2004	84	16.98	42.75	0	6	55	-
List A	42	30	6	432	46	18.00	96.86	0	0	11	-
T20s	9	7	4	50	18*	16.66	106.38	0	0	3	-

Bowling	Mat	Balls	Mdns	Runs	Wkts	BB	Ave	4wI	5wI	SR	Econ
First-class	91	15301	550	8263	316	8-57	26.14	-	17	48.42	3.24
List A	42	1863	24	1623	62	7-26	26.17	0	2	30.04	5.22
T20s	9	172	0	255	5	2-28	51.00	0	0	34.40	8.89

DANIAL IBRAHIM — RHB / RMF / RO / WO

FULL NAME: Danial Kashif Ibrahim
BORN: August 9, 2004, Burnley, Lancashire
SQUAD NO: 40
HEIGHT: 5ft 10in
NICKNAME: Ian
EDUCATION: Eastbourne College; Bede's Senior School, Hailsham, East Sussex
TEAMS: Sussex, England U19
ROLE: Allrounder
DEBUT: First-class: 2021; List A: 2021; T20: 2023

BEST BATTING: 100* Sussex vs Glamorgan, Hove, 2022
BEST BOWLING: 2-9 Sussex vs Worcestershire, Worcester, 2021

FIRST CRICKET CLUB? Preston Nomads CC, West Sussex
BEST PLAYER IN COUNTY CRICKET (EXCLUDING TEAMMATES)? James Vince
BEST PERFORMANCE AS A PRO? Scoring 55 on my first-class debut at Headingley in 2021
FAVOURITE FORMAT? Four-day cricket because those matches are the best to win
WHO WOULD YOU MOST AND LEAST LIKE TO HAVE A NET WITH? Marnus Labuschagne for both – he would be very annoying to bowl at with all his mannerisms, but it would be great to learn about batting because of his love of the game and how good he is
HOBBIES? Gaming
FAVOURITE TOY AS A KID? Power Rangers
WHICH PERSON INSPIRES YOU MOST? Giannis Antetokounmpo

Batting	Mat	Inns	NO	Runs	HS	Ave	SR	100	50	Ct	St
First-class	17	32	3	634	100*	21.86	42.95	1	3	8	-
List A	24	20	1	347	56	18.26	76.94	0	3	7	-
T20s	4	4	0	47	18	11.75	117.50	0	0	0	-

Bowling	Mat	Balls	Mdns	Runs	Wkts	BB	Ave	4wl	5wl	SR	Econ
First-class	17	877	16	555	7	2-9	79.28	-	0	125.28	3.79
List A	24	714	0	610	13	3-34	46.92	0	0	54.92	5.12
T20s	4	-	-	-	-	-	-	-	-	-	-

COLIN INGRAM LHB / LB / R1 / W0 / MVP18

FULL NAME: Colin Alexander Ingram
BORN: July 3, 1985, Port Elizabeth, SA
SQUAD NO: 41
HEIGHT: 5ft 10in
NICKNAME: Stingray
EDUCATION: Woodbridge College, SA
TEAMS: South Africa, Glamorgan, Adelaide Strikers, Delhi Daredevils, Eastern Province, Hobart Hurricanes, MI Cape Town, Oval Invincibles, Pretoria Capitals, Somerset, Warriors
ROLE: Batter
DEBUT: ODI: 2010; T20I: 2010; First-class: 2004; List A: 2005; T20: 2007

BEST BATTING: 257* Glamorgan vs Leicestershire, Cardiff, 2024
BEST BOWLING: 4-16 Eastern Province vs Boland, Port Elizabeth, 2006
COUNTY CAP: 2017 (Glamorgan)

FIRST CRICKET CLUB? Thornhill CC, Port Elizabeth, South Africa
EARLIEST CRICKETING MEMORY? Watching my dad play club cricket at Thornhill and my mom throwing balls to me
WHAT'S THE BIGGEST PRIZE IN DOMESTIC CRICKET? The MVP
THE KOOKABURRA BALL: YES OR NO? No, as I don't think it suits the county pitches. The Dukes adds something for the bowler and makes for a better contest between bat and ball
OPPONENT YOU MOST LOOK FORWARD TO PLAYING AGAINST? My old teammate David Lloyd – he's loud, he's got great chat and I look forward to the battle!
FAVOURITE WARM-UP SONG? Cotton Eyed Joe by Rednex
SPECIALITY SUBJECT IN A PUB QUIZ (EXCLUDING SPORT)? Woodwork and tools
ONE THING YOU WANT TO DO BEFORE YOU DIE: Climb a big mountain
SURPRISING FACT ABOUT YOU: I only wear barefoot shoes

Batting	Mat	Inns	NO	Runs	HS	Ave	SR	100	50	Ct	St
ODIs	31	29	3	843	124	32.42	82.32	3	3	12	-
T20Is	9	9	1	210	78	26.25	129.62	0	1	2	-
First-class	135	236	20	8979	257*	41.56	52.53	23	38	95	-
List A	206	198	23	8501	155	48.57	90.96	21	53	76	-
T20s	363	350	46	8672	127*	28.52	138.00	4	51	118	-

Bowling	Mat	Balls	Mdns	Runs	Wkts	BB	Ave	4wl	5wl	SR	Econ
ODIs	31	6	0	17	0	0-17	-	-	-	-	17.00
T20Is	9	-	-	-	-	-	-	-	-	-	-
First-class	135	3897	56	2352	56	4-16	42.00	-	0	69.58	3.62
List A	206	1620	3	1522	43	4-39	35.39	1	0	37.67	5.63
T20s	363	1001	1	1319	40	4-32	32.97	1	0	25.02	7.90

WILL JACKS

RHB / OB / R0 / W0

FULL NAME: William George Jacks
BORN: November 21, 1998, Chertsey, Surrey
SQUAD NO: 9
HEIGHT: 6ft 2in
NICKNAME: Jacko
EDUCATION: St George's College, Weybridge
TEAMS: England, Surrey, Oval Invincibles, Chattogram Challengers, Comilla Victorians, Hobart Hurricanes, Islamabad United, Pretoria Capitals, RC Bangalore
ROLE: Allrounder
DEBUT: Test: 2022; ODI: 2023; T20I: 2022; First-class: 2018; List A: 2018; T20: 2018

BEST BATTING: 150* Surrey vs Essex, The Oval, 2022
BEST BOWLING: 7-129 Surrey vs Nottinghamshire, Trent Bridge, 2024
COUNTY CAP: 2022

FIRST CRICKET CLUB? Valley End CC, Surrey
WHAT WOULD YOU DO IF YOU WERE IN CHARGE OF COUNTY CRICKET? Play more T20 games on the weekend
CHILDHOOD SPORTING HERO? Kevin Pietersen

Batting	Mat	Inns	NO	Runs	HS	Ave	SR	100	50	Ct	St
Tests	2	4	0	89	31	22.25	98.88	0	0	0	-
ODIs	15	15	0	468	94	31.20	100.64	0	4	6	-
T20Is	23	21	0	383	40	18.23	136.78	0	0	5	-
First-class	54	81	9	2455	150*	34.09	61.69	3	16	55	-
List A	37	36	0	974	121	27.05	97.98	1	6	19	-
T20s	202	191	11	5090	108*	28.27	156.23	4	34	86	-

Bowling	Mat	Balls	Mdns	Runs	Wkts	BB	Ave	4wI	5wI	SR	Econ
Tests	2	327	5	232	6	6-161	38.66	-	1	54.50	4.25
ODIs	15	234	1	225	5	3-22	45.00	0	0	46.80	5.76
T20Is	23	18	0	41	1	1-5	41.00	0	0	18.00	13.66
First-class	54	3389	71	1875	44	7-129	42.61	-	3	77.02	3.31
List A	37	716	2	648	16	3-22	40.50	0	0	44.75	5.43
T20s	202	1204	3	1461	64	4-15	22.82	1	0	18.81	7.28

LYNDON JAMES

RHB / RMF / R0 / W0

NOTTINGHAMSHIRE

FULL NAME: Lyndon Wallace James
BORN: December 27, 1998, Worksop, Nottinghamshire
SQUAD NO: 45
HEIGHT: 6ft 3in
NICKNAME: LJ
EDUCATION: Oakham School, Rutland
TEAMS: Nottinghamshire, England Lions
ROLE: Allrounder
DEBUT: First-class: 2018; List A: 2019; T20: 2021

BEST BATTING: 164* Nottinghamshire vs Durham, Trent Bridge, 2022
BEST BOWLING: 6-74 Nottinghamshire vs Surrey, The Oval, 2023
COUNTY CAP: 2024

FIRST CRICKET CLUB? Ordsall Bridon CC, Nottinghamshire
WHICH TEAMMATE HAS HAD THE BIGGEST IMPACT ON YOUR GAME? James Pattinson
WHAT PART OF THE SEASON DO YOU MOST ENJOY? Friday night T20s
WHICH AWAY GROUND DO YOU MOST ENJOY VISITING? The Oval
WHO IS THE MOST TALENTED U19 TEENAGER IN THE COUNTY GAME? Farhan Ahmed (Not)
IF YOU COULD PINCH A PLAYER FROM ANOTHER COUNTY, WHO WOULD IT BE? Jake Ball
WHAT DO YOU THINK OF THE CURRENT 50-OVER COMPETITION? From a Notts perspective, it would be nice to play more of our home games at Trent Bridge
WHO IS THE TOUGHEST BOWLER TO FACE? Mohammad Abbas – he rearranged my poles twice in the same game
WHAT'S THE SILLIEST OUTFIT YOU'VE EVER WORN? Dressing up as Baby Spice
CHOOSE A FANTASY SLIP CORDON TO SPEND A DAY IN THE FIELD WITH: Tiger Woods (wk), Cameron Smith, John Daly, Seve Ballesteros

Batting	Mat	Inns	NO	Runs	HS	Ave	SR	100	50	Ct	St
First-class	57	85	10	2440	164*	32.53	45.77	4	13	27	-
List A	30	27	2	632	82	25.28	81.65	0	5	15	-
T20s	29	24	5	303	51	15.94	109.38	0	1	9	-

Bowling	Mat	Balls	Mdns	Runs	Wkts	BB	Ave	4wI	5wI	SR	Econ
First-class	57	5059	135	2881	83	6-74	34.71	-	1	60.95	3.41
List A	30	504	0	537	21	5-48	25.57	1	1	24.00	6.39
T20s	29	219	0	370	11	3-31	33.63	0	0	19.90	10.13

KEATON JENNINGS — LHB / RM / R3 / W0 / MVP5

FULL NAME: Keaton Kent Jennings
BORN: June 19, 1992, Johannesburg, SA
SQUAD NO: 1
HEIGHT: 6ft 4in
NICKNAME: Jet
EDUCATION: King Edward VII School; University of South Africa
TEAMS: England, Lancashire, London Spirit, Durham, Gauteng, Perth Scorchers, South Africa U19
ROLE: Batter
DEBUT: Test: 2016; First-class: 2011; List A: 2012; T20: 2014

BEST BATTING: 318 Lancashire vs Somerset, Southport, 2022
BEST BOWLING: 3-37 Durham vs Sussex, Chester-le-Street, 2017
COUNTY CAP: 2018 (Lancashire)

FIRST CRICKET CLUB? Pirates CC, Johannesburg, South Africa
FAMILY TIES? My brother Dylan, uncle Kenneth and father Ray have all played first-class cricket in South Africa
EARLIEST CRICKETING MEMORY? Playing with my dad back in South Africa
WHAT'S THE BIGGEST PRIZE IN DOMESTIC CRICKET? The County Championship
THE KOOKABURRA BALL: YES OR NO? Yes, it's a good challenge as an opener and as a captain in the field
OPPONENT YOU MOST LOOK FORWARD TO PLAYING AGAINST? My former Durham teammate Mark Wood. It's always a good challenge
FAVOURITE WARM-UP SONG? Take Me Home, Country Roads by John Denver
ONE THING YOU WANT TO DO BEFORE YOU DIE: Go to the Glastonbury festival
SURPRISING FACT ABOUT YOU: I have a master's in business
FILM YOU CAN WATCH OVER AND OVER: Gladiator

Batting	Mat	Inns	NO	Runs	HS	Ave	SR	100	50	Ct	St
Tests	17	32	1	781	146*	25.19	42.49	2	1	17	-
First-class	187	317	20	11421	318	38.45	47.79	31	42	168	-
List A	92	91	18	3314	139	45.39	83.79	8	20	41	-
T20s	102	83	19	2040	108	31.87	129.44	1	9	22	-

Bowling	Mat	Balls	Mdns	Runs	Wkts	BB	Ave	4wI	5wI	SR	Econ
Tests	17	73	1	55	0	0-2	-	-	-	-	4.52
First-class	187	1761	41	988	30	3-37	32.93	-	0	58.70	3.36
List A	92	690	2	670	11	2-19	60.90	0	0	62.72	5.82
T20s	102	510	0	628	22	4-37	28.54	1	0	23.18	7.38

CALEB JEWELL — LHB / WK / R0 / W0

DERBYSHIRE

FULL NAME: Caleb Paul Jewell
BORN: April 21, 1997, Hobart, Australia
SQUAD NO: TBC
TEAMS: Derbyshire, Australia U19, Hobart Hurricanes, Tasmania
ROLE: Batter
DEBUT: First-class: 2016; List A: 2016; T20: 2018

BEST BATTING: 227 Tasmania vs Western Australia, Hobart, 2024

NOTES: The Australian opening bat is set for his first season of county cricket and is due to be available throughout the campaign and across all formats. He was part of the Hobart Hurricanes side that won their first Big Bash title in January, making 164 runs in seven knocks including a career-best 76 in a last-ball win over Brisbane Heat. Jewell has a solid red-ball record, too, notching his maiden first-class double-century for Tasmania in the 2023/24 Sheffield Shield. Mickey Arthur, Derbyshire's head of cricket, said: "Caleb is a player I've had my eye on for some time, and everyone I have spoken to about him has said what a good player he is. Chief selector for Cricket Australia, George Bailey, and Ian Bell in particular spoke very highly of his ability." Jewell added: "I'm looking forward to getting my first taste of county cricket with Derbyshire, to show what I can do in all formats and help the club win matches. There are plenty of Australian players who have made their mark in England, and I want to be next"

Batting	Mat	Inns	NO	Runs	HS	Ave	SR	100	50	Ct	St
First-class	47	87	3	2580	227	30.71	53.73	6	11	27	-
List A	45	44	3	1416	137	34.53	90.94	5	5	18	1
T20s	60	58	2	1210	76	21.60	125.64	0	6	23	-
Bowling	Mat	Balls	Mdns	Runs	Wkts	BB	Ave	4wI	5wI	SR	Econ
First-class	47	-	-	-	-	-	-	-	-	-	-
List A	45	-	-	-	-	-	-	-	-	-	-
T20s	60	-	-	-	-	-	-	-	-	-	-

MICHAEL JONES   RHB / OB / R0 / W0

FULL NAME: Michael Alexander Jones
BORN: January 5, 1998, Ormskirk, Lancashire
SQUAD NO: TBC
HEIGHT: 6ft 3in
NICKNAME: Conqs
EDUCATION: Ormskirk School; Myerscough College, Preston; Edge Hill University, Ormskirk
TEAMS: Scotland, Lancashire, Durham, Northern Superchargers
ROLE: Batter
DEBUT: ODI: 2018; T20I: 2022; First-class: 2018; List A: 2018; T20: 2022

BEST BATTING: 206 Durham vs Middlesex, Chester-le-Street, 2022

MOST EXCITING DAY AS A CRICKETER? The World Cup Qualifier between Scotland and West Indies at Harare in 2018. We fell five runs short of a win which would have meant qualification for the 2019 World Cup
WHAT WOULD YOU DO IF YOU WERE IN CHARGE OF COUNTY CRICKET? Introduce free hits for no-balls in first-class cricket
CHILDHOOD SPORTING HERO? Steven Gerrard

Batting	Mat	Inns	NO	Runs	HS	Ave	SR	100	50	Ct	St
ODIs	16	14	0	385	87	27.50	67.30	0	3	4	-
T20Is	11	11	1	224	86	22.40	136.58	0	1	6	-
First-class	40	66	4	2053	206	33.11	51.89	3	12	15	-
List A	32	30	1	746	119	25.72	74.82	1	4	10	-
T20s	56	52	7	1082	86	24.04	135.41	0	2	18	-

Bowling	Mat	Balls	Mdns	Runs	Wkts	BB	Ave	4wI	5wI	SR	Econ
ODIs	16	-	-	-	-	-	-	-	-	-	-
T20Is	11	-	-	-	-	-	-	-	-	-	-
First-class	40	6	0	1	0	0-1	-	-	-	-	1.00
List A	32	-	-	-	-	-	-	-	-	-	-
T20s	56	-	-	-	-	-	-	-	-	-	-

ROB JONES RHB / LB / R0 / W0

WORCESTERSHIRE

FULL NAME: Robert Peter Jones
BORN: November 3, 1995, Warrington, Cheshire
SQUAD NO: 88
HEIGHT: 5ft 11in
NICKNAME: Jonah
EDUCATION: Bridgewater High School, Warrington; Priestley College
TEAMS: Worcestershire, England U19, Lancashire
ROLE: Batter
DEBUT: First-class: 2016; List A: 2018; T20: 2017

BEST BATTING: 122 Lancashire vs Middlesex, Lord's, 2019
BEST BOWLING: 1-4 Lancashire vs Northamptonshire, Old Trafford, 2021

FIRST CRICKET CLUB? Stretton CC, Warrington, Cheshire
EARLIEST CRICKETING MEMORY? Playing with my dad on Anglesey
WHAT'S THE BIGGEST PRIZE IN DOMESTIC CRICKET? Winning the County Championship
THE KOOKABURRA BALL: YES OR NO? Yes, because it doesn't nip as much
OPPONENT YOU MOST LOOK FORWARD TO PLAYING AGAINST? Tom Bailey
FAVOURITE WARM-UP SONG? Dance Tonight by Paul McCartney
HOW MANY HOURS DO YOU SPEND ON YOUR PHONE A DAY? Three
SPECIALITY SUBJECT IN A PUB QUIZ (EXCLUDING SPORT)? Westies
ONE THING YOU WANT TO DO BEFORE YOU DIE: Climb all the Munros
HOBBY YOU WOULD LIKE TO LEARN: The tin whistle
WHICH PUBLIC FIGURE INSPIRES YOU (EXCLUDING SPORTSPEOPLE)? Bob Mortimer
SURPRISING FACT ABOUT YOU: I collect whisky

Batting	Mat	Inns	NO	Runs	HS	Ave	SR	100	50	Ct	St
First-class	59	89	8	2190	122	27.03	43.91	3	9	71	-
List A	46	39	7	1253	122	39.15	74.22	1	9	23	-
T20s	41	28	15	432	61*	33.23	113.08	0	1	18	-
Bowling	Mat	Balls	Mdns	Runs	Wkts	BB	Ave	4wI	5wI	SR	Econ
First-class	59	114	3	50	2	1-4	25.00	-	0	57.00	2.63
List A	46	122	0	122	2	1-3	61.00	0	0	61.00	6.00
T20s	41	6	0	10	0	0-10	-	-	-	-	10.00

CHRIS JORDAN   RHB / RFM / R0 / W1

FULL NAME: Christopher James Jordan
BORN: October 4, 1988, Christ Church, Barbados
SQUAD NO: 34
HEIGHT: 6ft
EDUCATION: Combermere School, Barbados; Dulwich College, London
TEAMS: England, Surrey, Southern Brave, Barbados, Hobart Hurricanes, Mumbai Indians, Punjab Kings, Sussex, Sydney Sixers
ROLE: Allrounder
DEBUT: Test: 2014; ODI: 2013; T20I: 2013; First-class: 2007; List A: 2007; T20: 2008

BEST BATTING: 73 Surrey vs Somerset, Taunton, 2022 (T20)
BEST BOWLING: 4-6 England vs West Indies, Basseterre, 2019 (T20)
COUNTY CAP: 2014 (Sussex)

FIRST CRICKET CLUB? Spartan Juniors CC, Barbados
NOTES: After nearly a decade at Sussex, Jordan re-joined his former club ahead of the 2022 season and captained Surrey's T20 side to the quarter-finals in his first year back at The Oval, finishing as the club's leading wicket-taker in the competition. He took Surrey one stage further in 2023 as they reached Finals Day and repeated the trick again last summer without being able to get his hands on the trophy

Batting	Mat	Inns	NO	Runs	HS	Ave	SR	100	50	Ct	St
Tests	8	11	1	180	35	18.00	56.25	0	0	14	-
ODIs	35	24	9	184	38*	12.26	87.20	0	0	19	-
T20Is	95	57	25	439	36	13.71	129.11	0	0	48	-
First-class	114	159	23	3443	166	25.31	-	3	15	137	-
List A	85	57	15	648	55	15.42	-	0	1	45	-
T20s	396	240	102	2358	73	17.08	131.51	0	3	199	-

Bowling	Mat	Balls	Mdns	Runs	Wkts	BB	Ave	4wI	5wI	SR	Econ
Tests	8	1530	74	752	21	4-18	35.80	-	0	72.85	2.94
ODIs	35	1660	5	1660	46	5-29	36.08	0	1	36.08	6.00
T20Is	95	1953	2	2847	108	4-6	26.36	4	0	18.08	8.74
First-class	114	18986	582	10730	335	7-43	32.02	-	10	56.67	3.39
List A	85	3840	17	3682	122	5-28	30.18	1	2	31.47	5.75
T20s	396	7874	8	11318	416	4-6	27.20	7	0	18.92	8.62

ARI KARVELAS — RHB / RMF / RO / WO

FULL NAME: Aristides Karvelas
BORN: March 20, 1994, Alberton, Transvaal, South Africa
SQUAD NO: 36
HEIGHT: 6ft 5in
EDUCATION: St Benedict's College, Johannesburg; University of South Africa
TEAMS: Greece, Sussex, Central Gauteng, Gauteng
ROLE: Bowler
DEBUT: T20I: 2022; First-class: 2018; List A: 2018; T20: 2022

BEST BATTING: 57 Sussex vs Middlesex, Lord's, 2022
BEST BOWLING: 6-71 Gauteng vs North West, Potchefstroom, 2018

FIRST CRICKET CLUB? Alberton CC, Gauteng, South Africa
THE KOOKABURRA BALL: YES OR NO? No, the ball doesn't suit English wickets
OPPONENT YOU MOST LOOK FORWARD TO PLAYING AGAINST? Dan Worrall – he's someone who has helped his team win the County Championship and I look forward to learning about how he goes about things
FAVOURITE WARM-UP SONG? Africa by Toto
HOW MANY HOURS DO YOU SPEND ON YOUR PHONE A DAY? 2.5-3
SPECIALITY SUBJECT IN A PUB QUIZ (EXCLUDING SPORT)? History
WHICH PUBLIC FIGURE INSPIRES YOU (EXCLUDING SPORTSPEOPLE)? Nelson Mandela
SURPRISING FACT ABOUT YOU: I've been in a TV advert with Virat Kohli
FILM YOU CAN WATCH OVER AND OVER: Bad Boys

Batting	Mat	Inns	NO	Runs	HS	Ave	SR	100	50	Ct	St
T20Is	1	1	0	10	10	10.00	50.00	0	0	0	-
First-class	27	36	6	475	57	15.83	59.82	0	2	9	-
List A	29	18	4	177	33	12.64	93.65	0	0	3	-
T20s	9	6	3	23	10	7.66	54.76	0	0	2	-

Bowling	Mat	Balls	Mdns	Runs	Wkts	BB	Ave	4wI	5wI	SR	Econ
T20Is	1	18	0	10	0	0-10	-	-	-	-	3.33
First-class	27	4237	165	2211	86	6-71	25.70	-	2	49.26	3.13
List A	29	1371	19	1129	44	5-16	25.65	2	1	31.15	4.94
T20s	9	155	0	241	10	4-20	24.10	1	0	15.50	9.32

BEN KELLAWAY   RHB / OB / R0 / W0

FULL NAME: Benjamin Ian Kellaway
BORN: January 5, 2004, Newport, Wales
SQUAD NO: 8
HEIGHT: 6ft 2in
NICKNAME: Kellers
EDUCATION: Chepstow Comprehensive
School; Clifton College; Cardiff university
TEAMS: Glamorgan
ROLE: Allrounder
DEBUT: First-class: 2023; List A: 2023; T20: 2023

GLAMORGAN

BEST BATTING: 36 Glamorgan vs Derbyshire, Derby, 2024
BEST BOWLING: 5-142 Glamorgan vs Sussex, Hove, 2024

FIRST CRICKET CLUB? Chepstow CC, Monmouthshire
EARLIEST CRICKETING MEMORY? Softball cricket at Chepstow
WHAT'S THE BIGGEST PRIZE IN DOMESTIC CRICKET? The T20 Blast
THE KOOKABURRA BALL: YES OR NO? Yes, it grips well for spinners and doesn't move as much when batting
OPPONENT YOU MOST LOOK FORWARD TO PLAYING AGAINST? Jimmy Anderson
FAVOURITE WARM-UP SONG? We Found Love by Rihanna
HOW MANY HOURS DO YOU SPEND ON YOUR PHONE A DAY? Five
SPECIALITY SUBJECT IN A PUB QUIZ (EXCLUDING SPORT)? Biology and physiology
WHICH PUBLIC FIGURE INSPIRES YOU (EXCLUDING SPORTSPEOPLE)? Ed Sheeran
SURPRISING FACT ABOUT YOU: I held the high jump record at secondary school
FILM YOU CAN WATCH OVER AND OVER: Step Brothers

Batting	Mat	Inns	NO	Runs	HS	Ave	SR	100	50	Ct	St
First-class	6	8	0	80	36	10.00	43.24	0	0	4	-
List A	14	11	1	317	82	31.70	106.37	0	3	5	-
T20s	9	9	2	44	11	6.28	89.79	0	0	5	-

Bowling	Mat	Balls	Mdns	Runs	Wkts	BB	Ave	4wI	5wI	SR	Econ
First-class	6	587	11	330	12	5-142	27.50	-	1	48.91	3.37
List A	14	606	2	554	24	3-33	23.08	0	0	25.25	5.48
T20s	9	54	0	85	1	1-5	85.00	0	0	54.00	9.44

ROB KEOGH

RHB / OB / R0 / W0

NORTHAMPTONSHIRE

FULL NAME: Robert Ian Keogh
BORN: October 21, 1991, Dunstable, Bedfordshire
SQUAD NO: 14
HEIGHT: 6ft 2in
NICKNAME: Keezy
EDUCATION: Queensbury Upper School, Dunstable; Dunstable College
TEAMS: Northamptonshire
ROLE: Allrounder
DEBUT: First-class: 2012; List A: 2010; T20: 2011

BEST BATTING: 221 Northamptonshire vs Hampshire, Southampton, 2013
BEST BOWLING: 9-52 Northamptonshire vs Glamorgan, Northampton, 2016
COUNTY CAP: 2019; BENEFIT: 2024

FIRST CRICKET CLUB? Dunstable Town CC, Bedfordshire
WHAT'S THE BIGGEST PRIZE IN DOMESTIC CRICKET? The County Championship
THE KOOKABURRA BALL: YES OR NO? Don't mind either way as long as it's the same all season
OPPONENT YOU MOST LOOK FORWARD TO PLAYING AGAINST? My former Northants teammate Emilio Gay
HOW MANY HOURS DO YOU SPEND ON YOUR PHONE A DAY? Four
SPECIALITY SUBJECT IN A PUB QUIZ (EXCLUDING SPORT)? Beaches in Perth
HOBBY YOU WOULD LIKE TO LEARN: DIY
SURPRISING FACT ABOUT YOU: I'm the best footballer in the Northants squad (not that surprising because we have some shockers)
FILM YOU CAN WATCH OVER AND OVER: I'm not a movie person

Batting	Mat	Inns	NO	Runs	HS	Ave	SR	100	50	Ct	St
First-class	134	222	13	6476	221	30.98	53.07	17	21	28	1
List A	70	64	5	1879	134	31.84	89.43	3	14	16	-
T20s	88	60	18	1096	59*	26.09	117.59	0	4	35	-

Bowling	Mat	Balls	Mdns	Runs	Wkts	BB	Ave	4wI	5wI	SR	Econ
First-class	134	11513	288	6620	165	9-52	40.12	-	4	69.77	3.45
List A	70	1671	3	1531	30	4-49	51.03	1	0	55.70	5.49
T20s	88	318	0	439	16	3-30	27.43	0	0	19.87	8.28

LOUIS KIMBER

RHB / OB / WK / R0 / W0

FULL NAME: Louis Philip James Kimber
BORN: February 24, 1997, Scunthorpe, Lincolnshire
SQUAD NO: 17
HEIGHT: 6ft 3in
NICKNAME: Melmo
EDUCATION: William Farr Church of England School, Lincoln; Loughborough University
TEAMS: Leicestershire, Birmingham Phoenix
ROLE: Batter
DEBUT: First-class: 2019; List A: 2021; T20: 2021

BEST BATTING: 243 Leicestershire vs Sussex, Hove, 2024
BEST BOWLING: 1-8 Leicestershire vs Middlesex, Leicester, 2022

FIRST CRICKET CLUB? Lindum CC, Lincolnshire
FAMILY TIES? My younger brother Nick played for Surrey until leaving the club last year
EARLIEST CRICKETING MEMORY? Playing with my two brothers at Lindum CC
WHAT'S THE BIGGEST PRIZE IN DOMESTIC CRICKET? The T20 Blast
THE KOOKABURRA BALL: YES OR NO? Yes
OPPONENT YOU MOST LOOK FORWARD TO PLAYING AGAINST? Kane Williamson
FAVOURITE WARM-UP SONG? Luther by Kendrick Lamar
HOW MANY HOURS DO YOU SPEND ON YOUR PHONE A DAY? Three
SPECIALITY SUBJECT IN A PUB QUIZ (EXCLUDING SPORT)? Geography
ONE THING YOU WANT TO DO BEFORE YOU DIE: Watch Arsenal win the Champions League

Batting	Mat	Inns	NO	Runs	HS	Ave	SR	100	50	Ct	St
First-class	36	58	3	1511	243	27.47	60.80	2	8	28	-
List A	31	28	4	833	102	34.70	104.64	1	6	11	-
T20s	37	32	5	539	59*	19.96	153.12	0	4	20	-

Bowling	Mat	Balls	Mdns	Runs	Wkts	BB	Ave	4wI	5wI	SR	Econ
First-class	36	824	12	586	8	1-8	73.25	-	0	103.00	4.26
List A	31	245	1	246	9	4-61	27.33	1	0	27.22	6.02
T20s	37	60	0	97	1	1-23	97.00	0	0	60.00	9.70

SAMMY KING

RHB / RMF / R0 / W0

FULL NAME: Samuel Isaac Michael King
BORN: January 12, 2003, Nottingham
SQUAD NO: 94
HEIGHT: 6ft 4in
NICKNAME: Kingy
EDUCATION: Nottingham High School;
University of Nottingham
TEAMS: Nottinghamshire
ROLE: Allrounder
DEBUT: List A: 2021; T20: 2024

FIRST CRICKET CLUB? Gedling Colliery CC, Nottingham
BEST DELIVERY YOU HAVE EVER BOWLED? To Ben Slater, caught second slip, see ya duck
BEST PERFORMANCE AS A PRO? My 120 against Leicestershire Second XI at Uppingham in 2022
GREATEST PERFORMANCE YOU HAVE WITNESSED? Alex Hales hitting 187 not out against Surrey in the 2017 one-day final at Lord's
FAVOURITE FORMAT? T20 – it's all flair
WHO WOULD YOU MOST AND LEAST LIKE TO HAVE A NET WITH? Most – Muttiah Muralitharan, to see how good he was. Least – Marchant de Lange, because he's rapid
DESCRIBE YOURSELF IN THREE WORDS: Funny, tall, humble
HOBBIES? Touch rugby
FAVOURITE TOY AS A KID? Shrek
WHAT WOULD BE YOUR PERFECT BREAKFAST? Milkshake and fruit
WHICH PERSON INSPIRES YOU MOST? Ant Botha

Batting	Mat	Inns	NO	Runs	HS	Ave	SR	100	50	Ct	St
List A	4	4	0	62	37	15.50	71.26	0	0	2	-
T20s	1	1	0	44	44	44.00	176.00	0	0	1	-

Bowling	Mat	Balls	Mdns	Runs	Wkts	BB	Ave	4wI	5wI	SR	Econ
List A	4	-	-	-	-	-	-	-	-	-	-
T20s	1	-	-	-	-	-	-	-	-	-	-

FRED KLAASSEN

RHB / LMF / RO / WO

FULL NAME: Frederick Jack Klaassen
BORN: November 13, 1992, Haywards Heath, Sussex
SQUAD NO: 18
HEIGHT: 6ft 5in
NICKNAME: TFD
EDUCATION: University of Otago, Dunedin, New Zealand
TEAMS: Netherlands, Kent, Manchester Originals
ROLE: Bowler
DEBUT: ODI: 2018; T20I: 2018; First-class: 2019; List A: 2017; T20: 2018

BEST BATTING: 14* Kent vs Loughborough MCCU, Canterbury, 2019
BEST BOWLING: 4-44 Kent vs Middlesex, Canterbury, 2020

FIRST CRICKET CLUB? Cornwall CC, Auckland, New Zealand
WHO IS THE MOST TALENTED U19 TEENAGER IN THE COUNTY GAME? Jaydn Denly (Kent)
IF YOU COULD PINCH A PLAYER FROM ANOTHER COUNTY, WHO WOULD IT BE? Bas de Leede
BEST DELIVERY YOU HAVE EVER FACED? A bumper from Duanne Olivier
BEST PERFORMANCE AS A PRO? My five-fer for Netherlands against Uganda at Bulawayo in the T20 World Cup Qualifier last year – Associate hero!
GREATEST PERFORMANCE YOU HAVE WITNESSED? James Anderson's 7-19 against Kent at Old Trafford in 2021
FAVOURITE FORMAT? T20 (I'm not a purist)
WHAT DO YOU THINK OF THE CURRENT 50-OVER COMPETITION? Add the Dutchies!

Batting	Mat	Inns	NO	Runs	HS	Ave	SR	100	50	Ct	St
ODIs	19	15	7	68	13	8.50	58.62	0	0	5	-
T20Is	39	15	5	45	13	4.50	84.90	0	0	17	-
First-class	5	8	3	45	14*	9.00	17.44	0	0	3	-
List A	34	25	13	97	13	8.08	57.05	0	0	12	-
T20s	105	29	14	85	13	5.66	94.44	0	0	40	-

Bowling	Mat	Balls	Mdns	Runs	Wkts	BB	Ave	4wI	5wI	SR	Econ
ODIs	19	1047	12	753	32	3-23	23.53	0	0	32.71	4.31
T20Is	39	804	0	1008	43	5-19	23.44	0	1	18.69	7.52
First-class	5	689	11	422	9	4-44	46.88	-	0	76.55	3.67
List A	34	1711	19	1346	50	3-23	26.92	0	0	34.22	4.72
T20s	105	2119	3	2964	115	5-19	25.77	2	1	18.42	8.39

TOM KOHLER-CADMORE   RHB / WK / R1 / W0

SOMERSET

FULL NAME: Tom Kohler-Cadmore
BORN: August 19, 1994, Chatham, Kent
SQUAD NO: 32
HEIGHT: 6ft 2in
NICKNAME: Pepsi
EDUCATION: Malvern College
TEAMS: Somerset, Welsh Fire, England Lions, Jaffna Kings, Northern Superchargers, Peshawar Zalmi, Rajasthan Royals, Rangpur Riders, Sydney Thunder, Trent Rockets, Worcestershire, Yorkshire
ROLE: Batter
DEBUT: First-class: 2014; List A: 2013; T20: 2014

BEST BATTING: 176 Yorkshire vs Leeds/Bradford MCCU, Weetwood, 2019

COUNTY CAP: 2019 (Yorkshire)

BIGGEST INFLUENCE ON YOUR DEVELOPMENT AS A CRICKETER (EXCLUDING PARENTS)? My school coaches Noel Brett and Mark Hardinges – they put in so many hours of training with me, as did my Worcester coaches
WHICH AWAY GROUND DO YOU MOST ENJOY VISITING? Always enjoy the trip to London for a four-day game at Lord's
IF YOU COULD PINCH A PLAYER FROM ANOTHER COUNTY, WHO WOULD IT BE? Matt Fisher
WHO IS THE TOUGHEST BOWLER TO FACE? Ben Coad or Sam Cook – both don't miss and move the ball both ways
FAVOURITE FORMAT? T20
SURPRISING FACT ABOUT YOU? I've been called the songbird of my generation by people who have heard me sing

Batting	Mat	Inns	NO	Runs	HS	Ave	SR	100	50	Ct	St
First-class	100	166	10	5126	176	32.85	54.73	11	23	136	1
List A	56	54	1	1808	164	34.11	86.79	3	10	29	-
T20s	228	223	24	5694	127	28.61	138.40	1	40	114	3

Bowling	Mat	Balls	Mdns	Runs	Wkts	BB	Ave	4wl	5wl	SR	Econ
First-class	100	-	-	-	-	-	-	-	-	-	-
List A	56	-	-	-	-	-	-	-	-	-	-
T20s	228	-	-	-	-	-	-	-	-	-	-

DANNY LAMB

RHB / RMF / R0 / W0

FULL NAME: Daniel John Lamb
BORN: September 7, 1995, Preston, Lancashire
SQUAD NO: 10
HEIGHT: 6ft
NICKNAME: Sherman
EDUCATION: St Michael's CE High School, Chorley; Cardinal Newman College, Preston; Edge Hill University, Ormskirk
TEAMS: Sussex, Gloucestershire, Lancashire, Somerset
ROLE: Allrounder
DEBUT: First-class: 2018; List A: 2017; T20: 2017

BEST BATTING: 134 Sussex vs Leicestershire, Leicester, 2024
BEST BOWLING: 4-55 Lancashire vs Yorkshire, Headingley, 2020

FIRST CRICKET CLUB? Hoghton CC, Lancashire
BEST PLAYER IN COUNTY CRICKET (EXCLUDING TEAMMATES)? James Vince
WHICH COUNTY PLAYER WOULD YOU MOST LIKE TO GO FOR A DRINK WITH? Luke Fletcher
BEST PERFORMANCE AS A PRO? Scoring 86 not out against Sussex at Sedbergh School in the 2021 One-Day Cup
FAVOURITE FORMAT? T20
HOBBIES? Hiking – completing the Wainwrights
WHAT WOULD BE YOUR PERFECT BREAKFAST? Smashed avocado on toast
WHICH PERSON INSPIRES YOU MOST? Tiger Woods
SURPRISING FACT ABOUT YOU? I was Blackburn Rovers Academy goalkeeper from U9 to U16 level

Batting	Mat	Inns	NO	Runs	HS	Ave	SR	100	50	Ct	St
First-class	33	45	8	1102	134	29.78	51.61	2	5	12	-
List A	26	17	6	390	86*	35.45	127.45	0	2	14	-
T20s	68	40	12	403	40	14.39	110.41	0	0	10	-

Bowling	Mat	Balls	Mdns	Runs	Wkts	BB	Ave	4wI	5wI	SR	Econ
First-class	33	3830	121	2044	63	4-55	32.44	-	0	60.79	3.20
List A	26	1235	6	1211	36	5-30	33.63	0	1	34.30	5.88
T20s	68	1081	1	1662	51	3-23	32.58	0	0	21.19	9.22

TOM LAMMONBY
LHB / LM / RO / WO

SOMERSET

FULL NAME: Thomas Alexander Lammonby
BORN: June 2, 2000, Exeter, Devon
SQUAD NO: 15
HEIGHT: 6ft
NICKNAME: Lammers
EDUCATION: Exeter School
TEAMS: Somerset, England Lions, Hobart Hurricanes, Karachi Kings, Manchester Originals, Oval Invincibles
ROLE: Batter
DEBUT: First-class: 2020; List A: 2023; T20: 2019

BEST BATTING: 116 Somerset vs Essex, Lord's, 2020
BEST BOWLING: 3-35 Somerset vs Essex, Chelmsford, 2022

FIRST CRICKET CLUB? Exeter CC, Devon
BIGGEST CRICKETING REGRET? Not playing at the 2018 U19 World Cup because of injury
MOST EXCITING DAY AS A CRICKETER? Scoring a hundred in the Bob Willis Trophy final at Lord's in 2020
WHO WOULD YOU MOST AND LEAST LIKE TO HAVE A NET WITH? Most – Ricky Ponting. Least – Morné Morkel
MAKE ONE PREDICTION FOR THE FUTURE OF CRICKET: It will grow in Europe
CHILDHOOD SPORTING HERO? Ricky Ponting
HOBBIES? Squash – as a kid I played in competitions all around the country

Batting	Mat	Inns	NO	Runs	HS	Ave	SR	100	50	Ct	St
First-class	61	107	8	3134	116	31.65	49.36	7	13	44	-
List A	1	1	0	6	6	6.00	30.00	0	0	0	-
T20s	79	59	11	904	90	18.83	140.59	0	1	44	-

Bowling	Mat	Balls	Mdns	Runs	Wkts	BB	Ave	4wI	5wI	SR	Econ
First-class	61	1052	29	630	11	3-35	57.27	-	0	95.63	3.59
List A	1	-	-	-	-	-	-	-	-	-	-
T20s	79	299	2	458	15	2-32	30.53	0	0	19.93	9.19

TOM LATHAM

LHB / RM / RO / WO

FULL NAME: Thomas William Maxwell Latham
BORN: April 2, 1992, Christchurch, New Zealand
SQUAD NO: TBC
HEIGHT: 5ft 6in
EDUCATION: Lincoln University, Christchurch
TEAMS: New Zealand, Warwickshire, Canterbury, Durham, Kent, Surrey
ROLE: Batter/wicketkeeper
DEBUT: Test: 2014; ODI: 2012; T20I: 2012; First-class: 2010; List A: 2011; T20: 2012

BEST BATTING: 264* New Zealand vs Sri Lanka, Wellington, 2018
BEST BOWLING: 1-7 New Zealanders vs Cricket Australia XI, Sydney, 2015

FAMILY TIES? My father Rod played cricket for New Zealand in the 1990s
CRICKETING HEROES? Mike Hussey – fellow left-hand top-order batter, always enjoyed the way he played and how he loves cricket so much. Brendon McCullum – admired how he went out and smashed the ball everywhere
NOTES: New Zealand's Test skipper joins Warwickshire on a one-year multi-format deal for the 2025 summer. "The New Zealand team has limited conflict with our domestic cricket calendar next season," said Gavin Larsen, who stepped down as Warwickshire performance director over the winter. "In this modern cricket world it's rare to have a player of Tom's quality and experience agree to join, and be available, for an entire season"

Batting	Mat	Inns	NO	Runs	HS	Ave	SR	100	50	Ct	St
Tests	88	158	6	5834	264*	38.38	47.49	13	31	101	-
ODIs	157	144	18	4361	145*	34.61	85.67	8	26	133	17
T20Is	26	23	3	516	65*	25.80	108.86	0	3	15	4
First-class	167	291	18	11446	264*	41.92	50.10	26	62	221	1
List A	240	220	27	6896	145*	35.73	86.01	11	41	213	24
T20s	111	100	7	2706	110	29.09	129.90	1	18	53	6

Bowling	Mat	Balls	Mdns	Runs	Wkts	BB	Ave	4wI	5wI	SR	Econ
Tests	88	-	-	-	-	-	-	-	-	-	-
ODIs	157	-	-	-	-	-	-	-	-	-	-
T20Is	26	-	-	-	-	-	-	-	-	-	-
First-class	167	26	0	18	1	1-7	18.00	-	0	26.00	4.15
List A	240	-	-	-	-	-	-	-	-	-	-
T20s	111	-	-	-	-	-	-	-	-	-	-

TOM LAWES

RHB / RMF / RO / WO

SURREY

FULL NAME: Thomas Edward Lawes
BORN: December 25, 2002, Singapore
SQUAD NO: 30
HEIGHT: 6ft 1in
EDUCATION: Cranleigh School, Surrey
TEAMS: Surrey, Northern Superchargers, England Lions
ROLE: Bowler
DEBUT: First-class: 2022; List A: 2022; T20: 2022

BEST BATTING: 58 Surrey vs Durham, The Oval, 2024
BEST BOWLING: 5-22 Surrey vs Kent, The Oval, 2023

WHICH COUNTY PLAYER WOULD YOU MOST LIKE TO GO FOR A DRINK WITH? Chris Woakes – he's a similar type of player as me so it'd be good to chat
BEST DELIVERY YOU HAVE EVER BOWLED? Bowling Finlay Bean of Yorkshire with an in-swinger from round the wicket in a Championship match at The Oval in 2022
GREATEST PERFORMANCE YOU HAVE WITNESSED? Will Jacks' 150 not out at The Oval against Essex in 2022
FAVOURITE FORMAT? First-class cricket
HOBBIES? Fishing
FAVOURITE TOY AS A KID? Play-Doh
WHAT WOULD BE YOUR PERFECT BREAKFAST? Pancakes with bacon and syrup
WHICH PERSON INSPIRES YOU MOST? Andrew Flintoff
SURPRISING FACT ABOUT YOU: I was born in Singapore

Batting	Mat	Inns	NO	Runs	HS	Ave	SR	100	50	Ct	St
First-class	25	31	6	415	58	16.60	48.99	0	2	8	-
List A	9	8	1	324	75	46.28	97.88	0	4	2	-
T20s	14	7	3	29	12	7.25	87.87	0	0	7	-

Bowling	Mat	Balls	Mdns	Runs	Wkts	BB	Ave	4wI	5wI	SR	Econ
First-class	25	3134	85	1803	74	5-22	24.36	-	3	42.35	3.45
List A	9	378	1	399	8	2-20	49.87	0	0	47.25	6.33
T20s	14	208	0	400	8	2-17	50.00	0	0	26.00	11.53

DAN LAWRENCE RHB / OB / R1 / W0 / MVP38

FULL NAME: Daniel William Lawrence
BORN: July 12, 1997, Whipps Cross, Essex
SQUAD NO: 28
EDUCATION: Trinity Catholic High School, Woodford Green, London
TEAMS: England, Surrey, Brisbane Heat, Essex, London Spirit, Melbourne Stars
ROLE: Batter
DEBUT: Test: 2021; First-class: 2015; List A: 2016; T20: 2015

BEST BATTING: 175 Surrey vs Worcestershire, Worcester, 2024
BEST BOWLING: 4-91 Surrey vs Lancashire, Old Trafford, 2024
COUNTY CAP: 2017 (Essex)

FAMILY TIES? My dad is the groundsman at Chingford CC and played at the club for many years. My great uncle played for England
CHILDHOOD SPORTING HERO? David Beckham

Batting	Mat	Inns	NO	Runs	HS	Ave	SR	100	50	Ct	St
Tests	14	27	2	671	91	26.84	55.63	0	4	6	-
First-class	132	211	17	7097	175	36.58	55.29	17	32	94	-
List A	28	25	0	670	115	26.80	89.09	1	4	9	-
T20s	149	139	11	3154	93	24.64	140.24	0	20	53	-

Bowling	Mat	Balls	Mdns	Runs	Wkts	BB	Ave	4wl	5wl	SR	Econ
Tests	14	258	11	133	3	1-0	44.33	-	0	86.00	3.09
First-class	132	2556	59	1517	35	4-91	43.34	-	0	73.02	3.56
List A	28	573	0	597	11	3-35	54.27	0	0	52.09	6.25
T20s	149	975	0	1290	57	4-20	22.63	2	0	17.10	7.93

JACK LEACH

LHB / SLA / RO / W3

FULL NAME: Matthew Jack Leach
BORN: June 22, 1991, Taunton, Somerset
SQUAD NO: 17
HEIGHT: 6ft
NICKNAME: Nut
EDUCATION: Bishop Fox's Community School; Richard Huish College; Cardiff Metropolitan University
TEAMS: England, Somerset
ROLE: Bowler
DEBUT: Test: 2018; First-class: 2012; List A: 2012; T20: 2021

BEST BATTING: 92 England vs Ireland, Lord's, 2019
BEST BOWLING: 8-85 Somerset vs Essex, Taunton, 2018
COUNTY CAP: 2017

FIRST CRICKET CLUB? Taunton Deane CC, Somerset
EARLIEST CRICKETING MEMORY? Watching Somerset at the County Ground
THE KOOKABURRA BALL: YES OR NO? No, use the same ball for the whole competition
GREATEST PERFORMANCE YOU HAVE WITNESSED? Marcus Trescothick's 13-ball fifty in a T20 in 2010
WHAT WOULD YOU DO IF YOU WERE IN CHARGE OF COUNTY CRICKET? Change the lbw law so that you can be given out even if you are hit outside the line
SURPRISING FACT ABOUT YOU: I wrote a letter to Marcus Trescothick asking for advice when I was about 10 years old. He sent me a long reply and I still have the letter. What a man

Batting	Mat	Inns	NO	Runs	HS	Ave	SR	100	50	Ct	St
Tests	39	59	22	498	92	13.45	37.33	0	1	18	-
First-class	151	208	62	2057	92	14.08	40.08	0	3	59	-
List A	27	8	4	45	18	11.25	55.55	0	0	17	-
T20s	7	1	0	0	0	0.00	0.00	0	0	3	-

Bowling	Mat	Balls	Mdns	Runs	Wkts	BB	Ave	4wI	5wI	SR	Econ
Tests	39	9402	308	4838	142	5-66	34.07	-	5	66.21	3.08
First-class	151	29934	1168	13926	495	8-85	28.13	-	31	60.47	2.79
List A	27	1361	8	1030	36	6-26	28.61	0	1	37.80	4.54
T20s	7	138	0	186	11	3-28	16.90	0	0	12.54	8.08

JACK LEANING
RHB / OB / R0 / W0

FULL NAME: Jack Andrew Leaning
BORN: October 18, 1993, Bristol
SQUAD NO: 34
HEIGHT: 6ft
EDUCATION: Archbishop Holgate's School, York; York College
TEAMS: Kent, England U19, Yorkshire
ROLE: Batter
DEBUT: First-class: 2013; List A: 2012; T20: 2013

BEST BATTING: 220* Kent vs Sussex, Canterbury, 2020
BEST BOWLING: 3-64 Kent vs Lancashire, Canterbury, 2023
COUNTY CAP: 2016 (Yorkshire); 2021 (Kent)

FIRST CRICKET CLUB? Heworth CC, York, North Yorkshire
WHICH TEAMMATE HAS HAD THE BIGGEST IMPACT ON YOUR GAME? Tim Bresnan – he guided me through my early years at Yorkshire and always fought my corner if things weren't going well. And I scored my first three hundreds batting with him
IF YOU COULD PINCH A PLAYER FROM ANOTHER COUNTY, WHO WOULD IT BE? Dan Worrall
HOW IS BAZBALL AFFECTING CHAMPIONSHIP CRICKET? It's encouraging more freedom and a desire to move the game forward in pursuit of victory
WHAT DO YOU THINK OF THE CURRENT 50-OVER COMPETITION? I think it's in a good state, helping young players make the transition to the first team
WHAT'S THE SILLIEST OUTFIT YOU'VE EVER WORN? A giant duck costume

Batting	Mat	Inns	NO	Runs	HS	Ave	SR	100	50	Ct	St
First-class	123	202	22	6047	220*	33.59	43.37	11	31	120	-
List A	70	62	9	1765	137*	33.30	80.66	3	9	36	-
T20s	111	94	23	1921	81*	27.05	130.32	0	7	62	-

Bowling	Mat	Balls	Mdns	Runs	Wkts	BB	Ave	4wI	5wI	SR	Econ
First-class	123	3244	58	2155	36	3-64	59.86	-	0	90.11	3.98
List A	70	639	1	564	14	5-22	40.28	0	1	45.64	5.29
T20s	111	414	0	535	23	3-15	23.26	0	0	18.00	7.75

DOM LEECH

RHB / RMF / R0 / W0

FULL NAME: Dominic James Leech
BORN: January 10, 2001, Middlesbrough
SQUAD NO: TBC
EDUCATION: Nunthorpe Academy, Middlesbrough; Queen Ethelburga's School, York
TEAMS: Northamptonshire, England U19, Yorkshire
ROLE: Bowler
DEBUT: First-class: 2020; List A: 2023; T20: 2022

BEST BATTING: 32 Yorkshire vs Gloucestershire, Headingley, 2023
BEST BOWLING: 3-78 Yorkshire vs Gloucestershire, Headingley, 2023

NOTES: The 24-year-old pace bowler joined Northamptonshire at the end of last season on a three-year contract. A tall seamer who has played twice for England U19, Leech has come through the ranks at Yorkshire and represented the county in all three formats without ever making the breakthrough at Headingley. He took four wickets in five Championship appearances in 2024, two of them for Yorkshire and the other three for his new club. "I am thrilled to be joining Northamptonshire and I'm really looking forward to becoming a multi-format cricketer and progressing my game over the next three years with the help of the coaching team here," said Leech. "I would like to thank Yorkshire CCC for the last eight years having helped me progress from the academy to first team"

Batting	Mat	Inns	NO	Runs	HS	Ave	SR	100	50	Ct	St
First-class	10	12	1	66	32	6.00	28.44	0	0	2	-
List A	9	6	3	74	23	24.66	61.66	0	0	1	-
T20s	7	2	1	1	1*	1.00	33.33	0	0	0	-

Bowling	Mat	Balls	Mdns	Runs	Wkts	BB	Ave	4wI	5wI	SR	Econ
First-class	10	826	15	627	11	3-78	57.00	-	0	75.09	4.55
List A	9	366	3	385	11	3-48	35.00	0	0	33.27	6.31
T20s	7	109	0	141	8	3-13	17.62	0	0	13.62	7.76

ALEX LEES

LHB / LB / R3 / WO

FULL NAME: Alexander Zak Lees
BORN: April 14, 1993, Halifax, Yorkshire
SQUAD NO: 19
HEIGHT: 6ft 3in
NICKNAME: Leesy
EDUCATION: Holy Trinity Senior School, Halifax
TEAMS: England, Durham, Yorkshire
ROLE: Batter
DEBUT: Test: 2022; First-class: 2010; List A: 2011; T20: 2013

BEST BATTING: 275* Yorkshire vs Derbyshire, Chesterfield, 2013
BEST BOWLING: 2-51 Yorkshire vs Middlesex, Lord's, 2016
COUNTY CAP: 2014 (Yorkshire)

FIRST CRICKET CLUB? Bradshaw & Illingworth CC, Halifax
CHILDHOOD SPORTING HERO? Brian Lara
SURPRISING FACT ABOUT YOU: I do a bit of magic on the side
NOTES: Lees was announced as Durham's new club captain in December, replacing Scott Borthwick as red-ball skipper alongside his existing role as leader of the 50-over and T20 sides. He also signed a new three-year contract with the club. On becoming club captain, Lees said: "This opportunity to captain Durham gives me an opportunity to put some real focus into the red-ball team, building on the foundations that we have built over the last few years. I am very settled in the North East, the region is fantastic for myself and the family, this is home now and long may that continue, and I am really excited to see what the next three years have to offer"

Batting	Mat	Inns	NO	Runs	HS	Ave	SR	100	50	Ct	St
Tests	10	19	0	453	67	23.84	43.06	0	2	6	-
First-class	176	301	19	10829	275*	38.40	50.06	28	51	112	-
List A	79	74	6	2810	144	41.32	80.44	6	21	31	-
T20s	91	87	11	2154	95*	28.34	122.59	0	13	29	-

Bowling	Mat	Balls	Mdns	Runs	Wkts	BB	Ave	4wI	5wI	SR	Econ
Tests	10	-	-	-	-	-	-	-	-	-	-
First-class	176	67	1	96	3	2-51	32.00	-	0	22.33	8.59
List A	79	-	-	-	-	-	-	-	-	-	-
T20s	91	-	-	-	-	-	-	-	-	-	-

ARCHIE LENHAM

RHB / LB / RO / WO

SUSSEX

FULL NAME: Archie David Lenham
BORN: July 23, 2004, Eastbourne, Sussex
SQUAD NO: 41
HEIGHT: 5ft 7in
NICKNAME: Catch
EDUCATION: Bede's Senior School, Hailsham, East Sussex
TEAMS: Sussex, England U19
ROLE: Bowler
DEBUT: First-class: 2021; List A: 2021; T20: 2021

BEST BATTING: 48 Sussex vs Leicestershire, Leicester, 2022
BEST BOWLING: 4-84 Sussex vs Leicestershire, Leicester, 2022

FIRST CRICKET CLUB? Eastbourne CC, East Sussex
FAMILY TIES? My grandfather Les Lenham played for Sussex in the 1950s and '60s, and my dad Neil played for the club in the 1980s and '90s
BEST PLAYER IN COUNTY CRICKET (EXCLUDING TEAMMATES)? James Vince
BEST DELIVERY YOU HAVE EVER BOWLED? A leg-spinner to Colin Ackermann which spun to hit his off stump
BEST PERFORMANCE AS A PRO? Taking four wickets at Cardiff in the T20 Blast in 2021
FAVOURITE FORMAT? Four-day cricket – the hardest format
FAVOURITE TOY AS A KID? Lego
WHAT WOULD BE YOUR PERFECT BREAKFAST? A Full English

Batting	Mat	Inns	NO	Runs	HS	Ave	SR	100	50	Ct	St
First-class	7	12	2	206	48	20.60	38.07	0	0	2	-
List A	20	15	6	143	31	15.88	72.58	0	0	4	-
T20s	24	6	5	15	7*	15.00	44.11	0	0	5	-

Bowling	Mat	Balls	Mdns	Runs	Wkts	BB	Ave	4wI	5wI	SR	Econ
First-class	7	835	10	528	7	4-84	75.42	-	0	119.28	3.79
List A	20	874	1	832	20	4-59	41.60	1	0	43.70	5.71
T20s	24	366	0	501	14	4-26	35.78	1	0	26.14	8.21

NED LEONARD

RHB / RFM / R0 / W0

FULL NAME: Edward Owen Leonard
BORN: August 15, 2002, Hammersmith, London
SQUAD NO: TBC
HEIGHT: 6ft 2in
NICKNAME: Deadly
EDUCATION: Millfield School, Somerset
TEAMS: Glamorgan, England U19, Somerset
ROLE: Bowler
DEBUT: First-class: 2021; List A: 2021; T20: 2022

GLAMORGAN

BEST BATTING: 15 Glamorgan vs Derbyshire, Derby, 2024
BEST BOWLING: 2-42 Glamorgan vs Gloucestershire, Cardiff, 2024

BIGGEST INFLUENCE ON YOUR DEVELOPMENT AS A CRICKETER (EXCLUDING PARENTS)?
Mark Garaway – director of cricket at Millfield School
MOST EXCITING DAY AS A CRICKETER? Signing my first professional contract at Somerset
WHAT WOULD YOU DO IF YOU WERE IN CHARGE OF COUNTY CRICKET? Remove the free-hit rule from T20 and one-day formats, allow three bouncers per over
CHILDHOOD SPORTING HERO? Jonny Wilkinson

Batting	Mat	Inns	NO	Runs	HS	Ave	SR	100	50	Ct	St
First-class	7	10	6	46	15	11.50	50.54	0	0	2	-
List A	15	8	4	73	32	18.25	148.97	0	0	6	-
T20s	1	0	-	-	-	-	-	-	-	0	-

Bowling	Mat	Balls	Mdns	Runs	Wkts	BB	Ave	4wI	5wI	SR	Econ
First-class	7	884	22	579	8	2-42	72.37	-	0	110.50	3.92
List A	15	635	2	685	13	3-40	52.69	0	0	48.84	6.47
T20s	1	12	0	8	1	1-8	8.00	0	0	12.00	4.00

JAKE LIBBY

RHB / OB / R2 / W0

WORCESTERSHIRE

FULL NAME: Jacob Daniel Libby
BORN: January 3, 1993, Plymouth, Devon
SQUAD NO: 2
HEIGHT: 5ft 8in
NICKNAME: Libs
EDUCATION: Plymouth College; Truro College, Cornwall; Cardiff Metropolitan University
TEAMS: Worcestershire, Northamptonshire, Nottinghamshire
ROLE: Batter
DEBUT: First-class: 2014; List A: 2019; T20: 2018

BEST BATTING: 215 Worcestershire vs Sussex, Hove, 2022
BEST BOWLING: 2-10 Worcestershire vs Middlesex, Worcester, 2022

FIRST CRICKET CLUB? Menheniot & Looe CC, Cornwall
WHICH TEAMMATE HAS HAD THE BIGGEST IMPACT ON YOUR GAME? Joe Leach – a fountain of knowledge and experience
WHAT PART OF THE SEASON DO YOU MOST ENJOY? September because it's crunch time (and the golf season is just around the corner!)
WHICH AWAY GROUND DO YOU MOST ENJOY VISITING? Taunton – the ground where I grew up watching the game and I get some Cornish folk support there
WHO IS THE MOST TALENTED U19 TEENAGER IN THE COUNTY GAME? Olly Cox (Wor)
IF YOU COULD PINCH A PLAYER FROM ANOTHER COUNTY, WHO WOULD IT BE? Brett Hutton
WHO IS THE TOUGHEST BOWLER TO FACE? My four-month-old baby

Batting	Mat	Inns	NO	Runs	HS	Ave	SR	100	50	Ct	St
First-class	115	197	16	6727	215	37.16	47.97	17	30	45	-
List A	40	37	9	1611	126*	57.53	87.84	2	14	12	-
T20s	54	47	8	1167	78*	29.92	123.49	0	5	15	-

Bowling	Mat	Balls	Mdns	Runs	Wkts	BB	Ave	4wl	5wl	SR	Econ
First-class	115	1099	20	634	9	2-10	70.44	-	0	122.11	3.46
List A	40	273	1	244	6	2-47	40.66	0	0	45.50	5.36
T20s	54	54	0	77	1	1-11	77.00	0	0	54.00	8.55

JAKE LINTOTT

RHB / SLW / R0 / W0

FULL NAME: Jacob Benedict Lintott
BORN: April 22, 1993, Taunton, Somerset
SQUAD NO: 23
HEIGHT: 5ft 11in
NICKNAME: Linsanity
EDUCATION: Queen's College, Taunton
TEAMS: Warwickshire, Barbados Royals, Fortune Barisal, Gloucestershire, Hampshire, Southern Brave
ROLE: Bowler
DEBUT: First-class: 2021; List A: 2022; T20: 2017

BEST BATTING: 78 Warwickshire vs Essex, Chelmsford, 2023
BEST BOWLING: 3-10 Warwickshire vs Lancashire, Old Trafford, 2024

FIRST CRICKET CLUB? Taunton St Andrews CC, Somerset
BIGGEST INFLUENCE ON YOUR DEVELOPMENT AS A CRICKETER (EXCLUDING PARENTS)?
Piers McBride, my county age-group coach at Somerset. He was very supportive of me since I was 13 and still works with me now at my club Clevedon CC
WHAT WOULD YOU CHANGE ABOUT THE STRUCTURE OF THE COUNTY SEASON? One-Day Cup: three regions, 10 games per team plus knockout stages, played in April/May. Championship: three divisions (10 games each), played in June and September. T20: three regions (10 games plus knockout stages) played in July. The Hundred: played in August. Everyone's a winner – higher-quality Championship cricket (played in the warmer months and with fewer games), everyone plays in the 50-over comp, T20 and The Hundred during the school holidays
WHO WOULD YOU MOST LIKE TO HAVE A NET WITH? Shane Warne (my childhood hero)
HOBBIES? Exeter City FC

Batting	Mat	Inns	NO	Runs	HS	Ave	SR	100	50	Ct	St
First-class	3	4	0	110	78	27.50	73.33	0	1	2	-
List A	26	17	8	255	28	28.33	81.73	0	0	8	-
T20s	93	35	12	236	41	10.26	102.60	0	0	41	-

Bowling	Mat	Balls	Mdns	Runs	Wkts	BB	Ave	4wI	5wI	SR	Econ
First-class	3	384	3	211	6	3-10	35.16	-	0	64.00	3.29
List A	26	1228	4	1150	39	5-37	29.48	0	1	31.48	5.61
T20s	93	1835	0	2372	105	4-20	22.59	2	0	17.47	7.75

JOSH LITTLE

RHB / LFM / R0 / W0

MIDDLESEX

FULL NAME: Joshua Brian Little
BORN: November 1, 1999, Dublin, Ireland
SQUAD NO: 82
TEAMS: Ireland, Middlesex, Dambulla Giants, Gujarat Titans, Leinster Lightning, Manchester Originals, Pretoria Capitals, Trinbago Knight Riders, Welsh Fire
ROLE: Bowler
DEBUT: ODI: 2019; T20I: 2016; First-class: 2018; List A: 2018; T20: 2016

BEST BATTING: 27* Leinster Lightning vs Northern Knights, Dublin, 2021 (T20)
BEST BOWLING: 5-13 Manchester Originals vs Oval Invincibles, Old Trafford, 2022 (T20/Hundred)

NOTES: Ireland's exciting pace-bowling talent has signed up with Middlesex on a multi-format deal, although he is expected to feature mostly in the T20 Blast. While final details of the deal remain subject to Cricket Ireland issuing a No Objection Certificate, the contract opens up the possibility of Little developing his red-ball game, following his controversial absence from Ireland's Test team for the Lord's Test in 2023. To date, Little has claimed 139 international wickets across both white-ball formats but has yet to make his Test bow. A regular presence on the franchise circuit, he made his IPL debut for Gujarat Titans in 2023 and will bring pace and left-arm angle to Middlesex's ranks

Batting	Mat	Inns	NO	Runs	HS	Ave	SR	100	50	Ct	St
ODIs	39	15	5	81	29	8.10	93.10	0	0	5	-
T20Is	72	32	20	132	22*	11.00	85.71	0	0	18	-
First-class	6	6	2	68	27	17.00	62.38	0	0	1	-
List A	61	23	8	137	29	9.13	84.56	0	0	11	-
T20s	136	54	37	220	27*	12.94	88.70	0	0	45	-

Bowling	Mat	Balls	Mdns	Runs	Wkts	BB	Ave	4wI	5wI	SR	Econ
ODIs	39	1877	12	1929	58	6-36	33.25	3	1	32.36	6.16
T20Is	72	1586	3	1978	82	4-23	24.12	2	0	19.34	7.48
First-class	6	441	12	320	6	3-95	53.33	-	0	73.50	4.35
List A	61	2730	23	2615	81	6-36	32.28	3	1	33.70	5.74
T20s	136	2821	5	3642	158	5-13	23.05	3	1	17.85	7.74

LIAM LIVINGSTONE RHB / OB / LB / R0 / W0

FULL NAME: Liam Stephen Livingstone
BORN: August 4, 1993, Barrow-in-Furness, Cumbria
SQUAD NO: 7
HEIGHT: 6ft 2in
EDUCATION: Chetwynde School, Cumbria
TEAMS: England, Lancashire, Birmingham Phoenix, Karachi Kings, MI Cape Town, Perth Scorchers, Peshawar Zalmi, Pretoria Capitals, Punjab Kings, Rajasthan Royals
ROLE: Allrounder
DEBUT: Test: 2022; ODI: 2021; T20I: 2018; First-class: 2016; List A: 2015; T20: 2015

LANCASHIRE

BEST BATTING: 224 Lancashire vs Warwickshire, Old Trafford, 2017
BEST BOWLING: 6-52 Lancashire vs Surrey, Old Trafford, 2017
COUNTY CAP: 2017

FIRST CRICKET CLUB? Barrow CC, Cumbria
WHAT PART OF THE SEASON DO YOU MOST ENJOY? The T20 phase
WHICH AWAY GROUND DO YOU MOST ENJOY VISITING? The Oval
WHO IS THE TOUGHEST BOWLER TO FACE? Jasprit Bumrah
CHOOSE A FANTASY SLIP CORDON TO SPEND A DAY IN THE FIELD WITH: David Beckham (wk), Tiger Woods, Kevin Hart
SURPRISING FACT ABOUT YOU: I once scored 350 in a club game

Batting	Mat	Inns	NO	Runs	HS	Ave	SR	100	50	Ct	St
Tests	1	2	1	16	9	16.00	88.88	0	0	0	-
ODIs	39	36	6	932	124*	31.06	108.12	1	4	15	-
T20Is	60	47	9	955	103	25.13	148.98	1	2	26	-
First-class	63	96	15	3085	224	38.08	59.55	7	15	74	-
List A	94	82	9	2484	129	34.02	102.55	2	14	40	-
T20s	300	276	32	6772	103	27.75	143.59	2	35	119	-

Bowling	Mat	Balls	Mdns	Runs	Wkts	BB	Ave	4wI	5wI	SR	Econ
Tests	1	-	-	-	-	-	-	-	-	-	-
ODIs	39	968	2	982	25	3-16	39.28	0	0	38.72	6.08
T20Is	60	576	1	838	33	3-17	25.39	0	0	17.45	8.72
First-class	63	3375	112	1552	43	6-52	36.09	-	1	78.48	2.75
List A	94	2273	3	2116	48	3-16	44.08	0	0	47.35	5.58
T20s	300	2366	1	3364	128	4-17	26.28	2	0	18.48	8.53

DAVID LLOYD

RHB / RM / R0 / W0

DERBYSHIRE

FULL NAME: David Liam Lloyd
BORN: June 15, 1992, St Asaph, Denbighshire, Wales
SQUAD NO: 46
HEIGHT: 5ft 9in
NICKNAME: Dai
EDUCATION: Darland High School, Wrexham; Shrewsbury School
TEAMS: Derbyshire, Glamorgan, Welsh Fire
ROLE: Batter
DEBUT: First-class: 2012; List A: 2014; T20: 2014

BEST BATTING: 313* Glamorgan vs Derbyshire, Cardiff, 2022
BEST BOWLING: 4-11 Glamorgan vs Kent, Cardiff, 2021
COUNTY CAP: 2022 (Glamorgan)

FIRST CRICKET CLUB? Brymbo CC, Clwyd, Wales
WHAT'S THE BIGGEST PRIZE IN DOMESTIC CRICKET? The County Championship
THE KOOKABURRA BALL: YES OR NO? Not bothered
OPPONENT YOU MOST LOOK FORWARD TO PLAYING AGAINST? Chris Cooke – a close friend from our time together at Glamorgan
HOW MANY HOURS DO YOU SPEND ON YOUR PHONE A DAY? Hours? About 10 mins I'd say
SPECIALITY SUBJECT IN A PUB QUIZ (EXCLUDING SPORT)? Football
ONE THING YOU WANT TO DO BEFORE YOU DIE: Fly a plane
HOBBY YOU WOULD LIKE TO LEARN: Chess
WHICH PUBLIC FIGURE INSPIRES YOU (EXCLUDING SPORTSPEOPLE)? Jamie Oliver
SURPRISING FACT ABOUT YOU: I have a degree in Economics
FILM YOU CAN WATCH OVER AND OVER: The Longest Yard

Batting	Mat	Inns	NO	Runs	HS	Ave	SR	100	50	Ct	St
First-class	118	202	17	5538	313*	29.93	62.74	6	26	62	-
List A	63	55	3	1426	92	27.42	86.58	0	10	18	-
T20s	92	85	4	1947	97*	24.03	132.99	0	12	20	-

Bowling	Mat	Balls	Mdns	Runs	Wkts	BB	Ave	4wI	5wI	SR	Econ
First-class	118	7413	160	4716	108	4-11	43.66	-	0	68.63	3.81
List A	63	913	4	909	22	5-53	41.31	1	1	41.50	5.97
T20s	92	126	0	187	6	2-13	31.16	0	0	21.00	8.90

ROB LORD

RHB / RFM / R0 / W0

FULL NAME: Robert Lord
BORN: May 4, 2001, Salford, Lancashire
SQUAD NO: 4
EDUCATION: St Ambrose Barlow School;
Myerscough College
TEAMS: Nottinghamshire
ROLE: Bowler
DEBUT: First-class: 2024; List A: 2024

BEST BATTING: 31 Nottinghamshire vs Warwickshire, Trent Bridge, 2024
BEST BOWLING: 3-42 Nottinghamshire vs Kent, Canterbury, 2024

FIRST CRICKET CLUB? Clifton CC, Ashbourne, Derby
EARLIEST CRICKETING MEMORY? Watching my dad
WHAT'S THE BIGGEST PRIZE IN DOMESTIC CRICKET? It's a toss-up between the T20 Blast and the County Championship
THE KOOKABURRA BALL: YES OR NO? I'm not sure – I made my debut using the Kookaburra ball and I didn't mind bowling with it
OPPONENT YOU MOST LOOK FORWARD TO PLAYING AGAINST? Anybody that has played international cricket
HOW MANY HOURS DO YOU SPEND ON YOUR PHONE A DAY? Too many
ONE THING YOU WANT TO DO BEFORE YOU DIE: A triathalon
FILM YOU CAN WATCH OVER AND OVER: Most of the Marvel films

Batting	Mat	Inns	NO	Runs	HS	Ave	SR	100	50	Ct	St
First-class	4	5	0	63	31	12.60	49.21	0	0	2	-
List A	5	3	2	26	12*	26.00	100.00	0	0	2	-

Bowling	Mat	Balls	Mdns	Runs	Wkts	BB	Ave	4wI	5wI	SR	Econ
First-class	4	397	9	278	10	3-42	27.80	-	0	39.70	4.20
List A	5	261	1	249	11	5-45	22.63	0	1	23.72	5.72

FULL NAME: Adam Lyth
BORN: September 25, 1987, Whitby, Yorkshire
SQUAD NO: 9
HEIGHT: 5ft 9in
EDUCATION: Caedmon School; Whitby Community School
TEAMS: England, Yorkshire, Multan Sultans, Northern Superchargers, Perth Scorchers, Rangpur Riders, Trent Rockets
ROLE: Batter
DEBUT: Test: 2015; First-class: 2007; List A: 2006; T20: 2008

BEST BATTING: 251 Yorkshire vs Lancashire, Old Trafford, 2014
BEST BOWLING: 4-56 Yorkshire vs Northamptonshire, Northampton, 2024
COUNTY CAP: 2010; BENEFIT: 2021

FIRST CRICKET CLUB? Scarborough CC, North Yorkshire
FAMILY TIES? My brother and dad played for Scarborough and my grandad played for Whitby CC
WHICH COUNTY PLAYER WOULD YOU MOST LIKE TO GO FOR A DRINK WITH? Callum Parkinson makes me laugh all the time
BEST PERFORMANCE AS A PRO? Scoring a Test hundred
GREATEST PERFORMANCE YOU HAVE WITNESSED? Darren Lehmann's triple hundred in his final match for Yorkshire at Headingley in 2006
FAVOURITE FORMAT? T20
DESCRIBE YOURSELF IN THREE WORDS: Funny, thick, honest
WHAT WOULD BE YOUR PERFECT BREAKFAST? Poached eggs on toast
WHICH PERSON INSPIRES YOU MOST? David Beckham
SURPRISING FACT ABOUT YOU: I had trials with Manchester City

Batting	Mat	Inns	NO	Runs	HS	Ave	SR	100	50	Ct	St
Tests	7	13	0	265	107	20.38	50.09	1	0	8	-
First-class	236	394	18	14737	251	39.19	-	37	74	317	-
List A	122	115	8	3765	144	35.18	93.84	5	18	55	-
T20s	210	200	6	4817	161	24.82	143.70	1	32	102	-
Bowling	Mat	Balls	Mdns	Runs	Wkts	BB	Ave	4wI	5wI	SR	Econ
Tests	7	6	1	0	0	0-0	-	-	-	-	0.00
First-class	236	3597	97	2058	46	4-56	44.73	-	0	78.19	3.43
List A	122	360	1	373	6	2-27	62.16	0	0	60.00	6.21
T20s	210	529	0	684	25	5-31	27.36	0	1	21.16	7.75

WAYNE MADSEN

RHB / OB / R7 / W0

FULL NAME: Wayne Lee Madsen
BORN: January 2, 1984, Durban, South Africa
SQUAD NO: 77
HEIGHT: 5ft 11in
NICKNAME: Psycho
EDUCATION: Highbury Preparatory School; Kearsney College; University of South Africa
TEAMS: Italy, Derbyshire, Dolphins, Joburg Super Kings, KwaZulu-Natal, Manchester Originals, Multan Sultans, Rangpur Riders
ROLE: Batter
DEBUT: T20I: 2023; First-class: 2004; List A: 2004; T20: 2010

BEST BATTING: 231* Derbyshire vs Northamptonshire, Northampton, 2012
BEST BOWLING: 3-45 KwaZulu-Natal vs Eastern Province, Port Elizabeth, 2008
COUNTY CAP: 2011; BENEFIT: 2017

FIRST CRICKET CLUB? Crusaders CC, Durban, South Africa. I got a golden duck on debut
EARLIEST CRICKETING MEMORY? Beach cricket
THE KOOKABURRA BALL? YES OR NO? Yes (I'm a batter)
OPPONENT YOU MOST LOOK FORWARD TO PLAYING AGAINST? Kane Williamson at Middlesex – I love watching him bat, although hopefully not for long against us!
FAVOURITE WARM-UP SONG? Lionheart (Fearless) by Joel Corry & Tom Grennan
HOW MANY HOURS DO YOU SPEND ON YOUR PHONE A DAY? Two to three
SPECIALITY SUBJECT IN A PUB QUIZ (EXCLUDING SPORT)? Geography
ONE THING YOU WANT TO DO BEFORE YOU DIE: Dive with great whites
HOBBY YOU WOULD LIKE TO LEARN: Drawing
WHICH PUBLIC FIGURE INSPIRES YOU (EXCLUDING SPORTSPEOPLE)? Nelson Mandela
SURPRISING FACT ABOUT YOU: I once held the Guinness world record for the most cricket bat taps in one minute (282)
FILM YOU CAN WATCH OVER AND OVER: Gladiator

Batting	Mat	Inns	NO	Runs	HS	Ave	SR	100	50	Ct	St
T20Is	4	4	0	95	52	23.75	141.79	0	1	4	-
First-class	239	421	30	15909	231*	40.68	52.77	39	88	285	-
List A	117	109	19	3819	138	42.43	92.35	8	21	79	-
T20s	201	193	31	4965	109*	30.64	135.39	2	31	80	-

Bowling	Mat	Balls	Mdns	Runs	Wkts	BB	Ave	4wI	5wI	SR	Econ
T20Is	4	-	-	-	-	-	-	-	-	-	-
First-class	239	3636	110	1948	38	3-45	51.26	-	0	95.68	3.21
List A	117	740	9	606	18	3-27	33.66	0	0	41.11	4.91
T20s	201	593	1	810	22	2-20	36.81	0	0	26.95	8.19

SAQIB MAHMOOD

RHB / RF / RO / WO

FULL NAME: Saqib Mahmood
BORN: February 25, 1997, Birmingham
SQUAD NO: 25
HEIGHT: 6ft 3in
NICKNAME: Saq
EDUCATION: Matthew Moss High School, Rochdale
TEAMS: England, Lancashire, Oval Invincibles, Peshawar Zalmi, Sydney Thunder
ROLE: Bowler
DEBUT: Test: 2022; ODI: 2020; T20I: 2019; First-class: 2016; List A: 2016; T20: 2015

BEST BATTING: 49 England vs West Indies, Grenada, 2022
BEST BOWLING: 5-47 Lancashire vs Yorkshire, Old Trafford, 2021
COUNTY CAP: 2021

NOTES: The England seamer, now 28, has been plagued by injury in recent seasons but was back in the thick of it last summer, taking a full part in Lancashire's T20 Blast campaign and playing a starring role in the Hundred final for Oval Invincibles. Mahmood also returned to England's white-ball sides over the winter. He signed a new three-year white-ball contract with Lancashire last year, although the deal does allow for the possibility of four-day cricket if circumstances allow. Mahmood said: "While this is a white-ball contract, I still have an ambition to play red-ball cricket for England again and for Lancashire in the County Championship, which is still the biggest test of skill and fitness outside of Test match cricket, and there are options within this contract for that to happen"

Batting	Mat	Inns	NO	Runs	HS	Ave	SR	100	50	Ct	St
Tests	2	2	1	52	49	52.00	41.93	0	0	1	-
ODIs	13	6	3	29	12	9.66	58.00	0	0	2	-
T20Is	19	9	4	35	12	7.00	77.77	0	0	2	-
First-class	32	40	18	362	49	16.45	36.05	0	0	5	-
List A	42	19	9	147	45	14.70	79.45	0	0	9	-
T20s	83	26	15	81	12	7.36	74.31	0	0	11	-

Bowling	Mat	Balls	Mdns	Runs	Wkts	BB	Ave	4wI	5wI	SR	Econ
Tests	2	366	17	137	6	2-21	22.83	-	0	61.00	2.24
ODIs	13	633	5	558	17	4-42	32.82	1	0	37.23	5.28
T20Is	19	378	2	586	21	4-34	27.90	1	0	18.00	9.30
First-class	32	5077	166	2586	85	5-47	30.42	-	1	59.72	3.05
List A	42	2008	16	1875	71	6-37	26.40	2	3	28.28	5.60
T20s	83	1638	5	2340	111	4-14	21.08	4	0	14.75	8.57

YOUSEF MAJID

LHB / SLA / R0 / W0

FULL NAME: Yousef Majid
BORN: September 8, 2003, Slough, Buckinghamshire
SQUAD NO: 68
EDUCATION: Cranleigh School
TEAMS: Surrey, England U19
ROLE: Bowler
DEBUT: First-class: 2024; List A: 2022

BEST BATTING: 5 Surrey vs Essex, Chelmsford, 2024
BEST BOWLING: 2-128 Surrey vs Essex, Chelmsford, 2024

NOTES: The left-arm spinner was initially given a short-term professional contract at Surrey for the duration of the 2022 One-Day Cup after he took 10 wickets in two Second XI Championship games, which included a second innings 6-54 at Radlett against Middlesex. He impressed during that tournament, taking a wicket with his fifth ball, and nine scalps in eight matches at an economy-rate of 5.57. In August he was called up to play for England U19 against Sri Lanka and in December was selected to play for the same side against Australia at Brisbane in January, playing in two Youth ODIs and the only Youth T20I. Majid was awarded a full-time professional contract for 2023 by Surrey but injury curtailed his season after three wicket-less outings in the One-Day Cup. He did show some ability with the bat, scoring 29 from 97 balls in a 90-run tenth-wicket partnership with Tommy Ealham that got Surrey to within seven runs of a famous Second XI Championship victory against Hampshire. Majid started his cricket journey in the Berkshire pathway, before switching to Surrey at U16 level while attending Cranleigh School, the alma mater of Ollie Pope, Stuart Meaker and Tom Lawes. He made his first-class debut last summer

Batting	Mat	Inns	NO	Runs	HS	Ave	SR	100	50	Ct	St
First-class	1	1	0	5	5	5.00	13.88	0	0	0	-
List A	19	13	5	31	7	3.87	39.24	0	0	4	-

Bowling	Mat	Balls	Mdns	Runs	Wkts	BB	Ave	4wI	5wI	SR	Econ
First-class	1	180	0	128	2	2-128	64.00	-	0	90.00	4.26
List A	19	852	2	786	15	3-74	52.40	0	0	56.80	5.53

DAWID MALAN

LHB / LB / R3 / W0

YORKSHIRE

FULL NAME: Dawid Johannes Malan
BORN: September 3, 1987, Roehampton
SQUAD NO: 29
HEIGHT: 6ft
EDUCATION: University of South Africa
TEAMS: England, Yorkshire, Boland, Hobart Hurricanes, Oval Invincibles, Middlesex, Multan Sultans, Peshawar Zalmi, Punjab Kings, Sunrisers Eastern Cape, Trent Rockets
ROLE: Batter
DEBUT: Test: 2017; ODI: 2019; T20I: 2017; First-class: 2006; List A: 2006; T20: 2006

BEST BATTING: 219 Yorkshire vs Derbyshire, Headingley, 2020
BEST BOWLING: 5-61 Middlesex vs Lancashire, Liverpool, 2012
COUNTY CAP: 2010 (Middlesex); 2020 (Yorkshire); BENEFIT: 2019 (Middlesex)

FAMILY TIES? My dad Dawid played for Transvaal B and Western Province B and my brother Charl played for MCC Young Cricketers and Loughborough MCCU
CHILDHOOD SPORTING HERO? Gary Kirsten
SURPRISING FACT ABOUT YOU: I love to go to the cinema by myself

Batting	Mat	Inns	NO	Runs	HS	Ave	SR	100	50	Ct	St
Tests	22	39	0	1074	140	27.53	40.96	1	9	13	-
ODIs	30	30	4	1450	140	55.76	97.44	6	7	11	-
T20Is	62	60	8	1892	103*	36.38	132.49	1	16	22	-
First-class	212	363	21	13201	219	38.59	53.50	30	68	205	-
List A	178	174	25	6561	185*	44.03	86.46	16	32	62	-
T20s	361	354	56	9925	117	33.30	129.36	5	67	126	-
Bowling	Mat	Balls	Mdns	Runs	Wkts	BB	Ave	4wl	5wl	SR	Econ
Tests	22	222	4	131	2	2-33	65.50	-	0	111.00	3.54
ODIs	30	15	0	17	1	1-5	17.00	0	0	15.00	6.80
T20Is	62	12	0	27	1	1-27	27.00	0	0	12.00	13.50
First-class	212	4249	81	2556	63	5-61	40.57	-	1	67.44	3.60
List A	178	1362	2	1327	41	4-25	32.36	1	0	33.21	5.84
T20s	361	567	1	722	23	2-10	31.39	0	0	24.65	7.64

ZEN MALIK

RHB / LB / RO / WO

FULL NAME: Zen-Ul-Abideen Malik
BORN: April 9, 1998, Stoke-on-Trent, Staffordshire
SQUAD NO: 8
HEIGHT: 5ft 9in
NICKNAME: Zenchen
EDUCATION: Malvern College
TEAMS: Warwickshire, England U19
ROLE: Batter
DEBUT: List A: 2024

WARWICKSHIRE

FIRST CRICKET CLUB? Burslem CC, Stoke-on-Trent
EARLIEST CRICKETING MEMORY? Watching my dad
WHAT'S THE BIGGEST PRIZE IN DOMESTIC CRICKET? The County Championship
THE KOOKABURRA BALL: YES OR NO? Yes, it makes batting easier!
OPPONENT YOU MOST LOOK FORWARD TO PLAYING AGAINST? Anyone with international experience to test myself against the best
FAVOURITE WARM-UP SONG? Homecoming by Kanye West
HOW MANY HOURS DO YOU SPEND ON YOUR PHONE A DAY? Three to five
SPECIALITY SUBJECT IN A PUB QUIZ (EXCLUDING SPORT)? Geography
ONE THING YOU WANT TO DO BEFORE YOU DIE: Hajj
HOBBY YOU WOULD LIKE TO LEARN: Chess
WHICH PUBLIC FIGURE INSPIRES YOU (EXCLUDING SPORTSPEOPLE)? Sam Youkilis
SURPRISING FACT ABOUT YOU: I changed the spelling of my name when I was six
FILM YOU CAN WATCH OVER AND OVER: Léon: The Professional

Batting	Mat	Inns	NO	Runs	HS	Ave	SR	100	50	Ct	St
List A	2	2	0	2	1	1.00	22.22	0	0	1	-
Bowling	Mat	Balls	Mdns	Runs	Wkts	BB	Ave	4wl	5wl	SR	Econ
List A	2	-	-	-	-	-	-	-	-	-	-

BEN MARTINDALE

LHB / RM / RO / WO

NOTTINGHAMSHIRE

FULL NAME: Benjamin John Richardson Martindale
BORN: December 12, 2002, Nottingham
SQUAD NO: 95
HEIGHT: 5ft 11in
NICKNAME: Tindale
EDUCATION: Nottingham High School
TEAMS: Nottinghamshire
ROLE: Allrounder
DEBUT: List A: 2022; T20: 2024

WHICH COUNTY PLAYER WOULD YOU MOST LIKE TO GO FOR A DRINK WITH? Dane Paterson – that energy…
BEST DELIVERY YOU HAVE EVER FACED? The ones that were too quick to see
BEST PERFORMANCE AS A PRO? To be continued…
GREATEST PERFORMANCE YOU HAVE WITNESSED? Suryakumar Yadav's 117 against England in the T20I at Trent Bridge in 2022
FAVOURITE FORMAT? First-class cricket – a win is a massive reward for the effort put in
DESCRIBE YOURSELF IN THREE WORDS: Chilled, flair, particular
HOBBIES? Playing the guitar
FAVOURITE TOY AS A KID? A McDonald's Happy Meal karaoke machine which only played Jason Derulo's 'Whatcha Say'
WHAT WOULD BE YOUR PERFECT BREAKFAST? An omelette, smoothie, tropical fruit and yoghurt

Batting	Mat	Inns	NO	Runs	HS	Ave	SR	100	50	Ct	St
List A	8	8	0	180	55	22.50	63.60	0	1	4	-
T20s	7	6	0	78	44	13.00	90.69	0	0	3	-
Bowling	Mat	Balls	Mdns	Runs	Wkts	BB	Ave	4wi	5wi	SR	Econ
List A	8	12	0	13	0	0-13	-	-	-	-	6.50
T20s	7	-	-	-	-	-	-	-	-	-	-

NATHAN MCANDREW — RHB / RFM / R0 / W0

FULL NAME: Nathan John McAndrew
BORN: July 14, 1993, Bankstown, New South Wales, Australia
SQUAD NO: 43
TEAMS: Sussex, Auckland, Australia A, New South Wales, South Australia, Sydney Thunder, Warwickshire
ROLE: Bowler
DEBUT: First-class: 2016; List A: 2019; T20: 2016

BEST BATTING: 92 Australia A vs Sri Lanka A, Hambantota, 2022
BEST BOWLING: 7-11 South Australia vs Western Australia, Perth, 2025

NOTES: Sussex have secured McAndrew's services for the third year in a row, the Australian allrounder returning to Hove to play in the County Championship and the T20 Blast throughout June and July. "We are delighted that Nathan will be returning to Hove for the 2025 season," said Sussex head coach Paul Farbrace. "He has been fantastic for us in both forms over the last two seasons. He brings a wealth of experience and sets very high standards around the group." A relatively late developer, McAndrew made his first-class debut for Auckland in New Zealand in 2015 before falling off the radar and barely appearing in any professional cricket until a breakout Big Bash campaign for Sydney Thunder in 2020/21, since when he has gone from strength to strength

Batting	Mat	Inns	NO	Runs	HS	Ave	SR	100	50	Ct	St
First-class	54	82	15	1775	92	26.49	50.80	0	9	18	-
List A	20	18	2	233	55	14.56	116.50	0	1	7	-
T20s	88	57	26	513	32*	16.54	162.85	0	0	30	-

Bowling	Mat	Balls	Mdns	Runs	Wkts	BB	Ave	4wl	5wl	SR	Econ
First-class	54	10444	366	5410	213	7-11	25.39	-	12	49.03	3.10
List A	20	970	8	983	25	5-40	39.32	0	1	38.80	6.08
T20s	88	1641	0	2494	81	5-16	30.79	1	1	20.25	9.11

FREDDIE McCANN

LHB / OB / R0 / W0

NOTTINGHAMSHIRE

FULL NAME: Freddie William McCann
BORN: April 19, 2005, Nottingham
SQUAD NO: 44
HEIGHT: 6ft 3in
NICKNAME: Fmac
EDUCATION: Toothill Comprehensive School; Trent College
TEAMS: Nottinghamshire, England Lions
ROLE: Batter
DEBUT: First-class: 2024; List A: 2024; T20: 2024

BEST BATTING: 154 Nottinghamshire vs Surrey, Trent Bridge, 2024
BEST BOWLING: 1-6 Nottinghamshire vs Essex, Chelmsford, 2024

FIRST CRICKET CLUB? Papplewick & Linby CC, Nottingham
EARLIEST CRICKETING MEMORY? Winning a Kwik Cricket final for school
THE KOOKABURRA BALL: YES OR NO? Yes, it brings a balance between batters and bowlers throughout the season
OPPONENT YOU MOST LOOK FORWARD TO PLAYING AGAINST? Harry Moore, we're good mates off the pitch so would be entertaining to come up against him in the middle
HOW MANY HOURS DO YOU SPEND ON YOUR PHONE A DAY? Two
ONE THING YOU WANT TO DO BEFORE YOU DIE: Play in the Boxing Day Test match with my parents watching
HOBBY YOU WOULD LIKE TO LEARN: Pilates
SURPRISING FACT ABOUT YOU: I can do magic tricks
FILM YOU CAN WATCH OVER AND OVER: Interstellar

Batting	Mat	Inns	NO	Runs	HS	Ave	SR	100	50	Ct	St
First-class	6	9	0	360	154	40.00	54.38	2	1	8	-
List A	8	8	0	168	48	21.00	75.33	0	0	8	-
T20s	1	1	0	48	48	48.00	150.00	0	0	1	-

Bowling	Mat	Balls	Mdns	Runs	Wkts	BB	Ave	4wI	5wI	SR	Econ
First-class	6	306	5	208	2	1-6	104.00	-	0	153.00	4.07
List A	8	196	1	188	1	1-48	188.00	0	0	196.00	5.75
T20s	1	-	-	-	-	-	-	-	-	-	-

JAMIE MCILROY

RHB / LFM / R0 / W0

FULL NAME: Jamie Peter McIlroy
BORN: June 19, 1994, Hereford
SQUAD NO: 35
HEIGHT: 6ft 3in
NICKNAME: Macca
EDUCATION: Builth Wells High School, Powys; Coleg Powys, Newtown
TEAMS: Glamorgan
ROLE: Bowler
DEBUT: First-class: 2020; List A: 2022; T20: 2022

BEST BATTING: 30* Glamorgan vs Yorkshire, Cardiff, 2023
BEST BOWLING: 5-34 Glamorgan vs Worcestershire, Worcester, 2023

FIRST CRICKET CLUB? Builth Wells CC, Powys
BIGGEST INFLUENCE ON YOUR DEVELOPMENT AS A CRICKETER (EXCLUDING PARENTS)?
Ed Price, my former Herefordshire U17 coach. He was the first person to teach me how to correctly swing a ball and control it with the wrist position
MOST EXCITING DAY AS A CRICKETER? Hard to choose between winning the Minor Counties national knockout cup with Herefordshire and signing my first professional contract at Glamorgan
WHAT WOULD YOU DO IF YOU WERE IN CHARGE OF COUNTY CRICKET? Come up with more incentives to entice spectators, push to get more games on the television
CHILDHOOD SPORTING HERO? Ryan Giggs

Batting	Mat	Inns	NO	Runs	HS	Ave	SR	100	50	Ct	St
First-class	17	18	8	93	30*	9.30	36.90	0	0	2	-
List A	18	8	7	44	13	44.00	54.32	0	0	4	-
T20s	25	8	5	11	7*	3.66	64.70	0	0	8	-

Bowling	Mat	Balls	Mdns	Runs	Wkts	BB	Ave	4wl	5wl	SR	Econ
First-class	17	2453	79	1244	28	5-34	44.42	-	1	87.60	3.04
List A	18	824	18	603	21	3-33	28.71	0	0	39.23	4.39
T20s	25	518	0	804	32	4-36	25.12	1	0	16.18	9.31

CONOR MCKERR RHB / RFM / R0 / W0

NOTTINGHAMSHIRE

FULL NAME: Conor McKerr
BORN: January 19, 1998, Johannesburg, South Africa
SQUAD NO: TBC
HEIGHT: 6ft 6in
NICKNAME: Tree
EDUCATION: St John's College, Johannesburg
TEAMS: Nottinghamshire, Derbyshire, Kent, South Africa U19, Surrey, Yorkshire
ROLE: Bowler
DEBUT: First-class: 2017; List A: 2019; T20: 2021

BEST BATTING: 37 Surrey vs Warwickshire, The Oval, 2022
BEST BOWLING: 5-54 Derbyshire vs Northamptonshire, Northampton, 2017

FIRST CRICKET CLUB? Randburg CC, Johannesburg
BIGGEST INFLUENCE ON YOUR DEVELOPMENT AS A CRICKETER (EXCLUDING PARENTS)?
Alec Stewart – he gave me the chance to be a professional cricketer
WHAT WOULD YOU CHANGE ABOUT THE STRUCTURE OF THE COUNTY SEASON? Each
format to be started and finished in one block
WHO WOULD YOU MOST LIKE TO HAVE A NET WITH? Graeme Smith
MAKE ONE PREDICTION FOR THE FUTURE OF CRICKET: Test cricket will always be the
pinnacle of the game
MOST BEAUTIFUL THING YOU HAVE EVER SEEN? Clouds moving in reverse

Batting	Mat	Inns	NO	Runs	HS	Ave	SR	100	50	Ct	St
First-class	26	28	5	284	37	12.34	41.45	0	0	8	-
List A	39	31	7	393	71	16.37	91.82	0	1	6	-
T20s	21	11	6	38	10	7.60	95.00	0	0	7	-

Bowling	Mat	Balls	Mdns	Runs	Wkts	BB	Ave	4wI	5wI	SR	Econ
First-class	26	3153	87	1927	62	5-54	31.08	-	2	50.85	3.66
List A	39	1768	5	1829	60	4-32	30.48	3	0	29.46	6.20
T20s	21	342	0	587	17	2-19	34.52	0	0	20.11	10.29

BEN MCKINNEY LHB / OB / R0 / W0

FULL NAME: Ben Stewart McKinney
BORN: October 4, 2004, Sunderland
SQUAD NO: 9
HEIGHT: 6ft 7in
NICKNAME: Kinny
EDUCATION: Park View Academy, Chester-le-Street; Seaham High School, Durham
TEAMS: Durham, England Lions, Tuskers
ROLE: Batter
DEBUT: First-class: 2023; List A: 2023; T20: 2024

BEST BATTING: 121 Durham vs Nottinghamshire, Chester-le-Street, 2024

WHICH TEAMMATE HAS HAD THE BIGGEST IMPACT ON YOUR GAME? Alex Lees – he keeps things simple and has his own way of scoring big hundreds
WHAT PART OF THE SEASON DO YOU MOST ENJOY? The red-ball phases as I love to impact and win games over a longer period of time
WHICH AWAY GROUND DO YOU MOST ENJOY VISITING? Hove – it's a lovely place to bat and I made my senior debut there in April 2023
WHO IS THE MOST TALENTED U19 TEENAGER IN THE COUNTY GAME? Farhan Ahmed (Not)
IF YOU COULD PINCH A PLAYER FROM ANOTHER COUNTY, WHO WOULD IT BE?
Liam Dawson
WHO IS THE TOUGHEST BOWLER TO FACE? Matthew Potts – he bowls aggressively and nips the ball both ways
WHAT'S THE SILLIEST OUTFIT YOU'VE EVER WORN? A hot-dog costume
CHOOSE A FANTASY SLIP CORDON TO SPEND A DAY IN THE FIELD WITH: God (wk), Ricky Gervais, Lee Cattermole, Lionel Messi

Batting	Mat	Inns	NO	Runs	HS	Ave	SR	100	50	Ct	St
First-class	10	17	1	550	121	34.37	86.75	2	1	4	-
List A	10	10	0	308	115	30.80	80.83	1	1	3	-
T20s	7	5	0	89	40	17.80	127.14	0	0	4	-

Bowling	Mat	Balls	Mdns	Runs	Wkts	BB	Ave	4wI	5wI	SR	Econ
First-class	10	-	-	-	-	-	-	-	-	-	-
List A	10	-	-	-	-	-	-	-	-	-	-
T20s	7	-	-	-	-	-	-	-	-	-	-

LEWIS MCMANUS

RHB / WK / R0 / W0

FULL NAME: Lewis David McManus
BORN: October 9, 1994, Poole, Dorset
SQUAD NO: 15
HEIGHT: 5ft 8in
NICKNAME: Lewy
EDUCATION: Clayesmore School,
Bournemouth; University of Exeter
TEAMS: Northamptonshire, England U19,
Hampshire
ROLE: Wicketkeeper/batter
DEBUT: First-class: 2015; List A: 2016; T20: 2016

BEST BATTING: 168 Northamptonshire vs Glamorgan, Cardiff, 2024

FIRST CRICKET CLUB? Broadstone CC, Poole, Dorset
BEST DELIVERY YOU HAVE EVER FACED? Any juicy half-volley which has met the middle of my bat
BEST PERFORMANCE AS A PRO? My 132 not out for Hampshire against Surrey in 2016
GREATEST PERFORMANCE YOU HAVE WITNESSED? Kyle Abbott's 17 for 86 for against Somerset at the Ageas Bowl in 2019
FAVOURITE FORMAT? The County Championship because it's the hardest and most rewarding
DESCRIBE YOURSELF IN THREE WORDS: Disciplined, motivated, passionate
FAVOURITE TOY AS A KID? A football
WHAT WOULD BE YOUR PERFECT BREAKFAST? Poached eggs, avocado and halloumi

Batting	Mat	Inns	NO	Runs	HS	Ave	SR	100	50	Ct	St
First-class	89	128	19	2955	168*	27.11	48.75	2	14	208	23
List A	60	51	8	1161	107	27.00	89.44	1	4	46	13
T20s	103	83	24	1005	60*	17.03	133.46	0	2	60	22

Bowling	Mat	Balls	Mdns	Runs	Wkts	BB	Ave	4wI	5wI	SR	Econ
First-class	89	-	-	-	-	-	-	-	-	-	-
List A	60	-	-	-	-	-	-	-	-	-	-
T20s	103	-	-	-	-	-	-	-	-	-	-

RILEY MEREDITH

RHB / RF / RO / WO

FULL NAME: Riley Patrick Meredith
BORN: June 21, 1996, Bellerive, Tasmania, Australia
SQUAD NO: 12
TEAMS: Australia, Somerset, Hobart Hurricanes, Mumbai Indians, Punjab Kings, Tasmania
ROLE: Bowler
DEBUT: ODI: 2021; T20I: 2021; First-class: 2017; List A: 2017; T20: 2018

BEST BATTING: 10 Hobart Hurricanes vs Adelaide Strikers, Melbourne, 2022 (T20)
BEST BOWLING: 4-12 Somerset vs Middlesex, Lord's, 2024 (T20)

NOTES: The Australian international fast bowler has re-signed with Somerset for the entirety of the club's Vitality Blast group stage, and potentially a quarter-final fixture should they get there. In the competition last year, he impressed with his pace and energy, picking up 14 wickets at an average of 22.78 to help drive Somerset to Finals Day. A well-travelled T20 gun-for-hire, he has represented Mumbai Indians in the IPL and last winter took three wickets in the Big Bash final as his hometown club, Hobart Hurricanes, clinched their inaugural BBL title. In all he claimed 16 wickets across the tournament. Somerset's director of cricket, Andy Hurry is thrilled to welcome back their spearhead. "We were all extremely impressed with how Riley performed on the field last year and by how he seamlessly he fitted into the group," he said

Batting	Mat	Inns	NO	Runs	HS	Ave	SR	100	50	Ct	St
ODIs	1	1	1	0	0*	-	0.00	0	0	0	-
T20Is	6	0	-	-	-	-	-	-	-	0	-
First-class	34	49	28	245	44	11.66	35.81	0	0	9	-
List A	37	18	10	61	16	7.62	58.65	0	0	13	-
T20s	114	20	11	36	10	4.00	97.29	0	0	17	-

Bowling	Mat	Balls	Mdns	Runs	Wkts	BB	Ave	4wI	5wI	SR	Econ
ODIs	1	30	0	36	0	0-36	-	-	-	-	7.20
T20Is	6	137	0	222	9	3-48	24.66	0	0	15.22	9.72
First-class	34	5664	174	3364	101	5-96	33.30	-	2	56.07	3.56
List A	37	1878	14	1610	52	5-26	30.96	2	1	36.11	5.14
T20s	114	2483	1	3473	145	4-12	23.95	2	0	17.12	8.39

ED MIDDLETON

RHB / LB / R0 / W0

GLOUCESTERSHIRE

FULL NAME: Edward William Osborne Middleton
BORN: December 28, 2000, Exeter
SQUAD NO: 55
HEIGHT: 6ft 4in
NICKNAME: Middo
EDUCATION: King's College, Taunton; Oxford Brookes University
TEAMS: Gloucestershire
ROLE: Allrounder
DEBUT: First-class: 2023

BEST BATTING: 39* Gloucestershire vs Derbyshire, Bristol, 2023
BEST BOWLING: 3-92 Gloucestershire vs Leicestershire, Leicester, 2024

FIRST CRICKET CLUB? Clyst St George CC, Exeter
EARLIEST CRICKETING MEMORY? Heading to a Saturday game to watch Dad and playing in the nets all day
WHAT'S THE BIGGEST PRIZE IN DOMESTIC CRICKET? Division One of the County Championship
THE KOOKABURRA BALL: YES OR NO? Yes, to encourage high-pace bowling and high-quality spin to take 20 wickets
FAVOURITE WARM-UP SONG? Greenlight by Pitbull
HOW MANY HOURS DO YOU SPEND ON YOUR PHONE A DAY? 3.5 hours
SPECIALITY SUBJECT IN A PUB QUIZ (EXCLUDING SPORT)? Geography
ONE THING YOU WANT TO DO BEFORE YOU DIE: A skydive
HOBBY YOU WOULD LIKE TO LEARN: Fishing
FILM YOU CAN WATCH OVER AND OVER: Shrek 2

Batting	Mat	Inns	NO	Runs	HS	Ave	SR	100	50	Ct	St
First-class	6	9	4	116	39*	23.20	35.36	0	0	0	-

Bowling	Mat	Balls	Mdns	Runs	Wkts	BB	Ave	4wl	5wl	SR	Econ
First-class	6	733	19	445	9	3-92	49.44	-	0	81.44	3.64

FLETCHA MIDDLETON
RHB / OB / R0 / W0

FULL NAME: Fletcha Scott Middleton
BORN: January 21, 2002, Southampton
SQUAD NO: 19
HEIGHT: 5ft 9in
EDUCATION: Wyvern College, Eastleigh
TEAMS: Hampshire
ROLE: Batter
DEBUT: First-class: 2022; List A: 2021; T20: 2024

BEST BATTING: 116 Hampshire vs Warwickshire, Southampton, 2024

WHICH TEAMMATE HAS HAD THE BIGGEST IMPACT ON YOUR GAME? There's two: James Vince and Nick Gubbins, both great role models
WHAT PART OF THE SEASON DO YOU MOST ENJOY? The start
WHICH AWAY GROUND DO YOU MOST ENJOY VISITING? Old Trafford – a good wicket and nice changing rooms
WHO IS THE MOST TALENTED U19 TEENAGER IN THE COUNTY GAME? Eddie Jack (Ham)
IF YOU COULD PINCH A PLAYER FROM ANOTHER COUNTY, WHO WOULD IT BE? Ollie Pope
HOW IS BAZBALL AFFECTING CHAMPIONSHIP CRICKET? Ask me again in five years
WHO IS THE TOUGHEST BOWLER TO FACE? Gareth Berg
WHAT KEEPS YOU AWAKE AT NIGHT? TikTok
WHAT'S THE SILLIEST OUTFIT YOU'VE EVER WORN? Dressing up as a banana
CHOOSE A FANTASY SLIP CORDON TO SPEND A DAY IN THE FIELD WITH: Jesus (wk), Sachin Tendulkar, Mila Kunis

Batting	Mat	Inns	NO	Runs	HS	Ave	SR	100	50	Ct	St
First-class	28	46	1	1278	116	28.40	46.74	2	8	20	-
List A	30	30	2	883	100	31.53	82.44	1	6	16	-
T20s	2	2	0	34	18	17.00	121.42	0	0	0	
Bowling	Mat	Balls	Mdns	Runs	Wkts	BB	Ave	4wI	5wI	SR	Econ
First-class	28	-	-	-	-	-	-	-	-	-	-
List A	30	-	-	-	-	-	-	-	-	-	-
T20s	2	-	-	-	-	-	-	-	-	-	-

BEN MIKE

RHB / RFM / RO / WO

LEICESTERSHIRE

FULL NAME: Benjamin Wentworth Munro Mike
BORN: August 24, 1998, Nottingham
SQUAD NO: 8
HEIGHT: 6ft 1in
NICKNAME: Benny
EDUCATION: Loughborough Grammar School
TEAMS: Leicestershire, Warwickshire, Yorkshire
ROLE: Bowler
DEBUT: First-class: 2018; List A: 2018; T20: 2019

BEST BATTING: 99* Leicestershire vs Middlesex, Lord's, 2022
BEST BOWLING: 5-22 Leicestershire vs Middlesex, Leicester, 2022

FIRST CRICKET CLUB? Radcliffe-On-Trent CC, Nottingham
BIGGEST INFLUENCE ON YOUR DEVELOPMENT AS A CRICKETER (EXCLUDING PARENTS)?
Dips Patel at Leicestershire and Brad Spencer in Perth
WHAT'S THE BIGGEST PRIZE IN DOMESTIC CRICKET? The County Championship
OPPONENT YOU MOST LOOK FORWARD TO PLAYING AGAINST? My old friend
Callum Parkinson
FAVOURITE WARM-UP SONG? Drift by Teejay
HOW MANY HOURS DO YOU SPEND ON YOUR PHONE A DAY? Three
SPECIALITY SUBJECT IN A PUB QUIZ (EXCLUDING SPORT)? History
ONE THING YOU WANT TO DO BEFORE YOU DIE: Visit New York
HOBBY YOU WOULD LIKE TO LEARN: Speak Spanish
WHICH PUBLIC FIGURE INSPIRES YOU (EXCLUDING SPORTSPEOPLE)? Martin Luther King
FILM YOU CAN WATCH OVER AND OVER: Fast & Furious

Batting	Mat	Inns	NO	Runs	HS	Ave	SR	100	50	Ct	St
First-class	47	72	7	1639	99*	25.21	54.96	0	11	10	-
List A	19	17	4	221	41	17.00	73.17	0	0	5	-
T20s	67	54	18	669	37	18.58	144.80	0	0	31	-

Bowling	Mat	Balls	Mdns	Runs	Wkts	BB	Ave	4wI	5wI	SR	Econ
First-class	47	5523	113	4025	106	5-22	37.97	-	2	52.10	4.37
List A	19	636	1	806	23	4-40	35.04	1	0	27.65	7.60
T20s	67	922	1	1552	57	4-22	27.22	1	0	16.17	10.09

CRAIG MILES — RHB / RFM / RO / W3

FULL NAME: Craig Neil Miles
BORN: July 20, 1994, Swindon, Wiltshire
SQUAD NO: 18
HEIGHT: 6ft 4in
NICKNAME: Milo
EDUCATION: Bradon Forest School, Purton, Wiltshire; SGS Filton College, Bristol
TEAMS: Warwickshire, Durham, Glamorgan, Gloucestershire, Northern Superchargers
ROLE: Bowler
DEBUT: First-class: 2011; List A: 2011; T20: 2013

WARWICKSHIRE

BEST BATTING: 62* Gloucestershire vs Worcestershire, Cheltenham, 2014
BEST BOWLING: 6-63 Gloucestershire vs Northamptonshire, Northampton, 2015
COUNTY CAP: 2011 (Gloucestershire)

FIRST CRICKET CLUB? Purton CC, Swindon
FAMILY TIES? My older brother Adam has played for Cardiff MCCU and for New Zealand side Otago in first-class cricket
MOST EXCITING DAY AS A CRICKETER? Beating Surrey in the 2015 One-Day Cup final at Lord's when I was with Gloucestershire
WHAT WOULD YOU DO IF YOU WERE IN CHARGE OF COUNTY CRICKET? Allow the second new ball after 60 overs, bring back the 40-over format
CHILDHOOD SPORTING HERO? Wayne Rooney
SURPRISING FACT ABOUT YOU: I played football for Swindon Town Academy until I was 13

Batting	Mat	Inns	NO	Runs	HS	Ave	SR	100	50	Ct	St
First-class	107	143	24	1850	62*	15.54	44.19	0	5	35	-
List A	50	18	6	152	31*	12.66	80.85	0	0	9	-
T20s	61	19	11	58	11*	7.25	75.32	0	0	34	-

Bowling	Mat	Balls	Mdns	Runs	Wkts	BB	Ave	4wI	5wI	SR	Econ
First-class	107	16613	479	10211	360	6-63	28.36	-	18	46.14	3.68
List A	50	2126	9	2213	60	4-29	36.88	1	0	35.43	6.24
T20s	61	1080	1	1596	67	4-29	23.82	1	0	16.11	8.86

GUS MILLER

RHB / RFM / R0 / W0

NORTHAMPTONSHIRE

FULL NAME: Augustus Horatio Miller
BORN: January 8, 2002, Oxford
SQUAD NO: 24
HEIGHT: 6ft 2in
NICKNAME: The Big Bird
EDUCATION: Bedford School
TEAMS: Northamptonshire
ROLE: Allrounder
DEBUT: First-class: 2024; List A: 2022; T20: 2022

BEST BATTING: 42 Northamptonshire Vs Derbyshire, Northampton, 2024

FIRST CRICKET CLUB? Oxford Downs CC, Witney, Oxfordshire
EARLIEST CRICKETING MEMORY? Playing at my local village club
WHAT'S THE BIGGEST PRIZE IN DOMESTIC CRICKET? The County Championship
THE KOOKABURRA BALL: YES OR NO? Yes, it brings other aspects of the game into play, such as more spin-friendly wickets, which isn't something we typically play on much
HOW MANY HOURS DO YOU SPEND ON YOUR PHONE A DAY? Four
SPECIALITY SUBJECT IN A PUB QUIZ (EXCLUDING SPORT)? Economics
ONE THING YOU WANT TO DO BEFORE YOU DIE: Hit a nine-darter
HOBBY YOU WOULD LIKE TO LEARN: Elite coffee art
SURPRISING FACT ABOUT YOU: I'm a grade five on the saxophone
FILM YOU CAN WATCH OVER AND OVER: The Wolf of Wall Street

Batting	Mat	Inns	NO	Runs	HS	Ave	SR	100	50	Ct	St
First-class	5	8	0	162	42	20.25	54.72	0	0	0	-
List A	13	12	5	258	73	36.85	93.47	0	1	4	-
T20s	7	4	2	21	8*	10.50	161.53	0	0	2	-

Bowling	Mat	Balls	Mdns	Runs	Wkts	BB	Ave	4wI	5wI	SR	Econ
First-class	5	174	4	160	0	0-13	-	-	-	-	5.51
List A	13	228	2	228	3	1-19	76.00	0	0	76.00	6.00
T20s	7	6	0	12	0	0-12	-	-	-	-	12.00

TYMAL MILLS

RHB / LF

FULL NAME: Tymal Solomon Mills
BORN: August 12, 1992, Dewsbury, Yorkshire
SQUAD NO: 7
HEIGHT: 6ft 1in
EDUCATION: Mildenhall College of Technology, Suffolk; Uni of East London
TEAMS: England, Sussex, Southern Brave, Essex, Hobart Hurricanes, Islamabad United, Mumbai Indians, Perth Scorchers, Peshawar Zalmi, RC Bangalore
ROLE: Bowler
DEBUT: T20I: 2016; First-class: 2011; List A: 2011; T20: 2012

BEST BATTING: 27 Sussex vs Gloucestershire, Hove, 2021 (T20)
BEST BOWLING: 4-13 Southern Brave vs Welsh Fire, Cardiff, 2023 (T20/Hundred)

FIRST CRICKET CLUB? Tunddenham CC, Suffolk
EARLIEST CRICKETING MEMORY? Making my club debut for Tuddenham against Gazeley CC
WHAT'S THE BIGGEST PRIZE IN DOMESTIC CRICKET? Division One of the County Championship
THE KOOKABURRA BALL: YES OR NO? Yes, it brings other types of bowlers into the game
GREATEST PERFORMANCE YOU HAVE WITNESSED? I was stood at mid-on as David Masters took 8-10 for Essex against Leicestershire at Southend back in 2011
HOBBIES? I'm a big NFL fan
CHOOSE A FANTASY SLIP CORDON TO SPEND A DAY IN THE FIELD WITH: Ricky Gervais (wk), Daniel Ricciardo, Eric Cartman, Ari Gold
SURPRISING FACT ABOUT YOU: I started playing cricket aged 14
FILM YOU CAN WATCH OVER AND OVER: Hamilton

Batting	Mat	Inns	NO	Runs	HS	Ave	SR	100	50	Ct	St
T20Is	15	5	2	8	7	2.66	66.66	0	0	2	-
First-class	32	38	15	260	31*	11.30	57.77	0	0	9	-
List A	23	9	5	7	3*	1.75	31.81	0	0	3	-
T20s	235	54	26	160	27	5.71	92.48	0	0	38	-

Bowling	Mat	Balls	Mdns	Runs	Wkts	BB	Ave	4wI	5wI	SR	Econ
T20Is	15	304	0	461	14	3-27	32.92	0	0	21.71	9.09
First-class	32	3530	108	2008	55	4-25	36.50	-	0	64.18	3.41
List A	23	790	1	787	22	3-23	35.77	0	0	35.90	5.97
T20s	235	4875	3	6713	289	4-13	23.22	7	0	16.86	8.26

MATT MILNES

RHB / RFM / R0 / W1

FULL NAME: Matthew Edward Milnes
BORN: July 29, 1994, Nottingham
SQUAD NO: 4
HEIGHT: 6ft 1in
NICKNAME: Mad Dog
EDUCATION: West Bridgford School, Nottinghamshire; Durham University
TEAMS: Yorkshire, England Lions, Kent, Nottinghamshire, Oval Invincibles, Welsh Fire
ROLE: Bowler
DEBUT: First-class: 2014; List A: 2019; T20: 2019

BEST BATTING: 78 Kent vs Yorkshire, Canterbury, 2021
BEST BOWLING: 6-53 Kent vs Leicestershire, Leicester, 2021
COUNTY CAP: 2021 (Kent)

FIRST CRICKET CLUB? Plumtree CC, Nottinghamshire
BIGGEST INFLUENCE ON YOUR DEVELOPMENT AS A CRICKETER (EXCLUDING PARENTS)? My brother – I spent days on end bowling to him in the garden while he blocked half-volleys. Never got a bat either
WHAT WOULD YOU CHANGE ABOUT THE STRUCTURE OF THE COUNTY SEASON? T20 to be played in one block with the knockout stage straight after the group stage
BIGGEST CRICKETING REGRET? Not being a left-arm spinner who bats No.5
HOBBIES? Football – you can't beat being on the terraces for a non-league game

Batting	Mat	Inns	NO	Runs	HS	Ave	SR	100	50	Ct	St
First-class	49	74	21	1055	78	19.90	44.57	0	4	19	-
List A	12	7	1	101	26	16.83	112.22	0	0	5	-
T20s	47	18	10	64	14*	8.00	130.61	0	0	13	-

Bowling	Mat	Balls	Mdns	Runs	Wkts	BB	Ave	4wI	5wI	SR	Econ
First-class	49	7667	240	4428	153	6-53	28.94	-	4	50.11	3.46
List A	12	575	1	647	19	5-79	34.05	0	1	30.26	6.75
T20s	47	891	0	1381	45	5-22	30.68	1	1	19.80	9.29

MATTHEW MONTGOMERY RHB / OB / R0 / W0

NOTTINGHAMSHIRE

FULL NAME: Matthew Montgomery
BORN: May 10, 2000, Johannesburg, South Africa
SQUAD NO: 14
HEIGHT: 6ft
NICKNAME: Monty
EDUCATION: Clifton College, Durban, South Africa; Loughborough University
TEAMS: Germany, Nottinghamshire, KwaZulu-Natal, South Africa U19
ROLE: Batter
DEBUT: T20I: 2023;
First-class: 2019; List A: 2019; T20: 2018

BEST BATTING: 178 Nottinghamshire vs Durham, Trent Bridge, 2022
BEST BOWLING: 1-0 Nottinghamshire vs Kent, Canterbury, 2023

FIRST CRICKET CLUB? Delta CC, Durban, South Africa
WHICH AWAY GROUND DO YOU MOST ENJOY VISITING? Lord's
IF YOU COULD PINCH A PLAYER FROM ANOTHER COUNTY, WHO WOULD IT BE?
Simon Harmer
WHAT DO YOU THINK OF THE CURRENT 50-OVER COMPETITION? There's not enough support for it
FAVOURITE FORMAT? 50-over cricket – it has many different phases and incorporates aspects of all formats
HOBBIES? Go-karting

Batting	Mat	Inns	NO	Runs	HS	Ave	SR	100	50	Ct	St
T20Is	1	1	0	13	13	13.00	68.42	0	0	0	-
First-class	23	39	2	1121	178	30.29	45.34	2	3	24	-
List A	35	32	5	1129	104	41.81	86.77	1	8	19	-
T20s	31	28	4	486	51	20.25	114.35	0	2	13	-

Bowling	Mat	Balls	Mdns	Runs	Wkts	BB	Ave	4wI	5wI	SR	Econ
T20Is	1	18	0	21	0	0-21	-	-	-	-	7.00
First-class	23	180	3	132	3	1-0	44.00	-	0	60.00	4.40
List A	35	492	3	494	7	2-38	70.57	0	0	70.28	6.02
T20s	31	164	0	238	5	1-5	47.60	0	0	32.80	8.70

HARRY MOORE RHB / RFM / RO / WO

FULL NAME: Harry John Moore
BORN: April 26, 2007, Derby
SQUAD NO: 16
HEIGHT: 6ft 7in
EDUCATION: Repton School, Derbyshire
TEAMS: Derbyshire, England Lions
ROLE: Bowler
DEBUT: First-class: 2024; List A: 2023

BEST BATTING: 32 Derbyshire vs Middlesex, Derby, 2024
BEST BOWLING: 3-55 Derbyshire vs Middlesex, Derby, 2024

FIRST CRICKET CLUB? Clifton CC, Ashbourne, Derbyshire
EARLIEST CRICKETING MEMORY? Training with my dad in the nets at my club
WHAT'S THE BIGGEST PRIZE IN DOMESTIC CRICKET? A win in the County Championship
THE KOOKABURRA BALL: YES OR NO? Yes – as a bowler it makes you concentrate more
OPPONENT YOU MOST LOOK FORWARD TO PLAYING AGAINST? Freddie McCann – he's a good mate and we always enjoy a battle
HOW MANY HOURS DO YOU SPEND ON YOUR PHONE A DAY? Four
SPECIALITY SUBJECT IN A PUB QUIZ (EXCLUDING SPORT)? Video games
HOBBY YOU WOULD LIKE TO LEARN: Fishing
WHICH PUBLIC FIGURE INSPIRES YOU (EXCLUDING SPORTSPEOPLE)? Will Smith
SURPRISING FACT ABOUT YOU: I LOVE milkshakes
FILM YOU CAN WATCH OVER AND OVER: Bad Boys

Batting	Mat	Inns	NO	Runs	HS	Ave	SR	100	50	Ct	St
First-class	3	4	1	48	32	16.00	46.15	0	0	0	-
List A	10	6	2	86	40	21.50	98.85	0	0	4	-

Bowling	Mat	Balls	Mdns	Runs	Wkts	BB	Ave	4wI	5wI	SR	Econ
First-class	3	252	11	143	6	3-55	23.83	-	0	42.00	3.40
List A	10	504	2	446	12	3-45	37.16	0	0	42.00	5.30

TOM MOORES

LHB / WK / R0 / W0

FULL NAME: Thomas James Moores
BORN: September 4, 1996, Brighton, Sussex
SQUAD NO: 23
HEIGHT: 5ft 9in
EDUCATION: Loughborough Grammar
School; Millfield School, Somerset
TEAMS: Nottinghamshire, England Lions,
Jaffna Stallions, Kandy Warriors, Lancashire,
Multan Sultans, Rangpur Riders, Sylhet
Strikers, Trent Rockets
ROLE: Wicketkeeper/batter
DEBUT: First-class: 2016; List A: 2016; T20: 2016

NOTTINGHAMSHIRE

BEST BATTING: 106 Nottinghamshire vs Yorkshire, Trent Bridge, 2020

COUNTY CAP: 2021 (Nottinghamshire)

FIRST CRICKET CLUB? Barrow Town CC, Leicestershire. The club gave me my first
opportunity to play men's cricket
FAMILY TIES? My father Peter played for Sussex and was England head coach. He's now my
coach at Nottinghamshire
CHILDHOOD SPORTING HERO? Adam Gilchrist. The first-ever bat I had was a Puma Ballistic,
which Gilchrist used to score his hundreds in the 2006 Perth Ashes Test and the 2007 World
Cup final

Batting	Mat	Inns	NO	Runs	HS	Ave	SR	100	50	Ct	St
First-class	78	122	7	2681	106	23.31	51.11	2	8	220	5
List A	29	26	6	776	76	38.80	111.97	0	5	27	5
T20s	147	128	29	2311	80*	23.34	131.90	0	8	72	23
Bowling	Mat	Balls	Mdns	Runs	Wkts	BB	Ave	4wl	5wl	SR	Econ
First-class	78	8	0	6	0	0-1	-	-	-	-	4.50
List A	29	-	-	-	-	-	-	-	-	-	-
T20s	147	-	-	-	-	-	-	-	-	-	-

DANIEL MORIARTY

LHB / SLA / R0 / W0

YORKSHIRE

FULL NAME: Daniel Thornhill Moriarty
BORN: December 2, 1999, Reigate, Surrey
SQUAD NO: 11
HEIGHT: 6ft 2in
NICKNAME: Mozza
EDUCATION: Rondesbosch Boy's High School, Cape Town
TEAMS: Yorkshire, South Africa U19, Southern Brave, Surrey
ROLE: Bowler
DEBUT: First-class: 2020; List A: 2021; T20: 2020

BEST BATTING: 29 Surrey vs Sri Lanka Development XI, Guildford, 2022
BEST BOWLING: 6-60 Surrey vs Sussex, The Oval, 2020

FIRST CRICKET CLUB? Western Province CC, Cape Town
BIGGEST INFLUENCE ON YOUR DEVELOPMENT AS A CRICKETER (EXCLUDING PARENTS)?
Gareth Batty – he helped me understand my game in more depth
WHO WOULD YOU MOST LIKE TO HAVE A NET WITH? Daniel Vettori
MAKE ONE PREDICTION FOR THE FUTURE OF CRICKET: It will become more skilful, competitive and will be played at a higher intensity
MOST BEAUTIFUL THING YOU HAVE EVER SEEN? Sunrise after hiking up Lion's Head mountain in Cape Town

Batting	Mat	Inns	NO	Runs	HS	Ave	SR	100	50	Ct	St
First-class	21	21	9	121	29	10.08	37.57	0	0	3	-
List A	25	14	5	83	16*	9.22	56.84	0	0	9	-
T20s	50	10	6	41	9*	10.25	91.11	0	0	4	-

Bowling	Mat	Balls	Mdns	Runs	Wkts	BB	Ave	4wI	5wI	SR	Econ
First-class	21	4220	124	2212	61	6-60	36.26	-	6	69.18	3.14
List A	25	1235	10	1032	32	4-30	32.25	1	0	38.59	5.01
T20s	50	980	1	1239	46	4-25	26.93	1	0	21.30	7.58

JACK MORLEY

LHB / SLA / R0 / W0

FULL NAME: Jack Peter Morley
BORN: June 25, 2001, Rochdale, Lancashire
SQUAD NO: 18
HEIGHT: 5ft 11in
NICKNAME: Morles
EDUCATION: Siddal Moor Sports College, Heywood, Greater Manchester; Myerscough College, Preston, Lancashire
TEAMS: Derbyshire, England U19, Lancashire
ROLE: Bowler
DEBUT: First-class: 2020; List A: 2021; T20: 2024

BEST BATTING: 28 Derbyshire vs Sussex, Derby, 2024
BEST BOWLING: 5-69 Lancashire vs Somerset, Southport, 2022

FIRST CRICKET CLUB? Heywood CC, Rochdale
EARLIEST CRICKETING MEMORY? The 2005 Ashes
WHAT'S THE BIGGEST PRIZE IN DOMESTIC CRICKET? The County Championship
THE KOOKABURRA BALL: YES OR NO? Yes
BEST PERFORMANCE AS A PRO? Taking my first red-ball five fer against Somerset at Southport in 2022
WHO IS THE MOST TALENTED U19 TEENAGER IN THE COUNTY GAME? Charlie Barnard (Lan)

Batting	Mat	Inns	NO	Runs	HS	Ave	SR	100	50	Ct	St
First-class	15	18	3	51	28	3.40	16.24	0	0	5	-
List A	23	7	4	23	10*	7.66	52.27	0	0	5	-
T20s	1	0	-	-	-	-	-	-	-	0	-

Bowling	Mat	Balls	Mdns	Runs	Wkts	BB	Ave	4wI	5wI	SR	Econ
First-class	15	2639	70	1320	44	5-69	30.00	-	1	59.97	3.00
List A	23	1018	8	832	26	3-40	32.00	0	0	39.15	4.90
T20s	1	12	0	19	0	0-19	-	-	-	-	9.50

DAN MOUSLEY

LHB / OB / R0 / W0 / MVP22

WARWICKSHIRE

FULL NAME: Daniel Richard Mousley
BORN: July 8, 2001, Birmingham
SQUAD NO: 80
HEIGHT: 6ft 2in
NICKNAME: Mousetrap
EDUCATION: Bablake School, Coventry
TEAMS: England, Warwickshire, Birmingham Phoenix, Burgher Recreation Club, Peshawar Zalmi
ROLE: Allrounder
DEBUT: ODI: 2024; T20I: 2024; First-class: 2019; List A: 2021; T20: 2020

BEST BATTING: 94 Warwickshire vs Kent, Edgbaston, 2023
BEST BOWLING: 3-43 England Lions vs India A, Ahmedabad, 2024

FIRST CRICKET CLUB? Nether Whitacre CC, Coleshill, Warwickshire
WHICH TEAMMATE HAS HAD THE BIGGEST IMPACT ON YOUR GAME? Sam Hain for batting – he makes it look easy. Danny Briggs is a bowling genius and I love badgering him!
WHAT PART OF THE SEASON DO YOU MOST ENJOY? T20 games in front of the big crowds
HOW IS BAZBALL AFFECTING CHAMPIONSHIP CRICKET? It's been brilliiant – teams are risking losing in order to win and it's making it more entertaining to watch
WHO IS THE TOUGHEST BOWLER TO FACE? Dan Worrall
CHOOSE A FANTASY SLIP CORDON TO SPEND A DAY IN THE FIELD WITH: Paul McGrath (wk), Freddie Flintoff, Unai Emery, Jack Carson

Batting	Mat	Inns	NO	Runs	HS	Ave	SR	100	50	Ct	St
ODIs	3	3	1	69	57	34.50	80.23	0	1	1	-
T20Is	4	1	0	8	8	8.00	133.33	0	0	4	-
First-class	34	56	4	1349	94	25.94	53.87	0	11	21	-
List A	12	12	1	407	105	37.00	92.50	1	3	7	-
T20s	73	64	7	1185	68	20.78	127.14	0	8	43	-

Bowling	Mat	Balls	Mdns	Runs	Wkts	BB	Ave	4wI	5wI	SR	Econ
ODIs	3	12	0	17	0	0-17	-	-	-	-	8.50
T20Is	4	54	0	82	2	2-29	41.00	0	0	27.00	9.11
First-class	34	458	8	307	8	3-43	38.37	-	0	57.25	4.02
List A	12	264	3	195	7	3-32	27.85	0	0	37.71	4.43
T20s	73	932	0	1133	57	4-28	19.87	2	0	16.35	7.29

TAWANDA MUYEYE — RHB / OB / R0 / W0

FULL NAME: Tawanda Sean Muyeye
BORN: March 5, 2001, Harare, Zimbabwe
SQUAD NO: 14
HEIGHT: 6ft
NICKNAME: BAM
EDUCATION: Eastbourne College, East Sussex; The Open University, Milton Keynes
TEAMS: Kent, Oval Invincibles, Melbourne Renegades
ROLE: Batter
DEBUT: First-class: 2021; List A: 2021; T20: 2022

BEST BATTING: 211 Kent vs Worcestershire, Worcester, 2024
BEST BOWLING: 2-70 Kent vs Hampshire, Canterbury, 2022

FIRST CRICKET CLUB? Mountaineers, Mutare, Zimbabwe
EARLIEST CRICKETING MEMORY? Playing in the backyard with my brother
WHAT'S THE BIGGEST PRIZE IN DOMESTIC CRICKET? The County Championship
THE KOOKABURRA BALL: YES OR NO? I'm indifferent
FAVOURITE WARM-UP SONG? The Rapture Pt.III by Black Coffee
HOW MANY HOURS DO YOU SPEND ON YOUR PHONE A DAY? Six
SPECIALITY SUBJECT IN A PUB QUIZ (EXCLUDING SPORT)? Music
ONE THING YOU WANT TO DO BEFORE YOU DIE: Play cricket for England and in the IPL
HOBBY YOU WOULD LIKE TO LEARN: Play the saxophone
WHICH PUBLIC FIGURE INSPIRES YOU (EXCLUDING SPORTSPEOPLE)? Barack Obama
SURPRISING FACT ABOUT YOU: I like to read and swim in the ocean
FILM YOU CAN WATCH OVER AND OVER: Pretty Woman

Batting	Mat	Inns	NO	Runs	HS	Ave	SR	100	50	Ct	St
First-class	28	49	2	1557	211	33.12	64.12	2	8	22	-
List A	11	10	1	221	40	24.55	97.35	0	0	2	-
T20s	40	38	0	721	73	18.97	139.45	0	5	18	-

Bowling	Mat	Balls	Mdns	Runs	Wkts	BB	Ave	4wI	5wI	SR	Econ
First-class	28	329	3	204	3	2-70	68.00	-	0	109.66	3.72
List A	11	60	0	33	1	1-17	33.00	0	0	60.00	3.30
T20s	40	-	-	-	-	-	-	-	-	-	-

SAM NORTHEAST

RHB / OB / R6 / W0

FULL NAME: Sam Alexander Northeast
BORN: October 16, 1989, Ashford, Kent
SQUAD NO: 16
HEIGHT: 5ft 11in
NICKNAME: Chumley
EDUCATION: Harrow School, London
TEAMS: Glamorgan, England Lions, Hampshire, Kent, Nottinghamshire, Yorkshire
ROLE: Batter
DEBUT: First-class: 2007; List A: 2007; T20: 2010

BEST BATTING: 410* Glamorgan vs Leicestershire, Leicester, 2022
BEST BOWLING: 1-60 Kent vs Gloucestershire, Cheltenham, 2013
COUNTY CAP: 2022 (Glamorgan); 2012 (Kent)

FIRST CRICKET CLUB? Sandwich Town CC, Kent
WHICH TEAMMATE HAS HAD THE BIGGEST IMPACT ON YOUR GAME? Rob Key at Kent
WHICH AWAY GROUND DO YOU MOST ENJOY VISITING? Lord's
WHO IS THE MOST TALENTED U19 TEENAGER IN THE COUNTY GAME? Jaydn Denly (Ken)
IF YOU COULD PINCH A PLAYER FROM ANOTHER COUNTY, WHO WOULD IT BE?
Daniel Bell-Drummond
HOW IS BAZBALL AFFECTING CHAMPIONSHIP CRICKET? It's hugely affecting it, all the way down to the pathways
WHO IS THE TOUGHEST BOWLER TO FACE? Sunil Narine – a wizard
WHAT KEEPS YOU AWAKE AT NIGHT? My daughter
CHOOSE A FANTASY SLIP CORDON TO SPEND A DAY IN THE FIELD WITH: Adam Gilchrist (wk), Ricky Ponting, Viv Richards, Don Bradman

Batting	Mat	Inns	NO	Runs	HS	Ave	SR	100	50	Ct	St
First-class	223	376	34	13678	410*	39.99	56.33	32	65	114	-
List A	124	116	14	3786	177*	37.11	80.16	6	22	44	-
T20s	162	150	19	4007	114	30.58	126.88	1	28	48	-
Bowling	Mat	Balls	Mdns	Runs	Wkts	BB	Ave	4wl	5wl	SR	Econ
First-class	223	230	4	181	1	1-60	181.00	-	0	230.00	4.72
List A	124	-	-	-	-	-	-	-	-	-	-
T20s	162	-	-	-	-	-	-	-	-	-	-

FERGUS O'NEILL

RHB / RFM / R0 / W0

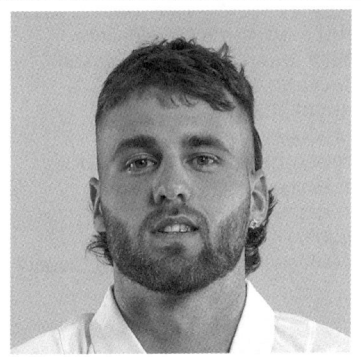

FULL NAME: Fergus Patrick O'Neill
BORN: January 27, 2001, Tauranga, New Zealand
SQUAD NO: TBC
TEAMS: Nottinghamshire, Melbourne Renegades, Victoria
ROLE: Bowler
DEBUT: First-class: 2022; List A: 2022; T20: 2024

NOTTINGHAMSHIRE

BEST BATTING: 70* Victoria vs New South Wales, Melbourne, 2023
BEST BOWLING: 5-28 Victoria vs South Australia, Adelaide, 2023

NOTES: The signing of O'Neill, a tall, strapping quick bowler with an outstanding first-class record, is a coup for Notts and could be the start of a long and fruitful partnership. Across the 2023/24 first-class season, he claimed 40 wickets in the Sheffield Shield for Victoria to take him to the edge of international honours; at the end of that campaign he was named the Bradman Young Cricketer of the Year at Australia's end-of-season awards. Due to visa restrictions, he is only available for three home Championship games and one away fixture at Edgbaston, though Peter Moores, the club's head coach, is convinced that he will have an impact even in a short space of time. "It's really exciting to get Fergus on board as a player who has enjoyed real success over the last couple of seasons at Victoria, and I hope this is just the start of Notts' relationship with him"

Batting	Mat	Inns	NO	Runs	HS	Ave	SR	100	50	Ct	St
First-class	28	45	8	759	70*	20.51	59.29	0	1	8	-
List A	17	10	3	113	25*	16.14	73.85	0	0	4	-
T20s	10	7	2	54	16*	10.80	96.42	0	0	3	-

Bowling	Mat	Balls	Mdns	Runs	Wkts	BB	Ave	4wI	5wI	SR	Econ
First-class	28	5377	271	2219	112	5-28	19.81	-	5	48.00	2.47
List A	17	852	5	694	26	4-22	26.69	1	0	32.76	4.88
T20s	10	201	1	241	10	3-16	24.10	0	0	20.10	7.19

MARCUS O'RIORDAN

RHB / OB / R0 / W0

FULL NAME: Marcus Kevin O'Riordan
BORN: January 25, 1998, Pembury, Kent
SQUAD NO: 55
HEIGHT: 5ft 10in
NICKNAME: Ray
EDUCATION: Holmewood House School, Tunbridge Wells; Tonbridge School
TEAMS: Kent
ROLE: Allrounder
DEBUT: First-class: 2019; List A: 2021; T20: 2019

BEST BATTING: 102* Kent vs Sri Lanka Development XI, Canterbury, 2022
BEST BOWLING: 3-50 Kent vs Sussex, Canterbury, 2020

FIRST CRICKET CLUB? Tunbridge Wells CC, Kent
BEST PLAYER IN COUNTY CRICKET (EXCLUDING TEAMMATES)? Simon Harmer
BEST PERFORMANCE AS A PRO? My maiden first-class hundred for Kent against Sri Lanka Development XI in 2022
GREATEST PERFORMANCE YOU HAVE WITNESSED? Darren Stevens's 237 against Yorkshire in 2019
FAVOURITE FORMAT? The Championship – that is the competition I'd most like to win
WHAT WOULD BE YOUR PERFECT BREAKFAST? Poached eggs and avocado on toast followed by coffee and an almond croissant
WHICH PERSON INSPIRES YOU MOST? Rafael Nadal
SURPRISING FACT ABOUT YOU: I never had to commute to school

Batting	Mat	Inns	NO	Runs	HS	Ave	SR	100	50	Ct	St
First-class	19	27	4	631	102*	27.43	46.87	1	1	9	-
List A	13	12	1	211	60	19.18	85.77	0	2	5	-
T20s	17	15	1	168	33	12.00	134.40	0	0	4	-

Bowling	Mat	Balls	Mdns	Runs	Wkts	BB	Ave	4wl	5wl	SR	Econ
First-class	19	1151	21	749	14	3-50	53.50	-	0	82.21	3.90
List A	13	169	0	193	4	3-36	48.25	0	0	42.25	6.85
T20s	17	202	0	272	10	2-24	27.20	0	0	20.20	8.07

FULL NAME: William Peter O'Rourke
BORN: August 6, 2001, Kingston upon Thames, Surrey
SQUAD NO: TBC
HEIGHT: 6ft 4in
TEAMS: New Zealand, Yorkshire, Canterbury
ROLE: Bowler
DEBUT: Test: 2024; ODI: 2023: T20I: 2024; First-class: 2022; List A: 2022; T20: 2022

BEST BATTING: 10 Canterbury vs Auckland, Christchurch, 2022 (T20)
BEST BOWLING: 4-23 Canterbury vs Northern Districts, Hamilton, 2024 (T20)

NOTES: The tall, imposing Kiwi fast bowler has burst onto the international scene over the last 18 months and is already a key member for his country in all formats of the game. O'Rourke now joins Yorkshire for the group phase of this summer's T20 Blast for what will be his first stint in county cricket. "As soon as we were aware that there was potential to bring Will into the club, we knew we wanted to confirm it as soon as possible," said Anthony McGrath, Yorkshire's head coach. "With his frame and height, he has a release point which will provide a key point of difference for our attack. He's young, hungry to succeed and able to extract both pace and bounce from all types of pitches"

Batting	Mat	Inns	NO	Runs	HS	Ave	SR	100	50	Ct	St
Tests	10	18	12	18	5*	3.00	9.32	0	0	5	-
ODIs	14	4	2	6	3*	3.00	40.00	0	0	2	-
T20Is	3	1	0	0	0	0.00	0.00	0	0	0	-
First-class	26	34	22	86	17*	7.16	20.33	0	0	11	-
List A	35	18	8	70	16	7.00	41.66	0	0	9	-
T20s	36	7	5	23	10	11.50	104.54	0	0	9	-

Bowling	Mat	Balls	Mdns	Runs	Wkts	BB	Ave	4wI	5wI	SR	Econ
Tests	10	1424	52	893	36	5-34	24.80	-	2	39.55	3.76
ODIs	14	682	2	681	20	4-43	34.05	1	0	34.10	5.99
T20Is	3	72	0	85	4	3-27	21.25	0	0	18.00	7.08
First-class	26	4309	166	2374	91	5-34	26.08	-	2	47.35	3.30
List A	35	1656	16	1433	57	6-20	25.14	2	1	29.05	5.19
T20s	36	693	0	906	36	4-23	25.16	1	0	19.25	7.84

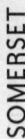

ALFIE OGBOURNE RHB / LMF / R0 / W0

SOMERSET

FULL NAME: Alfie Richard James Ogborne
BORN: July 15, 2003, Yeovil
SQUAD NO: 3
HEIGHT: 6ft 3in
NICKNAME: Oggers
EDUCATION: Ansford Academy; Richard Huish College
TEAMS: Somerset, Kent
ROLE: Bowler
DEBUT: First-class: 2023; List A: 2022

BEST BATTING: 12 Somerset vs Warwickshire, Edgbaston, 2024
BEST BOWLING: 2-56 Somerset vs Hampshire, Taunton, 2023

FIRST CRICKET CLUB? Sparkford CC, Somerset
EARLIEST CRICKETING MEMORY? Taking a catch off my dad's bowling at fine leg
WHAT'S THE BIGGEST PRIZE IN DOMESTIC CRICKET? The County Championship
THE KOOKABURRA BALL: YES OR NO? Yes, it's a new challenge which provides teams and players with different scenarios and opportunities
FAVOURITE WARM-UP SONG? Rhyme Dust by Dom Dolla
HOW MANY HOURS DO YOU SPEND ON YOUR PHONE A DAY? Four
ONE THING YOU WANT TO DO BEFORE YOU DIE: Play for England
HOBBY YOU WOULD LIKE TO LEARN: Fishing
WHICH PUBLIC FIGURE INSPIRES YOU (EXCLUDING SPORTSPEOPLE)? Jesus
SURPRISING FACT ABOUT YOU: I love socialising
FILM YOU CAN WATCH OVER AND OVER: The Chronicles of Narnia

Batting	Mat	Inns	NO	Runs	HS	Ave	SR	100	50	Ct	St
First-class	4	7	2	31	12	6.20	24.60	0	0	3	-
List A	12	5	2	47	27*	15.66	55.29	0	0	6	-

Bowling	Mat	Balls	Mdns	Runs	Wkts	BB	Ave	4wl	5wl	SR	Econ
First-class	4	506	12	343	8	2-56	42.87	-	0	63.25	4.06
List A	12	519	5	504	14	3-49	36.00	0	0	37.07	5.82

FULL NAME: Felix Spencer Organ
BORN: June 2, 1999, Sydney, Australia
SQUAD NO: 3
HEIGHT: 5ft 10in
NICKNAME: Fe
EDUCATION: Canford School, Dorset
TEAMS: Hampshire, England U19
ROLE: Allrounder
DEBUT: First-class: 2017; List A: 2018; T20: 2020

HAMPSHIRE

BEST BATTING: 118 Hampshire vs Gloucestershire, Cheltenham, 2022
BEST BOWLING: 6-67 Hampshire vs Lancashire, Southport, 2023

FIRST CRICKET CLUB? St Cross Symondians CC, Winchester, Hampshire
WHICH TEAMMATE HAS HAD THE BIGGEST IMPACT ON YOUR GAME? Liam Dawson
WHICH AWAY GROUND DO YOU MOST ENJOY VISITING? The Oval – great wicket, great crowds
WHO IS THE MOST TALENTED U19 TEENAGER IN THE COUNTY GAME? Dom Kelly (Ham)
WHO IS THE TOUGHEST BOWLER TO FACE? Mohammad Abbas
WHAT KEEPS YOU AWAKE AT NIGHT? Netflix
CHOOSE A FANTASY SLIP CORDON TO SPEND A DAY IN THE FIELD WITH: Kevin Hart (wk), Dwayne Johnson, Steven Gerrard, Nelson Mandela

Batting	Mat	Inns	NO	Runs	HS	Ave	SR	100	50	Ct	St
First-class	50	82	5	1711	118	22.22	45.15	3	7	20	-
List A	34	29	5	585	79	24.37	83.21	0	4	13	-
T20s	5	4	0	24	9	6.00	82.75	0	0	1	-

Bowling	Mat	Balls	Mdns	Runs	Wkts	BB	Ave	4wI	5wI	SR	Econ
First-class	50	3074	87	1658	60	6-67	27.63	-	3	51.23	3.23
List A	34	1264	8	1014	19	3-39	53.36	0	0	66.52	4.81
T20s	5	66	0	75	3	2-21	25.00	0	0	22.00	6.81

ALI ORR

HAMPSHIRE

FULL NAME: Alastair Graham Hamilton Orr
BORN: April 6, 2001, Eastbourne, Sussex
SQUAD NO: 27
HEIGHT: 6ft
NICKNAME: Boat
EDUCATION: Bede's Senior School, Hailsham, East Sussex; Loughborough University
TEAMS: Hampshire, Sussex
ROLE: Batter
DEBUT: First-class: 2021; List A: 2021; T20: 2022

BEST BATTING: 198 Sussex vs Glamorgan, Hove, 2022

FIRST CRICKET CLUB? Eastbourne CC, East Sussex
EARLIEST CRICKETING MEMORY? Scoring my first-ever hundred for Eastbourne
WHAT'S THE BIGGEST PRIZE IN DOMESTIC CRICKET? Division One of the County Championship
THE KOOKABURRA BALL: YES OR NO? Yes, it brings variety to the game
FAVOURITE WARM-UP SONG? Shotput by Still Woozy
HOW MANY HOURS DO YOU SPEND ON YOUR PHONE A DAY? Two
SPECIALITY SUBJECT IN A PUB QUIZ (EXCLUDING SPORT)? Countries of the world (I know every one)
ONE THING YOU WANT TO DO BEFORE YOU DIE: Surf in Bali
WHICH PUBLIC FIGURE INSPIRES YOU (EXCLUDING SPORTSPEOPLE)? Piers Morgan
FILM YOU CAN WATCH OVER AND OVER: Catch Me If You Can

Batting	Mat	Inns	NO	Runs	HS	Ave	SR	100	50	Ct	St
First-class	32	59	2	2113	198	37.07	50.85	5	8	12	-
List A	14	14	0	670	206	47.85	90.78	2	3	5	-
T20s	15	15	0	273	41	18.20	140.72	0	0	8	-

Bowling	Mat	Balls	Mdns	Runs	Wkts	BB	Ave	4wl	5wl	SR	Econ
First-class	32	18	0	12	0	0-12	-	-	-	-	4.00
List A	14	-	-	-	-	-	-	-	-	-	-
T20s	15	-	-	-	-	-	-	-	-	-	-

FULL NAME: Craig Overton
BORN: April 10, 1994, Barnstaple, Devon
SQUAD NO: 12
HEIGHT: 6ft 5in
NICKNAME: Goober
EDUCATION: West Buckland School, Devon
TEAMS: England, Somerset, Southern Brave,
Sunrisers Eastern Cape
ROLE: Allrounder
DEBUT: Test: 2017; ODI: 2018;
First-class: 2012; List A: 2012; T20: 2014

BEST BATTING: 138 Somerset vs Hampshire, Taunton, 2016
BEST BOWLING: 7-57 Somerset vs Essex, Taunton, 2022
COUNTY CAP: 2016

FIRST CRICKET CLUB? North Devon CC, Bideford
WHO IS THE MOST TALENTED U19 TEENAGER IN THE COUNTY GAME? Ben McKinney (Dur)
IF YOU COULD PINCH A PLAYER FROM ANOTHER COUNTY, WHO WOULD IT BE?
Keaton Jennings
HOW IS BAZBALL AFFECTING CHAMPIONSHIP CRICKET? Players are definitely trying to take
the game forward at every opportunity
WHAT DO YOU THINK OF THE CURRENT 50-OVER COMPETITION? It has its purpose, though
I do think we should all be playing in it
WHAT'S THE SILLIEST OUTFIT YOU'VE EVER WORN? An Avatar costume
SURPRISING FACT ABOUT YOU: I own two racehorses with trainer Harry Derham

Batting	Mat	Inns	NO	Runs	HS	Ave	SR	100	50	Ct	St
Tests	8	14	2	182	41*	15.16	43.85	0	0	7	-
ODIs	7	5	2	68	32	22.66	89.47	0	0	4	-
First-class	136	200	28	3740	138	21.74	64.70	1	16	123	-
List A	75	55	18	824	66*	22.27	113.96	0	2	33	-
T20s	117	58	23	508	42	14.51	128.28	0	0	81	-

Bowling	Mat	Balls	Mdns	Runs	Wkts	BB	Ave	4wI	5wI	SR	Econ
Tests	8	1472	43	760	21	3-14	36.19	-	0	70.09	3.09
ODIs	7	308	2	291	5	2-23	58.20	0	0	61.60	5.66
First-class	136	23116	915	11371	470	7-57	24.19	-	17	49.18	2.95
List A	75	3444	31	3056	95	5-18	32.16	1	1	36.25	5.32
T20s	117	2265	8	3111	120	4-25	25.92	1	0	18.87	8.24

JAMIE OVERTON   RHB / RF / R0 / W0

SURREY

FULL NAME: Jamie Overton
BORN: April 10, 1994, Barnstaple, Devon
SQUAD NO: 88
HEIGHT: 6ft 5in
NICKNAME: J
EDUCATION: West Buckland School, Devon
TEAMS: England, Surrey, Adelaide Strikers, Manchester Originals, Northamptonshire, Somerset
ROLE: Allrounder
DEBUT: Test: 2022;
First-class: 2012; List A: 2012; T20: 2015

BEST BATTING: 120 Somerset vs Warwickshire, Edgbaston, 2020
BEST BOWLING: 6-61 Surrey vs Yorkshire, Scarborough, 2022
COUNTY CAP: 2023 (Surrey)

FIRST CRICKET CLUB? North Devon CC, Bideford
FAMILY TIES? My dad played for Devon and my twin brother Craig plays for Somerset
BIGGEST INFLUENCE ON YOUR DEVELOPMENT AS A CRICKETER (EXCLUDING PARENTS)? Clifford Dark, my club coach at North Devon CC. He offered me the opportunity to play at a higher age-group level and gave me lots of confidence
WHAT WOULD YOU CHANGE ABOUT THE STRUCTURE OF THE COUNTY SEASON? Not have first-class games during the white-ball competitions
HOBBIES? Horse racing
MOST BEAUTIFUL THING YOU HAVE EVER SEEN? Watching horses galloping on a crisp winter morning

Batting	Mat	Inns	NO	Runs	HS	Ave	SR	100	50	Ct	St
Tests	1	1	0	97	97	97.00	71.32	0	1	0	-
ODIs	5	5	0	81	32	16.20	101.25	0	0	1	-
T20Is	12	8	2	50	19	8.33	106.38	0	0	6	-
First-class	96	134	27	2336	120	21.83	78.70	1	13	73	-
List A	47	36	8	480	40*	17.14	112.14	0	0	20	-
T20s	162	114	38	1590	83*	20.92	158.05	0	1	87	-

Bowling	Mat	Balls	Mdns	Runs	Wkts	BB	Ave	4wI	5wI	SR	Econ
Tests	1	222	4	146	2	1-61	73.00	-	0	111.00	3.94
ODIs	5	144	0	150	4	2-27	37.50	0	0	36.00	6.25
T20Is	12	136	0	186	11	3-20	16.90	0	0	12.36	8.20
First-class	96	12439	346	7239	235	6-61	30.80	-	6	52.93	3.49
List A	47	1806	6	1891	61	4-42	31.00	3	0	29.60	6.28
T20s	162	2109	0	3180	118	5-47	26.94	2	1	17.87	9.04

CALLUM PARKINSON RHB / SLA / R0 / W1

FULL NAME: Callum Francis Parkinson
BORN: October 24, 1996, Bolton, Lancashire
SQUAD NO: 17
HEIGHT: 5ft 8in
NICKNAME: Parky
EDUCATION: Bolton School; Canon Slade, Bolton
TEAMS: Durham, Northern Superchargers, England Lions, Derbyshire, Leicestershire
ROLE: Bowler
DEBUT: First-class: 2016; List A: 2017; T20: 2017

BEST BATTING: 75 Leicestershire vs Kent, Canterbury, 2017
BEST BOWLING: 8-148 Leicestershire vs Worcestershire, Worcester, 2017

FIRST CRICKET CLUB? Heaton CC, Bolton
EARLIEST CRICKETING MEMORY? Watching my brother climb a tree while I was playing for Heaton U9s
WHAT'S THE BIGGEST PRIZE IN DOMESTIC CRICKET? The County Championship
THE KOOKABURRA BALL: YES OR NO? Yes – because it means you have to bowl more spin
OPPONENT YOU MOST LOOK FORWARD TO PLAYING AGAINST? My brother Matt. As nerve-racking as it is, it's also always a good chuckle
FAVOURITE WARM-UP SONG? Feliz Navidad
HOW MANY HOURS DO YOU SPEND ON YOUR PHONE A DAY? Four
SPECIALITY SUBJECT IN A PUB QUIZ (EXCLUDING SPORT)? World War 2
ONE THING YOU WANT TO DO BEFORE YOU DIE: Watch Bolton in Europe
HOBBY YOU WOULD LIKE TO LEARN: Spinning the cricket pellet
WHICH PUBLIC FIGURE INSPIRES YOU (EXCLUDING SPORTSPEOPLE)? Dick Winters (a WW2 general)

Batting	Mat	Inns	NO	Runs	HS	Ave	SR	100	50	Ct	St
First-class	74	108	24	1426	75	16.97	36.45	0	1	16	-
List A	14	12	4	226	52*	28.25	88.62	0	1	2	-
T20s	126	64	36	317	27*	11.32	92.96	0	0	23	-

Bowling	Mat	Balls	Mdns	Runs	Wkts	BB	Ave	4wI	5wI	SR	Econ
First-class	74	14076	387	7898	191	8-148	41.35	-	7	73.69	3.36
List A	14	612	0	631	6	2-42	105.16	0	0	102.00	6.18
T20s	126	2593	4	3261	148	4-20	22.03	3	0	17.52	7.54

MATT PARKINSON

RHB / LB / R0 / W0

KENT

FULL NAME: Matthew William Parkinson
BORN: October 24, 1996, Bolton, Lancashire
SQUAD NO: 28
HEIGHT: 5ft 9in
NICKNAME: Daddy
EDUCATION: Canon Slade School, Bolton
TEAMS: England, Kent, Durham, Eagles, Lancashire, Manchester Originals
ROLE: Bowler
DEBUT: Test: 2022; ODI: 2020; T20I: 2019; First-class: 2016; List A: 2018; T20: 2017

BEST BATTING: 48 Kent vs Essex, Canterbury, 2024
BEST BOWLING: 7-126 Lancashire vs Kent, Canterbury, 2021
COUNTY CAP: 2019 (Lancashire)

FIRST CRICKET CLUB? Heaton CC, Bolton
EARLIEST CRICKETING MEMORY? Climbing trees at Heaton CC
WHAT'S THE BIGGEST PRIZE IN DOMESTIC CRICKET? The County Championship
THE KOOKABURRA BALL: YES OR NO? Yes, but at the right time. It wasn't good in April – needs the summer months
OPPONENT YOU MOST LOOK FORWARD TO PLAYING AGAINST? My twin Callum, as it's nice to see him
SPECIALITY SUBJECT IN A PUB QUIZ (EXCLUDING SPORT)? History
SURPRISING FACT ABOUT YOU: I have fake teeth
FILM YOU CAN WATCH OVER AND OVER: Outlaw King

Batting	Mat	Inns	NO	Runs	HS	Ave	SR	100	50	Ct	St
Tests	1	1	0	8	8	8.00	100.00	0	0	0	-
ODIs	5	1	1	7	7*	-	87.50	0	0	1	-
T20Is	6	4	0	5	5	1.25	45.45	0	0	1	-
First-class	67	79	25	550	48	10.18	32.52	0	0	15	-
List A	45	22	14	125	19	15.62	50.40	0	0	6	-
T20s	116	28	10	81	18	4.50	78.64	0	0	14	-

Bowling	Mat	Balls	Mdns	Runs	Wkts	BB	Ave	4wI	5wI	SR	Econ
Tests	1	93	0	47	1	1-47	47.00	-	0	93.00	3.03
ODIs	5	208	0	203	5	2-28	40.60	0	0	41.60	5.85
T20Is	6	120	0	198	7	4-47	28.28	1	0	17.14	9.90
First-class	67	11965	331	6180	209	7-126	29.56	-	8	57.24	3.09
List A	45	2208	7	1952	76	5-51	25.68	5	2	29.05	5.30
T20s	116	2277	0	2929	155	4-9	18.89	7	0	14.69	7.71

RISHI PATEL

RHB / LB / R1 / W0

FULL NAME: Rishi Ketan Patel
BORN: July 26, 1998, Chigwell, Essex
SQUAD NO: 26
HEIGHT: 6ft 2in
NICKNAME: Yogi
EDUCATION: Brentwood School, Essex
TEAMS: Leicestershire, Birmingham Phoenix, Essex
ROLE: Batter
DEBUT: First-class: 2019; List A: 2019; T20: 2021

LEICESTERSHIRE

BEST BATTING: 179 Leicestershire vs Glamorgan, Cardiff, 2023

FIRST CRICKET CLUB? Ilford CC, London
EARLIEST CRICKETING MEMORY? Grandad throwing balls to me in the garden
WHAT'S THE BIGGEST PRIZE IN DOMESTIC CRICKET? Winning the County Championship
THE KOOKABURRA BALL: YES OR NO? Yes, it brings spinners into the game earlier
OPPONENT YOU MOST LOOK FORWARD TO PLAYING AGAINST? Kane Williamson – I love to watch him bat and also to learn from him
FAVOURITE WARM-UP SONG? The Greatest Show by Hugh Jackman
HOW MANY HOURS DO YOU SPEND ON YOUR PHONE A DAY? 2.5
ONE THING YOU WANT TO DO BEFORE YOU DIE: Swim in the Great Barrier Reef
HOBBY YOU WOULD LIKE TO LEARN: Speak Italian
WHICH PUBLIC FIGURE INSPIRES YOU (EXCLUDING SPORTSPEOPLE)? Sir Alan Bates
SURPRISING FACT ABOUT YOU: I've never been to a concert
FILM YOU CAN WATCH OVER AND OVER: Any of the Harry Potter movies

Batting	Mat	Inns	NO	Runs	HS	Ave	SR	100	50	Ct	St
First-class	47	79	3	2525	179	33.22	53.75	5	9	27	-
List A	30	30	1	790	161	27.24	85.59	2	3	19	-
T20s	58	55	2	1235	104	23.30	136.31	2	2	17	-

Bowling	Mat	Balls	Mdns	Runs	Wkts	BB	Ave	4wI	5wI	SR	Econ
First-class	47	-	-	-	-	-	-	-	-	-	-
List A	30	-	-	-	-	-	-	-	-	-	-
T20s	58	-	-	-	-	-	-	-	-	-	-

RYAN PATEL

LHB / RM / R0 / W0

SURREY

FULL NAME: Ryan Patel
BORN: October 26, 1997, Sutton, Surrey
SQUAD NO: 26
HEIGHT: 5ft 10in
NICKNAME: Pat
EDUCATION: Whitgift School, Croydon
TEAMS: Surrey, England U19
ROLE: Batter
DEBUT: First-class: 2017; List A: 2019; T20: 2019

BEST BATTING: 134 Surrey vs Durham, The Oval, 2024
BEST BOWLING: 6-5 Surrey vs Somerset, Guildford, 2018
COUNTY CAP: 2024

FIRST CRICKET CLUB? Old Rutlishians CC, London
BIGGEST INFLUENCE ON YOUR DEVELOPMENT AS A CRICKETER (EXCLUDING PARENTS)?
Sid Lahiri, director of the Rajasthan Royals Academy in Cobham who has also worked with
Surrey age-group sides
MOST EXCITING DAY AS A CRICKETER? Winning the County Championship in 2018, 2022,
2023 and 2024
GREATEST PERFORMANCE YOU HAVE WITNESSED? Kumar Sangakkara's double-hundred
against Essex at Chelmsford in 2017
CHILDHOOD SPORTING HERO? Thierry Henry

Batting	Mat	Inns	NO	Runs	HS	Ave	SR	100	50	Ct	St
First-class	62	96	8	2665	134	30.28	45.30	5	9	41	-
List A	36	34	3	1423	131	45.90	94.80	4	8	16	-
T20s	8	4	1	12	5*	4.00	80.00	0	0	1	-

Bowling	Mat	Balls	Mdns	Runs	Wkts	BB	Ave	4wI	5wI	SR	Econ
First-class	62	2098	45	1214	22	6-5	55.18	-	1	95.36	3.47
List A	36	397	1	394	8	2-65	49.25	0	0	49.62	5.95
T20s	8	21	0	36	0	0-8	-	-	-	-	10.28

SAMIT PATEL

RHB / SLA / R4 / W0

FULL NAME: Samit Rohit Patel
BORN: November 30, 1984, Leicester
SQUAD NO: 21
HEIGHT: 5ft 8in
NICKNAME: Slippery
EDUCATION: Worksop College
TEAMS: England, Derbyshire, Glamorgan, Melbourne Renegades, Nottinghamshire, Sylhet Strikers, Trent Rockets, Trinbago Knight Riders, Wellington
ROLE: Allrounder
DEBUT: Test: 2012; ODI: 2008; T20I: 2011; First-class: 2002; List A: 2002; T20: 2003

BEST BATTING: 257* Nottinghamshire vs Gloucestershire, Bristol, 2017
BEST BOWLING: 7-68 Nottinghamshire vs Hampshire, Southampton, 2011
COUNTY CAP: 2008 (Nottinghamshire); **BENEFIT:** 2017 (Nottinghamshire)

FIRST CRICKET CLUB? Kimberley Institute CC, Nottinghamshire
BEST DELIVERY YOU HAVE EVER BOWLED OR FACED? Both were in the Test match against Pakistan at Karachi in 2015. I bowled Sarfraz Ahmed with a ball that pitched on leg and hit off, after Yasir Shah had bowled me in the exact same way
WHAT WOULD BE YOUR PERFECT BREAKFAST? A bacon sandwich
WHICH PERSON INSPIRES YOU MOST? Sachin Tendulkar

Batting	Mat	Inns	NO	Runs	HS	Ave	SR	100	50	Ct	St
Tests	6	9	0	151	42	16.77	44.67	0	0	3	-
ODIs	36	22	7	482	70*	32.13	93.23	0	1	7	-
T20Is	18	14	2	189	67	15.75	109.24	0	1	3	-
First-class	231	376	20	12692	257*	35.65	62.71	26	64	140	-
List A	253	218	35	6342	136*	34.65	85.04	8	33	72	-
T20s	414	342	71	6673	90*	24.62	124.96	0	35	113	-

Bowling	Mat	Balls	Mdns	Runs	Wkts	BB	Ave	4wI	5wI	SR	Econ
Tests	6	858	23	421	7	2-27	60.14	-	0	122.57	2.94
ODIs	36	1187	4	1091	24	5-41	45.45	0	1	49.45	5.51
T20Is	18	252	0	321	7	2-6	45.85	0	0	36.00	7.64
First-class	231	26909	964	13650	357	7-68	38.23	-	5	75.37	3.04
List A	253	8737	32	7830	236	6-13	33.17	3	2	37.02	5.37
T20s	414	7589	6	9173	352	4-5	26.05	3	0	21.55	7.25

DANE PATERSON

RHB / RFM / R0 / W2

MIDDLESEX

FULL NAME: Dane Paterson
BORN: April 4, 1989, Cape Town, South Africa
SQUAD NO: 32
TEAMS: South Africa, Middlesex, Cape Cobras, Dolphins, Eastern Province, Jozi Stars, KwaZulu-Natal, Nottinghamshire, Paarl Rocks, South Western Districts, Western Province
ROLE: Bowler
DEBUT: Test: 2020; ODI: 2017; T20I: 2017; First-class: 2009; List A: 2009; T20: 2013

BEST BATTING: 59 KwaZulu-Natal vs Free State, Bloemfontein, 2013
BEST BOWLING: 8-52 Nottinghamshire vs Worcestershire, Trent Bridge, 2022

NOTES: The 36-year-old South African seamer begins anew at Middlesex following four summers at Notts, for whom he has taken 180 first-class wickets at 23.25. Paterson is scheduled to be available for the first seven rounds of the County Championship. "We are really pleased to get this signing secured as Dane is a player that will bring an enormous amount of quality to our pace attack and is someone that can make a real impact for us in the first half of the season," said Middlesex director of cricket Alan Coleman. "He has proven throughout the four years he spent with Nottinghamshire that he has all the attributes needed to succeed in English conditions, and he brings with him a wealth of experience, built up over many years on both the domestic and international stages"

Batting	Mat	Inns	NO	Runs	HS	Ave	SR	100	50	Ct	St
Tests	7	11	3	101	39*	12.62	91.81	0	0	2	-
ODIs	4	0	-	-	-	-	-	-	-	2	-
T20Is	8	2	1	5	4*	5.00	250.00	0	0	1	-
First-class	167	206	61	1713	59	11.81	69.60	0	1	48	-
List A	118	55	19	415	29	11.52	101.96	0	0	33	-
T20s	106	38	17	175	24*	8.33	120.68	0	0	25	-
Bowling	Mat	Balls	Mdns	Runs	Wkts	BB	Ave	4wI	5wI	SR	Econ
Tests	7	1319	43	656	25	5-61	26.24	-	2	52.76	2.98
ODIs	4	209	1	217	4	3-44	54.25	0	0	52.25	6.22
T20Is	8	179	0	265	9	4-32	29.44	1	0	19.88	8.88
First-class	167	27997	1014	14394	610	8-52	23.59	-	24	45.89	3.08
List A	118	5632	64	4963	162	5-19	30.63	6	1	34.76	5.28
T20s	106	2084	7	2791	110	4-24	25.37	3	0	18.94	8.03

FULL NAME: Liam Anthony Patterson-White
BORN: November 8, 1998, Sunderland, County Durham
SQUAD NO: 87
HEIGHT: 6ft
NICKNAME: Patto
EDUCATION: Worksop College, Nottinghamshire
TEAMS: Nottinghamshire, England Lions, Northamptonshire
ROLE: Bowler
DEBUT: First-class: 2019; List A: 2021; T20: 2024

BEST BATTING: 101 Nottinghamshire vs Somerset, Taunton, 2021
BEST BOWLING: 5-41 Nottinghamshire vs Hampshire, Southampton, 2021

FIRST CRICKET CLUB? Bashford Mill CC, Nottingham
WHICH TEAMMATE HAS HAD THE BIGGEST IMPACT ON YOUR GAME? Luke Fletcher – in cricket he's been a father figure for me
WHICH AWAY GROUND DO YOU MOST ENJOY VISITING? Taunton – the crowd and atmosphere is the best around
WHO IS THE MOST TALENTED U19 TEENAGER IN THE COUNTY GAME? Farhan Ahmed (Not)
IF YOU COULD PINCH A PLAYER FROM ANOTHER COUNTY, WHO WOULD IT BE? Sam Billings
HOW IS BAZBALL AFFECTING CHAMPIONSHIP CRICKET? Players are attempting to be more aggressive in approach in order to get picked for higher honours, which is both a benefit and a hindrance to the County Championship
WHAT DO YOU THINK OF THE CURRENT 50-OVER COMPETITION? A great opportunity for young players but it should get more financial backing so that games are staged at the big grounds
WHO IS THE TOUGHEST BOWLER TO FACE? Chris Rushworth
WHAT KEEPS YOU AWAKE AT NIGHT? Failing to reach my potential

Batting	Mat	Inns	NO	Runs	HS	Ave	SR	100	50	Ct	St
First-class	48	69	8	1329	101	21.78	54.22	1	6	21	-
List A	30	24	3	441	62*	21.00	99.77	0	1	13	-
T20s	10	7	2	121	44*	24.20	142.35	0	0	2	-

Bowling	Mat	Balls	Mdns	Runs	Wkts	BB	Ave	4wI	5wI	SR	Econ
First-class	48	8098	255	4014	116	5-41	34.60	-	5	69.81	2.97
List A	30	1345	7	1112	41	5-19	27.12	0	2	32.80	4.96
T20s	10	120	0	142	7	2-9	20.28	0	0	17.14	7.10

DAVID PAYNE

RHB / LFM / R0 / W0 / MVP45

GLOUCESTERSHIRE

FULL NAME: David Alan Payne
BORN: February 15, 1991, Poole, Dorset
SQUAD NO: 14
HEIGHT: 6ft 3in
NICKNAME: Sid
EDUCATION: Lytchett Minster Secondary &
Sixth Form, Poole, Dorset
TEAMS: England, Gloucestershire, Welsh Fire,
Adelaide Strikers, Perth Scorchers
ROLE: Bowler
DEBUT: ODI: 2022;
First-class: 2011; List A: 2009; T20: 2010

BEST BATTING: 28 Welsh Fire vs Oval Invincibles, Cardiff, 2024 (Hundred)
BEST BOWLING: 5-24 Gloucestershire vs Middlesex, Richmond, 2015 (T20)
COUNTY CAP: 2011

FIRST CRICKET CLUB? Parley CC, Dorset
WHAT'S THE BIGGEST PRIZE IN DOMESTIC CRICKET? The T20 Blast
THE KOOKABURRA BALL: YES OR NO? Yes, it's good to have experience with it in case you
get called up for England and have to use it abroad
OPPONENT YOU MOST LOOK FORWARD TO PLAYING AGAINST? Jake Ball for the catch-up
FAVOURITE WARM-UP SONG? Jerusalema by Master KG
ONE THING YOU WANT TO DO BEFORE YOU DIE: Play golf at Augusta
HOBBY YOU WOULD LIKE TO LEARN: Carpentry
SURPRISING FACT ABOUT YOU: I hate tea
FILM YOU CAN WATCH OVER AND OVER: Remember the Titans, The Blind Side, Coach Carter
plus many, many more
NOTES: Payne is on a white-ball contract at Gloucestershire

Batting	Mat	Inns	NO	Runs	HS	Ave	SR	100	50	Ct	St
ODIs	1	0	-	-	-	-	-	-	-	0	-
First-class	115	142	47	1779	67*	18.72	46.55	0	6	40	-
List A	70	29	18	222	40	20.18	83.14	0	0	20	-
T20s	196	57	24	234	28	7.09	114.70	0	0	43	-

Bowling	Mat	Balls	Mdns	Runs	Wkts	BB	Ave	4wl	5wl	SR	Econ
ODIs	1	54	0	38	1	1-38	38.00	0	0	54.00	4.22
First-class	115	18791	642	9705	328	6-26	29.58	-	6	57.28	3.09
List A	70	3074	19	2928	115	7-29	25.46	4	3	26.73	5.71
T20s	196	3975	11	5386	249	5-24	21.63	4	1	15.96	8.12

DILLON PENNINGTON

RHB / RFM / R0 / W0

FULL NAME: Dillon Pennington
BORN: February 26, 1999, Shrewsbury, Shropshire
SQUAD NO: 18
HEIGHT: 6ft 4in
NICKNAME: Dill
EDUCATION: Wrekin College, Shropshire; University of Worcester
TEAMS: Nottinghamshire, Birmingham Phoenix, England Lions, Northern Superchargers, Worcestershire
ROLE: Bowler
DEBUT: First-class: 2018; List A: 2018; T20: 2018

NOTTINGHAMSHIRE

BEST BATTING: 56 Worcestershire vs Essex, Chelmsford, 2021
BEST BOWLING: 5-32 Worcestershire vs Derbyshire, Worcester, 2021

FIRST CRICKET CLUB? Shrewsbury CC, Shropshire
WHICH TEAMMATE HAS HAD THE BIGGEST IMPACT ON YOUR GAME? Josh Tongue
WHAT PART OF THE SEASON DO YOU MOST ENJOY? April
IF YOU COULD PINCH A PLAYER FROM ANOTHER COUNTY, WHO WOULD IT BE? Ben Raine
WHAT DO YOU THINK OF THE CURRENT 50-OVER COMPETITION? I really like it
FAVOURITE FORMAT? The County Championship – I enjoy the challenge of having to compete over long periods of time
WHO IS THE TOUGHEST BOWLER TO FACE? Joe Leach – the shin-hunter
WHAT'S THE SILLIEST OUTFIT YOU'VE EVER WORN? Dressing up as an Oompa Loompa
SURPRISING FACT ABOUT YOU: When I was growing up I washed lawnmowers

Batting	Mat	Inns	NO	Runs	HS	Ave	SR	100	50	Ct	St
First-class	54	74	16	612	56	10.55	46.89	0	1	13	-
List A	18	11	5	109	35	18.16	87.20	0	0	5	-
T20s	61	22	13	68	10*	7.55	91.89	0	0	19	-

Bowling	Mat	Balls	Mdns	Runs	Wkts	BB	Ave	4wl	5wl	SR	Econ
First-class	54	8679	290	4749	173	5-32	27.45	-	2	50.16	3.28
List A	18	919	4	915	31	5-67	29.51	0	1	29.64	5.97
T20s	61	1051	5	1582	55	4-9	28.76	2	0	19.10	9.03

MICHAEL PEPPER

RHB / WK / R0 / W0 / MVP9

ESSEX

FULL NAME: Michael-Kyle Steven Pepper
BORN: June 25, 1998, Harlow, Essex
SQUAD NO: 19
HEIGHT: 5ft 11in
NICKNAME: Peps
EDUCATION: The Perse School, Cambridge
TEAMS: Essex, London Spirit, Northern Superchargers
ROLE: Batter/wicketkeeper
DEBUT: First-class: 2018; List A: 2021; T20: 2018

BEST BATTING: 115 Essex vs Nottinghamshire, Chelmsford, 2024

FIRST CRICKET CLUB? Wendens Ambo CC, Saffron Walden
NOTES: Once seen as a successor to keeper Adam Wheater, Pepper has recast himself as an explosive top-order batter for Essex in white-ball cricket. The 26-year-old finished as the club's leading run-scorer in the 2022 edition of the T20 Blast, hitting 439 runs at a strike-rate of 163, and followed up with another 409 runs the following summer, behind only Daniel Sams. Last year he was even better, finishing as the third-highest runscorer in the competition with 535 runs including two hundreds – his first in the format – form that led England to call Pepper up as cover for the white-ball series in the Caribbean before Christmas. He also enjoyed his best red-ball season to date in 2024, scoring over 500 runs in 10 matches and registering his first two centuries in the longer version of the game

Batting	Mat	Inns	NO	Runs	HS	Ave	SR	100	50	Ct	St
First-class	25	38	4	946	115	27.82	67.18	2	4	57	1
List A	7	5	0	134	63	26.80	120.72	0	1	0	-
T20s	96	94	10	2237	120*	26.63	151.04	2	11	36	2
Bowling	Mat	Balls	Mdns	Runs	Wkts	BB	Ave	4wl	5wl	SR	Econ
First-class	25	-	-	-	-	-	-	-	-	-	-
List A	7	-	-	-	-	-	-	-	-	-	-
T20s	96	-	-	-	-	-	-	-	-	-	-

ANDERSON PHILLIP

RHB / RFM / RO / WO

FULL NAME: Anderson Phillip
BORN: August 22, 1996, Trinidad
SQUAD NO: 48
TEAMS: West Indies, Lancashire, Trinbago
Knight Riders, Trinidad & Tobago
ROLE: Bowler
DEBUT: Test: 2022; ODI: 2021;
First-class: 2017; List A: 2019; T20: 2016

BEST BATTING: 63* Trinidad & Tobago vs Jamaica, Tarouba, 2023
BEST BOWLING: 6-19 Trinidad & Tobago vs Windward Islands, Tarouba, 2020

NOTES: The Trinidadian pace bowler has re-signed for Lancashire for the 2025 season after playing three Championship matches last summer in which he took 15 wickets at 23.93 but couldn't prevent the club suffering relegation. Phillip is set to be available for 11 Championship matches until the end of July and his contract also includes the option to play in the Blast. He was included on the West Indies' tour of Pakistan in January but didn't feature in the two-Test series. He made the most recent of his seven international appearances in 2022, in a Test match at Adelaide, where he made 43 as a nightwatchman. "We were hugely impressed by Anderson's performances during the final three matches of last season and jumped at the opportunity to bring him back for a longer spell next season," said Mark Chilton, Lancashire's director of cricket. "He displayed a really good attitude during his time with us and we believe that he has all the right attributes for a fast bowler – with room to still grow and improve his game"

Batting	Mat	Inns	NO	Runs	HS	Ave	SR	100	50	Ct	St
Tests	2	3	1	53	43	26.50	51.45	0	0	0	-
ODIs	5	2	1	22	21*	22.00	88.00	0	0	2	-
First-class	39	57	17	555	63*	13.87	49.20	0	1	17	-
List A	30	8	3	65	21*	13.00	90.27	0	0	9	-
T20s	20	6	5	12	6*	12.00	66.66	0	0	3	-

Bowling	Mat	Balls	Mdns	Runs	Wkts	BB	Ave	4wI	5wI	SR	Econ
Tests	2	276	4	212	3	2-30	70.66	-	0	92.00	4.60
ODIs	5	195	0	207	4	2-50	51.75	0	0	48.75	6.36
First-class	39	5200	148	3229	133	6-19	24.27	-	7	39.09	3.72
List A	30	1143	10	1121	40	4-44	28.02	1	0	28.57	5.88
T20s	20	264	0	416	10	3-38	41.60	0	0	26.40	9.45

ED POLLOCK

LHB / OB / R0 / W0

FULL NAME: Edward John Pollock
BORN: July 10, 1995, High Wycombe, Buckinghamshire
SQUAD NO: 7
HEIGHT: 5ft 10in
EDUCATION: Royal Grammar School, Worcester; Shrewsbury School; Durham University
TEAMS: Worcestershire, Warwickshire
ROLE: Batter
DEBUT: First-class: 2015; List A: 2018; T20: 2017

BEST BATTING: 113 Worcestershire vs Middlesex, Northwood, 2022

FIRST CRICKET CLUB? Barnt Green CC, Worcestershire. Andy and Grant Flower have both played for the club

FAMILY TIES? My dad and brother have both captained Cambridge University

BEST PERFORMANCE AS A PRO? My Championship hundred against Middlesex at Northwood three summers ago

GREATEST PERFORMANCE YOU HAVE WITNESSED? Ben Stokes at New Road in 2022

HOW IS BAZBALL AFFECTING CHAMPIONSHIP CRICKET? It's making my dismissals look normal!

FAVOURITE FORMAT? The County Championship

WHO IS THE TOUGHEST BOWLER TO FACE? Jeetan Patel in the nets

CHOOSE A FANTASY SLIP CORDON TO SPEND A DAY IN THE FIELD WITH: Tiger Woods (wk), Brian Lara, Jimmy Carr, Emma Watson

Batting	Mat	Inns	NO	Runs	HS	Ave	SR	100	50	Ct	St
First-class	27	43	1	1085	113	25.83	62.78	2	5	19	-
List A	44	42	1	1100	180	26.82	105.66	2	4	12	-
T20s	85	80	10	1394	77	19.91	153.69	0	7	22	-

Bowling	Mat	Balls	Mdns	Runs	Wkts	BB	Ave	4wl	5wl	SR	Econ
First-class	27	-	-	-	-	-	-	-	-	-	-
List A	44	-	-	-	-	-	-	-	-	-	-
T20s	85	-	-	-	-	-	-	-	-	-	-

OLLIE POPE

RHB / WK / R2 / W0

FULL NAME: Oliver John Douglas Pope
BORN: January 2, 1998, Chelsea, Middlesex
SQUAD NO: 32
HEIGHT: 5ft 10in
NICKNAME: Pope-dog
EDUCATION: Cranleigh School, Surrey
TEAMS: England, Surrey, London Spirit, Adelaide Strikers, Welsh Fire
ROLE: Batter
DEBUT: Test: 2018;
First-class: 2017; List A: 2016; T20: 2017

BEST BATTING: 274 Surrey vs Glamorgan, The Oval, 2021

COUNTY CAP: 2018

FIRST CRICKET CLUB? Grayshott CC, Hampshire
MOST BEAUTIFUL THING YOU HAVE EVER SEEN? Clapham Common in south London
HOBBIES? The guitar
WHO WOULD YOU MOST AND LEAST LIKE TO HAVE A NET WITH? Most – AB de Villiers (just to watch him). Least – Chris Woakes (too good)

Batting	Mat	Inns	NO	Runs	HS	Ave	SR	100	50	Ct	St
Tests	55	97	5	3130	205	34.02	63.68	7	15	73	1
First-class	114	183	17	7603	274	45.80	65.49	21	29	151	1
List A	31	28	5	767	93*	33.34	79.48	0	5	9	-
T20s	70	67	12	1505	99*	27.36	131.09	0	5	29	3

Bowling	Mat	Balls	Mdns	Runs	Wkts	BB	Ave	4wI	5wI	SR	Econ
Tests	55	-	-	-	-	-	-	-	-	-	-
First-class	114	6	0	10	0	0-10	-	-	-	-	10.00
List A	31	-	-	-	-	-	-	-	-	-	-
T20s	70	-	-	-	-	-	-	-	-	-	-

JAMIE PORTER

RHB / RMF / R0 / W6

ESSEX

FULL NAME: James Alexander Porter
BORN: May 25, 1993, Leytonstone, Essex
SQUAD NO: 44
HEIGHT: 6ft 1in
NICKNAME: Ports
EDUCATION: Oaks Park High School, Ilford;
Epping Forest College, Essex
TEAMS: Essex, England Lions
ROLE: Bowler
DEBUT: First-class: 2014; List A: 2015; T20: 2017

BEST BATTING: 34 Essex vs Glamorgan, Cardiff, 2015
BEST BOWLING: 7-41 Essex vs Worcestershire, Chelmsford, 2018
COUNTY CAP: 2015

FIRST CRICKET CLUB? Old Parksonians CC, Ilford, Essex
EARLIEST CRICKETING MEMORY? The 2005 Ashes
WHAT'S THE BIGGEST PRIZE IN DOMESTIC CRICKET? Division One of the
County Championship
THE KOOKABURRA BALL: YES OR NO? Yes but in the middle of the summer. It's a terrible
ball if it gets wet
OPPONENT YOU MOST LOOK FORWARD TO PLAYING AGAINST? My ex-teammate Dan
Lawrence because I'm going to hit him on the pad first ball
FAVOURITE WARM-UP SONG? Singin' in the Rain by Gene Kelly
SPECIALITY SUBJECT IN A PUB QUIZ (EXCLUDING SPORT)? Black holes (space)
ONE THING YOU WANT TO DO BEFORE YOU DIE: Hit a century break in snooker
WHICH PUBLIC FIGURE INSPIRES YOU (EXCLUDING SPORTSPEOPLE)? Joe Rogan
SURPRISING FACT ABOUT YOU: I scored a hundred before I took a five-fer
FILM YOU CAN WATCH OVER AND OVER: Top Gun

Batting	Mat	Inns	NO	Runs	HS	Ave	SR	100	50	Ct	St
First-class	138	158	67	537	34	5.90	24.73	0	0	41	-
List A	44	19	12	58	10*	8.28	49.15	0	0	8	-
T20s	25	6	5	5	1*	5.00	71.42	0	0	6	-

Bowling	Mat	Balls	Mdns	Runs	Wkts	BB	Ave	4wI	5wI	SR	Econ
First-class	138	22653	773	12147	522	7-41	23.27	-	21	43.39	3.21
List A	44	2082	19	1666	47	4-29	35.44	4	0	44.29	4.80
T20s	25	421	0	636	19	4-20	33.47	2	0	22.15	9.06

MATTHEW POTTS   RHB / RFM / R0 / W2

FULL NAME: Matthew James Potts
BORN: October 29, 1998, Sunderland, County Durham
SQUAD NO: 35
HEIGHT: 6ft 2in
NICKNAME: Harry
EDUCATION: St Robert of Newminster Catholic School, Sunderland
TEAMS: England, Durham, Northern Superchargers, MI Cape Town
ROLE: Bowler
DEBUT: Test: 2022; ODI: 2022; First-class: 2017; List A: 2018; T20: 2019

DURHAM

BEST BATTING: 149* Durham vs Warwickshire, Edgbaston, 2024
BEST BOWLING: 9-68 Durham vs Lancashire, Chester-le-Street, 2024

FIRST CRICKET CLUB? Philadelphia CC, Tyne & Wear
WHICH TEAMMATE HAS HAD THE BIGGEST IMPACT ON YOUR GAME? Ollie Robinson
WHAT PART OF THE SEASON DO YOU MOST ENJOY? The first day
WHICH AWAY GROUND DO YOU MOST ENJOY VISITING? Lord's
WHO IS THE MOST TALENTED U19 TEENAGER IN THE COUNTY GAME? Ben McKinney (Dur)
WHAT KEEPS YOU AWAKE AT NIGHT? Facing Mark Wood in the nets

Batting	Mat	Inns	NO	Runs	HS	Ave	SR	100	50	Ct	St
Tests	10	13	3	86	21	8.60	51.19	0	0	8	-
ODIs	9	6	5	45	15*	45.00	72.58	0	0	3	-
First-class	60	76	15	1127	149*	18.47	49.23	1	3	26	-
List A	19	10	5	98	30	19.60	71.53	0	0	6	-
T20s	62	23	11	203	40*	16.91	127.67	0	0	19	-

Bowling	Mat	Balls	Mdns	Runs	Wkts	BB	Ave	4wI	5wI	SR	Econ
Tests	10	2041	78	1060	36	4-13	29.44	-	0	56.69	3.11
ODIs	9	300	3	293	10	4-38	29.30	1	0	30.00	5.86
First-class	60	11591	418	5896	243	9-68	24.26	-	10	47.69	3.05
List A	19	684	7	667	26	4-38	25.65	2	0	26.30	5.85
T20s	62	1164	1	1651	63	3-8	26.20	0	0	18.47	8.51

NICK POTTS — RHB / RFM / R0 / W0

DERBYSHIRE

FULL NAME: Nicholas James Potts
BORN: July 17, 2002, Burton-on-Trent, Staffordshire
SQUAD NO: 26
HEIGHT: 6ft 1in
EDUCATION: De Ferrers Academy, Burton-on-Trent
TEAMS: Derbyshire
ROLE: Bowler
DEBUT: First-class: 2022; List A: 2022

BEST BATTING: 13 Derbyshire vs Leicestershire, Derby, 2022
BEST BOWLING: 4-50 Derbyshire vs Nottinghamshire, Trent Bridge, 2022

FIRST CRICKET CLUB? Dunstall CC, Staffordshire
EARLIEST CRICKETING MEMORY? Playing in the garden aged five
WHAT'S THE BIGGEST PRIZE IN DOMESTIC CRICKET? The County Championship
THE KOOKABURRA BALL: YES OR NO? No – it doesn't suit English conditions and creates an imbalance between bat and ball
OPPONENT YOU MOST LOOK FORWARD TO PLAYING AGAINST? Jimmy Anderson – I'd love to see him bowl from up close
FAVOURITE WARM-UP SONG? How We Do by Game
HOW MANY HOURS DO YOU SPEND ON YOUR PHONE A DAY? Three
SPECIALITY SUBJECT IN A PUB QUIZ (EXCLUDING SPORT)? Geography
ONE THING YOU WANT TO DO BEFORE YOU DIE: Get a 147 in snooker
HOBBY YOU WOULD LIKE TO LEARN: Surfing
WHICH PUBLIC FIGURE INSPIRES YOU (EXCLUDING SPORTSPEOPLE)? David Attenborough
SURPRISING FACT ABOUT YOU: I can solve a Rubix cube in 30 seconds
FILM YOU CAN WATCH OVER AND OVER: Interstellar

Batting	Mat	Inns	NO	Runs	HS	Ave	SR	100	50	Ct	St
First-class	8	9	1	58	13	7.25	40.84	0	0	2	-
List A	7	6	5	13	6*	13.00	72.22	0	0	2	-

Bowling	Mat	Balls	Mdns	Runs	Wkts	BB	Ave	4wI	5wI	SR	Econ
First-class	8	935	16	646	15	4-50	43.06	-	0	62.33	4.14
List A	7	264	0	316	5	2-63	63.20	0	0	52.80	7.18

FULL NAME: Thomas James Prest
BORN: March 24, 2003, Wimborne, Dorset
SQUAD NO: 24
HEIGHT: 6ft
NICKNAME: Tim
EDUCATION: Canford School, Dorset
TEAMS: Hampshire, England Lions
ROLE: Batter
DEBUT: First-class: 2021; List A: 2021; T20: 2021

HAMPSHIRE

BEST BATTING: 156 Hampshire vs Essex, Southampton, 2024
BEST BOWLING: 2-32 Hampshire vs Surrey, Southampton, 2023

FIRST CRICKET CLUB? Broadstone CC, Poole, Dorset
EARLIEST CRICKETING MEMORY? The 2005 Ashes
WHAT'S THE BIGGEST PRIZE IN DOMESTIC CRICKET? The County Championship
THE KOOKABURRA BALL: YES OR NO? Yes – better for batting!
FAVOURITE WARM-UP SONG? Sonder by Barry Can't Swim
HOW MANY HOURS DO YOU SPEND ON YOUR PHONE A DAY? Five
SPECIALITY SUBJECT IN A PUB QUIZ (EXCLUDING SPORT)? History
FILM YOU CAN WATCH OVER AND OVER: Law Abiding Citizen

Batting	Mat	Inns	NO	Runs	HS	Ave	SR	100	50	Ct	St
First-class	18	24	2	808	156	36.72	69.05	4	1	12	-
List A	39	39	2	1166	181	31.51	85.29	2	7	11	-
T20s	37	37	2	749	64	21.40	123.39	0	5	13	-

Bowling	Mat	Balls	Mdns	Runs	Wkts	BB	Ave	4wI	5wI	SR	Econ
First-class	18	279	3	191	4	2-32	47.75	-	0	69.75	4.10
List A	39	407	0	355	13	3-41	27.30	0	0	31.30	5.23
T20s	37	36	0	43	2	1-8	21.50	0	0	18.00	7.16

LHUAN-DRE PRETORIUS

LHB / WK

HAMPSHIRE

FULL NAME: Lhuan-dre Gilbert Pretorius
BORN: March 27, 2006, Potchefstroom, South Africa
SQUAD NO: TBC
TEAMS: Hampshire, Northerns, Paarl Royals, South Africa U19
ROLE: Batter/wicketkeeper
DEBUT: First-class: 2024; List A: 2023; T20: 2024

BEST BATTING: 97 Paarl Royals vs Sunrisers Eastern Cape, Paarl, 2025 (T20)

NOTES: An aggressive opener who keeps wicket, Pretorius has been signed by Hampshire for the T20 Blast following an impressive 2024/25 season for Paarl Royals in his native South Africa. The left-hander finished as the top scorer in the SA20, with 397 runs in 12 matches at a strike-rate of 166.80, including an audacious 97 on his Royals debut. That match was against Sunrisers Eastern Cape, who are coached by Hampshire head coach Adrian Birrell and who's XI featured Hawks allrounder Liam Dawson. Known for his idiosyncratic backlift, Pretorius was also South Africa's leading run-scorer in the 2023/24 U19 World Cup, scoring 287 runs at an average of 57.40. "Lhuan-dre impressed with his batting during the recent SA20 and played a number of eye-catching innings against some of the best bowlers in the world," said Giles White, Hampshire's director of cricket. "He's a special talent with a big future and we are delighted that he is joining us"

Batting	Mat	Inns	NO	Runs	HS	Ave	SR	100	50	Ct	St
First-class	1	1	0	120	120	120.00	65.21	1	0	0	-
List A	13	13	1	565	120	47.08	113.00	2	3	10	-
T20s	33	33	0	911	97	27.60	147.17	0	6	16	1

Bowling	Mat	Balls	Mdns	Runs	Wkts	BB	Ave	4wI	5wI	SR	Econ
First-class	1	-	-	-	-	-	-	-	-	-	-
List A	13	30	1	19	1	1-8	19.00	0	0	30.00	3.80
T20s	33	-	-	-	-	-	-	-	-	-	-

MIGAEL PRETORIUS · RHB / RFM / RO / WO

FULL NAME: Migael Pretorius
BORN: March 24, 1995, Vereeniging, Gauteng, South Africa
SQUAD NO: 27
TEAMS: Somerset, Durham, Free State, Jamaica Tallawahs, Knights, Lions, Northerns, North West, Pretoria Capitals, Titans
ROLE: Allrounder
DEBUT: First-class: 2016; List A: 2015; T20: 2017

BEST BATTING: 109* North West vs Eastern Provinces, Potchefstroom, 2023
BEST BOWLING: 6-38 Northerns vs Northern Cape, Pretoria, 2017

NOTES: South African bowling allrounder Migael Pretorius has re-signed for Somerset after impressing in his debut season for the club. The 30-year-old played in eight Championship fixtures last year, scoring 324 runs at an average of 32.40, including an impressive knock of 95 not out against Notts, and took 23 wickets, completing an impressive all-round campaign. He is expected to be available across all three formats for the duration of the summer. Pretorius has taken over 200 first-class wickets at an average well under 30, alongside more than 2,000 runs batting in the lower order. Andy Hurry, director of cricket at Somerset, was delighted to have the South African return for the new season: "Following his time with us during 2024, Migael knows what it means to represent the club and understands what we are aspiring to achieve here. He has a proven ability to impact games, and he will add further all-round quality as well as depth to our already impressive seam attack. Understanding how demanding the season is for teams competing across all three competitions, we feel that squad depth will be a vital factor for us"

Batting	Mat	Inns	NO	Runs	HS	Ave	SR	100	50	Ct	St
First-class	69	91	13	2158	109*	27.66	73.20	1	14	18	-
List A	43	29	5	339	33	14.12	99.41	0	0	7	-
T20s	85	56	17	398	38*	10.20	125.94	0	0	15	-

Bowling	Mat	Balls	Mdns	Runs	Wkts	BB	Ave	4wI	5wI	SR	Econ
First-class	69	10604	392	5626	201	6-38	27.99	-	6	52.75	3.18
List A	43	1996	22	1594	61	4-21	26.13	4	0	32.72	4.79
T20s	85	1638	5	2362	96	4-14	24.60	3	0	17.06	8.65

OLLIE PRICE

RHB / OB / R0 / W0 / MVP50

GLOUCESTERSHIRE

FULL NAME: Oliver Joseph Price
BORN: June 12, 2001, Oxford
SQUAD NO: 67
HEIGHT: 6ft 4in
NICKNAME: Frube
EDUCATION: Magdalen College School, Oxford; Durham University
TEAMS: Gloucestershire, England Lions
ROLE: Allrounder
DEBUT: First-class: 2021; List A: 2021; T20: 2022

BEST BATTING: 147 Gloucestershire vs Yorkshire, Bristol, 2024
BEST BOWLING: 3-40 Gloucestershire vs Leicestershire, Bristol, 2023

WHICH TEAMMATE HAS HAD THE BIGGEST IMPACT ON YOUR GAME? My brother Tom, having played and trained so much together. Also Graeme van Buuren – great guy to have in your dressing room
WHAT PART OF THE SEASON DO YOU MOST ENJOY? The Chetenham festival
WHO IS THE MOST TALENTED U19 TEENAGER IN THE COUNTY GAME? Max Dunne (Glo)
IF YOU COULD PINCH A PLAYER FROM ANOTHER COUNTY, WHO WOULD IT BE?
Dan Worrall
HOW IS BAZBALL AFFECTING CHAMPIONSHIP CRICKET? More sixes, less draws
WHO IS THE TOUGHEST BOWLER TO FACE? Zaman Akhter in the nets – horrible!
WHAT KEEPS YOU AWAKE AT NIGHT? The nip-backer
CHOOSE A FANTASY SLIP CORDON TO SPEND A DAY IN THE FIELD WITH: Jack Russell (wk), Jürgen Klopp, Ricky Ponting, Zafar Gohar
SURPRISING FACT ABOUT YOU: I've coached cricket in Argentina

Batting	Mat	Inns	NO	Runs	HS	Ave	SR	100	50	Ct	St
First-class	39	69	3	2003	147	30.34	45.62	4	11	47	-
List A	27	27	5	1053	116*	47.86	85.88	2	5	21	-
T20s	25	22	5	316	46	18.58	124.40	0	0	14	-

Bowling	Mat	Balls	Mdns	Runs	Wkts	BB	Ave	4wl	5wl	SR	Econ
First-class	39	2245	38	1531	23	3-40	66.56	-	0	97.60	4.09
List A	27	408	0	395	10	2-12	39.50	0	0	40.80	5.80
T20s	25	245	0	378	20	3-21	18.90	0	0	12.25	9.25

FULL NAME: Thomas James Price
BORN: January 2, 2000, Oxford
SQUAD NO: 53
EDUCATION: Magdalen College School, Oxford
TEAMS: Gloucestershire
ROLE: Bowler
DEBUT: First-class: 2020; List A: 2019; T20: 2022

BEST BATTING: 109 Gloucestershire vs Worcestershire, Worcester, 2023
BEST BOWLING: 8-27 Gloucestershire vs Warwickshire, Bristol, 2022

NOTES: A seam-bowling allrounder, Price was handed his first professional contract by Gloucestershire in January 2020 and repaid the club with some outstanding bowling performances in 2022, including a stunning return of 8-27 against Warwickshire at Bristol. In all he claimed 32 Championship wickets at an average of 20.09 that season. Price was less effective with the ball in red-ball cricket the following summer but registered his maiden first-class hundred in the four-day match against Worcestershire at New Road. The 21-year-old also shone in the One-Day Cup, taking 13 wickets at 22.07 to help Gloucestershire reach the semi-finals. A back injury kept him on the sidelines for most of the 2024 season, but he returned to action in September to play all three T20 knockout matches, including the final which Gloucestershire won to seal their first-ever Blast title. His brother is Ollie Price, who is also on the books at Bristol, one of three sibling pairs currently at the club

Batting	Mat	Inns	NO	Runs	HS	Ave	SR	100	50	Ct	St
First-class	29	46	10	949	109	26.36	53.19	1	3	10	-
List A	16	13	2	229	45	20.81	99.13	0	0	5	-
T20s	9	5	0	63	25	12.60	128.57	0	0	6	-

Bowling	Mat	Balls	Mdns	Runs	Wkts	BB	Ave	4wI	5wI	SR	Econ
First-class	29	3878	132	2265	75	8-27	30.20	-	4	51.70	3.50
List A	16	745	8	691	19	4-26	36.36	2	0	39.21	5.56
T20s	9	114	0	178	2	1-22	89.00	0	0	57.00	9.36

LUKE PROCTER

LHB / RM / R0 / W0

NORTHAMPTONSHIRE

FULL NAME: Luke Anthony Procter
BORN: June 24, 1988, Oldham, Lancashire
SQUAD NO: 2
HEIGHT: 5ft 11in
NICKNAME: Dickson
EDUCATION: Counthill School, Oldham
TEAMS: Northamptonshire, Lancashire
ROLE: Allrounder
DEBUT: First-class: 2010; List A: 2009; T20: 2011

BEST BATTING: 144* Northamptonshire vs Warwickshire, Northampton, 2022
BEST BOWLING: 7-71 Lancashire vs Surrey, Liverpool, 2012
COUNTY CAP: 2020 (Northamptonshire)

FIRST CRICKET CLUB? Oldham CC, Lancashire
WHICH TEAMMATE HAS HAD THE BIGGEST IMPACT ON YOUR GAME? Simon Kerrigan – he always notices anything out of the ordinary
WHAT PART OF THE SEASON DO YOU MOST ENJOY? April to June – that's when you feel you get into the rhythm of playing with back-to-back Championship matches
WHICH AWAY GROUND DO YOU MOST ENJOY VISITING? Old Trafford – it was home for 12 years
IF YOU COULD PINCH A PLAYER FROM ANOTHER COUNTY, WHO WOULD IT BE?
Josh Bohannon
HOW IS BAZBALL AFFECTING CHAMPIONSHIP CRICKET? Positively – every team is looking to make a game no matter the situation
WHO IS THE TOUGHEST BOWLER TO FACE? Sam Cook – his consistency makes you play at good balls
SURPRISING FACT ABOUT YOU: I'm a qualified electrician

Batting	Mat	Inns	NO	Runs	HS	Ave	SR	100	50	Ct	St
First-class	149	240	30	7269	144*	34.61	43.48	8	42	42	-
List A	56	44	14	904	97	30.13	82.78	0	5	10	-
T20s	37	24	7	240	25*	14.11	102.12	0	0	10	-

Bowling	Mat	Balls	Mdns	Runs	Wkts	BB	Ave	4wI	5wI	SR	Econ
First-class	149	10647	344	6014	167	7-71	36.01	-	4	63.75	3.38
List A	56	1514	6	1422	36	4-34	39.50	1	0	42.05	5.63
T20s	37	296	0	438	14	3-22	31.28	0	0	21.14	8.87

MATT QUINN

RHB / RMF / RO / WO

FULL NAME: Matthew Richard Quinn
BORN: February 28, 1993, Auckland, New Zealand
SQUAD NO: 64
HEIGHT: 6ft 4in
NICKNAME: Quinny
EDUCATION: Sacred Heart College, Auckland; Auckland University of Technology
TEAMS: Kent, Auckland, Essex, New Zealand U19
ROLE: Bowler
DEBUT: First-class: 2013; List A: 2013; T20: 2012

BEST BATTING: 50 Auckland vs Canterbury, Auckland, 2013
BEST BOWLING: 7-76 Essex vs Gloucestershire, Cheltenham, 2016

FIRST CRICKET CLUB? Cornwall CC, Auckland – the largest cricket club in New Zealand
BEST DELIVERY YOU HAVE EVER BOWLED? Getting Joe Root caught down the leg side
BEST PERFORMANCE AS A PRO? Hitting Marnus Labuschagne first ball for six over wide long-on
GREATEST PERFORMANCE YOU HAVE WITNESSED? Ben Compton getting a 60 on a snake pit at Hampshire in 2022
FAVOURITE FORMAT? The County Championship because it's proper cricket
DESCRIBE YOURSELF IN THREE WORDS: County cricket battler
HOBBIES? Motorbikes (when not in the UK)
FAVOURITE TOY AS A KID? Nintendo Game Boy Advanced
WHICH PERSON INSPIRES YOU MOST? Luke Skywalker
SURPRISING FACT ABOUT YOU: I can't bat

Batting	Mat	Inns	NO	Runs	HS	Ave	SR	100	50	Ct	St
First-class	61	81	25	606	50	10.82	50.62	0	1	13	-
List A	47	28	14	166	36	11.85	75.79	0	0	9	-
T20s	74	13	11	29	8*	14.50	100.00	0	0	14	-

Bowling	Mat	Balls	Mdns	Runs	Wkts	BB	Ave	4wI	5wI	SR	Econ
First-class	61	10868	389	5709	192	7-76	29.73	-	2	56.60	3.15
List A	47	2222	19	2318	59	4-71	39.28	1	0	37.66	6.25
T20s	74	1458	2	2150	75	4-20	28.66	2	0	19.44	8.84

BEN RAINE

LHB / RMF / R0 / W4 / MVP39

FULL NAME: Benjamin Alexander Raine
BORN: September 14, 1991, Sunderland
SQUAD NO: 44
HEIGHT: 6ft
NICKNAME: Ranger
EDUCATION: St Aidan's Catholic Academy, Sunderland
TEAMS: Durham, Leicestershire, Manchester Originals, Northern Superchargers, Otago
ROLE: Bowler
DEBUT: First-class: 2011; List A: 2011; T20: 2014

BEST BATTING: 103* Durham vs Worcestershire, Chester-le-Street, 2022
BEST BOWLING: 6-27 Durham vs Sussex, Hove, 2019
COUNTY CAP: 2018 (Leicestershire)

FIRST CRICKET CLUB? Murton CC, County Durham
BIGGEST INFLUENCE ON YOUR DEVELOPMENT AS A CRICKETER (EXCLUDING PARENTS)? Lloyd Tennant at Leicestershire – he encouraged me to take bowling seriously, which shaped my career
MOST EXCITING DAY AS A CRICKETER? Winning in three days at Lord's in 2019
BIGGEST CRICKETING REGRET? Taking far too long to realise that it doesn't really matter if I have a bad game
WHAT WOULD YOU DO IF YOU WERE IN CHARGE OF COUNTY CRICKET? Go back to a 40-over competition and play it in March and April
HOBBIES? Call of Duty (video game)

Batting	Mat	Inns	NO	Runs	HS	Ave	SR	100	50	Ct	St
First-class	135	197	28	3920	103*	23.19	51.36	1	19	30	-
List A	31	22	2	409	83	20.45	102.76	0	1	9	-
T20s	137	95	20	1391	113	18.54	131.10	1	4	25	-

Bowling	Mat	Balls	Mdns	Runs	Wkts	BB	Ave	4wl	5wl	SR	Econ
First-class	135	24695	976	11949	461	6-27	25.91	-	14	53.56	2.90
List A	31	1400	11	1309	34	4-30	38.50	1	0	41.17	5.61
T20s	137	2278	3	3183	132	5-21	24.11	1	1	17.25	8.38

ADIL RASHID

RHB / LB / R0 / W2

FULL NAME: Adil Usman Rashid
BORN: February 17, 1988, Bradford
SQUAD NO: 3
HEIGHT: 5ft 8in
EDUCATION: Heaton School, Bradford;
Bellevue Sixth Form College, Bradford
TEAMS: England, Yorkshire, Northern
Superchargers, Adelaide Strikers, Pretoria
Capitals, Punjab Kings, South Australia,
Sunrisers Hyderabad
ROLE: Allrounder
DEBUT: Test: 2015; ODI: 2009; T20I: 2009;
First-class: 2006; List A: 2006; T20: 2008

BEST BATTING: 36* Yorkshire vs Uva Next, Johannesburg, 2012 (T20)
BEST BOWLING: 4-2 England vs West Indies, Dubai, 2021 (T20)
COUNTY CAP: 2008; BENEFIT: 2018

CHILDHOOD SPORTING HERO? Shane Warne
SURPRISING FACT ABOUT YOU: I have a big FIFA (video game) rivalry with Moeen Ali
NOTES: Rashid is on a white-ball contract with Yorkshire

Batting	Mat	Inns	NO	Runs	HS	Ave	SR	100	50	Ct	St
Tests	19	33	5	540	61	19.28	42.51	0	2	4	-
ODIs	149	79	25	934	69	17.29	96.18	0	1	48	-
T20Is	124	41	20	155	22	7.38	88.57	0	0	36	-
First-class	175	251	41	6822	180	32.48	-	10	37	79	-
List A	266	161	49	2051	71	18.31	90.67	0	2	86	-
T20s	324	138	53	970	36*	11.41	106.35	0	0	84	-

Bowling	Mat	Balls	Mdns	Runs	Wkts	BB	Ave	4wl	5wl	SR	Econ
Tests	19	3816	50	2390	60	5-49	39.83	-	2	63.60	3.75
ODIs	149	7517	14	7058	215	5-27	32.82	9	2	34.96	5.63
T20Is	124	2600	5	3190	131	4-2	24.35	3	0	19.84	7.36
First-class	175	29901	610	17949	512	7-107	35.05	-	20	58.40	3.60
List A	266	12574	29	11496	360	5-27	31.93	12	3	34.92	5.48
T20s	324	6646	12	8242	362	4-2	22.76	10	0	18.35	7.44

LUIS REECE

LHB / LMF / R1 / W1

FULL NAME: Luis Michael Reece
BORN: August 4, 1990, Taunton
SQUAD NO: 10
HEIGHT: 6ft 2in
NICKNAME: Lu da wrench
EDUCATION: St Michael's School; Myerscough College; Leeds Metropolitan University
TEAMS: Derbyshire, Chittagong Vikings, Dhaka Platoon, Lancashire, London Spirit
ROLE: Allrounder
DEBUT: First-class: 2012; List A: 2011; T20: 2016

BEST BATTING: 201* Derbyshire vs Nottinghamshire, Trent Bridge, 2023
BEST BOWLING: 7-20 Derbyshire vs Gloucestershire, Derby, 2018
COUNTY CAP: 2019 (Derbyshire)

FIRST CRICKET CLUB? Vernon Carus CC, Lancashire
EARLIEST CRICKETING MEMORY? Watching my dad on a Saturday
WHAT'S THE BIGGEST PRIZE IN DOMESTIC CRICKET? The County Championship
THE KOOKABURRA BALL: YES OR NO? No – it produces rubbish cricket
OPPONENT YOU MOST LOOK FORWARD TO PLAYING AGAINST? My old teammate Sam Conners
FAVOURITE WARM-UP SONG? Greenlight by Pitbull
HOW MANY HOURS DO YOU SPEND ON YOUR PHONE A DAY? Two
SPECIALITY SUBJECT IN A PUB QUIZ (EXCLUDING SPORT)? Films
ONE THING YOU WANT TO DO BEFORE YOU DIE: Run the London marathon
HOBBY YOU WOULD LIKE TO LEARN: Fly a plane
WHICH PUBLIC FIGURE INSPIRES YOU (EXCLUDING SPORTSPEOPLE)? Ryan Reynolds
SURPRISING FACT ABOUT YOU: I played chess at national level
FILM YOU CAN WATCH OVER AND OVER: The last Harry Potter film

Batting	Mat	Inns	NO	Runs	HS	Ave	SR	100	50	Ct	St
First-class	112	199	19	6292	201*	34.95	49.62	13	34	49	-
List A	63	59	6	1904	136	35.92	84.09	3	12	19	-
T20s	101	98	5	2040	97*	21.93	130.18	0	16	43	-

Bowling	Mat	Balls	Mdns	Runs	Wkts	BB	Ave	4wl	5wl	SR	Econ
First-class	112	9166	339	4942	161	7-20	30.69	-	4	56.93	3.23
List A	63	1547	3	1549	37	4-35	41.86	2	0	41.81	6.00
T20s	101	733	0	1067	33	3-33	32.33	0	0	22.21	8.73

MATTHEW REVIS
RHB / RM / RO / WO

FULL NAME: Matthew Liam Revis
BORN: November 15, 2001, Steeton, Yorkshire
SQUAD NO: 77
EDUCATION: Ilkley Grammar School; Sedbergh School
TEAMS: Yorkshire
ROLE: Allrounder
DEBUT: First-class: 2019; List A: 2021; T20: 2020

BEST BATTING: 106 Yorkshire vs Derbyshire, Scarborough, 2023
BEST BOWLING: 5-50 Yorkshire vs Glamorgan, Cardiff, 2023

NOTES: A talented allrounder who progressed through Yorkshire's youth pathways and Academy, Revis made his Championship debut for the White Rose as an opening batter back in 2019 aged just 17, since when he has developed into an effective middle-order stroke-maker and medium-fast bowler. A product of Sedbergh School, which also produced teammates Harry Brook and George Hill, Revis established himself in Yorkshire's Championship side as a genuine allrounder in 2023, registering his maiden first-class century and five-wicket haul. In so doing, he became just the fourth uncapped Yorkshire player to score a hundred and take a five-fer in the same Championship season since the turn of the millennium. Revis is also a talented white-ball performer and was a regular presence in Yorkshire's side across all formats last year. Along with Hill and Jordan Thompson, he is part of a battery of seam-bowling allrounders that give the county strength in depth, something that should benefit them as they return to Division One after an absence of two years

Batting	Mat	Inns	NO	Runs	HS	Ave	SR	100	50	Ct	St
First-class	27	38	10	893	106	31.89	46.97	2	3	16	-
List A	31	28	6	625	58*	28.40	89.28	0	4	14	-
T20s	40	22	5	255	42	15.00	114.34	0	0	13	-

Bowling	Mat	Balls	Mdns	Runs	Wkts	BB	Ave	4wI	5wI	SR	Econ
First-class	27	2548	72	1652	41	5-50	40.29	-	1	62.14	3.89
List A	31	1158	7	1148	33	4-54	34.78	2	0	35.09	5.94
T20s	40	564	0	923	29	2-10	31.82	0	0	19.44	9.81

JAMES REW

LHB / WK / R1 / W0 / MVP36

SOMERSET

FULL NAME: James Edward Kenneth Rew
BORN: January 11, 2004, Lambeth, Surrey
SQUAD NO: 55
EDUCATION: King's College, Taunton
TEAMS: Somerset, England Lions
ROLE: Batter/wicketkeeper
DEBUT: First-class: 2021; List A: 2021; T20: 2022

BEST BATTING: 221 Somerset vs Hampshire, Taunton, 2023

NOTES: The 21-year-old keeper/batter has made an extraordinary start to his Somerset career since he first took the gloves from the now retired Steven Davies midway through the 2022 season, passing 1,000 runs in his first full Championship campaign in 2023 and being named the PCA Young Player of the Year. Rew made his England Lions debut in 2023 and was part of the Lions squad that shadowed the Test team in India early in 2024. He signed a contract extension in October 2023 that keeps him at Taunton until the end of the 2026 season. After a difficult start to the 2024 season, Rew was back to his best later in the summer, scoring two red-ball hundreds and going well in the One-Day Cup

Batting	Mat	Inns	NO	Runs	HS	Ave	SR	100	50	Ct	St
First-class	40	66	11	2305	221	41.90	52.64	8	7	106	5
List A	31	31	3	1106	114	39.50	89.19	2	7	32	-
T20s	3	3	1	115	62*	57.50	132.18	0	1	0	-
Bowling	Mat	Balls	Mdns	Runs	Wkts	BB	Ave	4wI	5wI	SR	Econ
First-class	40	6	0	1	0	0-1	-	-	-	-	1.00
List A	31	-	-	-	-	-	-	-	-	-	-
T20s	3	-	-	-	-	-	-	-	-	-	-

WILL RHODES
LHB / RM / R0 / W0 / MVP29

DURHAM

FULL NAME: William Michael Harry Rhodes
BORN: March 2, 1995, Nottingham
SQUAD NO: 15
HEIGHT: 6ft 1in
NICKNAME: Codhead
EDUCATION: Cottingham High School, Hull
TEAMS: Durham, England U19, Essex, Warwickshire, Yorkshire
ROLE: Allrounder
DEBUT: First-class: 2015; List A: 2013; T20: 2013

BEST BATTING: 207 Warwickshire vs Worcestershire, Worcester, 2020
BEST BOWLING: 5-17 Warwickshire vs Essex, Chelmsford, 2019
COUNTY CAP: 2020 (Warwickshire)

FIRST CRICKET CLUB? Cottingham CC, East Riding of Yorkshire
WHICH COUNTY PLAYER WOULD YOU MOST LIKE TO GO FOR A DRINK WITH? Jack Leaning
GREATEST PERFORMANCE YOU HAVE WITNESSED? Liam Norwell's nine-fer against
Hampshire at the end of the 2022 season
FAVOURITE FORMAT? The County Championship
HOBBIES? Long dog walks followed by a roast and pint in a country pub
WHAT WOULD BE YOUR PERFECT BREAKFAST? A Full English minus the mushrooms
and tomatoes

Batting	Mat	Inns	NO	Runs	HS	Ave	SR	100	50	Ct	St
First-class	113	183	10	6224	207	35.97	50.12	12	26	79	-
List A	66	60	5	1779	113	32.34	80.38	1	9	29	-
T20s	56	51	6	659	79	14.64	122.03	0	1	15	-

Bowling	Mat	Balls	Mdns	Runs	Wkts	BB	Ave	4wI	5wI	SR	Econ
First-class	113	6814	259	3509	99	5-17	35.44	-	2	68.82	3.08
List A	66	1453	2	1441	35	3-22	41.17	0	0	41.51	5.95
T20s	56	493	0	741	36	4-34	20.58	1	0	13.69	9.01

JAMAL RICHARDS

RHB / RFM / R0 / W0

ESSEX

FULL NAME: Jamal Adrian Richards
BORN: March 3, 2004, Edmonton, London
SQUAD NO: 87
HEIGHT: 5ft 11in
NICKNAME: Jamaa
EDUCATION: Norlington School, London;
Waltham Forest College, London
TEAMS: Essex, England U19
ROLE: Bowler
DEBUT: First-class: 2023; List A: 2022

BEST BATTING: 17* Essex vs Ireland, Chelmsford, 2023
BEST BOWLING: 5-96 Essex vs Ireland, Chelmsford, 2023

NOTES: The England U19 international signed his first senior professional contract ahead of the 2023 season and is the latest in a line of quick bowlers to have graduated from the Essex Academy. His maiden first-team appeareance came in 2022 during the One-Day Cup competition in which he played all seven group games. At the end of that summer he was callled up by England U19 for the three-match ODI series against Sri Lanka, going on to play four times against during the subsequent 2022/23 tour of Australia. The following summer he impressed with a maiden five-wicket haul on his first-class debut against Ireland at Chelmsford and last year he was the Eagles' leading wicket-taker in the One-Day, with 15 scalps at an average of 24.86. Richards signed a one-year extension to his deal last November. "I'm really happy to stay at Essex for another year, the club where I've grown up and developed as a cricketer from childhood," he said. "Last season was really successful with the ball, and I'm keen to kick on and continue that progress during another season with the Eagles"

Batting	Mat	Inns	NO	Runs	HS	Ave	SR	100	50	Ct	St
First-class	1	2	2	19	17*	-	95.00	0	0	0	-
List A	19	17	6	255	46	23.18	90.10	0	0	2	-

Bowling	Mat	Balls	Mdns	Runs	Wkts	BB	Ave	4wl	5wl	SR	Econ
First-class	1	156	6	130	5	5-96	26.00	-	1	31.20	5.00
List A	19	747	8	696	23	5-31	30.26	0	1	32.47	5.59

OLLIE ROBINSON — RHB / WK / R1 / W0

FULL NAME: Oliver George Robinson
BORN: December 1, 1998, Sidcup, Kent
SQUAD NO: 21
HEIGHT: 5ft 8in
NICKNAME: Bob
EDUCATION: Hurstmere School, London;
Chislehurst & Sidcup Grammar, London
TEAMS: Durham, Northern Superchargers,
England Lions, Kent
ROLE: Batter/wicketkeeper
DEBUT: First-class: 2018; List A: 2017; T20: 2019

BEST BATTING: 198 Durham vs Essex, Chelmsford, 2024

COUNTY CAP: 2022 (Kent)

FIRST CRICKET CLUB? Sidcup CC, London
EARLIEST CRICKETING MEMORY? Watching Dad
WHAT'S THE BIGGEST PRIZE IN DOMESTIC CRICKET? The County Championship
THE KOOKABURRA BALL: YES OR NO? Yes – in early season
OPPONENT YOU MOST LOOK FORWARD TO PLAYING AGAINST? Matt Parkinson
FAVOURITE WARM-UP SONG? Any song by Luke Combs
SPECIALITY SUBJECT IN A PUB QUIZ (EXCLUDING SPORT)? World War 2
HOBBY YOU WOULD LIKE TO LEARN: Play the guitar
WHICH PUBLIC FIGURE INSPIRES YOU (EXCLUDING SPORTSPEOPLE)? Chris Martin (singer)
SURPRISING FACT ABOUT YOU: I love history
FILM YOU CAN WATCH OVER AND OVER: Step Brothers

Batting	Mat	Inns	NO	Runs	HS	Ave	SR	100	50	Ct	St
First-class	78	121	9	4174	198	37.26	67.99	9	23	233	12
List A	26	22	1	821	206*	39.09	100.36	1	4	14	1
T20s	77	67	12	1224	69*	22.25	126.83	0	6	31	9

Bowling	Mat	Balls	Mdns	Runs	Wkts	BB	Ave	4wI	5wI	SR	Econ
First-class	78	12	0	8	0	0-8	-	-	-	-	4.00
List A	26	-	-	-	-	-	-	-	-	-	-
T20s	77	-	-	-	-	-	-	-	-	-	-

OLLIE ROBINSON

RHB / RMF / R0 / W3

SUSSEX

FULL NAME: Oliver Edward Robinson
BORN: December 1, 1993, Margate, Kent
SQUAD NO: 25
HEIGHT: 6ft 5in
NICKNAME: The Rig
EDUCATION: King's School, Canterbury
TEAMS: England, Sussex, Hampshire, Trent Rockets, Yorkshire
ROLE: Bowler
DEBUT: Test: 2021;
First-class: 2015; List A: 2013; T20: 2014

BEST BATTING: 110 Sussex vs Durham, Chester-le-Street, 2015
BEST BOWLING: 9-78 Sussex vs Glamorgan, Cardiff, 2021
COUNTY CAP: 2019 (Sussex)

FIRST CRICKET CLUB? Margate CC, Kent
EARLIEST CRICKETING MEMORY? Blue stumps, blue bat, and an orange wind ball in the back garden with my dad and grandad when I was about three years old
WHAT'S THE BIGGEST PRIZE IN DOMESTIC CRICKET? The County Championship
THE KOOKABURRA BALL: YES OR NO? Yes, I think it develops different skills for both batting and bowling. But the time of year is key – the wickets should be harder
FAVOURITE WARM-UP SONG? Lose Yourself by Eminem
HOW MANY HOURS DO YOU SPEND ON YOUR PHONE A DAY? Two to three
HOBBY YOU WOULD LIKE TO LEARN: Being a coffee barista – my partner bought me lessons for my birthday
SURPRISING FACT ABOUT YOU: I have a stamp collection

Batting	Mat	Inns	NO	Runs	HS	Ave	SR	100	50	Ct	St
Tests	20	33	5	410	58	14.64	55.78	0	1	8	-
First-class	102	148	28	2353	110	19.60	61.38	1	8	31	-
List A	16	11	3	122	30	15.25	88.40	0	0	7	-
T20s	65	29	12	163	31	9.58	109.39	0	0	24	-

Bowling	Mat	Balls	Mdns	Runs	Wkts	BB	Ave	4wI	5wI	SR	Econ
Tests	20	3796	159	1742	76	5-49	22.92	-	3	49.94	2.75
First-class	102	19038	721	9269	435	9-78	21.30	-	23	43.76	2.92
List A	16	672	6	663	19	3-31	34.89	0	0	35.36	5.91
T20s	65	1230	2	1724	63	4-15	27.36	1	0	19.52	8.40

SAM ROBSON

RHB / LB / R3 / W0

FULL NAME: Samuel David Robson
BORN: July 1, 1989, Sydney, Australia
SQUAD NO: 12
HEIGHT: 6ft
NICKNAME: Bronco
EDUCATION: Marcellin College, Sydney
TEAMS: England, Middlesex, Australia U19
ROLE: Batter
DEBUT: Test: 2014;
First-class: 2009; List A: 2008; T20: 2011

MIDDLESEX

BEST BATTING: 253 Middlesex vs Sussex, Hove, 2021
BEST BOWLING: 4-46 Middlesex vs Nottinghamshire, Trent Bridge, 2023
COUNTY CAP: 2013

FIRST CRICKET CLUB? Randwick Junior CC, New South Wales, Australia
EARLIEST CRICKETING MEMORY? Watching my father Jim
WHAT'S THE BIGGEST PRIZE IN DOMESTIC CRICKET? The County Championship
THE KOOKABURRA BALL: YES OR NO? Yes! For a few games at least
FAVOURITE WARM-UP SONG? Fever to the Form by Nick Mulvey
HOW MANY HOURS DO YOU SPEND ON YOUR PHONE A DAY? Two
SPECIALITY SUBJECT IN A PUB QUIZ (EXCLUDING SPORT)? Geography
ONE THING YOU WANT TO DO BEFORE YOU DIE: Travel more
HOBBY YOU WOULD LIKE TO LEARN: A new language
FILM YOU CAN WATCH OVER AND OVER: Happy Gilmore

Batting	Mat	Inns	NO	Runs	HS	Ave	SR	100	50	Ct	St
Tests	7	11	0	336	127	30.54	44.50	1	1	5	-
First-class	214	379	29	13448	253	38.42	51.75	36	50	211	-
List A	46	44	2	1603	111	38.16	82.54	3	11	22	-
T20s	7	7	2	128	60	25.60	113.27	0	1	3	-

Bowling	Mat	Balls	Mdns	Runs	Wkts	BB	Ave	4wI	5wI	SR	Econ
Tests	7	-	-	-	-	-	-	-	-	-	-
First-class	214	819	9	621	17	4-46	36.52	-	0	48.17	4.54
List A	46	320	0	357	10	2-12	35.70	0	0	32.00	6.69
T20s	7	-	-	-	-	-	-	-	-	-	-

GARETH RODERICK RHB / WK / R0 / W0 / MVP33

WORCESTERSHIRE

FULL NAME: Gareth Hugh Roderick
BORN: August 29, 1991, Durban, South Africa
SQUAD NO: 9
HEIGHT: 6ft
NICKNAME: Rodders
EDUCATION: Maritzburg College, South Africa
TEAMS: Worcestershire, Gloucestershire, KwaZulu-Natal
ROLE: Batter/wicketkeeper
DEBUT: First-class: 2011; List A: 2011; T20: 2011

BEST BATTING: 172* Worcestershire vs Glamorgan, Cardiff, 2022

COUNTY CAP: 2013 (Gloucestershire)

FIRST CRICKET CLUB? Northwood Crusaders CC, Durban
BEST PLAYER IN COUNTY CRICKET (EXCLUDING TEAMMATES)? Simon Harmer
WHICH COUNTY PLAYER WOULD YOU MOST LIKE TO GO FOR A DRINK WITH? Charlie
Morris so that I can hear about his lawn treatments
BEST DELIVERY YOU HAVE EVER FACED? I can think more of a spell: Ryan Harris for Australia
A against Gloucestershire some years ago. But I survived it!
GREATEST PERFORMANCE YOU HAVE WITNESSED? Michael Klinger's hundred at
Headingley in the semi-final of the One-Day Cup in 2015
FAVOURITE FORMAT? The County Championship
DESCRIBE YOURSELF IN THREE WORDS: Relaxed, competitive, stubborn
HOBBIES? The NFL

Batting	Mat	Inns	NO	Runs	HS	Ave	SR	100	50	Ct	St
First-class	142	230	27	6907	172*	34.02	48.98	11	40	393	8
List A	79	69	7	2083	152*	33.59	83.58	5	10	78	10
T20s	62	41	11	443	39	14.76	125.49	0	0	36	2

Bowling	Mat	Balls	Mdns	Runs	Wkts	BB	Ave	4wI	5wI	SR	Econ
First-class	142	-	-	-	-	-	-	-	-	-	-
List A	79	-	-	-	-	-	-	-	-	-	-
T20s	62	-	-	-	-	-	-	-	-	-	-

TOM ROGERS   LHB / RMF

FULL NAME: Thomas Stewart Rogers
BORN: March3, 1994, Bruce, Australia
SQUAD NO: 10
TEAMS: Kent, Australia A, Hobart Hurricanes, Melbourne Renegades, Pretoria Capitals, Tasmania
ROLE: Allrounder
DEBUT: First-class: 2017; List A: 2017; T20: 2017

BEST BATTING: 49* Melbourne Renegades vs Perth Scorchers, Perth, 2025 (T20)
BEST BOWLING: 5-16 Melbourne Renegades vs Melbourne Stars, Melbourne, 2023 (T20)

NOTES: The Spitfires have re-signed Rogers for the Blast group stage after the Australian allrounder made six appearances in last season's competition. "During his short spell with us last year, Tom showed that he is a great contributor with not only the ball but with some quick runs in our lower order and some outstanding contributions in the field, too," said Simon Cook, Kent's director of cricket. "We're excited to see him work in tandem with Wes Agar as our overseas line-up in T20 cricket this coming summer." Rogers is a veteran of the Big Bash, having represented Hobart Hurricanes and Melbourne Renegades. He was the second-highest wicket-taker in the 2024/25 Big Bash, taking 16 wickets for the Renegades at an average of 19.12. He was also a valuable contributor with the bat, averaging 49.50 and hitting a career-best 49 not out against Perth Scorchers. On returning to Kent, Rogers said: "My time at Canterbury was short but sweet last summer so I'm raring to go. I'm excited to work with Adam Hollioake and put on that Spitfires shirt again in front of packed-out crowds"

Batting	Mat	Inns	NO	Runs	HS	Ave	SR	100	50	Ct	St
First-class	15	21	0	365	80	17.38	52.82	0	1	3	-
List A	33	21	5	261	38	16.31	71.90	0	0	16	-
T20s	67	38	22	314	49*	19.62	124.11	0	0	23	-

Bowling	Mat	Balls	Mdns	Runs	Wkts	BB	Ave	4wI	5wI	SR	Econ
First-class	15	1948	65	1048	47	4-9	22.29	-	0	41.44	3.22
List A	33	1567	8	1395	48	5-32	29.06	2	1	32.64	5.34
T20s	67	1432	1	2010	79	5-16	25.44	1	1	18.12	8.42

TOBY ROLAND-JONES RHB / RFM / RO / W4

FULL NAME: Tobias Skelton Roland-Jones
BORN: January 29, 1988, Ashford, Middlesex
SQUAD NO: 21
HEIGHT: 6ft 3in
NICKNAME: Rojo
EDUCATION: Hampton School, Greater London; University of Leeds
TEAMS: England, Middlesex
ROLE: Bowler
DEBUT: Test: 2017; ODI: 2017; First-class: 2010; List A: 2010; T20: 2011

BEST BATTING: 103* Middlesex vs Yorkshire, Lord's, 2015
BEST BOWLING: 7-52 Middlesex vs Gloucestershire, Northwood, 2019
COUNTY CAP: 2012; BENEFIT: 2024

FIRST CRICKET CLUB? Sunbury CC, Surrey
EARLIEST CRICKETING MEMORY? My first match for Sunbury aged seven
THE KOOKABURRA BALL: YES OR NO? No – improving pitches is the answer
OPPONENT YOU MOST LOOK FORWARD TO PLAYING AGAINST? Martin Andersson – a great and curious fella who I'm excited to see do well at Derbyshire (just not against us)
FAVOURITE WARM-UP SONG? Mountain At My Gates by Foals
HOW MANY HOURS DO YOU SPEND ON YOUR PHONE A DAY? Too long (still rubbish at replying to messages though)
WHICH PUBLIC FIGURE INSPIRES YOU (EXCLUDING SPORTSPEOPLE)? James Acaster
SURPRISING FACT ABOUT YOU: I had laser eye surgery in 2017 and it turned me colour blind
FILM YOU CAN WATCH OVER AND OVER: Silver Linings Playbook

Batting	Mat	Inns	NO	Runs	HS	Ave	SR	100	50	Ct	St
Tests	4	6	2	82	25	20.50	69.49	0	0	0	-
ODIs	1	1	1	37	37*	-	100.00	0	0	0	-
First-class	156	220	38	3890	103*	21.37	59.97	1	16	45	-
List A	81	49	15	690	65	20.29	94.39	0	1	13	-
T20s	61	36	13	326	40	14.17	124.42	0	0	18	-
Bowling	Mat	Balls	Mdns	Runs	Wkts	BB	Ave	4wI	5wI	SR	Econ
Tests	4	536	23	334	17	5-57	19.64	-	1	31.52	3.73
ODIs	1	42	2	34	1	1-34	34.00	0	0	42.00	4.85
First-class	156	27401	939	14233	574	7-52	24.79	-	32	47.73	3.11
List A	81	3761	34	3255	126	4-10	25.83	4	0	29.84	5.19
T20s	61	1212	0	1779	74	5-21	24.04	4	1	16.37	8.80

BILLY ROOT

LHB / OB / R0 / W0

FULL NAME: William Thomas Root
BORN: August 5, 1992, Sheffield
SQUAD NO: 7
HEIGHT: 5ft 11in
NICKNAME: Ferret
EDUCATION: Worksop College, Nottinghamshire; Leeds Metropolitan University
TEAMS: Glamorgan, Nottinghamshire
ROLE: Batter
DEBUT: First-class: 2015; List A: 2017; T20: 2017

BEST BATTING: 229 Glamorgan vs Northamptonshire, Northampton, 2019
BEST BOWLING: 3-29 Nottinghamshire vs Sussex, Hove, 2017
COUNTY CAP: 2021 (Glamorgan)

FIRST CRICKET CLUB? Sheffield Collegiate CC
EARLIEST CRICKETING MEMORY? On the outfield while my dad was playing
WHAT'S THE BIGGEST PRIZE IN DOMESTIC CRICKET? The County Championship
THE KOOKABURRA BALL: YES OR NO? No – let it swing so that there's less fielding to do
FAVOURITE WARM-UP SONG? Whatever Dan Douthwaite puts on
SPECIALITY SUBJECT IN A PUB QUIZ (EXCLUDING SPORT)? Lord of the Rings
ONE THING YOU WANT TO DO BEFORE YOU DIE: Go to Japan
HOBBY YOU WOULD LIKE TO LEARN: Play the piano
SURPRISING FACT ABOUT YOU: My right foot is bigger than my left
FILM YOU CAN WATCH OVER AND OVER: Happy Gilmore

Batting	Mat	Inns	NO	Runs	HS	Ave	SR	100	50	Ct	St
First-class	78	132	13	4023	229	33.80	54.29	7	17	23	-
List A	55	47	10	1604	113*	43.35	90.62	3	8	13	-
T20s	50	39	9	634	41*	21.13	111.81	0	0	18	-

Bowling	Mat	Balls	Mdns	Runs	Wkts	BB	Ave	4wI	5wI	SR	Econ
First-class	78	389	8	275	8	3-29	34.37	-	0	48.62	4.24
List A	55	292	0	310	6	2-36	51.66	0	0	48.66	6.36
T20s	50	18	0	37	0	0-6	-	-	-	-	12.33

JOE ROOT

RHB / OB / R3 / W0

YORKSHIRE

FULL NAME: Joseph Edward Root
BORN: December 30, 1990, Sheffield
SQUAD NO: 66
HEIGHT: 6ft
NICKNAME: Rootie
EDUCATION: King Ecgbert School, Sheffield;
Worksop College, Nottinghamshire
TEAMS: England, Yorkshire, Trent Rockets,
Paarl Royals, Rajasthan Royals, Sydney
Thunder
ROLE: Batter
DEBUT: Test: 2012; ODI: 2013; T20I: 2012;
First-class: 2010; List A: 2009; T20: 2011

BEST BATTING: 262 England vs Pakistan, Multan, 2024
BEST BOWLING: 5-8 England vs India, Ahmedabad, 2021
COUNTY CAP: 2012

FIRST CRICKET CLUB? Sheffield Collegiate CC
FAMILY TIES? My dad played club cricket and represented Nottinghamshire Second XI and
Colts. My brother Billy has played for Notts and is currently at Glamorgan
CHILDHOOD SPORTING HERO? Michael Vaughan

Batting	Mat	Inns	NO	Runs	HS	Ave	SR	100	50	Ct	St
Tests	152	278	23	12972	262	50.87	57.47	36	65	207	-
ODIs	177	166	23	6859	133*	47.96	87.03	17	41	86	-
T20Is	32	30	5	893	90*	35.72	126.30	0	5	18	-
First-class	225	394	34	18027	262	50.07	57.85	50	86	256	-
List A	215	203	29	8072	133*	46.39	85.81	18	49	98	-
T20s	119	109	22	2823	92*	32.44	128.96	0	17	54	-

Bowling	Mat	Balls	Mdns	Runs	Wkts	BB	Ave	4wl	5wl	SR	Econ
Tests	152	5851	159	3221	71	5-8	45.36	-	1	82.40	3.30
ODIs	177	1755	2	1732	28	3-52	61.85	0	0	62.67	5.92
T20Is	32	84	0	139	6	2-9	23.16	0	0	14.00	9.92
First-class	225	8568	245	4612	97	5-8	47.54	-	1	88.32	3.22
List A	215	2318	4	2209	41	3-52	53.87	0	0	56.53	5.71
T20s	119	717	0	974	34	2-7	28.64	0	0	21.08	8.15

ADAM ROSSINGTON

RHB / WK / R0 / W0

FULL NAME: Adam Matthew Rossington
BORN: May 5, 1993, Edgware, Middlesex
SQUAD NO: 17
HEIGHT: 6ft
NICKNAME: Rosso
EDUCATION: Belmont Preparatory School, Surrey; Mill Hill School, London
TEAMS: Essex, London Spirit, Durdanto Dhaka, England U19, Karachi Kings, Lahore Qalandars, Middlesex, Northamptonshire, Sunrisers Eastern Cape
ROLE: Batter/wicketkeeper
DEBUT: First-class: 2010; List A: 2012; T20: 2011

BEST BATTING: 138* Northamptonshire vs Sussex, Arundel, 2016

COUNTY CAP: 2019 (Northamptonshire); 2023 (Essex)

FIRST CRICKET CLUB? Barnet CC, London
BIGGEST CRICKETING REGRET? That I've never played in the Hong Kong Sixes
WHO WOULD YOU MOST AND LEAST LIKE TO HAVE A NET WITH? Most – Chris Gayle, to see some range hitting. Least – Mitchell Starc, because broken toes aren't fun
HOBBIES? Horse racing
MOST BEAUTIFUL THING YOU HAVE EVER SEEN? Scarborough beach
SURPRISING FACT ABOUT YOU: I can't ride a bicycle

Batting	Mat	Inns	NO	Runs	HS	Ave	SR	100	50	Ct	St
First-class	113	181	17	5446	138*	33.20	64.60	9	34	245	20
List A	49	44	7	1381	97	37.32	99.42	0	11	34	5
T20s	181	174	7	3506	95	20.99	145.23	0	18	82	33

Bowling	Mat	Balls	Mdns	Runs	Wkts	BB	Ave	4wI	5wI	SR	Econ
First-class	113	120	1	86	0	0-6	-	-	-	-	4.30
List A	49	-	-	-	-	-	-	-	-	-	-
T20s	181	-	-	-	-	-	-	-	-	-	-

JASON ROY

RHB / RM / R1 / W0

SURREY

FULL NAME: Jason Jonathan Roy
BORN: July 21, 1990, Durban, South Africa
SQUAD NO: 20
HEIGHT: 6ft
EDUCATION: Whitgift School, Croydon
TEAMS: England, Surrey, Delhi Daredevils, Dhaka Capitals, Kolkata Knight Riders, Oval Invincibles, Paarl Royals, Perth Scorchers, Quetta Gladiators, Sunrisers, Sydney Sixers, Sylhet Sixers, Trinbago Knight Riders
ROLE: Batter
DEBUT: Test: 2019; ODI: 2015; T20I: 2014; First-class: 2010; List A: 2008; T20: 2008

BEST BATTING: 143 Surrey vs Lancashire, The Oval, 2015
BEST BOWLING: 3-9 Surrey vs Gloucestershire, Bristol, 2014
COUNTY CAP: 2014

MOST EXCITING DAY AS A CRICKETER? There's been quite a few of them – winning the Championship with Surrey, making my England T20, ODI and Test debuts, scoring my first century for England in ODI cricket and winning the World Cup in 2019
CHILDHOOD SPORTING HERO? Jacques Kallis

Batting	Mat	Inns	NO	Runs	HS	Ave	SR	100	50	Ct	St
Tests	5	10	0	187	72	18.70	58.80	0	1	1	-
ODIs	116	110	3	4271	180	39.91	105.50	12	21	46	-
T20Is	64	64	1	1522	78	24.15	137.61	0	8	19	-
First-class	87	144	11	4850	143	36.46	80.75	9	23	75	-
List A	211	200	9	7252	180	37.96	105.74	19	36	84	-
T20s	389	382	16	9974	145*	27.25	140.16	6	65	183	-

Bowling	Mat	Balls	Mdns	Runs	Wkts	BB	Ave	4wl	5wl	SR	Econ
Tests	5	-	-	-	-	-	-	-	-	-	-
ODIs	116	-	-	-	-	-	-	-	-	-	-
T20Is	64	-	-	-	-	-	-	-	-	-	-
First-class	87	712	11	495	14	3-9	35.35	-	0	50.85	4.17
List A	211	6	0	12	0	0-12	-	-	-	-	12.00
T20s	389	18	0	39	1	1-23	39.00	0	0	18.00	13.00

CHRIS RUSHWORTH RHB / RFM / R0 / W7

FULL NAME: Christopher Rushworth
BORN: July 11, 1986, Sunderland
SQUAD NO: 22
HEIGHT: 6ft 2in
NICKNAME: Russian
EDUCATION: Castle View Comprehensive School, Sunderland
TEAMS: Warwickshire, Durham
ROLE: Bowler
DEBUT: First-class: 2010; List A: 2004; T20: 2011

WARWICKSHIRE

BEST BATTING: 57 Durham vs Kent, Canterbury, 2017
BEST BOWLING: 9-52 Durham vs Northamptonshire, Chester-le-Street, 2014
COUNTY CAP: 2023 (Warwickshire); **BENEFIT:** 2019 (Durham)

FIRST CRICKET CLUB? Hylton Colliery CC, Sunderland
FAMILY TIES? My brother Lee represented England U19 and my cousin Phil Mustard played for England, Durham and Gloucestershire
BIGGEST INFLUENCE ON YOUR DEVELOPMENT AS A CRICKETER (EXCLUDING PARENTS)?
Geoff Cook (former Durham coach) – he coached me when I was a young lad and then was there to hand me a second opportunity to play professional cricket
MOST EXCITING DAY AS A CRICKETER? The Lord's one-day final in 2014
BIGGEST CRICKETING REGRET? Trying to sweep Liam Dawson while my partner was on 99 at the other end. I was the last man. Oops
CHILDHOOD SPORTING HERO? Shaun Pollock

Batting	Mat	Inns	NO	Runs	HS	Ave	SR	100	50	Ct	St
First-class	174	229	78	1782	57	11.80	62.81	0	1	37	-
List A	87	38	19	215	38*	11.31	83.98	0	0	19	-
T20s	85	15	9	20	5	3.33	50.00	0	0	18	-

Bowling	Mat	Balls	Mdns	Runs	Wkts	BB	Ave	4wI	5wI	SR	Econ
First-class	174	30615	1181	15121	669	9-52	22.60	-	32	45.76	2.96
List A	87	3959	47	3416	140	5-31	24.40	3	2	28.27	5.17
T20s	85	1623	3	2121	78	3-14	27.19	0	0	20.80	7.84

JAMES SALES

RHB / RM / RO / WO

FULL NAME: James John Grimwood Sales
BORN: February 11, 2003, Northampton
SQUAD NO: 5
HEIGHT: 6ft
NICKNAME: Baby Jumby
EDUCATION: Wellingborough School, Northamptonshire
TEAMS: Northamptonshire, England U19
ROLE: Allrounder
DEBUT: First-class: 2021; List A: 2021; T20: 2022

BEST BATTING: 135 Northamptonshire vs Leicestershire, Northampton, 2024
BEST BOWLING: 4-24 Northamptonshire vs Nottinghamshire, Northampton, 2023

FIRST CRICKET CLUB? Overstone Park CC, Northampton
FAMILY TIES? My dad David also played for Northants
WHAT'S THE BIGGEST PRIZE IN DOMESTIC CRICKET? Winning the County Championship
THE KOOKABURRA BALL: YES OR NO? I'm not sure – nice to face, horrible to bowl with
OPPONENT YOU MOST LOOK FORWARD TO PLAYING AGAINST? Cameron Green
FAVOURITE WARM-UP SONG? The Days (Notion remix) by Chrystal
HOW MANY HOURS DO YOU SPEND ON YOUR PHONE A DAY? Five
SPECIALITY SUBJECT IN A PUB QUIZ (EXCLUDING SPORT)? Food types
ONE THING YOU WANT TO DO BEFORE YOU DIE: Play for England
HOBBY YOU WOULD LIKE TO LEARN: How to dance
WHICH PUBLIC FIGURE INSPIRES YOU (EXCLUDING SPORTSPEOPLE)? Fred Again
FILM YOU CAN WATCH OVER AND OVER: Marley & Me

Batting	Mat	Inns	NO	Runs	HS	Ave	SR	100	50	Ct	St
First-class	19	32	5	767	135	28.40	48.42	2	3	10	-
List A	21	17	7	258	35*	25.80	66.49	0	0	4	-
T20s	10	6	3	42	12	14.00	102.43	0	0	3	-

Bowling	Mat	Balls	Mdns	Runs	Wkts	BB	Ave	4wI	5wI	SR	Econ
First-class	19	684	14	549	11	4-24	49.90	-	0	62.18	4.81
List A	21	448	2	464	7	2-31	66.28	0	0	64.00	6.21
T20s	10	114	0	183	1	1-16	183.00	0	0	114.00	9.63

MATT SALISBURY — RHB / RMF / RO / WO

FULL NAME: Matthew Edward Thomas Salisbury
BORN: April 18, 1993, Chelmsford, Essex
SQUAD NO: 18
HEIGHT: 6ft 2in
NICKNAME: Great Wall
EDUCATION: Shenfield High School, Essex; Anglia Ruskin University, Cambridge
TEAMS: Leicestershire, Durham, Essex, Hampshire
ROLE: Bowler
DEBUT: First-class: 2012; List A: 2014; T20: 2014

BEST BATTING: 45 Durham vs Middlesex, Lord's, 2022
BEST BOWLING: 6-37 Durham vs Middlesex, Chester-le-Street, 2018

FIRST CRICKET CLUB? Shenfield CC, Essex
BEST DELIVERY YOU HAVE EVER FACED? A Mitchell Starc in-swinging yorker
BEST PERFORMANCE AS A PRO? My 25 off 147 balls for Durham against Derbyshire in 2018 to help turn the match around after we'd been bowled out for 96 in the first innings
FAVOURITE FORMAT? Four-day cricket
NOTES: The former Durham and Essex seamer signed for the Foxes on a three-year deal in October 2022 and performed creditably the following season, despite only intermittent appeareances across the formats. He took his first five-wicket haul since 2018 during the extraordinary Championship match at Hove in which Leicestershire nearly pulled off a chase of 499 – Salisbury was the not-out batter when Chris Wright was bowled with the Foxes just 16 runs short of the target. The 31-year-old played just five Championship matches last summer alongside a handful of games in the One-Day Cup

Batting	Mat	Inns	NO	Runs	HS	Ave	SR	100	50	Ct	St
First-class	54	77	16	528	45	8.65	30.91	0	0	6	-
List A	24	5	4	10	5*	10.00	34.48	0	0	4	-
T20s	12	5	4	4	1*	4.00	30.76	0	0	2	-

Bowling	Mat	Balls	Mdns	Runs	Wkts	BB	Ave	4wI	5wI	SR	Econ
First-class	54	8098	263	4816	141	6-37	34.15	-	2	57.43	3.56
List A	24	985	4	896	28	4-55	32.00	1	0	35.17	5.45
T20s	12	244	1	382	13	2-19	29.38	0	0	18.76	9.39

PHIL SALT

RHB / WK / R0 / W0

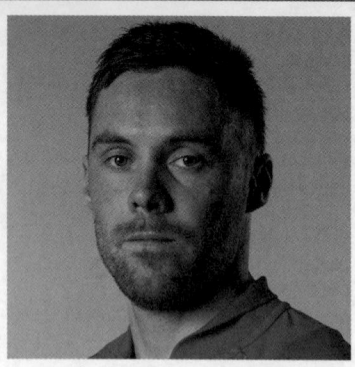

FULL NAME: Philip Dean Salt
BORN: August 28, 1996, Bodelwyddan, Denbighshire, Wales
SQUAD NO: 7
HEIGHT: 6ft
EDUCATION: Harrison College, Barbados; Reed's School, Surrey
TEAMS: England, Lancashire, Manchester Originals, Adelaide Strikers, Kolkata Knight Riders, Pretoria Capitals, Sussex
ROLE: Batter/wicketkeeper
DEBUT: ODI: 2021; T20I: 2022; First-class: 2016; List A: 2015; T20: 2016

BEST BATTING: 148 Sussex vs Derbyshire, Hove, 2018
BEST BOWLING: 1-32 Sussex vs Warwickshire, Hove, 2018

FIRST CRICKET CLUB? St Asaph CC, North Wales
EARLIEST CRICKETING MEMORY? Playing at St Asaph and Andrew Flintoff's testimonial at Old Trafford
WHAT'S THE BIGGEST PRIZE IN DOMESTIC CRICKET? Winning the Roses clash
OPPONENT YOU MOST LOOK FORWARD TO PLAYING AGAINST? Jofra Archer
FAVOURITE WARM-UP SONG? The Boys in Blue
HOBBY YOU WOULD LIKE TO LEARN: Beekeeping
SURPRISING FACT ABOUT YOU: I once fed Dan Douthwaite's homework to his German Shepard, Storm
FILM YOU CAN WATCH OVER AND OVER: Trainspotting

Batting	Mat	Inns	NO	Runs	HS	Ave	SR	100	50	Ct	St
ODIs	33	31	0	988	122	31.87	114.75	1	5	16	-
T20Is	43	40	5	1193	119	34.08	164.32	3	5	29	2
First-class	52	85	3	2749	148	33.52	71.96	6	14	75	4
List A	49	47	1	1482	137*	32.21	111.17	2	7	21	-
T20s	276	267	21	6679	119	27.15	155.18	3	43	148	14

Bowling	Mat	Balls	Mdns	Runs	Wkts	BB	Ave	4wI	5wI	SR	Econ
ODIs	33	-	-	-	-	-	-	-	-	-	-
T20Is	43	-	-	-	-	-	-	-	-	-	-
First-class	52	54	2	32	1	1-32	32.00	-	0	54.00	3.55
List A	49	-	-	-	-	-	-	-	-	-	-
T20s	276	-	-	-	-	-	-	-	-	-	-

DANIEL SAMS

RHB / LFM

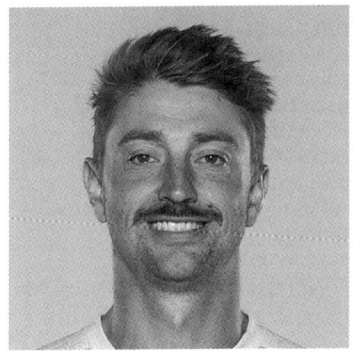

FULL NAME: Daniel Richard Sams
BORN: October 27, 1992, Milperra, New South Wales, Australia
SQUAD NO: 95
TEAMS: Australia, Nottinghamshire, Trent Rockets, Canterbury, Delhi Capitals, Essex, Karachi Kings, Mumbai Indians, New South Wales, Royal Challengers Bangalore, Sydney Sixers, Sydney Thunder
ROLE: Allrounder
DEBUT: T20I: 2020;
First-class: 2017; List A: 2018; T20: 2017

BEST BATTING: 98* Sydney Thunder vs Melbourne Renegades, Melbourne, 2022 (T20)
BEST BOWLING: 5-30 Sydney Thunder vs Brisbane Heat, Brisbane, 2023 (T20)

NOTES: After three seasons at Chelmsford, the all-action Australian allrounder has signed to play for Nottinghamshire in this summer's T20 Blast competition – a major boost for an Outlaws side that finished bottom of their group last year. Sams is already a familar face in Nottingham, having helped Trent Rockets to the Hundred title in 2022. The 32-year-old brings a wealth of T20 experience to the Outlaws squad having played in all the major franchise tournaments around the world as well as representing his country on 10 occasions. "It was a priority for us to bring in an experienced overseas player who can contribute with bat and ball," said Peter Moores, Nottinghamshire's head coach. "Dan is the perfect player in that respect – he has a unique skill set to that which we've already got in our squad, and he'll be a great support to Joe Clarke as captain. He's got the added bonus of having played T20 cricket in England and knowing what it asks of you, as well as handling the pressure of franchise cricket around the world"

Batting	Mat	Inns	NO	Runs	HS	Ave	SR	100	50	Ct	St
T20Is	10	7	3	106	41	26.50	170.96	0	0	4	-
First-class	5	10	0	255	88	25.50	91.07	0	2	2	-
List A	19	16	0	392	62	24.50	101.03	0	2	5	-
T20s	181	148	31	1964	98*	16.78	151.07	0	7	70	-

Bowling	Mat	Balls	Mdns	Runs	Wkts	BB	Ave	4wI	5wI	SR	Econ
T20Is	10	180	0	305	7	2-33	43.57	0	0	25.71	10.16
First-class	5	928	34	494	13	4-55	38.00	-	0	71.38	3.19
List A	19	789	2	692	24	5-46	28.83	0	1	32.87	5.26
T20s	181	3606	6	5334	218	5-30	24.46	7	1	16.54	8.87

BEN SANDERSON

RHB / RMF / R0 / W3

FULL NAME: Ben William Sanderson
BORN: January 3, 1989, Sheffield
SQUAD NO: 26
HEIGHT: 6ft
NICKNAME: Sandoooo
EDUCATION: Ecclesfield School, Sheffield; Sheffield College
TEAMS: Northamptonshire, England U19, Yorkshire
ROLE: Bowler
DEBUT: First-class: 2008; List A: 2010; T20: 2010

BEST BATTING: 46 Northamptonshire vs Kent, Northampton, 2023
BEST BOWLING: 8-73 Northamptonshire vs Gloucestershire, Northampton, 2016
COUNTY CAP: 2018 (Northamptonshire)

FIRST CRICKET CLUB? Whitley Hall CC, Sheffield
WHAT'S THE BIGGEST PRIZE IN DOMESTIC CRICKET? The County Championship
THE KOOKABURRA BALL: YES OR NO? No, it's not suited to our pitches
FAVOURITE WARM-UP SONG? Pump It Up by Endor
HOW MANY HOURS DO YOU SPEND ON YOUR PHONE A DAY? Two
SPECIALITY SUBJECT IN A PUB QUIZ (EXCLUDING SPORT)? Horse racing
ONE THING YOU WANT TO DO BEFORE YOU DIE: Score a hundred
SURPRISING FACT ABOUT YOU: I'm not as grumpy as I look. I was 6ft 4in when I started out at Northants
FILM YOU CAN WATCH OVER AND OVER: Wonka

Batting	Mat	Inns	NO	Runs	HS	Ave	SR	100	50	Ct	St
First-class	110	148	42	999	46	9.42	48.37	0	0	13	-
List A	53	27	8	169	31	8.89	61.90	0	0	13	-
T20s	88	25	15	74	12*	7.40	76.28	0	0	19	-

Bowling	Mat	Balls	Mdns	Runs	Wkts	BB	Ave	4wI	5wI	SR	Econ
First-class	110	20220	869	9047	401	8-73	22.56	-	21	50.42	2.68
List A	53	2171	28	1909	67	3-17	28.49	0	0	32.40	5.27
T20s	88	1735	3	2519	102	4-15	24.69	3	0	17.00	8.71

GURINDER SANDHU

LHB / RFM / R0 / W0

FULL NAME: Gurinder Singh Sandhu
BORN: June 14, 1993, Blacktown, New South Wales, Australia
SQUAD NO: TBC
TEAMS: Australia, Sussex, Delhi Daredevils, Melbourne Renegades, New South Wales, Queensland, Sydney Sixers, Sydney Thunder, Tasmania
ROLE: Bowler
DEBUT: ODI: 2015;
First-class: 2013; List A: 2013; T20: 2012

BEST BATTING: 97* New South Wales vs Tasmania, Sydney, 2015
BEST BOWLING: 6-57 Queensland vs South Australia, Adelaide, 2021

NOTES: Aussie seamer Gurinder Sandhu will head to the south coast for June and July and will be available for four Championship games as well as the T20 Blast. A tall, imposing bowler with One-Day International and IPL experience, Sandhu, who currently plays for Queensland and the Melbourne Renegades, will be one of four overseas seamers to feature at Hove over the course of this summer, joining Jayden Seales, Jaydev Unadkat and fellow countryman Nathan McAndrew. "He will add real skill and experience to our bowling attack," said Sussex head coach Paul Farbrace. "He is a vastly experienced performer and is very skillful with the ball. The fact that all four games are being played with a Kookaburra ball means he will be very comfortable with that type of ball"

Batting	Mat	Inns	NO	Runs	HS	Ave	SR	100	50	Ct	St
ODIs	2	0	-	-	-	-	-	-	-	0	-
First-class	55	71	9	1000	97*	16.12	44.56	0	2	22	-
List A	76	43	16	387	51	14.33	72.33	0	1	22	-
T20s	78	27	15	110	20*	9.16	97.34	0	0	19	-

Bowling	Mat	Balls	Mdns	Runs	Wkts	BB	Ave	4wI	5wI	SR	Econ
ODIs	2	120	0	107	3	2-49	35.66	0	0	40.00	5.35
First-class	55	9726	376	4604	151	6-57	30.49	-	5	64.41	2.84
List A	76	3801	37	3251	141	7-56	23.05	8	3	26.95	5.13
T20s	78	1489	2	2009	77	4-22	26.09	1	0	19.33	8.09

MITCHELL SANTNER

LHB / SLA

FULL NAME: Mitchell Josef Santner
BORN: February 5, 1992, Hamilton
SQUAD NO: TBC
HEIGHT: 6ft
EDUCATION: Hamilton Boys' High School, New Zealand
TEAMS: New Zealand, Surrey, Northern Superchargers, Barbados Tridents, Chennai SK, Northern Districts, Southern Brave, Worcestershire
ROLE: Allrounder
DEBUT: Test: 2015; ODI: 2015; T20I: 2015; First-class: 2011; List A: 2014; T20: 2014

BEST BATTING: 92* Northern Districts vs Canterbury, Hamilton, 2022 (T20)
BEST BOWLING: 4-11 New Zealand vs India, Nagpur, 2016 (T20)

NOTES: New Zealand's white-ball captain will join Surrey for the first eight matches of the T20 Blast, lining up alongside fellow Kiwi Nathan Smith. The skillful left-arm spinning allrounder has experience in the county game, having represented Worcestershire on 26 occasions in the T20 Blast. "Mitch will bring quality and experience to the Surrey side. He's a proven international cricketer who plays T20 cricket all over the world and has built an excellent skillset," said Alec Stewart, who is still working with Surrey in an advisory role despite having stepped down as the club's director of cricket last year. Santner also intends to be available to Surrey for the knockout stages of the competition in September should they get that far

Batting	Mat	Inns	NO	Runs	HS	Ave	SR	100	50	Ct	St
Tests	30	43	2	1066	126	26.00	46.96	1	4	22	-
ODIs	118	86	31	1438	67	26.14	90.78	0	3	50	-
T20Is	109	74	31	725	77*	16.86	120.23	0	1	43	-
First-class	65	102	6	2956	136	30.79	51.94	4	16	56	-
List A	148	113	33	2153	86	26.91	90.27	0	8	66	-
T20s	213	160	58	2335	92*	22.89	130.37	0	6	81	-

Bowling	Mat	Balls	Mdns	Runs	Wkts	BB	Ave	4wI	5wI	SR	Econ
Tests	30	5346	178	2526	74	7-53	34.13	-	2	72.24	2.83
ODIs	118	5607	24	4505	126	5-50	35.75	0	2	44.50	4.82
T20Is	109	2268	2	2661	120	4-11	22.17	3	0	18.90	7.03
First-class	65	10533	359	5112	134	7-53	38.14	-	3	78.60	2.91
List A	148	7035	36	5523	163	5-50	33.88	1	2	43.15	4.71
T20s	213	4391	5	5140	216	4-11	23.79	3	0	20.32	7.02

DANE SCHADENDORF   RHB / WK / R0 / W0

FULL NAME: Dane Schadendorf
BORN: July 31, 2002, Harare, Zimbabwe
SQUAD NO: 89
HEIGHT: 5ft 9in
NICKNAME: Shady
EDUCATION: Ruzawi School, Mashonaland East, Zimbabwe; St John's College, Harare
TEAMS: Nottinghamshire, Mountaineers, Zimbabwe U19
ROLE: Wicketkeeper/batter
DEBUT: First-class: 2021; List A: 2021

NOTTINGHAMSHIRE

BEST BATTING: 29 Nottinghamshire vs Kent, Canterbury, 2024

FIRST CRICKET CLUB? Caythorpe CC, Nottingham
BIGGEST INFLUENCE ON YOUR DEVELOPMENT AS A CRICKETER (EXCLUDING PARENTS)? My brother – I used to watch him play growing up and I always wanted to be up there playing with him. I've always remembered that and it pushes me to keep getting better
BEST PERFORMANCE AS A PRO? Twin hundreds against Leicestershire in the Second XI Championship in 2022
FAVOURITE FORMAT? T20 for the excitement
FAVOURITE TOY AS A KID? Transformers
WHAT WOULD BE YOUR PERFECT BREAKFAST? Oats and a protein shake
WHICH PERSON INSPIRES YOU MOST? Michael Jordan

Batting	Mat	Inns	NO	Runs	HS	Ave	SR	100	50	Ct	St
First-class	3	4	0	93	29	23.25	56.02	0	0	11	-
List A	30	26	4	410	47	18.63	81.51	0	0	20	5
Bowling	Mat	Balls	Mdns	Runs	Wkts	BB	Ave	4wI	5wI	SR	Econ
First-class	3	-	-	-	-	-	-	-	-	-	-
List A	30	-	-	-	-	-	-	-	-	-	-

GEORGE SCRIMSHAW   RHB / RMF / R0 / W0

FULL NAME: George Louis Sheridan Scrimshaw
BORN: February 10, 1998, Burton-on-Trent, Staffordshire
SQUAD NO: 98
HEIGHT: 6ft 7in
EDUCATION: Thomas Russell Junior School; John Taylor High School, Burton-on-Trent
TEAMS: England, Northamptonshire, Derbyshire, Welsh Fire, Worcestershire
ROLE: Bowler
DEBUT: ODI: 2023;
First-class: 2021; List A: 2021; T20: 2017

BEST BATTING: 19* Derbyshire vs Sussex, Hove, 2023
BEST BOWLING: 5-49 Derbyshire vs Sussex, Hove, 2023

FIRST CRICKET CLUB? Dunstall CC, Burton-upon-Trent, Staffordshire – aka Deer Park, home of the Stags
WHAT PART OF THE SEASON DO YOU MOST ENJOY? The T20 Blast
WHICH AWAY GROUND DO YOU MOST ENJOY VISITING? Edgbaston
FAVOURITE FORMAT? T20 – I love the speed of the game and performing in front of the big crowds
HOBBIES? Football
WHAT KEEPS YOU AWAKE AT NIGHT? Bowling six no-balls in two overs!
CHOOSE A FANTASY SLIP CORDON TO SPEND A DAY IN THE FIELD WITH: Tom DeLonge, Mark Hoppus, Travis Baker, Robert Smith
SURPRISING FACT ABOUT YOU: I once hit 16 sixes in a row in Kwik Cricket

Batting	Mat	Inns	NO	Runs	HS	Ave	SR	100	50	Ct	St
ODIs	1	0	-	-	-	-	-	-	-	0	-
First-class	10	15	9	47	19*	7.83	27.48	0	0	5	-
List A	5	2	2	13	13*	-	50.00	0	0	1	-
T20s	51	10	9	25	6*	25.00	62.50	0	0	5	-

Bowling	Mat	Balls	Mdns	Runs	Wkts	BB	Ave	4wI	5wI	SR	Econ
ODIs	1	52	0	66	3	3-66	22.00	0	0	17.33	7.61
First-class	10	973	19	755	20	5-49	37.75	-	1	48.65	4.65
List A	5	172	0	216	7	3-66	30.85	0	0	24.57	7.53
T20s	51	1050	0	1558	70	3-16	22.25	0	0	15.00	8.90

TOM SCRIVEN — RHB / RMF / RO / WO

FULL NAME: Thomas Antony Rhys Scriven
BORN: November 18, 1998, Oxford
SQUAD NO: 88
HEIGHT: 6ft 1in
NICKNAME: Skippy
EDUCATION: Magdalen College School, Oxford
TEAMS: Leicestershire, England U19, Hampshire
ROLE: Allrounder
DEBUT: First-class: 2020; List A: 2021; T20: 2018

LEICESTERSHIRE

BEST BATTING: 78 Leicestershire vs Sussex, Hove, 2023
BEST BOWLING: 4-30 Leicestershire vs Gloucestershire, Leicester, 2023

FIRST CRICKET CLUB? West Ilsley CC, Berkshire
BEST PLAYER IN COUNTY CRICKET (EXCLUDING TEAMMATES)? Simon Harmer
FAVOURITE FORMAT? Championship cricket
FAVOURITE TOY AS A KID? Toy soldiers
WHAT WOULD BE YOUR PERFECT BREAKFAST? A Full English
SURPRISING FACT ABOUT YOU: I've never eaten anything from Greggs

Batting	Mat	Inns	NO	Runs	HS	Ave	SR	100	50	Ct	St
First-class	29	43	8	962	78	27.48	56.12	0	8	6	-
List A	30	19	9	307	55	30.70	92.46	0	1	4	-
T20s	9	6	0	40	18	6.66	88.88	0	0	2	-

Bowling	Mat	Balls	Mdns	Runs	Wkts	BB	Ave	4wi	5wi	SR	Econ
First-class	29	3597	92	2061	61	4-30	33.78	-	0	58.96	3.43
List A	30	1151	7	1061	39	5-66	27.20	0	1	29.51	5.53
T20s	9	132	0	204	10	4-21	20.40	1	0	13.20	9.27

JAYDEN SEALES

LHB / RFM / R0 / W0

SUSSEX

FULL NAME: Jayden Nigel Tristan Seales
BORN: September 10, 2001, Trinidad & Tobago
SQUAD NO: 14
HEIGHT: 6ft 3in
NICKNAME: Big J
EDUCATION: Presentation College, Chaguanas, Trinidad & Tobago
TEAMS: West Indies, Sussex, Jaffna Kings, Trinbago Knight Riders, Trinidad & Tobago
ROLE: Bowler
DEBUT: Test: 2021; ODI: 2022; T20I: 2024; First-class: 2020; List A: 2021; T20: 2020

BEST BATTING: 33 Trinidad & Tobago vs Leeward Islands, Trinidad, 2022
BEST BOWLING: 6-61 West Indies vs South Africa, Guyana, 2024
COUNTY CAP: 2024

FIRST CRICKET CLUB? Queen's Park CC, Trinidad & Tobago
EARLIEST CRICKETING MEMORY? In the backyard aged three with my family
THE KOOKABURRA BALL: YES OR NO? Yes, it'll help the players adapt to when they go to countries that use the Kookaburra
OPPONENT YOU MOST LOOK FORWARD TO PLAYING AGAINST? Rory Burns –just to challenge myself against him
FAVOURITE WARM-UP SONG? Good Energy by Young Wylin'
ONE THING YOU WANT TO DO BEFORE YOU DIE: Get a drive in a F1 car
WHICH PUBLIC FIGURE INSPIRES YOU (EXCLUDING SPORTSPEOPLE)? Samuel L Jackson

Batting	Mat	Inns	NO	Runs	HS	Ave	SR	100	50	Ct	St
Tests	18	30	14	124	22	7.75	40.52	0	0	6	-
ODIs	17	6	2	22	16*	5.50	46.80	0	0	3	-
T20Is	1	1	1	4	4*	-	200.00	0	0	1	-
First-class	39	53	18	304	33	8.68	44.83	0	0	11	-
List A	29	7	3	23	16*	5.75	47.91	0	0	5	-
T20s	32	8	8	23	16*	-	143.75	0	0	17	-

Bowling	Mat	Balls	Mdns	Runs	Wkts	BB	Ave	4wI	5wI	SR	Econ
Tests	18	2937	98	1670	75	6-61	22.26	-	2	39.16	3.41
ODIs	17	720	5	713	13	4-22	54.84	1	0	55.38	5.94
T20Is	1	12	0	18	0	0-18	-	-	-	-	9.00
First-class	39	5786	193	3199	134	6-61	23.87	-	5	43.17	3.31
List A	29	1114	11	1072	23	4-22	46.60	1	0	48.43	5.77
T20s	32	512	2	780	33	4-13	23.63	1	0	15.51	9.14

HAMZA SHAIKH

RHB / LB / RO / WO

FULL NAME: Hamza Shaikh
BORN: May 29, 2006, Birmingham
SQUAD NO: 15
HEIGHT: 5ft 11in
NICKNAME: Hammer
EDUCATION: Eden Boys School, Birmingham
TEAMS: Warwickshire, England Lions
ROLE: Batter
DEBUT: First-class: 2024; List A: 2022

WARWICKSHIRE

BEST BATTING: 91 England Lions vs Sri Lankans, Worcester, 2024

FIRST CRICKET CLUB? Smethwick CC, West Midlands
EARLIEST CRICKETING MEMORY? Playing in an adult game with my dad
WHAT'S THE BIGGEST PRIZE IN DOMESTIC CRICKET? Winning the County Championship
THE KOOKABURRA BALL: YES OR NO? Yes, a lot of international cricket is played with the Kookaburra so it's good practice
OPPONENT YOU MOST LOOK FORWARD TO PLAYING AGAINST? Ben McKinney – I've played with him for England U19 and he looks like an unbelievable player
ONE THING YOU WANT TO DO BEFORE YOU DIE: Play for England
HOBBY YOU WOULD LIKE TO LEARN: Padel
WHICH PUBLIC FIGURE INSPIRES YOU (EXCLUDING SPORTSPEOPLE)? Chunkz
FILM YOU CAN WATCH OVER AND OVER: Extraction

Batting	Mat	Inns	NO	Runs	HS	Ave	SR	100	50	Ct	St
First-class	4	8	1	188	91	26.85	38.13	0	1	2	-
List A	17	14	3	258	39	23.45	73.92	0	0	4	-

Bowling	Mat	Balls	Mdns	Runs	Wkts	BB	Ave	4wl	5wl	SR	Econ
First-class	4	-	-	-	-	-	-	-	-	-	-
List A	17	-	-	-	-	-	-	-	-	-	-

JOSH SHAW

RHB / RMF / R0 / W0

GLOUCESTERSHIRE

FULL NAME: Joshua Shaw
BORN: January 3, 1996, Wakefield, Yorkshire
SQUAD NO: 5
HEIGHT: 6ft 1in
EDUCATION: Crofton Academy, West Yorkshire; Skills Exchange College, Wakefield
TEAMS: Gloucestershire, England U19, Yorkshire
ROLE: Bowler
DEBUT: First-class: 2016; List A: 2019; T20: 2015

BEST BATTING: 44 Gloucestershire vs Durham, Bristol, 2023
BEST BOWLING: 5-79 Gloucestershire vs Sussex, Bristol, 2016
COUNTY CAP: 2016 (Gloucestershire)

FIRST CRICKET CLUB? Wakefield Thornes CC, West Yorkshire
FAMILY TIES? My father Chris played for Yorkshire. We lived on the back of Streethouse CC so I was always around cricket from a young age
WHAT PART OF THE SEASON DO YOU MOST ENJOY? October!
WHICH AWAY GROUND DO YOU MOST ENJOY VISITING? New Road, Worcester
IF YOU COULD PINCH A PLAYER FROM ANOTHER COUNTY, WHO WOULD IT BE?
Zak Chappell
HOBBIES? Fishing. Don't mind picking up a book either
WHAT WOULD BE YOUR PERFECT BREAKFAST? Poached eggs, bacon, avocado, halloumi – all on top of sourdough
WHICH PERSON INSPIRES YOU MOST? James Anderson
WHAT KEEPS YOU AWAKE AT NIGHT? Hitting the top of off stump
SURPRISING FACT ABOUT YOU: I'd like to be a groundsman one day

Batting	Mat	Inns	NO	Runs	HS	Ave	SR	100	50	Ct	St
First-class	57	79	14	886	44	13.63	46.36	0	0	10	-
List A	18	9	1	20	8*	2.50	50.00	0	0	2	-
T20s	44	10	4	45	14	7.50	145.16	0	0	7	-

Bowling	Mat	Balls	Mdns	Runs	Wkts	BB	Ave	4wI	5wI	SR	Econ
First-class	57	7984	226	5002	130	5-79	38.47	-	2	61.41	3.75
List A	18	827	3	824	17	4-36	48.47	1	0	48.64	5.97
T20s	44	739	2	1041	43	3-27	24.20	0	0	17.18	8.45

DOM SIBLEY — RHB / OB / R1 / W0 / MVP35

FULL NAME: Dominic Peter Sibley
BORN: September 5, 1995, Epsom, Surrey
SQUAD NO: 45
HEIGHT: 6ft 3in
NICKNAME: Frocko
EDUCATION: Whitgift School, Croydon
TEAMS: England, Surrey, Khulna Tigers, Warwickshire
ROLE: Batter
DEBUT: Test: 2019;
First-class: 2013; List A: 2013; T20: 2016

BEST BATTING: 244 Warwickshire vs Kent, Canterbury, 2019
BEST BOWLING: 2-103 Surrey vs Hampshire, Southampton, 2016
COUNTY CAP: 2024 (Surrey)

FIRST CRICKET CLUB? Ashtead CC, Surrey
GREATEST PERFORMANCE YOU HAVE WITNESSED? Kevin Pietersen's hundred against South Africa in the 2012 Headingley Test
WHAT WOULD YOU DO IF YOU WERE IN CHARGE OF COUNTY CRICKET? Introduce free hits for no-balls in four-day cricket
BIGGEST CRICKETING REGRET? Playing while I did my A-Levels
SURPRISING FACT ABOUT YOU: I am half-French

Batting	Mat	Inns	NO	Runs	HS	Ave	SR	100	50	Ct	St
Tests	22	39	3	1042	133*	28.94	34.22	2	5	12	-
First-class	142	242	28	8412	244	39.30	40.60	22	43	113	-
List A	44	42	3	1215	149	31.15	83.44	5	2	22	-
T20s	47	44	4	1131	74*	28.27	123.47	0	8	22	

Bowling	Mat	Balls	Mdns	Runs	Wkts	BB	Ave	4wI	5wI	SR	Econ
Tests	22	6	0	7	0	0-7	-	-	-	-	7.00
First-class	142	387	8	286	4	2-103	71.50	-	0	96.75	4.43
List A	44	54	0	62	1	1-20	62.00	0	0	54.00	6.88
T20s	47	228	0	338	5	2-33	67.60	0	0	45.60	8.89

CHÉ SIMMONS

RHB / RFM / R0 / W0

FULL NAME: Ché Brendon Simmons
BORN: December 18, 2003
SQUAD NO: 99
HEIGHT: 6ft 2in
NICKNAME: Simz
EDUCATION: Combermere School, Bridgetown, Barbados; Sandwell College, West Midlands
TEAMS: Warwickshire
ROLE: Bowler
DEBUT: First-class: 2024

BEST BATTING: 17 Warwickshire vs Essex, Chelmsford, 2024
BEST BOWLING: 3-12 Warwickshire vs Essex, Chelmsford, 2024

BEST PLAYER IN COUNTY CRICKET (EXCLUDING TEAMMATES)? James Vince
WHICH COUNTY PLAYER WOULD YOU MOST LIKE TO GO FOR A DRINK WITH? Olly Stone
BEST DELIVERY YOU HAVE EVER BOWLED? A top-of-off nut I bowled to Dan Mousley in club cricket
FAVOURITE FORMAT? The T20 Blast for the entertainment
DESCRIBE YOURSELF IN THREE WORDS: Chilled, charismatic, positive
HOBBIES? Gaming
FAVOURITE TOY AS A KID? Fire trucks
WHAT WOULD BE YOUR PERFECT BREAKFAST? A Full English
SURPRISING FACT ABOUT YOU: I was a wicketkeeper at one point

Batting	Mat	Inns	NO	Runs	HS	Ave	SR	100	50	Ct	St
First-class	1	2	0	25	17	12.50	45.45	0	0	1	-

Bowling	Mat	Balls	Mdns	Runs	Wkts	BB	Ave	4wI	5wI	SR	Econ
First-class	1	122	3	71	5	3-12	14.20	-	0	24.40	3.49

JOHN SIMPSON — LHB / WK / R2 / W0 / MVP19

FULL NAME: John Andrew Simpson
BORN: July 13, 1988, Bury, Lancashire
SQUAD NO: 9
HEIGHT: 5ft 11in
NICKNAME: Yon
EDUCATION: St Gabriel's RC High School, Bury; Holy Cross College, Bury
TEAMS: England, Sussex, Middlesex, Northern Superchargers
ROLE: Wicketkeeper/batter
DEBUT: ODI: 2021; First-class: 2009; List A: 2009; T20: 2009

BEST BATTING: 205* Sussex vs Leicestershire, Leicester, 2024

COUNTY CAP: 2011 (Middlesex); 2024 (Sussex); **BENEFIT:** 2023 (Middlesex)

FIRST CRICKET CLUB? Ramsbottom CC, Greater Manchester
WHICH TEAMMATE HAS HAD THE BIGGEST IMPACT ON YOUR GAME? Sam Robson – we started our careers together at Middlesex
BEST PERFORMANCE AS A PRO? 79 not out to chase down 302 at Taunton during Middlesex's championship-winning season of 2016
GREATEST PERFORMANCE YOU HAVE WITNESSED? Mark Ramprakash scoring twin hundreds against Lancashire at The Oval in 2007
IF YOU COULD PINCH A PLAYER FROM ANOTHER COUNTY, WHO WOULD IT BE? James Vince
FAVOURITE FORMAT? Four-day cricket – still the pinnacle
DESCRIBE YOURSELF IN THREE WORDS: Hard-working, dedicated, leader
CHOOSE A FANTASY SLIP CORDON TO SPEND A DAY IN THE FIELD WITH: Tiger Woods (wk), Nelson Mandela, Brian Clough, Paul Gascoigne

Batting	Mat	Inns	NO	Runs	HS	Ave	SR	100	50	Ct	St
ODIs	3	2	0	20	17	10.00	64.51	0	0	9	-
First-class	215	340	49	10265	205*	35.27	48.62	15	56	668	40
List A	108	86	13	1953	85	26.75	87.57	0	10	104	21
T20s	180	158	26	2859	84*	21.65	129.42	0	10	94	30

Bowling	Mat	Balls	Mdns	Runs	Wkts	BB	Ave	4wI	5wI	SR	Econ
ODIs	3	-	-	-	-	-	-	-	-	-	-
First-class	215	18	0	23	0	0-2	-	-	-	-	7.66
List A	108	-	-	-	-	-	-	-	-	-	-
T20s	180	-	-	-	-	-	-	-	-	-	-

FATEH SINGH

LHB / SLA / RO / WO

WORCESTERSHIRE

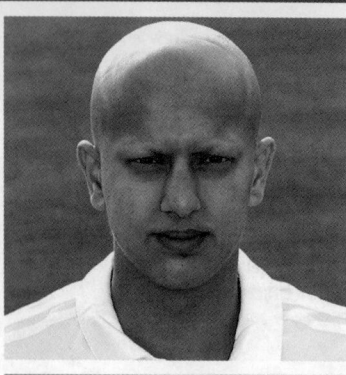

FULL NAME: Fateh Singh Landa
BORN: April 20, 2004, Nottingham
SQUAD NO: 1
HEIGHT: 6ft
NICKNAME: Fatz
EDUCATION: Trent College, Long Eaton
TEAMS: Worcestershire, England U19, Northamptonshire, Nottinghamshire
ROLE: Bowler
DEBUT: First-class: 2024; List A: 2021

BEST BATTING: 4 Northamptonshire vs Yorkshire, Headingley, 2024
BEST BOWLING: 3-193 Northamptonshire vs Yorkshire, Headingley, 2024

FIRST CRICKET CLUB? Cavaliers and Carrington CC, Nottingham
WHICH TEAMMATE HAS HAD THE BIGGEST IMPACT ON YOUR GAME? Liam Patterson-White – he's not too much older than me and we are very similar players. He's helped me settle into the professional environment
WHAT PART OF THE SEASON DO YOU MOST ENJOY? The middle of the season, when you're on the road a lot creating fun memories
WHICH AWAY GROUND DO YOU MOST ENJOY VISITING? Old Trafford – big and good for spinners
IF YOU COULD PINCH A PLAYER FROM ANOTHER COUNTY, WHO WOULD IT BE? Ben Stokes
HOW IS BAZBALL AFFECTING CHAMPIONSHIP CRICKET? It's forcing the pace and generating more results
WHO IS THE TOUGHEST BOWLER TO FACE? Marchant de Lange – he's very quick
WHAT KEEPS YOU AWAKE AT NIGHT? Netflix
WHAT'S THE SILLIEST OUTFIT YOU'VE EVER WORN? A lifeguard costume
CHOOSE A FANTASY SLIP CORDON TO SPEND A DAY IN THE FIELD WITH: Lionel Messi (wk), Harry Potter, Drake, Big Narstie

Batting	Mat	Inns	NO	Runs	HS	Ave	SR	100	50	Ct	St
First-class	1	1	0	4	4	4.00	36.36	0	0	0	-
List A	20	14	1	265	60	20.38	119.36	0	1	4	-

Bowling	Mat	Balls	Mdns	Runs	Wkts	BB	Ave	4wI	5wI	SR	Econ
First-class	1	240	0	193	3	3-193	64.33	-	0	80.00	4.82
List A	20	814	2	749	24	4-52	31.20	1	0	33.91	5.52

JAS SINGH

RHB / RFM / R0 / W0

FULL NAME: Jaskaran Singh
BORN: September 19, 2002, Denmark Hill, Surrey
SQUAD NO: 19
HEIGHT: 6ft 5in
NICKNAME: Jassy
EDUCATION: Wilmington Academy, Kent
TEAMS: Kent
ROLE: Bowler
DEBUT: First-class: 2021; List A: 2023; T20: 2022

BEST BATTING: 18 Kent vs Hampshire, Canterbury, 2024
BEST BOWLING: 4-51 Kent vs Sussex, Canterbury, 2021

FIRST CRICKET CLUB? Bexley CC, Kent
EARLIEST CRICKETING MEMORY? Playing for Bexley U9
WHAT'S THE BIGGEST PRIZE IN DOMESTIC CRICKET? The County Championship
THE KOOKABURRA BALL: YES OR NO? Yes – if there's bounce in the pitch
FAVOURITE WARM-UP SONG? You & Me by Disclosure (Flume remix)
HOW MANY HOURS DO YOU SPEND ON YOUR PHONE A DAY? Six
ONE THING YOU WANT TO DO BEFORE YOU DIE: Skydive
HOBBY YOU WOULD LIKE TO LEARN: How to deejay
FILM YOU CAN WATCH OVER AND OVER: The Wolf of Wall Street

Batting	Mat	Inns	NO	Runs	HS	Ave	SR	100	50	Ct	St
First-class	11	14	6	70	18	8.75	30.04	0	0	3	-
List A	5	4	3	24	19*	24.00	75.00	0	0	1	-
T20s	5	1	0	1	1	1.00	50.00	0	0	0	-

Bowling	Mat	Balls	Mdns	Runs	Wkts	BB	Ave	4wI	5wI	SR	Econ
First-class	11	1178	12	953	17	4-51	56.05	-	0	69.29	4.85
List A	5	210	0	227	5	3-74	45.40	0	0	42.00	6.48
T20s	5	66	0	136	5	3-27	27.20	0	0	13.20	12.36

YADVINDER SINGH

RHB / RMF / R0 / W0

WORCESTERSHIRE

FULL NAME: Yadvinder Singh Chahal
BORN: January 18, 1996, Rajasthan, India
SQUAD NO: 8
HEIGHT: 6ft
NICKNAME: Yadi
EDUCATION: Solihull College, West Midlands
TEAMS: Worcestershire
ROLE: Bowler
DEBUT: First-class: 2024

BEST BATTING: 14* Worcestershire vs Surrey, The Oval, 2024
BEST BOWLING: 4-103 Worcestershire vs Surrey, The Oval, 2024

FIRST CRICKET CLUB? Moseley CC, Solihull
EARLIEST CRICKETING MEMORY? Gully cricket in India
WHAT'S THE BIGGEST PRIZE IN DOMESTIC CRICKET? The County Championship
THE KOOKABURRA BALL: YES OR NO? I don't mind
HOW MANY HOURS DO YOU SPEND ON YOUR PHONE A DAY? Four to five
SPECIALITY SUBJECT IN A PUB QUIZ (EXCLUDING SPORT)? Geography
ONE THING YOU WANT TO DO BEFORE YOU DIE: Be happy
HOBBY YOU WOULD LIKE TO LEARN: Golf
WHICH PUBLIC FIGURE INSPIRES YOU (EXCLUDING SPORTSPEOPLE)? Diljit Dosanjh
SURPRISING FACT ABOUT YOU: I never gave up
FILM YOU CAN WATCH OVER AND OVER: Phir Hera Pheri 2
NOTES: In January 2024 Singh became the second member of the South Asian Cricket Academy
(SACA) to sign a professional contract with Worcestershire. The pace bowler emulated batter
Kashif Ali in signing for the county after an impressive trial period. Rajasthan-born Singh made
his first-class debut last year in the match against Surrey at The Oval in May

Batting	Mat	Inns	NO	Runs	HS	Ave	SR	100	50	Ct	St
First-class	1	2	1	14	14*	14.00	60.86	0	0	0	-

Bowling	Mat	Balls	Mdns	Runs	Wkts	BB	Ave	4wI	5wI	SR	Econ
First-class	1	165	1	146	4	4-103	36.50	-	0	41.25	5.30

BEN SLATER

LHB / OB / R1 / W0

FULL NAME: Benjamin Thomas Slater
BORN: August 26, 1991, Chesterfield, Derbyshire
SQUAD NO: 26
HEIGHT: 5ft 11in
NICKNAME: Slats
EDUCATION: Netherthorpe School, Staveley; Leeds Metropolitan University
TEAMS: Nottinghamshire, Derbyshire, Leicestershire, Southern Rocks
ROLE: Batter
DEBUT: First-class: 2012; List A: 2012; T20: 2012

NOTTINGHAMSHIRE

BEST BATTING: 225* Nottinghamshire vs Durham, Chester-le-Street, 2022
BEST BOWLING: 1-1 Nottinghamshire vs Middlesex, Trent Bridge, 2022
COUNTY CAP: 2021 (Nottinghamshire)

FIRST CRICKET CLUB? Chesterfield CC, Derbyshire
WHICH AWAY GROUND DO YOU MOST ENJOY VISITING? The Oval
WHO IS THE MOST TALENTED U19 TEENAGER IN THE COUNTY GAME? Farhan Ahmed (Not)
WHAT DO YOU THINK OF THE CURRENT 50-OVER COMPETITION? It's good, although more games need to be played at county grounds rather than outgrounds
CHOOSE A FANTASY SLIP CORDON TO SPEND A DAY IN THE FIELD WITH: Margot Robbie (wk), Jack Grealish, Corinna Kopf, David Beckham

Batting	Mat	Inns	NO	Runs	HS	Ave	SR	100	50	Ct	St
First-class	144	260	18	8343	225*	34.47	46.68	14	41	54	-
List A	68	65	8	3007	164	52.75	88.54	8	17	12	-
T20s	18	17	1	325	57	20.31	110.92	0	1	1	-

Bowling	Mat	Balls	Mdns	Runs	Wkts	BB	Ave	4wI	5wI	SR	Econ
First-class	144	423	13	238	3	1-1	79.33	-	0	141.00	3.37
List A	68	24	0	34	0	0-5	-	-	-	-	8.50
T20s	18	-	-	-	-	-	-	-	-	-	-

WILL SMEED

RHB / OB / R0 / W0

SOMERSET

FULL NAME: William Conrad Francis Smeed
BORN: October 26, 2001, Cambridge
SQUAD NO: 23
HEIGHT: 6ft
NICKNAME: Smeedy
EDUCATION: King's College, Taunton
TEAMS: Somerset, Birmingham Phoenix, England Lions, Pretoria Capitals, Quetta Gladiators, St Kitts & Nevis Patriots
ROLE: Batter
DEBUT: List A: 2022; T20: 2020

BEST BATTING: 101* Birmingham Phoenix vs Southern Brave, Edgbaston, 2022 (T20)

FIRST CRICKET CLUB? Glastonbury CC, Somerset
WHO WOULD YOU MOST LIKE TO HAVE A NET WITH? Chris Gayle – to see how hard he hits it
CHILDHOOD SPORTING HERO? Jonny Wilkinson
HOBBIES? Reading
NOTES: The 23-year-old top-order batter – who has not played first-class cricket – burst onto the scene in 2021 when scoring 385 runs in the T20 Blast and followed it up with another 407 the following summer. A short-format specialist who made his List A debut for England Lions in 2022, Smeed scored the first-ever century in The Hundred later that year before signing a deal with Somerset to play T20 cricket only. He then produced his best short-format campaign to date – 523 runs in 17 innings – as Somerset won the Blast for the second time in their history. Ahead of the 2025 season, Smeed amended his contract with the club to allow hom to play red-ball cricket. He said: "Watching how the team went about things in the Championship last year was great and some of the wins were absolutely insane. It would be crazy to not want to be a part of that team"

Batting	Mat	Inns	NO	Runs	HS	Ave	SR	100	50	Ct	St
List A	1	1	0	0	0	0.00	0.00	0	0	0	-
T20s	105	104	4	2626	101*	26.26	151.18	1	18	49	-

Bowling	Mat	Balls	Mdns	Runs	Wkts	BB	Ave	4wl	5wl	SR	Econ
List A	1	-	-	-	-	-	-	-	-	-	-
T20s	105	-	-	-	-	-	-	-	-	-	-

JAMIE SMITH

RHB / WK / R0 / W0

FULL NAME: Jamie Luke Smith
BORN: July 12, 2000, Epsom, Surrey
SQUAD NO: 11
HEIGHT: 6ft 2in
NICKNAME: Smudger
EDUCATION: Whitgift School, Croydon
TEAMS: England, Surrey, London Spirit,
Birmingham Phoenix
ROLE: Batter/wicketkeeper
DEBUT: Test: 2024; ODI: 2023; T20I: 2025;
First-class: 2019; List A: 2019; T20: 2018

BEST BATTING: 234* Surrey vs Gloucestershire, Bristol, 2022

COUNTY CAP: 2023

FIRST CRICKET CLUB? Sutton CC, Surrey
WHAT PART OF THE SEASON DO YOU MOST ENJOY? The first day
GREATEST PERFORMANCE YOU HAVE WITNESSED? An opening partnership of nearly 200
between Aaron Finch and Jason Roy in the T20 against Middlesex at The Oval in 2018
WHICH AWAY GROUND DO YOU MOST ENJOY VISITING? Lord's – it's close to home and you
always get treated well there (the lunches)
CHILDHOOD SPORTING HERO? Mark Noble
HOBBIES? Horse racing

Batting	Mat	Inns	NO	Runs	HS	Ave	SR	100	50	Ct	St
Tests	9	15	0	637	111	42.46	72.30	1	4	31	1
ODIs	10	9	0	157	49	17.44	91.27	0	0	7	-
T20Is	2	2	0	28	22	14.00	175.00	0	0	0	-
First-class	68	104	7	4070	234*	41.95	60.96	11	18	99	5
List A	25	21	2	582	85	30.63	84.59	0	3	20	2
T20s	87	72	13	1382	87	23.42	138.33	0	7	48	10

Bowling	Mat	Balls	Mdns	Runs	Wkts	BB	Ave	4wl	5wl	SR	Econ
Tests	9	-	-	-	-	-	-	-	-	-	-
ODIs	10	-	-	-	-	-	-	-	-	-	-
T20Is	2	-	-	-	-	-	-	-	-	-	-
First-class	68	-	-	-	-	-	-	-	-	-	-
List A	25	-	-	-	-	-	-	-	-	-	-
T20s	87	-	-	-	-	-	-	-	-	-	-

NATHAN SMITH

RHB / RMF / RO / WO

FULL NAME: Nathan Gregory Smith
BORN: July 15, 1998, Dunedin, New Zealand
SQUAD NO: TBC
TEAMS: New Zealand, Surrey, Otago, Wellington, Worcestershire
ROLE: Allrounder
DEBUT: Test: 2024; ODI: 2024;
First-class: 2016; List A: 2017; T20: 2016

BEST BATTING: 114 Otago vs Northern Districts, Dunedin, 2019
BEST BOWLING: 6-36 Wellington vs Canterbury, Rangiora, 2024

NOTES: Surrey have signed the New Zealand allrounder to play in the County Championship and the T20 Blast subject to his international committments. Smith made a strong impression for Worcestershire last summer and made both his Test and ODI debuts in 2024. "I loved my time at Worcestershire last year and I am extremely grateful for the opportunity they gave me to come and play county cricket," Smith said. "However, the chance to join one of the best counties in the country was one I couldn't turn down. I have only heard great things about the club, and I look forward to hopefully contributing to continuing the remarkable success the club has had in recent years. I am especially excited about the prospect of bowling on the Kia Oval wicket and linking up with the outstanding group of bowlers in the squad"

Batting	Mat	Inns	NO	Runs	HS	Ave	SR	100	50	Ct	St
Tests	2	4	0	80	42	20.00	66.66	0	0	0	-
ODIs	8	5	1	26	17	6.50	65.00	0	0	5	-
First-class	55	86	11	1999	114	26.65	49.28	1	13	26	-
List A	57	49	10	942	81	24.15	93.17	0	3	26	-
T20s	63	44	8	533	51*	14.80	128.12	0	1	23	-

Bowling	Mat	Balls	Mdns	Runs	Wkts	BB	Ave	4wI	5wI	SR	Econ
Tests	2	344	1	339	7	4-86	48.42	-	0	49.14	5.91
ODIs	8	270	4	314	7	2-43	44.85	0	0	38.57	6.97
First-class	55	8271	355	4062	151	6-36	26.90	-	6	54.77	2.94
List A	57	2305	22	2136	65	3-21	32.86	0	0	35.46	5.56
T20s	63	1166	3	1620	67	5-14	24.17	2	1	17.40	8.33

TOM SMITH

RHB / SLA

FULL NAME: Thomas Michael John Smith
BORN: August 29, 1987, Eastbourne, Sussex
SQUAD NO: 6
HEIGHT: 5ft 9in
NICKNAME: Smudge
EDUCATION: Seaford Head Community College, East Sussex; Sussex Downs College
TEAMS: Gloucestershire, Middlesex, Surrey, Sussex
ROLE: Bowler
DEBUT: First-class: 2007; List A: 2006; T20: 2007

GLOUCESTERSHIRE

BEST BATTING: 36* Middlesex vs Gloucestershire, Uxbridge, 2011 (T20)
BEST BOWLING: 5-16 Gloucestershire vs Birmingham Bears, Edgbaston, 2020 (T20)
COUNTY CAP: 2013 (Gloucestershire)

FIRST CRICKET CLUB? Eastbourne CC, East Sussex
WHICH TEAMMATE HAS HAD THE BIGGEST IMPACT ON YOUR GAME? James Kirtley – we both played at Eastbourne CC before we were teammates at Sussex. Someone I always looked up to and drew inspiration from
WHICH AWAY GROUND DO YOU MOST ENJOY VISITING? Hove – I grew up in East Sussex and have fond memories of sitting in the deckchairs with my dad in the 1990s
IF YOU COULD PINCH A PLAYER FROM ANOTHER COUNTY, WHO WOULD IT BE? Benny Howell – I miss discussing his 74 bowling variations when he was with us at Gloucestershire
WHAT DO YOU THINK OF THE CURRENT 50-OVER COMPETITION? Great shop window for young players – and keeps the older ones active!
WHO IS THE TOUGHEST BOWLER TO FACE? Liam Dawson
CHOOSE A FANTASY SLIP CORDON TO SPEND A DAY IN THE FIELD WITH: Ted Lasso (wk), Shane Warne, Michael Jordan, Vicky McClure
NOTES: Smith signed a new one-year T20 deal with Gloucestershire last November

Batting	Mat	Inns	NO	Runs	HS	Ave	SR	100	50	Ct	St
First-class	55	77	14	1422	84	22.57	37.38	0	4	17	-
List A	112	60	26	704	65	20.70	74.34	0	2	48	-
T20s	181	67	45	392	36*	17.81	110.73	0	0	59	-

Bowling	Mat	Balls	Mdns	Runs	Wkts	BB	Ave	4wI	5wI	SR	Econ
First-class	55	7469	166	4171	82	4-35	50.86	-	0	91.08	3.35
List A	112	4533	15	3929	103	4-26	38.14	1	0	44.00	5.20
T20s	181	3423	2	4226	188	5-16	22.47	1	3	18.20	7.40

ESSEX

SHANE SNATER　　RHB / RMF / R0 / W0 / MVP20

FULL NAME: Shane Snater
BORN: March 24, 1996, Harare, Zimbabwe
SQUAD NO: 29
EDUCATION: St John's College, Harare
TEAMS: Netherlands, Essex, Kent, Southern Rocks
ROLE: Bowler
DEBUT: ODI: 2018; T20I: 2018;
First-class: 2016; List A: 2017; T20: 2018

BEST BATTING: 83* Essex vs Kent, Canterbury, 2024
BEST BOWLING: 7-98 Essex vs Nottinghamshire, Trent Bridge, 2021
COUNTY CAP: 2022 (Essex)

NOTES: Essex signed the Netherlands seamer following a successful trial period at the club in 2018 and he appeared to have established himself as a key member of their highly regarded pace attack after taking 67 wickets across the 2021 and 2022 seasons. With four red-ball fifties, the 28-year-old also showed signs of becoming a genuine allrounder. After a fallow 2023, Snater was back to his best last summer, taking 41 red-ball wickets at an average of 22 as well as hitting three half-centuries. Snater grew up in Harare and represented Zimbabwe U17 but holds a Dutch passport and made his ODI and T20I debut for Netherlands in 2018, though he has not appeared for his country since 2022

Batting	Mat	Inns	NO	Runs	HS	Ave	SR	100	50	Ct	St
ODIs	4	4	1	33	17*	11.00	122.22	0	0	5	-
T20Is	13	6	1	18	10	3.60	112.50	0	0	2	-
First-class	48	63	12	1162	83*	22.78	75.06	0	8	9	-
List A	37	27	7	315	64	15.75	102.27	0	1	16	-
T20s	53	26	13	128	20*	9.84	119.62	0	0	20	-

Bowling	Mat	Balls	Mdns	Runs	Wkts	BB	Ave	4wI	5wI	SR	Econ
ODIs	4	150	1	188	2	1-41	94.00	0	0	75.00	7.52
T20Is	13	209	0	337	13	3-42	25.92	0	0	16.07	9.67
First-class	48	6025	222	3159	136	7-98	23.22	-	8	44.30	3.14
List A	37	1690	14	1546	53	5-29	29.16	1	2	31.88	5.48
T20s	53	812	1	1300	45	3-13	28.88	0	0	18.04	9.60

NATHAN SOWTER

RHB / LB

FULL NAME: Nathan Adam Sowter
BORN: October 12, 1992, Penrith, New South Wales, Australia
SQUAD NO: 72
HEIGHT: 5ft 11in
NICKNAME: Racing Snake
EDUCATION: Hills Sport High School, New South Wales
TEAMS: Durham, Oval Invincibles, Guyana Amazon Warriors, Middlesex
ROLE: Bowler
DEBUT: First-class: 2017; List A: 2016; T20: 2015

BEST BATTING: 37* Middlesex vs Somerset, Taunton, 2021 (T20)
BEST BOWLING: 5-15 Durham vs Northamptonshire, Northampton, 2023 (T20)

FIRST CRICKET CLUB? Rooty Hill RSL CC – a small club not far from where I grew up in western Sydney
WHAT'S THE BIGGEST PRIZE IN DOMESTIC CRICKET? The T20 Blast
THE KOOKABURRA BALL: YES OR NO? Yes, I like the feel of it as a spinner
HOW MANY HOURS DO YOU SPEND ON YOUR PHONE A DAY? Four
WHICH PUBLIC FIGURE INSPIRES YOU (EXCLUDING SPORTSPEOPLE)?
SURPRISING FACT ABOUT YOU: I'm a glazier by trade, and I used to own lizards
FILM YOU CAN WATCH OVER AND OVER: Hangover
NOTES: Sowter is on a white-ball contract with Durham

Batting	Mat	Inns	NO	Runs	HS	Ave	SR	100	50	Ct	St
First-class	13	23	4	292	57*	15.36	65.47	0	2	12	-
List A	19	12	3	134	31	14.88	76.13	0	0	17	-
T20s	149	48	21	246	37*	9.11	111.81	0	0	54	-

Bowling	Mat	Balls	Mdns	Runs	Wkts	BB	Ave	4wI	5wI	SR	Econ
First-class	13	1870	47	1032	20	3-42	51.60	-	0	93.50	3.31
List A	19	1008	0	928	36	6-62	25.77	3	1	28.00	5.52
T20s	149	2810	1	3623	160	5-15	22.64	4	1	17.56	7.73

MITCHELL STANLEY

RHB / RFM / R0 / W0

FULL NAME: Mitchell Terry Stanley
BORN: March 17, 2001, Telford, Shropshire
SQUAD NO: 38
HEIGHT: 6ft 4in
NICKNAME: Lurch
EDUCATION: Idsall School, Shifnal, Shropshire; Shrewsbury Sixth Form College
TEAMS: Lancashire, England Lions, Manchester Originals, Worcestershire
ROLE: Bowler
DEBUT: List A: 2024; T20: 2022

FIRST CRICKET CLUB? Shifnal CC, Shropshire
BEST PLAYER IN COUNTY CRICKET (EXCLUDING TEAMMATES)? Wayne Madsen
WHICH COUNTY PLAYER WOULD YOU MOST LIKE TO GO FOR A DRINK WITH? Mark Wood
– seems like a good laugh and has a lot of insight into bowling quick
BEST DELIVERY YOU HAVE EVER BOWLED? Bowling Alex Davies at Edgbaston in the T20
Blast a few summers ago. It swung away and hit the top of off, just what you practise to try to
do all the time
GREATEST PERFORMANCE YOU HAVE WITNESSED? Ben Stokes' innings against us at New
Road in 2022
FAVOURITE FORMAT? The T20 Blast
DESCRIBE YOURSELF IN THREE WORDS: All or nothing
HOBBIES? Cars
FAVOURITE TOY AS A KID? Hot Wheels cars
WHICH PERSON INSPIRES YOU MOST? Brett Lee

Batting	Mat	Inns	NO	Runs	HS	Ave	SR	100	50	Ct	St
List A	1	1	0	0	0	0.00	0.00	0	0	0	-
T20s	14	4	2	10	7	5.00	83.33	0	0	0	-

Bowling	Mat	Balls	Mdns	Runs	Wkts	BB	Ave	4wI	5wI	SR	Econ
List A	1	30	0	37	0	0-37	-	-	-	-	7.40
T20s	14	196	1	333	12	2-24	27.75	0	0	16.33	10.19

CAMERON STEEL

RHB / LB / RO / WO

FULL NAME: Cameron Tate Steel
BORN: September 13, 1995, Greenbrae, California, USA
SQUAD NO: 44
HEIGHT: 5ft 10in
NICKNAME: Moggy
EDUCATION: Millfield Prep School, Somerset; Scotch College, Perth, Australia; Durham University
TEAMS: Surrey, Durham, Hampshire
ROLE: Allrounder
DEBUT: First-class: 2014; List A: 2017; T20: 2017

BEST BATTING: 224 Durham vs Leicestershire, Leicester, 2017
BEST BOWLING: 5-25 Surrey vs Lancashire, Old Trafford, 2024

FIRST CRICKET CLUB? Glastonbury CC, Somerset
WHICH COUNTY PLAYER WOULD YOU MOST LIKE TO GO FOR A DRINK WITH? Umesh Yadav – he owes me one
BEST DELIVERY YOU HAVE EVER BOWLED? My waist-high full toss to get Luke Wright caught at deep square in a four-day game at Arundel in 2018
BEST PERFORMANCE AS A PRO? My rendition of 'Insomnia' for Surrey's initiation song
GREATEST PERFORMANCE YOU HAVE WITNESSED? Dan Worrall's performance of 'Test Cricket Died' after winning the Championship in 2022 (see Twitter)
FAVOURITE FORMAT? The Championship – nothing beats four days away in Northampton
DESCRIBE YOURSELF IN THREE WORDS: English American Australian
FAVOURITE TOY AS A KID? My Thomas the Tank Engine train set
WHAT WOULD BE YOUR PERFECT BREAKFAST? Eggs on toast and a croissant
SURPRISING FACT ABOUT YOU: I was the U9 West of England chess champion

Batting	Mat	Inns	NO	Runs	HS	Ave	SR	100	50	Ct	St
First-class	64	104	5	2651	224	26.77	41.47	4	12	30	-
List A	37	34	5	589	77	20.31	79.59	0	5	15	-
T20s	24	16	6	165	37	16.50	122.22	0	0	12	-

Bowling	Mat	Balls	Mdns	Runs	Wkts	BB	Ave	4wI	5wI	SR	Econ
First-class	64	2904	35	1971	60	5-25	32.85	-	2	48.40	4.07
List A	37	1269	5	1193	41	4-33	29.09	4	0	30.95	5.64
T20s	24	264	0	436	12	3-41	36.33	0	0	22.00	9.90

GRANT STEWART

RHB / RFM / R0 / W0

FULL NAME: Grant Stewart
BORN: February 19, 1994, Kalgoorlie, Western Australia, Australia
SQUAD NO: 9
HEIGHT: 6ft 3in
NICKNAME: Stewie
EDUCATION: All Saints College, New South Wales; University of Newcastle, NSW
TEAMS: Italy, Kent, Sussex
ROLE: Allrounder
DEBUT: T20I: 2021; First-class: 2017; List A: 2018; T20: 2018

BEST BATTING: 103 Kent vs Middlesex, Canterbury, 2018
BEST BOWLING: 6-22 Kent vs Middlesex, Canterbury, 2018

BIGGEST INFLUENCE ON YOUR DEVELOPMENT AS A CRICKETER (EXCLUDING PARENTS)?
My older brothers
MOST EXCITING DAY AS A CRICKETER? My first-class debut for Kent against Glamorgan at Canterbury in 2017
CHILDHOOD SPORTING HERO? Steve Waugh
SURPRISING FACT ABOUT YOU: I was a wicketkeeper until I was 16

Batting	Mat	Inns	NO	Runs	HS	Ave	SR	100	50	Ct	St
T20Is	14	13	0	360	76	27.69	162.89	0	3	5	-
First-class	47	75	9	1568	103	23.75	68.53	1	9	6	-
List A	50	39	3	728	78	20.22	103.85	0	4	17	-
T20s	74	54	18	669	76	18.58	146.71	0	3	16	-
Bowling	Mat	Balls	Mdns	Runs	Wkts	BB	Ave	4wl	5wl	SR	Econ
T20Is	14	204	1	185	10	3-29	18.50	0	0	20.40	5.44
First-class	47	6058	182	3433	88	6-22	39.01	-	2	68.84	3.40
List A	50	1745	26	1472	49	4-42	30.04	1	0	35.61	5.06
T20s	74	1241	1	1878	73	4-48	25.72	1	0	17.00	9.07

BEN STOKES

LHB / RFM / RO / WO

FULL NAME: Benjamin Andrew Stokes
BORN: June 4, 1991, Christchurch, NZ
SQUAD NO: 38
HEIGHT: 6ft 2in
NICKNAME: Stokesie
EDUCATION: Cockermouth School, Cumbria
TEAMS: England, Durham, Northern Superchargers, Canterbury, Chennai Super Kings, Melbourne Renegades, Rajasthan Royals, Rising Pune Supergiant
ROLE: Allrounder
DEBUT: Test: 2013; ODI: 2011; T20I: 2011; First-class: 2010; List A: 2009; T20: 2010

DURHAM

BEST BATTING: 258 England vs South Africa, Cape Town, 2016
BEST BOWLING: 7-67 Durham vs Sussex, Chester-le-Street, 2014

FIRST CRICKET CLUB? Cockermouth CC, Cumbria
SURPRISING FACT ABOUT YOU: My father played one Test match for New Zealand in rugby league. I was a right-handed batter when I was younger

Batting	Mat	Inns	NO	Runs	HS	Ave	SR	100	50	Ct	St
Tests	110	198	9	6719	258	35.55	59.71	13	35	112	-
ODIs	114	99	15	3463	182	41.22	95.68	5	24	55	-
T20Is	43	36	9	585	52*	21.66	128.00	0	1	22	-
First-class	193	329	17	10898	258	34.92	-	22	56	156	-
List A	184	162	24	5303	182	38.42	97.17	9	30	85	-
T20s	162	148	24	3027	107*	24.41	132.87	1	10	74	-

Bowling	Mat	Balls	Mdns	Runs	Wkts	BB	Ave	4wI	5wI	SR	Econ
Tests	110	12252	359	6797	210	6-22	32.36	-	4	58.34	3.32
ODIs	114	3110	8	3137	74	5-61	42.39	1	1	42.02	6.05
T20Is	43	612	1	856	26	3-26	32.92	0	0	23.53	8.39
First-class	193	21156	602	12166	407	7-67	29.89	-	8	51.98	3.45
List A	184	4774	23	4597	137	5-61	33.55	3	1	34.84	5.77
T20s	162	2034	3	2875	93	4-16	30.91	2	0	21.87	8.48

OLLY STONE

RHB / RF / R0 / W0

NOTTINGHAMSHIRE

FULL NAME: Oliver Peter Stone
BORN: October 9, 1993, Norwich
SQUAD NO: 9
HEIGHT: 6ft 2in
EDUCATION: Thorpe St Andrew High School, Norwich; Moulton College, Northamptonshire
TEAMS: England, Notts, London Spirit, Melbourne Stars, MI Cape Town, Multan Sultans, Northants, Warwickshire
ROLE: Bowler
DEBUT: Test: 2019; ODI: 2018; T20I: 2022; First-class: 2012; List A: 2012; T20: 2011

BEST BATTING: 90 Northamptonshire vs Lancashire, Trent Bridge, 2024
BEST BOWLING: 8-80 Warwickshire vs Sussex, Edgbaston, 2018
COUNTY CAP: 2020 (Warwickshire)

FIRST CRICKET CLUB? Vauxhall Mallards CC, Norfolk. Home of the ducks
GREATEST PERFORMANCE YOU HAVE WITNESSED? David Willey's 27-ball 60 for my former county Northants in the 2013 final of the T20 Blast
SURPRISING FACT ABOUT YOU: My great-grandad created the Twix chocolate bar

Batting	Mat	Inns	NO	Runs	HS	Ave	SR	100	50	Ct	St
Tests	5	10	1	102	20	11.33	43.58	0	0	2	-
ODIs	10	6	3	24	9*	8.00	68.57	0	0	2	-
T20Is	1	1	0	0	0	0.00	0.00	0	0	0	-
First-class	54	75	14	1116	90	18.29	46.03	0	4	21	-
List A	36	19	11	137	24*	17.12	68.50	0	0	15	-
T20s	105	43	18	170	22*	6.80	91.89	0	0	33	-

Bowling	Mat	Balls	Mdns	Runs	Wkts	BB	Ave	4wI	5wI	SR	Econ
Tests	5	610	17	400	17	3-29	23.52	-	0	35.88	3.93
ODIs	10	394	2	399	9	4-85	44.33	1	0	43.77	6.07
T20Is	1	24	0	36	0	0-36	-	-	-	-	9.00
First-class	54	8229	232	4727	174	8-80	27.16	-	6	47.29	3.44
List A	36	1423	10	1325	32	4-71	41.40	2	0	44.46	5.58
T20s	105	2001	6	2905	109	4-14	26.65	3	0	18.35	8.71

MARK STONEMAN · LHB / OB / R6 / W0

FULL NAME: Mark Daniel Stoneman
BORN: June 26, 1987, Newcastle
SQUAD NO: TBC
HEIGHT: 5ft 10in
NICKNAME: Rocky
EDUCATION: Whickham Comprehensive School, Newcastle Upon Tyne
TEAMS: England, Hampshire, Durham, Middlesex, Surrey, Yorkshire
ROLE: Batter
DEBUT: Test: 2017; First-class: 2007; List A: 2008; T20: 2010

HAMPSHIRE

BEST BATTING: 197 Surrey vs Sussex, Guildford, 2017
BEST BOWLING: 1-34 Middlesex vs Sussex, Hove, 2022
COUNTY CAP: 2018 (Surrey); 2022 (Middlesex)

FIRST CRICKET CLUB? Burnopfield CC, Newcastle upon Tyne
FAMILY TIES? My grandfather played and umpired locally for many years and my dad played all over the north-east as a local pro
WHICH TEAMMATE HAS HAD THE BIGGEST IMPACT ON YOUR GAME? Dale Benkenstein after he asked me: "When are you going to start scoring some runs?"
WHICH AWAY GROUND DO YOU MOST ENJOY VISITING? The Riverside, Chester-le-Street – it smells like home
IF YOU COULD PINCH A PLAYER FROM ANOTHER COUNTY, WHO WOULD IT BE?
Dan Worrall
HOW IS BAZBALL AFFECTING CHAMPIONSHIP CRICKET? It isn't
WHO IS THE TOUGHEST BOWLER TO FACE? Mohammad Abbas – the ball shouldn't feel like it gets quicker off the pitch

Batting	Mat	Inns	NO	Runs	HS	Ave	SR	100	50	Ct	St
Tests	11	20	1	526	60	27.68	44.27	0	5	1	-
First-class	250	434	12	14448	197	34.23	56.37	31	73	106	-
List A	113	108	8	3809	144*	38.09	92.49	7	23	35	-
T20s	79	72	4	1349	89*	19.83	116.99	0	8	31	-

Bowling	Mat	Balls	Mdns	Runs	Wkts	BB	Ave	4wI	5wI	SR	Econ
Tests	11	-	-	-	-	-	-	-	-	-	-
First-class	250	467	2	354	1	1-34	354.00	-	0	467.00	4.54
List A	113	22	0	41	1	1-8	41.00	0	0	22.00	11.18
T20s	79	-	-	-	-	-	-	-	-	-	-

WILL SUTHERLAND

RHB / RFM / RO / WO

YORKSHIRE

FULL NAME: William James Sutherland
BORN: October 27, 1999, East Melbourne, Victoria, Australia
SQUAD NO: TBC
TEAMS: Australia, Yorkshire, Melbourne Renegades, Victoria
ROLE: Allrounder
DEBUT: ODI: 2024;
First-class: 2019; List A: 2017; T20: 2018

BEST BATTING: 100 Victoria vs South Australia, Adelaide, 2022
BEST BOWLING: 6-67 Victoria vs South Australia, Adelaide, 2020

NOTES: The 25-year-old Australian quick has signed for Yorkshire to play in eight T20 Blast group fixtures as well as two rounds of the County Championship. Sutherland, who has played two ODIs, has previously signed deals with Somerset and Essex only for both to have been botched because of injury. Yorkshire head coach Anthony McGrath said: "Will is someone I have admired for a long time and feel he can add something extra to our bowling attack for that middle period of the season as well as offering us an added dimension with the bat. I know the Australian selectors think highly of him, and they know a thing or two about allrounders, so I am confident Will can hit the ground running and deliver for us in both red and white-ball games." Sutherland's father James played briefly for Victoria before moving into administration as Cricket Australia's CEO, while his younger sister Annabel is one of the best young female players in the game

Batting	Mat	Inns	NO	Runs	HS	Ave	SR	100	50	Ct	St
ODIs	2	1	0	18	18	18.00	54.54	0	0	1	-
First-class	45	68	7	1112	100	18.22	55.02	1	2	43	-
List A	43	34	4	597	66	19.90	86.64	0	3	20	-
T20s	63	51	17	630	70	18.52	134.32	0	2	27	-

Bowling	Mat	Balls	Mdns	Runs	Wkts	BB	Ave	4wI	5wI	SR	Econ
ODIs	2	51	0	33	2	2-28	16.50	0	0	25.50	3.88
First-class	45	7597	331	3486	148	6-67	23.55	-	7	51.33	2.75
List A	43	2006	14	1861	62	5-45	30.01	1	1	32.35	5.56
T20s	63	932	2	1367	36	3-14	37.97	0	0	25.88	8.80

S

OLLIE SUTTON — LHB / LMF / RO / WO

FULL NAME: Oliver William Sutton
BORN: January 25, 2000, Sefton, Lancashire
SQUAD NO: 22
HEIGHT: 6ft 3in
NICKNAME: Sutz
EDUCATION: Range High School, Formby, Merseyside; Nottingham Trent University
TEAMS: Lancashire
ROLE: Bowler
DEBUT: List A: 2024

LANCASHIRE

FIRST CRICKET CLUB? Formby CC, Merseyside
EARLIEST CRICKETING MEMORY? Pairs cricket at U10 level
WHAT'S THE BIGGEST PRIZE IN DOMESTIC CRICKET? The County Championship
THE KOOKABURRA BALL: YES OR NO? No – not appropriate for English weather and conditions
OPPONENT YOU MOST LOOK FORWARD TO PLAYING AGAINST? Ben Aitchison – I grew up playing with him
FAVOURITE WARM-UP SONG? Back On 74 by Jungle
HOW MANY HOURS DO YOU SPEND ON YOUR PHONE A DAY? Two
SPECIALITY SUBJECT IN A PUB QUIZ (EXCLUDING SPORT)? Healthy food
ONE THING YOU WANT TO DO BEFORE YOU DIE: Go on safari in Africa
HOBBY YOU WOULD LIKE TO LEARN: Play an instrument
FILM YOU CAN WATCH OVER AND OVER: I prefer TV shows, so it's The Office

Batting	Mat	Inns	NO	Runs	HS	Ave	SR	100	50	Ct	St
List A	1	1	0	0	0	0.00	0.00	0	0	0	-

Bowling	Mat	Balls	Mdns	Runs	Wkts	BB	Ave	4wI	5wI	SR	Econ
List A	1	3	0	1	1	1-1	1.00	0	0	3.00	2.00

HARRY SWINDELLS

RHB / WK / R0 / W0

LEICESTERSHIRE

FULL NAME: Harry John Swindells
BORN: February 21, 1999, Leicester
SQUAD NO: 28
HEIGHT: 5ft 8in
NICKNAME: Dumbo
EDUCATION: Brockington College, Leicestershire; Lutterworth College; Loughborough College
TEAMS: Leicestershire, England U19
ROLE: Batter
DEBUT: First-class: 2019; List A: 2018; T20: 2018

BEST BATTING: 171* Leicestershire vs Somerset, Taunton, 2021

FIRST CRICKET CLUB? Narborough & Littlethorpe CC, Leicestershire
EARLIEST CRICKETING MEMORY? The 2005 Ashes
WHAT'S THE BIGGEST PRIZE IN DOMESTIC CRICKET? The County Championship
THE KOOKABURRA BALL: YES OR NO? Yes, yes, yes!
FAVOURITE WARM-UP SONG? The Fox (What Does The Fox Say?) by Ylvis
HOW MANY HOURS DO YOU SPEND ON YOUR PHONE A DAY? Three
SPECIALITY SUBJECT IN A PUB QUIZ (EXCLUDING SPORT)? Art
ONE THING YOU WANT TO DO BEFORE YOU DIE: Climb to Everest base camp
HOBBY YOU WOULD LIKE TO LEARN: Learn a new language (I speak Arabic)
SURPRISING FACT ABOUT YOU: I was in the paper the day after I was born
FILM YOU CAN WATCH OVER AND OVER: The Imitation Game

Batting	Mat	Inns	NO	Runs	HS	Ave	SR	100	50	Ct	St
First-class	43	67	5	1629	171*	26.27	45.00	2	8	75	3
List A	23	20	2	567	117*	31.50	84.24	1	4	16	3
T20s	36	31	4	521	63	19.29	112.77	0	3	14	3

Bowling	Mat	Balls	Mdns	Runs	Wkts	BB	Ave	4wl	5wl	SR	Econ
First-class	43	6	0	3	0	0-3	-	-	-	-	3.00
List A	23	-	-	-	-	-	-	-	-	-	-
T20s	36	-	-	-	-	-	-	-	-	-	-

JONATHAN TATTERSALL — RHB / WK / R0 / W0

FULL NAME: Jonathan Andrew Tattersall
BORN: December 15, 1994, Harrogate, Yorkshire
SQUAD NO: 12
HEIGHT: 5ft 8in
NICKNAME: Tatts
EDUCATION: King James's School, Knaresborough
TEAMS: Yorkshire, England U19, Gloucestershire, Surrey
ROLE: Wicketkeeper/batter
DEBUT: First-class: 2018; List A: 2013; T20: 2018

BEST BATTING: 180* Yorkshire vs Surrey, Scarborough, 2022
BEST BOWLING: 2-27 Yorkshire vs Lancashire, Old Trafford, 2022
COUNTY CAP: 2022 (Yorkshire)

FIRST CRICKET CLUB? Knaresborough CC, North Yorkshire
EARLIEST CRICKETING MEMORY? Playing in the drive with my brother
BIGGEST INFLUENCE ON YOUR DEVELOPMENT AS A CRICKETER (EXCLUDING PARENTS)?
Two people: Tim Boon who helped my batting while I was with England U19, and Yorkshire Academy coach Richard Damms who helped me understand the game better
THE KOOKABURRA BALL: YES OR NO? No, it's difficult to get a positive result unless the pitches are changed
OPPONENT YOU MOST LOOK FORWARD TO PLAYING AGAINST? Ed Barnard, I played with him for England U19 so it's nice to catch up
FAVOURITE WARM-UP SONG? Lady (Hear Me Tonight) by Modjo
HOW MANY HOURS DO YOU SPEND ON YOUR PHONE A DAY? 1.5
SPECIALITY SUBJECT IN A PUB QUIZ (EXCLUDING SPORT)? Quotes from the Harry Potter films
CHILDHOOD SPORTING HERO? Michael Vaughan
FILM YOU CAN WATCH OVER AND OVER: Anchorman

Batting	Mat	Inns	NO	Runs	HS	Ave	SR	100	50	Ct	St
First-class	65	99	13	3001	180*	34.89	47.61	4	14	153	11
List A	34	27	3	757	89	31.54	95.70	0	8	30	3
T20s	54	35	10	526	53*	21.04	123.76	0	1	36	6

Bowling	Mat	Balls	Mdns	Runs	Wkts	BB	Ave	4wI	5wI	SR	Econ
First-class	65	60	0	66	2	2-27	33.00	-	0	30.00	6.60
List A	34	-	-	-	-	-	-	-	-	-	-
T20s	54	-	-	-	-	-	-	-	-	-	-

JACK TAYLOR

RHB / OB / R0 / W0

GLOUCESTERSHIRE

FULL NAME: Jack Martin Robert Taylor
BORN: November 12, 1991, Banbury, Oxfordshire
SQUAD NO: 10
HEIGHT: 6ft
NICKNAME: JT
EDUCATION: Chipping Norton School, Oxfordshire
TEAMS: Gloucestershire
ROLE: Batter
DEBUT: First-class: 2010; List A: 2011; T20: 2011

BEST BATTING: 156 Gloucestershire vs Northamptonshire, Cheltenham, 2015
BEST BOWLING: 4-16 Gloucestershire vs Glamorgan, Bristol, 2016
COUNTY CAP: 2010

FIRST CRICKET CLUB? Great & Little Tew CC, Oxfordshire
EARLIEST CRICKETING MEMORY? Being in the nets all summer holiday while Dad and Grampy did the ground
WHAT'S THE BIGGEST PRIZE IN DOMESTIC CRICKET? The T20 Blast or County Championship, it's hard to say
THE KOOKABURRA BALL: YES OR NO? Yes – in the middle of the year on harder pitches. It means you have to use different types of skill to have success
OPPONENT YOU MOST LOOK FORWARD TO PLAYING AGAINST? Rashid Khan, the world's best T20 bowler
FAVOURITE WARM-UP SONG? Gbona by Burna Boy
HOW MANY HOURS DO YOU SPEND ON YOUR PHONE A DAY? Two
ONE THING YOU WANT TO DO BEFORE YOU DIE: Eat sushi in Japan
WHICH PUBLIC FIGURE INSPIRES YOU (EXCLUDING SPORTSPEOPLE)? Nelson Mandela
SURPRISING FACT ABOUT YOU: I like getting into bed at 7pm and I have four tattoos
FILM YOU CAN WATCH OVER AND OVER: Wedding Crashers

Batting	Mat	Inns	NO	Runs	HS	Ave	SR	100	50	Ct	St
First-class	91	141	9	3771	156	28.56	62.35	7	12	47	-
List A	85	69	14	2317	139*	42.12	114.25	3	18	36	-
T20s	143	118	29	1996	80*	22.42	138.61	0	5	57	-

Bowling	Mat	Balls	Mdns	Runs	Wkts	BB	Ave	4wI	5wI	SR	Econ
First-class	91	5878	145	3492	76	4-16	45.94	-	0	77.34	3.56
List A	85	1498	4	1346	41	4-31	32.82	2	0	36.53	5.39
T20s	143	718	0	986	27	4-16	36.51	1	0	26.59	8.23

JAMES TAYLOR

RHB / RFM / R0 / W0

FULL NAME: James Philip Arthur Taylor
BORN: January 19, 2001, Stoke-on-Trent, Staffordshire
SQUAD NO: 25
HEIGHT: 6ft 3in
NICKNAME: JT
EDUCATION: Trentham High School, Stoke-on-Trent; Newcastle-under-Lyme College, Staffordshire
TEAMS: Surrey, Derbyshire, England U19
ROLE: Bowler
DEBUT: First-class: 2017; List A: 2019; T20: 2020

SURREY

BEST BATTING: 31* Surrey vs Warwickshire, Edgbaston, 2022
BEST BOWLING: 3-19 Surrey vs Worcestershire, Worcester, 2024

FIRST CRICKET CLUB? Barlaston CC, Staffordshire. Always stay on the front foot because the wicket is slow and low at Barlaston
GREATEST PERFORMANCE YOU HAVE WITNESSED? Wayne Madsen's Championship hundred against Northants at Chesterfield in 2018. On a turning wicket, he made it look easy
WHAT WOULD YOU CHANGE ABOUT THE STRUCTURE OF THE COUNTY SEASON? Begin the season abroad
WHO WOULD YOU MOST AND LEAST LIKE TO HAVE A NET WITH? Most – James Anderson (to learn from him). Least – Mitchell Johnson (danger alert)
HOBBIES? Walking my dog

Batting	Mat	Inns	NO	Runs	HS	Ave	SR	100	50	Ct	St
First-class	12	14	5	140	31*	15.55	30.04	0	0	2	-
List A	9	7	6	31	10*	31.00	77.50	0	0	2	-
T20s	2	1	0	3	3	3.00	50.00	0	0	0	-

Bowling	Mat	Balls	Mdns	Runs	Wkts	BB	Ave	4wI	5wI	SR	Econ
First-class	12	1405	39	874	24	3-19	36.41	-	0	58.54	3.73
List A	9	415	3	404	13	3-43	31.07	0	0	31.92	5.84
T20s	2	12	0	34	1	1-6	34.00	0	0	12.00	17.00

T

GLOUCESTERSHIRE

FULL NAME: Matthew David Taylor
BORN: July 8, 1994, Banbury, Oxfordshire
SQUAD NO: 36
HEIGHT: 6ft 2in
NICKNAME: Bomber
EDUCATION: Chipping Norton Secondary School, Oxfordshire
TEAMS: Gloucestershire
ROLE: Bowler
DEBUT: First-class: 2013; List A: 2011; T20: 2015

BEST BATTING: 57* Gloucestershire vs Derbyshire, Derby, 2023
BEST BOWLING: 5-15 Gloucestershire vs Cardiff MCCU, Bristol, 2018
COUNTY CAP: 2013

FIRST CRICKET CLUB? Great & Little Tew CC, Oxfordshire
FAMILY TIES? My older brother Jack also plays for Gloucestershire. My dad and grandad both played Minor Counties for Oxfordshire
WHAT PART OF THE SEASON DO YOU MOST ENJOY? October!
WHICH AWAY GROUND DO YOU MOST ENJOY VISITING? Hove
WHO IS THE MOST TALENTED U19 TEENAGER IN THE COUNTY GAME? Archie Bailey (Glo)
HOW IS BAZBALL AFFECTING CHAMPIONSHIP CRICKET? We're seeing more shots
WHO IS THE TOUGHEST BOWLER TO FACE? Simon Harmer
WHAT KEEPS YOU AWAKE AT NIGHT? Knowing you've got to bowl tomorrow having just spent a whole day in the field
WHAT'S THE SILLIEST OUTFIT YOU'VE EVER WORN? Bill and Ben the Flowerpot Men

Batting	Mat	Inns	NO	Runs	HS	Ave	SR	100	50	Ct	St
First-class	82	108	38	983	57*	14.04	40.45	0	2	11	-
List A	40	16	8	151	51*	18.87	91.51	0	1	5	-
T20s	71	31	13	170	27	9.44	111.11	0	0	17	-

Bowling	Mat	Balls	Mdns	Runs	Wkts	BB	Ave	4wI	5wI	SR	Econ
First-class	82	12954	426	7243	218	5-15	33.22	-	7	59.42	3.35
List A	40	1802	15	1581	37	4-44	42.72	1	0	48.70	5.26
T20s	71	1363	1	1884	73	4-22	25.80	1	0	18.67	8.29

TOM TAYLOR
RHB / RMF / R0 / W0

FULL NAME: Thomas Alexander Ian Taylor
BORN: December 21, 1994, Stoke-on-Trent, Staffordshire
SQUAD NO: 12
HEIGHT: 6ft 3in
NICKNAME: TT
EDUCATION: Trentham High School, Stoke-on-Trent; Newcastle-under-Lyme College; Leeds Metropolitan University
TEAMS: Worcestershire, Derbyshire, Leicestershire, Northamptonshire
ROLE: Allrounder
DEBUT: First-class: 2014; List A 2014; T20: 2020

WORCESTERSHIRE

BEST BATTING: 80 Derbyshire vs Kent, Derby, 2016
BEST BOWLING: 6-28 Worcestershire vs Warwickshire, Worcester, 2024

FIRST CRICKET CLUB? Barlaston CC, Stoke-on-Trent, Staffordshire
BEST PLAYER IN COUNTY CRICKET (EXCLUDING TEAMMATES)? James Anderson
WHICH COUNTY PLAYER WOULD YOU MOST LIKE TO GO FOR A DRINK WITH? James Taylor at Surrey – always great to catch up with my baby brother
BEST DELIVERY YOU HAVE EVER BOWLED? Normally you don't get wickets with your best balls! But having Hashim Amla as my first-ever first-class wicket will always be special
BEST PERFORMANCE AS A PRO? My 50 not out on debut for Northants in a T20 at Edgbaston to help us qualify for the quarter-finals
GREATEST PERFORMANCE YOU HAVE WITNESSED? Mohammad Abbas taking match figures of 10-52 against Durham at Leicester in 2018
FAVOURITE FORMAT? T20 – the most exciting format
HOBBIES? Sketching
FAVOURITE TOY AS A KID? My Gameboy

Batting	Mat	Inns	NO	Runs	HS	Ave	SR	100	50	Ct	St
First-class	70	109	16	1787	80	19.21	48.25	0	9	21	-
List A	35	25	5	1009	112	50.45	111.00	2	7	17	-
T20s	61	42	18	435	50*	18.12	116.93	0	1	33	-

Bowling	Mat	Balls	Mdns	Runs	Wkts	BB	Ave	4wI	5wI	SR	Econ
First-class	70	10761	356	6102	196	6-28	31.13	-	6	54.90	3.40
List A	35	1604	11	1579	41	3-14	38.51	0	0	39.12	5.90
T20s	61	1085	0	1668	65	5-28	25.66	1	1	16.69	9.22

CHARLIE TEAR

RHB / WK / R0 / W0

SUSSEX

FULL NAME: Charles Joseph Tear
BORN: June 12, 2004, Chichester, Sussex
SQUAD NO: 28
HEIGHT: 5ft 9in
NICKNAME: Thierry
EDUCATION: Westbourne House School, Chichester; Seaford College, West Sussex
TEAMS: Scotland, Sussex, England U19
ROLE: Wicketkeeper/batter
DEBUT: ODI: 2024; T20I: 2024; First-class: 2022; List A: 2023; T20: 2024

BEST BATTING: 56 Sussex vs Glamorgan, Hove, 2022

WHICH TEAMMATE HAS HAD THE BIGGEST IMPACT ON YOUR GAME? Tom Alsop – very helpful in how to mentally approach batting
BEST PERFORMANCE AS A PRO? Scoring 56 in my first innings at Hove in 2022 against Glamorgan, including hitting Ajaz Patel for six fours in a row
GREATEST PERFORMANCE YOU HAVE WITNESSED? Shubman Gill's hundred for Glamorgan at Hove in 2022
FAVOURITE FORMAT? First-class cricket – it's more demanding technically and tactically which makes it more satisfying when you pull off a good performance
WHICH AWAY GROUND DO YOU MOST ENJOY VISITING? Headingley – because it reminds me of Ben Stokes's Ashes innings
CHOOSE A FANTASY SLIP CORDON TO SPEND A DAY IN THE FIELD WITH: Karl Pilkington (wk), Ricky Gervais, Mr Gilbert, Will Mckenzie

Batting	Mat	Inns	NO	Runs	HS	Ave	SR	100	50	Ct	St
ODIs	10	9	3	237	54*	39.50	68.49	0	2	2	-
T20Is	5	5	0	52	16	10.40	82.53	0	0	2	1
First-class	3	5	0	129	56	25.80	55.12	0	1	2	-
List A	17	16	3	324	54*	24.92	66.25	0	2	9	1
T20s	5	5	0	52	16	10.40	82.53	0	0	2	1
Bowling	Mat	Balls	Mdns	Runs	Wkts	BB	Ave	4wI	5wI	SR	Econ
ODIs	10	-	-	-	-	-	-	-	-	-	-
T20Is	5	-	-	-	-	-	-	-	-	-	-
First-class	3	-	-	-	-	-	-	-	-	-	-
List A	17	-	-	-	-	-	-	-	-	-	-
T20s	5	-	-	-	-	-	-	-	-	-	-

NOAH THAIN · RHB / RM / R0 / W0

FULL NAME: Noah Robin Mostyn Thain
BORN: January 13, 2005, Huntingdon, Cambridgeshire
SQUAD NO: 8
HEIGHT: 5ft 11in
NICKNAME: Stouters
EDUCATION: King's College School Cambridge; The Leys School, Cambridge
TEAMS: Essex, England U19
ROLE: Allrounder
DEBUT: First-class: 2023; List A: 2023

BEST BATTING: 36 Essex vs Ireland, Chelmsford, 2023
BEST BOWLING: 1-27 Essex vs Lancashire, Chelmsford, 2024

FIRST CRICKET CLUB? Thriplow CC, Cambridgeshire
WHAT'S THE BIGGEST PRIZE IN DOMESTIC CRICKET? The County Championship
THE KOOKABURRA BALL: YES OR NO? Yes – to help prepare for playing overseas
OPPONENT YOU MOST LOOK FORWARD TO PLAYING AGAINST? Charlie Barnard
FAVOURITE WARM-UP SONG? American Trilogy by Elvis Presley
HOW MANY HOURS DO YOU SPEND ON YOUR PHONE A DAY? Three
ONE THING YOU WANT TO DO BEFORE YOU DIE: Play in a band
HOBBY YOU WOULD LIKE TO LEARN: Surfing
WHICH PUBLIC FIGURE INSPIRES YOU (EXCLUDING SPORTSPEOPLE)? Fray Bentos
FILM YOU CAN WATCH OVER AND OVER: Good Will Hunting

Batting	Mat	Inns	NO	Runs	HS	Ave	SR	100	50	Ct	St
First-class	6	7	0	119	36	17.00	53.84	0	0	2	-
List A	14	14	2	386	83	32.16	76.89	0	4	3	-

Bowling	Mat	Balls	Mdns	Runs	Wkts	BB	Ave	4wI	5wI	SR	Econ
First-class	6	156	0	162	2	1-27	81.00	-	0	78.00	6.23
List A	14	330	1	364	4	1-24	91.00	0	0	82.50	6.61

SHARDUL THAKUR

RHB / RMF / R0 / W0

ESSEX

FULL NAME: Shardul Narendra Thakur
BORN: October 16, 1991, Palghar, Maharashtra, India
SQUAD NO: 54
TEAMS: India, Essex, Chennai Super Kings, Delhi Capitals, Kings XI Punjab, Kolkata Knight Riders, Mumbai, Rising Pune Supergiant
ROLE: Allrounder
DEBUT: Test: 2018; ODI: 2017; T20I: 2018; First-class: 2012; List A: 2014; T20: 2015

BEST BATTING: 119 Mumbia vs Jammu & Kashmir, Mumbai, 2025
BEST BOWLING: 7-61 India vs South Africa, Johannesburg, 2022

NOTES: Essex have secured the services of Indian medium-fast bowler Shardul Thakur for a seven-game spell at the start of the season. Thakur, 33, has been an effective strike bowler at Test level, taking 31 wickets in 11 matches despite being in and out of India's star-packed team since making his debut in 2018. His ability to swing the ball at a reasonable pace has helped him to pick up 298 wickets in 92 first-class matches at a healthy average of 27.52 (stats taken ahead of the 2025 season). Thakur's ability to bat lower down the order will also be a valuable asset for the Eagles. Chris Silverwood, Essex's new director of cricket, said: "We were very clear amongst ourselves that a high-quality quick bowler, with lower-order batting ability, was a key target for the club this winter"

Batting	Mat	Inns	NO	Runs	HS	Ave	SR	100	50	Ct	St
Tests	11	18	1	331	67	19.47	63.40	0	4	5	-
ODIs	47	25	6	329	50*	17.31	105.11	0	1	9	-
T20Is	25	6	3	69	22*	23.00	181.57	0	0	7	-
First-class	92	128	7	2492	119	20.59	69.04	2	16	28	-
List A	118	68	18	998	92	19.96	112.26	0	4	27	-
T20s	168	60	21	441	68	11.30	128.94	0	1	50	-

Bowling	Mat	Balls	Mdns	Runs	Wkts	BB	Ave	4wI	5wI	SR	Econ
Tests	11	1449	36	880	31	7-61	28.38	-	1	46.74	3.64
ODIs	47	1940	10	2014	65	4-37	30.98	3	0	29.84	6.22
T20Is	25	506	0	772	33	4-27	23.39	1	0	15.33	9.15
First-class	92	15306	505	8203	298	7-61	27.52	-	15	51.36	3.21
List A	118	5196	36	5029	180	4-19	27.93	9	0	28.86	5.80
T20s	168	3403	3	5064	189	4-25	26.79	3	0	18.00	8.92

JORDAN THOMPSON

LHB / RMF / R0 / W0

FULL NAME: Jordan Aaron Thompson
BORN: October 9, 1996, Leeds
SQUAD NO: 44
HEIGHT: 6ft 1in
NICKNAME: Lizard
EDUCATION: Benton Park School, Leeds
TEAMS: Yorkshire, Karachi Kings, Hobart Hurricanes, London Spirit, Northern Superchargers, Trent Rockets
ROLE: Allrounder
DEBUT: First-class: 2019; List A: 2019; T20: 2018

BEST BATTING: 98 Yorkshire vs Nottinghamshire, Trent Bridge, 2020
BEST BOWLING: 5-31 Yorkshire vs Leicestershire, Headingley, 2020
COUNTY CAP: 2022

FIRST CRICKET CLUB? Guiseley CC, West Yorkshire
BEST PLAYER IN COUNTY CRICKET (EXCLUDING TEAMMATES)? James Vince
WHICH COUNTY PLAYER WOULD YOU MOST LIKE TO GO FOR A DRINK WITH? Tom Lammonby – he's got decent chat for a southerner
BEST DELIVERY YOU HAVE EVER BOWLED OR FACED? An away-swinging nip-backer to Marnus Labuschagne
BEST PERFORMANCE AS A PRO? My 50 off 18 balls in the 2022 Blast semi-final against Lancashire
GREATEST PERFORMANCE YOU HAVE WITNESSED? Eoin Morgan's 87 not out to chase down 144 in the Abu Dhabi T10 in 2022
FAVOURITE FORMAT? T20 – I love playing in front of big crowds
DESCRIBE YOURSELF IN THREE WORDS: Passionate, joker, competitive
WHAT WOULD BE YOUR PERFECT BREAKFAST? Poached eggs, bacon and avocado on a white muffin

Batting	Mat	Inns	NO	Runs	HS	Ave	SR	100	50	Ct	St
First-class	57	78	7	1534	98	21.60	64.61	0	9	17	-
List A	1	0	-	-	-	-	-	-	-	0	-
T20s	115	88	23	1087	74	16.72	152.66	0	5	40	-

Bowling	Mat	Balls	Mdns	Runs	Wkts	BB	Ave	4wl	5wl	SR	Econ
First-class	57	8452	309	4662	170	5-31	27.42	-	4	49.71	3.30
List A	1	30	0	43	0	0-43	-	-	-	-	8.60
T20s	115	1878	0	2947	119	5-21	24.76	5	1	15.78	9.41

DERBYSHIRE

ALEX THOMSON — RHB / OB / R0 / W0

FULL NAME: Alexander Thomas Thomson
BORN: October 30, 1993, Stoke-on-Trent, Staffordshire
SQUAD NO: 15
HEIGHT: 6ft 5in
NICKNAME: Grizz
EDUCATION: Denstone College, Uttoxeter, Staffordshire; Cardiff Metropolitan University
TEAMS: Derbyshire, Warwickshire
ROLE: Allrounder
DEBUT: First-class: 2014; List A: 2018; T20: 2018

BEST BATTING: 54 Derbyshire vs Worcestershire, Derby, 2022
BEST BOWLING: 7-65 Derbyshire vs Glamorgan, Cardiff, 2024

FIRST CRICKET CLUB? Leek CC, Staffordshire
WHICH AWAY GROUND DO YOU MOST ENJOY VISITING? Scarborough
WHO IS THE MOST TALENTED U19 TEENAGER IN THE COUNTY GAME? Harry Moore (Der)
IF YOU COULD PINCH A PLAYER FROM ANOTHER COUNTY, WHO WOULD IT BE? Graham Clark
WHICH PUBLIC FIGURE INSPIRES YOU (EXCLUDING SPORTSPEOPLE)? Matthew Bowcock
FILM YOU CAN WATCH OVER AND OVER: Coach Carter

Batting	Mat	Inns	NO	Runs	HS	Ave	SR	100	50	Ct	St
First-class	47	64	5	996	54	16.88	46.26	0	2	18	-
List A	26	21	7	441	68*	31.50	90.74	0	2	7	-
T20s	33	18	9	184	28	20.44	135.29	0	0	6	-

Bowling	Mat	Balls	Mdns	Runs	Wkts	BB	Ave	4wI	5wI	SR	Econ
First-class	47	7461	211	4095	104	7-65	39.37	-	5	71.74	3.29
List A	26	1050	2	981	31	3-25	31.64	0	0	33.87	5.60
T20s	33	582	0	827	24	4-35	34.45	1	0	24.25	8.52

BLAIR TICKNER

RHB / RMF / R0 / W0

FULL NAME: Blair Marshall Tickner
BORN: October 13, 1993, Napier, Hawke's Bay, New Zealand
SQUAD NO: 13
TEAMS: New Zealand, Derbyshire, Central Districts
ROLE: Bowler
DEBUT: Test: 2023; ODI: 2022; T20I: 2019; First-class: 2015; List A: 2016; T20: 2016

BEST BATTING: 47 Derbyshire vs Sussex, Derby, 2024
BEST BOWLING: 5-23 Central Districts vs Canterbury, Napier, 2018

NOTES: The New Zealand fast bowler has been re-signed by Derbyshire and is due to be available across all formats for the duration of the season. Tickner had to cut short his stint at the club last summer after his wife was diagnosed with leukaemia. The 31-year-old has played for his country in all formats and made his Test debut against England in 2023. In New Zealand he plays for Central Districts. Derbyshire head of cricket Mickey Arthur said: "We never got to see the best of Blair in his first spell with us, there was a lot going on off the field, but he was the consummate professional and we were always eager to bring him back for 2025. His record deserved to be better last season, we dropped chances off his bowling and if we take those, his average comes right down. With the likes of Zak Chappell, Harry Moore, Pat Brown and Blair all vying to take the new ball, I'm very excited about our attack in 2025"

Batting	Mat	Inns	NO	Runs	HS	Ave	SR	100	50	Ct	St
Tests	3	3	2	13	8	13.00	22.41	0	0	1	-
ODIs	13	7	5	16	6*	8.00	57.14	0	0	5	-
T20Is	18	4	2	11	5*	5.50	47.82	0	0	2	-
First-class	80	91	35	738	47	13.17	34.97	0	0	33	-
List A	67	31	18	172	24*	13.23	64.90	0	0	21	-
T20s	99	18	10	52	22	6.50	88.13	0	0	21	-

Bowling	Mat	Balls	Mdns	Runs	Wkts	BB	Ave	4wI	5wI	SR	Econ
Tests	3	635	10	435	12	4-100	36.25	-	0	52.91	4.11
ODIs	13	623	4	679	16	4-50	42.43	1	0	38.93	6.53
T20Is	18	341	0	536	19	4-27	28.21	1	0	17.94	9.43
First-class	80	14386	407	8282	236	5-23	35.09	-	5	60.95	3.45
List A	67	3232	23	2931	93	4-37	31.51	4	0	34.75	5.44
T20s	99	2063	3	3055	130	5-19	23.50	5	1	15.86	8.88

JOSH TONGUE

RHB / RMF / R0 / W0

NOTTINGHAMSHIRE

FULL NAME: Joshua Charles Tongue
BORN: November 15, 1997, Redditch, Worcestershire
SQUAD NO: TBC
HEIGHT: 6ft 4in
EDUCATION: King's School, Worcester; Christopher Whitehead Language College, Worcester
TEAMS: England, Nottinghamshire, Manchester Originals, Worcestershire
ROLE: Bowler
DEBUT: Test: 2023; First-class: 2016; List A: 2017; T20: 2017

BEST BATTING: 45* Worcestershire vs Nottinghamshire, Worcester, 2022
BEST BOWLING: 6-97 Worcestershire vs Glamorgan, Worcester, 2017

FIRST CRICKET CLUB? Redditch CC, Worcestershire
BIGGEST INFLUENCE ON YOUR DEVELOPMENT AS A CRICKETER (EXCLUDING PARENTS)?
Former Worcestershire allrounder Gavin Haynes – he was my first coach at the club's Academy and he's happy to help out even now
WHICH TEAMMATE HAS HAD THE BIGGEST IMPACT ON YOUR GAME? Joe Leach
WHAT PART OF THE SEASON DO YOU MOST ENJOY? The first game of the season
WHICH AWAY GROUND DO YOU MOST ENJOY VISITING? The Oval
WHO IS THE TOUGHEST BOWLER TO FACE? Pat Cummins
WHAT KEEPS YOU AWAKE AT NIGHT? A crying baby
CHOOSE A FANTASY SLIP CORDON TO SPEND A DAY IN THE FIELD WITH: Margot Robbie (wk), Ted Lasso, Conor McGregor, Tyson Fury

Batting	Mat	Inns	NO	Runs	HS	Ave	SR	100	50	Ct	St
Tests	2	2	0	20	19	10.00	66.66	0	0	1	-
First-class	51	66	16	640	45*	12.80	46.14	0	0	6	-
List A	15	8	3	99	34	19.80	103.12	0	0	3	-
T20s	15	3	2	4	2*	4.00	100.00	0	0	5	-

Bowling	Mat	Balls	Mdns	Runs	Wkts	BB	Ave	4wI	5wI	SR	Econ
Tests	2	456	13	257	10	5-66	25.70	-	1	45.60	3.38
First-class	51	8038	221	4562	177	6-97	25.77	-	9	45.41	3.40
List A	15	631	0	728	16	2-35	45.50	0	0	39.43	6.92
T20s	15	250	0	397	15	3-32	26.46	0	0	16.66	9.52

REECE TOPLEY   RHB / LFM / R0 / W0

FULL NAME: Reece James William Topley
BORN: February 21, 1994, Ipswich
SQUAD NO: 24
HEIGHT: 6ft 7in
EDUCATION: Royal Hospital School, Suffolk
TEAMS: England, Surrey, Durban's Super Giants, Essex, Hampshire, Melbourne Renegades, Northern Superchargers, Oval Invincibles, RC Bangalore, Sussex, Sylhet Strikers
ROLE: Bowler
DEBUT: ODI: 2015; T20I: 2015;
First-class: 2011; List A: 2011; T20: 2012

BEST BATTING: 16 Hampshire vs Yorkshire, Southampton, 2017
BEST BOWLING: 6-29 Essex vs Worcestershire, Chelmsford, 2013
COUNTY CAP: 2013 (Essex)

FAMILY TIES? My father Don played for Essex and Surrey and also coached Zimbabwe. My uncle Peter played for Kent
BIGGEST INFLUENCE ON YOUR DEVELOPMENT AS A CRICKETER (EXCLUDING PARENTS)? Chris Silverwood, my bowling coach when I was at Essex
CHILDHOOD SPORTING HERO? Kobe Bryant
SURPRISING FACT ABOUT YOU: I speak Spanish

Batting	Mat	Inns	NO	Runs	HS	Ave	SR	100	50	Ct	St
ODIs	30	14	11	35	15*	11.66	50.00	0	0	7	-
T20Is	35	10	8	17	9	8.50	85.00	0	0	6	-
First-class	46	54	22	132	16	4.12	20.56	0	0	8	-
List A	75	26	18	82	19	10.25	57.34	0	0	18	-
T20s	190	44	34	117	14*	11.70	90.69	0	0	35	-

Bowling	Mat	Balls	Mdns	Runs	Wkts	BB	Ave	4wI	5wI	SR	Econ
ODIs	30	1392	17	1257	47	6-24	26.74	2	1	29.61	5.41
T20Is	35	706	0	978	33	3-22	29.63	0	0	21.39	8.31
First-class	46	7932	273	4382	163	6-29	26.88	-	8	48.66	3.31
List A	75	3487	26	3213	124	6-24	25.91	10	1	28.12	5.52
T20s	190	3804	5	5338	230	4-20	23.20	5	0	16.53	8.41

LIAM TREVASKIS

RHB / SLA / RO / WO

LEICESTERSHIRE

FULL NAME: Liam Trevaskis
BORN: April 18, 1999, Carlisle, Cumberland
SQUAD NO: 80
HEIGHT: 5ft 10in
NICKNAME: T-rev
EDUCATION: Queen Elizabeth Grammar School, Penrith, Cumbria
TEAMS: Leicestershire, Durham, England U19
ROLE: Allrounder
DEBUT: First-class: 2017; List A: 2019; T20: 2017

BEST BATTING: 88 Durham vs Sussex, Hove, 2022
BEST BOWLING: 5-78 Durham vs Gloucestershire, Bristol, 2021

FIRST CRICKET CLUB? Penrith CC, Cumbria
EARLIEST CRICKETING MEMORY? My first-ever session at Penrith CC at five years old
WHAT'S THE BIGGEST PRIZE IN DOMESTIC CRICKET? Division One of the County Championship
THE KOOKABURRA BALL: YES OR NO? Yes, but it has to be in the middle of the year
FAVOURITE WARM-UP SONG? Coal by Dylan Gossett
HOW MANY HOURS DO YOU SPEND ON YOUR PHONE A DAY? Three
SPECIALITY SUBJECT IN A PUB QUIZ (EXCLUDING SPORT)? Film quotes
HOBBY YOU WOULD LIKE TO LEARN: Axe-throwing
SURPRISING FACT ABOUT YOU: I broke my neck and didn't know
FILM YOU CAN WATCH OVER AND OVER: Step Brothers

Batting	Mat	Inns	NO	Runs	HS	Ave	SR	100	50	Ct	St
First-class	34	51	11	1291	88	32.27	43.48	0	10	14	-
List A	42	35	7	647	76*	23.10	88.14	0	4	11	-
T20s	68	45	19	379	31*	14.57	125.08	0	0	41	-

Bowling	Mat	Balls	Mdns	Runs	Wkts	BB	Ave	4wI	5wI	SR	Econ
First-class	34	3929	127	2075	38	5-78	54.60	-	2	103.39	3.16
List A	42	1801	9	1610	45	4-50	35.77	2	0	40.02	5.36
T20s	68	1252	1	1659	56	4-16	29.62	1	0	22.35	7.95

ASHTON TURNER

RHB / OB / RO / WO

FULL NAME: Ashton James Turner
BORN: January 25, 1993, Perth, Australia
SQUAD NO: TBC
TEAMS: Australia, Lancashire, Durham, Lucknow Super Giants, Manchester Originals, Perth Scorchers, Pretoria Capitals, Rajasthan Royals, Western Australia
ROLE: Batter
DEBUT: ODI: 2019; T20I: 2017;
First-class: 2013; List A: 2013; T20: 2013

BEST BATTING: 84* Perth Scorchers vs Sydney Sixers, Perth, 2023 (T20)
BEST BOWLING: 3-20 Durham vs Warwickshire, Edgbaston, 2023 (T20)

NOTES: Lancashire have signed the Australian batter for the first eight games of the Blast. Turner, who is also a handy spin bowler, will also be available for three Championship matches during his time at Old Trafford. He has spent the past three English summers playing T20 for Durham, scoring 693 runs in 36 matches at an average of 33 and claiming nine wickets with his off-breaks. He has a wealth of white-ball experience, having played 28 times for Australia between 2017 and 2023 and had two stints in the IPL. "To have the opportunity to join one of the biggest clubs in England is a really exciting one for me," Turner said. "The Blast is a competition that I have loved playing in, while testing myself in the County Championship is something I have always wanted to do, so I can't wait for that"

Batting	Mat	Inns	NO	Runs	HS	Ave	SR	100	50	Ct	St
ODIs	9	7	1	192	84*	32.00	120.00	0	1	4	-
T20Is	19	14	5	110	24	12.22	83.96	0	0	7	-
First-class	57	92	10	2880	128	35.12	54.54	5	13	67	-
List A	75	70	14	1834	100	32.75	96.52	1	10	41	-
T20s	214	185	52	3428	84*	25.77	141.47	0	16	86	-

Bowling	Mat	Balls	Mdns	Runs	Wkts	BB	Ave	4wI	5wI	SR	Econ
ODIs	9	84	1	60	2	1-23	30.00	0	0	42.00	4.28
T20Is	19	78	0	82	4	2-12	20.50	0	0	19.50	6.30
First-class	57	1112	36	599	12	6-111	49.91	-	1	92.66	3.23
List A	75	613	2	573	16	2-14	35.81	0	0	38.31	5.60
T20s	214	664	0	833	34	3-20	24.50	0	0	19.52	7.52

JOHN TURNER

RHB / RFM / R0 / W0

FULL NAME: John Andrew Turner
BORN: April 10, 2001, Leicester
SQUAD NO: 6
HEIGHT: 6ft 1in
NICKNAME: JT
EDUCATION: Hilton College, Johannesburg; Exeter University
TEAMS: England, Hampshire, Trent Rockets, Paarl Royals
ROLE: Bowler
DEBUT: ODI: 2024; T20I: 2024; First-class: 2022; List A: 2021; T20: 2023

BEST BATTING: 7 Hampshire vs Essex, Southampton, 2023
BEST BOWLING: 5-31 Hampshire vs Sri Lanka Development XI, 2022

WHICH TEAMMATE HAS HAD THE BIGGEST IMPACT ON YOUR GAME? I have to give you three: Keith Barker, Kyle Abbott and Nathan Ellis – they have all taken me under their wing and helped me develop different aspects of my game
WHAT PART OF THE SEASON DO YOU MOST ENJOY? The T20 Blast
WHICH AWAY GROUND DO YOU MOST ENJOY VISITING? The Oval – great place for a fast bowler because of the wicket. And it's always fun being in London
WHO IS THE MOST TALENTED U19 TEENAGER IN THE COUNTY GAME? Dom Kelly (Ham)
WHAT DO YOU THINK OF THE CURRENT 50-OVER COMPETITION? A great competition which offers inexperienced players the chance to play against quality opponents
WHAT'S THE SILLIEST OUTFIT YOU'VE EVER WORN? An elephant costume
CHOOSE A FANTASY SLIP CORDON TO SPEND A DAY IN THE FIELD WITH: Nelson Mandela (wk), James Bond, Andrew Flintoff

Batting	Mat	Inns	NO	Runs	HS	Ave	SR	100	50	Ct	St
ODIs	2	1	1	2	2*	-	40.00	0	0	0	-
T20Is	2	0	-	-	-	-	-	-	-	0	-
First-class	5	6	1	11	7	2.20	36.66	0	0	0	-
List A	19	10	7	36	12	12.00	45.56	0	0	2	-
T20s	29	6	5	8	3*	8.00	66.66	0	0	4	-

Bowling	Mat	Balls	Mdns	Runs	Wkts	BB	Ave	4wI	5wI	SR	Econ
ODIs	2	66	0	68	2	2-42	34.00	0	0	33.00	6.18
T20Is	2	36	0	64	1	1-42	64.00	0	0	36.00	10.66
First-class	5	507	15	278	14	5-31	19.85	-	1	36.21	3.28
List A	19	791	7	665	37	5-25	17.97	2	2	21.37	5.04
T20s	29	553	2	755	43	4-23	17.55	1	0	12.86	8.19

ZAIN UL HASSAN　　　LHB / RM / RO / WO

FULL NAME: Zain ul Hassan
BORN: October 28, 2000, Islamabad, Punjab, Pakistan
SQUAD NO: 27
HEIGHT: 5ft 9in
NICKNAME: Zazu
EDUCATION: Pedmore Technical College, Stourbridge; King Edward VI College
TEAMS: Glamorgan, Worcestershire
ROLE: Allrounder
DEBUT: First-class: 2023; List A: 2018; T20: 2023

GLAMORGAN

BEST BATTING: 69 Glamorgan vs Derbyshire, Derby, 2023
BEST BOWLING: 2-18 Glamorgan vs Worcestershire, Worcester, 2023

FIRST CRICKET CLUB? Stourbridge CC, West Midlands
WHAT'S THE BIGGEST PRIZE IN DOMESTIC CRICKET? Winning the County Championship
THE KOOKABURRA BALL: YES OR NO? Yes, you have to adapt to it so it brings in new skills
OPPONENT YOU MOST LOOK FORWARD TO PLAYING AGAINST? Zen Malik – we've played together for a long time, he's a good friend and a quality player
FAVOURITE WARM-UP SONG? Not Like Us by Kendrick Lamar
HOW MANY HOURS DO YOU SPEND ON YOUR PHONE A DAY? Six
SPECIALITY SUBJECT IN A PUB QUIZ (EXCLUDING SPORT)? General knowledge
ONE THING YOU WANT TO DO BEFORE YOU DIE: A skydive
HOBBY YOU WOULD LIKE TO LEARN: Padel
SURPRISING FACT ABOUT YOU: I broke my leg playing cricket
FILM YOU CAN WATCH OVER AND OVER: The Avengers

Batting	Mat	Inns	NO	Runs	HS	Ave	SR	100	50	Ct	St
First-class	15	26	2	618	69	25.75	40.10	0	2	3	-
List A	5	5	2	47	26*	15.66	70.14	0	0	0	-
T20s	3	2	1	14	11	14.00	155.55	0	0	1	-

Bowling	Mat	Balls	Mdns	Runs	Wkts	BB	Ave	4wI	5wI	SR	Econ
First-class	15	1338	36	713	8	2-18	89.12	-	0	167.25	3.19
List A	5	168	0	186	7	4-25	26.57	1	0	24.00	6.64
T20s	3	54	0	114	0	0-23	-	-	-	-	12.66

ANDY UMEED

RHB / LB / RO / WO

SOMERSET

FULL NAME: Andrew Robert Isaac Umeed
BORN: April 19, 1996, Glasgow
SQUAD NO: 1
HEIGHT: 6ft 1in
EDUCATION: The High School of Glasgow
TEAMS: Scotland, Somerset, Warwickshire
ROLE: Batter
DEBUT: ODI: 2024;
First-class: 2015; List A: 2018

BEST BATTING: 113 Warwickshire vs Lancashire, Edgbaston, 2017
BEST BOWLING: 1-3 Somerset vs Warwickshire, Edgbaston, 2024

NOTES: After four years out of the professional game, the former Warwickshire batter returned to the big time in 2022 after signing a deal with Somerset which lasts until the end of this season. "I'm really grateful for this opportunity and it means everything to me – being a cricketer is all I've ever wanted to do," said the 27-year-old after agreeing terms with the club. Umeed was limited to a bit-part role in red-ball cricket in 2023 but produced some scintillating form in the One-Day Cup which brought him a staggering 613 runs in just eight innings with three hundreds, including an unbeaten 172 off 147 balls at Derby. He was underwhelming across formats last summer

Batting	Mat	Inns	NO	Runs	HS	Ave	SR	100	50	Ct	St
ODIs	5	4	1	138	98*	46.00	99.28	0	1	1	-
First-class	30	52	3	1074	113	21.91	43.78	2	2	24	-
List A	29	28	3	1375	172*	55.00	89.81	4	8	9	-
Bowling	Mat	Balls	Mdns	Runs	Wkts	BB	Ave	4wI	5wI	SR	Econ
ODIs	5	-	-	-	-	-	-	-	-	-	-
First-class	30	325	4	233	3	1-3	77.66	-	0	108.33	4.30
List A	29	60	0	37	4	3-31	9.25	0	0	15.00	3.70

JAYDEV UNADKAT

RHB / LFM / R0 / W0

FULL NAME: Jaydev Dipakbhai Unadkat
BORN: October 18, 1991, Porbandar, Saurashtra, India
SQUAD NO: 91
TEAMS: India, Sussex, Delhi Daredevils, Kolkata Knight Riders, Lucknow Super Giants, Mumbai Indians, Royal Challengers Bangalore, Saurashtra, Sunrisers
ROLE: Bowler
DEBUT: Test: 2010; ODI: 2013; T20I: 2016; First-class: 2010; List A: 2010: T20: 2010

BEST BATTING: 92 Saurashtra vs Jammu & Kashmir, Jammu, 2015
BEST BOWLING: 8-39 Saurashtra vs Delhi, Rajkot, 2023
COUNTY CAP: 2024

NOTES: The experienced Indian left-arm swing bowler and IPL stalwart is a popular part of the set-up at Hove. It was his starring role at the backend of 2024 that helped clinch Sussex the Division Two title. Unadkat played the final five games, taking 22 wickets at an average of 14.4, performances which earned him a two-year red-ball extension that will kick in for the final stages of this campaign. Coach Paul Farbrace welcomed Unadkat's return for the business end of their first season back in the top tier since 2015. "Everyone at Hove is very pleased and excited that Jaydev has signed a two-year extension and will be returning to the club for the next two seasons," he told the club's website. "Jaydev's quality on the pitch has been so evident for everyone else to see, but just as importantly his qualities as a person make him one of the most popular and nicest guys any team could wish for"

Batting	Mat	Inns	NO	Runs	HS	Ave	SR	100	50	Ct	St
Tests	4	5	2	36	14*	12.00	40.44	0	0	3	-
ODIs	8	0	-	-	-	-	-	-	-	1	-
T20Is	10	0	-	-	-	-	-	-	-	3	-
First-class	127	163	36	2133	92	16.79	51.04	0	8	53	-
List A	130	69	14	643	57	11.69	78.51	0	1	33	-
T20s	199	77	41	562	58*	15.61	130.09	0	1	59	-

Bowling	Mat	Balls	Mdns	Runs	Wkts	BB	Ave	4wI	5wI	SR	Econ
Tests	4	474	17	231	3	2-50	77.00	-	0	158.00	2.92
ODIs	8	342	5	225	9	4-41	25.00	1	0	38.00	3.94
T20Is	10	208	0	301	14	3-38	21.50	0	0	14.85	8.68
First-class	127	20921	787	10340	447	8-39	23.13	-	24	46.80	2.96
List A	130	6811	97	5385	185	5-23	29.10	6	3	36.81	4.74
T20s	199	4232	7	5659	234	5-25	24.18	3	2	18.08	8.02

LOGAN VAN BEEK

RHB / RFM / R0 / W0

FULL NAME: Logan Verjus van Beek
BORN: September 7, 1990, Christchurch, New Zealand
SQUAD NO: TBC
HEIGHT: 6ft
EDUCATION: University of Canterbury, New Zealand
TEAMS: Netherlands, Leicestershire, Canterbury, Derbyshire, Wellington, Worcestershire
ROLE: Allrounder
DEBUT: ODI: 2021; T20I: 2014; First-class: 2010; List A: 2010; T20: 2012

BEST BATTING: 111* Canterbury vs Otago, Christchurch, 2015
BEST BOWLING: 6-46 Canterbury vs Otago, Christchurch, 2015

FIRST CRICKET CLUB? Old Boys Collegians CC, Christchurch, New Zealand
EARLIEST CRICKETING MEMORY? Backyard cricket with my grandpa
WHAT'S THE BIGGEST PRIZE IN DOMESTIC CRICKET? Winning the T20 Blast
THE KOOKABURRA BALL: YES OR NO? No, because the majority of pitches are on the slow side. Plus I'm a bowler!
OPPONENT YOU MOST LOOK FORWARD TO PLAYING AGAINST? Any Kiwis
SPECIALITY SUBJECT IN A PUB QUIZ (EXCLUDING SPORT)? Modern history
ONE THING YOU WANT TO DO BEFORE YOU DIE: Have a big family
SURPRISING FACT ABOUT YOU: I wanted to be a Michael Jackson back-up dancer when I was a kid
FILM YOU CAN WATCH OVER AND OVER: Independence Day

Batting	Mat	Inns	NO	Runs	HS	Ave	SR	100	50	Ct	St
ODIs	33	32	10	477	59	21.68	80.03	0	1	17	-
T20Is	31	19	6	100	23	7.69	80.00	0	0	18	-
First-class	85	122	25	2411	111*	24.85	52.47	2	11	56	-
List A	150	117	28	1694	136	19.03	85.98	1	5	80	-
T20s	170	98	34	858	61*	13.40	124.16	0	2	87	-

Bowling	Mat	Balls	Mdns	Runs	Wkts	BB	Ave	4wl	5wl	SR	Econ
ODIs	33	1713	15	1612	46	4-24	35.04	3	0	37.23	5.64
T20Is	31	558	2	698	36	4-27	19.38	1	0	15.50	7.50
First-class	85	13393	412	7495	236	6-46	31.75	-	9	56.75	3.35
List A	150	6590	56	6291	194	6-18	32.42	7	1	33.96	5.72
T20s	170	3136	5	4388	177	4-15	24.79	3	0	17.71	8.39

GRAEME VAN BUUREN — RHB / SLA / RO / WO

FULL NAME: Graeme Lourens van Buuren
BORN: August 22, 1990, Pretoria, South Africa
SQUAD NO: 12
HEIGHT: 5ft 7in
NICKNAME: GV
EDUCATION: Pretoria Boys High School, South Africa
TEAMS: Gloucestershire, Birmingham Phoenix, Northerns, Titans, South Africa U19
ROLE: Allrounder
DEBUT: First-class: 2010; List A: 2010; T20: 2011

GLOUCESTERSHIRE

BEST BATTING: 235 Northerns vs Eastern Province, Centurion, 2015
BEST BOWLING: 4-12 Northerns vs South Western Districts, Oudtshoorn, 2013
COUNTY CAP: 2016

FIRST CRICKET CLUB? Tuks CC, Pretoria, South Africa
MOST EXCITING DAY AS A CRICKETER? Winning promotion with Gloucestershire in 2019
WHAT WOULD YOU DO IF YOU WERE IN CHARGE OF COUNTY CRICKET? Keep with the current Championship structure, look at staging tournaments in Dubai
CHILDHOOD SPORTING HERO? AB de Villiers
NOTES: After three years as Gloucestershire club captain, van Buuren stepped down from the role in January, with Cameron Bancroft taking over in four-day cricket and Jack Taylor continuing to lead in the white-ball formats

Batting	Mat	Inns	NO	Runs	HS	Ave	SR	100	50	Ct	St
First-class	129	203	32	6977	235	40.80	62.47	15	41	70	-
List A	94	83	15	1964	119*	28.88	82.90	2	8	28	-
T20s	88	66	22	993	64	22.56	120.65	0	4	37	-

Bowling	Mat	Balls	Mdns	Runs	Wkts	BB	Ave	4wI	5wI	SR	Econ
First-class	129	7563	223	3772	110	4-12	34.29	-	0	68.75	2.99
List A	94	3027	11	2448	76	5-35	32.21	2	1	39.82	4.85
T20s	88	1178	0	1421	53	5-8	26.81	0	1	22.22	7.23

TIMM VAN DER GUGTEN — RHB / RFM / RO / W1

GLAMORGAN

FULL NAME: Timm van der Gugten
BORN: February 25, 1991, Sydney, Australia
SQUAD NO: 64
HEIGHT: 6ft 2in
EDUCATION: St Pius X College, Sydney; Swinburne University, Melbourne
TEAMS: Netherlands, Glamorgan, Birmingham Phoenix, Hobart Hurricanes, New South Wales, Northern Districts, Tasmania, Trent Rockets
ROLE: Bowler
DEBUT: ODI: 2012; T20I: 2012; First-class: 2011; List A: 2011; T20: 2012

BEST BATTING: 85* Glamorgan vs Yorkshire, Headingley, 2021
BEST BOWLING: 7-42 Glamorgan vs Kent, Cardiff, 2018
COUNTY CAP: 2018

FIRST CRICKET CLUB? Normanhurst-Warrawee CC, New South Wales, Australia
BEST DELIVERY YOU HAVE EVER FACED? An off-cutter from a left-armer which got me for a golden duck. When the ball was halfway down the wicket, the keeper said 'bowled', and I was
FAVOURITE FORMAT? Four-day cricket because of the tactics it involves. Nothing better than executing a plan
DESCRIBE YOURSELF IN THREE WORDS: Dad, happy, curious
HOBBIES? Crosswords

Batting	Mat	Inns	NO	Runs	HS	Ave	SR	100	50	Ct	St
ODIs	14	9	2	118	49	16.85	69.41	0	0	1	-
T20Is	49	15	5	168	40*	16.80	135.48	0	0	12	-
First-class	87	119	37	1658	85*	20.21	47.96	0	7	23	-
List A	82	49	16	613	49	18.57	86.33	0	0	13	-
T20s	138	62	23	555	48	14.23	137.37	0	0	36	-

Bowling	Mat	Balls	Mdns	Runs	Wkts	BB	Ave	4wI	5wI	SR	Econ
ODIs	14	510	10	291	14	5-24	20.78	0	1	36.42	3.42
T20Is	49	913	1	1150	52	3-9	22.11	0	0	17.55	7.55
First-class	87	15018	518	7796	285	7-42	27.35	-	15	52.69	3.11
List A	82	3652	57	3050	94	5-24	32.44	2	2	38.85	5.01
T20s	138	2578	9	3595	159	5-21	22.61	4	1	16.21	8.36

RICARDO VASCONCELOS

LHB / WK / R0 / W0

FULL NAME: Ricardo Surrador Vasconcelos
BORN: October 27, 1997, Johannesburg, South Africa
SQUAD NO: 27
HEIGHT: 5ft 5in
NICKNAME: Vasco
EDUCATION: St Stithians College, Johannesburg; Stellenbosch University, Western Cape
TEAMS: Northamptonshire, Boland, South Africa U19
ROLE: Batter/wicketkeeper
DEBUT: First-class: 2016; List A: 2016; T20: 2017

BEST BATTING: 185* Northamptonshire vs Glamorgan, Northampton, 2021

COUNTY CAP: 2021

FIRST CRICKET CLUB? Old Edwardians CC, Johannesburg
THE KOOKABURRA BALL: YES OR NO? Yes, but at the right time of year. It's used in other parts of the world, so if you want to make that step you are going to need to have the experience and skill to play with it
OPPONENT YOU MOST LOOK FORWARD TO PLAYING AGAINST? My former Northants teammate Emilio Gay
FAVOURITE WARM-UP SONG? Saif Zaib is usually on the speaker so whatever he's playing
HOW MANY HOURS DO YOU SPEND ON YOUR PHONE A DAY? Four to five
SPECIALITY SUBJECT IN A PUB QUIZ (EXCLUDING SPORT)? Board games
ONE THING YOU WANT TO DO BEFORE YOU DIE: Skydive
HOBBY YOU WOULD LIKE TO LEARN: Carpentry
SURPRISING FACT ABOUT YOU: I'm Portuguese but can't speak the language
FILM YOU CAN WATCH OVER AND OVER: The Shawshank Redemption

Batting	Mat	Inns	NO	Runs	HS	Ave	SR	100	50	Ct	St
First-class	84	151	9	4797	185*	33.78	56.69	10	22	133	7
List A	56	55	2	1657	112	31.26	81.70	4	8	36	3
T20s	48	47	4	1162	78*	27.02	124.67	0	5	27	2

Bowling	Mat	Balls	Mdns	Runs	Wkts	BB	Ave	4wI	5wI	SR	Econ
First-class	84	45	0	43	0	0-0	-	-	-	-	5.73
List A	56	-	-	-	-	-	-	-	-	-	-
T20s	48	-	-	-	-	-	-	-	-	-	-

ARCHIE VAUGHAN — RHB / OB / R0 / W0

SOMERSET

FULL NAME: Archie Matthew Vaughan
BORN: December 9, 2005, Sheffield
SQUAD NO: 66
HEIGHT: 6ft 3in
NICKNAME: Conductor
EDUCATION: Millfield School, Somerset
TEAMS: Somerset, England U19
ROLE: Allrounder
DEBUT: First-class: 2024; List A: 2024

BEST BATTING: 68 Somerset vs Lancashire, Old Trafford, 2024
BEST BOWLING: 6-102 Somerset vs Surrey, Taunton, 2024

FIRST CRICKET CLUB? Sheffield Collegiate CC, Sheffield
EARLIEST CRICKETING MEMORY? Playing with my dad in the garden
WHAT'S THE BIGGEST PRIZE IN DOMESTIC CRICKET? The County Championship
THE KOOKABURRA BALL: YES OR NO? Yes
OPPONENT YOU MOST LOOK FORWARD TO PLAYING AGAINST? Surrey
FAVOURITE WARM-UP SONG? Can't Stop by Red Hot Chilli Peppers
HOW MANY HOURS DO YOU SPEND ON YOUR PHONE A DAY? 2.5
SPECIALITY SUBJECT IN A PUB QUIZ (EXCLUDING SPORT)? Music
ONE THING YOU WANT TO DO BEFORE YOU DIE: Make a hole-in-one
SURPRISING FACT ABOUT YOU: I can play the piano (a bit)
FILM YOU CAN WATCH OVER AND OVER: The Hangover

Batting	Mat	Inns	NO	Runs	HS	Ave	SR	100	50	Ct	St
First-class	4	8	1	236	68	33.71	51.64	0	1	1	-
List A	7	4	2	72	32*	36.00	116.12	0	0	1	-

Bowling	Mat	Balls	Mdns	Runs	Wkts	BB	Ave	4wI	5wI	SR	Econ
First-class	4	766	37	302	15	6-102	20.13	-	2	51.06	2.36
List A	7	90	0	63	3	1-7	21.00	0	0	30.00	4.20

KYLE VERREYNNE
RHB / WK / R0 / W0

FULL NAME: Kyle Verreynne
BORN: May 12, 1997, Pretoria, South Africa
SQUAD NO: 7
TEAMS: South Africa, Nottinghamshire, Cape Cobras, Cape Town Blitz, Joburg Super Kings, Paarl Rocks, Pretoria Capitals, Western Province
ROLE: Batter/wicketkeeper
DEBUT: Test: 2021; ODI: 2020; First-class: 2015; List A: 2015; T20: 2016

NOTTINGHAMSHIRE

BEST BATTING: 216* Cape Cobras vs Warriors, Cape Town, 2021

NOTES: South Africa's first-choice Test keeper only managed three Championship games for Notts last season but played a useful hand in the club's successful push to avoid the drop, keeping tidily – he is one of the international game's most adept glovemen – and making 148 not out against Warwickshire and an unbeaten half-century against Surrey. Verreynne is expected to be available for 12 of the club's 14 first-class fixtures this summer and will want to be exposed to English conditions as much as possible ahead of the World Test Championship final against Australia in early June. Of his experiences last year, he said: "I thought the competition was of a really good standard – when you've played international cricket, you still want to be tested at domestic level, so I really enjoyed adapting to English conditions. I know the challenge could be different next year in the early part of the summer, but I'm sure that will be beneficial to me"

Batting	Mat	Inns	NO	Runs	HS	Ave	SR	100	50	Ct	St
Tests	24	37	4	1060	136*	32.12	58.20	4	3	70	7
ODIs	19	16	2	533	95	38.07	90.64	0	5	11	1
First-class	91	138	20	5872	216*	49.76	63.59	13	33	270	20
List A	69	58	6	1934	114*	37.19	92.84	3	13	77	10
T20s	82	74	12	1620	116*	26.12	132.24	1	4	37	5

Bowling	Mat	Balls	Mdns	Runs	Wkts	BB	Ave	4wI	5wI	SR	Econ
Tests	24	-	-	-	-	-	-	-	-	-	-
ODIs	19	-	-	-	-	-	-	-	-	-	-
First-class	91	-	-	-	-	-	-	-	-	-	-
List A	69	-	-	-	-	-	-	-	-	-	-
T20s	82	-	-	-	-	-	-	-	-	-	-

JAMES VINCE   RHB / RM / R3 / W0 / MVP2

HAMPSHIRE

FULL NAME: James Michael Vince
BORN: March 14, 1991, Cuckfield, Sussex
SQUAD NO: 14
HEIGHT: 6ft 2in
NICKNAME: JV
EDUCATION: Warminster School, Wiltshire
TEAMS: England, Hampshire, Southern Brave, Auckland, Karachi Kings, Multan Sultans, Paarl Rocks, Quetta Gladiators, Rangpur Riders, Sydney Sixers, Sydney Thunder
ROLE: Batter
DEBUT: Test: 2016; ODI: 2015; T20I: 2015; First-class: 2009; List A: 2009; T20: 2010

BEST BATTING: 129* Hampshire vs Somerset, Taunton, 2022 (T20)
BEST BOWLING: 1-5 Hampshire vs Middlesex, Richmond, 2013 (T20)
COUNTY CAP: 2013

FIRST CRICKET CLUB? Erlestoke CC, Wiltshire
WHICH AWAY GROUND DO YOU MOST ENJOY VISITING? Edgbaston – it has the best dressing rooms, good food and generally a good wicket
HOW IS BAZBALL AFFECTING CHAMPIONSHIP CRICKET? Not much, though the approach of a few players has changed to fit the Bazball mould
WHAT DO YOU THINK OF THE CURRENT 50-OVER COMPETITION? I would like to see it have its own window with all players available
CHOOSE A FANTASY SLIP CORDON TO SPEND A DAY IN THE FIELD WITH: Ricky Gervais (wk), Tiger Woods, Lionel Messi, Donald Trump
NOTES: In January Hampshire announced that Vince will not play red-ball cricket this summer and instead feature only in the T20 Blast

Batting	Mat	Inns	NO	Runs	HS	Ave	SR	100	50	Ct	St
Tests	13	22	0	548	83	24.90	49.81	0	3	8	-
ODIs	25	22	0	616	102	28.00	87.62	1	3	10	-
T20Is	17	17	0	463	59	27.23	128.25	0	2	7	-
First-class	216	359	27	13340	240	40.18	62.53	30	58	211	-
List A	148	138	7	5199	190	39.68	97.10	10	25	57	-
T20s	419	407	43	11647	129*	31.99	135.02	6	73	229	-
Bowling	Mat	Balls	Mdns	Runs	Wkts	BB	Ave	4wI	5wI	SR	Econ
Tests	13	24	1	13	0	0-0	-	-	-	-	3.25
ODIs	25	42	0	38	1	1-18	38.00	0	0	42.00	5.42
T20Is	17	-	-	-	-	-	-	-	-	-	-
First-class	216	1778	36	1141	24	5-41	47.54	-	1	74.08	3.85
List A	148	174	0	162	3	1-18	54.00	0	0	58.00	5.58
T20s	419	78	0	87	3	1-5	29.00	0	0	26.00	6.69

MITCH WAGSTAFF

LHB / LB / RO / WO

FULL NAME: Mitchell David Wagstaff
BORN: September 2, 2003, Derby
SQUAD NO: 22
HEIGHT: 6ft 3in
NICKNAME: Waggy
EDUCATION: John Port School, Derby; Trent College, Nottingham
TEAMS: Derbyshire
ROLE: Allrounder
DEBUT: First-class: 2023; List A: 2021; T20: 2024

BEST BATTING: 78 Derbyshire vs Glamorgan, Cardiff, 2023
BEST BOWLING: 2-24 Derbyshire vs Leicestershire, Leicester, 2024

FIRST CRICKET CLUB? Mickleover CC, Derby
EARLIEST CRICKETING MEMORY? Watching my dad
WHAT'S THE BIGGEST PRIZE IN DOMESTIC CRICKET? The County Championship Division One title
THE KOOKABURRA BALL: YES OR NO? Yes – it brings a different challenge to the games
OPPONENT YOU MOST LOOK FORWARD TO PLAYING AGAINST? Joe Root – one of the best
FAVOURITE WARM-UP SONG? Greenlight by Pitbull
HOW MANY HOURS DO YOU SPEND ON YOUR PHONE A DAY? Three
SPECIALITY SUBJECT IN A PUB QUIZ (EXCLUDING SPORT)? Movie quotes
WHICH PUBLIC FIGURE INSPIRES YOU (EXCLUDING SPORTSPEOPLE)? Kevin Hart
SURPRISING FACT ABOUT YOU: I used to play football for Derby Academy
FILM YOU CAN WATCH OVER AND OVER: Hustle

Batting	Mat	Inns	NO	Runs	HS	Ave	SR	100	50	Ct	St
First-class	6	9	0	213	78	23.66	52.59	0	2	2	-
List A	8	6	0	76	36	12.66	81.72	0	0	1	-
T20s	6	2	2	1	1*	-	33.33	0	0	4	-

Bowling	Mat	Balls	Mdns	Runs	Wkts	BB	Ave	4wI	5wI	SR	Econ
First-class	6	342	9	166	4	2-24	41.50	-	0	85.50	2.91
List A	8	102	1	80	2	1-37	40.00	0	0	51.00	4.70
T20s	6	102	0	142	1	1-31	142.00	0	0	102.00	8.35

MATTHEW WAITE

RHB / RFM / RO / WO

WORCESTERSHIRE

FULL NAME: Matthew James Waite
BORN: December 24, 1995, Leeds
SQUAD NO: 6
HEIGHT: 6ft 1in
NICKNAME: Pingu
EDUCATION: Brigshaw High School, West Yorkshire
TEAMS: Worcestershire, Yorkshire
ROLE: Allrounder
DEBUT: First-class: 2017; List A: 2014; T20: 2015

BEST BATTING: 109* Worcestershire vs Derbyshire, Derby, 2023
BEST BOWLING: 5-16 Yorkshire vs Leeds/Bradford MCCU, Weetwood, 2019

FIRST CRICKET CLUB? Methley CC, Leeds
BEST PLAYER IN COUNTY CRICKET (EXCLUDING TEAMMATES)? Ben Coad
BEST DELIVERY YOU HAVE EVER BOWLED? I ran in, tripped up, it bounced three times and Haseeb Hameed hit it for four
GREATEST PERFORMANCE YOU HAVE WITNESSED? Harry Brook and Jordan Thompson sharing a stand of 141 for Yorkshire against Worcestershire at Headingley during the 2022 T20 Blast. Yorkshire were 15 for 4 at one point!
WHAT WOULD BE YOUR PERFECT BREAKFAST? A Full English

Batting	Mat	Inns	NO	Runs	HS	Ave	SR	100	50	Ct	St
First-class	37	56	8	1390	109*	28.95	63.32	2	7	11	-
List A	36	29	7	696	71	31.63	95.47	0	1	4	-
T20s	38	25	7	252	40	14.00	133.33	0	0	5	-

Bowling	Mat	Balls	Mdns	Runs	Wkts	BB	Ave	4wI	5wI	SR	Econ
First-class	37	4651	165	2548	84	5-16	30.33	-	1	55.36	3.28
List A	36	1423	10	1350	48	5-59	28.12	1	1	29.64	5.69
T20s	38	469	1	742	30	5-21	24.73	1	1	15.63	9.49

ROMAN WALKER

RHB / RFM / R0 / W0

FULL NAME: Roman Isaac Walker
BORN: August 6, 2000, Wrexham, Clwyd, Wales
SQUAD NO: 49
HEIGHT: 6ft 3in
NICKNAME: Stroller
EDUCATION: Ysgol Bryn Alyn, Wrexham
TEAMS: Leicestershire, England U19, Glamorgan
ROLE: Bowler
DEBUT: First-class: 2022; List A: 2019; T20: 2019

BEST BATTING: 64 Leicestershire vs Glamorgan, Leicester, 2022
BEST BOWLING: 3-84 Leicestershire vs Derbyshire, Derby, 2022

FIRST CRICKET CLUB? Bersham CC, Wrexham
EARLIEST CRICKETING MEMORY? Bowling in the nets aged six
WHAT'S THE BIGGEST PRIZE IN DOMESTIC CRICKET? The T20 Blast trophy
THE KOOKABURRA BALL: YES OR NO? No, it's too easy to manufacture high-scoring games with a Kookaburra. The Dukes, even on a flat deck, leaves something to the imagination at least
OPPONENT YOU MOST LOOK FORWARD TO PLAYING AGAINST? Ethan Bamber – nicest man in cricket
FAVOURITE WARM-UP SONG? Italian Horror by Kasabian
HOW MANY HOURS DO YOU SPEND ON YOUR PHONE A DAY? Two
ONE THING YOU WANT TO DO BEFORE YOU DIE: Watch an F1 race from the paddock
HOBBY YOU WOULD LIKE TO LEARN: Fishing
WHICH PUBLIC FIGURE INSPIRES YOU (EXCLUDING SPORTSPEOPLE)? Bob Mortimer
SURPRISING FACT ABOUT YOU: I'm related to Gene Wilder
FILM YOU CAN WATCH OVER AND OVER: Hot Fuzz

Batting	Mat	Inns	NO	Runs	HS	Ave	SR	100	50	Ct	St
First-class	3	6	1	103	64	20.60	48.58	0	1	1	-
List A	16	11	4	113	23	16.14	76.87	0	0	6	-
T20s	15	9	3	29	19*	4.83	82.85	0	0	3	-

Bowling	Mat	Balls	Mdns	Runs	Wkts	BB	Ave	4wI	5wI	SR	Econ
First-class	3	438	13	285	7	3-84	40.71	-	0	62.57	3.90
List A	16	683	1	689	19	6-43	36.26	0	1	35.94	6.05
T20s	15	287	0	443	19	3-15	23.31	0	0	15.10	9.26

PAUL WALTER

LHB / LMF / RO / WO

FULL NAME: Paul Ian Walter
BORN: May 28, 1994, Basildon, Essex
SQUAD NO: 22
HEIGHT: 6ft 7in
EDUCATION: Billericay School, Essex
TEAMS: Essex, Brisbane Heat, Manchester Originals, Peshawar Zalmi, Sharjah Warriors
ROLE: Allrounder
DEBUT: First-class: 2016; List A: 2017; T20: 2016

BEST BATTING: 141 Essex vs Yorkshire, Chelmsford, 2022
BEST BOWLING: 3-20 Essex vs Lancashire, Blackpool, 2023
COUNTY CAP: 2023

NOTES: The tall alrounder signed a new three-year contract with Essex after an excellent 2022 season in which he made his maiden first-class hundred and was one of the their leading lights in the T20 Blast. The 30-year-old, who has been a consistent member of Manchester Originals in The Hundred, was nevertheless a surprise pick in Australia's Big Bash and took 17 wickets to help Brisbane Heat to the title in the 2023/24 season down under, though he was less effective in his second year in the BBL over the winter. For Essex, his multi-format talents were on display again last summer, with a second first-class hundred in the Championship coming alongside 20 wickets in the T20 Blast

Batting	Mat	Inns	NO	Runs	HS	Ave	SR	100	50	Ct	St
First-class	53	74	9	2344	141	36.06	50.95	2	13	24	-
List A	16	13	3	253	50	25.30	95.47	0	1	7	-
T20s	155	130	25	2094	78	19.94	140.91	0	7	78	-

Bowling	Mat	Balls	Mdns	Runs	Wkts	BB	Ave	4wI	5wI	SR	Econ
First-class	53	1990	47	1159	31	3-20	37.38	-	0	64.19	3.49
List A	16	368	1	434	14	4-37	31.00	1	0	26.28	7.07
T20s	155	1772	3	2647	105	3-20	25.20	0	0	16.87	8.96

HARRISON WARD

LHB / OB / R0 / W0

FULL NAME: Harrison David Ward
BORN: October 25, 1999, Oxford
SQUAD NO: 35
HEIGHT: 6ft 2in
NICKNAME: Indy
EDUCATION: St Edward's School, Oxford;
Cardiff Metropolitan University
TEAMS: Sussex, England U19
ROLE: Batter
DEBUT: First-class: 2021; List A: 2021; T20: 2021

BEST BATTING: 19 Sussex vs Derbyshire, Hove, 2021

FIRST CRICKET CLUB? Abingdon Vale CC, Oxfordshire
WHICH TEAMMATE HAS HAD THE BIGGEST IMPACT ON YOUR GAME? Jack Carson – he
helped me out when I was out of the professional game
WHAT PART OF THE SEASON DO YOU MOST ENJOY? The T20 Blast
WHO IS THE MOST TALENTED U19 TEENAGER IN THE COUNTY GAME? Henry Rogers (Sus)
WHAT DO YOU THINK OF THE CURRENT 50-OVER COMPETITION? I would like to see the
National Counties involved
WHO IS THE TOUGHEST BOWLER TO FACE? Sunil Narine – just can't pick him
WHAT KEEPS YOU AWAKE AT NIGHT? A red Dukes ball
CHOOSE A FANTASY SLIP CORDON TO SPEND A DAY IN THE FIELD WITH: Shane Warne,
Dennis Rodman, George Best, Tiger Woods

Batting	Mat	Inns	NO	Runs	HS	Ave	SR	100	50	Ct	St
First-class	4	7	0	32	19	4.57	22.37	0	0	2	-
List A	12	12	0	215	37	17.91	93.47	0	0	2	-
T20s	39	38	4	792	68	23.29	143.21	0	5	13	-

Bowling	Mat	Balls	Mdns	Runs	Wkts	BB	Ave	4wl	5wl	SR	Econ
First-class	4	6	0	2	0	0-2	-	-	-	-	2.00
List A	12	66	0	87	0	0-18	-	-	-	-	7.90
T20s	39	13	0	16	1	1-5	16.00	0	0	13.00	7.38

RAPHY WEATHERALL

RHB / RFM / RO / WO

FULL NAME: Raphael Alexander Weatherall
BORN: October 24, 2004, Kendal, Westmorland
SQUAD NO: 84
HEIGHT: 6ft 4in
NICKNAME: Bestie
EDUCATION: Dr Challoner's Grammar School, Amersham; University of Exeter
TEAMS: Northamptonshire, England U19
ROLE: Bowler
DEBUT: First-class: 2024; List A: 2024; T20: 2024

BEST BATTING: 13 Northamptonshire vs Glamorgan, Cardiff, 2024
BEST BOWLING: 2-55 Northamptonshire vs Glamorgan, Northampton, 2024

FIRST CRICKET CLUB? Ballinger Waggonners CC, Great Missenden, Buckinghamshire
THE KOOKABURRA BALL: YES OR NO? No – as a bowler, I didn't have the best experience with it last year
OPPONENT YOU MOST LOOK FORWARD TO PLAYING AGAINST? Riley Meredith of Somerset – he is an inspiring example of the speeds I want to eventually bowl at, and playing against him will be a good opportunity to learn
FAVOURITE WARM-UP SONG? 1973 by James Blunt
HOW MANY HOURS DO YOU SPEND ON YOUR PHONE A DAY? Three to four
HOBBY YOU WOULD LIKE TO LEARN: Speak Spanish
WHICH PUBLIC FIGURE INSPIRES YOU (EXCLUDING SPORTSPEOPLE)? Shane Gillis
SURPRISING FACT ABOUT YOU: I'm a quarter Colombian
FILM YOU CAN WATCH OVER AND OVER: The Hangover

Batting	Mat	Inns	NO	Runs	HS	Ave	SR	100	50	Ct	St
First-class	4	4	1	15	13	5.00	27.77	0	0	1	-
List A	5	4	4	15	12*	-	71.42	0	0	2	-
T20s	9	1	1	21	21*	-	100.00	0	0	2	-

Bowling	Mat	Balls	Mdns	Runs	Wkts	BB	Ave	4wI	5wI	SR	Econ
First-class	4	426	8	320	6	2-55	53.33	-	0	71.00	4.50
List A	5	187	0	218	6	4-50	36.33	1	0	31.16	6.99
T20s	9	127	0	243	11	4-50	22.09	1	0	11.54	11.48

JOE WEATHERLEY   RHB / OB / R0 / W0

FULL NAME: Joe James Weatherley
BORN: January 19, 1997, Winchester, Hampshire
SQUAD NO: 5
HEIGHT: 6ft 2in
NICKNAME: Lord
EDUCATION: King Edward VI School, Southampton; The Open University, Milton Keynes
TEAMS: Hampshire, England U19, Kent, Southern Brave
ROLE: Batter
DEBUT: First-class: 2016; List A: 2016; T20: 2016

BEST BATTING: 168 Hampshire vs Somerset, Southampton, 2022
BEST BOWLING: 1-2 Hampshire vs Nottinghamshire, Southampton, 2018

FIRST CRICKET CLUB? St Cross Symondians CC, Winchester, Hampshire
EARLIEST CRICKETING MEMORY? The 2005 Ashes
WHAT'S THE BIGGEST PRIZE IN DOMESTIC CRICKET? The County Championship
THE KOOKABURRA BALL: YES OR NO? Yes, because it tests different skills
OPPONENT YOU MOST LOOK FORWARD TO PLAYING AGAINST? My ex-teammate Mason Crane
FAVOURITE WARM-UP SONG? Supersonic by Oasis
HOW MANY HOURS DO YOU SPEND ON YOUR PHONE A DAY? Three to four
SPECIALITY SUBJECT IN A PUB QUIZ (EXCLUDING SPORT)? Music
ONE THING YOU WANT TO DO BEFORE YOU DIE: Play golf at Augusta
HOBBY YOU WOULD LIKE TO LEARN: How to cook well
SURPRISING FACT ABOUT YOU: My dad played at Wimbledon in the 1972 Championships

Batting	Mat	Inns	NO	Runs	HS	Ave	SR	100	50	Ct	St
First-class	63	101	4	2344	168	24.16	42.96	2	11	52	-
List A	33	32	4	908	105*	32.42	74.00	2	5	13	-
T20s	85	77	12	1830	71	28.15	127.70	0	7	30	-

Bowling	Mat	Balls	Mdns	Runs	Wkts	BB	Ave	4wI	5wI	SR	Econ
First-class	63	396	7	268	5	1-2	53.60	-	0	79.20	4.06
List A	33	327	7	221	8	4-25	27.62	1	0	40.87	4.05
T20s	85	6	0	9	0	0-9	-	-	-	-	9.00

BEAU WEBSTER

RHB / RM / OB / R0 / W0

WARWICKSHIRE

FULL NAME: Beau Jacob Webster
BORN: December 1, 1993, Snug, Hobart, Tasmania, Australia
SQUAD NO: TBC
TEAMS: Australia, Warwickshire, Essex, Gloucestershire, Hobart Hurricanes, Melbourne Stars, Melbourne Renegades, Tasmania
ROLE: Allrounder
DEBUT: Test: 2025;
First-class: 2014; List A: 2016; T20: 2017

BEST BATTING: 187 Tasmania vs Western Australia, Hobart, 2020
BEST BOWLING: 6-100 Gloucestershire vs Derbyshire, Bristol, 2024

NOTES: Australia's latest Test allrounder will feature for Warwickshire in both the Championship and the T20 Blast during a three-month stint starting in early May. Webster scored a half-century on Test debut against India during the winter and so far in his fledgling career has taken Test wickets bowling both seam and spin. "Having played Birmingham league cricket in the past, I have great memories of the people and the area," said Webster upon signing. "I played some Championship cricket last summer with Gloucestershire and loved the challenge of the competition." First team coach Mark Robinson added: "We're delighted Beau has chosen to become a Bear. Since we first approached him he has made his international debut which shows how highly regarded he is by Australia's selectors"

Batting	Mat	Inns	NO	Runs	HS	Ave	SR	100	50	Ct	St
Tests	3	4	1	150	57	50.00	59.76	0	1	7	-
First-class	98	167	21	5603	187	38.37	54.20	12	27	136	
List A	56	50	6	1334	121	30.31	77.10	1	7	34	-
T20s	96	82	16	1816	78	27.51	119.23	0	12	52	-

Bowling	Mat	Balls	Mdns	Runs	Wkts	BB	Ave	4wI	5wI	SR	Econ
Tests	3	133	5	72	3	2-6	24.00	-	0	44.33	3.24
First-class	98	10083	279	5760	156	6-100	36.92	-	2	64.63	3.42
List A	56	1599	11	1454	49	6-17	29.67	0	1	32.63	5.45
T20s	96	828	1	1034	25	4-29	41.36	1	0	33.12	7.49

LUKE WELLS

LHB / OB / R2 / W0 / MVP7

FULL NAME: Luke William Peter Wells
BORN: December 29, 1990, Eastbourne, Sussex
SQUAD NO: 3
HEIGHT: 6ft 4in
NICKNAME: Dave
EDUCATION: St Bede's, Hailsham, East Sussex; Loughborough University
TEAMS: Lancashire, Welsh Fire, Colombo, England Lions, Lahore Qalandars, Sussex
ROLE: Allrounder
DEBUT: First-class: 2010; List A: 2010; T20: 2011

BEST BATTING: 258 Sussex vs Durham, Hove, 2017
BEST BOWLING: 5-25 Lancashire vs Northamptonshire, Northampton, 2023
COUNTY CAP: 2016 (Sussex); 2022 (Lancashire)

FIRST CRICKET CLUB? Glynde & Beddingham CC, Sussex
WHICH TEAMMATE HAS HAD THE BIGGEST IMPACT ON YOUR GAME? Murray Goodwin at Sussex – the intensity of his training and his ruthlessness when batting left a lasting impression on me
IF YOU COULD PINCH A PLAYER FROM ANOTHER COUNTY, WHO WOULD IT BE? A fully fit Jofra Archer
HOW IS BAZBALL AFFECTING CHAMPIONSHIP CRICKET? Players who aspire to play for England know that runs alone aren't sufficient – they have to score at a higher rate. Except that's hard to do on many county surfaces
WHO IS THE TOUGHEST BOWLER TO FACE? Previously without doubt Darren Stevens. Now it's probably Sam Cook – skilful wobble seam, swing both ways, extremely accurate and quick enough

Batting	Mat	Inns	NO	Runs	HS	Ave	SR	100	50	Ct	St
First-class	195	320	21	10733	258	35.89	48.16	26	45	107	-
List A	44	37	1	778	88	21.61	84.10	0	5	14	-
T20s	72	66	8	1049	66	18.08	138.20	0	5	29	-

Bowling	Mat	Balls	Mdns	Runs	Wkts	BB	Ave	4wl	5wl	SR	Econ
First-class	195	7718	157	4442	116	5-25	38.29	-	2	66.53	3.45
List A	44	1032	2	900	23	3-19	39.13	0	0	44.86	5.23
T20s	72	907	0	1168	37	2-19	31.56	0	0	24.51	7.72

TOM WESTLEY

ESSEX

FULL NAME: Thomas Westley
BORN: March 13, 1989, Cambridge
SQUAD NO: 21
HEIGHT: 6ft 2in
NICKNAME: Westie
EDUCATION: Linton Valley College, South Cambridgeshire; Hills Road College, Cambridge; Durham University
TEAMS: England, Essex, Bloomfield Cricket & Athletic Club
ROLE: Batter
DEBUT: Test: 2017;
First-class: 2007; List A: 2006; T20: 2010

BEST BATTING: 254 Essex vs Worcestershire, Chelmsford, 2016
BEST BOWLING: 4-55 Durham MCCU vs Durham, Durham University, 2010
COUNTY CAP: 2013

FIRST CRICKET CLUB? Weston Colville CC, Cambridgeshire
EARLIEST CRICKETING MEMORY? My dad and uncle playing in the village
WHAT'S THE BIGGEST PRIZE IN DOMESTIC CRICKET? Winning Division One of the County Championship
THE KOOKABURRA BALL: YES OR NO? Not fussed
OPPONENT YOU MOST LOOK FORWARD TO PLAYING AGAINST? Jack Leach – I like it when he cleans his glasses while batting
HOW MANY HOURS DO YOU SPEND ON YOUR PHONE A DAY? Two hours and 46 minutes
SPECIALITY SUBJECT IN A PUB QUIZ (EXCLUDING SPORT)? Harry Potter
WHICH PUBLIC FIGURE INSPIRES YOU (EXCLUDING SPORTSPEOPLE)? Ricky Gervais
SURPRISING FACT ABOUT YOU: I studied Harry Potter academically
FILM YOU CAN WATCH OVER AND OVER: Zog and the Flying Doctors

Batting	Mat	Inns	NO	Runs	HS	Ave	SR	100	50	Ct	St
Tests	5	9	1	193	59	24.12	42.60	0	1	1	-
First-class	240	400	29	13421	254	36.17	50.05	29	61	138	-
List A	120	114	7	4017	134	37.54	88.22	7	32	30	-
T20s	111	99	11	2569	109*	29.19	129.22	2	10	42	-

Bowling	Mat	Balls	Mdns	Runs	Wkts	BB	Ave	4wI	5wI	SR	Econ
Tests	5	24	0	12	0	0-12	-	-	-	-	3.00
First-class	240	5305	125	2775	62	4-55	44.75	-	0	85.56	3.13
List A	120	2036	5	1712	43	4-60	39.81	1	0	47.34	5.04
T20s	111	246	0	310	8	2-27	38.75	0	0	30.75	7.56

JAMES WHARTON RHB / OB / R0 / W0

FULL NAME: James Henry Wharton
BORN: February 1, 2001, Huddersfield
SQUAD NO: 23
HEIGHT: 6ft 5in
NICKNAME: Pumba
EDUCATION: Holmfirth High School;
Greenhead College, Huddersfield
TEAMS: Yorkshire
ROLE: Batter
DEBUT: First-class: 2022; List A: 2023; T20: 2020

YORKSHIRE

BEST BATTING: 285 Yorkshire vs Northamptonshire, Headingley, 2024
BEST BOWLING: 1-1 Yorkshire vs Glamorgan, Cardiff, 2023

FIRST CRICKET CLUB? Holmfirth CC, West Yorkshire
EARLIEST CRICKETING MEMORY? Hitting balls down the hallway with my dad
THE KOOKABURRA BALL: YES OR NO? No, in England we should always use a Dukes
OPPONENT YOU MOST LOOK FORWARD TO PLAYING AGAINST? Ryan Patel (I want to hear his laugh)
FAVOURITE WARM-UP SONG? Gangsta's Paradise by Coolio
HOW MANY HOURS DO YOU SPEND ON YOUR PHONE A DAY? Four hours and 31 minutes
SPECIALITY SUBJECT IN A PUB QUIZ (EXCLUDING SPORT)? National flags
ONE THING YOU WANT TO DO BEFORE YOU DIE: Drive an old Porsche down the Amalfi coast
HOBBY YOU WOULD LIKE TO LEARN: Become a padel expert
SURPRISING FACT ABOUT YOU: I don't have any earlobes
FILM YOU CAN WATCH OVER AND OVER: The Dark Knight

Batting	Mat	Inns	NO	Runs	HS	Ave	SR	100	50	Ct	St
First-class	18	30	2	1227	285	43.82	63.14	2	6	11	-
List A	12	12	2	320	71	32.00	72.07	0	3	12	-
T20s	15	14	1	289	111*	22.23	133.17	1	1	6	-

Bowling	Mat	Balls	Mdns	Runs	Wkts	BB	Ave	4wI	5wI	SR	Econ
First-class	18	85	1	128	1	1-1	128.00	-	0	85.00	9.03
List A	12	-	-	-	-	-	-	-	-	-	-
T20s	15	-	-	-	-	-	-	-	-	-	-

BRAD WHEAL

RHB / RFM / R0 / W0

FULL NAME: Bradley Thomas James Wheal
BORN: August 28, 1996, Durban, South Africa
SQUAD NO: 58
HEIGHT: 5ft 11in
NICKNAME: Whealy
EDUCATION: Clifton School, Durban
TEAMS: Scotland, Hampshire, Glamorgan,
Gloucestershire, London Spirit, Warwickshire
ROLE: Bowler
DEBUT: ODI: 2016; T20I: 2016;
First-class: 2015; List A: 2016; T20: 2016

BEST BATTING: 61 Hampshire vs Kent, Canterbury, 2024
BEST BOWLING: 6-51 Hampshire vs Nottinghamshire, Trent Bridge, 2016

FIRST CRICKET CLUB? Berea Rovers CC, Durban, South Africa
EARLIEST CRICKETING MEMORY? Learning to bowl in my driveway with the neighbours
THE KOOKABURRA BALL: YES OR NO? Yes, it's good in mid to late season when conditions
are drier and the ball reverse-swings
OPPONENT YOU MOST LOOK FORWARD TO PLAYING AGAINST? My old teammate
Ian Holland
FAVOURITE WARM-UP SONG? Unwritten by Natasha Bedingfield
HOW MANY HOURS DO YOU SPEND ON YOUR PHONE A DAY? One
ONE THING YOU WANT TO DO BEFORE YOU DIE: Climb Mount Kilimanjaro
SURPRISING FACT ABOUT YOU: I've surfed since I was eight
FILM YOU CAN WATCH OVER AND OVER: A Million Ways to Die in the West

Batting	Mat	Inns	NO	Runs	HS	Ave	SR	100	50	Ct	St
ODIs	18	9	3	49	24	8.16	62.82	0	0	3	-
T20Is	23	7	5	18	8*	9.00	90.00	0	0	7	-
First-class	50	62	22	484	61	12.10	28.86	0	1	16	-
List A	46	27	12	138	24	9.20	64.78	0	0	9	-
T20s	69	16	8	48	16	6.00	87.27	0	0	15	-
Bowling	Mat	Balls	Mdns	Runs	Wkts	BB	Ave	4wI	5wI	SR	Econ
ODIs	18	873	15	623	27	3-34	23.07	0	0	32.33	4.28
T20Is	23	462	1	657	22	3-20	29.86	0	0	21.00	8.53
First-class	50	6804	204	3963	116	6-51	34.16	-	1	58.65	3.49
List A	46	2102	26	1769	71	5-47	24.91	2	1	29.60	5.04
T20s	69	1361	3	1954	86	5-38	22.72	2	1	15.82	8.61

JACK WHITE

LHB / RFM / R0 / W0

FULL NAME: Curtley-Jack White
BORN: February 19, 1992, Kendal, Cumberland
SQUAD NO: TBC
HEIGHT: 6ft 2in
EDUCATION: Ullswater Community College, Penrith, Cumbria; Queen Elizabeth Grammar School, Penrith
TEAMS: Yorkshire, Northamptonshire
ROLE: Bowler
DEBUT: First-class: 2020; List A: 2021; T20: 2024

BEST BATTING: 59 Northamptonshire vs Kent, Northampton, 2023
BEST BOWLING: 6-38 Northamptonshire vs Essex, Northampton, 2022

FIRST CRICKET CLUB? Penrith CC, Cumbria
WHICH TEAMMATE HAS HAD THE BIGGEST IMPACT ON YOUR GAME? Simon Kerrigan – a keen observer
WHAT PART OF THE SEASON DO YOU MOST ENJOY? The first game
WHICH AWAY GROUND DO YOU MOST ENJOY VISITING? The Oval
WHO IS THE TOUGHEST BOWLER TO FACE? Mohammad Abbas
HOBBIES? Fly fishing
WHAT KEEPS YOU AWAKE AT NIGHT? Traffic
SURPRISING FACT ABOUT YOU: I've ridden a snow mobile to the Russian border

Batting	Mat	Inns	NO	Runs	HS	Ave	SR	100	50	Ct	St
First-class	35	52	24	226	59	8.07	52.92	0	1	3	-
List A	24	11	2	93	29	10.33	71.53	0	0	5	-
T20s	4	0	-	-	-	-	-	-	-	2	-

Bowling	Mat	Balls	Mdns	Runs	Wkts	BB	Ave	4wl	5wl	SR	Econ
First-class	35	5764	221	2871	114	6-38	25.18	-	5	50.56	2.98
List A	24	1034	12	856	30	4-20	28.53	1	0	34.46	4.96
T20s	4	72	0	99	5	3-16	19.80	0	0	14.40	8.25

ROSS WHITELEY

LHB / LM / RO / WO

DERBYSHIRE

FULL NAME: Ross Andrew Whiteley
BORN: September 13, 1988, Sheffield
SQUAD NO: 44
HEIGHT: 6ft 2in
NICKNAME: Rossco
EDUCATION: Repton School, Derbyshire;
Leeds Metropolitan University
TEAMS: Derbyshire, Welsh Fire, Brisbane
Heat, England Lions, Hampshire, Multan
Sultans, Oval Invincibles, Southern Brave,
Sylhet Sixers, Worcestershire
ROLE: Batter
DEBUT: First-class: 2008; List A: 2008; T20: 2011

BEST BATTING: 130* Derbyshire vs Kent, Derby, 2011
BEST BOWLING: 2-6 Derbyshire vs Hampshire, Derby, 2012
COUNTY CAP: 2013 (Worcestershire)

FIRST CRICKET CLUB? Eckington CC, South Yorkshire
WHAT'S THE BIGGEST PRIZE IN DOMESTIC CRICKET? The Hundred
THE KOOKABURRA BALL: YES OR NO? The white one, yes. The red one, no
OPPONENT YOU MOST LOOK FORWARD TO PLAYING AGAINST? Brett D'Oliveira, my old
teammate, so I can try to hit him for six
FAVOURITE WARM-UP SONG? Lose Yourself by Eminem
HOW MANY HOURS DO YOU SPEND ON YOUR PHONE A DAY? Two
SPECIALITY SUBJECT IN A PUB QUIZ (EXCLUDING SPORT)? Neuroscience
ONE THING YOU WANT TO DO BEFORE YOU DIE: Create something that will have a positive
impact on people's lives
HOBBY YOU WOULD LIKE TO LEARN: Reading my fiancée's mind
SURPRISING FACT ABOUT YOU? To date I'm the only English cricketer to hit six sixes in an
over in a professional game
FILM YOU CAN WATCH OVER AND OVER: My Dog: An Unconditional Love Story

Batting	Mat	Inns	NO	Runs	HS	Ave	SR	100	50	Ct	St
First-class	92	150	14	3738	130*	27.48	49.72	3	22	60	-
List A	83	73	11	1727	131	27.85	97.40	1	11	24	-
T20s	225	197	48	3364	91*	22.57	136.58	0	6	86	-

Bowling	Mat	Balls	Mdns	Runs	Wkts	BB	Ave	4wl	5wl	SR	Econ
First-class	92	3073	42	2143	42	2-6	51.02	-	0	73.16	4.18
List A	83	507	0	563	14	4-58	40.21	1	0	36.21	6.66
T20s	225	204	0	316	10	3-23	31.60	0	0	20.40	9.29

DAVID WILLEY

LHB / LFM / R0 / W0

FULL NAME: David Jonathan Willey
BORN: February 28, 1990, Northampton
SQUAD NO: 23
HEIGHT: 6ft 1in
NICKNAME: Will Mildman
EDUCATION: Northampton School for Boys
TEAMS: England, Northamptonshire, CSK, Durban's Super Giants, Lucknow Super Giants, Multan Sultans, Northern Superchargers, Perth Scorchers, RCB, Welsh Fire, Yorkshire
ROLE: Allrounder
DEBUT: ODI: 2015; T20I: 2015; First-class: 2009; List A: 2009; T20: 2009

BEST BATTING: 104* Northamptonshire vs Gloucestershire, Northampton, 2015
BEST BOWLING: 5-29 Northamptonshire vs Gloucestershire, Northampton, 2011
COUNTY CAP: 2013 (Northamptonshire); 2016 (Yorkshire)

FIRST CRICKET CLUB? Old Northamptonians CC, Northampton
FAMILY TIES? My dad Peter played for England, Northamptonshire and Leicestershire
WHAT PART OF THE SEASON DO YOU MOST ENJOY? The Hundred
WHICH AWAY GROUND DO YOU MOST ENJOY VISITING? Edgbaston – great atmosphere
IF YOU COULD PINCH A PLAYER FROM ANOTHER COUNTY, WHO WOULD IT BE? Moeen Ali
WHAT DO YOU THINK OF THE CURRENT 50-OVER COMPETITION? It should have a knockout format
HOBBIES? Baking and gardening

Batting	Mat	Inns	NO	Runs	HS	Ave	SR	100	50	Ct	St
ODIs	73	46	19	663	51	24.55	95.67	0	2	27	-
T20Is	43	26	11	226	33*	15.06	130.63	0	0	17	-
First-class	77	108	16	2515	104*	27.33	63.75	2	14	18	-
List A	156	111	27	2145	167	25.53	97.05	3	7	53	-
T20s	324	238	51	4257	118	22.76	133.69	2	17	141	-

Bowling	Mat	Balls	Mdns	Runs	Wkts	BB	Ave	4wl	5wl	SR	Econ
ODIs	73	3230	34	2975	100	5-30	29.75	4	1	32.30	5.52
T20Is	43	865	1	1180	51	4-7	23.13	1	0	16.96	8.18
First-class	77	10745	348	5895	198	5-29	29.77	-	6	54.26	3.29
List A	156	6021	54	5617	188	5-30	29.87	7	2	32.02	5.59
T20s	324	5795	14	7560	327	4-7	23.11	4	0	17.72	7.82

WILL WILLIAMS — RHB / RMF / R0 / W0

LANCASHIRE

FULL NAME: William Salter Austen Williams
BORN: October 6, 1992, Christchurch, Canterbury, New Zealand
SQUAD NO: 30
HEIGHT: 6ft 3in
NICKNAME: Billy
EDUCATION: Christchurch Boys' High School, New Zealand
TEAMS: Lancashire, Canterbury
ROLE: Bowler
DEBUT: First-class: 2012; List A: 2017; T20: 2017

BEST BATTING: 61 Lancashire vs Surrey, The Oval, 2023
BEST BOWLING: 5-26 Canterbury vs Northern Districts, Rangiora, 2020

FIRST CRICKET CLUB? Diamond Harbour CC, Canterbury, New Zealand
WHAT'S THE BIGGEST PRIZE IN DOMESTIC CRICKET? Winning the County Championship
THE KOOKABURRA BALL: YES OR NO? Yes, when the wickets have a little pace and bounce in them
FAVOURITE WARM-UP SONG? Any song by Greatest Showman
HOW MANY HOURS DO YOU SPEND ON YOUR PHONE A DAY? Three
SPECIALITY SUBJECT IN A PUB QUIZ (EXCLUDING SPORT)? Geography
ONE THING YOU WANT TO DO BEFORE YOU DIE: Fly a jet plane
WHICH PUBLIC FIGURE INSPIRES YOU (EXCLUDING SPORTSPEOPLE)? Chris Martin
SURPRISING FACT ABOUT YOU: I am qualified to teach aerobatics in New Zealand and hold a commercial pilot's licence
FILM YOU CAN WATCH OVER AND OVER: Shooter

Batting	Mat	Inns	NO	Runs	HS	Ave	SR	100	50	Ct	St
First-class	73	98	28	882	61	12.60	30.23	0	1	31	-
List A	58	33	14	188	19*	9.89	72.58	0	0	24	-
T20s	37	13	10	76	29*	25.33	128.81	0	0	27	-

Bowling	Mat	Balls	Mdns	Runs	Wkts	BB	Ave	4wI	5wI	SR	Econ
First-class	73	12033	573	4781	207	5-26	23.09	-	3	58.13	2.38
List A	58	2733	30	2292	78	4-20	29.38	3	0	35.03	5.03
T20s	37	493	0	787	30	5-12	26.23	0	1	16.43	9.57

KANE WILLIAMSON   RHB / OB / R0 / W0

FULL NAME: Kane Stuart Williamson
BORN: August 8, 1990, Tauranga, New Zealand
SQUAD NO: 87
HEIGHT: 5ft 8in
EDUCATION: Tauranga Boys College, Bay of Plenty, New Zealand
TEAMS: New Zealand, Middlesex, London Spirit, Barbados Tridents, Durban's Super Giants, Gloucestershire, Gujarat Titans, Northern Districts, Sunrisers Hyderabad, Yorkshire
ROLE: Batter
DEBUT: Test: 2010; ODI: 2010; T20I: 2011; First-class: 2007; List A: 2007; T20: 2009

BEST BATTING: 284* Northern Districts vs Wellington, Lincoln, 2011
BEST BOWLING: 5-75 Northern Districts vs Canterbury, Christchurch, 2009
COUNTY CAP: 2011 (Gloucestershire)

NOTES: One of New Zealand's finest returns to English domestic cricket after signing a deal with Middlesex that takes in at least 10 T20 group games and five Championship matches in the second half of the summer. Williamson, now 34, has had previous spells with Gloucestershire and Yorkshire but hasn't played county cricket since 2018. New Zealand's highest Test run-scorer is also vastly experienced at T20 level, having played in the IPL as well as the premier franchise competitions in South Africa and West Indies. He will also turn out for London Spirit in The Hundred this summer. "I've played a bit of county cricket in the past, but not for a number of years now, so when this opportunity arose with Middlesex it was a really exciting prospect," said Williamson. "There's a good balance of youth and experience in the Middlesex squad, which is great, and I'm really excited to join up with the team, meet the players in the squad and helping out wherever I can"

Batting	Mat	Inns	NO	Runs	HS	Ave	SR	100	50	Ct	St
Tests	105	186	17	9276	251	54.88	51.78	33	37	90	-
ODIs	173	165	18	7235	148	49.21	81.72	15	47	74	-
T20Is	93	90	13	2575	95	33.44	123.08	0	18	45	-
First-class	174	301	24	14151	284*	51.08	52.10	43	65	155	-
List A	235	223	26	9399	148	47.71	81.27	19	59	102	-
T20s	262	250	41	6675	101*	31.93	122.45	1	47	114	-

Bowling	Mat	Balls	Mdns	Runs	Wkts	BB	Ave	4wI	5wI	SR	Econ
Tests	105	2151	48	1207	30	4-44	40.23	-	0	71.70	3.36
ODIs	173	1467	2	1310	37	4-22	35.40	1	0	39.64	5.35
T20Is	93	118	0	164	6	2-16	27.33	0	0	19.66	8.33
First-class	174	6624	175	3721	86	5-75	43.26	-	1	77.02	3.37
List A	235	2756	7	2383	67	5-51	35.56	1	1	41.13	5.18
T20s	262	770	1	909	30	3-33	30.30	0	0	25.66	7.08

CHRIS WOAKES

RHB / RFM / R0 / W3

WARWICKSHIRE

FULL NAME: Christopher Roger Woakes
BORN: March 2, 1989, Birmingham
SQUAD NO: 19
HEIGHT: 6ft 1in
NICKNAME: Wiz
EDUCATION: Barr Beacon Language College
TEAMS: England, Warwickshire, Welsh Fire,
Birmingham Phoenix, Delhi Capitals, Durban's
Super Giants, KKR, Punjab Kings, RCB, Sydney
Thunder, Wellington
ROLE: Allrounder
DEBUT: Test: 2013; ODI: 2011; T20I: 2011;
First-class: 2006; List A: 2007; T20: 2008

BEST BATTING: 152* Warwickshire vs Derbyshire, Derby, 2013
BEST BOWLING: 9-36 Warwickshire vs Durham, Edgbaston, 2016
COUNTY CAP: 2009

FAMILY TIES? My brothers played Birmingham League cricket
CHILDHOOD SPORTING HERO? Jacques Kallis
SURPRISING FACT ABOUT YOU: I won a keep-uppy competition when I was 10
(70 keepy-ups)

Batting	Mat	Inns	NO	Runs	HS	Ave	SR	100	50	Ct	St
Tests	57	92	17	1970	137*	26.26	53.41	1	7	29	-
ODIs	122	88	24	1524	95*	23.81	89.12	0	6	50	-
T20Is	33	17	8	147	37	16.33	125.64	0	0	12	-
First-class	178	266	55	6685	152*	31.68	-	10	26	77	-
List A	204	141	40	2265	95*	22.42	89.52	0	7	67	-
T20s	167	100	49	1031	57*	20.21	128.87	0	2	64	-

Bowling	Mat	Balls	Mdns	Runs	Wkts	BB	Ave	4wI	5wI	SR	Econ
Tests	57	10133	380	5112	181	6-17	28.24	-	5	55.98	3.02
ODIs	122	5737	52	5193	173	6-45	30.01	11	3	33.16	5.43
T20Is	33	611	1	822	31	3-4	26.51	0	0	19.70	8.07
First-class	178	30507	1146	15546	606	9-36	25.65	-	22	50.34	3.05
List A	204	9005	93	8169	251	6-45	32.54	13	3	35.87	5.44
T20s	167	3251	5	4468	177	4-21	25.24	1	0	18.36	8.24

CHRIS WOOD

RHB / LMF / R0 / W0

FULL NAME: Christopher Philip Wood
BORN: June 27, 1990, Basingstoke, Hampshire
SQUAD NO: 25
HEIGHT: 6ft 3in
NICKNAME: Nuts
EDUCATION: St Lawrence CE Primary School; Amery Hill School; Alton College, Hampshire
TEAMS: Hampshire, Birmingham Phoenix, England U19, London Spirit
ROLE: Bowler
DEBUT: First-class: 2010; List A: 2010; T20: 2010

BEST BATTING: 31 Hampshire vs Middlesex, Radlett, 2023 (T20)
BEST BOWLING: 5-32 Hampshire vs Somerset, Taunton, 2018 (T20)
COUNTY CAP: 2018; BENEFIT: 2024

FIRST CRICKET CLUB? Liphook & Ripsley CC, West Sussex
WHAT'S THE BIGGEST PRIZE IN DOMESTIC CRICKET? The County Championship
THE KOOKABURRA BALL: YES OR NO? No, the Dukes is a better ball
FAVOURITE WARM-UP SONG? Changing by Sigma featuring Paloma Faith
HOW MANY HOURS DO YOU SPEND ON YOUR PHONE A DAY? Four
ONE THING YOU WANT TO DO BEFORE YOU DIE: Travel New Zealand
WHICH PUBLIC FIGURE INSPIRES YOU (EXCLUDING SPORTSPEOPLE)? Donald Trump
SURPRISING FACT ABOUT YOU: I played football at semi-pro level
FILM YOU CAN WATCH OVER AND OVER: Law Abiding Citizen
NOTES: Wood signed a new one-year deal (white-ball only) last September

Batting	Mat	Inns	NO	Runs	HS	Ave	SR	100	50	Ct	St
First-class	43	62	6	1326	105*	23.67	64.65	1	6	14	-
List A	79	45	14	400	41	12.90	96.85	0	0	24	-
T20s	205	78	30	554	31	11.54	112.37	0	0	47	-

Bowling	Mat	Balls	Mdns	Runs	Wkts	BB	Ave	4wI	5wI	SR	Econ
First-class	43	6169	255	3174	105	5-39	30.22	-	3	58.75	3.08
List A	79	3304	20	2964	106	5-22	27.96	2	2	31.16	5.38
T20s	205	4129	5	5652	214	5-32	26.41	4	1	19.29	8.21

LUKE WOOD

LHB / LMF / RO / WO

FULL NAME: Luke Wood
BORN: August 2, 1995, Sheffield
SQUAD NO: 14
HEIGHT: 5ft 9in
EDUCATION: Portland Comprehensive School; Outwood Post 16 Centre Worksop
TEAMS: England, Lancashire, Melbourne Stars, Mumbai Indians, Nottinghamshire, Peshawar Zalmi, Sylhet Strikers, Trent Rockets, Worcestershire
ROLE: Bowler
DEBUT: ODI: 2022; T20I: 2022; First-class: 2014; List A: 2016; T20: 2016

BEST BATTING: 119 Lancashire vs Kent, Canterbury, 2021
BEST BOWLING: 5-40 Nottinghamshire vs Cambridge MCCU, Cambridge, 2016

FIRST CRICKET CLUB? Cuckney CC, Nottinghamshire
THE KOOKABURRA BALL: YES OR NO? Yes, because it provides a test for different conditions
OPPONENT YOU MOST LOOK FORWARD TO PLAYING AGAINST? Tom Moores, he's a best mate and it's always a good contest
FAVOURITE WARM-UP SONG? Some form of drum and bass or techno
HOW MANY HOURS DO YOU SPEND ON YOUR PHONE A DAY? Five to six
ONE THING YOU WANT TO DO BEFORE YOU DIE: Go skiing
WHICH PUBLIC FIGURE INSPIRES YOU (EXCLUDING SPORTSPEOPLE)? David Goggins
SURPRISING FACT ABOUT YOU: I'm a twin
FILM YOU CAN WATCH OVER AND OVER: Step Brothers

Batting	Mat	Inns	NO	Runs	HS	Ave	SR	100	50	Ct	St
ODIs	2	1	0	10	10	10.00	100.00	0	0	0	-
T20Is	5	1	0	3	3	3.00	75.00	0	0	1	-
First-class	62	90	16	1884	119	25.45	59.20	2	7	19	-
List A	6	4	2	83	52	41.50	116.90	0	1	0	-
T20s	165	69	33	382	33*	10.61	118.63	0	0	54	-
Bowling	Mat	Balls	Mdns	Runs	Wkts	BB	Ave	4wl	5wl	SR	Econ
ODIs	2	60	0	59	0	0-59	-	-	-	-	5.90
T20Is	5	108	0	174	8	3-24	21.75	0	0	13.50	9.66
First-class	62	8391	232	4851	137	5-40	35.40	-	3	61.24	3.46
List A	6	186	1	184	5	2-36	36.80	0	0	37.20	5.93
T20s	165	3175	3	4472	165	5-50	27.10	1	1	19.24	8.45

MARK WOOD

RHB / RF / R0 / W0

FULL NAME: Mark Andrew Wood
BORN: January 11, 1990, Ashington, Northumberland
SQUAD NO: 33
HEIGHT: 6ft
EDUCATION: Ashington High School; Newcastle College
TEAMS: England, Durham, Chennai Super Kings, Lucknow Super Giants
ROLE: Bowler
DEBUT: Test: 2015; ODI: 2015; T20I: 2015; First-class: 2011; List A: 2011; T20: 2013

BEST BATTING: 72* Durham vs Kent, Chester-le-Street, 2017
BEST BOWLING: 6-37 England vs Australia, Hobart, 2022

FAMILY TIES? My dad Derek and uncle Neil played for Ashington CC and Minor Counties for Northumberland
CHILDHOOD SPORTING HERO? Steve Harmison
SURPRISING FACT ABOUT YOU: I was in the Newcastle United FC Academy

Batting	Mat	Inns	NO	Runs	HS	Ave	SR	100	50	Ct	St
Tests	37	62	11	807	52	15.82	70.72	0	1	8	-
ODIs	70	29	16	168	43*	12.92	100.59	0	0	14	-
T20Is	38	7	5	27	10*	13.50	96.42	0	0	5	-
First-class	78	126	23	1973	72*	19.15	60.00	0	5	17	-
List A	104	45	21	230	43*	9.58	92.00	0	0	24	-
T20s	63	20	11	134	27*	14.88	108.06	0	0	11	-

Bowling	Mat	Balls	Mdns	Runs	Wkts	BB	Ave	4wI	5wI	SR	Econ
Tests	37	6544	196	3621	119	6-37	30.42	-	5	54.99	3.31
ODIs	70	3506	19	3266	80	4-33	40.82	2	0	43.82	5.58
T20Is	38	776	1	1093	54	3-9	20.24	0	0	14.37	8.45
First-class	78	12662	363	6944	255	6-37	27.23	-	13	49.65	3.29
List A	104	4885	30	4406	126	4-33	34.96	2	0	38.76	5.41
T20s	63	1292	2	1770	85	5-14	20.82	1	1	15.20	8.21

DAN WORRALL

RHB / RFM / RO / W1 / MVP24

SURREY

FULL NAME: Daniel James Worrall
BORN: July 10, 1991, Melbourne, Australia
SQUAD NO: 8
HEIGHT: 5ft 11in
NICKNAME: Franky
EDUCATION: University of Melbourne
TEAMS: Australia, Surrey, London Spirit,
Adelaide Strikers, Gloucestershire,
Melbourne Stars, South Australia, Sunrisers
Eastern Cape
ROLE: Bowler
DEBUT: ODI: 2016;
First-class: 2012; List A: 2012; T20: 2014

BEST BATTING: 51 Surrey vs Lancashire, The Oval, 2023
BEST BOWLING: 7-64 South Australia vs Western Australia, Adelaide, 2018
COUNTY CAP: 2018 (Gloucestershire); 2023 (Surrey)

WHICH COUNTY PLAYER WOULD YOU MOST LIKE TO GO FOR A DRINK WITH? Ian Cockbain
– that man knows where to find the best taps
BEST DELIVERY YOU HAVE EVER FACED? Anything on middle stump is too good for me
BEST PERFORMANCE AS A PRO? Speaking more generally, it would be winning the County
Championship with Surrey over the last two seasons
GREATEST PERFORMANCE YOU HAVE WITNESSED? Will Jacks hitting 150 not out against
Essex at The Oval in the Championship two summers ago
FAVOURITE FORMAT? T20 – the crowds at The Oval are great fun
DESCRIBE YOURSELF IN THREE WORDS: Right arm over
HOBBIES? The guitar
WHAT WOULD BE YOUR PERFECT BREAKFAST? Poached eggs and avocado (after a sleep-in)
WHICH PERSON INSPIRES YOU MOST? Bruce Wayne

Batting	Mat	Inns	NO	Runs	HS	Ave	SR	100	50	Ct	St
ODIs	3	1	1	6	6*	-	150.00	0	0	1	-
First-class	96	136	48	1197	51	13.60	54.83	0	2	25	-
List A	43	23	11	128	31*	10.66	80.50	0	0	15	-
T20s	107	37	23	172	62*	12.28	105.52	0	1	26	-

Bowling	Mat	Balls	Mdns	Runs	Wkts	BB	Ave	4wl	5wl	SR	Econ
ODIs	3	158	0	171	1	1-43	171.00	0	0	158.00	6.49
First-class	96	19554	779	9463	373	7-64	25.36	-	16	52.42	2.90
List A	43	2161	20	1944	50	5-62	38.88	2	1	43.22	5.39
T20s	107	2116	6	2725	97	4-23	28.09	1	0	21.81	7.72

CHRIS WRIGHT
RHB / RMF / RO / W2

FULL NAME: Christopher Julian Clement Wright
BORN: July 14, 1985, Chipping Norton, Oxfordshire
SQUAD NO: 31
HEIGHT: 6ft 3in
NICKNAME: Dog
EDUCATION: Eggars Grammar School, Alton
TEAMS: Leicestershire, England Lions, Essex, Middlesex, Tamil Union, Warwickshire
ROLE: Bowler
DEBUT: First-class: 2004; List A: 2004; T20: 2004

BEST BATTING: 87 Leicestershire vs Derbyshire, Derby, 2021
BEST BOWLING: 7-53 Leicestershire vs Gloucestershire, Bristol, 2021
COUNTY CAP: 2013 (Warwickshire); 2021 (Leicestershire)

FIRST CRICKET CLUB? Liphook & Ripsley CC, Hampshire
WHICH TEAMMATE HAS HAD THE BIGGEST IMPACT ON YOUR GAME? My old Hampshire teammate Keith Barker – we love talking bowling together
IF YOU COULD PINCH A PLAYER FROM ANOTHER COUNTY, WHO WOULD IT BE? Keith Barker
HOW IS BAZBALL AFFECTING CHAMPIONSHIP CRICKET? Some teams play more shots and have a more aggressive outlook, but otherwise nothing too noticeable. I think it becomes more apparent when conditions are good like in Test cricket
WHO IS THE TOUGHEST BOWLER TO FACE? Anybody I face in the nets – I feel trapped there! And any leg-spinner
WHAT KEEPS YOU AWAKE AT NIGHT? Batting in the nets
CHOOSE A FANTASY SLIP CORDON TO SPEND A DAY IN THE FIELD WITH: James Foster (wk), Varun Chopra, Rikki Clarke, Ian Bell

Batting	Mat	Inns	NO	Runs	HS	Ave	SR	100	50	Ct	St
First-class	205	272	62	3945	87	18.78	50.71	0	14	40	-
List A	135	54	26	323	42	11.53	-	0	0	22	-
T20s	62	16	9	30	6*	4.28	90.90	0	0	13	-

Bowling	Mat	Balls	Mdns	Runs	Wkts	BB	Ave	4wl	5wl	SR	Econ
First-class	205	33461	1018	19121	590	7-53	32.40	-	19	56.71	3.42
List A	135	5623	41	5100	145	6-35	35.17	1	1	38.77	5.44
T20s	62	1222	0	1834	53	4-24	34.60	2	0	23.05	9.00

ROB YATES

LHB / OB / R0 / W0 / MVP15

WARWICKSHIRE

FULL NAME: Robert Michael Yates
BORN: September 19, 1999, Solihull, Warwickshire
SQUAD NO: 17
HEIGHT: 6ft 2in
NICKNAME: Robot
EDUCATION: Warwick School; University of Birmingham
TEAMS: Warwickshire, England Lions
ROLE: Batter
DEBUT: First-class: 2019; List A: 2019; T20: 2020

BEST BATTING: 228* Warwickshire vs Kent, Canterbury, 2023
BEST BOWLING: 4-37 Warwickshire vs Hampshire, Southampton, 2024
COUNTY CAP: 2023

FIRST CRICKET CLUB? Moseley CC, Solihull, West Midlands
BEST DELIVERY YOU HAVE EVER FACED? A Dan Mousley double-bounce ball in the nets. I was bowled, middle stump
GREATEST PERFORMANCE YOU HAVE WITNESSED? Adam Hose smashing a T20 hundred for the Bears against the Pears in 2022
FAVOURITE FORMAT? Four-day cricket
DESCRIBE YOURSELF IN THREE WORDS: Quiet, determined, hungry
HOBBIES? Racquet sports
SURPRISING FACT ABOUT YOU: My dad, grandad and great grandad are all named Rob

Batting	Mat	Inns	NO	Runs	HS	Ave	SR	100	50	Ct	St
First-class	70	114	7	3357	228*	31.37	-	10	12	100	-
List A	32	31	0	1186	114	38.25	85.20	3	7	29	-
T20s	35	35	1	842	71	24.76	134.29	0	7	14	-

Bowling	Mat	Balls	Mdns	Runs	Wkts	BB	Ave	4wl	5wl	SR	Econ
First-class	70	2224	64	1180	24	4-37	49.16	-	0	92.66	3.18
List A	32	496	2	465	5	1-27	93.00	0	0	99.20	5.62
T20s	35	60	0	79	1	1-13	79.00	0	0	60.00	7.90

SAIF ZAIB

LHB / SLA / R0 / W0 / MVP43

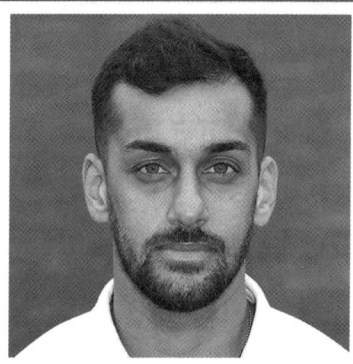

FULL NAME: Saif Ali Zaib
BORN: May 22, 1998, High Wycombe, Buckinghamshire
SQUAD NO: 18
HEIGHT: 5ft 8in
NICKNAME: Danger
EDUCATION: Royal Grammar School, High Wycombe
TEAMS: Northamptonshire, Northern Superchargers, Southern Rocks
ROLE: Allrounder
DEBUT: First-class: 2015; List A: 2014; T20: 2017

BEST BATTING: 135 Northamptonshire vs Sussex, Northampton, 2021
BEST BOWLING: 6-115 Northamptonshire vs Loughborough MCCU, Northampton, 2017

FIRST CRICKET CLUB? High Wycombe CC, Buckinghamshire
WHAT'S THE BIGGEST PRIZE IN DOMESTIC CRICKET? The T20 Blast
THE KOOKABURRA BALL: YES OR NO? Yes
FAVOURITE WARM-UP SONG? Forever by Chris Brown
HOW MANY HOURS DO YOU SPEND ON YOUR PHONE A DAY? Too many
HOBBY YOU WOULD LIKE TO LEARN: Darts
FILM YOU CAN WATCH OVER AND OVER: Forrest Gump

Batting	Mat	Inns	NO	Runs	HS	Ave	SR	100	50	Ct	St
First-class	60	96	6	2459	135	27.32	50.88	3	12	19	-
List A	35	28	1	791	136	29.29	92.73	1	4	9	-
T20s	74	62	12	1266	92	25.32	141.76	0	7	35	-

Bowling	Mat	Balls	Mdns	Runs	Wkts	BB	Ave	4wI	5wI	SR	Econ
First-class	60	2314	57	1487	35	6-115	42.48	-	2	66.11	3.85
List A	35	1146	5	1023	30	4-23	34.10	1	0	38.20	5.35
T20s	74	302	0	402	12	3-12	33.50	0	0	25.16	7.98

fairfield books

Recommended reading from Fairfield Books

Fairfield Books was set up in 1997 by Stephen Chalke to publish his work and that of fellow cricket writers. In 2020 it was taken over by the publishers of *Wisden Cricket Monthly* and *The Nightwatchman*, with the aim of continuing the tradition of publishing excellent and interesting titles. 11 Fairfield titles have won national Book of the Year awards, including two winning *Wisden*'s book of the year. The following cricket titles are amongst those available to buy via our website, over the phone or by post. For postal orders, please refer to our website or give us a call to confirm prices.

2025
· *Cricket Changed My Life: Eleven Personal Journeys* by Annie Chave
· *Sticky Dogs and Stardust: When the Legends Played in the Leagues – The Second Innings* by Scott Oliver

2024
· *Blood on the Tracks – England in Australia: The 1974/75 Ashes* by David Tossell
· *A Striking Summer: How Cricket United a Divided Nation* by Stephen Brenkley
· *One Hell of a Life: Brian Close – Daring Defiant and Daft* by Stephen Chalke
· *LARA: The England Chronicles* by Brian Lara

2023
· *Son of Grace: Frank Worrell – A Biography* by Vaneisa Baksh
· *Balls to Fly: Ricky Ellcock – An Autobiography* by Ricky Ellcock
· *Footprints: David Foot's Lifetime of Writing* by Stephen Chalke
· *Sticky Dogs and Stardust: When the Legends Played in the Leagues* by Scott Oliver

2022
· *Summer Days Promise* by Paul Edwards
· *Being Geoffrey Boycott: A First and Second-Hand Account of 108 Test Caps* by Geoffrey Boycott & Jon Hotten

2021
· *Who Only Cricket Know: Hutton's Men in the West Indies 1953/54* by David Woodhouse

Fairfield Books Ltd, Bedser Stand, Fourth Floor, The Kia Oval, London SE11 5SS
W: www.fairfieldbooks.co.uk   **E:** contact@fairfieldbooks.co.uk   **T:** 0203 006 5790

Women's
Players

GEORGIA ADAMS

RHB / OB / MVP4

HAMPSHIRE

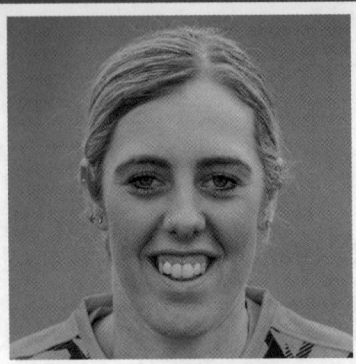

FULL NAME: Georgia Louise Adams
BORN: October 4, 1993, Chesterfield, Derbyshire
SQUAD NO: 1
HEIGHT: 5ft 10in
EDUCATION: Brighton College; Loughborough University
TEAMS: England, Hampshire, Southern Brave, Adelaide Strikers, Loughborough Lightning, NSW, Oval Invincibles, Southern Vipers, Sussex, Sydney Thunder
ROLE: Allrounder
DEBUT: T20I: 2024; List A: 2009; T20: 2009

BEST BATTING: 154* Southern Vipers vs Western Storm, Southampton, 2020
BEST BOWLING: 4-30 Southern Vipers vs Central Sparks, Wormsley, 2023

FIRST CRICKET CLUB? Henfield CC, West Sussex
EARLIEST CRICKETING MEMORY? Watching my dad (Chris) play for Sussex at Hove
WHAT WILL YOU MISS ABOUT REGIONAL CRICKET? The branding and kit
WHAT EXCITES YOU ABOUT THE NEW COUNTY STRUCTURE? Aligning with a men's team and county to create a bigger fan base and better resources
OPPONENT YOU MOST LOOK FORWARD TO PLAYING AGAINST? Georgia Elwiss – she's my best friend so it gives me a great excuse to visit her for a few days! (And she makes good coffee)
FAVOURITE WARM-UP SONG? Fireball by Pitbull
HOW MANY HOURS DO YOU SPEND ON YOUR PHONE A DAY? Three
SPECIALITY SUBJECT IN A PUB QUIZ (EXCLUDING SPORT)? Music
ONE THING YOU WANT TO DO BEFORE YOU DIE: Look at the Northern Lights
HOBBY YOU WOULD LIKE TO LEARN: Barista training to improve my latte art
WHICH PUBLIC FIGURE INSPIRES YOU (EXCLUDING SPORTSPEOPLE)? Adele
SURPRISING FACT ABOUT YOU: I have a tattoo of Simba
FILM YOU CAN WATCH OVER AND OVER: The Lion King

Batting	Mat	Inns	NO	Runs	HS	Ave	SR	100	50	Ct	St
T20Is	2	2	0	39	23	19.50	125.80	0	0	2	-
List A	129	124	9	3787	154*	32.93	71.06	3	26	69	-
T20s	195	171	29	3245	88*	22.85	105.66	0	17	87	-

Bowling	Mat	Balls	Mdns	Runs	Wkts	BB	Ave	4wI	5wI	SR	Econ
T20Is	2	30	0	29	0	0-13	-	-	-	-	5.80
List A	129	3374	23	2375	103	4-30	23.05	3	0	32.75	4.22
T20s	195	1395	1	1538	75	4-11	20.50	2	0	18.60	6.61

ELLIE ANDERSON   RHB / RFM

FULL NAME: Ellie Jane Anderson
BORN: October 30, 2003, Wolverhampton, Staffordshire
SQUAD NO: 45
HEIGHT: 5ft 6in
NICKNAME: Jimmy
EDUCATION: Oldbury Wells School, Bridgnorth, Shropshire; Bromsgrove School, Worcestershire
TEAMS: Somerset, Central Sparks, England U19, Western Storm, Worcestershire
ROLE: Bowler
DEBUT: List A: 2019; T20: 2018

BEST BATTING: 67* Worcestershire vs Oxfordshire, Flagge Meadow, 2024
BEST BOWLING: 3-9 Worcestershire vs Dorset, Bromsgrove, 2024

FIRST CRICKET CLUB? Alveley CC, Shropshire
EARLIEST CRICKETING MEMORY? Not wanting to go to training when I was about eight. But I did go and had a great time and now I'm here
WHAT WILL YOU MISS ABOUT REGIONAL CRICKET? Having our own team identity and values unique to our region
WHAT EXCITES YOU ABOUT THE NEW COUNTY STRUCTURE? Having more fans in the grounds and a bigger interest in our team. Plus telling people you play for a county is easier to explain than playing for a region!
OPPONENT YOU MOST LOOK FORWARD TO PLAYING AGAINST? Davina Perrin – we always tend to have a bit of a battle (but no hard feelings afterwards)
FAVOURITE WARM-UP SONG? Delilah (pull me out of this) by Fred Again
HOW MANY HOURS DO YOU SPEND ON YOUR PHONE A DAY? Three and a bit
HOBBY YOU WOULD LIKE TO LEARN: How to sing

Batting	Mat	Inns	NO	Runs	HS	Ave	SR	100	50	Ct	St
List A	16	10	2	182	67*	22.75	-	0	2	1	-
T20s	28	9	3	23	8	3.83	60.52	0	0	4	-

Bowling	Mat	Balls	Mdns	Runs	Wkts	BB	Ave	4wl	5wl	SR	Econ
List A	16	451	4	432	14	3-9	30.85	0	0	32.21	5.74
T20s	28	428	0	482	24	4-9	24.10	1	0	21.40	6.75

EMILY ARLOTT

RHB / RMF / MVP28

BIRMINGHAM BEARS

FULL NAME: Emily Louise Arlott
BORN: February 23, 1998, King's Lynn, Norfolk
SQUAD NO: 37
HEIGHT: 6ft
NICKNAME: Arlo
EDUCATION: John Masefield High School, Ledbury, Herefordshire
TEAMS: Birmingham Bears, Birmingham Phoenix, Central Sparks, Western Australia, Worcestershire
ROLE: Bowler
DEBUT: List A: 2013; T20: 2013

BEST BATTING: 63 Central Sparks vs Sunrisers, Worcester, 2022
BEST BOWLING: 5-29 Central Sparks vs Southern Vipers, Hove, 2021

FIRST CRICKET CLUB? Eastnor CC, Ledbury, Herefordshire
EARLIEST CRICKETING MEMORY? Bowling at my brother in the Eastnor nets
WHAT WILL YOU MISS ABOUT REGIONAL CRICKET? The Central Sparks family
WHAT EXCITES YOU ABOUT THE NEW COUNTY STRUCTURE? Being part of the Bears and growing a new fan base there
OPPONENT YOU MOST LOOK FORWARD TO PLAYING AGAINST? Marie Kelly
FAVOURITE WARM-UP SONG? Any song by Chase & Status
HOW MANY HOURS DO YOU SPEND ON YOUR PHONE A DAY? Two to three
SPECIALITY SUBJECT IN A PUB QUIZ (EXCLUDING SPORT)? The 1% Club
ONE THING YOU WANT TO DO BEFORE YOU DIE: Travel the world with my fiancé
HOBBY YOU WOULD LIKE TO LEARN: Cook properly
SURPRISING FACT ABOUT YOU: I am related to John Arlott
FILM YOU CAN WATCH OVER AND OVER: Any Marvel film

Batting	Mat	Inns	NO	Runs	HS	Ave	SR	100	50	Ct	St
List A	79	63	7	582	63	10.39	-	0	1	34	-
T20s	104	79	26	939	54	17.71	-	0	1	25	-

Bowling	Mat	Balls	Mdns	Runs	Wkts	BB	Ave	4wI	5wI	SR	Econ
List A	79	3071	44	2267	80	5-29	28.33	3	1	38.38	4.42
T20s	104	1754	8	1898	96	4-21	19.97	2	0	18.46	6.49

HOLLIE ARMITAGE — RHB / LB / MVP7

FULL NAME: Hollie Jade Armitage
BORN: June 14, 1997, Huddersfield
SQUAD NO: 57
HEIGHT: 5ft 9in
EDUCATION: Honley High School, West Yorkshire; Loughborough College
TEAMS: England, Durham, Northern Superchargers, Central Districts, Northern Diamonds, South Australia, Sydney Sixers, Tasmania, Yorkshire
ROLE: Allrounder
DEBUT: ODI: 2024; T20I: 2024; List A: 2013; T20: 2013

BEST BATTING: 131* Northern Diamonds vs Western Storm, Taunton, 2022
BEST BOWLING: 4-17 Yorkshire vs Berkshire, Finchampstead, 2016

FIRST CRICKET CLUB? Meltham CC, Kirklees, West Yorkshire
BEST PLAYER IN DOMESTIC CRICKET (EXCLUDING TEAMMATES)? Nat Sciver-Brunt
BEST PERFORMANCE AS A PRO? 131 not out against Western Storm at Taunton in 2022
GREATEST PERFORMANCE YOU HAVE WITNESSED? Lauren Winfield-Hill hitting 96 off 51 balls in a T20 against Lightning at Loughborough in 2022
FAVOURITE FORMAT? T20 because it's quick
DESCRIBE YOURSELF IN THREE WORDS: Enthusiastic, driven, funny
WHAT WOULD BE YOUR PERFECT BREAKFAST? Eggs on sourdough with chilli jam
SURPRISING FACT ABOUT YOU: I was student of the year in my final year of university

Batting	Mat	Inns	NO	Runs	HS	Ave	SR	100	50	Ct	St
ODIs	3	3	0	78	44	26.00	84.78	0	0	1	-
T20Is	3	3	0	5	4	1.66	50.00	0	0	1	-
List A	104	102	11	2948	131*	32.39	74.70	6	16	39	-
T20s	150	144	15	2977	97	23.07	109.69	0	15	52	-

Bowling	Mat	Balls	Mdns	Runs	Wkts	BB	Ave	4wI	5wI	SR	Econ
ODIs	3	-	-	-	-	-	-	-	-	-	-
T20Is	3	-	-	-	-	-	-	-	-	-	-
List A	104	1441	10	1251	52	4-17	24.05	1	0	27.71	5.20
T20s	150	680	2	693	34	4-27	20.38	1	0	20.00	6.11

HANNAH BAKER

BIRMINGHAM BEARS

FULL NAME: Hannah Louise Baker
BORN: February 3, 2004, West Midlands
SQUAD NO: 3
HEIGHT: 5ft 5in
NICKNAME: Bakes
EDUCATION: King Edwards VI College, Stourbridge
TEAMS: England, Birmingham Bears, Birmingham Phoenix, Central Sparks, Warwickshire, Welsh Fire, Worcestershire
ROLE: Bowler
DEBUT: ODI: 2024; List A: 2019; T20: 2018

BEST BATTING: 12 England A vs New Zealand A, Dunedin, 2024
BEST BOWLING: 5-45 Central Sparks vs South East Stars, Beckenham, 2024

FIRST CRICKET CLUB? Beacon CC, Cornwall
EARLIEST CRICKETING MEMORY? Getting the better of my dad and brother in the back yard
WHAT WILL YOU MISS ABOUT REGIONAL CRICKET? The lovely kits of Central Sparks
WHAT EXCITES YOU ABOUT THE NEW COUNTY STRUCTURE? Being part of one club with the men's team
OPPONENT YOU MOST LOOK FORWARD TO PLAYING AGAINST? Eve Jones – she's like a big sister to me and has always been an idol
FAVOURITE WARM-UP SONG? Baby by Justin Bieber
HOW MANY HOURS DO YOU SPEND ON YOUR PHONE A DAY? Four
SPECIALITY SUBJECT IN A PUB QUIZ (EXCLUDING SPORT)? Paddington Bear
HOBBY YOU WOULD LIKE TO LEARN: The guitar
SURPRISING FACT ABOUT YOU: I can tie my shoelaces in under two seconds
FILM YOU CAN WATCH OVER AND OVER: The Spy Who Loved Me

Batting	Mat	Inns	NO	Runs	HS	Ave	SR	100	50	Ct	St
ODIs	2	1	1	3	3*	-	100.00	0	0	0	-
List A	37	17	6	64	12	5.81	48.48	0	0	6	-
T20s	65	18	9	29	6*	3.22	64.44	0	0	12	-

Bowling	Mat	Balls	Mdns	Runs	Wkts	BB	Ave	4wI	5wI	SR	Econ
ODIs	2	78	0	77	1	1-53	77.00	0	0	78.00	5.92
List A	37	1577	5	1298	37	5-45	35.08	0	1	42.62	4.93
T20s	65	1063	0	1198	56	4-14	22.60	2	0	20.05	6.76

GRACE BALLINGER   LHB / LM / MVP50

FULL NAME: Grace Ballinger
BORN: April 3, 2002, Birmingham
SQUAD NO: 1
HEIGHT: 5ft 9in
NICKNAME: G Banger
EDUCATION: Plantsbrook School, Sutton Coldfield, Birmingham; Loughborough Univeristy
TEAMS: The Blaze, Northern Superchargers, Leicestershire, London Spirit, Warwickshire
ROLE: Bowler
DEBUT: List A: 2020; T20: 2018

BEST BATTING: 25 The Blaze vs South East Stars, Leicester, 2024
BEST BOWLING: 5-29 Lightning vs Thunder, Loughborough, 2022

FIRST CRICKET CLUB? Sutton Coldfield CC, Birmingham
EARLIEST CRICKETING MEMORY? Watching my dad at Highcroft CC in Birmingham
OPPONENT YOU MOST LOOK FORWARD TO PLAYING AGAINST? The team I'm most looking forward to coming up against is Durham at their place – that's my favourite away ground as an opening bowler
FAVOURITE WARM-UP SONG? Work It by Missy Elliott
SPECIALITY SUBJECT IN A PUB QUIZ (EXCLUDING SPORT)? Music
ONE THING YOU WANT TO DO BEFORE YOU DIE: Score a red-ball ton (as a nightwatchman)
HOBBY YOU WOULD LIKE TO LEARN: How to DJ so that I can go back-to-back with my older brother in Birmingham

Batting	Mat	Inns	NO	Runs	HS	Ave	SR	100	50	Ct	St
List A	38	23	15	128	25	16.00	46.37	0	0	9	-
T20s	67	27	11	252	59*	15.75	69.23	0	2	5	-

Bowling	Mat	Balls	Mdns	Runs	Wkts	BB	Ave	4wI	5wI	SR	Econ
List A	38	1642	22	1303	48	5-29	27.14	3	1	34.20	4.76
T20s	67	1101	6	1179	44	3-6	26.79	0	0	25.02	6.42

TAMMY BEAUMONT

RHB / WK / MVP43

FULL NAME: Tamsin Tilley Beaumont
BORN: March 11, 1991, Dover, Kent
SQUAD NO: 12
HEIGHT: 5ft 2in
EDUCATION: Sir Roger Manwood's School, Kent; Loughborough University
TEAMS: England, The Blaze, Welsh Fire, Adelaide Strikers, Kent, London Spirit, Melbourne Renegades, Southern Vipers, Surrey Stars, Sydney Thunder
ROLE: Batter
DEBUT: Test: 2013; ODI: 2009; T20I: 2009; List A: 2007; T20: 2008

BEST BATTING: 168* England vs Pakistan, Taunton, 2016

WHICH TEAMMATE HAS HAD THE BIGGEST IMPACT ON YOUR GAME? Danni Wyatt-Hodge for the way she sees the game and her fearless approach regardless of the situation. Sometimes I wish I was more like her

WHICH GROUND DO YOU MOST ENJOY VISITING? The Adelaide Oval – a stunning venue with the right blend of modern and historical parts. And you can't beat the pink sunsets over the ground

CHOOSE A FANTASY SLIP CORDON TO SPEND A DAY IN THE FIELD WITH: Kumar Sangakkara (wk), Stephen Fry, Me, Andrew Flintoff

Batting	Mat	Inns	NO	Runs	HS	Ave	SR	100	50	Ct	St
Tests	11	18	0	612	208	34.00	48.76	1	2	13	-
ODIs	127	117	12	4274	168*	40.70	75.43	10	23	36	4
T20Is	104	88	11	1859	116	24.14	108.96	1	10	14	4
List A	253	234	29	8195	168*	39.97	70.10	14	52	105	33
T20s	320	297	34	6532	118	24.83	-	3	27	63	25

Bowling	Mat	Balls	Mdns	Runs	Wkts	BB	Ave	4wl	5wl	SR	Econ
Tests	11	-	-	-	-	-	-	-	-	-	-
ODIs	127	-	-	-	-	-	-	-	-	-	-
T20Is	104	-	-	-	-	-	-	-	-	-	-
List A	253	-	-	-	-	-	-	-	-	-	-
T20s	320	-	-	-	-	-	-	-	-	-	-

LAUREN BELL   RHB / RFM

FULL NAME: Lauren Katie Bell
BORN: January 2, 2001, Swindon, Wiltshire
SQUAD NO: 63
HEIGHT: 6ft 1in
NICKNAME: Belly
EDUCATION: Bradfield College;
Loughborough University
TEAMS: England, Hampshire, Southern Brave,
Berkshire, Middlesex, Southern Vipers,
Sydney Thunder, UP Warriorz
ROLE: Bowler
DEBUT: Test: 2022; ODI: 2022; T20I: 2022;
List A: 2015; T20: 2015

BEST BATTING: 36 Berkshire vs Surrey, Maidenhead, 2018
BEST BOWLING: 5-37 England vs New Zealand, Bristol, 2024

FIRST CRICKET CLUB: Hungerford CC, Berkshire
WHICH TEAMMATE HAS HAD THE BIGGEST IMPACT ON YOUR GAME? Kate Cross, my
bowling partner
WHO IS THE TOUGHEST BOWLER TO FACE IN DOMESTIC CRICKET? Georgia Adams
WHAT KEEPS YOU AWAKE AT NIGHT? TikTok
WHAT'S THE SILLIEST OUTFIT YOU'VE EVER WORN? I once dressed up as a pea
CHOOSE A FANTASY SLIP CORDON TO SPEND A DAY IN THE FIELD WITH: Taylor Swift (wk),
Shrek, David Beckham, Barbie

Batting	Mat	Inns	NO	Runs	HS	Ave	SR	100	50	Ct	St
Tests	5	8	6	19	8	9.50	23.17	0	0	2	-
ODIs	19	8	3	27	11*	5.40	50.00	0	0	6	-
T20Is	29	1	0	0	0	0.00	0.00	0	0	5	-
List A	64	38	10	243	36	8.67	-	0	0	12	-
T20s	123	34	11	201	35	8.73	75.56	0	0	19	-

Bowling	Mat	Balls	Mdns	Runs	Wkts	BB	Ave	4wI	5wI	SR	Econ
Tests	5	750	22	434	18	4-27	24.11	-	0	41.66	3.47
ODIs	19	929	3	836	34	5-37	24.58	1	1	27.32	5.39
T20Is	29	608	0	736	37	4-12	19.89	1	0	16.43	7.26
List A	64	2858	29	2182	97	5-37	22.49	4	1	29.46	4.58
T20s	123	2265	6	2609	123	4-10	21.21	3	0	18.41	6.91

OLIVIA BELL

RHB / OB

LANCASHIRE

FULL NAME: Olivia Niamh Bell
BORN: November 12, 2003, Stockport, Cheshire
SQUAD NO: 4
HEIGHT: 5ft 4in
NICKNAME: Belly
EDUCATION: Stockport School, Cheshire; Aquinas College, Stockport; UA92, Old Trafford
TEAMS: Scotland, Lancashire, Thunder
ROLE: Bowler
DEBUT: ODI: 2023; T20I: 2022; List A: 2023; T20: 2022

BEST BATTING: 22 Lancashire vs North East Warriors, Croston, 2024
BEST BOWLING: 4-19 Lancashire vs North East Warriors, Croston, 2024

FIRST CRICKET CLUB? Stockport Georgians CC, Manchester
EARLIEST CRICKETING MEMORY? Playing at U6 level at my local club
WHAT WILL YOU MISS ABOUT REGIONAL CRICKET? It grew a lot over the last few years and should not be forgotten
WHAT EXCITES YOU ABOUT THE NEW COUNTY STRUCTURE? Being aligned with the men's game, hopefully increasing the fans and public engagement with the women's domestic game
OPPONENT YOU MOST LOOK FORWARD TO PLAYING AGAINST? Kathryn Bryce – I play with her at Scotland. She's always a prize wicket
FAVOURITE WARM-UP SONG? Escapism by RAYE
HOW MANY HOURS DO YOU SPEND ON YOUR PHONE A DAY? Two to three
ONE THING YOU WANT TO DO BEFORE YOU DIE: A huge charity fundraising event
SURPRISING FACT ABOUT YOU: I love reading and taking naps – not really a fan of going out clubbing or anything like that
FILM YOU CAN WATCH OVER AND OVER: Little Women

Batting	Mat	Inns	NO	Runs	HS	Ave	SR	100	50	Ct	St
ODIs	6	5	2	32	15*	10.66	44.44	0	0	1	-
T20Is	9	2	2	5	3*	-	45.45	0	0	2	-
List A	13	10	3	84	22	12.00	42.00	0	0	3	-
T20s	21	9	4	29	7	5.80	-	0	0	4	-

Bowling	Mat	Balls	Mdns	Runs	Wkts	BB	Ave	4wI	5wI	SR	Econ
ODIs	6	288	7	160	3	1-15	53.33	0	0	96.00	3.33
T20Is	9	192	1	194	12	2-18	16.16	0	0	16.00	6.06
List A	13	661	19	369	22	4-19	16.77	3	0	30.04	3.34
T20s	21	433	3	409	31	4-37	13.19	1	0	13.96	5.66

MAIA BOUCHIER

RHB / RM

FULL NAME: Maia Emily Bouchier
BORN: December 5, 1998, Kensington, London
SQUAD NO: 14
HEIGHT: 5ft 9in
EDUCATION: Rugby School, Warwickshire; Oxford Brookes University
TEAMS: England, Hampshire, Southern Brave, Auckland, Melbourne Stars, Middlesex, Southern Vipers, Western Australia
ROLE: Batter
DEBUT: Test: 2024; ODI: 2023; T20I: 2021; List A: 2014; T20: 2014

BEST BATTING: 100* England vs New Zealand, Worcester, 2024
BEST BOWLING: 3-24 Middlesex vs Warwickshire, Wellesbourne, 2014

FIRST CRICKET CLUB? Primrose Hill CC, London
EARLIEST CRICKETING MEMORY? Being dressed in full whites aged about four, and playing cricket with my South African family in Cape Town
WHAT WILL YOU MISS ABOUT REGIONAL CRICKET? The Vipers name and brand
WHAT EXCITES YOU ABOUT THE NEW COUNTY STRUCTURE? Better facilities and funding, and more opportunities to play the longer formats
OPPONENT YOU MOST LOOK FORWARD TO PLAYING AGAINST? Tilly Corteen-Coleman – she has been a teammate and I'd love to get in the battle with her
FAVOURITE WARM-UP SONG? Houdini by Dua Lipa
ONE THING YOU WANT TO DO BEFORE YOU DIE: Run a marathon
WHICH PUBLIC FIGURE INSPIRES YOU (EXCLUDING SPORTSPEOPLE)? David Attenborough
FILM YOU CAN WATCH OVER AND OVER: Interstellar

Batting	Mat	Inns	NO	Runs	HS	Ave	SR	100	50	Ct	St
Tests	2	4	0	129	126	32.25	68.61	1	0	0	-
ODIs	17	15	2	482	100*	37.07	106.87	1	2	4	-
T20Is	44	37	6	722	91	23.29	122.16	0	3	12	-
List A	87	80	9	2243	100*	31.59	81.32	1	14	34	-
T20s	197	180	28	3217	93	21.16	-	0	9	84	-

Bowling	Mat	Balls	Mdns	Runs	Wkts	BB	Ave	4wI	5wI	SR	Econ
Tests	2	-	-	-	-	-	-	-	-	-	-
ODIs	17	-	-	-	-	-	-	-	-	-	-
T20Is	44	-	-	-	-	-	-	-	-	-	-
List A	87	568	4	389	16	3-24	24.31	0	0	35.50	4.10
T20s	197	234	1	236	12	3-18	19.66	0	0	19.50	6.05

GEORGIE BOYCE

RHB / RM

FULL NAME: Georgie Eva Burton Boyce
BORN: October 4, 1998, Nottingham
SQUAD NO: 4
HEIGHT: 5ft 6in
EDUCATION: The Holgate Academy, Hucknall, Nottinghamshire; Loughborough University
TEAMS: The Blaze, Lancashire, Lancashire Thunder, Manchester Originals, Nottinghamshire, Thunder
ROLE: Batter
DEBUT: List A: 2014; T20: 2013

BEST BATTING: 104 The Blaze vs Sunrisers, Loughborough, 2023
BEST BOWLING: 2-20 Lancashire vs Yorkshire, Harrogate, 2019

FIRST CRICKET CLUB? Notts & Arnold CC, Nottingham
EARLIEST CRICKETING MEMORY? Taking part in a Chance to Shine event with Jenny Gunn
WHAT EXCITES YOU ABOUT THE NEW COUNTY STRUCTURE? Beating Notts
FAVOURITE WARM-UP SONG? Anything but rap
HOW MANY HOURS DO YOU SPEND ON YOUR PHONE A DAY? Too many
SPECIALITY SUBJECT IN A PUB QUIZ (EXCLUDING SPORT)? Friends (TV series)
ONE THING YOU WANT TO DO BEFORE YOU DIE: Climb to Everest Base Camp
SURPRISING FACT ABOUT YOU: I have been riding motorbikes since I was four
FILM YOU CAN WATCH OVER AND OVER: Any musical

Batting	Mat	Inns	NO	Runs	HS	Ave	SR	100	50	Ct	St
List A	69	68	3	1544	104	23.75	-	1	8	15	-
T20s	94	88	9	1918	96*	24.27	-	0	13	15	-

Bowling	Mat	Balls	Mdns	Runs	Wkts	BB	Ave	4wI	5wI	SR	Econ
List A	69	444	6	308	6	2-20	51.33	0	0	74.00	4.16
T20s	94	234	0	236	8	2-3	29.50	0	0	29.25	6.05

CHLOE BREWER

RHB / RM

FULL NAME: Chloe Brewer
BORN: July 12, 2002
SQUAD NO: 2
HEIGHT: 5ft 7in
NICKNAME: Brew
EDUCATION: Sir William Perkins's School, Surrey; The Magna Carta School, Staines
TEAMS: Birmingham Bears, Birmingham Phoenix, Central Sparks, Surrey, South East Stars
ROLE: Batter
DEBUT: List A: 2019; T20: 2019

BEST BATTING: 79 South East Stars vs Southern Vipers, The Oval, 2020
BEST BOWLING: 1-26 South East Stars vs Sunrisers, Chelmsford, 2020

FIRST CRICKET CLUB? Shepperton CC, Surrey
EARLIEST CRICKETING MEMORY? Playing at school
WHAT EXCITES YOU ABOUT THE NEW COUNTY STRUCTURE? Playing under the name of a club which has a base we can call home
HOW MANY HOURS DO YOU SPEND ON YOUR PHONE A DAY? Three
SPECIALITY SUBJECT IN A PUB QUIZ (EXCLUDING SPORT)? Music
ONE THING YOU WANT TO DO BEFORE YOU DIE: Climb Mount Kilimanjaro
SURPRISING FACT ABOUT YOU: I'm converting a van
FILM YOU CAN WATCH OVER AND OVER: How to Lose a Guy in 10 Days

Batting	Mat	Inns	NO	Runs	HS	Ave	SR	100	50	Ct	St
List A	27	25	1	541	79	22.54	68.39	0	4	7	-
T20s	18	13	0	123	41	9.46	78.84	0	0	4	-
Bowling	Mat	Balls	Mdns	Runs	Wkts	BB	Ave	4wl	5wl	SR	Econ
List A	27	60	1	55	1	1-26	55.00	0	0	60.00	5.50
T20s	18	28	0	47	1	1-21	47.00	0	0	28.00	10.07

KATHRYN BRYCE

RHB / RM / MVP1

FULL NAME: Kathryn Emma Bryce
BORN: November 17, 1997, Edinburgh
SQUAD NO: 17
HEIGHT: 5ft 4in
EDUCATION: Loughborough University
TEAMS: Scotland, The Blaze, Manchester Originals, Derbyshire, Gujarat Giants, Hobart Hurricanes, Loughborough Lightning, Trent Rockets, Warwickshire
ROLE: Allrounder
DEBUT: ODI: 2023; T20I: 2018; List A: 2017; T20: 2017

BEST BATTING: 162 Lightning vs Central Sparks, Loughborough, 2021
BEST BOWLING: 5-29 Lightning vs Northern Diamonds, Chester-le-Street, 2020

FIRST CRICKET CLUB? Watsonian CC, Edinburgh
EARLIEST CRICKETING MEMORY? Playing with my sister in Granny's back garden
WHAT WILL YOU MISS ABOUT REGIONAL CRICKET? Representing a wider area
WHAT EXCITES YOU ABOUT THE NEW COUNTY STRUCTURE? Sharing an identity with a county and being able to connect with the Nottinghamshire supporters
FAVOURITE WARM-UP SONG? Wagon Wheel by Darius Rucker
HOW MANY HOURS DO YOU SPEND ON YOUR PHONE A DAY? I don't want to know
SPECIALITY SUBJECT IN A PUB QUIZ (EXCLUDING SPORT)? Musicals
ONE THING YOU WANT TO DO BEFORE YOU DIE: Go to Antarctica
HOBBY YOU WOULD LIKE TO LEARN: Play the piano
WHICH PUBLIC FIGURE INSPIRES YOU (EXCLUDING SPORTSPEOPLE)? Michelle Obama
FILM YOU CAN WATCH OVER AND OVER: Mamma Mia!

Batting	Mat	Inns	NO	Runs	HS	Ave	SR	100	50	Ct	St
ODIs	5	5	0	301	83	60.20	86.00	0	4	2	-
T20Is	49	47	13	1273	73*	37.44	103.74	0	10	27	-
List A	78	75	9	1987	162	30.10	68.96	3	12	33	-
T20s	185	160	50	3449	79*	31.35		-	25	68	-

Bowling	Mat	Balls	Mdns	Runs	Wkts	BB	Ave	4wl	5wl	SR	Econ
ODIs	5	168	2	100	5	2-12	20.00	0	0	33.60	3.57
T20Is	49	949	10	727	48	4-8	15.14	2	0	19.77	4.59
List A	78	2969	56	1854	81	5-29	22.88	4	1	36.65	3.74
T20s	185	3026	25	2887	149	5-13	19.37	4	1	20.30	5.72

SARAH BRYCE — RHB / WK / MVP15

FULL NAME: Sarah Jennifer Bryce
BORN: January 8, 2000, Edinburgh
SQUAD NO: 8
HEIGHT: 5ft 7in
NICKNAME: Sazzle
EDUCATION: Loughborough University
TEAMS: Scotland, The Blaze, Welsh Fire, Delhi Capitals, Kent, Lightning, Nottinghamshire, Oval Invincibles, Sydney Sixers
ROLE: Wicketkeeper/batter
DEBUT: ODI: 2023; T20I: 2018; List A: 2019; T20: 2018

BEST BATTING: 136* Lightning vs Central Sparks, Leicester, 2020

FIRST CRICKET CLUB? Watsonian CC, Edinburgh
EARLIEST CRICKETING MEMORY? Playing in the garden with my dad and sister
WHAT WILL YOU MISS ABOUT REGIONAL CRICKET? Being connected to the whole region
WHAT EXCITES YOU ABOUT THE NEW COUNTY STRUCTURE? Being fully integrated into Nottinghamshire CCC
HOW MANY HOURS DO YOU SPEND ON YOUR PHONE A DAY? Two hours and 30 minutes
SPECIALITY SUBJECT IN A PUB QUIZ (EXCLUDING SPORT)? Musicals
WHICH PUBLIC FIGURE INSPIRES YOU (EXCLUDING SPORTSPEOPLE)? Michelle Obama
FILM YOU CAN WATCH OVER AND OVER: Pitch Perfect

Batting	Mat	Inns	NO	Runs	HS	Ave	SR	100	50	Ct	St
ODIs	5	5	0	171	84	34.20	71.54	0	1	5	3
T20Is	58	58	13	1290	67	28.66	106.52	0	4	29	33
List A	70	68	5	1986	136*	31.52	70.07	1	14	49	23
T20s	179	159	42	3353	101*	28.65	-	1	15	73	86
Bowling	Mat	Balls	Mdns	Runs	Wkts	BB	Ave	4wl	5wl	SR	Econ
ODIs	5	-	-	-	-	-	-	-	-	-	-
T20Is	58	-	-	-	-	-	-	-	-	-	-
List A	70	-	-	-	-	-	-	-	-	-	-
T20s	179	-	-	-	-	-	-	-	-	-	-

ALICE CAPSEY

RHB / OB

SURREY

FULL NAME: Alice Rose Capsey
BORN: August 11, 2004, Redhill, Surrey
SQUAD NO: 26
HEIGHT: 5ft 4in
EDUCATION: Bede's Senior School,
Hailsham, East Sussex; Lancing College,
West Sussex
TEAMS: England, Surrey, Oval Invincibles,
Delhi Capitals, Melbourne Renegades, South
East Stars
ROLE: Batter
DEBUT: ODI: 2022; T20I: 2022;
List A: 2019; T20: 2019

BEST BATTING: 78 South East Stars vs Lightning, Beckenham, 2021
BEST BOWLING: 6-28 South East Stars vs Western Storm, Bristol, 2023

FIRST CRICKET CLUB? Capel CC, Surrey
BEST PLAYER IN DOMESTIC CRICKET (EXCLUDING TEAMMATES)? Ella McCaughan
BEST PERFORMANCE AS A PRO? 80 not out for Melbourne Stars against Hobart Hurricanes in
the 2022/23 Big Bash
FAVOURITE FORMAT? T20 – quick and exciting
FAVOURITE TOY AS A KID? A football
WHAT WOULD BE YOUR PERFECT BREAKFAST? Smashed avocado and eggs on toast

Batting	Mat	Inns	NO	Runs	HS	Ave	SR	100	50	Ct	St
ODIs	23	17	2	283	44	18.86	73.31	0	0	6	-
T20Is	38	36	3	707	67*	21.42	119.42	0	4	13	-
List A	42	36	4	660	78	20.62	73.74	0	3	12	-
T20s	156	141	9	2860	80*	21.66	124.13	0	14	54	-

Bowling	Mat	Balls	Mdns	Runs	Wkts	BB	Ave	4wI	5wI	SR	Econ
ODIs	23	282	4	215	8	3-22	26.87	0	0	35.25	4.57
T20Is	38	132	0	147	6	2-4	24.50	0	0	22.00	6.68
List A	42	833	6	664	26	6-28	25.53	0	1	32.03	4.78
T20s	156	1673	1	1891	97	5-25	19.49	0	1	17.24	6.78

AMARA CARR   RHB / WK

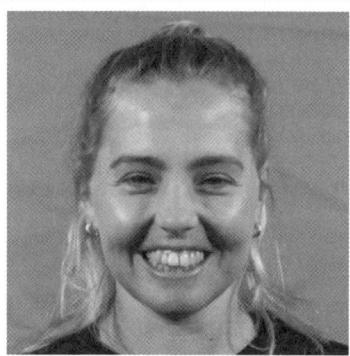

FULL NAME: Amara Danielle Carr
BORN: April 17, 1994, Plymouth, Devon
SQUAD NO: 17
HEIGHT: 5ft 2in
NICKNAME: Mars
EDUCATION: University of Essex
TEAMS: Essex, Devon, Manchester Originals, Middlesex, Somerset, Sunrisers
ROLE: Wicketkeeper/batter
DEBUT: List A: 2008; T20: 2009

ESSEX

BEST BATTING: 105 Devon vs Middlesex, Eastcote, 2019

FIRST CRICKET CLUB: Mount Wise CC, Plymouth, Devon
EARLIEST CRICKETING MEMORY? Saturdays down the cricket club
WHAT EXCITES YOU ABOUT THE NEW COUNTY STRUCTURE? The T20 Blast double headers
ONE THING YOU WANT TO DO BEFORE YOU DIE: Climb a mountain
HOBBY YOU WOULD LIKE TO LEARN: Spanish
CHOOSE A FANTASY SLIP CORDON TO SPEND A DAY IN THE FIELD WITH: Adam Gilchrist (wk), Lissy Macleod, Ryan Reynolds, Will Smith
FILM YOU CAN WATCH OVER AND OVER: Coach Carter

Batting	Mat	Inns	NO	Runs	HS	Ave	SR	100	50	Ct	St
List A	128	116	11	2028	105	19.31	-	1	8	68	44
T20s	85	67	15	939	52	18.05	-	0	2	20	37
Bowling	Mat	Balls	Mdns	Runs	Wkts	BB	Ave	4wI	5wI	SR	Econ
List A	128	-	-	-	-	-	-	-	-	-	-
T20s	85	-	-	-	-	-	-	-	-	-	-

DARCEY CARTER

RHB / OB

LANCASHIRE

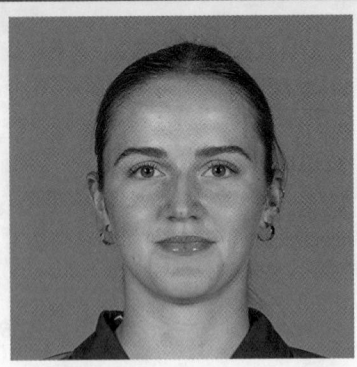

FULL NAME: Darcey Elizabeth Morris Carter
BORN: May 31, 2005, Sidcup, Kent
SQUAD NO: TBC
HEIGHT: 5ft 9in
NICKNAME: DC
EDUCATION: Canterbury Academy
TEAMS: Scotland, Lancashire, Kent, South East Stars, Thunder
ROLE: Allrounder
DEBUT: ODI: 2023; T20I: 2023; List A: 2023; T20: 2022

BEST BATTING: 86 Scotland vs Netherlands, Amstelveen, 2024
BEST BOWLING: 3-20 Scotland vs Papua New Guinea, Amstelveen, 2024

FIRST CRICKET CLUB? Bapchild CC, Sittingbourne, Kent
EARLIEST CRICKETING MEMORY? Watching my dad play
WHAT EXCITES YOU ABOUT THE NEW COUNTY STRUCTURE? The T20 Blast double headers
FAVOURITE WARM-UP SONG? Who's That Girl? by Eve
HOW MANY HOURS DO YOU SPEND ON YOUR PHONE A DAY? Six
ONE THING YOU WANT TO DO BEFORE YOU DIE: Go skydiving
HOBBY YOU WOULD LIKE TO LEARN: How to juggle
FILM YOU CAN WATCH OVER AND OVER: The Lion King

Batting	Mat	Inns	NO	Runs	HS	Ave	SR	100	50	Ct	St
ODIs	9	9	0	200	86	22.22	73.80	0	1	4	-
T20Is	21	20	3	354	54*	20.82	98.88	0	2	5	-
List A	15	15	0	221	86	14.73	66.16	0	1	7	-
T20s	33	22	3	414	54*	21.78	101.97	0	2	9	-
Bowling	Mat	Balls	Mdns	Runs	Wkts	BB	Ave	4wI	5wI	SR	Econ
ODIs	9	370	3	265	7	3-20	37.85	0	0	52.85	4.29
T20Is	21	228	0	222	16	3-11	13.87	0	0	14.25	5.84
List A	15	592	4	453	13	3-20	34.84	0	0	45.53	4.59
T20s	33	418	1	366	26	3-11	14.07	0	0	16.07	5.25

KELLY CASTLE RHB / RMF

FULL NAME: Kelly Shannon Castle
BORN: September 4, 1997, Southend-on-Sea, Essex
SQUAD NO: 7
HEIGHT: 5ft 9in
NICKNAME: KC
EDUCATION: The King Edmund School, Rochford, Essex; Anglia Ruskin University
TEAMS: Essex, Sunrisers
ROLE: Bowler
DEBUT: List A: 2012; T20: 2011

ESSEX

BEST BATTING: 52 Sunrisers vs Lightning, Loughborough, 2021
BEST BOWLING: 5-18 Essex vs Scotland, Billericay, 2015

FIRST CRICKET CLUB? Rayleigh CC, Wickford, Essex
EARLIEST CRICKETING MEMORY? Playing ASDA Kwik Cricket on the outfield at Headingley
WHAT EXCITES YOU ABOUT THE NEW COUNTY STRUCTURE? Having somewhere to call home
FAVOURITE WARM-UP SONG? Lyla by Oasis
HOW MANY HOURS DO YOU SPEND ON YOUR PHONE A DAY? Three
SPECIALITY SUBJECT IN A PUB QUIZ (EXCLUDING SPORT)? Music – any genre, any decade
ONE THING YOU WANT TO DO BEFORE YOU DIE: Perform on Broadway
WHICH PUBLIC FIGURE INSPIRES YOU (EXCLUDING SPORTSPEOPLE)? Dolly Parton – the queen of country music and a strong independent woman
SURPRISING FACT ABOUT YOU: I helped my brother win a game show
FILM YOU CAN WATCH OVER AND OVER: Any Harry Potter film

Batting	Mat	Inns	NO	Runs	HS	Ave	SR	100	50	Ct	St
List A	72	62	6	652	52	11.64	-	0	1	16	-
T20s	84	76	19	894	75	15.68	84.90	0	2	25	-

Bowling	Mat	Balls	Mdns	Runs	Wkts	BB	Ave	4wI	5wI	SR	Econ
List A	72	1882	27	1282	48	5-18	26.70	0	1	39.20	4.08
T20s	84	1205	4	1107	57	3-6	19.42	0	0	21.14	5.51

KIRA CHATHLI

RHB / WK

FULL NAME: Kira Meghan Chathli
BORN: July 29, 1999, Southwark, Surrey
SQUAD NO: 20
HEIGHT: 5ft 5in
NICKNAME: KC
EDUCATION: Sydenham High School,
London; University College London
TEAMS: Surrey, Oval Invincibles, South East
Stars
ROLE: Batter/wicketkeeper
DEBUT: List A: 2013; T20: 2014

BEST BATTING: 86* South East Stars vs Western Storm, Beckenham, 2024

WHICH PART OF THE SEASON DO YOU MOST ENJOY? April and May
WHICH GROUND DO YOU MOST ENJOY VISITING? Lord's
WHO IS THE MOST TALENTED TEENAGER IN WOMEN'S DOMESTIC CRICKET? Jemima Spence
IF YOU COULD PINCH A PLAYER FROM ANOTHER TEAM, WHO WOULD IT BE? Sarah Bryce
WHO IS THE TOUGHEST BOWLER TO FACE IN DOMESTIC CRICKET? Sarah Glenn
WHAT ONE THING WOULD YOU CHANGE ABOUT WOMEN'S CRICKET IN ENGLAND? Bring in
some red-ball cricket
WHAT'S THE SILLIEST OUTFIT YOU'VE EVER WORN? I stick to tracksuits
SURPRISING FACT ABOUT YOU: I am a vegetarian who eats tuna

Batting	Mat	Inns	NO	Runs	HS	Ave	SR	100	50	Ct	St
List A	46	43	2	874	86*	21.31	65.96	0	7	31	2
T20s	59	40	13	439	36	16.25	-	0	0	16	9
Bowling	Mat	Balls	Mdns	Runs	Wkts	BB	Ave	4wi	5wi	SR	Econ
List A	46	-	-	-	-	-	-	-	-	-	-
T20s	59	-	-	-	-	-	-	-	-	-	-

ELLA CLARIDGE

RHB / WK

FULL NAME: Ella Caterina Claridge
BORN: September 28, 2002, Aylesbury, Buckinghamshire
SQUAD NO: 33
HEIGHT: 5ft 8in
EDUCATION: Cedars Upper School, Bedfordshire; Loughborough University
TEAMS: USA, The Blaze, Buckinghamshire, Leicestershire, Lightning
ROLE: Wicketkeeper/batter
DEBUT: ODI: 2024; List A: 2017; T20: 2017

BEST BATTING: 71 The Blaze vs South East Stars, Beckenham, 2024

FIRST CRICKET CLUB? Leighton Buzzard Town CC, Bedfordshire
EARLIEST CRICKETING MEMORY? Watching my dad on a Saturday afternoon at the local club
WHAT WILL YOU MISS ABOUT REGIONAL CRICKET? Playing at lots of different grounds
WHAT EXCITES YOU ABOUT THE NEW COUNTY STRUCTURE? More double headers with the men
OPPONENT YOU MOST LOOK FORWARD TO PLAYING AGAINST? Lauren Bell – it's a great challenge against such a good bowler
FAVOURITE WARM-UP SONG? Power by Kanye West
HOW MANY HOURS DO YOU SPEND ON YOUR PHONE A DAY? Four
SPECIALITY SUBJECT IN A PUB QUIZ (EXCLUDING SPORT)? Science
HOBBY YOU WOULD LIKE TO LEARN: How to shuffle cards
WHICH PUBLIC FIGURE INSPIRES YOU (EXCLUDING SPORTSPEOPLE)? Michelle Obama
SURPRISING FACT ABOUT YOU: I can juggle with four balls
FILM YOU CAN WATCH OVER AND OVER: The Hunger Games: Catching Fire

Batting	Mat	Inns	NO	Runs	HS	Ave	SR	100	50	Ct	St
ODIs	5	5	1	79	49*	19.75	81.44	0	0	2	-
List A	38	36	6	828	71	27.60	79.69	0	3	16	8
T20s	52	47	6	894	96	21.80	-	0	6	10	11

Bowling	Mat	Balls	Mdns	Runs	Wkts	BB	Ave	4wl	5wl	SR	Econ
ODIs	5	-	-	-	-	-	-	-	-	-	-
List A	38	-	-	-	-	-	-	-	-	-	-
T20s	52	-	-	-	-	-	-	-	-	-	-

ALICE CLARKE LHB / WK

LANCASHIRE

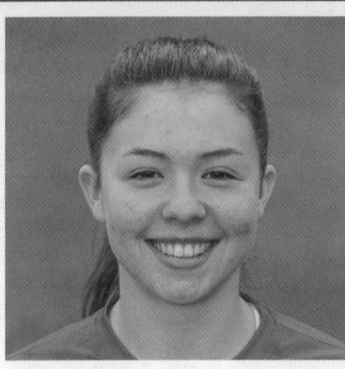

FULL NAME: Alice Clarke
BORN: August 4, 2001, Blackburn, Lancashire
SQUAD NO: 35
HEIGHT: 5ft 5in
TEAMS: Lancashire, Cumbria, Thunder
ROLE: Wicketkeeper/batter
DEBUT: List A: 2020; T20: 2018

BEST BATTING: 62 Lancashire vs North East Warriors, Croston, 2024

NOTES: The 23-year-old wicketkeeper-batter signed her first professional deal at Old Trafford last November ahead of the new-look domestic season in which Lancashire are one of eight counties who will play in Tier One this summer. Clarke, who bats in the top order, had previously held a pay-as-you-play contract with Lancashire but is now on a full-time deal until the end of 2025. She has made six senior appearances for Lancashire, five of them last year, with her top score of 41 coming during the final match of the season against Western Storm. Once of Accrington CC, Clarke has also played for the Red Rose at U15 and U17 level and impressed during her time in the club's Academy before moving into the senior set-up. "It is a proud moment to sign my first professional contract with Lancashire and I am looking forward to the opportunity which lies ahead," she said. "It was brilliant to play some first-team cricket in the regional competitions last season, now I want to push on and hopefully cement my place in the side for 2025." David Thorley, director of cricket performance at Lancashire, added: "Alice has been in and around our set-up for a while now and it was great to see her kick on last season, play regular first-team cricket during the second half of the campaign and really improve her game to earn this contract"

Batting	Mat	Inns	NO	Runs	HS	Ave	SR	100	50	Ct	St
List A	8	8	0	174	62	21.75	58.38	0	1	3	2
T20s	26	25	6	432	75*	22.73	-	0	2	4	4

Bowling	Mat	Balls	Mdns	Runs	Wkts	BB	Ave	4wl	5wl	SR	Econ
List A	8	-	-	-	-	-	-	-	-	-	-
T20s	26	-	-	-	-	-	-	-	-	-	-

DANIELLE COLLINS

LHB / RM

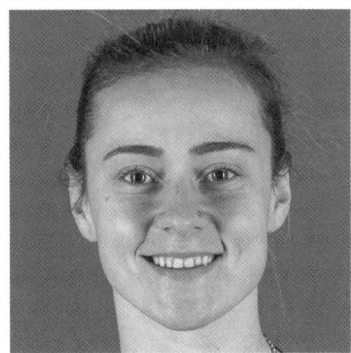

FULL NAME: Danielle Louise Collins
BORN: June 7, 2000, Bury, Lancashire, England
SQUAD NO: 30
HEIGHT: 5ft 7in
EDUCATION: The Elton High School; Bury College
TEAMS: Lancashire, Thunder, Cumbria
ROLE: Batter
DEBUT: List A: 2019; T20: 2018

BEST BATTING: 32 Thunder vs Western Storm, Old Trafford, 2022

WHICH TEAMMATE HAS HAD THE BIGGEST IMPACT ON YOUR GAME? Ellie Threlkeld – she's always pushing me to be a better cricketer and person
WHICH GROUND DO YOU MOST ENJOY VISITING? Headingley – it's always nice to beat Yorkshire in Yorkshire
WHO IS THE MOST TALENTED TEENAGER IN WOMEN'S DOMESTIC CRICKET? Mahika Gaur
IF YOU COULD PINCH A PLAYER FROM ANOTHER TEAM, WHO WOULD IT BE? Georgia Adams
WHO IS THE TOUGHEST BOWLER TO FACE IN DOMESTIC CRICKET? Lauren Filer – she's quick
WHAT KEEPS YOU AWAKE AT NIGHT? TV, thinking and music
CHOOSE A FANTASY SLIP CORDON TO SPEND A DAY IN THE FIELD WITH: Adele (wk), Alastair Cook, Cristiano Ronaldo, Tyson Fury

Batting	Mat	Inns	NO	Runs	HS	Ave	SR	100	50	Ct	St
List A	32	29	5	326	32	13.58	51.82	0	0	4	-
T20s	54	41	8	439	51	13.30	81.29	0	1	9	-

Bowling	Mat	Balls	Mdns	Runs	Wkts	BB	Ave	4wI	5wI	SR	Econ
List A	32	18	0	20	0	0-20	-	-	-	-	6.66
T20s	54	6	0	16	0	0-16	-	-	-	-	16.00

KATE COPPACK

RHB / RMF

ESSEX

FULL NAME: Kate Louise Coppack
BORN: August 30, 1994, Chester, Cheshire
SQUAD NO: 11
HEIGHT: 5ft 4in
NICKNAME: Coppie
EDUCATION: University of Nottingham; University of New South Wales, Sydney; BPP Law School, Leeds
TEAMS: Essex, Berkshire, Cheshire, Middlesex, Sunrisers
ROLE: Allrounder
DEBUT: List A: 2009; T20: 2009

BEST BATTING: 56 Cheshire vs Suffolk, Woodford, 2015
BEST BOWLING: 6-28 Cheshire vs Somerset, Warrington, 2011

FIRST CRICKET CLUB? Chester Boughton Hall CC, Chester
EARLIEST CRICKETING MEMORY? Freddie Flintoff bowling in the 2005 Ashes
WHAT WILL YOU MISS ABOUT REGIONAL CRICKET? Playing at lots of great county grounds within our region
WHAT EXCITES YOU ABOUT THE NEW COUNTY STRUCTURE? The T20 Blast double headers
FAVOURITE WARM-UP SONG? Kids by MGMT
HOW MANY HOURS DO YOU SPEND ON YOUR PHONE A DAY? 1.5
ONE THING YOU WANT TO DO BEFORE YOU DIE: Renovate a campervan
HOBBY YOU WOULD LIKE TO LEARN: Play the banjo
SURPRISING FACT ABOUT YOU: I once worked as a human billboard in Australia
FILM YOU CAN WATCH OVER AND OVER: Forrest Gump

Batting	Mat	Inns	NO	Runs	HS	Ave	SR	100	50	Ct	St
List A	80	55	16	545	56	13.97	62.14	0	1	15	-
T20s	78	49	11	618	51	16.26	-	0	1	12	-

Bowling	Mat	Balls	Mdns	Runs	Wkts	BB	Ave	4wI	5wI	SR	Econ
List A	80	2834	46	2056	88	6-28	23.36	3	1	32.20	4.35
T20s	78	1292	8	1061	60	3-11	17.68	0	0	21.53	4.92

FULL NAME: Emma Corney
BORN: September 15, 2003
SQUAD NO: 21
HEIGHT: 5ft 5in
NICKNAME: Corndog
EDUCATION: St Peter's Lympstone, Devon; Exeter School
TEAMS: Somerset, Devon, Western Storm
ROLE: Batter
DEBUT: List A: 2019; T20: 2019

BEST BATTING: 82 Devon vs Warwickshire, Exeter, 2024
BEST BOWLING: 1-16 Western Storm vs Sunrisers, Bristol, 2020

FIRST CRICKET CLUB? Woodbury CC, East Devon
WHAT WILL YOU MISS ABOUT REGIONAL CRICKET? Playing at the different venues around the south-west of England
WHAT EXCITES YOU ABOUT THE NEW COUNTY STRUCTURE? Making Taunton a fortress and building our fanbase
OPPONENT YOU MOST LOOK FORWARD TO PLAYING AGAINST? Sophia Smale – she always has plenty of chat, and she's a fellow Chelsea fan
FAVOURITE WARM-UP SONG? The Less I Know the Better by Tame Impala
HOW MANY HOURS DO YOU SPEND ON YOUR PHONE A DAY? 1.5
SPECIALITY SUBJECT IN A PUB QUIZ (EXCLUDING SPORT)? M5 service stations
ONE THING YOU WANT TO DO BEFORE YOU DIE: Travel South America
HOBBY YOU WOULD LIKE TO LEARN: Surfing
WHICH PUBLIC FIGURE INSPIRES YOU (EXCLUDING SPORTSPEOPLE)? Miranda Hart
SURPRISING FACT ABOUT YOU: I'm a summer-only golfer
FILM YOU CAN WATCH OVER AND OVER: Cars

Batting	Mat	Inns	NO	Runs	HS	Ave	SR	100	50	Ct	St
List A	34	29	1	714	82	25.50	61.97	0	4	3	-
T20s	27	25	4	662	64	31.52	101.84	0	2	4	-

Bowling	Mat	Balls	Mdns	Runs	Wkts	BB	Ave	4wI	5wI	SR	Econ
List A	34	138	0	114	2	1-16	57.00	0	0	69.00	4.95
T20s	27	36	0	23	2	2-15	11.50	0	0	18.00	3.83

TILLY CORTEEN-COLEMAN — LHB / SLA / MVP48

FULL NAME: Matilda Rose Corteen-Coleman
BORN: August 23, 2007, Canterbury, Kent
SQUAD NO: 21
HEIGHT: 5ft 8in
NICKNAME: Tilly Con Carne
EDUCATION: Kent College Canterbury
TEAMS: Surrey, Southern Brave, Kent, South East Stars
ROLE: Bowler
DEBUT: List A: 2024; T20: 2024

BEST BATTING: 1* South East Stars vs The Blaze, Beckenham, 2024
BEST BOWLING: 3-33 South East Stars vs Southern Vipers, Beckenham, 2024

FIRST CRICKET CLUB? St Lawrence & Highland Court CC, Kent
EARLIEST CRICKETING MEMORY? In the garden with my brother: I was batting and he said he was going to bowl "the rhino". He bowled it as fast as he could straight at me and it hit me in the face without bouncing
WHAT WILL YOU MISS ABOUT REGIONAL CRICKET? All the funny kits, and the Stars' team song
WHAT EXCITES YOU ABOUT THE NEW COUNTY STRUCTURE? Lots, in particular playing for Surrey and having The Oval as home
FAVOURITE WARM-UP SONG? Greenlight by Pitbull
HOW MANY HOURS DO YOU SPEND ON YOUR PHONE A DAY? Four
ONE THING YOU WANT TO DO BEFORE YOU DIE: Play for England
HOBBY YOU WOULD LIKE TO LEARN: Sign language
FILM YOU CAN WATCH OVER AND OVER: I don't watch movies – more of a series gal

Batting	Mat	Inns	NO	Runs	HS	Ave	SR	100	50	Ct	St
List A	9	6	2	4	1*	1.00	36.36	0	0	1	-
T20s	19	6	5	8	4*	8.00	42.10	0	0	4	-

Bowling	Mat	Balls	Mdns	Runs	Wkts	BB	Ave	4wI	5wI	SR	Econ
List A	9	416	3	253	10	3-33	25.30	0	0	41.60	3.64
T20s	19	383	1	399	22	5-19	18.13	0	1	17.40	6.25

AYLISH CRANSTONE

LHB / LM

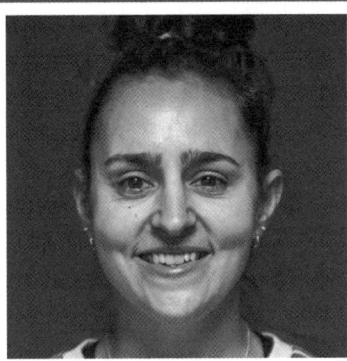

FULL NAME: Aylish Cranstone
BORN: August 28, 1994, Guildford, Surrey
SQUAD NO: 28
HEIGHT: 5ft 2in
EDUCATION: Weydon School, Farnham, Surrey; University of Exeter
TEAMS: Surrey, Devon, Hampshire, Oval Invincibles, South East Stars, Surrey Stars
ROLE: Batter
DEBUT: List A: 2008; T20: 2010

BEST BATTING: 134* Devon vs Essex, Dunmow, 2016
BEST BOWLING: 5-5 Devon vs Leicestershire, Bolham, 2016

WHICH PART OF THE SEASON DO YOU MOST ENJOY? June and July – the height of the season when things are hotting up
WHICH GROUND DO YOU MOST ENJOY VISITING? Chelmsford – there's always glorious sunshine at Chelmsford!
WHO IS THE TOUGHEST BOWLER TO FACE IN DOMESTIC CRICKET? Eva Gray – my former teammate and a great competitor
WHAT'S THE SILLIEST OUTFIT YOU'VE EVER WORN? Dressing up as a curling stone for a curling social at university
CHOOSE A FANTASY SLIP CORDON TO SPEND A DAY IN THE FIELD WITH: Amara Carr (wk), Elastigirl, Ben Stokes, Spiderman
SURPRISING FACT ABOUT YOU: I learned to scuba dive aged 12

Batting	Mat	Inns	NO	Runs	HS	Ave	SR	100	50	Ct	St
List A	111	107	12	2638	134*	27.76	-	1	15	30	-
T20s	93	73	16	1194	78*	20.94	102.75	0	6	21	-

Bowling	Mat	Balls	Mdns	Runs	Wkts	BB	Ave	4wI	5wI	SR	Econ
List A	111	883	16	662	23	5-5	28.78	0	1	38.39	4.49
T20s	93	153	1	120	8	3-17	15.00	0	0	19.12	4.70

KATE CROSS

RHB / RMF / MVP37

LANCASHIRE

FULL NAME: Kathryn Laura Cross
BORN: October 3, 1991, Manchester
SQUAD NO: 16
HEIGHT: 5ft 7in
EDUCATION: Bury Grammar School;
University of Leeds
TEAMS: England, Lancashire, Northern
Superchargers, Brisbane Heat, Manchester
Originals, Perth Scorchers, Royal Challengers
Bangalore, Thunder, Western Australia
ROLE: Bowler
DEBUT: Test: 2014; ODI: 2013; T20I: 2013;
List A: 2005; T20: 2008

BEST BATTING: 86 Lancashire vs Devon, Southport, 2010
BEST BOWLING: 6-30 England vs Ireland, Belfast, 2024

FIRST CRICKET CLUB: Heywood CC, Greater Manchester
WHICH TEAMMATE HAS HAD THE BIGGEST IMPACT ON YOUR GAME? Lauren Bell – her
energy and willingness to learn and try new skills has been really refreshing
WHICH PART OF THE SEASON DO YOU MOST ENJOY? Meeting up for the first day of the
international summer
WHAT'S THE SILLIEST OUTFIT YOU'VE EVER WORN? A Bugs Bunny costume (mum even
gave me a carrot to eat)
CHOOSE A FANTASY SLIP CORDON TO SPEND A DAY IN THE FIELD WITH: MS Dhoni (wk),
Kate Middleton, Luke Littler, Kevin Sinfield
SURPRISING FACT ABOUT YOU: I carry a lucky little pig with me wherever I play

Batting	Mat	Inns	NO	Runs	HS	Ave	SR	100	50	Ct	St
Tests	8	13	4	58	16	6.44	37.90	0	0	2	-
ODIs	72	34	12	271	38*	12.31	70.38	0	0	15	-
T20Is	18	4	2	3	2	1.50	42.85	0	0	4	-
List A	204	143	24	1784	86	14.99	-	0	6	70	-
T20s	171	102	28	893	59	12.06	-	0	1	53	-

Bowling	Mat	Balls	Mdns	Runs	Wkts	BB	Ave	4wI	5wI	SR	Econ
Tests	8	1464	52	768	25	4-63	30.72	-	0	58.56	3.14
ODIs	72	3192	40	2343	98	6-30	23.90	3	3	32.57	4.40
T20Is	18	350	0	427	14	2-18	30.50	0	0	25.00	7.32
List A	204	8803	165	5696	257	6-30	22.16	10	4	34.25	3.88
T20s	171	3285	13	3689	143	4-20	25.79	1	0	22.97	6.73

NAOMI DATTANI

LHB / LMF

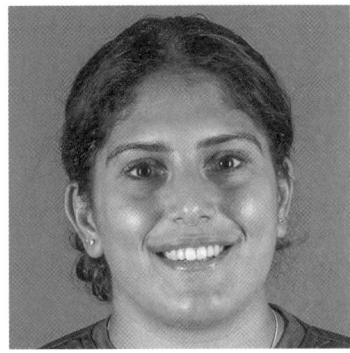

FULL NAME: Naomi Dilip Dattani
BORN: April 28, 1994, Ealing, London
SQUAD NO: 11
HEIGHT: 5ft 4in
EDUCATION: Greenford High School, Ealing; Loughborough University
TEAMS: Hampshire, Southern Brave, London Spirit, Middlesex, Sunrisers, Surrey Stars, Thunder, Trent Rockets, Western Australia, Western Storm
ROLE: Allrounder
DEBUT: List A: 2008; T20: 2009

BEST BATTING: 82 Thunder vs Western Storm, Old Trafford, 2023
BEST BOWLING: 5-21 Southern Vipers vs Sunrisers, Southampton, 2024

FIRST CRICKET CLUB? Perivale Phoenicians CC, London
EARLIEST CRICKETING MEMORY? Constantly searching for the balls in the hedges or neighbours' garden while playing with my older brother
WHAT WILL YOU MISS ABOUT REGIONAL CRICKET? The way it has its own history and culture even stretching back to the Kia Super League days, building new brands and bringing fans to the game
WHAT EXCITES YOU ABOUT THE NEW COUNTY STRUCTURE? Being part of one club with the men's team, and more fans understanding who we play for and can follow our games through double headers
OPPONENT YOU MOST LOOK FORWARD TO PLAYING AGAINST? Cordelia Griffith – she's competitive on the field but also a good friend off it
FAVOURITE WARM-UP SONG? Any song by Burna Boy
HOW MANY HOURS DO YOU SPEND ON YOUR PHONE A DAY? Four hours
HOBBY YOU WOULD LIKE TO LEARN: How to dance
WHICH PUBLIC FIGURE INSPIRES YOU (EXCLUDING SPORTSPEOPLE)? Michelle Obama
FILM YOU CAN WATCH OVER AND OVER: Bend it Like Beckham

Batting	Mat	Inns	NO	Runs	HS	Ave	SR	100	50	Ct	St
List A	112	93	2	1480	82	16.26	-	0	4	49	-
T20s	136	105	17	1475	71	16.76	91.16	0	6	36	-

Bowling	Mat	Balls	Mdns	Runs	Wkts	BB	Ave	4wl	5wl	SR	Econ
List A	112	3328	20	2945	78	5-51	37.75	3	1	42.66	5.30
T20s	136	1311	6	1602	57	3-9	28.10	0	0	23.00	7.33

ALICE DAVIDSON-RICHARDS   RHB / RFM / MVP6

SURREY

FULL NAME: Alice Natica Davidson-Richards
BORN: May 29, 1994, Tunbridge Wells, Kent
SQUAD NO: 24
HEIGHT: 5ft 9in
NICKNAME: ADR
EDUCATION: Epsom College, Surrey; University of Leeds
TEAMS: England, Surrey, Northern Superchargers, Kent, Otago, South East Stars, Yorkshire Diamonds
ROLE: Allrounder
DEBUT: Test: 2022; ODI: 2018; T20I: 2018; List A: 2010; T20: 2010

BEST BATTING: 101 South East Stars vs The Blaze, Beckenham, 2023
BEST BOWLING: 4-18 Kent vs Nottinghamshire, Nottingham, 2017

FIRST CRICKET CLUB? Tunbridge Wells CC, Kent
EARLIEST CRICKETING MEMORY? Being at the nets with Dad
WHAT WILL YOU MISS ABOUT REGIONAL CRICKET? The shorter commute
WHAT EXCITES YOU ABOUT THE NEW COUNTY STRUCTURE? The lunches at The Oval
OPPONENT YOU MOST LOOK FORWARD TO PLAYING AGAINST? Freya Davies – I'm her maid of honour
FAVOURITE WARM-UP SONG? I'm Coming Out by Diana Ross
SPECIALITY SUBJECT IN A PUB QUIZ (EXCLUDING SPORT)? Human physiology
HOBBY YOU WOULD LIKE TO LEARN: Gardening
FILM YOU CAN WATCH OVER AND OVER: Lord of the Rings

Batting	Mat	Inns	NO	Runs	HS	Ave	SR	100	50	Ct	St
Tests	1	1	0	107	107	107.00	55.15	1	0	0	-
ODIs	6	5	2	65	50*	21.66	59.09	0	1	4	-
T20Is	8	5	1	46	24	11.50	80.70	0	0	2	-
List A	121	96	12	2378	101	28.30	65.94	1	20	48	-
T20s	172	143	35	2324	80	21.51	0	7	60	-

Bowling	Mat	Balls	Mdns	Runs	Wkts	BB	Ave	4wI	5wI	SR	Econ
Tests	1	84	2	43	1	1-39	43.00	-	0	84.00	3.07
ODIs	6	138	1	117	6	3-35	19.50	0	0	23.00	5.08
T20Is	8	72	0	90	4	3-5	22.50	0	0	18.00	7.50
List A	121	3666	39	2588	103	4-18	25.12	3	0	35.59	4.23
T20s	172	2290	7	2656	133	4-11	19.96	4	0	17.21	6.95

FREYA DAVIES

RHB / RFM / MVP29

FULL NAME: Freya Ruth Davies
BORN: October 27, 1995, Chichester, Sussex
SQUAD NO: 61
HEIGHT: 5ft 9in
NICKNAME: Frey-Frey
EDUCATION: Brighton College; University of Exeter
TEAMS: England, Hampshire, Welsh Fire, London Spirit, South East Stars, Southern Vipers, Sussex, Western Storm
ROLE: Bowler
DEBUT: ODI: 2019; T20I: 2019; List A: 2012; T20: 2010

BEST BATTING: 32 Sussex vs Lancashire, Heywood, 2019
BEST BOWLING: 6-10 Sussex vs Derbyshire, Derby, 2018

FIRST CRICKET CLUB? Singleton CC, West Sussex
EARLIEST CRICKETING MEMORY? Nearly being hit by a tile from the roof of a clubhouse after my dad hit a six
WHAT EXCITES YOU ABOUT THE NEW COUNTY STRUCTURE? Consistently playing at first-class grounds, hopefully with bigger crowds
OPPONENT YOU MOST LOOK FORWARD TO PLAYING AGAINST? Alice Davidson-Richards, because we're such good friends and know each other's games so well. It is always fun battling against her
FAVOURITE WARM-UP SONG? A Bar Song (Tipsy) by Shaboozey
SPECIALITY SUBJECT IN A PUB QUIZ (EXCLUDING SPORT)? Scrubs (the TV show)
ONE THING YOU WANT TO DO BEFORE YOU DIE: Travel to New York around Christmas
SURPRISING FACT ABOUT YOU: I have a law degree and have completed my Legal Practice Course (LPC)
FILM YOU CAN WATCH OVER AND OVER: Dodgeball

Batting	Mat	Inns	NO	Runs	HS	Ave	SR	100	50	Ct	St
ODIs	9	5	2	13	10*	4.33	30.95	0	0	4	-
T20Is	26	1	1	1	1*	-	100.00	0	0	6	-
List A	73	40	16	286	32	11.91	40.45	0	0	19	-
T20s	163	42	18	199	27*	8.29	65.89	0	0	24	-

Bowling	Mat	Balls	Mdns	Runs	Wkts	BB	Ave	4wI	5wI	SR	Econ
ODIs	9	423	4	311	10	2-36	31.10	0	0	42.30	4.41
T20Is	26	468	1	534	23	4-23	23.21	1	0	20.34	6.84
List A	73	3407	74	2179	82	6-10	26.57	1	1	41.54	3.83
T20s	163	3064	10	3308	150	4-8	22.05	5	0	20.42	6.47

GEORGIA DAVIS

RHB / OB / MVP32

BIRMINGHAM BEARS

FULL NAME: Georgia Katie Davis
BORN: June 3, 1999, Birmingham
SQUAD NO: 64
HEIGHT: 5ft 4in
NICKNAME: G
EDUCATION: Moor Hall Primary School, Birmingham; The Arthur Terry School; Staffordshire University
TEAMS: England, Birmingham Bears, Welsh Fire, Central Sparks, Warwickshire, Trent Rockets, Yorkshire Diamonds
ROLE: Allrounder
DEBUT: ODI: 2024; List A: 2015; T20: 2015

BEST BATTING: 52* Central Sparks vs South East Stars, Beckenham, 2022
BEST BOWLING: 6-23 Central Sparks vs Western Storm, Taunton, 2024

FIRST CRICKET CLUB? Walmley CC, West Midlands
EARLIEST CRICKETING MEMORY? Playing Kwik Cricket at Walmley CC every Friday night
WHAT WILL YOU MISS ABOUT REGIONAL CRICKET? Playing at New Road
OPPONENT YOU MOST LOOK FORWARD TO PLAYING AGAINST? Hollie Armitage – she's always a challenge to come up against
FAVOURITE WARM-UP SONG? Kisses by BL3SS
HOW MANY HOURS DO YOU SPEND ON YOUR PHONE A DAY? Four
SPECIALITY SUBJECT IN A PUB QUIZ (EXCLUDING SPORT)? Picture round
ONE THING YOU WANT TO DO BEFORE YOU DIE: Travel around Thailand
HOBBY YOU WOULD LIKE TO LEARN: Darts
WHICH PUBLIC FIGURE INSPIRES YOU (EXCLUDING SPORTSPEOPLE)? Michelle Obama
SURPRISING FACT ABOUT YOU: I was a police officer for three years
FILM YOU CAN WATCH OVER AND OVER: The Heat

Batting	Mat	Inns	NO	Runs	HS	Ave	SR	100	50	Ct	St
ODIs	1	0	-	-	-	-	-	-	-	0	-
List A	58	39	8	263	52*	8.48	-	0	1	12	-
T20s	92	40	22	251	44*	13.94	-	0	0	14	-

Bowling	Mat	Balls	Mdns	Runs	Wkts	BB	Ave	4wI	5wI	SR	Econ
ODIs	1	23	0	19	2	2-19	9.50	0	0	11.50	4.95
List A	58	2549	32	1628	89	6-23	18.29	5	1	28.64	3.83
T20s	92	1719	10	1529	107	5-14	14.42	1	1	16.21	5.33

CHARLIE DEAN RHB / OB / MVP30

FULL NAME: Charlotte Ellen Dean
BORN: December 22, 2000, Burton-upon-Trent, Staffordshire
SQUAD NO: 24
HEIGHT: 5ft 6in
NICKNAME: Deano
EDUCATION: Portsmouth Grammar School; University of Southampton
TEAMS: England, Somerset, London Spirit, Hampshire, Southern Vipers
ROLE: Bowler
DEBUT: Test: 2022; ODI: 2021; T20I: 2022; List A: 2016; T20: 2016

BEST BATTING: 73 Hampshire vs Kent, Andover, 2018
BEST BOWLING: 5-31 England vs Sri Lanka, Leicester, 2023

FIRST CRICKET CLUB? Havant CC, Hampshire
WHAT WILL YOU MISS ABOUT REGIONAL CRICKET? Donning the orange with my Vipers teammates
WHAT EXCITES YOU ABOUT THE NEW COUNTY STRUCTURE? Bigger crowds and more opportunity both on and off the pitch (hopefully)
OPPONENT YOU MOST LOOK FORWARD TO PLAYING AGAINST? Issy Wong – so I can see her cats
ONE THING YOU WANT TO DO BEFORE YOU DIE: Go to Japan
HOBBY YOU WOULD LIKE TO LEARN: Crocheting
WHICH PUBLIC FIGURE INSPIRES YOU (EXCLUDING SPORTSPEOPLE)? Taylor Swift
SURPRISING FACT ABOUT YOU: I broke my wrist as a kid because my wardrobe fell on me
FILM YOU CAN WATCH OVER AND OVER: Shrek

Batting	Mat	Inns	NO	Runs	HS	Ave	SR	100	50	Ct	St
Tests	3	6	1	41	20*	8.20	37.61	0	0	0	-
ODIs	40	25	7	359	47*	19.94	67.48	0	0	16	-
T20Is	39	14	4	138	34	13.80	107.81	0	0	6	-
List A	89	69	10	1350	73	22.88	-	0	4	39	-
T20s	128	82	27	955	64*	17.36	-	0	2	36	-

Bowling	Mat	Balls	Mdns	Runs	Wkts	BB	Ave	4wI	5wI	SR	Econ
Tests	3	408	6	249	7	4-68	35.57	-	0	58.28	3.66
ODIs	40	1904	15	1478	71	5-31	20.81	6	1	26.81	4.65
T20Is	39	798	1	924	50	4-19	18.48	2	0	15.96	6.94
List A	89	4278	49	2989	143	5-31	20.90	8	1	29.91	4.19
T20s	128	2490	11	2630	140	5-19	18.78	3	1	17.78	6.33

LEAH DOBSON

RHB

DURHAM

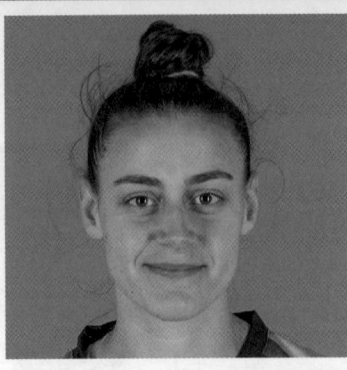

FULL NAME: Leah Christie Dobson
BORN: October 6, 2001, Scarborough
SQUAD NO: 10
HEIGHT: 5ft 8in
NICKNAME: Dobbo
EDUCATION: Norton College, North Yorkshire
TEAMS: Durham, Northern Diamonds, Northern Superchargers, Yorkshire
ROLE: Batter
DEBUT: List A: 2019; T20: 2018

BEST BATTING: 68* Northern Diamonds vs Western Storm, Taunton, 2023

FIRST CRICKET CLUB? Sherburn CC, Malton, North Yorkshire
WHAT WILL YOU MISS ABOUT REGIONAL CRICKET? My old teammates
WHAT EXCITES YOU ABOUT THE NEW COUNTY STRUCTURE? Playing T20 games alongside the men's competition
OPPONENT YOU MOST LOOK FORWARD TO PLAYING AGAINST? Chloe Brewer – so that we can catch up over a coffee
FAVOURITE WARM-UP SONG? We Found Love by Rihanna
SPECIALITY SUBJECT IN A PUB QUIZ (EXCLUDING SPORT)? Populations round the world
ONE THING YOU WANT TO DO BEFORE YOU DIE: Swim with turtles
HOBBY YOU WOULD LIKE TO LEARN: Juggling
WHICH PUBLIC FIGURE INSPIRES YOU (EXCLUDING SPORTSPEOPLE)? Kate Middleton
FILM YOU CAN WATCH OVER AND OVER: Camp Rock 2: The Final Jam

Batting	Mat	Inns	NO	Runs	HS	Ave	SR	100	50	Ct	St
List A	31	26	3	461	68*	20.04	68.80	0	2	4	-
T20s	41	34	5	384	55	13.24	83.66	0	1	12	-
Bowling	Mat	Balls	Mdns	Runs	Wkts	BB	Ave	4wi	5wi	SR	Econ
List A	31	-	-	-	-	-	-	-	-	-	-
T20s	41	-	-	-	-	-	-	-	-	-	-

ARIANA DOWSE

RHB / WK

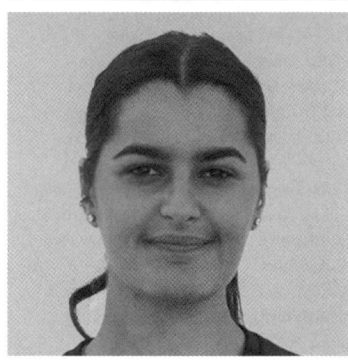

FULL NAME: Ariana Dowse
BORN: February 8, 2001, Eastbourne, Sussex
SQUAD NO: 83
HEIGHT: 5ft 6in
NICKNAME: Ari Potter
EDUCATION: Bede's School, Eastbourne;
Solent University, Southampton
TEAMS: Essex, Berkshire, Hampshire,
Sunrisers, Sussex
ROLE: Wicketkeeper/batter
DEBUT: List A: 2017; T20: 2017

ESSEX

BEST BATTING: 105 Sunrisers vs The Blaze, Loughborough, 2023

FIRST CRICKET CLUB? Hastings CC, East Sussex
EARLIEST CRICKETING MEMORY? Being taken out of rounders at school to try cricket for the first time
OPPONENT YOU MOST LOOK FORWARD TO PLAYING AGAINST? Maia Bouchier – just to see how she goes about her batting after a successful season playing for England
HOW MANY HOURS DO YOU SPEND ON YOUR PHONE A DAY? Six
SPECIALITY SUBJECT IN A PUB QUIZ (EXCLUDING SPORT)? Harry Potter
ONE THING YOU WANT TO DO BEFORE YOU DIE: Travel
HOBBY YOU WOULD LIKE TO LEARN: I want to improve my art, so drawing, painting etc. And scrapbooking
WHICH PUBLIC FIGURE INSPIRES YOU (EXCLUDING SPORTSPEOPLE)? Michelle Obama
FILM YOU CAN WATCH OVER AND OVER: Any Harry Potter film

Batting	Mat	Inns	NO	Runs	HS	Ave	SR	100	50	Ct	St
List A	27	22	3	227	105	11.94	61.68	1	0	11	7
T20s	34	18	1	147	37	8.64	62.82	0	0	14	12

Bowling	Mat	Balls	Mdns	Runs	Wkts	BB	Ave	4wI	5wI	SR	Econ
List A	27	-	-	-	-	-	-	-	-	-	-
T20s	34	-	-	-	-	-	-	-	-	-	-

SOPHIA DUNKLEY   RHB / LB / MVP10

FULL NAME: Sophia Ivy Dunkley
BORN: July 16, 1998, Lambeth, Surrey
SQUAD NO: 47
HEIGHT: 5ft 6in
EDUCATION: Mill Hill School, London;
Loughborough University
TEAMS: England, Surrey, Welsh Fire, Gujarat
Giants, Lancashire Thunder, Melbourne Stars,
Middlesex, South East Stars, Southern Brave,
Surrey Stars
ROLE: Batter
DEBUT: Test: 2021; ODI: 2021; T20I: 2018;
List A: 2013; T20: 2012

BEST BATTING: 138 Middlesex vs Worcestershire, Mill Hill, 2019
BEST BOWLING: 4-7 Middlesex vs Yorkshire, Harrogate, 2017

FIRST CRICKET CLUB? Finchley CC, London
WHICH TEAMMATE HAS HAD THE BIGGEST IMPACT ON YOUR GAME? Danni Wyatt-Hodge – I
love batting with her, she makes me laugh all the time
WHICH PART OF THE SEASON DO YOU MOST ENJOY? I love the month of June
WHICH GROUND DO YOU MOST ENJOY VISITING? Mount Maunganui in New Zealand.
Beautiful place to play and tour
IF YOU COULD PINCH A PLAYER FROM ANOTHER TEAM, WHO WOULD IT BE?
Grace Scrivens
WHO IS THE TOUGHEST BOWLER TO FACE IN DOMESTIC CRICKET? Linsey Smith
WHAT KEEPS YOU AWAKE AT NIGHT? The jumper I can't seem to find!
WHAT'S THE SILLIEST OUTFIT YOU'VE EVER WORN? A vet outfit

Batting	Mat	Inns	NO	Runs	HS	Ave	SR	100	50	Ct	St
Tests	6	10	1	228	74*	25.33	53.90	0	1	1	-
ODIs	34	32	2	789	107	26.30	81.84	1	5	3	-
T20Is	64	52	9	986	61*	22.93	120.53	0	4	15	-
List A	87	80	13	2333	138	34.82	-	6	13	32	-
T20s	202	183	23	3516	77*	21.97	-	0	19	54	-

Bowling	Mat	Balls	Mdns	Runs	Wkts	BB	Ave	4wI	5wI	SR	Econ
Tests	6	18	0	22	0	0-9	-	-	-	-	7.33
ODIs	34	3	0	1	1	1-1	1.00	0	0	3.00	2.00
T20Is	64	24	0	13	1	1-6	13.00	0	0	24.00	3.25
List A	87	1893	46	1090	57	4-7	19.12	3	0	33.21	3.45
T20s	202	1082	3	1098	61	4-24	18.00	1	0	17.73	6.08

SOPHIE ECCLESTONE | RHB / SLA

FULL NAME: Sophie Ecclestone
BORN: May 6, 1999, Chester, Cheshire
SQUAD NO: 19
HEIGHT: 5ft 10in
NICKNAME: Eccles
EDUCATION: Helsby High School, Cheshire
TEAMS: England, Lancashire, Manchester Originals, Cheshire, Lancashire Thunder, Sydney Sixers, Thunder, UP Warriorz
ROLE: Bowler
DEBUT: Test: 2017; ODI: 2016; T20I: 2016; List A: 2013; T20: 2014

BEST BATTING: 74 Thunder vs Central Sparks, Old Trafford, 2023
BEST BOWLING: 6-12 Lancashire vs Warwickshire, Birmingham, 2017

FIRST CRICKET CLUB? Alvanley CC, Cheshire
WHICH TEAMMATE HAS HAD THE BIGGEST IMPACT ON YOUR GAME? Lauren Bell – she always has a smile on her face and enjoys the game
WHO IS THE MOST TALENTED TEENAGER IN WOMEN'S DOMESTIC CRICKET? Liberty Heap
WHO IS THE TOUGHEST BOWLER TO FACE IN DOMESTIC CRICKET? Hannah Rainey
WHAT WAKES YOU UP IN THE MORNING? The Manchester city skyline
WHAT KEEPS YOU AWAKE AT NIGHT? Monopoly Go
CHOOSE A FANTASY SLIP CORDON TO SPEND A DAY IN THE FIELD WITH: Justin Bieber (wk), Taylor Swift, Phil Jagielka, Tom Cruise

Batting	Mat	Inns	NO	Runs	HS	Ave	SR	100	50	Ct	St
Tests	9	14	3	196	35	17.81	42.24	0	0	7	-
ODIs	72	49	13	377	33*	10.47	69.30	0	0	22	-
T20Is	96	40	23	285	33*	16.76	126.66	0	0	30	-
List A	123	95	22	1044	74	14.30	67.00	0	4	38	-
T20s	240	145	54	1217	47*	13.37	-	0	0	77	-

Bowling	Mat	Balls	Mdns	Runs	Wkts	BB	Ave	4wI	5wI	SR	Econ
Tests	9	2509	97	1190	40	5-63	29.75	-	3	62.72	2.84
ODIs	72	3876	74	2385	120	6-36	19.87	3	2	32.30	3.69
T20Is	96	2132	10	2089	137	4-18	15.24	2	0	15.56	5.87
List A	123	6388	153	3629	215	6-12	16.87	9	4	29.71	3.40
T20s	240	5349	18	5348	321	5-15	16.66	7	1	16.66	5.99

BETHAN ELLIS RHB / RMF

BIRMINGHAM BEARS

FULL NAME: Bethan Louisa Ellis
BORN: July 7, 1999, Leamington Spa, Warwickshire
SQUAD NO: 14
HEIGHT: 5ft 6in
NICKNAME: Bellis
EDUCATION: University of Birmingham; Loughborough University
TEAMS: Birmingham Bears, Central Sparks, Derbyshire, Lightning, Shropshire, Warwickshire, Worcestershire
ROLE: Allrounder
DEBUT: List A: 2015; T20: 2016

BEST BATTING: 74 Warwickshire vs Kent, Beckenham, 2019
BEST BOWLING: 4-20 Worcestershire vs Wales, Griffithstown, 2017

FIRST CRICKET CLUB? Leamington CC, Warwickshire
EARLIEST CRICKETING MEMORY? Playing in the back garden with my dad and brother
WHAT EXCITES YOU ABOUT THE NEW COUNTY STRUCTURE? Representing my home county once again
OPPONENT YOU MOST LOOK FORWARD TO PLAYING AGAINST? Any of my previous teammates
FAVOURITE WARM-UP SONG? Weekend in Paradise by Jamie Webster
HOW MANY HOURS DO YOU SPEND ON YOUR PHONE A DAY? Three hours
SPECIALITY SUBJECT IN A PUB QUIZ (EXCLUDING SPORT)? Gavin and Stacey
ONE THING YOU WANT TO DO BEFORE YOU DIE: See the Northern Lights
HOBBY YOU WOULD LIKE TO LEARN: Painting
WHICH PUBLIC FIGURE INSPIRES YOU (EXCLUDING SPORTSPEOPLE)? Emmeline Pankhurst
SURPRISING FACT ABOUT YOU: I am a twin
FILM YOU CAN WATCH OVER AND OVER: Miss Congeniality (first and second films)

Batting	Mat	Inns	NO	Runs	HS	Ave	SR	100	50	Ct	St
List A	52	41	7	784	74	23.05	55.88	0	6	14	-
T20s	56	44	16	551	57*	19.67	-	0	2	11	-

Bowling	Mat	Balls	Mdns	Runs	Wkts	BB	Ave	4wl	5wl	SR	Econ
List A	52	1321	22	911	35	4-20	26.02	1	0	37.74	4.13
T20s	56	665	1	670	46	4-21	14.56	2	0	14.45	6.04

GEORGIA ELWISS

RHB / RM / MVP18

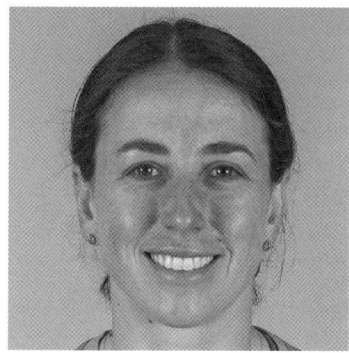

FULL NAME: Georgia Amanda Elwiss
BORN: May 31, 1991, Wolverhampton
SQUAD NO: TBC
HEIGHT: 5ft 7in
NICKNAME: Gelwiss
EDUCATION: Wolverhampton Girls' High School; Loughborough University
TEAMS: England, The Blaze, Welsh Fire, Birmingham Phoenix, Melbourne Stars, Southern Vipers, Staffordshire, Sussex
ROLE: Allrounder
DEBUT: Test: 2015; ODI: 2011; T20I: 2011; List A: 2004; T20: 2005

BEST BATTING: 115 Southern Vipers vs South East Stars, Hove, 2022
BEST BOWLING: 6-17 Sussex vs Somerset, Bath, 2016

FIRST CRICKET CLUB? Wolverhampton CC, West Midlands
WHAT WILL YOU MISS ABOUT REGIONAL CRICKET? Playing for the Charlotte Edwards Cup and the Rachael Heyhoe Flint Trophy
WHAT EXCITES YOU ABOUT THE NEW COUNTY STRUCTURE? Alignment with the counties
OPPONENT YOU MOST LOOK FORWARD TO PLAYING AGAINST? Georgia Adams – I haven't come up against her for a while
FAVOURITE WARM-UP SONG? Higher by The Saturdays
SPECIALITY SUBJECT IN A PUB QUIZ (EXCLUDING SPORT)? Marks & Spencer food halls
ONE THING YOU WANT TO DO BEFORE YOU DIE: An Ironman Triathlon
HOBBY YOU WOULD LIKE TO LEARN: How to fly a plane
SURPRISING FACT ABOUT YOU: I enjoy running
FILM YOU CAN WATCH OVER AND OVER: The Grinch

Batting	Mat	Inns	NO	Runs	HS	Ave	SR	100	50	Ct	St
Tests	4	6	1	145	46	29.00	28.54	0	0	1	-
ODIs	36	24	5	388	77	20.42	73.20	0	2	11	-
T20Is	14	5	2	29	18	9.66	96.66	0	0	3	-
List A	199	152	30	3259	115	26.71	-	4	15	54	-
T20s	197	151	33	2414	80*	20.45	-	0	8	50	-

Bowling	Mat	Balls	Mdns	Runs	Wkts	BB	Ave	4wl	5wl	SR	Econ
Tests	4	174	5	91	1	1-40	91.00	-	0	174.00	3.13
ODIs	36	1097	19	679	26	3-17	26.11	0	0	42.19	3.71
T20Is	14	163	0	161	8	2-9	20.12	0	0	20.37	5.92
List A	199	7350	198	4038	189	6-17	21.36	3	3	38.88	3.29
T20s	197	3031	8	3330	142	4-16	23.45	1	0	21.34	6.59

TASH FARRANT

LHB / LMF

SURREY

FULL NAME: Natasha Eleni Farrant
BORN: May 29, 1996, Athens, Greece
SQUAD NO: 53
HEIGHT: 5ft 5in
NICKNAME: Faz
EDUCATION: Sevenoaks School;
Loughborough University
TEAMS: England, Surrey, Kent, Oval
Invincibles, South East Stars, Southern Vipers,
Western Australia
ROLE: Bowler
DEBUT: ODI: 2013; T20I: 2013;
List A: 2012; T20: 2012

BEST BATTING: 94 South East Stars vs Southern Vipers, Beckenham, 2024
BEST BOWLING: 6-16 Kent vs Staffordshire, Beckenham, 2016

FIRST CRICKET CLUB? Holmesdale CC, Sevenoaks, Kent
BEST DELIVERY YOU HAVE BOWLED? Bowling Sarah Taylor through the gate for Southern Vipers against Surrey Stars in the Kia Super League in 2018
BEST PERFORMANCE AS A PRO? Giving a bit of a speech and taking four wickets for Oval Invincibles in the 2021 Hundred eliminator to get us back in the game against Birmingham Phoenix
GREATEST PERFORMANCE YOU HAVE WITNESSED? Danni Wyatt-Hodge's hundred in the T20 against India at Mumbai in 2018
FAVOURITE FORMAT? T20 – comes thick and fast. I love being under pressure with the ball and racing around in the field
FAVOURITE TOY AS A KID? Pokémon cards
WHICH PERSON INSPIRES YOU MOST? Lydia Greenway
SURPRISING FACT ABOUT YOU? I always wear matching sets of pyjamas

Batting	Mat	Inns	NO	Runs	HS	Ave	SR	100	50	Ct	St
ODIs	6	4	1	42	22	14.00	61.76	0	0	1	-
T20Is	18	4	3	7	3*	7.00	43.75	0	0	4	-
List A	66	42	7	655	94	18.71	64.91	0	3	13	-
T20s	121	61	17	415	37	9.43	-	0	0	28	-
Bowling	Mat	Balls	Mdns	Runs	Wkts	BB	Ave	4wI	5wI	SR	Econ
ODIs	6	253	0	190	5	2-31	38.00	0	0	50.60	4.50
T20Is	18	388	2	405	15	2-15	27.00	0	0	25.86	6.26
List A	66	3057	70	1893	92	6-16	20.57	4	3	33.22	3.71
T20s	121	2420	12	2344	135	4-10	17.36	1	0	17.92	5.81

LAUREN FILER RHB / RFM

DURHAM

FULL NAME: Lauren Louise Filer
BORN: December 22, 2000, Bristol
SQUAD NO: 24
HEIGHT: 5ft 10in
NICKNAME: Big Fil
EDUCATION: Cardiff Metropolitan University
TEAMS: England, Durham, Manchester Originals, London Spirit, Somerset, Welsh Fire, Western Storm
ROLE: Bowler
DEBUT: Test: 2023; ODI: 2023; T20I: 2024; List A: 2018; T20: 2018

BEST BATTING: 58* Western Storm vs Central Sparks, Bristol, 2022
BEST BOWLING: 3-10 England vs Ireland, Belfast, 2024

WHICH TEAMMATE HAS HAD THE BIGGEST IMPACT ON YOUR GAME? Heather Knight – she's allowed me to play an attacking role and backed me to do well
WHICH GROUND DO YOU MOST ENJOY VISITING? Trent Bridge – good atmosphere and the pitch generally offers pace and bounce
WHO IS THE MOST TALENTED TEENAGER IN WOMEN'S DOMESTIC CRICKET? Katie Jones – definitely a keeper to look out for
WHAT WAKES YOU UP IN THE MORNING? Taking Barney for a walk
WHAT KEEPS YOU AWAKE AT NIGHT? My dog Barney
CHOOSE A FANTASY SLIP CORDON TO SPEND A DAY IN THE FIELD WITH: Romesh Ranganathan (wk), Freddie Flintoff, Benedict Cumberbatch, Jürgen Klopp

Batting	Mat	Inns	NO	Runs	HS	Ave	SR	100	50	Ct	St
Tests	4	8	1	41	14	5.85	41.00	0	0	1	-
ODIs	15	6	2	24	8*	6.00	58.53	0	0	3	-
T20Is	8	2	1	6	4*	6.00	60.00	0	0	2	-
List A	51	30	11	164	58*	8.63	67.48	0	1	10	-
T20s	65	30	11	171	21*	9.00	86.80	0	0	9	-

Bowling	Mat	Balls	Mdns	Runs	Wkts	BB	Ave	4wI	5wI	SR	Econ
Tests	4	588	12	396	9	2-49	44.00	-	0	65.33	4.04
ODIs	15	587	4	494	24	3-10	20.58	0	0	24.45	5.04
T20Is	8	162	0	187	5	2-17	37.40	0	0	32.40	6.92
List A	51	1939	15	1681	60	3-10	28.01	0	0	32.31	5.20
T20s	65	1081	5	1183	48	3-8	24.64	0	0	22.52	6.56

SURREY

FULL NAME: Phoebe Antonia Franklin
BORN: February 18, 1998, Greenwich, Kent
SQUAD NO: 10
HEIGHT: 5ft 6in
NICKNAME: Pheebo
EDUCATION: Chislehurst & Sidcup Grammar
School, Bexley; Loughborough University
TEAMS: Surrey, Welsh Fire, Birmingham
Phoenix, Kent, South East Stars
ROLE: Allrounder
DEBUT: List A: 2015; T20: 2014

BEST BATTING: 37 South East Stars vs Central Sparks, Beckenham, 2022
BEST BOWLING: 3-18 South East Stars vs Sunrisers, Radlett, 2023

FIRST CRICKET CLUB? Old Colfeians CC, London
EARLIEST CRICKETING MEMORY? Playing Kwik Cricket with my sister at primary school
WHAT EXCITES YOU ABOUT THE NEW COUNTY STRUCTURE? Playing at world-class venues
and the double headers with the men
FAVOURITE WARM-UP SONG? Girlz Wanna Have Fun by MATTN
HOW MANY HOURS DO YOU SPEND ON YOUR PHONE A DAY? Two
SPECIALITY SUBJECT IN A PUB QUIZ (EXCLUDING SPORT)? Music (guess the intro)
HOBBY YOU WOULD LIKE TO LEARN: To become a more advanced French speaker
WHICH PUBLIC FIGURE INSPIRES YOU (EXCLUDING SPORTSPEOPLE)? Michelle Obama
SURPRISING FACT ABOUT YOU: I've never broken a bone
FILM YOU CAN WATCH OVER AND OVER: Grown Ups

Batting	Mat	Inns	NO	Runs	HS	Ave	SR	100	50	Ct	St
List A	53	45	5	662	37	16.55	72.66	0	0	29	-
T20s	83	69	11	1034	53	17.82	101.77	0	5	21	-
Bowling	Mat	Balls	Mdns	Runs	Wkts	BB	Ave	4wI	5wI	SR	Econ
List A	53	1180	6	920	34	3-18	27.05	0	0	34.70	4.67
T20s	83	598	0	721	27	3-14	26.70	0	0	22.14	7.23

KATHERINE FRASER — RHB / OB

FULL NAME: Katherine Joan Grainne Fraser
BORN: April 9, 2005, Edinburgh, Scotland
SQUAD NO: 70
HEIGHT: 5ft 4in
EDUCATION: The Mary Erskine School, Edinburgh
TEAMS: Scotland, Durham, Northern Diamonds
ROLE: Allrounder
DEBUT: ODI: 2024; T20I: 2019; List A: 2018; T20: 2019

DURHAM

BEST BATTING: 74* Scotland vs Papua New Guinea, Utrecht, 2024
BEST BOWLING: 3-37 Northern Diamonds vs Sunrisers, Chelmsford, 2024

FIRST CRICKET CLUB? Boroughmuir CC, Edinburgh
WHAT WILL YOU MISS ABOUT REGIONAL CRICKET? Playing alongside my Diamonds teammates
WHAT EXCITES YOU ABOUT THE NEW COUNTY STRUCTURE? The opportunity to improve standards
OPPONENT YOU MOST LOOK FORWARD TO PLAYING AGAINST? Any of my former Diamonds
FAVOURITE WARM-UP SONG? Since U Been Gone by Kelly Clarkson
HOW MANY HOURS DO YOU SPEND ON YOUR PHONE A DAY? Three
SPECIALITY SUBJECT IN A PUB QUIZ (EXCLUDING SPORT)? National flags
ONE THING YOU WANT TO DO BEFORE YOU DIE: Travel in Canada
HOBBY YOU WOULD LIKE TO LEARN: Padel
WHICH PUBLIC FIGURE INSPIRES YOU (EXCLUDING SPORTSPEOPLE)? Michelle Obama
SURPRISING FACT ABOUT YOU: I've flown a plane
FILM YOU CAN WATCH OVER AND OVER: Mamma Mia!

Batting	Mat	Inns	NO	Runs	HS	Ave	SR	100	50	Ct	St
ODIs	6	6	2	152	74*	38.00	77.15	0	1	3	-
T20Is	41	19	5	92	14*	6.57	65.24	0	0	8	-
List A	18	17	4	238	74*	18.30	-	0	1	7	-
T20s	70	39	11	269	30	9.60	-	0	0	14	-

Bowling	Mat	Balls	Mdns	Runs	Wkts	BB	Ave	4wI	5wI	SR	Econ
ODIs	6	237	1	145	7	2-20	20.71	0	0	33.85	3.67
T20Is	41	706	3	620	43	4-19	14.41	1	0	16.41	5.26
List A	18	455	2	295	11	3-37	26.81	0	0	41.36	3.89
T20s	70	1183	5	1089	67	4-18	16.25	2	0	17.65	5.52

ABBEY FREEBORN   RHB / WK / MVP24

BIRMINGHAM BEARS

FULL NAME: Abigail Johanna Freeborn
BORN: November 12, 1996, Eastbourne, Sussex
SQUAD NO: 27
HEIGHT: 5ft 7in
EDUCATION: Loughborough University; Lewes College; Bishop Bell CofE, Eastbourne
TEAMS: Birmingham Bears, London Spirit, Birmingham Phoenix, Central Sparks, Lightning, Staffordshire, Sussex, Trent Rockets, Yorkshire
ROLE: Wicketkeeper/batter
DEBUT: List A: 2013; T20: 2013

BEST BATTING: 107* Central Sparks vs Sunrisers, Chelmsford, 2023

FIRST CRICKET CLUB? Hastings & St Leonards Priory CC, East Sussex
EARLIEST CRICKETING MEMORY? My first-ever practice aged 11 when I could not understand how to run between the wickets as a pair
WHAT WILL YOU MISS ABOUT REGIONAL CRICKET? The teas at New Road
WHAT EXCITES YOU ABOUT THE NEW COUNTY STRUCTURE? Playing in the T20 Blast and having more double-headers with the men
OPPONENT YOU MOST LOOK FORWARD TO PLAYING AGAINST? Ami Campbell because it's always nice to catch up
FAVOURITE WARM-UP SONG? Dance Monkey by Tones and I
HOW MANY HOURS DO YOU SPEND ON YOUR PHONE A DAY? Five – working on reducing it
SPECIALITY SUBJECT IN A PUB QUIZ (EXCLUDING SPORT)? European capital cities
ONE THING YOU WANT TO DO BEFORE YOU DIE: Swim with sharks
HOBBY YOU WOULD LIKE TO LEARN: Rock climbing
WHICH PUBLIC FIGURE INSPIRES YOU (EXCLUDING SPORTSPEOPLE)? Riley Hemson
SURPRISING FACT ABOUT YOU: I am obsessed with real survival stories
FILM YOU CAN WATCH OVER AND OVER: Mamma Mia! Here We Go Again

Batting	Mat	Inns	NO	Runs	HS	Ave	SR	100	50	Ct	St
List A	85	73	12	1730	107*	28.36	63.16	1	6	63	18
T20s	108	81	18	1278	71*	20.28	97.40	0	4	31	34
Bowling	Mat	Balls	Mdns	Runs	Wkts	BB	Ave	4wI	5wI	SR	Econ
List A	85	-	-	-	-	-	-	-	-	-	-
T20s	108	-	-	-	-	-	-	-	-	-	-

JO GARDNER   RHB / OB / MVP40

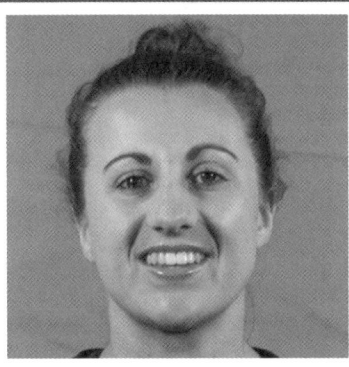

FULL NAME: Jo-Anne Lynda Gardner
BORN: March 25, 1997, Newport, Isle of Wight
SQUAD NO: 14
HEIGHT: 5ft 6in
NICKNAME: Joey G
EDUCATION: Loughborough University
TEAMS: Essex, Oval Invincibles, Northamptonshire, Trent Rockets, Loughborough Lightning, Sunrisers, Warwickshire
ROLE: Allrounder
DEBUT: List A: 2011; T20: 2011

ESSEX

BEST BATTING: 86 Northamptonshire vs Cheshire, Horton, 2016
BEST BOWLING: 6-21 Northamptonshire vs Oxfordshire, Chesterton, 2013

FIRST CRICKET CLUB? Great Houghton CC, Northampton
EARLIEST CRICKETING MEMORY? Playing in the back garden with my dad and brother
WHAT EXCITES YOU ABOUT THE NEW COUNTY STRUCTURE? Having more visibility and being aligned with the men
FAVOURITE WARM-UP SONG? Set My Heart on Fire by Majestic, The Jammin Kid and Celine Dion
SPECIALITY SUBJECT IN A PUB QUIZ (EXCLUDING SPORT)? Geography
ONE THING YOU WANT TO DO BEFORE YOU DIE: Run a marathon
HOBBY YOU WOULD LIKE TO LEARN: Sports photography
SURPRISING FACT ABOUT YOU: I don't like tomatoes but was once paid to taste ketchup
FILM YOU CAN WATCH OVER AND OVER: A Star is Born

Batting	Mat	Inns	NO	Runs	HS	Ave	SR	100	50	Ct	St
List A	97	84	16	1332	86	19.58	-	0	6	29	-
T20s	116	90	27	1145	79*	18.17	-	0	3	36	-

Bowling	Mat	Balls	Mdns	Runs	Wkts	BB	Ave	4wl	5wl	SR	Econ
List A	97	2223	35	1531	70	6-21	21.87	0	3	31.75	4.13
T20s	116	1076	8	1051	36	3-25	29.19	0	0	29.88	5.86

MAHIKA GAUR

RHB / LFM

LANCASHIRE

FULL NAME: Mahika Gaur
BORN: March 9, 2006, Reading
SQUAD NO: 18
HEIGHT: 6ft 1in
NICKNAME: Meeks
EDUCATION: Sedbergh School, Cumbria;
Dubai College, UAE
TEAMS: England, Lancashire, Cumbria,
Manchester Originals, Thunder, UAE
ROLE: Bowler
DEBUT: ODI: 2023; T20I: 2019;
List A: 2023; T20: 2019

BEST BATTING: 11 Thunder vs Northern Diamonds, Chester-le-Street, 2024
BEST BOWLING: 3-26 England vs Sri Lanka, Chester-le-Street, 2023

WHICH PART OF THE SEASON DO YOU MOST ENJOY? The Hundred
WHICH GROUND DO YOU MOST ENJOY VISITING? New Road – they do great food there,
particularly the gnocchi
WHO IS THE TOUGHEST BOWLER TO FACE IN DOMESTIC CRICKET? Sophie Ecclestone
WHAT ONE THING WOULD YOU CHANGE ABOUT WOMEN'S CRICKET IN ENGLAND?
Schedule some red-ball games
WHAT KEEPS YOU AWAKE AT NIGHT? Assignments from school
WHAT'S THE SILLIEST OUTFIT YOU'VE EVER WORN? Dressing up as Donald Trump for
Halloween – I went all out, with the wig and everything else

Batting	Mat	Inns	NO	Runs	HS	Ave	SR	100	50	Ct	St
ODIs	2	0	-	-	-	-	-	-	-	0	-
T20Is	19	3	1	11	6*	5.50	122.22	0	0	4	-
List A	12	7	1	41	11	6.83	47.67	0	0	1	-
T20s	44	11	4	24	6*	3.42	80.00	0	0	5	-
Bowling	Mat	Balls	Mdns	Runs	Wkts	BB	Ave	4wI	5wI	SR	Econ
ODIs	2	74	0	55	4	3-26	13.75	0	0	18.50	4.45
T20Is	19	354	1	304	9	3-21	33.77	0	0	39.33	5.15
List A	12	482	5	358	14	3-26	25.57	0	0	34.42	4.45
T20s	44	814	4	830	28	3-21	29.64	0	0	29.07	6.11

KATIE GEORGE   RHB / LFM / MVP21

FULL NAME: Katie Louise George
BORN: April 7, 1999, Haywards Heath, Sussex
SQUAD NO: 99
HEIGHT: 5ft 6in
EDUCATION: The Mountbatten School, Hampshire; Richard Taunton Sixth Form
TEAMS: England, Birmingham Bears, Trent Rockets, Central Sparks, Hampshire, Manchester Originals, Southern Vipers, Welsh Fire, Western Storm, Yorkshire Diamonds
ROLE: Allrounder
DEBUT: ODI: 2018; T20I: 2018; List A: 2013; T20: 2015

BEST BATTING: 80 Hampshire vs Nottinghamshire, Nettleworth, 2019
BEST BOWLING: 5-50 Central Sparks vs Western Storm, Worcester, 2024

FIRST CRICKET CLUB? Poole Town CC, Dorset
EARLIEST CRICKETING MEMORY? Watching Test cricket on TV with my dad
WHAT EXCITES YOU ABOUT THE NEW COUNTY STRUCTURE? Wearing the bear and ragged staff
HOW MANY HOURS DO YOU SPEND ON YOUR PHONE A DAY? Two to three
SPECIALITY SUBJECT IN A PUB QUIZ (EXCLUDING SPORT)? Random football players
ONE THING YOU WANT TO DO BEFORE YOU DIE: Travel
HOBBY YOU WOULD LIKE TO LEARN: The guitar

Batting	Mat	Inns	NO	Runs	HS	Ave	SR	100	50	Ct	St
ODIs	2	1	0	9	9	9.00	47.36	0	0	1	-
T20Is	5	1	0	0	0	0.00	0.00	0	0	0	-
List A	66	57	5	1145	80	22.01	-	0	7	30	-
T20s	110	83	19	897	53	14.01	-	0	2	45	-

Bowling	Mat	Balls	Mdns	Runs	Wkts	BB	Ave	4wI	5wI	SR	Econ
ODIs	2	75	0	70	4	3-36	17.50	0	0	18.75	5.60
T20Is	5	78	0	117	2	1-22	58.50	0	0	39.00	9.00
List A	66	2391	34	1683	70	5-50	24.04	3	1	34.15	4.22
T20s	110	1296	6	1457	54	4-36	26.98	1	0	24.00	6.74

DANI GIBSON

RHB / RMF

FULL NAME: Danielle Rose Gibson
BORN: April 30, 2001, Cheltenham, Gloucestershire
SQUAD NO: 28
HEIGHT: 5ft 6in
NICKNAME: Kimmy K
EDUCATION: Hartpury College, Gloucestershire
TEAMS: England, Somerset, London Spirit, Adelaide Strikers, Gloucestershire, Wales, Western Storm
ROLE: Allrounder
DEBUT: T20I: 2023; List A: 2015; T20: 2014

BEST BATTING: 76 Western Storm vs Northern Diamonds, Taunton, 2022
BEST BOWLING: 5-17 Gloucestershire vs Cornwall, Falmouth, 2017

FIRST CRICKET CLUB: Dumbleton CC, Evesham, Gloucestershire
WHICH GROUND DO YOU MOST ENJOY VISITING? Lord's – good food
WHO IS THE MOST TALENTED TEENAGER IN WOMEN'S DOMESTIC CRICKET? Katie Jones
IF YOU COULD PINCH A PLAYER FROM ANOTHER TEAM, WHO WOULD IT BE? Bess Heath
WHO IS THE TOUGHEST BOWLER TO FACE IN DOMESTIC CRICKET? Lauren Bell – she hoops the ball
WHAT ONE THING WOULD YOU CHANGE ABOUT WOMEN'S CRICKET IN ENGLAND?
Introduce a multi-day format
WHAT KEEPS YOU AWAKE AT NIGHT? TikTok
WHAT'S THE SILLIEST OUTFIT YOU'VE EVER WORN? A Severus Snape costume
CHOOSE A FANTASY SLIP CORDON TO SPEND A DAY IN THE FIELD WITH: Voldemort (wk), Harry Redknapp, Romesh Ranganathan, The Queen
SURPRISING FACT ABOUT YOU: I'm an introvert

Batting	Mat	Inns	NO	Runs	HS	Ave	SR	100	50	Ct	St
T20Is	22	15	5	147	41*	14.70	124.57	0	0	8	-
List A	49	45	4	845	76	20.60	-	0	6	20	-
T20s	127	99	23	1370	62	18.02	132.75	0	2	61	-

Bowling	Mat	Balls	Mdns	Runs	Wkts	BB	Ave	4wI	5wI	SR	Econ
T20Is	22	276	0	339	10	2-22	33.90	0	0	27.60	7.36
List A	49	1508	13	1156	54	5-17	21.40	2	1	27.92	4.59
T20s	127	1827	6	2137	93	4-23	22.97	1	0	19.64	7.01

SARAH GLENN — RHB / LB

FULL NAME: Sarah Glenn
BORN: August 27, 1999, Derby
SQUAD NO: 3
HEIGHT: 5ft 10in
EDUCATION: Trent College, Long Eaton; The Open University, Milton Keynes
TEAMS: England, The Blaze, London Spirit, Brisbane Heat, Central Sparks, Derbyshire, Loughborough Lightning, Northern Districts, Perth Scorchers, Trent Rockets
ROLE: Bowler
DEBUT: ODI: 2019; T20I: 2019; List A: 2013; T20: 2013

THE BLAZE

BEST BATTING: 72 Derbyshire vs Essex, Southend-on-Sea, 2018
BEST BOWLING: 4-17 Worcestershire vs Wales, Pontarddulais, 2019

FIRST CRICKET CLUB? Denby CC, Ripley, Derbyshire
WHICH TEAMMATE HAS HAD THE BIGGEST IMPACT ON YOUR GAME? Heather Knight
WHICH GROUND DO YOU MOST ENJOY VISITING? Newlands in South Africa
WHO IS THE MOST TALENTED TEENAGER IN WOMEN'S DOMESTIC CRICKET? Charis Pavely
WHO IS THE TOUGHEST BOWLER TO FACE IN DOMESTIC CRICKET? Phoebe Franklin
WHAT WAKES YOU UP IN THE MORNING? My dog
WHAT KEEPS YOU AWAKE AT NIGHT? Knowing I have to get up early and dreading it!
WHAT'S THE SILLIEST OUTFIT YOU'VE EVER WORN? Dressing up as Nessa from Gavin and Stacey
CHOOSE A FANTASY SLIP CORDON TO SPEND A DAY IN THE FIELD WITH: Adele (wk), Grace Barry, Peter Kay, Karl Pilkington

Batting	Mat	Inns	NO	Runs	HS	Ave	SR	100	50	Ct	St
ODIs	17	6	2	65	22*	16.25	81.25	0	0	4	-
T20Is	72	20	12	134	26	16.75	119.64	0	0	11	-
List A	66	49	9	955	72	23.87	71.75	0	5	19	-
T20s	205	106	35	917	43*	12.91	-	0	0	41	-

Bowling	Mat	Balls	Mdns	Runs	Wkts	BB	Ave	4wI	5wI	SR	Econ
ODIs	17	733	7	526	20	4-18	26.30	1	0	36.65	4.30
T20Is	72	1430	3	1434	89	4-12	16.11	4	0	16.06	6.01
List A	66	2822	54	1723	84	4-17	20.51	5	0	33.59	3.66
T20s	205	3795	9	3767	218	4-12	17.27	8	0	17.40	5.95

KIRSTIE GORDON

RHB / SLA / MVP3

THE BLAZE

FULL NAME: Kirstie Louise Gordon
BORN: October 20, 1997, Huntly, Aberdeenshire, Scotland
SQUAD NO: 24
HEIGHT: 5ft 5in
EDUCATION: Loughborough University
TEAMS: England, The Blaze, Trent Rockets, Birmingham Phoenix, Kent, Loughborough Lightning, Nottinghamshire, Otago, Scotland
ROLE: Bowler
DEBUT: Test: 2019; T20I: 2018; List A: 2012; T20: 2014

BEST BATTING: 60* Scotland vs Staffordshire, Oakamoor, 2015
BEST BOWLING: 5-18 Nottinghamshire vs Warwickshire, Nottingham, 2018

FIRST CRICKET CLUB? Huntly CC, Aberdeenshire
EARLIEST CRICKETING MEMORY? Playing with my mum and cousin in Fala Park (close to Edinburgh) when I was three
WHAT WILL YOU MISS ABOUT REGIONAL CRICKET? The legacy of the teams – some of them go back to Kia Super League days
WHAT EXCITES YOU ABOUT THE NEW COUNTY STRUCTURE? More T20 double headers with the men
OPPONENT YOU MOST LOOK FORWARD TO PLAYING AGAINST? Hollie Armitage – a great friend and a great player who I enjoy trying to get out
HOW MANY HOURS DO YOU SPEND ON YOUR PHONE A DAY? Five
ONE THING YOU WANT TO DO BEFORE YOU DIE: Climb Kilimanjaro
WHICH PUBLIC FIGURE INSPIRES YOU (EXCLUDING SPORTSPEOPLE)? The Obamas
SURPRISING FACT ABOUT YOU: I enjoy cleaning the bathroom
FILM YOU CAN WATCH OVER AND OVER: Any of the five Bourne movies

Batting	Mat	Inns	NO	Runs	HS	Ave	SR	100	50	Ct	St
Tests	1	0	-	-	-	-	-	-	-	0	-
T20Is	5	1	1	1	1*	-	100.00	0	0	0	-
List A	93	68	19	680	60*	13.87	-	0	1	35	-
T20s	152	62	20	391	29	9.30	-	0	0	53	-

Bowling	Mat	Balls	Mdns	Runs	Wkts	BB	Ave	4wI	5wI	SR	Econ
Tests	1	220	8	119	3	2-50	39.66	-	0	73.33	3.24
T20Is	5	114	1	98	8	3-16	12.25	0	0	14.25	5.15
List A	93	5015	113	2766	150	5-18	18.44	8	2	33.43	3.30
T20s	152	3232	10	3097	187	5-12	16.56	2	1	17.28	5.74

PHOEBE GRAHAM   RHB / RMF

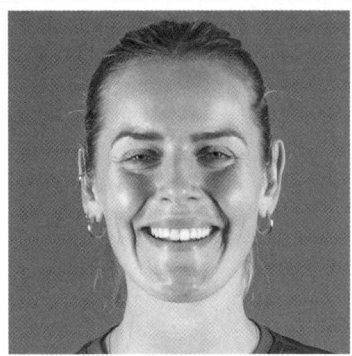

FULL NAME: Phoebe Claire Graham
BORN: October 23, 1991, Steeton, Yorkshire
SQUAD NO: 17
HEIGHT: 5ft 11in
NICKNAME: PG
EDUCATION: University of Exeter
TEAMS: Lancashire, Manchester Originals, Berkshire, Devon, Northern Diamonds, Northern Districts, Northern Superchargers, Nottinghamshire, Thunder, Western Storm, Yorkshire
ROLE: Bowler
DEBUT: List A: 2010; T20: 2010

BEST BATTING: 29* Northern Diamonds vs Thunder, Liverpool, 2020
BEST BOWLING: 3-14 Berkshire vs Worcestershire, Maidenhead, 2019

FIRST CRICKET CLUB? Guiseley CC, Leeds
WHAT WILL YOU MISS ABOUT REGIONAL CRICKET? The names of the competitions
WHAT EXCITES YOU ABOUT THE NEW COUNTY STRUCTURE? Being part of Lancashire CCC
OPPONENT YOU MOST LOOK FORWARD TO PLAYING AGAINST? Katie Levick – she's got some high-quality chat
FAVOURITE WARM-UP SONG? Wacca Wacca by Shakira
HOW MANY HOURS DO YOU SPEND ON YOUR PHONE A DAY? A couple
SPECIALITY SUBJECT IN A PUB QUIZ (EXCLUDING SPORT)? Counties in the UK
ONE THING YOU WANT TO DO BEFORE YOU DIE: Go on a safari
HOBBY YOU WOULD LIKE TO LEARN: A new language
SURPRISING FACT ABOUT YOU: I have cycled to Italy
FILM YOU CAN WATCH OVER AND OVER: Any in the Bridget Jones series

Batting	Mat	Inns	NO	Runs	HS	Ave	SR	100	50	Ct	St
List A	72	43	10	251	29*	7.60	52.07	0	0	10	-
T20s	76	33	14	207	26*	10.89	97.18	0	0	15	-

Bowling	Mat	Balls	Mdns	Runs	Wkts	BB	Ave	4wI	5wI	SR	Econ
List A	72	2312	23	1756	48	3-14	36.58	0	0	48.16	4.55
T20s	76	1342	9	1393	61	3-8	22.83	0	0	22.00	6.22

EVA GRAY

RHB / RMF / MVP39

ESSEX

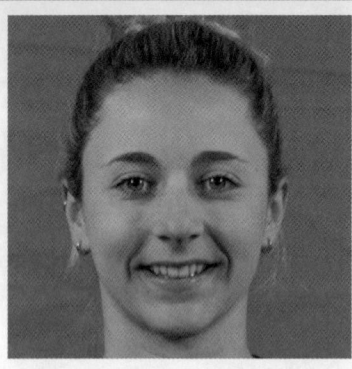

FULL NAME: Eva Gray
BORN: May 24, 2000
SQUAD NO: 10
HEIGHT: 5ft 4in
EDUCATION: Kingston Grammar School, London; University of Birmingham
TEAMS: Essex, London Spirit, Oval Invincibles, South East Stars, Sunrisers, Surrey, Surrey Stars
ROLE: Bowler
DEBUT: List A: 2016; T20: 2014

BEST BATTING: 52* Surrey vs Essex, Cobham, 2018
BEST BOWLING: 4-31 Sunrisers vs The Blaze, Loughborough, 2023

EARLIEST CRICKETING MEMORY? Playing in wellies in the back garden
WHAT WILL YOU MISS ABOUT REGIONAL CRICKET? The legacy we had built as the Sunrisers
WHAT EXCITES YOU ABOUT THE NEW COUNTY STRUCTURE? Hopefully equal opportunities and platform as the men have
OPPONENT YOU MOST LOOK FORWARD TO PLAYING AGAINST? Aylish Cranstone – we have lots of history and it's always a nice battle!
SPECIALITY SUBJECT IN A PUB QUIZ (EXCLUDING SPORT)? Geography
ONE THING YOU WANT TO DO BEFORE YOU DIE: A skydive
HOBBY YOU WOULD LIKE TO LEARN: Play the guitar
SURPRISING FACT ABOUT YOU: I have a law degree
FILM YOU CAN WATCH OVER AND OVER: A Star is Born

Batting	Mat	Inns	NO	Runs	HS	Ave	SR	100	50	Ct	St
List A	50	41	6	367	52*	10.48	57.07	0	1	15	-
T20s	92	49	16	358	34*	10.84	96.75	0	0	16	-

Bowling	Mat	Balls	Mdns	Runs	Wkts	BB	Ave	4wI	5wI	SR	Econ
List A	50	1722	18	1198	53	4-31	22.60	1	0	32.49	4.17
T20s	92	1154	0	1393	51	4-16	27.31	1	0	22.62	7.24

DANI GREGORY   RHB / LB

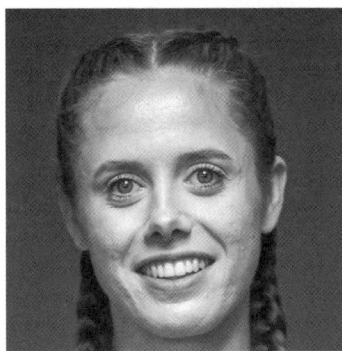

SURREY

FULL NAME: Danielle Lucy Gregory
BORN: December 4, 1998, Frimley, Surrey
SQUAD NO: 19
HEIGHT: 5ft 6in
NICKNAME: Greggo
EDUCATION: Weydon School, Farnham,
Surrey; Alton College, Hampshire; University
of Chichester, Sussex
TEAMS: Surrey, Manchester Originals, Oval
Invincibles, South East Stars
ROLE: Bowler
DEBUT: List A: 2019; T20: 2018

BEST BATTING: 20* South East Stars vs Southern Vipers, Southampton, 2023
BEST BOWLING: 4-12 South East Stars vs Sunrisers, Radlett, 2023

FIRST CRICKET CLUB? Rowledge CC, Surrey
EARLIEST CRICKETING MEMORY? Being hit in the face with a bat while wicketkeeping
WHAT EXCITES YOU ABOUT THE NEW COUNTY STRUCTURE? Playing all our home T20
games at The Oval
FAVOURITE WARM-UP SONG? The Champion – Carrie Underwood
SPECIALITY SUBJECT IN A PUB QUIZ (EXCLUDING SPORT)? Grey's Anatomy
HOBBY YOU WOULD LIKE TO LEARN: Speak another language
SURPRISING FACT ABOUT YOU: I have a master's degree in performance analysis
FILM YOU CAN WATCH OVER AND OVER: The Blind Side

Batting	Mat	Inns	NO	Runs	HS	Ave	SR	100	50	Ct	St
List A	54	31	16	88	20*	5.86	34.78	0	0	5	-
T20s	69	14	5	34	12*	3.77	58.62	0	0	11	-

Bowling	Mat	Balls	Mdns	Runs	Wkts	BB	Ave	4wl	5wl	SR	Econ
List A	54	2060	5	1593	50	4-12	31.86	3	0	41.20	4.63
T20s	69	1154	3	1257	57	4-7	22.05	2	0	20.24	6.53

JODI GREWCOCK   LHB / LB

ESSEX

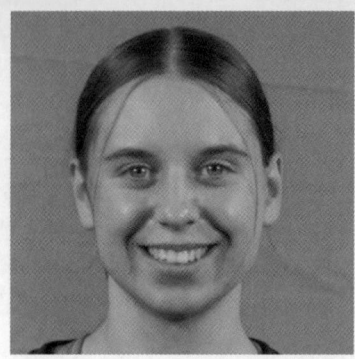

FULL NAME: Jodie Louise Grewcock
BORN: November 30, 2004, Leicester
SQUAD NO: 9
HEIGHT: 5ft 5in
NICKNAME: Jbizz
EDUCATION: Guilsborough Academy,
Northamptonshire
TEAMS: Essex, England U19,
Northamptonshire, Sunrisers
ROLE: Allrounder
DEBUT: List A: 2019; T20: 2018

BEST BATTING: 76 Sunrisers vs Southern Vipers, Chelmsford, 2023
BEST BOWLING: 4-45 Sunrisers vs Southern Vipers, Chelmsford, 2023

FIRST CRICKET CLUB? Market Harborough CC, Leicestershire
WHAT EXCITES YOU ABOUT THE NEW COUNTY STRUCTURE? Having an established home
base and being aligned with the men's setup (double headers etc…)
OPPONENT YOU MOST LOOK FORWARD TO PLAYING AGAINST? Mady Villiers
SPECIALITY SUBJECT IN A PUB QUIZ (EXCLUDING SPORT)? Animals
SURPRISING FACT ABOUT YOU: I have never been on a rollercoaster and I used to compete
nationally in trampolining
CHOOSE A FANTASY SLIP CORDON TO SPEND A DAY IN THE FIELD WITH: Sarah Taylor (wk),
Steve Smith, Mark Waugh, Cameron Green

Batting	Mat	Inns	NO	Runs	HS	Ave	SR	100	50	Ct	St
List A	33	26	3	653	76	28.39	64.20	0	5	11	-
T20s	33	30	7	562	65	24.43	89.06	0	1	10	-
Bowling	Mat	Balls	Mdns	Runs	Wkts	BB	Ave	4wl	5wl	SR	Econ
List A	33	1139	12	772	37	4-45	20.86	1	0	30.78	4.06
T20s	33	276	0	248	9	2-11	27.55	0	0	30.66	5.39

CORDELIA GRIFFITH   RHB / RM

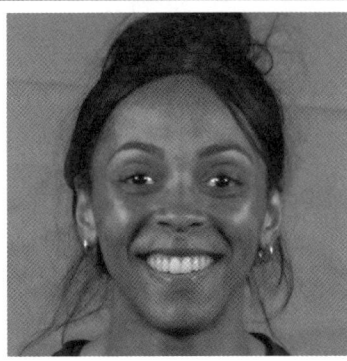

FULL NAME: Cordelia Lauren Griffith
BORN: September 19, 1995, Islington, London
SQUAD NO: 6
HEIGHT: 5ft 5in
EDUCATION: Chigwell School, Essex; Durham University
TEAMS: Essex, London Spirit, Middlesex, Oval Invincibles, Manchester Originals, Sunrisers, Surrey Stars, Yorkshire Diamonds
ROLE: Batter
DEBUT: List A: 2010; T20: 2010

BEST BATTING: 155* Essex vs Suffolk, Long Melford, 2018
BEST BOWLING: 1-6 Essex vs Berkshire, Sindlesham, 2013

FIRST CRICKET CLUB? Loughton CC, Essex
EARLIEST CRICKETING MEMORY? Playing in the garden with my dad
WHAT EXCITES YOU ABOUT THE NEW COUNTY STRUCTURE? The double headers in the T20 Blast
FAVOURITE WARM-UP SONG? Set My Heart on Fire by Majestic, The Jammin Kid and Celine Dion
HOW MANY HOURS DO YOU SPEND ON YOUR PHONE A DAY? Four hours
SPECIALITY SUBJECT IN A PUB QUIZ (EXCLUDING SPORT)? Music
ONE THING YOU WANT TO DO BEFORE YOU DIE: A skydive
HOBBY YOU WOULD LIKE TO LEARN: Play the piano
WHICH PUBLIC FIGURE INSPIRES YOU (EXCLUDING SPORTSPEOPLE)? Michelle Obama
SURPRISING FACT ABOUT YOU: I have a law degree and a master's in international law
FILM YOU CAN WATCH OVER AND OVER: Bridesmaids

Batting	Mat	Inns	NO	Runs	HS	Ave	SR	100	50	Ct	St
List A	72	69	3	2101	155*	31.83	-	3	13	21	-
T20s	104	90	10	1470	73	18.37	98.13	0	7	23	-

Bowling	Mat	Balls	Mdns	Runs	Wkts	BB	Ave	4wI	5wI	SR	Econ
List A	72	271	3	192	7	1-6	27.42	0	0	38.71	4.25
T20s	104	150	0	167	2	1-12	83.50	0	0	75.00	6.68

ALEX GRIFFITHS   RHB / RMF

SOMERSET

FULL NAME: Alexandra Clare Griffiths
BORN: June 12, 2002, Swansea
SQUAD NO: 25
HEIGHT: 5ft 7in
NICKNAME: Ali G
EDUCATION: Dyffryn Comprehensive
School, Port Talbot, Wales; Cardiff
Metropolitan University
TEAMS: Somerset, Wales, Western Storm,
Welsh Fire
ROLE: Allrounder
DEBUT: List A: 2016; T20: 2016

BEST BATTING: 80 Western Storm vs Sunrisers, Bristol, 2020
BEST BOWLING: 2-2 Wales vs Essex, Griffithstown, 2019

FIRST CRICKET CLUB? Port Talbot CC, Swansea
WHAT WILL YOU MISS ABOUT REGIONAL CRICKET? Representing more than one county
WHAT EXCITES YOU ABOUT THE NEW COUNTY STRUCTURE? Playing for Somerset and
getting into the club culture
OPPONENT YOU MOST LOOK FORWARD TO PLAYING AGAINST? Lauren Filer – she was with
us at Western Storm but has now moved to Durham, so it will be nice to have a catch-up
FAVOURITE WARM-UP SONG? Let's Go Back by Jungle
HOW MANY HOURS DO YOU SPEND ON YOUR PHONE A DAY? Four hours and 10 minutes
ONE THING YOU WANT TO DO BEFORE YOU DIE: A skydive
HOBBY YOU WOULD LIKE TO LEARN: I would like to rediscover the guitar
WHICH PUBLIC FIGURE INSPIRES YOU (EXCLUDING SPORTSPEOPLE)? Claudia Winkleman
FILM YOU CAN WATCH OVER AND OVER: Any Harry Potter movie

Batting	Mat	Inns	NO	Runs	HS	Ave	SR	100	50	Ct	St
List A	62	57	3	1016	80	18.81	60.40	0	4	17	-
T20s	72	47	5	476	50	11.33	93.33	0	1	14	-

Bowling	Mat	Balls	Mdns	Runs	Wkts	BB	Ave	4wI	5wI	SR	Econ
List A	62	1280	9	1154	28	2-2	41.21	0	0	45.71	5.40
T20s	72	537	1	692	25	3-12	27.68	0	0	21.48	7.73

JOSIE GROVES

RHB / LB

FULL NAME: Josephine Paige Groves
BORN: September 5, 2004, Milton Keynes, Buckinghamshire
SQUAD NO: 5
HEIGHT: 5ft 8in
NICKNAME: Jos
EDUCATION: Royal Latin School, Buckingham
TEAMS: The Blaze, Trent Rockets, England U19, Northamptonshire
ROLE: Bowler
DEBUT: List A: 2019; T20: 2019

BEST BATTING: 55 Lightning vs Southern Vipers, Derby, 2022
BEST BOWLING: 3-39 The Blaze vs Central Sparks, Edgbaston, 2023

FIRST CRICKET CLUB? Stony Stratford CC, Milton Keynes, Buckinghamshire
EARLIEST CRICKETING MEMORY? Softball training on Friday night at my local school
WHAT EXCITES YOU ABOUT THE NEW COUNTY STRUCTURE? The women's game becoming more competitive at all levels
OPPONENT YOU MOST LOOK FORWARD TO PLAYING AGAINST? Tilly Corteen-Coleman – we have funny battles on and off the field
FAVOURITE WARM-UP SONG? Any song by McFly
HOW MANY HOURS DO YOU SPEND ON YOUR PHONE A DAY? Six
SPECIALITY SUBJECT IN A PUB QUIZ (EXCLUDING SPORT)? Musicals
ONE THING YOU WANT TO DO BEFORE YOU DIE: Visit every continent
HOBBY YOU WOULD LIKE TO LEARN: Learn to communicate in Makaton
FILM YOU CAN WATCH OVER AND OVER: Hamilton

Batting	Mat	Inns	NO	Runs	HS	Ave	SR	100	50	Ct	St
List A	22	14	3	115	55	10.45	72.78	0	1	7	-
T20s	47	27	8	257	68	13.52	106.19	0	1	9	-

Bowling	Mat	Balls	Mdns	Runs	Wkts	BB	Ave	4wI	5wI	SR	Econ
List A	22	792	6	712	25	3-39	28.48	0	0	31.68	5.39
T20s	47	625	3	574	40	3-7	14.35	0	0	15.62	5.51

NANCY HARMAN

RHB / LB

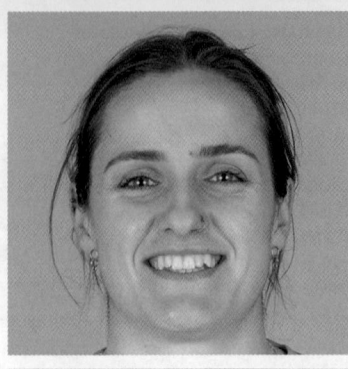

FULL NAME: Nancy Holly Harman
BORN: July 11, 1999, Worthing, Sussex
SQUAD NO: 25
HEIGHT: 5ft 6in
EDUCATION: Brighton College; Loughborough University
TEAMS: Hampshire, Leicestershire, Lightning, London Spirit, Southern Vipers, Sussex, Trent Rockets
ROLE: Allrounder
DEBUT: List A: 2017; T20: 2017

BEST BATTING: 49* Sussex vs Hampshire, Brighton, 2024
BEST BOWLING: 6-40 Sussex vs Warwickshire, Brighton, 2019

FIRST CRICKET CLUB? Brighton & Hove CC
WHAT WILL YOU MISS ABOUT REGIONAL CRICKET? The brand and culture we had built around the Vipers
WHAT EXCITES YOU ABOUT THE NEW COUNTY STRUCTURE? Lots of double headers at first-class grounds. Telling non-cricket fans who I play for and not being met with a look of confusion!
OPPONENT YOU MOST LOOK FORWARD TO PLAYING AGAINST? Alice Davidson-Richards – a smart player who clinched the 50-over semi-final against us for South East Stars in 2024 and had a brilliant run of form at the end of last season
HOW MANY HOURS DO YOU SPEND ON YOUR PHONE A DAY? Apple tells me it's three hours and 20 minutes
SPECIALITY SUBJECT IN A PUB QUIZ (EXCLUDING SPORT)? Chemistry
ONE THING YOU WANT TO DO BEFORE YOU DIE: Walk all 214 of Alfred Wainwright's Lakeland Fells in the Lake District. Done 36 so far…
WHICH PUBLIC FIGURE INSPIRES YOU (EXCLUDING SPORTSPEOPLE)? The late psychologist Daniel Kahneman. His work has forever changed our thinking
SURPRISING FACT ABOUT YOU: I can do the whole rap in the Moana song You're Welcome
FILM YOU CAN WATCH OVER AND OVER: Honestly none, I'm a terrible re-watcher

Batting	Mat	Inns	NO	Runs	HS	Ave	SR	100	50	Ct	St
List A	33	28	10	299	49*	16.61	67.49	0	0	8	-
T20s	67	47	15	499	43	15.59	87.54	0	0	22	1

Bowling	Mat	Balls	Mdns	Runs	Wkts	BB	Ave	4wI	5wI	SR	Econ
List A	33	705	6	623	28	6-40	22.25	1	1	25.17	5.30
T20s	67	773	3	736	40	4-10	18.40	1	0	19.32	5.71

LIBERTY HEAP

RHB / OB

FULL NAME: Liberty Nicole Heap
BORN: September 16, 2003, Burnley
SQUAD NO: 39
HEIGHT: 5ft 6in
NICKNAME: Berty
EDUCATION: Stonyhurst College, Clitheroe, Lancashire
TEAMS: Lancashire, Cumbria, England U19, Thunder
ROLE: Allrounder
DEBUT: List A: 2019; T20: 2019

BEST BATTING: 36* Thunder vs Western Storm, Old Trafford, 2022
BEST BOWLING: 3-34 Thunder vs Lightning, Old Trafford, 2020

FIRST CRICKET CLUB? Lowerhouse CC, Burnley, Lancashire
WHAT WILL YOU MISS ABOUT REGIONAL CRICKET? The excitement of getting the first glimpses of the professional women's game and the buzz that created
WHAT EXCITES YOU ABOUT THE NEW COUNTY STRUCTURE? Having more fixtures in general and more double headers – always exciting when a crowd is in
FAVOURITE WARM-UP SONG? Any song by Artic Monkeys – I was convinced they made us win whenever we listened to them
HOW MANY HOURS DO YOU SPEND ON YOUR PHONE A DAY? Five to six
ONE THING YOU WANT TO DO BEFORE YOU DIE: A skydive
HOBBY YOU WOULD LIKE TO LEARN: DIY renovation/building
WHICH PUBLIC FIGURE INSPIRES YOU (EXCLUDING SPORTSPEOPLE)? Billie Eilish
SURPRISING FACT ABOUT YOU: I'm a better darts player with my left hand even though I do everything else right-handed and right-footed
FILM YOU CAN WATCH OVER AND OVER: Step Brothers

Batting	Mat	Inns	NO	Runs	HS	Ave	SR	100	50	Ct	St
List A	19	17	1	192	36*	12.00	74.13	0	0	3	-
T20s	25	21	3	294	46	16.33	85.71	0	0	7	-

Bowling	Mat	Balls	Mdns	Runs	Wkts	BB	Ave	4wl	5wl	SR	Econ
List A	19	336	5	258	15	3-34	17.20	0	0	22.40	4.60
T20s	25	91	0	115	3	2-17	38.33	0	0	30.33	7.58

BESS HEATH

RHB / WK / MVP44

FULL NAME: Bess Alice May Heath
BORN: August 20, 2001, Chesterfield, Derbyshire
SQUAD NO: 25
HEIGHT: 5ft 6in
NICKNAME: Bam Bam
TEAMS: England, Durham, Northern Superchargers, Northern Diamonds, Brisbane Heat, Derbyshire, Melbourne Stars, Yorkshire
ROLE: Wicketkeeper/batter
DEBUT: ODI: 2023; T20I: 2023; List A: 2015; T20: 2014

BEST BATTING: 114 Derbyshire vs Norfolk, Spondon, 2016

FIRST CRICKET CLUB? Baslow CC, Derbyshire
WHAT ONE THING WOULD YOU CHANGE ABOUT WOMEN'S CRICKET IN ENGLAND? Create space for the longer version of the game
MOST BEAUTIFUL THING YOU HAVE EVER SEEN? My doggies Poppy and Coco
HOBBIES? Doing up Land Rovers
MAKE ONE PREDICTION FOR THE FUTURE OF CRICKET: Women's and men's cricket will be on an equal footing
SURPRISING FACT ABOUT YOU: I used to be a tree surgeon

Batting	Mat	Inns	NO	Runs	HS	Ave	SR	100	50	Ct	St
ODIs	4	4	1	59	33*	19.66	100.00	0	0	3	1
T20Is	4	3	0	6	3	2.00	46.15	0	0	2	-
List A	66	60	11	1582	114	32.28	99.06	2	11	39	6
T20s	133	120	23	1757	60	18.11	-	0	9	32	22

Bowling	Mat	Balls	Mdns	Runs	Wkts	BB	Ave	4wI	5wI	SR	Econ
ODIs	4	-	-	-	-	-	-	-	-	-	-
T20Is	4	-	-	-	-	-	-	-	-	-	-
List A	66	-	-	-	-	-	-	-	-	-	-
T20s	133	-	-	-	-	-	-	-	-	-	-

LUCY HIGHAM RHB / OB / MVP33

FULL NAME: Lucy Florence Higham
BORN: October 17, 1997, Leicester
SQUAD NO: 7
HEIGHT: 5ft 3in
EDUCATION: Leicester Grammar School;
Loughborough University
TEAMS: The Blaze, Northern Superchargers,
Leicestershire, Loughborough Lightning,
Nottinghamshire, Trent Rockets
ROLE: Bowler
DEBUT: List A: 2013; T20: 2013

BEST BATTING: 74 Leicestershire vs Northamptonshire, Northampton, 2015
BEST BOWLING: 5-19 The Blaze vs Central Sparks, Trent Bridge, 2023

FIRST CRICKET CLUB? Houghton & Thurnby CC, Leicester
EARLIEST CRICKETING MEMORY? Playing on the local park with friends
WHAT WILL YOU MISS ABOUT REGIONAL CRICKET? I think it will take me a while to stop calling teams by their regional names!
WHAT EXCITES YOU ABOUT THE NEW COUNTY STRUCTURE? Everyone being part of the county brand and having access to the facilities. And being able to learn from the male pros
HOW MANY HOURS DO YOU SPEND ON YOUR PHONE A DAY? Five
SPECIALITY SUBJECT IN A PUB QUIZ (EXCLUDING SPORT)? Music
ONE THING YOU WANT TO DO BEFORE YOU DIE: See wild penguins in the flesh
SURPRISING FACT ABOUT YOU: I can play a few songs on the guitar
FILM YOU CAN WATCH OVER AND OVER: The Blindside

Batting	Mat	Inns	NO	Runs	HS	Ave	SR	100	50	Ct	St
List A	94	80	9	1048	74	14.76	50.31	0	3	33	-
T20s	126	68	15	819	53	15.45	-	0	1	29	-

Bowling	Mat	Balls	Mdns	Runs	Wkts	BB	Ave	4wI	5wI	SR	Econ
List A	94	3639	47	2430	103	5-19	23.59	1	1	35.33	4.00
T20s	126	1624	6	1601	76	4-16	21.06	1	0	21.36	5.91

NIAMH HOLLAND

RHB / RM

SOMERSET

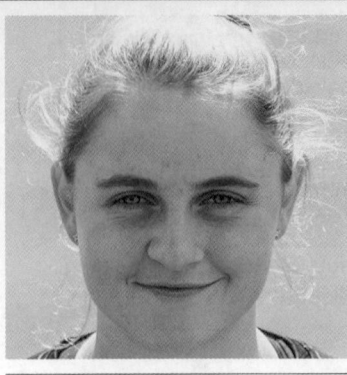

FULL NAME: Niamh Fiona Holland
BORN: October 27, 2004, Yeovil, Somerset
SQUAD NO: 27
HEIGHT: 5ft 5in
NICKNAME: Nevo
EDUCATION: Richard Huish College, Taunton; Wellington School, Somerset
TEAMS: Somerset, England U19, London Spirit, Western Storm
ROLE: Allrounder
DEBUT: List A: 2019; T20: 2019

BEST BATTING: 44 Western Storm vs Southern Vipers, Street, 2023
BEST BOWLING: 2-17 Western Storm vs Central Sparks, Bristol, 2022

WHICH TEAMMATE HAS HAD THE BIGGEST IMPACT ON YOUR GAME? Sophie Luff – a mentor who has helped me integrate into the first team
WHICH PART OF THE SEASON DO YOU MOST ENJOY? The Hundred
WHO IS THE MOST TALENTED TEENAGER IN WOMEN'S DOMESTIC CRICKET? Katie Jones
IF YOU COULD PINCH A PLAYER FROM ANOTHER TEAM, WHO WOULD IT BE? Lizzie Scott
WHO IS THE TOUGHEST BOWLER TO FACE IN DOMESTIC CRICKET? Lauren Filer
WHAT ONE THING WOULD YOU CHANGE ABOUT WOMEN'S CRICKET IN ENGLAND? Play more at Test grounds to attract more attention
WHAT'S THE SILLIEST OUTFIT YOU'VE EVER WORN? A Barbie costume
CHOOSE A FANTASY SLIP CORDON TO SPEND A DAY IN THE FIELD WITH: 50 Cent (wk), GK Barry, Harry Potter

Batting	Mat	Inns	NO	Runs	HS	Ave	SR	100	50	Ct	St
List A	41	34	4	340	44	11.33	55.37	0	0	6	-
T20s	41	33	6	301	32	11.14	80.69	0	0	5	-
Bowling	Mat	Balls	Mdns	Runs	Wkts	BB	Ave	4wI	5wI	SR	Econ
List A	41	600	5	604	16	2-17	37.75	0	0	37.50	6.04
T20s	41	489	0	559	29	3-11	19.96	0	0	17.46	6.85

SCARLETT HUGHES

LHB / WK

FULL NAME: Scarlett Talulla Ava Hughes
BORN: June 18, 2002, Cambridge
SQUAD NO: TBC
HEIGHT: 5ft 5in
EDUCATION: London School of Economics (LSE)
TEAMS: The Blaze, Essex, Sunrisers
ROLE: Wicketkeeper/batter
DEBUT: List A: 2017; T20: 2019

BEST BATTING: 15 Essex vs Middlesex, Coggeshall, 2024

FIRST CRICKET CLUB? Saffron Walden CC, Essex
EARLIEST CRICKETING MEMORY? Helping my dad set out the cones and drills for the boys' training sessions at SWCC
OPPONENT YOU MOST LOOK FORWARD TO PLAYING AGAINST? Mia Rogers – we've grown up playing together and this will be the first time she's the opposition and not my teammate!
FAVOURITE WARM-UP SONG? Our Song by Taylor Swift
HOW MANY HOURS DO YOU SPEND ON YOUR PHONE A DAY? Three
SPECIALITY SUBJECT IN A PUB QUIZ (EXCLUDING SPORT)? Science
ONE THING YOU WANT TO DO BEFORE YOU DIE: Thru-hike the Triple Crown
SURPRISING FACT ABOUT YOU: I've got a 570-day 'streak' on Duolingo (language app). And counting…
FILM YOU CAN WATCH OVER AND OVER: Notting Hill

Batting	Mat	Inns	NO	Runs	HS	Ave	SR	100	50	Ct	St
List A	12	9	1	48	15	6.00	31.57	0	0	11	4
T20s	32	27	4	386	70	16.78	106.04	0	2	14	15

Bowling	Mat	Balls	Mdns	Runs	Wkts	BB	Ave	4wI	5wI	SR	Econ
List A	12	-	-	-	-	-	-	-	-	-	-
T20s	32	-	-	-	-	-	-	-	-	-	-

LAURA JACKSON

RHB / RM

SOMERSET

FULL NAME: Laura Elizabeth Jackson
BORN: December 27, 1997
SQUAD NO: 4
HEIGHT: 5ft 7in
NICKNAME: Jacko
EDUCATION: Ormskirk High School, Lancashire
TEAMS: Somerset, Cheshire, Cumbria, Lancashire, Manchester Originals, Thunder
ROLE: Bowler
DEBUT: List A: 2015; T20: 2015

BEST BATTING: 30 Thunder vs Central Sparks, Worcester, 2021
BEST BOWLING: 7-9 Cumbria vs Scotland A, Kirkby Stephen, 2019

FIRST CRICKET CLUB? Halsall CC, Ormskirk, West Lancashire
EARLIEST CRICKETING MEMORY? Playing 'diamond cricket' at my primary school in year five
WHAT WILL YOU MISS ABOUT REGIONAL CRICKET? The team names
WHAT EXCITES YOU ABOUT THE NEW COUNTY STRUCTURE? Belonging to a county
OPPONENT YOU MOST LOOK FORWARD TO PLAYING AGAINST? Sophia Turner – she's my bestie and we get very competitive against each other
FAVOURITE WARM-UP SONG? Glue by Bicep
HOW MANY HOURS DO YOU SPEND ON YOUR PHONE A DAY? Two to three
SPECIALITY SUBJECT IN A PUB QUIZ (EXCLUDING SPORT)? Excel spreadsheets
ONE THING YOU WANT TO DO BEFORE YOU DIE: Build or renovate my dream house
HOBBY YOU WOULD LIKE TO LEARN: How to be a lash and brow technician
WHICH PUBLIC FIGURE INSPIRES YOU (EXCLUDING SPORTSPEOPLE)? Sandra Bullock
SURPRISING FACT ABOUT YOU: I can still do a front handspring
FILM YOU CAN WATCH OVER AND OVER: We're the Millers

Batting	Mat	Inns	NO	Runs	HS	Ave	SR	100	50	Ct	St
List A	37	27	6	197	30	9.38	36.82	0	0	10	-
T20s	59	35	17	280	53	15.55	66.98	0	1	10	-

Bowling	Mat	Balls	Mdns	Runs	Wkts	BB	Ave	4wI	5wI	SR	Econ
List A	37	1315	25	857	42	7-9	20.40	1	1	31.30	3.91
T20s	59	883	8	818	42	3-5	19.47	0	0	21.02	5.55

GRACE JOHNSON   RHB / RM

FULL NAME: Grace May Johnson
BORN: December 21, 2004, Burnley, Lancashire
SQUAD NO: TBC
HEIGHT: 5ft 7in
NICKNAME: Pluto
EDUCATION: Unity College, Burnley; Burnley College
TEAMS: Lancashire, Cumbria, Thunder
ROLE: Allrounder
DEBUT: List A: 2024; T20: 2021

BEST BATTING: 27 Thunder vs The Blaze, Sale, 2024
BEST BOWLING: 3-22 Lancashire vs Yorkshire, Castleford, 2024

FIRST CRICKET CLUB? Lowerhouse CC, Burnley, Lancashire
EARLIEST CRICKETING MEMORY? Playing at primary school
WHAT EXCITES YOU ABOUT THE NEW COUNTY STRUCTURE? More trophies to play for
FAVOURITE WARM-UP SONG? Hotel Room Service by Pitbull
HOW MANY HOURS DO YOU SPEND ON YOUR PHONE A DAY? Four to five
SPECIALITY SUBJECT IN A PUB QUIZ (EXCLUDING SPORT)? Disney
ONE THING YOU WANT TO DO BEFORE YOU DIE: Swim with sharks
WHICH PUBLIC FIGURE INSPIRES YOU (EXCLUDING SPORTSPEOPLE)? Michelle Obama
SURPRISING FACT ABOUT YOU: I'm one of five women in the world who wear a men's large helmet
FILM YOU CAN WATCH OVER AND OVER: Wicked

Batting	Mat	Inns	NO	Runs	HS	Ave	SR	100	50	Ct	St
List A	5	5	0	69	27	13.80	60.00	0	0	0	-
T20s	21	11	2	96	36*	10.66	79.33	0	0	7	-

Bowling	Mat	Balls	Mdns	Runs	Wkts	BB	Ave	4wI	5wI	SR	Econ
List A	5	192	5	88	8	3-22	11.00	0	0	24.00	2.75
T20s	21	330	0	289	16	2-14	18.06	0	0	20.62	5.25

AMY JONES   RHB / WK

THE BLAZE

FULL NAME: Amy Ellen Jones
BORN: June 13, 1993, Solihull, Warwickshire
SQUAD NO: TBC
HEIGHT: 5ft 9in
EDUCATION: John Willmott School;
Loughborough College
TEAMS: England, The Blaze, Birmingham
Phoenix, Central Sparks, Loughborough
Lightning, Perth Scorchers, Warwickshire,
Western Australia
ROLE: Wicketkeeper/batter
DEBUT: Test: 2019; ODI: 2013; T20I: 2013;
List A: 2008; T20: 2010

BEST BATTING: 163* Central Sparks vs Western Storm, Edgbaston, 2021

FIRST CRICKET CLUB: Walmley CC, West Midlands
WHICH TEAMMATE HAS HAD THE BIGGEST IMPACT ON YOUR GAME? Heather Knight – she
has always encouraged me to play with confidence and helped me to become more of a
leader within the England team
WHICH PART OF THE SEASON DO YOU MOST ENJOY? The last game of the season and the
feeling of being close to a well-earned rest
WHO IS THE MOST TALENTED TEENAGER IN WOMEN'S DOMESTIC CRICKET? Seren Smale
WHAT'S THE SILLIEST OUTFIT YOU'VE EVER WORN? A lobster costume
CHOOSE A FANTASY SLIP CORDON TO SPEND A DAY IN THE FIELD WITH: Me (wk), Adele,
Viktor Hovland, Margot Robbie

Batting	Mat	Inns	NO	Runs	HS	Ave	SR	100	50	Ct	St
Tests	8	13	0	188	64	14.46	47.95	0	1	20	-
ODIs	97	81	10	2137	94	30.09	83.05	0	14	78	19
T20Is	117	95	19	1592	89	20.94	122.36	0	5	51	43
List A	197	178	23	4993	163*	32.21	-	6	28	150	77
T20s	311	278	43	5565	89	23.68	-	0	23	127	122
Bowling	Mat	Balls	Mdns	Runs	Wkts	BB	Ave	4wI	5wI	SR	Econ
Tests	8	-	-	-	-	-	-	-	-	-	-
ODIs	97	-	-	-	-	-	-	-	-	-	-
T20Is	117	-	-	-	-	-	-	-	-	-	-
List A	197	-	-	-	-	-	-	-	-	-	-
T20s	311	-	-	-	-	-	-	-	-	-	-

EMMA JONES   RHB / RMF

FULL NAME: Emma Wing Sum Jones
BORN: August 8, 2002, Hatfield, Hertfordshire
SQUAD NO: 88
HEIGHT: 5ft 9in
EDUCATION: Felsted School, Essex; Cambridge University
TEAMS: Surrey, Essex, Hertfordshire, South East Stars
ROLE: Allrounder
DEBUT: List A: 2017; T20: 2021

SURREY

BEST BATTING: 47 South East Stars vs Northern Diamonds, Chester-le-Street, 2024
BEST BOWLING: 1-13 South East Stars vs Sunrisers, Beckenham, 2024

WHICH TEAMMATE HAS HAD THE BIGGEST IMPACT ON YOUR GAME?
Alice Davidson-Richards
DESCRIBE YOUR CAREER IN THREE WORDS: Fresh, fun, feet-breaking
WHICH PART OF THE SEASON DO YOU MOST ENJOY? The early season
WHICH GROUND DO YOU MOST ENJOY VISITING? Trent Bridge, where I made my debut for the Stars
IF YOU COULD PINCH A PLAYER FROM ANOTHER TEAM, WHO WOULD IT BE? Chloe Brewer
WHO IS THE TOUGHEST BOWLER TO FACE IN DOMESTIC CRICKET? Sarah Glenn
WHAT WAKES YOU UP IN THE MORNING? The joy and excitement of a new day, and needing to pee
WHAT KEEPS YOU AWAKE AT NIGHT? Being too warm
WHAT'S THE SILLIEST OUTFIT YOU'VE EVER WORN? A carboard tree costume for the genetics department of the Wizard of Oz pantomime at university last year

Batting	Mat	Inns	NO	Runs	HS	Ave	SR	100	50	Ct	St
List A	10	10	1	124	47	13.77	73.37	0	0	5	-
T20s	28	20	9	244	46*	22.18	129.78	0	0	9	-

Bowling	Mat	Balls	Mdns	Runs	Wkts	BB	Ave	4wl	5wl	SR	Econ
List A	10	168	1	164	2	1-13	82.00	0	0	84.00	5.85
T20s	28	270	0	377	11	2-13	34.27	0	0	24.54	8.37

J

EVE JONES — LHB / SLA / MVP 13

LANCASHIRE

FULL NAME: Evelyn Jones
BORN: August 8, 1992, Shrewsbury, Shropshire
SQUAD NO: 11
HEIGHT: 5ft 8in
EDUCATION: Oxford Brookes University
TEAMS: Lancashire, Manchester Originals, Central Sparks, Warwickshire, Birmingham Phoenix, Canterbury, Loughborough Lightning, Melbourne Renegades, Shropshire, Staffordshire, Thunder
ROLE: Batter
DEBUT: List A: 2008; T20: 2010

BEST BATTING: 136* Central Sparks vs Thunder, Old Trafford, 2024
BEST BOWLING: 6-29 Shropshire vs Northumberland, Madeley, 2011

FIRST CRICKET CLUB? Whitchurch CC, Shropshire
WHAT WILL YOU MISS ABOUT REGIONAL CRICKET? Good times and great people
WHAT EXCITES YOU ABOUT THE NEW COUNTY STRUCTURE? Being part of a big club and having increased equality with the men. It feels like we belong to something special
OPPONENT YOU MOST LOOK FORWARD TO PLAYING AGAINST? Hannah Baker – she's like a little sister to me
FAVOURITE WARM-UP SONG? Any song by Sam Fender
HOW MANY HOURS DO YOU SPEND ON YOUR PHONE A DAY? Four
SPECIALITY SUBJECT IN A PUB QUIZ (EXCLUDING SPORT)? Travel
ONE THING YOU WANT TO DO BEFORE YOU DIE: Win a major trophy
HOBBY YOU WOULD LIKE TO LEARN: DIY
SURPRISING FACT ABOUT YOU: I have a degree in fine art
FILM YOU CAN WATCH OVER AND OVER: The Inbetweeners (not so much the movie, more the series)

Batting	Mat	Inns	NO	Runs	HS	Ave	SR	100	50	Ct	St
List A	124	120	16	3815	136*	36.68	-	7	22	46	-
T20s	166	157	15	3370	93*	23.73	97.45	0	14	44	-

Bowling	Mat	Balls	Mdns	Runs	Wkts	BB	Ave	4wI	5wI	SR	Econ
List A	124	1161	26	784	26	6-29	30.15	1	1	44.65	4.05
T20s	166	437	0	466	19	3-14	24.52	0	0	23.00	6.39

HANNAH JONES   LHB / SLA

FULL NAME: Hannah Emily Jones
BORN: February 10, 1999, Manchester
SQUAD NO: 7
HEIGHT: 5ft 5in
EDUCATION: St Thomas More RC College,
Manchester; Myerscough College,
Lancashire
TEAMS: Lancashire, Manchester Originals,
Thunder
ROLE: Bowler
DEBUT: List A: 2014; T20: 2014

BEST BATTING: 26* Thunder vs South East Stars, Blackpool, 2024
BEST BOWLING: 5-33 Thunder vs South East Stars, Beckenham, 2021

FIRST CRICKET CLUB: Denton St Lawrence CC, Manchester
DESCRIBE YOUR CAREER IN THREE WORDS: Opportunity, memories, grateful
WHICH PART OF THE SEASON DO YOU MOST ENJOY? The middle of the season when there
are a lot of games
IF YOU COULD PINCH A PLAYER FROM ANOTHER TEAM, WHO WOULD IT BE?
Nat Sciver-Brunt
WHO IS THE TOUGHEST BOWLER TO FACE IN DOMESTIC CRICKET? Kathryn Bryce
WHAT ONE THING WOULD YOU CHANGE ABOUT WOMEN'S CRICKET IN ENGLAND? Greater
equality between the men's and women's game. It's improving but could be better…

Batting	Mat	Inns	NO	Runs	HS	Ave	SR	100	50	Ct	St
List A	55	33	18	139	26*	9.26	45.42	0	0	9	-
T20s	53	11	7	39	17	9.75	66.10	0	0	11	-
Bowling	Mat	Balls	Mdns	Runs	Wkts	BB	Ave	4wI	5wI	SR	Econ
List A	55	2519	44	1589	62	5-33	25.62	1	1	40.62	3.78
T20s	53	1016	3	888	47	3-17	18.89	0	0	21.61	5.24

KATIE JONES RB / WK

SOMERSET

FULL NAME: Katherine Abigail Jones
BORN: December 28, 2005
SQUAD NO: 38
HEIGHT: 5ft 4in
NICKNAME: Joner
EDUCATION: Denmark Road High School, Gloucester; Pate's Grammar School, Cheltenham
TEAMS: Lancashire, England U19, Gloucestershire, Western Storm
ROLE: Wicketkeeper
DEBUT: List A: 2023; T20: 2021

BEST BATTING: 32 Western Storm vs Central Sparks, Taunton, 2023

FIRST CRICKET CLUB? Dumbleton CC, Gloucestershire
EARLIEST CRICKETING MEMORY? Playing on a Friday night with the boys and whacking them all over the place
WHAT WILL YOU MISS ABOUT REGIONAL CRICKET? Being able to call three incredible grounds my home ground
WHAT EXCITES YOU ABOUT THE NEW COUNTY STRUCTURE? Having a permanent home, knowing where we are training and playing, and hopefully building a crowd and reputation at Taunton
HOW MANY HOURS DO YOU SPEND ON YOUR PHONE A DAY? Two to three
SPECIALITY SUBJECT IN A PUB QUIZ (EXCLUDING SPORT)? Coffee
ONE THING YOU WANT TO DO BEFORE YOU DIE: See Adele live
HOBBY YOU WOULD LIKE TO LEARN: Cook for fine dining
FILM YOU CAN WATCH OVER AND OVER: Any Harry Potter film

Batting	Mat	Inns	NO	Runs	HS	Ave	SR	100	50	Ct	St
List A	14	8	0	111	32	13.87	71.15	0	0	7	5
T20s	17	13	3	178	40	17.80	92.70	0	0	4	15

Bowling	Mat	Balls	Mdns	Runs	Wkts	BB	Ave	4wI	5wI	SR	Econ
List A	14	-	-	-	-	-	-	-	-	-	-
T20s	17	-	-	-	-	-	-	-	-	-	-

MARIE KELLY

RHB / RM / MVP49

FULL NAME: Marie Kelly
BORN: February 9, 1996, Birmingham
SQUAD NO: 23
HEIGHT: 5ft 7in
NICKNAME: MK
EDUCATION: Loughborough University
TEAMS: The Blaze, Northern Superchargers, Birmingham Phoenix, Central Sparks, Loughborough Lightning, Southern Vipers, Trent Rockets, Trinbago Knight Riders, Warwickshire
ROLE: Batter
DEBUT: List A: 2011; T20: 2012

BEST BATTING: 64 Warwickshire vs Lancashire, Newton-le-Willows, 2018
BEST BOWLING: 4-13 Warwickshire vs Surrey, Wellesbourne, 2013

FIRST CRICKET CLUB? Earlswood CC, Solihull, Warwickshire
WHAT WILL YOU MISS ABOUT REGIONAL CRICKET? Representing the whole of the East Midlands
WHAT EXCITES YOU ABOUT THE NEW COUNTY STRUCTURE? A more permanent base at Trent Bridge and being connected with Notts
OPPONENT YOU MOST LOOK FORWARD TO PLAYING AGAINST? Alexa Stonehouse – she always makes me laugh with her facial expressions
FAVOURITE WARM-UP SONG? Any song by Gyptian
HOW MANY HOURS DO YOU SPEND ON YOUR PHONE A DAY? Six (at least)
SPECIALITY SUBJECT IN A PUB QUIZ (EXCLUDING SPORT)? Biology
HOBBY YOU WOULD LIKE TO LEARN: To play the piano
WHICH PUBLIC FIGURE INSPIRES YOU (EXCLUDING SPORTSPEOPLE)? Malala Yousafzai
SURPRISING FACT ABOUT YOU: I weighed three pounds and four ounces when I was born
FILM YOU CAN WATCH OVER AND OVER: Mean Girls

Batting	Mat	Inns	NO	Runs	HS	Ave	SR	100	50	Ct	St
List A	102	96	6	1923	64	21.36	-	0	12	41	-
T20s	118	107	17	2005	100*	22.27	-	1	9	56	-

Bowling	Mat	Balls	Mdns	Runs	Wkts	BB	Ave	4wl	5wl	SR	Econ
List A	102	1140	15	774	33	4-13	23.45	1	0	34.54	4.07
T20s	118	597	3	564	35	4-30	16.11	1	0	17.05	5.66

FREYA KEMP

HAMPSHIRE

FULL NAME: Freya Grace Kemp
BORN: April 21, 2005, Westminster
SQUAD NO: 6
HEIGHT: 5ft 10in
EDUCATION: Cumnor House Sussex; Bede's
Senior School, Hailsham, East Sussex
TEAMS: England, Hampshire, Southern Brave,
Southern Vipers, Sussex
ROLE: Allrounder
DEBUT: ODI: 2022; T20I: 2022;
List A: 2022; T20: 2019

BEST BATTING: 80 England A vs New Zealand A, Nelson, 2024
BEST BOWLING: 2-7 England vs Ireland, Belfast, 2024

FIRST CRICKET CLUB? Ditching CC, Sussex
WHAT WILL YOU MISS ABOUT REGIONAL CRICKET? Representing my home county, Sussex
WHAT EXCITES YOU ABOUT THE NEW COUNTY STRUCTURE? Creating new memories
with Hampshire
FAVOURITE WARM-UP SONG? Adrenaline Rush by Sigma
HOW MANY HOURS DO YOU SPEND ON YOUR PHONE A DAY? Four
SPECIALITY SUBJECT IN A PUB QUIZ (EXCLUDING SPORT)? Name the song
ONE THING YOU WANT TO DO BEFORE YOU DIE: Go heli-skiing
HOBBY YOU WOULD LIKE TO LEARN: Get really good at padel
WHICH PUBLIC FIGURE INSPIRES YOU (EXCLUDING SPORTSPEOPLE)? The Queen
SURPRISING FACT ABOUT YOU: I have two miniature dachshunds
FILM YOU CAN WATCH OVER AND OVER: Home Alone

Batting	Mat	Inns	NO	Runs	HS	Ave	SR	100	50	Ct	St
ODIs	5	5	0	111	65	22.20	121.97	0	1	1	-
T20Is	25	15	7	145	51*	18.12	129.46	0	1	3	-
List A	24	23	4	635	80	33.42	117.15	0	3	8	-
T20s	88	70	21	898	60	18.32	130.14	0	4	21	-
Bowling	Mat	Balls	Mdns	Runs	Wkts	BB	Ave	4wI	5wI	SR	Econ
ODIs	5	138	2	135	6	2-7	22.50	0	0	23.00	5.86
T20Is	25	324	0	427	21	2-14	20.33	0	0	15.42	7.90
List A	24	216	3	179	8	2-7	22.37	0	0	27.00	4.97
T20s	88	765	0	948	40	2-11	23.70	0	0	19.12	7.43

MICHAELA KIRK

RHB / OB

FULL NAME: Michaela Louise Kirk
BORN: June 30, 1999, Johannesburg, South Africa
SQUAD NO: 25
HEIGHT: 5ft 3in
NICKNAME: Kirky
EDUCATION: Cornwall Hill College, Centurion, South Africa; Arden University (online)
TEAMS: The Blaze, Lightning, Northerns, Nottinghamshire, Trent Rockets
ROLE: Batter
DEBUT: List A: 2013; T20: 2012

BEST BATTING: 58 Northerns vs Boland, Hammanskraal, 2018
BEST BOWLING: 4-0 Northerns vs Easterns, Bloemfontein, 2018

FIRST CRICKET CLUB? Sinoville CC, Pretoria, South Africa
WHAT EXCITES YOU ABOUT THE NEW COUNTY STRUCTURE? The new opportunities that it will open for the women's game
OPPONENT YOU MOST LOOK FORWARD TO PLAYING AGAINST? Heather Knight – she's a very good competitor and I enjoy watching her bat
FAVOURITE WARM-UP SONG? Heat Waves by Glass Animals
HOW MANY HOURS DO YOU SPEND ON YOUR PHONE A DAY? Three
SPECIALITY SUBJECT IN A PUB QUIZ (EXCLUDING SPORT)? TV and film
ONE THING YOU WANT TO DO BEFORE YOU DIE: Run a marathon
HOBBY YOU WOULD LIKE TO LEARN: Barista skills – so I can make a good coffee at home
WHICH PUBLIC FIGURE INSPIRES YOU (EXCLUDING SPORTSPEOPLE)? Michelle Obama
SURPRISING FACT ABOUT YOU: I once broke my collarbone diving for the ball during a cricket game
FILM YOU CAN WATCH OVER AND OVER: Grown Ups

Batting	Mat	Inns	NO	Runs	HS	Ave	SR	100	50	Ct	St
List A	64	60	4	1017	58	18.16	53.35	0	3	28	4
T20s	53	37	7	712	62	23.73	98.75	0	2	22	1

Bowling	Mat	Balls	Mdns	Runs	Wkts	BB	Ave	4wI	5wI	SR	Econ
List A	64	1046	21	612	27	4-0	22.66	2	0	38.74	3.51
T20s	53	318	2	246	11	2-5	22.36	0	0	28.90	4.64

HEATHER KNIGHT   RHB / OB / MVP19

FULL NAME: Heather Clare Knight
BORN: December 26, 1990, Plymouth
SQUAD NO: 5
HEIGHT: 5ft 7in
EDUCATION: Plymstock School, Plymouth;
Cardiff University
TEAMS: England, Somerset, London Spirit,
Berkshire, Devon, Hobart Hurricanes, RC
Bangalore, Sydney Thunder, Tasmania,
Western Storm
ROLE: Batter
DEBUT: Test: 2011; ODI: 2010; T20I: 2010;
List A: 2008; T20: 2009

BEST BATTING: 190 Devon vs Oxfordshire, Bovey Tracey, 2008
BEST BOWLING: 5-14 Berkshire vs Warwickshire, Sindlesham, 2014

FIRST CRICKET CLUB? Plymstock CC, Plymouth
WHICH PERFORMANCE WERE YOU MOST PROUD OF LAST SEASON? My 75 not out in the
50-over chase against Australia at Bristol, winning by two wickets
WHICH TEAMMATE HAS HAD THE BIGGEST IMPACT ON YOUR GAME? Danni Wyatt
WHO IS THE MOST TALENTED TEENAGER IN WOMEN'S DOMESTIC CRICKET? Mahika Gaur
IF YOU COULD PINCH A PLAYER FROM ANOTHER TEAM, WHO WOULD IT BE? Charlie Dean
WHAT ONE THING WOULD YOU CHANGE ABOUT WOMEN'S CRICKET IN ENGLAND? Bring in
some red-ball cricket
WHAT KEEPS YOU AWAKE AT NIGHT? Seagulls if you stay in Worcester
WHAT'S THE SILLIEST OUTFIT YOU'VE EVER WORN? Dressing up as a red crayon
CHOOSE A FANTASY SLIP CORDON TO SPEND A DAY IN THE FIELD WITH: Ruth Bader
Ginsburg (wk), Freddie Mercury, Thierry Henry

Batting	Mat	Inns	NO	Runs	HS	Ave	SR	100	50	Ct	St
Tests	14	25	2	970	168*	42.17	48.47	2	5	12	-
ODIs	149	142	27	4037	106	35.10	72.47	2	26	48	-
T20Is	129	115	29	2222	108*	25.83	120.43	1	7	36	-
List A	239	232	41	8800	190	46.07	-	16	53	87	-
T20s	348	328	64	8496	111	32.18	-	3	49	100	-
Bowling	Mat	Balls	Mdns	Runs	Wkts	BB	Ave	4wI	5wI	SR	Econ
Tests	14	419	16	171	7	2-7	24.42	-	0	59.85	2.44
ODIs	149	1923	17	1396	56	5-26	24.92	1	1	34.33	4.35
T20Is	129	585	0	571	21	3-9	27.19	0	0	27.85	5.85
List A	239	4747	67	3179	138	5-14	23.03	2	2	34.39	4.01
T20s	348	3166	3	3463	140	3-4	24.73	0	0	22.61	6.56

EMMA LAMB — RHB / RM

FULL NAME: Emma Louise Lamb
BORN: December 16, 1997, Preston, Lancashire
SQUAD NO: 6
HEIGHT: 5ft 7in
EDUCATION: Cardinal Newman College, Preston; Edge Hill University, Ormskirk, Lancashire
TEAMS: England, Lancashire, Manchester Originals, Lancashire Thunder, Thunder
ROLE: Allrounder
DEBUT: Test: 2022; ODI: 2022; T20I: 2021; List A: 2012; T20: 2012

BEST BATTING: 121 Thunder vs Western Storm, Bristol, 2021
BEST BOWLING: 4-39 Lancashire vs Warwickshire, Newton-le-Willows, 2018

FIRST CRICKET CLUB? Chorley CC, Lancashire
EARLIEST CRICKETING MEMORY? Batting against my brother
WHAT EXCITES YOU ABOUT THE NEW COUNTY STRUCTURE? The opportunity for more contracts and more competitive cricket
OPPONENT YOU MOST LOOK FORWARD TO PLAYING AGAINST? Alice Davidson-Richards
FAVOURITE WARM-UP SONG? My Humps by Black Eyed Peas
SPECIALITY SUBJECT IN A PUB QUIZ (EXCLUDING SPORT)? Darts
ONE THING YOU WANT TO DO BEFORE YOU DIE: Travel New Zealand
HOBBY YOU WOULD LIKE TO LEARN: Riding a hobby horse
WHICH PUBLIC FIGURE INSPIRES YOU (EXCLUDING SPORTSPEOPLE)? Greta Thunberg
SURPRISING FACT ABOUT YOU: I am 13-per-cent Scandinavian
FILM YOU CAN WATCH OVER AND OVER: Inside Out

Batting	Mat	Inns	NO	Runs	HS	Ave	SR	100	50	Ct	St
Tests	2	3	0	76	38	25.33	53.90	0	0	2	-
ODIs	14	13	0	396	102	30.46	86.46	1	2	2	-
T20Is	1	1	1	0	0*	-	0.00	0	0	0	-
List A	102	100	10	3160	121	35.11	67.55	4	20	18	-
T20s	141	136	18	3083	119*	26.12	-	2	13	31	-

Bowling	Mat	Balls	Mdns	Runs	Wkts	BB	Ave	4wl	5wl	SR	Econ
Tests	2	12	0	7	0	0-7	-	-	-	-	3.50
ODIs	14	108	0	96	3	3-42	32.00	0	0	36.00	5.33
T20Is	1	-	-	-	-	-	-	-	-	-	-
List A	102	1391	24	1029	41	4-39	25.09	1	0	33.92	4.43
T20s	141	1571	10	1669	86	5-5	19.40	3	1	18.26	6.37

KATIE LEVICK

RHB / LB / MVP35

DURHAM

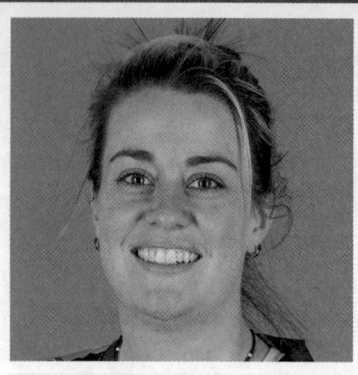

FULL NAME: Katie Ann Levick
BORN: July 17, 1991, Sheffield
SQUAD NO: 23
HEIGHT: 5ft 7in
NICKNAME: Lev
EDUCATION: Ecclesfield School, Sheffield;
Thomas Rotherham College, South
Yorkshire; Sheffield Hallam University
TEAMS: Durham, Birmingham Phoenix,
Northern Diamonds, Northern Superchargers,
Yorkshire
ROLE: Bowler
DEBUT: List A: 2008; T20: 2010

BEST BATTING: 30* Yorkshire vs Berkshire, Harrogate, 2017
BEST BOWLING: 6-25 Yorkshire vs Lancashire, Harrogate, 2015

FIRST CRICKET CLUB? Upper Haugh CC, Rotherham, South Yorkshire
EARLIEST CRICKETING MEMORY? Watching my brother Adam (he was a better cricketer than me)
WHAT WILL YOU MISS ABOUT REGIONAL CRICKET? I will always miss and treasure my Diamonds girls
WHAT EXCITES YOU ABOUT THE NEW COUNTY STRUCTURE? Being the first set of professional women cricketers to represent Durham and the north-east
OPPONENT YOU MOST LOOK FORWARD TO PLAYING AGAINST? Beth Langston – she's one of life's great people
FAVOURITE WARM-UP SONG? Absolutely Everybody by Vanessa Amorosi
HOW MANY HOURS DO YOU SPEND ON YOUR PHONE A DAY? Too many
SPECIALITY SUBJECT IN A PUB QUIZ (EXCLUDING SPORT)? RuPaul's Drag Race
ONE THING YOU WANT TO DO BEFORE YOU DIE: Befriend Taylor Swift
WHICH PUBLIC FIGURE INSPIRES YOU (EXCLUDING SPORTSPEOPLE)? Dolly Parton
FILM YOU CAN WATCH OVER AND OVER: Bridesmaids

Batting	Mat	Inns	NO	Runs	HS	Ave	SR	100	50	Ct	St
List A	133	67	32	295	30*	8.42	44.22	0	0	22	-
T20s	148	50	18	127	13	3.96	-	0	0	12	-

Bowling	Mat	Balls	Mdns	Runs	Wkts	BB	Ave	4wI	5wI	SR	Econ
List A	133	6307	119	3698	203	6-25	18.21	10	3	31.06	3.51
T20s	148	2952	10	2915	185	5-15	15.75	2	3	15.95	5.92

AILSA LISTER RHB / WK

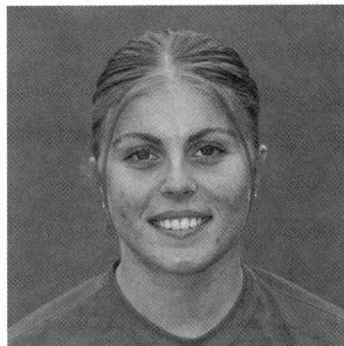

FULL NAME: Ailsa Kirsty Lister
BORN: April 8, 2004, Elgin, Moray, Scotland
SQUAD NO: 32
HEIGHT: 5ft 5in
NICKNAME: Scotty
EDUCATION: The Gordon Schools, Huntly, Scotland
TEAMS: Scotland, Lancashire, Thunder
ROLE: Wicketkeeper/batter
DEBUT: ODI: 2023; T20I: 2021; List A: 2019; T20: 2021

BEST BATTING: 47 Scotland vs Ireland, Almeria, 2023

FIRST CRICKET CLUB? Huntly CC, Aberdeenshire
EARLIEST CRICKETING MEMORY? Playing in the garden with my older brother
WHAT EXCITES YOU ABOUT THE NEW COUNTY STRUCTURE? Feeling more connected to our county and club, and ultimately growing the game across the country with the tier system
OPPONENT YOU MOST LOOK FORWARD TO PLAYING AGAINST? Kathryn Bryce. As Scotland captain, it's always nice to play against her. However, she did pretty well against us last year so I'd like to get one over her!
FAVOURITE WARM-UP SONG? Chelsea Dagger by The Fratellis
HOW MANY HOURS DO YOU SPEND ON YOUR PHONE A DAY? Anything between three and five
SPECIALITY SUBJECT IN A PUB QUIZ (EXCLUDING SPORT)? Musicals
ONE THING YOU WANT TO DO BEFORE YOU DIE: A skydive
HOBBY YOU WOULD LIKE TO LEARN: Play the guitar
FILM YOU CAN WATCH OVER AND OVER: Miss Congeniality

Batting	Mat	Inns	NO	Runs	HS	Ave	SR	100	50	Ct	St
ODIs	4	4	0	80	47	20.00	72.72	0	0	1	-
T20Is	38	32	3	530	68*	18.27	129.58	0	4	10	1
List A	7	7	0	108	47	15.42	55.95	0	0	3	-
T20s	49	41	4	794	117*	21.45	-	1	4	15	5

Bowling	Mat	Balls	Mdns	Runs	Wkts	BB	Ave	4wI	5wI	SR	Econ
ODIs	4	-	-	-	-	-	-	-	-	-	-
T20Is	38	-	-	-	-	-	-	-	-	-	-
List A	7	-	-	-	-	-	-	-	-	-	-
T20s	49	-	-	-	-	-	-	-	-	-	-

SOPHIE LUFF • RHB / RM / MVP31

SOMERSET

FULL NAME: Sophie Natasha Luff
BORN: December 6, 1993, Taunton, Somerset
SQUAD NO: 63
HEIGHT: 5ft 2in
NICKNAME: Queen of Somerset, Miss Logical
EDUCATION: Kings of Wessex Academy,
Somerset; Cardiff Metropolitan University
TEAMS: Somerset, London Spirit, New South
Wales, Welsh Fire, Western Storm
ROLE: Batter
DEBUT: List A: 2009; T20: 2010

BEST BATTING: 157* Western Storm vs Sunrisers, Bristol, 2021
BEST BOWLING: 1-27 Western Storm vs Sunrisers, Bristol, 2020

FIRST CRICKET CLUB? Weston-super-Mare CC, Somerset
WHAT WILL YOU MISS ABOUT REGIONAL CRICKET? The Western Storm identity, as well as connecting with so many people and fans across three counties
WHAT EXCITES YOU ABOUT THE NEW COUNTY STRUCTURE? Representing my home county. Being one club and hopefully getting good crowds. And the commercial and marketing opportunities that come with being a county team
OPPONENT YOU MOST LOOK FORWARD TO PLAYING AGAINST? Eve Jones in Lancashire colours
FAVOURITE WARM-UP SONG? Alive by Chase & Status
SPECIALITY SUBJECT IN A PUB QUIZ (EXCLUDING SPORT)? National flags
ONE THING YOU WANT TO DO BEFORE YOU DIE: Go to the Caribbean
HOBBY YOU WOULD LIKE TO LEARN: Perfecting my latte art
WHICH PUBLIC FIGURE INSPIRES YOU (EXCLUDING SPORTSPEOPLE)? Vanessa Shanessa Jenkins
FILM YOU CAN WATCH OVER AND OVER: Bend It Like Beckham

Batting	Mat	Inns	NO	Runs	HS	Ave	SR	100	50	Ct	St
List A	130	128	29	4233	157*	42.75	-	7	27	39	-
T20s	154	134	39	2693	78	28.34	-	0	10	46	-

Bowling	Mat	Balls	Mdns	Runs	Wkts	BB	Ave	4wl	5wl	SR	Econ
List A	130	296	1	261	2	1-27	130.50	0	0	148.00	5.29
T20s	154	197	0	238	8	2-12	29.75	0	0	24.62	7.24

RYANA MACDONALD-GAY   RHB / RMF / MVP16

FULL NAME: Ryana Lucelle MacDonald-Gay
BORN: February 12, 2004, Maidstone, Kent
SQUAD NO: 29
HEIGHT: 5ft 5in
NICKNAME: Macca
EDUCATION: Tonbridge Grammar School, Kent; Loughborough University
TEAMS: England, Surrey, Oval Invincibles, Kent, South East Stars
ROLE: Bowler
DEBUT: Test: 2024; ODI: 2024; T20I: 2024; List A: 2019; T20: 2019

BEST BATTING: 54* South East Stars vs Lightning, Leicester, 2022
BEST BOWLING: 5-31 South East Stars vs The Blaze, Leicester, 2024

FIRST CRICKET CLUB? Addington CC, Kent
WHAT WILL YOU MISS ABOUT REGIONAL CRICKET? Being a Star and wearing the bumble-bee yellow
WHAT EXCITES YOU ABOUT THE NEW COUNTY STRUCTURE? Being part of a two-team club under the Surrey name
OPPONENT YOU MOST LOOK FORWARD TO PLAYING AGAINST? There are a lot of young players this year so it will be exciting to see what they bring to the table
FAVOURITE WARM-UP SONG? Time of Our Lives by Pitbull & Ne-Yo
HOW MANY HOURS DO YOU SPEND ON YOUR PHONE A DAY? Five!
SPECIALITY SUBJECT IN A PUB QUIZ (EXCLUDING SPORT)? Rom-coms
WHICH PUBLIC FIGURE INSPIRES YOU (EXCLUDING SPORTSPEOPLE)? Simon Squibb
FILM YOU CAN WATCH OVER AND OVER: Two Weeks Notice

Batting	Mat	Inns	NO	Runs	HS	Ave	SR	100	50	Ct	St
Tests	2	4	1	22	15*	7.33	18.64	0	0	0	-
ODIs	2	1	0	17	17	17.00	130.76	0	0	1	-
T20Is	1	0	-	-	-	-	-	-	-	0	-
List A	35	31	9	419	54*	19.04	72.36	0	2	17	-
T20s	60	27	12	202	40*	13.46	93.08	0	0	16	-

Bowling	Mat	Balls	Mdns	Runs	Wkts	BB	Ave	4wI	5wI	SR	Econ
Tests	2	210	7	131	3	2-50	43.66	-	0	70.00	3.74
ODIs	2	66	0	52	1	1-30	52.00	0	0	66.00	4.72
T20Is	1	12	0	25	1	1-25	25.00	0	0	12.00	12.50
List A	35	1233	12	1010	50	5-31	20.20	3	1	24.66	4.91
T20s	60	730	2	893	51	4-16	17.50	2	0	14.31	7.33

ESMAE MACGREGOR

RHB / RM

ESSEX

FULL NAME: Esmae Isabel MacGregor
BORN: July 31, 2004
SQUAD NO: 8
HEIGHT: 5ft 7in
NICKNAME: Es
EDUCATION: Littlegarth School, Colchester;
Ipswich School; Loughborough University
TEAMS: Essex, Sunrisers
ROLE: Bowler
DEBUT: List A: 2023; T20: 2021

BEST BATTING: 20* Sunrisers vs South East Stars, Northampton, 2024
BEST BOWLING: 1-16 Sunrisers vs Western Storm, Cardiff, 2024

FIRST CRICKET CLUB? Colchester CC
EARLIEST CRICKETING MEMORY? My first training session when I was 13
WHAT EXCITES YOU ABOUT THE NEW COUNTY STRUCTURE? Continuing to play alongside
the girls with so much room for growth as we align with the men's set-up
OPPONENT YOU MOST LOOK FORWARD TO PLAYING AGAINST? Bethan Miles – good to get
some house rivalry!
HOW MANY HOURS DO YOU SPEND ON YOUR PHONE A DAY? Three
HOBBY YOU WOULD LIKE TO LEARN: Skiing
FILM YOU CAN WATCH OVER AND OVER: Top Gun: Maverick

Batting	Mat	Inns	NO	Runs	HS	Ave	SR	100	50	Ct	St
List A	8	3	2	22	20*	22.00	44.00	0	0	4	-
T20s	12	2	0	4	3	2.00	36.36	0	0	2	-
Bowling	Mat	Balls	Mdns	Runs	Wkts	BB	Ave	4wl	5wl	SR	Econ
List A	8	210	1	187	4	1-16	46.75	0	0	52.50	5.34
T20s	12	223	0	211	13	2-5	16.23	0	0	17.15	5.67

LISSY MACLEOD

RHB / OB

FULL NAME: Alice Jessamy Macleod
BORN: May 14, 1994, Ascot, Berkshire
SQUAD NO: 44
HEIGHT: 5ft 11in
NICKNAME: Lissy
EDUCATION: Wellington College, Berkshire;
Exeter University
TEAMS: Essex, Berkshire, Southern Vipers,
Sunrisers, Sussex, Welsh Fire, Western Storm
ROLE: Allrounder
DEBUT: List A: 2008; T20: 2009

BEST BATTING: 107 Berkshire vs Lancashire, Wigan, 2015
BEST BOWLING: 4-26 Berkshire vs Middlesex, Harrow-on-the-Hill, 2015

FIRST CRICKET CLUB? Taplow CC, Buckinghamshire
WHAT WILL YOU MISS ABOUT REGIONAL CRICKET? What we built as a brand new team –
our own identity as a group and watching that grow each year
WHAT EXCITES YOU ABOUT THE NEW COUNTY STRUCTURE? Being aligned with the men
should help with some of the practical difficulties we faced previously
OPPONENT YOU MOST LOOK FORWARD TO PLAYING AGAINST? Fritha Morris – she's an
exciting player and a good friend off the field. Always plays with the right attitude
FAVOURITE WARM-UP SONG? Wagon Wheel by Darius Rucker
HOW MANY HOURS DO YOU SPEND ON YOUR PHONE A DAY? Four
SPECIALITY SUBJECT IN A PUB QUIZ (EXCLUDING SPORT)? The Office (US version)
ONE THING YOU WANT TO DO BEFORE YOU DIE: A round trip around Scandinavia
HOBBY YOU WOULD LIKE TO LEARN: Woodwork
WHICH PUBLIC FIGURE INSPIRES YOU (EXCLUDING SPORTSPEOPLE)? Gisèle Pelicot
SURPRISING FACT ABOUT YOU: I am also an English teacher and head of girls' cricket at
Felsted School
FILM YOU CAN WATCH OVER AND OVER: Ocean's Eleven

Batting	Mat	Inns	NO	Runs	HS	Ave	SR	100	50	Ct	St
List A	110	109	11	2496	107	25.46	-	1	14	35	-
T20s	99	94	14	1515	82*	18.93	-	0	7	22	-

Bowling	Mat	Balls	Mdns	Runs	Wkts	BB	Ave	4wI	5wI	SR	Econ
List A	110	3422	41	2411	75	4-26	32.14	2	0	45.62	4.22
T20s	99	1274	5	1132	56	4-11	20.21	1	0	22.75	5.33

ABTAHA MAQSOOD

RHB / LB

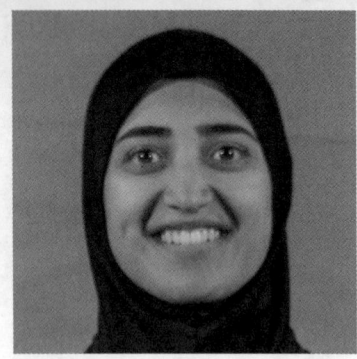

FULL NAME: Abtaha Mahin Maqsood
BORN: June 11, 1999, Glasgow
SQUAD NO: 18
HEIGHT: 5ft 8in
NICKNAME: Abs
EDUCATION: University of Glasgow
TEAMS: Scotland, Essex, Birmingham Phoenix, Middlesex, Sunrisers
ROLE: Bowler
DEBUT: ODI: 2023; T20I: 2018; List A: 2014; T20: 2015

BEST BATTING: 14 Sunrisers vs The Blaze, Chelmsford, 2023
BEST BOWLING: 5-30 Sunrisers vs Southern Vipers, Southampton, 2023

FIRST CRICKET CLUB? Poloc CC, Glasgow
EARLIEST CRICKETING MEMORY? Playing in the garden with my dad and brothers
WHAT EXCITES YOU ABOUT THE NEW COUNTY STRUCTURE? Playing more double headers with the men
SPECIALITY SUBJECT IN A PUB QUIZ (EXCLUDING SPORT)? Marvel movies
ONE THING YOU WANT TO DO BEFORE YOU DIE: Play in a 50-over World Cup
SURPRISING FACT ABOUT YOU: I'm a black belt in Taekwondo
FILM YOU CAN WATCH OVER AND OVER: Pitch Perfect

Batting	Mat	Inns	NO	Runs	HS	Ave	SR	100	50	Ct	St
ODIs	8	5	1	12	6*	3.00	36.36	0	0	3	-
T20Is	57	16	8	38	9	4.75	55.07	0	0	15	-
List A	40	25	6	69	14	3.63	-	0	0	9	-
T20s	124	36	16	78	9	3.90	49.05	0	0	26	-

Bowling	Mat	Balls	Mdns	Runs	Wkts	BB	Ave	4wI	5wI	SR	Econ
ODIs	8	372	3	245	19	4-30	12.89	2	0	19.57	3.95
T20Is	57	1040	4	953	54	3-8	17.64	0	0	19.25	5.49
List A	40	1353	14	909	52	5-30	17.48	3	1	26.01	4.03
T20s	124	2068	7	2049	101	3-8	20.28	0	0	20.47	5.94

EMMA MARLOW — RHB / OB

FULL NAME: Emma Kate Marlow
BORN: April 12, 2004, Harrogate
SQUAD NO: 7
HEIGHT: 5ft 6in
EDUCATION: Western Primary School; Harrogate Grammar School
TEAMS: Durham, England U19, Northern Diamonds, Yorkshire
ROLE: Allrounder
DEBUT: List A: 2022; T20: 2021

BEST BATTING: 25* Northern Diamonds vs Southern Vipers, Arundel, 2023
BEST BOWLING: 3-40 Northern Diamonds vs Sunrisers, Headingley, 2022

FIRST CRICKET CLUB? Beckwithshaw CC, Harrogate, North Yorkshire
EARLIEST CRICKETING MEMORY? Watching my day play village cricket on the weekend
WHAT WILL YOU MISS ABOUT REGIONAL CRICKET? Playing with my old teammates
WHAT EXCITES YOU ABOUT THE NEW COUNTY STRUCTURE? More double headers
FAVOURITE WARM-UP SONG? All Too Well by Taylor Swift
HOW MANY HOURS DO YOU SPEND ON YOUR PHONE A DAY? Four
SPECIALITY SUBJECT IN A PUB QUIZ (EXCLUDING SPORT)? Music
ONE THING YOU WANT TO DO BEFORE YOU DIE: Travel to South America
WHICH PUBLIC FIGURE INSPIRES YOU (EXCLUDING SPORTSPEOPLE)? Taylor Swift
SURPRISING FACT ABOUT YOU: I can speak Spanish
FILM YOU CAN WATCH OVER AND OVER: Pitch Perfect

Batting	Mat	Inns	NO	Runs	HS	Ave	SR	100	50	Ct	St
List A	30	27	4	583	63	25.34	63.36	0	3	8	-
T20s	21	16	3	188	51	14.46	85.84	0	1	6	-

Bowling	Mat	Balls	Mdns	Runs	Wkts	BB	Ave	4wI	5wI	SR	Econ
List A	30	478	3	395	10	3-40	39.50	0	0	47.80	4.95
T20s	21	228	0	188	9	2-12	20.88	0	0	25.33	4.94

CASSIDY MCCARTHY

RHB / RMF

THE BLAZE

FULL NAME: Cassidy Mae McCarthy
BORN: July 23, 2002, Crowborough, Sussex
SQUAD NO: 6
HEIGHT: 5ft 8in
NICKNAME: Cass
EDUCATION: St Gregory's Secondary School;
Loughborough University
TEAMS: The Blaze, Sussex, Trent Rockets
ROLE: Bowler
DEBUT: List A: 2017; T20: 2018

BEST BATTING: 12 The Blaze vs South East Stars, Beckenham, 2023
BEST BOWLING: 3-17 Sussex vs Hampshire, Totten, 2019

FIRST CRICKET CLUB? Bells Yew Green CC, Tunbridge Wells, Kent
EARLIEST CRICKETING MEMORY? Beach cricket with my family in Cornwall
WHAT WILL YOU MISS ABOUT REGIONAL CRICKET? Representing each county of the region on the big stage
WHAT EXCITES YOU ABOUT THE NEW COUNTY STRUCTURE? The increase in double headers
FAVOURITE WARM-UP SONG? No Regrets by Dappy
HOW MANY HOURS DO YOU SPEND ON YOUR PHONE A DAY? Six (but maybe more!)
SPECIALITY SUBJECT IN A PUB QUIZ (EXCLUDING SPORT)? A 'finish the lyrics' round
ONE THING YOU WANT TO DO BEFORE YOU DIE: Visit all seven continents
WHICH PUBLIC FIGURE INSPIRES YOU (EXCLUDING SPORTSPEOPLE)? David Attenborough
SURPRISING FACT ABOUT YOU: I'm half Irish
FILM YOU CAN WATCH OVER AND OVER: Mamma Mia!

Batting	Mat	Inns	NO	Runs	HS	Ave	SR	100	50	Ct	St
List A	24	11	1	67	12	6.70	98.52	0	0	7	-
T20s	25	4	0	14	10	3.50	93.33	0	0	0	-

Bowling	Mat	Balls	Mdns	Runs	Wkts	BB	Ave	4wl	5wl	SR	Econ
List A	24	556	2	451	13	3-17	34.69	0	0	42.76	4.86
T20s	25	200	1	225	10	4-28	22.50	1	0	20.00	6.75

ELLA McCAUGHAN

RHB / LB

FULL NAME: Ella May McCaughan
BORN: September 26, 2002, Southampton
SQUAD NO: 8
HEIGHT: 5ft 7in
NICKNAME: Macca
EDUCATION: Seaford Head School, East Sussex; University of Southampton
TEAMS: Hampshire, Welsh Fire, Southern Vipers, Sussex
ROLE: Batter
DEBUT: List A: 2018; T20: 2018

BEST BATTING: 83 Southern Vipers vs Northern Diamonds, Southampton, 2024

FIRST CRICKET CLUB? Seaford CC, East Sussex
WHAT WILL YOU MISS ABOUT REGIONAL CRICKET? Playing for the Vipers – we created a great legacy
WHAT EXCITES YOU ABOUT THE NEW COUNTY STRUCTURE? Seeing how the new teams match up and how the tier structure might raise standards across the country
OPPONENT YOU MOST LOOK FORWARD TO PLAYING AGAINST? Emily Windsor – to catch up
FAVOURITE WARM-UP SONG? This Charming Man by The Smiths
HOW MANY HOURS DO YOU SPEND ON YOUR PHONE A DAY? A couple of hours
SPECIALITY SUBJECT IN A PUB QUIZ (EXCLUDING SPORT)? Music
ONE THING YOU WANT TO DO BEFORE YOU DIE: Score a hundred three times in a row for Hampshire
WHICH PUBLIC FIGURE INSPIRES YOU (EXCLUDING SPORTSPEOPLE)? Olivia Dean
SURPRISING FACT ABOUT YOU: I have a scuba diving licence and used to live in Germany
FILM YOU CAN WATCH OVER AND OVER: Love Actually

Batting	Mat	Inns	NO	Runs	HS	Ave	SR	100	50	Ct	St
List A	60	55	1	1218	83	22.55	57.97	0	6	16	-
T20s	56	46	9	666	52*	18.00	85.93	0	1	11	-

Bowling	Mat	Balls	Mdns	Runs	Wkts	BB	Ave	4wl	5wl	SR	Econ
List A	60	-	-	-	-	-	-	-	-	-	-
T20s	56	52	0	63	4	3-6	15.75	0	0	13.00	7.26

FLO MILLER

RHB / RM

FULL NAME: Florence Hebe Miller
BORN: February 26, 2004, Oxford
SQUAD NO: 4
HEIGHT: 5ft 7in
EDUCATION: The Manor Preparatory School, Oxfordshire; Bedford Girls' School; Loughborough University
TEAMS: Essex, Northamptonshire, Sunrisers
ROLE: Batter
DEBUT: List A: 2019; T20: 2019

BEST BATTING: 47* Sunrisers vs Southern Vipers, Radlett, 2024

FIRST CRICKET CLUB? Oxford Downs CC, Oxfordshire
EARLIEST CRICKETING MEMORY? Playing in the garden
WHAT EXCITES YOU ABOUT THE NEW COUNTY STRUCTURE? It's making the women's game more professional
HOW MANY HOURS DO YOU SPEND ON YOUR PHONE A DAY? Five
ONE THING YOU WANT TO DO BEFORE YOU DIE: Travel to as many countries as possible
HOBBY YOU WOULD LIKE TO LEARN: Speak Spanish
SURPRISING FACT ABOUT YOU: I've got my scuba PADI certificate
CHOOSE A FANTASY SLIP CORDON TO SPEND A DAY IN THE FIELD WITH: Tana Mongeau (wk), Katie Price, Brooke Schofield, Ramona Singer
FILM YOU CAN WATCH OVER AND OVER: The Devil Wears Prada

Batting	Mat	Inns	NO	Runs	HS	Ave	SR	100	50	Ct	St
List A	25	17	4	277	47*	21.30	85.75	0	0	7	-
T20s	44	36	9	470	53*	17.40	84.07	0	1	12	-
Bowling	Mat	Balls	Mdns	Runs	Wkts	BB	Ave	4wl	5wl	SR	Econ
List A	25	-	-	-	-	-	-	-	-	-	-
T20s	44	-	-	-	-	-	-	-	-	-	-

ALICE MONAGHAN

RHB / RM

FULL NAME: Alice Zoe Monaghan
BORN: March 20, 2000, Basingstoke, Hampshire
SQUAD NO: 66
HEIGHT: 5ft 6in
EDUCATION: Testbourne Community School, Whitchurch; Peter Symonds College, Winchester; Loughborough University
TEAMS: Surrey, Manchester Originals, Hampshire, London Spirit, Southern Vipers, Yorkshire Diamonds
ROLE: Bowler
DEBUT: List A: 2016; T20: 2016

BEST BATTING: 43* Hampshire vs Leicestershire, Cove, 2016
BEST BOWLING: 4-22 Hampshire vs Staffordshire, Cove, 2017

FIRST CRICKET CLUB? Overton CC, Hampshire
WHAT WILL YOU MISS ABOUT REGIONAL CRICKET? The reputation and community that we created at Southern Vipers
WHAT EXCITES YOU ABOUT THE NEW COUNTY STRUCTURE? Playing at The Oval so much!
FAVOURITE WARM-UP SONG? Tambourine by Eve
HOW MANY HOURS DO YOU SPEND ON YOUR PHONE A DAY? Four
SPECIALITY SUBJECT IN A PUB QUIZ (EXCLUDING SPORT)? Music
ONE THING YOU WANT TO DO BEFORE YOU DIE: Learn jiu-jitsu
HOBBY YOU WOULD LIKE TO LEARN: How to throw a boomerang
WHICH PUBLIC FIGURE INSPIRES YOU (EXCLUDING SPORTSPEOPLE)? Grace Beverley
SURPRISING FACT ABOUT YOU: I am three-quarters Irish
FILM YOU CAN WATCH OVER AND OVER: Cool Runnings

Batting	Mat	Inns	NO	Runs	HS	Ave	SR	100	50	Ct	St
List A	50	32	9	275	43*	11.95	-	0	0	20	-
T20s	77	49	11	394	44*	10.36	-	0	0	22	-

Bowling	Mat	Balls	Mdns	Runs	Wkts	BB	Ave	4wI	5wI	SR	Econ
List A	50	641	5	547	15	4-22	36.46	1	0	42.73	5.12
T20s	77	470	1	518	19	2-7	27.26	0	0	24.73	6.61

KALEA MOORE

RHB / OB

SURREY

FULL NAME: Kalea Moore
BORN: March 27, 2003, Greenwich, Kent
SQUAD NO: 27
HEIGHT: 5ft 3in
NICKNAME: Denise
EDUCATION: The John Roan School, London;
St Lawrence College, Kent; University of Kent
TEAMS: Surrey, Southern Brave, Kent,
Northern Superchargers, South East Stars
ROLE: Allrounder
DEBUT: List A: 2019; T20: 2019

BEST BATTING: 52* South East Stars vs Southern Vipers, Beckenham, 2024
BEST BOWLING: 3-10 South East Stars vs Northern Diamonds, Chester-le-Street, 2024

FIRST CRICKET CLUB? Greenwich CC, London
EARLIEST CRICKETING MEMORY? Aside from playing with my dad, getting my tooth knocked out in a county game aged 13
WHAT WILL YOU MISS ABOUT REGIONAL CRICKET? It represents the place where my career took root and got me to where I am now
WHAT EXCITES YOU ABOUT THE NEW COUNTY STRUCTURE? Larger crowds
OPPONENT YOU MOST LOOK FORWARD TO PLAYING AGAINST? Grace Scrivens, as I enjoy the battle bowling against her as a left-hand bat. We have watched each other grow since we were 10
FAVOURITE WARM-UP SONG? Anything upbeat and vibey
HOW MANY HOURS DO YOU SPEND ON YOUR PHONE A DAY? Too many (working on bringing it down)
SPECIALITY SUBJECT IN A PUB QUIZ (EXCLUDING SPORT)? Reciting (roughly) from Harry Potter films
HOBBY YOU WOULD LIKE TO LEARN: How to sing
WHICH PUBLIC FIGURE INSPIRES YOU (EXCLUDING SPORTSPEOPLE)? Anna Sitar
FILM YOU CAN WATCH OVER AND OVER: She's the Man

Batting	Mat	Inns	NO	Runs	HS	Ave	SR	100	50	Ct	St
List A	27	22	5	289	52*	17.00	57.80	0	1	6	-
T20s	64	31	11	324	57*	16.20	93.64	0	1	14	-

Bowling	Mat	Balls	Mdns	Runs	Wkts	BB	Ave	4wI	5wI	SR	Econ
List A	27	894	4	718	25	3-10	28.72	0	0	35.76	4.81
T20s	64	968	2	1080	51	4-10	21.17	1	0	18.98	6.69

FI MORRIS   RHB / OB / MVP11

FULL NAME: Fritha Mary Kie Morris
BORN: January 31, 1994, Reading, Berkshire
SQUAD NO: 31
HEIGHT: 5ft 6in
NICKNAME: Frith
EDUCATION: University of Exeter
TEAMS: Lancashire, Manchester Originals, Berkshire, Gloucestershire, Hampshire, Oxfordshire, Southern Brave, Southern Vipers, Thunder, Welsh Fire, Western Storm
ROLE: Allrounder
DEBUT: List A: 2008; T20: 2009

BEST BATTING: 127 Gloucestershire vs Oxfordshire, Charlbury, 2011
BEST BOWLING: 6-35 Thunder vs The Blaze, Sale, 2024

FIRST CRICKET CLUB? Charlbury CC, Chipping Norton, Oxfordshire
EARLIEST CRICKETING MEMORY? Hitting apples in my grandma's garden
WHAT WILL YOU MISS ABOUT REGIONAL CRICKET? The kits
WHAT EXCITES YOU ABOUT THE NEW COUNTY STRUCTURE? Not that much changes for us at Lancashire!
OPPONENT YOU MOST LOOK FORWARD TO PLAYING AGAINST? Lissy MacLeod (so I can catch up with Sue on the sideline)
FAVOURITE WARM-UP SONG? Backbone by Stormzy
HOW MANY HOURS DO YOU SPEND ON YOUR PHONE A DAY? Two
SPECIALITY SUBJECT IN A PUB QUIZ (EXCLUDING SPORT)? Friends (TV series)
ONE THING YOU WANT TO DO BEFORE YOU DIE: Go to Glastonbury
HOBBY YOU WOULD LIKE TO LEARN: How to DJ
WHICH PUBLIC FIGURE INSPIRES YOU (EXCLUDING SPORTSPEOPLE)? Adele
SURPRISING FACT ABOUT YOU: I've got six older siblings
FILM YOU CAN WATCH OVER AND OVER: Demon Eye

Batting	Mat	Inns	NO	Runs	HS	Ave	SR	100	50	Ct	St
List A	100	94	9	1899	127	22.34	-	1	7	34	-
T20s	135	104	14	1308	50	14.53	-	0	1	32	-

Bowling	Mat	Balls	Mdns	Runs	Wkts	BB	Ave	4wI	5wI	SR	Econ
List A	100	4393	75	2785	134	6-35	20.78	8	2	32.78	3.80
T20s	135	2348	14	2279	127	5-7	17.94	2	1	18.48	5.82

SOPHIE MORRIS

LHB / SLA

LANCASHIRE

FULL NAME: Sophie Morris
BORN: January 2, 2004, Wirral, Cheshire
SQUAD NO: 3
HEIGHT: 5ft 5in
EDUCATION: Hilbre High School, West Kirby;
Caldy Grange Grammar School, Birkenhead
TEAMS: Lancashire, Thunder
ROLE: Bowler
DEBUT: List A: 2023; T20: 2022

BEST BATTING: 2* Thunder vs Central Sparks, Worcester, 2023
BEST BOWLING: 3-31 Thunder vs Central Sparks, Worcester, 2024

FIRST CRICKET CLUB? Upton CC, Wirrall, Merseyside
EARLIEST CRICKETING MEMORY? Playing on the beach with my brother
WHAT EXCITES YOU ABOUT THE NEW COUNTY STRUCTURE? More games!
FAVOURITE WARM-UP SONG? Gold Dust by DJ Fresh
HOW MANY HOURS DO YOU SPEND ON YOUR PHONE A DAY? Three
SPECIALITY SUBJECT IN A PUB QUIZ (EXCLUDING SPORT)? Geography
ONE THING YOU WANT TO DO BEFORE YOU DIE: Join the Barmy Army and travel all over the world watching England
HOBBY YOU WOULD LIKE TO LEARN: Sports massage therapy
FILM YOU CAN WATCH OVER AND OVER: I hate movies!

Batting	Mat	Inns	NO	Runs	HS	Ave	SR	100	50	Ct	St
List A	8	6	4	4	2*	2.00	13.33	0	0	0	-
T20s	12	2	0	7	4	3.50	53.84	0	0	3	-
Bowling	Mat	Balls	Mdns	Runs	Wkts	BB	Ave	4wi	5wi	SR	Econ
List A	8	406	1	258	10	3-31	25.80	0	0	40.60	3.81
T20s	12	252	0	215	14	3-13	15.35	0	0	18.00	5.11

FULL NAME: Sophie Elizabeth Naseem Munro
BORN: August 31, 2001, Lincoln
SQUAD NO: 22
HEIGHT: 5ft 8in
EDUCATION: Lincoln Minster School; Loughborough University
TEAMS: Essex, London Spirit, Lightning, Nottinghamshire, Sunrisers, The Blaze, Trent Rockets, Yorkshire Diamonds
ROLE: Bowler
DEBUT: List A: 2017; T20: 2017

ESSEX

BEST BATTING: 50 Lightning vs Thunder, Loughborough, 2022
BEST BOWLING: 5-24 Warwickshire vs Middlesex, Mill Hill, 2017

FIRST CRICKET CLUB? Lindum CC, Lincolnshire
FAVOURITE WARM-UP SONG? Any song by Fred Again
HOW MANY HOURS DO YOU SPEND ON YOUR PHONE A DAY? Far too many
ONE THING YOU WANT TO DO BEFORE YOU DIE: Visit as many countries as I can
HOBBY YOU WOULD LIKE TO LEARN: Surfing
SURPRISING FACT ABOUT YOU: I am part-English, part-Australian, part-Pakistani, part-Scottish
FILM YOU CAN WATCH OVER AND OVER: Chalet Girl

Batting	Mat	Inns	NO	Runs	HS	Ave	SR	100	50	Ct	St
List A	59	42	12	444	50	14.80	59.83	0	1	9	-
T20s	78	45	12	294	59*	8.90	-	0	1	15	-

Bowling	Mat	Balls	Mdns	Runs	Wkts	BB	Ave	4wI	5wI	SR	Econ
List A	59	2070	29	1505	72	5-24	20.90	2	2	28.75	4.36
T20s	78	1165	5	1312	59	4-23	22.23	2	0	19.74	6.75

TARA NORRIS — LHB / LFM / MVP36

LANCASHIRE

FULL NAME: Tara Gabriella Norris
BORN: June 4, 1998, Philadelphia, USA
SQUAD NO: 24
HEIGHT: 5ft 7in
EDUCATION: Portslade Aldridge Community Academy, Brighton; Loughborough University
TEAMS: USA, Lancashire, London Spirit, Delhi Capitals, Melbourne Rengades, Southern Brave, Southern Vipers, Sussex, Thunder
ROLE: Bowler
DEBUT: ODI: 2024; T20I: 2021; List A: 2014; T20: 2014

BEST BATTING: 53* Thunder vs The Blaze, Sale, 2024
BEST BOWLING: 4-14 Southern Vipers vs Thunder, Sale, 2021

FIRST CRICKET CLUB? Horsham CC, East Sussex
EARLIEST CRICKETING MEMORY? Taking a hat-trick at a school fair
WHAT WILL YOU MISS ABOUT REGIONAL CRICKET? The journey of how it all started
WHAT EXCITES YOU ABOUT THE NEW COUNTY STRUCTURE? Having a real sense of being part of a club
OPPONENT YOU MOST LOOK FORWARD TO PLAYING AGAINST? Lauren Winfield-Hill – always a great challenge coming up against her
FAVOURITE WARM-UP SONG? Temperature by Sean Paul
ONE THING YOU WANT TO DO BEFORE YOU DIE: Set up a sports or cricket charity
WHICH PUBLIC FIGURE INSPIRES YOU (EXCLUDING SPORTSPEOPLE)? Malala Yousafzai
SURPRISING FACT ABOUT YOU: I'd love to write a book one day
FILM YOU CAN WATCH OVER AND OVER: Pretty Women

Batting	Mat	Inns	NO	Runs	HS	Ave	SR	100	50	Ct	St
ODIs	5	3	1	59	31	29.50	109.25	0	0	1	-
T20Is	5	3	1	15	13	7.50	65.21	0	0	0	-
List A	86	57	19	618	53*	16.26	66.81	0	2	30	-
T20s	105	48	17	366	59*	11.80	79.91	0	1	28	-

Bowling	Mat	Balls	Mdns	Runs	Wkts	BB	Ave	4wi	5wi	SR	Econ
ODIs	5	252	1	182	7	3-55	26.00	0	0	36.00	4.33
T20Is	5	108	4	31	4	2-4	7.75	0	0	27.00	1.72
List A	86	3570	39	2532	96	4-14	26.37	4	0	37.18	4.25
T20s	105	1533	8	1590	80	5-29	19.87	2	1	19.16	6.22

CHARIS PAVELY   LHB / SLA

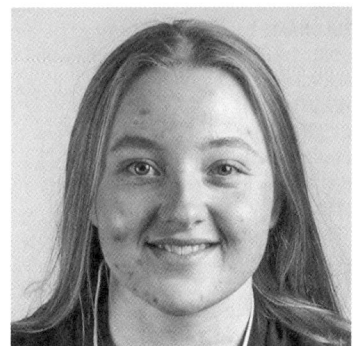

FULL NAME: Charis Rebekah Pavely
BORN: October 25, 2004, Redditch, Worcestershire
SQUAD NO: 28
HEIGHT: 5ft 3in
NICKNAME: Pavs
EDUCATION: Bromsgrove School, Worcestershire
TEAMS: England, Birmingham Bears, Birmingham Phoenix, Central Sparks, Worcestershire
ROLE: Allrounder
DEBUT: T20I: 2024; List A: 2023; T20: 2021

BEST BATTING: 57* Central Sparks vs South East Stars, Guildford, 2023
BEST BOWLING: 4-31 Central Sparks vs Southern Vipers, Worcester, 2024

FIRST CRICKET CLUB? Bromsgrove CC, Worcestershire
EARLIEST CRICKETING MEMORY? Lunchtime cricket at school
WHAT WILL YOU MISS ABOUT REGIONAL CRICKET? Playing at lots of different grounds in our region
WHAT EXCITES YOU ABOUT THE NEW COUNTY STRUCTURE? The one-club mentality
OPPONENT YOU MOST LOOK FORWARD TO PLAYING AGAINST? Niamh Holland
FAVOURITE WARM-UP SONG? Daydream Believer by The Monkees
HOW MANY HOURS DO YOU SPEND ON YOUR PHONE A DAY? Five
SPECIALITY SUBJECT IN A PUB QUIZ (EXCLUDING SPORT)? Music
ONE THING YOU WANT TO DO BEFORE YOU DIE: Beat my dad at golf
WHICH PUBLIC FIGURE INSPIRES YOU (EXCLUDING SPORTSPEOPLE)? Ben Francis
SURPRISING FACT ABOUT YOU: I won my first game of poker against a professional poker player with a 7-2
FILM YOU CAN WATCH OVER AND OVER: The Parent Trap

Batting	Mat	Inns	NO	Runs	HS	Ave	SR	100	50	Ct	St
T20Is	2	2	0	9	8	4.50	112.50	0	0	1	-
List A	13	10	3	166	57*	23.71	70.63	0	1	5	-
T20s	38	29	10	191	33*	10.05	90.09	0	0	16	-

Bowling	Mat	Balls	Mdns	Runs	Wkts	BB	Ave	4wi	5wi	SR	Econ
T20Is	2	48	0	53	3	3-19	17.66	0	0	16.00	6.62
List A	13	297	5	189	15	4-31	12.60	1	0	19.80	3.81
T20s	38	472	1	548	24	3-19	26.09	0	0	22.47	6.96

DAVINA PERRIN

RHB / LB / MVP34

BIRMINGHAM BEARS

FULL NAME: Davina Sarah T Perrin
BORN: September 8, 2006, Wolverhampton
SQUAD NO: 8
HEIGHT: 5ft 6in
NICKNAME: Dav
EDUCATION: Tettenhall College, Wolverhampton; Sandwell College, West Midlands
TEAMS: Birmingham Bears, Northern Superchargers, Central Sparks, Staffordshire, England U19
ROLE: Batter
DEBUT: List A: 2021; T20: 2021

BEST BATTING: 50 Central Sparks vs Northern Diamonds, Scarborough, 2024
BEST BOWLING: 3-26 Central Sparks vs Sunrisers, Worcester, 2022

FIRST CRICKET CLUB? Fordhouses CC, Wolverhampton
EARLIEST CRICKETING MEMORY? An U9 wind-ball tournament. I played the first few games, then got cold and spent the final game on the sidelines being fed biscuits and cake by a mum who wrapped me in a blanket
WHAT WILL YOU MISS ABOUT REGIONAL CRICKET? The way it represented the whole region. As a girl who grew up playing for a Minor County (Staffordshire), it was really nice to feel as though that area was still being represented
WHAT EXCITES YOU ABOUT THE NEW COUNTY STRUCTURE? The one-club-two-team structure
FAVOURITE WARM-UP SONG? Dive by Olivia Dean
HOW MANY HOURS DO YOU SPEND ON YOUR PHONE A DAY? Four
SPECIALITY SUBJECT IN A PUB QUIZ (EXCLUDING SPORT)? The Hunger Games
ONE THING YOU WANT TO DO BEFORE YOU DIE: A skydive
HOBBY YOU WOULD LIKE TO LEARN: Spray-painting
WHICH PUBLIC FIGURE INSPIRES YOU (EXCLUDING SPORTSPEOPLE)? Doechii
SURPRISING FACT ABOUT YOU: I got bumped up a year at school

Batting	Mat	Inns	NO	Runs	HS	Ave	SR	100	50	Ct	St
List A	30	26	2	514	50	21.41	64.81	0	2	6	-
T20s	38	33	2	646	87	20.83	117.88	0	3	14	-

Bowling	Mat	Balls	Mdns	Runs	Wkts	BB	Ave	4wI	5wI	SR	Econ
List A	30	60	0	65	3	3-26	21.66	0	0	20.00	6.50
T20s	38	132	0	122	6	2-21	20.33	0	0	22.00	5.54

CHARLEY PHILLIPS

RHB / RMF

FULL NAME: Charley Nicola Phillips
BORN: May 7, 2003
SQUAD NO: TBC
HEIGHT: 5ft 7in
NICKNAME: Chaz
EDUCATION: The Holt School, Berkshire; Reading Blue Coat School
TEAMS: The Blaze, Hertfordshire
ROLE: Bowler
DEBUT: List A: 2024; T20: 2021

BEST BOWLING: 3-22 Hertfordshire vs Berkshire, Finchampstead, 2024

FIRST CRICKET CLUB? Sonning CC, Reading, Berkshire
EARLIEST CRICKETING MEMORY? Getting to the national finals of a Kwik Cricket tournament at primary school
WHAT EXCITES YOU ABOUT THE NEW COUNTY STRUCTURE? Having one place to call home
FAVOURITE WARM-UP SONG? We Didn't Start the Fire by Billy Joel
SURPRISING FACT ABOUT YOU: I've ridden horses all my life

Batting	Mat	Inns	NO	Runs	HS	Ave	SR	100	50	Ct	St
List A	1	1	0	0	0	0.00	0.00	0	0	0	-
T20s	19	6	4	30	11*	15.00	56.60	0	0	2	-

Bowling	Mat	Balls	Mdns	Runs	Wkts	BB	Ave	4wI	5wI	SR	Econ
List A	1	28	0	22	3	3-22	7.33	0	0	9.33	4.71
T20s	19	342	1	287	12	4-10	23.91	1	0	28.50	5.03

GRACE POTTS

RHB / RMF

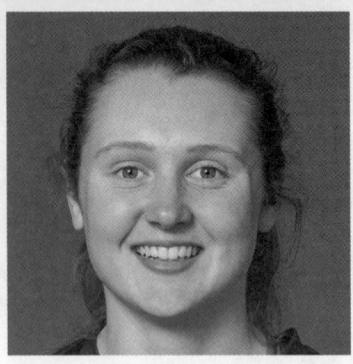

FULL NAME: Grace Elizabeth Ann Potts
BORN: July 12, 2002, Newcastle-under-Lyme, Staffordshire
SQUAD NO: 9
HEIGHT: 6ft
NICKNAME: Pottsy
EDUCATION: Newcastle-under-Lyme School, Staffordshire; Loughborough University
TEAMS: Lancashire, Trent Rockets, Central Sparks, Manchester Originals, Staffordshire
ROLE: Bowler
DEBUT: List A: 2018; T20: 2018

BEST BATTING: 30* England A vs New Zealand A, Dunedin, 2024
BEST BOWLING: 3-38 Central Sparks vs The Blaze, Chesterfield, 2024

FIRST CRICKET CLUB? Stone CC, Staffordshire
EARLIEST CRICKETING MEMORY? Watching my brother at our local club
WHAT WILL YOU MISS ABOUT REGIONAL CRICKET? Playing at different grounds across the region we were representing
WHAT EXCITES YOU ABOUT THE NEW COUNTY STRUCTURE? Bigger crowds (hopefully)
OPPONENT YOU MOST LOOK FORWARD TO PLAYING AGAINST? Hollie Armitage – it's always a good challenge against one of the best batters in the women's domestic game
FAVOURITE WARM-UP SONG? Stumblin' In by Cyril
SPECIALITY SUBJECT IN A PUB QUIZ (EXCLUDING SPORT)? Movies
ONE THING YOU WANT TO DO BEFORE YOU DIE: A skydive
HOBBY YOU WOULD LIKE TO LEARN: Baking
WHICH PUBLIC FIGURE INSPIRES YOU (EXCLUDING SPORTSPEOPLE)? Michelle Obama
SURPRISING FACT ABOUT YOU: I used to play hockey and netball at county level
FILM YOU CAN WATCH OVER AND OVER: A Few Good Men

Batting	Mat	Inns	NO	Runs	HS	Ave	SR	100	50	Ct	St
List A	42	23	13	166	30*	16.60	47.02	0	0	14	-
T20s	54	14	7	56	12	8.00	78.87	0	0	9	-

Bowling	Mat	Balls	Mdns	Runs	Wkts	BB	Ave	4wl	5wl	SR	Econ
List A	42	1711	28	1239	38	3-38	32.60	0	0	45.02	4.34
T20s	54	923	1	1006	41	4-36	24.53	1	0	22.51	6.53

HANNAH RAINEY RHB / RMF

FULL NAME: Hannah Rainey
BORN: June 2, 1997, Tower Hamlets, Essex
SQUAD NO: 26
HEIGHT: 5ft 9in
NICKNAME: Rainos
EDUCATION: The Mary Erskine School, Edinburgh; University of Edinburgh
TEAMS: Scotland, Lancashire, Cumbria
ROLE: Bowler
DEBUT: ODI: 2023; T20I: 2018; List A: 2017; T20: 2018

LANCASHIRE

BEST BATTING: 14 Scotland A vs Leicestershire, Barkby, 2019
BEST BOWLING: 5-41 Scotland vs Ireland, Almeria, 2023

FIRST CRICKET CLUB? Carlton CC, Edinburgh
EARLIEST CRICKETING MEMORY? Kwik Cricket at Carlton CC after school on Wednesdays
WHAT EXCITES YOU ABOUT THE NEW COUNTY STRUCTURE? Being fully integrated into a club and more double headers in the T20 Blast
OPPONENT YOU MOST LOOK FORWARD TO PLAYING AGAINST? Any of my Scotland teammates
FAVOURITE WARM-UP SONG? Can't Hold Us by Macklemore & Ryan Lewis
HOW MANY HOURS DO YOU SPEND ON YOUR PHONE A DAY? Three
SPECIALITY SUBJECT IN A PUB QUIZ (EXCLUDING SPORT)? Animal facts
ONE THING YOU WANT TO DO BEFORE YOU DIE: Complete an Ironman
WHICH PUBLIC FIGURE INSPIRES YOU (EXCLUDING SPORTSPEOPLE)? Michelle Obama
SURPRISING FACT ABOUT YOU: I am a fully qualified veterinary surgeon specialising in farm animals
FILM YOU CAN WATCH OVER AND OVER: Where the Crawdads Sing

Batting	Mat	Inns	NO	Runs	HS	Ave	SR	100	50	Ct	St
ODIs	4	4	2	12	8*	6.00	34.28	0	0	1	-
T20Is	37	9	3	12	5*	2.00	27.27	0	0	4	-
List A	16	11	3	40	14	5.00	-	0	0	2	-
T20s	55	14	5	19	5*	2.11	-	0	0	4	-

Bowling	Mat	Balls	Mdns	Runs	Wkts	BB	Ave	4wI	5wI	SR	Econ
ODIs	4	158	2	141	9	5-41	15.66	0	1	17.55	5.35
T20Is	37	492	2	422	22	3-15	19.18	0	0	22.36	5.14
List A	16	416	3	314	16	5-41	19.62	0	1	26.00	4.52
T20s	55	708	4	623	29	3-15	21.48	0	0	24.41	5.27

MOLLIE ROBBINS   RHB / RM

SOMERSET

FULL NAME: Mollie Joy Robbins
BORN: October 4, 1998, Bristol
SQUAD NO: 14
HEIGHT: 5ft 10in
NICKNAME: Robbo
EDUCATION: John Cabot Academy, Bristol
TEAMS: Somerset, Gloucestershire, Western Storm
ROLE: Bowler
DEBUT: List A: 2013; T20: 2014

BEST BATTING: 12* Gloucestershire vs Buckinghamshire, Marshfield, 2019
BEST BOWLING: 5-19 Gloucestershire vs Dorset, Bournemouth, 2019

FIRST CRICKET CLUB? Hanham CC, South Gloucestershire
WHAT WILL YOU MISS ABOUT REGIONAL CRICKET? Not being able to play at the home of Gloucestershire CCC
WHAT EXCITES YOU ABOUT THE NEW COUNTY STRUCTURE? Having a permanent base at Taunton and playing in front of being crowds (particularly for the double headers)
OPPONENT YOU MOST LOOK FORWARD TO PLAYING AGAINST? Sophia Smale – I played with her at Western Storm. She's a good friend and loves a send-off!
FAVOURITE WARM-UP SONG? Fireball by Pitbull
HOW MANY HOURS DO YOU SPEND ON YOUR PHONE A DAY? At a wild guess, two
ONE THING YOU WANT TO DO BEFORE YOU DIE: Visit New York
SURPRISING FACT ABOUT YOU: I went backpacking across Southeast Asia
FILM YOU CAN WATCH OVER AND OVER: Monsters, Inc

Batting	Mat	Inns	NO	Runs	HS	Ave	SR	100	50	Ct	St
List A	39	26	11	69	12*	4.60	30.39	0	0	7	-
T20s	44	29	8	257	47	12.23	81.84	0	0	8	-

Bowling	Mat	Balls	Mdns	Runs	Wkts	BB	Ave	4wI	5wI	SR	Econ
List A	39	1283	34	892	47	5-19	18.97	1	1	27.29	4.17
T20s	44	658	8	482	22	2-3	21.90	0	0	29.90	4.39

PAIGE SCHOLFIELD

RHB / RM / MVP9

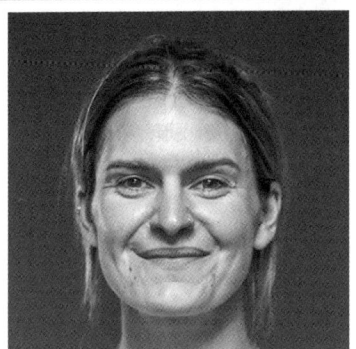

FULL NAME: Paige Jamie Scholfield
BORN: December 19, 1995, Durban, South Africa
SQUAD NO: 7
HEIGHT: 5ft 7in
EDUCATION: Beacon Academy, East Sussex; Loughborough College
TEAMS: England, Surrey, Sussex, Oval Invincibles, Loughborough Lightning, South East Stars, Southern Vipers
ROLE: Batter
DEBUT: ODI: 2024; T20I: 2024; List A: 2012; T20: 2013

SURREY

BEST BATTING: 134* South East Stars vs Western Storm, Bristol, 2023
BEST BOWLING: 3-16 Southern Vipers vs Thunder, Sale, 2021

FIRST CRICKET CLUB? Bells Yew Green CC, Tunbridge Wells, Kent
EARLIEST CRICKETING MEMORY? Playing at school aged 13
WHAT EXCITES YOU ABOUT THE NEW COUNTY STRUCTURE? Growing the women's game
FAVOURITE WARM-UP SONG? Pocketful of Sunshine by Natasha Bedingfield
SPECIALITY SUBJECT IN A PUB QUIZ (EXCLUDING SPORT)? Food
ONE THING YOU WANT TO DO BEFORE YOU DIE: Scuba diving on the Gold Coast
HOBBY YOU WOULD LIKE TO LEARN: Playing the guitar
FILM YOU CAN WATCH OVER AND OVER: The Lion King (original version)

Batting	Mat	Inns	NO	Runs	HS	Ave	SR	100	50	Ct	St
ODIs	3	3	0	59	31	19.66	101.72	0	0	0	-
T20Is	2	2	0	36	34	18.00	150.00	0	0	0	-
List A	95	79	12	1668	134*	24.89	81.88	2	6	40	-
T20s	127	110	19	1542	73*	16.94	112.39	0	5	44	1

Bowling	Mat	Balls	Mdns	Runs	Wkts	BB	Ave	4wI	5wI	SR	Econ
ODIs	3	-	-	-	-	-	-	-	-	-	-
T20Is	2	-	-	-	-	-	-	-	-	-	-
List A	95	1893	19	1357	51	3-16	26.60	0	0	37.11	4.30
T20s	127	920	2	1017	48	3-12	21.18	0	0	19.16	6.63

NAT SCIVER-BRUNT

RHB / RMF / MVP47

THE BLAZE

FULL NAME: Natalie Ruth Sciver-Brunt
BORN: August 20, 1992, Tokyo, Japan
SQUAD NO: 10
HEIGHT: 5ft 10in
EDUCATION: Epsom College, Surrey;
Loughborough University
TEAMS: England, The Blaze, Surrey, Trent
Rockets, Melbourne Stars, Mumbai Indians,
Northern Diamonds, Perth Scorchers,
Surrey Stars
ROLE: Allrounder
DEBUT: Test: 2014; ODI: 2013; T20I: 2013;
List A: 2010; T20: 2010

BEST BATTING: 180* Surrey vs Derbyshire, Spondon, 2018
BEST BOWLING: 5-27 Surrey vs Lancashire, Urmston, 2015

FIRST CRICKET CLUB: Stoke d'Abernon CC, Surrey
WHICH TEAMMATE HAS HAD THE BIGGEST IMPACT ON YOUR GAME? Katherine Sciver-Brunt
– she has shown me how to take myself seriously
WHICH GROUND DO YOU MOST ENJOY VISITING? The Oval – my second home ground!
IF YOU COULD PINCH A PLAYER FROM ANOTHER TEAM, WHO WOULD IT BE? Lauren Filer
WHO IS THE TOUGHEST BOWLER TO FACE IN DOMESTIC CRICKET? Kelly Castle – reading
her pace is hard
WHAT KEEPS YOU AWAKE AT NIGHT? The rain
WHAT'S THE SILLIEST OUTFIT YOU'VE EVER WORN? Dressing up as a star
CHOOSE A FANTASY SLIP CORDON TO SPEND A DAY IN THE FIELD WITH: Adele (wk), David
Beckham, Beyoncé, Jessica Ennis-Hill

Batting	Mat	Inns	NO	Runs	HS	Ave	SR	100	50	Ct	St
Tests	12	20	1	883	169*	46.47	54.91	2	5	10	-
ODIs	115	102	19	3811	148*	45.91	94.63	9	22	48	-
T20Is	132	126	28	2789	82	28.45	118.17	0	16	65	-
List A	188	174	32	6427	180*	45.26	-	14	35	84	-
T20s	328	316	79	7787	96*	32.85	-	0	46	142	-
Bowling	Mat	Balls	Mdns	Runs	Wkts	BB	Ave	4wl	5wl	SR	Econ
Tests	12	1057	44	461	12	3-41	38.41	-	0	88.08	2.61
ODIs	115	3356	36	2477	79	4-59	31.35	1	0	42.48	4.42
T20Is	132	1902	3	2096	90	4-15	23.28	2	0	21.13	6.61
List A	188	5900	72	4172	140	5-27	29.80	1	1	42.14	4.24
T20s	328	5112	10	6051	244	4-15	24.79	4	0	20.95	7.10

LIZZIE SCOTT   RHB / RFM

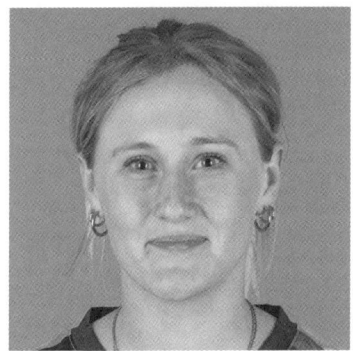

FULL NAME: Lizzie Eleanor Scott
BORN: September 1, 2004, Hexham, Northumberland
SQUAD NO: 2
TEAMS: Durham, Northern Diamonds, Northumberland, Oval Invincibles, England U19
ROLE: Bowler
DEBUT: List A: 2016; T20: 2016

DURHAM

BEST BATTING: 58 Northumberland vs Durham, Durham, 2017
BEST BOWLING: 5-24 Northumberland vs Scotland A, Alnwick, 2019

FIRST CRICKET CLUB? Maften CC, Newcastle upon Tyne
EARLIEST CRICKETING MEMORY? Hiding under the covers at my mum's cricket match when I was six
WHAT WILL YOU MISS ABOUT REGIONAL CRICKET? Playing with teammates from a large region
WHAT EXCITES YOU ABOUT THE NEW COUNTY STRUCTURE? The chance to develop a stronger fanbase
FAVOURITE WARM-UP SONG? Fight For This Love by Cheryl Cole
HOW MANY HOURS DO YOU SPEND ON YOUR PHONE A DAY? Four
SPECIALITY SUBJECT IN A PUB QUIZ (EXCLUDING SPORT)? Coffee
HOBBY YOU WOULD LIKE TO LEARN: How to crochet
WHICH PUBLIC FIGURE INSPIRES YOU (EXCLUDING SPORTSPEOPLE)? Bob Dylan
SURPRISING FACT ABOUT YOU: I can play the piano
FILM YOU CAN WATCH OVER AND OVER: Billy Elliot

Batting	Mat	Inns	NO	Runs	HS	Ave	SR	100	50	Ct	St
List A	36	27	7	254	58	12.70	-	0	1	2	-
T20s	25	22	7	321	49	21.40	-	0	0	3	-

Bowling	Mat	Balls	Mdns	Runs	Wkts	BB	Ave	4wl	5wl	SR	Econ
List A	36	1245	14	964	35	5-24	27.54	1	1	35.57	4.64
T20s	25	425	1	438	12	2-12	36.50	0	0	35.41	6.18

GRACE SCRIVENS   LB / OB / MVP5

ESSEX

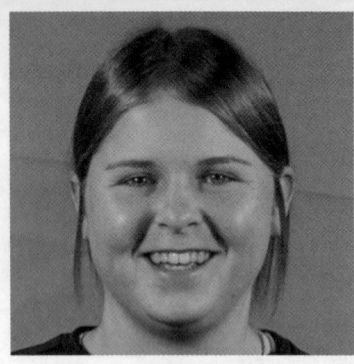

FULL NAME: Grace Elizabeth Scrivens
BORN: November 13, 2003, Kent
SQUAD NO: 29
HEIGHT: 5ft 11in
NICKNAME: Scriv
EDUCATION: Sutton Valence School, Maidstone, Kent
TEAMS: Essex, Trent Rockets, England U19, Kent, London Spirit, Melbourne Renegades, Sunrisers
ROLE: Allrounder
DEBUT: List A: 2019; T20: 2018

BEST BATTING: 118* Sunrisers vs Central Sparks, Kidderminster, 2024
BEST BOWLING: 4-20 Sunrisers vs Northern Diamonds, Headingley, 2022

FIRST CRICKET CLUB? Hollingbourne CC, Kent
WHAT WILL YOU MISS ABOUT REGIONAL CRICKET? The small, family feel that Sunrisers had
WHAT EXCITES YOU ABOUT THE NEW COUNTY STRUCTURE? Playing every game at Chelmsford as well as all the double headers
OPPONENT YOU MOST LOOK FORWARD TO PLAYING AGAINST? Georgia Adams – we had a good record against Southern Vipers last year
FAVOURITE WARM-UP SONG? Wagon Wheel by Darius Rucker
HOW MANY HOURS DO YOU SPEND ON YOUR PHONE A DAY? Five
SPECIALITY SUBJECT IN A PUB QUIZ (EXCLUDING SPORT)? Country music
ONE THING YOU WANT TO DO BEFORE YOU DIE: A skydive
HOBBY YOU WOULD LIKE TO LEARN: Coffee art
WHICH PUBLIC FIGURE INSPIRES YOU (EXCLUDING SPORTSPEOPLE)? Ant Middleton
SURPRISING FACT ABOUT YOU: I broke my leg on a trampoline aged four
FILM YOU CAN WATCH OVER AND OVER: Home Alone

Batting	Mat	Inns	NO	Runs	HS	Ave	SR	100	50	Ct	St
List A	51	49	4	1610	118*	35.77	67.73	2	12	19	-
T20s	78	72	16	1494	94*	26.67	103.24	0	10	16	-
Bowling	Mat	Balls	Mdns	Runs	Wkts	BB	Ave	4wI	5wI	SR	Econ
List A	51	1552	14	1149	30	4-20	38.30	2	0	51.73	4.44
T20s	78	572	0	630	24	4-33	26.25	1	0	23.83	6.60

CHLOE SKELTON   RHB / OB

FULL NAME: Chloe Skelton
BORN: June 20, 2001
SQUAD NO: 20
HEIGHT: 5ft 2in
NICKNAME: Skelts
EDUCATION: Dene Magna Secondary School; Hartpury College, Gloucestershire; Riverside Training, Hereford
TEAMS: Somerset, Gloucestershire, Western Storm
ROLE: Allrounder
DEBUT: List A: 2018; T20: 2018

BEST BATTING: 134* Gloucestershire vs Buckinghamshire, Amersham, 2018
BEST BOWLING: 5-29 Western Storm vs Sunrisers, Radlett, 2024

FIRST CRICKET CLUB? Newent CC, Gloucestershire
WHAT WILL YOU MISS ABOUT REGIONAL CRICKET? Not playing at the Cheltenham Festival
WHAT EXCITES YOU ABOUT THE NEW COUNTY STRUCTURE? Having a permanent home
OPPONENT YOU MOST LOOK FORWARD TO PLAYING AGAINST? Sophia Smale – it'll be great to catch up with a former teammate, and she's always a good laugh
FAVOURITE WARM-UP SONG? Fireball by Pitbull
HOW MANY HOURS DO YOU SPEND ON YOUR PHONE A DAY? Four
SPECIALITY SUBJECT IN A PUB QUIZ (EXCLUDING SPORT)? Films
ONE THING YOU WANT TO DO BEFORE YOU DIE: Go to New York
HOBBY YOU WOULD LIKE TO LEARN: How to cook
WHICH PUBLIC FIGURE INSPIRES YOU (EXCLUDING SPORTSPEOPLE)? Deborah Meaden
SURPRISING FACT ABOUT YOU: I'm from the Forest of Dean
FILM YOU CAN WATCH OVER AND OVER: Finding Nemo

Batting	Mat	Inns	NO	Runs	HS	Ave	SR	100	50	Ct	St
List A	47	35	15	567	134*	28.35	61.63	1	1	10	-
T20s	46	33	4	511	70*	17.62	68.31	0	1	15	-
Bowling	Mat	Balls	Mdns	Runs	Wkts	BB	Ave	4wl	5wl	SR	Econ
List A	47	1544	12	1225	45	5-29	27.22	0	2	34.31	4.76
T20s	46	573	1	593	29	4-24	20.44	1	0	19.75	6.20

SEREN SMALE — RHB / WK / MVP32

LANCASHIRE

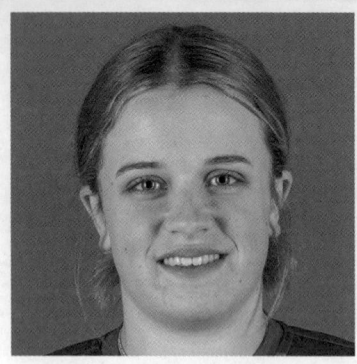

FULL NAME: Seren Anna Smale
BORN: December 13, 2004, Wrexham, Wales
SQUAD NO: 47
HEIGHT: 5ft 4in
NICKNAME: Sezza
EDUCATION: Ysgol Maes Garmon, Mold, Flintshire; Deeside Sixth Form
TEAMS: England, Lancashire, Birmingham Phoenix, Cheshire, Cumbria, Thunder
ROLE: Batter/wicketkeeper
DEBUT: T20I: 2024;
List A: 2021; T20: 2019

BEST BATTING: 99 Thunder vs Southern Vipers, Wormsley, 2024

FIRST CRICKET CLUB? Mold CC, Flintshire, Wales
EARLIEST CRICKETING MEMORY? Playing with my grandad in the nets after watching the cricket with him on the TV
WHAT EXCITES YOU ABOUT THE NEW COUNTY STRUCTURE? The increase in T20 double headers with the men
OPPONENT YOU MOST LOOK FORWARD TO PLAYING AGAINST? Lauren Filer – she bowls fast!
FAVOURITE WARM-UP SONG? Somedays by Sonny Fodera
HOW MANY HOURS DO YOU SPEND ON YOUR PHONE A DAY? Tooooooo many
SPECIALITY SUBJECT IN A PUB QUIZ (EXCLUDING SPORT)? The six times table
ONE THING YOU WANT TO DO BEFORE YOU DIE: Grow to 6ft
HOBBY YOU WOULD LIKE TO LEARN: Coffee art
WHICH PUBLIC FIGURE INSPIRES YOU (EXCLUDING SPORTSPEOPLE)? Adele
SURPRISING FACT ABOUT YOU: My first language is Welsh
FILM YOU CAN WATCH OVER AND OVER: Mamma Mia!

Batting	Mat	Inns	NO	Runs	HS	Ave	SR	100	50	Ct	St
T20Is	2	2	0	35	25	17.50	120.68	0	0	1	1
List A	28	28	0	796	99	28.42	69.03	0	6	7	1
T20s	44	35	7	672	121*	24.00	107.00	1	2	11	3

Bowling	Mat	Balls	Mdns	Runs	Wkts	BB	Ave	4wI	5wI	SR	Econ
T20Is	2	-	-	-	-	-	-	-	-	-	-
List A	28	-	-	-	-	-	-	-	-	-	-
T20s	44	-	-	-	-	-	-	-	-	-	-

FULL NAME: Sophia Ann Elizabeth Smale
BORN: December 8, 2004, Newport, Monmouthshire, Wales
SQUAD NO: 16
HEIGHT: 5ft 8in
NICKNAME: Noodles
EDUCATION: Haberdashers' Monmouth School for Girls
TEAMS: Essex, Oval Invincibles, England U19, Wales, Western Storm
ROLE: Allrounder
DEBUT: List A: 2022; T20: 2021

ESSEX

BEST BATTING: 59 Western Storm vs Northern Diamonds, Taunton, 2022
BEST BOWLING: 4-34 Western Storm vs Sunrisers, Cheltenham, 2023

FIRST CRICKET CLUB? Newport CC, Gwent
EARLIEST CRICKETING MEMORY? My first hard-ball game for Newport CC. I was about seven years old, running in and bowing seam as fast as I could. The seam bowling didn't last very long!
WHAT WILL YOU MISS ABOUT REGIONAL CRICKET? Playing at the different home grounds
WHAT EXCITES YOU ABOUT THE NEW COUNTY STRUCTURE? The one-club mentality and being properly integrated with the men's team
OPPONENT YOU MOST LOOK FORWARD TO PLAYING AGAINST? Chloe Skelton, one of my closest friends
FAVOURITE WARM-UP SONG? Point of View by DB Boulevard
HOW MANY HOURS DO YOU SPEND ON YOUR PHONE A DAY? Three hours and 15 minutes
HOBBY YOU WOULD LIKE TO LEARN: Hiking
WHICH PUBLIC FIGURE INSPIRES YOU (EXCLUDING SPORTSPEOPLE)? The Queen
SURPRISING FACT ABOUT YOU: I have a grade four at singing
FILM YOU CAN WATCH OVER AND OVER: Just Go With It

Batting	Mat	Inns	NO	Runs	HS	Ave	SR	100	50	Ct	St
List A	32	28	4	550	59	22.91	60.97	0	3	14	-
T20s	59	28	10	180	34	10.00	82.56	0	0	21	-

Bowling	Mat	Balls	Mdns	Runs	Wkts	BB	Ave	4wI	5wI	SR	Econ
List A	32	1450	10	1136	27	4-34	42.07	1	0	53.70	4.70
T20s	59	1060	5	1135	48	3-15	24.67	0	0	23.04	6.42

BRYONY SMITH

RHB / OB / MVP12

SURREY

FULL NAME: Bryony Frances Smith
BORN: December 12, 1997, Sutton, Surrey
SQUAD NO: 4
HEIGHT: 5ft 6in
NICKNAME: Bry
EDUCATION: St Andrews High School, London; Archbishop Tenison's Sixth Form
TEAMS: England, Surrey, Trent Rockets, Hobart Hurricanes, South East Stars, Surrey Stars, Welsh Fire
ROLE: Allrounder
DEBUT: ODI: 2019; T20I: 2018; List A: 2014; T20: 2014

BEST BATTING: 119* Surrey vs Essex, Cobham, 2018
BEST BOWLING: 5-33 Surrey vs Essex, Cobham, 2018

FIRST CRICKET CLUB? Wallington CC, London
WHAT WILL YOU MISS ABOUT REGIONAL CRICKET? The yellow kit
WHAT EXCITES YOU ABOUT THE NEW COUNTY STRUCTURE? Being able to play all our T20s at The Oval and creating stronger links with fans
OPPONENT YOU MOST LOOK FORWARD TO PLAYING AGAINST? Freya Davies – it's always a good battle against her with the new ball, and it's fun playing against your mate!
FAVOURITE WARM-UP SONG? Rockstar by Nickleback
HOW MANY HOURS DO YOU SPEND ON YOUR PHONE A DAY? Two
SPECIALITY SUBJECT IN A PUB QUIZ (EXCLUDING SPORT)? Episodes of Brooklyn Nine-Nine
ONE THING YOU WANT TO DO BEFORE YOU DIE: Go skydiving
WHICH PUBLIC FIGURE INSPIRES YOU (EXCLUDING SPORTSPEOPLE)? Nick Vujicic
SURPRISING FACT ABOUT YOU: I can balance a cricket bat on my nose
FILM YOU CAN WATCH OVER AND OVER: Miss Congeniality

Batting	Mat	Inns	NO	Runs	HS	Ave	SR	100	50	Ct	St
ODIs	1	0	-	-	-	-	-	-	-	0	-
T20Is	10	9	1	143	58	17.87	120.16	0	1	2	-
List A	83	79	5	2299	119*	31.06	-	3	14	23	-
T20s	157	150	7	2654	109*	18.55	-	1	11	38	1

Bowling	Mat	Balls	Mdns	Runs	Wkts	BB	Ave	4wI	5wI	SR	Econ
ODIs	1	48	0	20	1	1-20	20.00	0	0	48.00	2.50
T20Is	10	60	0	60	2	1-10	30.00	0	0	30.00	6.00
List A	83	2871	29	1914	79	5-33	24.22	0	1	36.34	4.00
T20s	157	1771	3	1970	84	4-14	23.45	2	0	21.08	6.67

LINSEY SMITH

LHB / SLA / MVP20

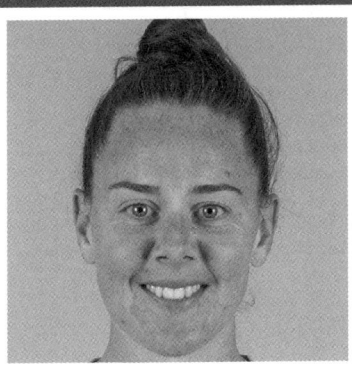

FULL NAME: Linsey Claire Neale Smith
BORN: March 10, 1995, Hillingdon, Middlesex
SQUAD NO: 59
HEIGHT: 5ft 2in
NICKNAME: Neal
EDUCATION: Loughborough University
TEAMS: England, Hampshire, Northern Superchargers, Berkshire, Melbourne Renegades, Northern Diamonds, Otago, Southern Vipers, Sussex, Sydney Sixers
ROLE: Bowler
DEBUT: T20I: 2018; List A: 2011; T20: 2011

BEST BATTING: 51 Southern Vipers vs South East Stars, Southampton, 2023
BEST BOWLING: 5-34 Northern Diamonds vs Western Storm, Chester-le-Street, 2021

FIRST CRICKET CLUB? Aston Rowant CC, Oxfordshire
EARLIEST CRICKETING MEMORY? Friday evenings down the local club with my brother and dad
WHAT WILL YOU MISS ABOUT REGIONAL CRICKET? Playing for the Charlotte Edwards Cup
OPPONENT YOU MOST LOOK FORWARD TO PLAYING AGAINST? Hollie Armitage – so I can reunite with my best mate
FAVOURITE WARM-UP SONG? Let's Get It Started by Black Eyed Peas
SPECIALITY SUBJECT IN A PUB QUIZ (EXCLUDING SPORT)? Elton John
ONE THING YOU WANT TO DO BEFORE YOU DIE: Watch Watford win the Premier League
HOBBY YOU WOULD LIKE TO LEARN: DIY
SURPRISING FACT ABOUT YOU: When I was younger I had a fear of buttons
FILM YOU CAN WATCH OVER AND OVER: Bend It Like Beckham

Batting	Mat	Inns	NO	Runs	HS	Ave	SR	100	50	Ct	St
T20Is	16	1	0	1	1	1.00	16.66	0	0	0	-
List A	91	69	12	715	51	12.54	-	0	1	25	-
T20s	202	83	27	533	34	9.51	-	0	0	50	-

Bowling	Mat	Balls	Mdns	Runs	Wkts	BB	Ave	4wI	5wI	SR	Econ
T20Is	16	354	1	376	19	3-18	19.78	0	0	18.63	6.37
List A	91	4649	111	2590	109	5-34	23.76	0	2	42.65	3.34
T20s	202	4130	14	3919	200	4-10	19.59	1	0	20.65	5.69

RHIANNA SOUTHBY

RHB / WK

FULL NAME: Rhianna Mae Southby
BORN: October 16, 2000, Hounslow, London
SQUAD NO: 17
HEIGHT: 5ft 2in
EDUCATION: Sparrow Farm Primary School, Feltham, London; Rivers Academy West London; Richmond upon Thames College
TEAMS: Hampshire, Southern Brave, South East Stars, Southern Vipers, Surrey, Surrey Stars
ROLE: Wicketkeeper
DEBUT: List A: 2016; T20: 2016

BEST BATTING: 54 South East Stars vs Western Storm, Cheltenham, 2022

FIRST CRICKET CLUB? Sunbury Cricket Club, Surrey

EARLIEST CRICKETING MEMORY? Putting on my brother's pads and learning how to hold a bat with my dad and brother

WHAT WILL YOU MISS ABOUT REGIONAL CRICKET? The identity and fan base – we had a good following at the Vipers

WHAT EXCITES YOU ABOUT THE NEW COUNTY STRUCTURE? There's been quite a bit of movement of players to different teams so it will be interesting to see how the new teams play together

FAVOURITE WARM-UP SONG? Feels This Good by Sigala

SPECIALITY SUBJECT IN A PUB QUIZ (EXCLUDING SPORT)? Song lyrics

ONE THING YOU WANT TO DO BEFORE YOU DIE: See the Northern Lights

WHICH PUBLIC FIGURE INSPIRES YOU (EXCLUDING SPORTSPEOPLE)? Niall Harbison – he set up a charity based in Thailand to help keep street dogs safe and find them homes. The charity has now expanded worldwide and has previously been supported by Liam Gallagher

FILM YOU CAN WATCH OVER AND OVER: Back to the Future

Batting	Mat	Inns	NO	Runs	HS	Ave	SR	100	50	Ct	St
List A	64	46	10	444	54	12.33	67.88	0	1	34	17
T20s	73	38	10	363	50	12.96	82.50	0	1	22	39
Bowling	Mat	Balls	Mdns	Runs	Wkts	BB	Ave	4wI	5wI	SR	Econ
List A	64	-	-	-	-	-	-	-	-	-	-
T20s	73	-	-	-	-	-	-	-	-	-	-

ALEXA STONEHOUSE
RHB / LMF / MVP45

FULL NAME: Alexa Kate Stonehouse
BORN: December 5, 2004, Ashford, Kent
SQUAD NO: 12
HEIGHT: 5ft 8in
NICKNAME: Pepper
EDUCATION: Canterbury Academy, Kent
TEAMS: Surrey, Trent Rockets, England U19, Kent, South East Stars
ROLE: Allrounder
DEBUT: List A: 2022; T20: 2021

SURREY

BEST BATTING: 51 South East Stars vs Sunrisers, Beckenham, 2023
BEST BOWLING: 4-27 South East Stars vs Northern Diamonds, Chester-le-Street, 2024

FIRST CRICKET CLUB? Whitstable CC, Kent
EARLIEST CRICKETING MEMORY? Playing with my brother
WHAT WILL YOU MISS ABOUT REGIONAL CRICKET? The South East Stars song
WHAT EXCITES YOU ABOUT THE NEW COUNTY STRUCTURE? The increase in T20 double headers with the men
OPPONENT YOU MOST LOOK FORWARD TO PLAYING AGAINST? Grace Scrivens, who I've played with since U11 level
FAVOURITE WARM-UP SONG? Hurtin' Me by Stefflon Don & French Montana
HOW MANY HOURS DO YOU SPEND ON YOUR PHONE A DAY? A couple
SPECIALITY SUBJECT IN A PUB QUIZ (EXCLUDING SPORT)? Clothing brands
ONE THING YOU WANT TO DO BEFORE YOU DIE: Go to an Adele concert
HOBBY YOU WOULD LIKE TO LEARN: Driving rally cars
FILM YOU CAN WATCH OVER AND OVER: Mid90s

Batting	Mat	Inns	NO	Runs	HS	Ave	SR	100	50	Ct	St
List A	31	28	1	405	51	15.00	61.08	0	1	1	-
T20s	45	12	7	87	22*	17.40	81.30	0	0	14	-

Bowling	Mat	Balls	Mdns	Runs	Wkts	BB	Ave	4wI	5wI	SR	Econ
List A	31	1014	13	806	33	4-27	24.42	1	0	30.72	4.76
T20s	45	551	1	622	22	3-13	28.27	0	0	25.04	6.77

AMU SURENKUMAR

RHB / RM

FULL NAME: Amuruthaa Surenkumar
BORN: October 24, 2006, Bournemouth
SQUAD NO: 10
HEIGHT: 5ft 5in
EDUCATION: Forest School, London; Rugby School, Warwickshire
TEAMS: Birmingham Bears, England A, Essex, Middlesex, Sunrisers
ROLE: Bowler
DEBUT: List A: 2023; T20: 2022

BEST BATTING: 25 Sunrisers vs Southern Vipers, Chelmsford, 2023
BEST BOWLING: 2-37 Sunrisers vs Western Storm, Cheltenham, 2023

FIRST CRICKET CLUB? North London CC
EARLIEST CRICKETING MEMORY? Playing in the hallway
WHAT EXCITES YOU ABOUT THE NEW COUNTY STRUCTURE? Playing for a team that has an established history
FAVOURITE WARM-UP SONG? Shella Verse by Sammy Virji & Flowdan
HOW MANY HOURS DO YOU SPEND ON YOUR PHONE A DAY? One
SPECIALITY SUBJECT IN A PUB QUIZ (EXCLUDING SPORT)? History
ONE THING YOU WANT TO DO BEFORE YOU DIE: Go skydiving
HOBBY YOU WOULD LIKE TO LEARN: Golf
WHICH PUBLIC FIGURE INSPIRES YOU (EXCLUDING SPORTSPEOPLE)? Michelle Obama
FILM YOU CAN WATCH OVER AND OVER: The Holiday

Batting	Mat	Inns	NO	Runs	HS	Ave	SR	100	50	Ct	St
List A	13	9	3	104	25	17.33	69.79	0	0	1	-
T20s	11	10	2	196	44	24.50	93.77	0	0	2	-

Bowling	Mat	Balls	Mdns	Runs	Wkts	BB	Ave	4wl	5wl	SR	Econ
List A	13	237	0	219	6	2-37	36.50	0	0	39.50	5.54
T20s	11	103	0	109	3	1-8	36.33	0	0	34.33	6.34

MARY TAYLOR RHB / RFM

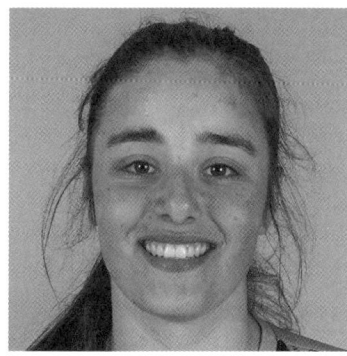

FULL NAME: Mary Louise Latham Taylor
BORN: October 7, 2004, Eastbourne, Sussex
SQUAD NO: 9
HEIGHT: 5ft 7in
NICKNAME: Meryl
EDUCATION: St Andrew's Prep, Eastbourne; Bede's Senior School
TEAMS: Hampshire, England U19, Southern Brave, Southern Vipers, Sussex
ROLE: Bowler
DEBUT: List A: 2022; T20: 2021

HAMPSHIRE

BEST BATTING: 16 Southern Vipers vs Thunder, Southport, 2023
BEST BOWLING: 4-39 Southern Vipers vs Thunder, Arundel, 2023

FIRST CRICKET CLUB? Eastbourne CC, East Sussex
EARLIEST CRICKETING MEMORY? Watching my grandad and brother play in the back garden and having no idea what was going on
WHAT EXCITES YOU ABOUT THE NEW COUNTY STRUCTURE? Playing in the new competitions
OPPONENT YOU MOST LOOK FORWARD TO PLAYING AGAINST? Mille Taylor (my sister)
FAVOURITE WARM-UP SONG? Footloose by Kenny Loggins
HOW MANY HOURS DO YOU SPEND ON YOUR PHONE A DAY? Six
SPECIALITY SUBJECT IN A PUB QUIZ (EXCLUDING SPORT)? History
ONE THING YOU WANT TO DO BEFORE YOU DIE: Visit New York
HOBBY YOU WOULD LIKE TO LEARN: Snowboarding
WHICH PUBLIC FIGURE INSPIRES YOU (EXCLUDING SPORTSPEOPLE)? King Charles III
SURPRISING FACT ABOUT YOU: I can do a Rubik's cube in two minutes
FILM YOU CAN WATCH OVER AND OVER: The Grand Budapest Hotel

Batting	Mat	Inns	NO	Runs	HS	Ave	SR	100	50	Ct	St
List A	24	14	8	66	16	11.00	80.48	0	0	5	-
T20s	34	17	4	285	82*	21.92	92.83	0	2	7	-

Bowling	Mat	Balls	Mdns	Runs	Wkts	BB	Ave	4wI	5wI	SR	Econ
List A	24	1069	6	929	25	4-39	37.16	1	0	42.76	5.21
T20s	34	537	2	549	24	3-6	22.87	0	0	22.37	6.13

ELLIE THRELKELD   RHB / WK

LANCASHIRE

FULL NAME: Eleanor Threlkeld
BORN: November 16, 1998, Knowsley, Lancashire
SQUAD NO: 21
HEIGHT: 5ft 6in
NICKNAME: Threlks
EDUCATION: Winstanley College, Wigan; Loughborough University
TEAMS: Lancashire, Manchester Originals, Lancashire Thunder, Thunder
ROLE: Wicketkeeper/batter
DEBUT: List A: 2014; T20: 2013

BEST BATTING: 107* Thunder vs Western Storm, Old Trafford, 2023

FIRST CRICKET CLUB? Rainford CC, St Helens, Merseyside
WHAT WILL YOU MISS ABOUT REGIONAL CRICKET? Being able to call ourselves the Thunderbirds
WHAT EXCITES YOU ABOUT THE NEW COUNTY STRUCTURE? The double headers at Old Trafford
OPPONENT YOU MOST LOOK FORWARD TO PLAYING AGAINST? Hollie Armitage – we're great friends and have had a good rivalry over the years while she was captaining the Diamonds
FAVOURITE WARM-UP SONG? Holiday by Dizzee Rascal
HOW MANY HOURS DO YOU SPEND ON YOUR PHONE A DAY? Hardly any, I'm terrible at replying
SPECIALITY SUBJECT IN A PUB QUIZ (EXCLUDING SPORT)? Gavin & Stacey
ONE THING YOU WANT TO DO BEFORE YOU DIE: Hire a campervan and travel round America
HOBBY YOU WOULD LIKE TO LEARN: Golf
SURPRISING FACT ABOUT YOU: I played for Liverpool FC for 10 years
FILM YOU CAN WATCH OVER AND OVER: The Inbetweeners Movie

Batting	Mat	Inns	NO	Runs	HS	Ave	SR	100	50	Ct	St
List A	85	81	11	1534	107*	21.91	58.52	1	7	47	34
T20s	140	112	28	1259	56*	14.98	-	0	4	41	77

Bowling	Mat	Balls	Mdns	Runs	Wkts	BB	Ave	4wI	5wI	SR	Econ
List A	85	-	-	-	-	-	-	-	-	-	-
T20s	140	-	-	-	-	-	-	-	-	-	-

PHOEBE TURNER · RHB / RM

FULL NAME: Phoebe Elisabeth Turner
BORN: August 8, 2003, Rotherham, Yorkshire
SQUAD NO: 17
HEIGHT: 5ft 8in
NICKNAME: Tina
EDUCATION: Thirsk High School, North Yorkshire
TEAMS: Durham, Northern Diamonds, Yorkshire
ROLE: Allrounder
DEBUT: List A: 2022; T20: 2021

BEST BATTING: 49* Northern Diamonds vs South East Stars, Chester-le-Street, 2024
BEST BOWLING: 6-20 Northern Diamonds vs Lancashire Thunder, Southport, 2024

FIRST CRICKET CLUB? Thirsk CC, North Yorkshire
EARLIEST CRICKETING MEMORY? Playing street cricket with my brothers
WHAT EXCITES YOU ABOUT THE NEW COUNTY STRUCTURE? Playing alongside the men in front of even bigger crowds
OPPONENT YOU MOST LOOK FORWARD TO PLAYING AGAINST? Any of the overseas players
FAVOURITE WARM-UP SONG? Rave Out by Charlotte Plank, Skepsis & Turno
HOW MANY HOURS DO YOU SPEND ON YOUR PHONE A DAY? Eight
SPECIALITY SUBJECT IN A PUB QUIZ (EXCLUDING SPORT)? Music from 2000-2020
ONE THING YOU WANT TO DO BEFORE YOU DIE: Skydive
HOBBY YOU WOULD LIKE TO LEARN: How to DJ
WHICH PUBLIC FIGURE INSPIRES YOU (EXCLUDING SPORTSPEOPLE)? Tina Turner
SURPRISING FACT ABOUT YOU: I used to play basketball for North Yorkshire
FILM YOU CAN WATCH OVER AND OVER: Mamma Mia!

Batting	Mat	Inns	NO	Runs	HS	Ave	SR	100	50	Ct	St
List A	30	26	5	215	49*	10.23	59.88	0	0	7	-
T20s	17	14	2	165	30*	13.75	82.91	0	0	9	-

Bowling	Mat	Balls	Mdns	Runs	Wkts	BB	Ave	4wI	5wI	SR	Econ
List A	30	786	8	658	28	6-20	23.50	0	1	28.07	5.02
T20s	17	66	0	55	2	1-12	27.50	0	0	33.00	5.00

REBECCA TYSON

LHB / SLA

FULL NAME: Rebecca Elizabeth Ann Tyson
BORN: June 26, 2000
SQUAD NO: 35
HEIGHT: 5ft 7in
NICKNAME: Bex
EDUCATION: Longdean School, Hertfordshire
TEAMS: Hampshire, Middlesex, Southern Vipers
ROLE: Bowler
DEBUT: List A: 2015; T20: 2015

BEST BATTING: 40 Hertfordshire vs Cambridgeshire & Huntingdonshire, Sawston, 2017
BEST BOWLING: 5-23 Hertfordshire vs Buckinghamshire, Knebworth, 2017

FIRST CRICKET CLUB? Leverstock Green CC, Hemel Hempstead, Hertfordshire
EARLIEST CRICKETING MEMORY? Playing U11 boys' cricket
WHAT EXCITES YOU ABOUT THE NEW COUNTY STRUCTURE? The televised games and (hopefully) the big crowds. Busy season ahead!
OPPONENT YOU MOST LOOK FORWARD TO PLAYING AGAINST? Heather Knight – because she just might have helped me get this contract at Hampshire!
FAVOURITE WARM-UP SONG? Can't Stop by Red Hot Chili Peppers
HOW MANY HOURS DO YOU SPEND ON YOUR PHONE A DAY? Three or four
ONE THING YOU WANT TO DO BEFORE YOU DIE: Go to Australia
HOBBY YOU WOULD LIKE TO LEARN: Play the guitar
WHICH PUBLIC FIGURE INSPIRES YOU (EXCLUDING SPORTSPEOPLE)? Harry Styles
SURPRISING FACT ABOUT YOU: I used to bowl left-arm pace until four years ago
FILM YOU CAN WATCH OVER AND OVER: Any of the Harry Potter films

Batting	Mat	Inns	NO	Runs	HS	Ave	SR	100	50	Ct	St
List A	22	16	5	139	40	12.63	53.87	0	0	6	-
T20s	39	26	11	311	67*	20.73	85.91	0	1	9	-

Bowling	Mat	Balls	Mdns	Runs	Wkts	BB	Ave	4wI	5wI	SR	Econ
List A	22	679	17	382	24	5-23	15.91	1	1	28.29	3.37
T20s	39	641	10	525	46	4-8	11.41	2	0	13.93	4.91

MADY VILLIERS   RHB / OB / MVP27

FULL NAME: Mady Kate Villiers
BORN: August 26, 1998, Havering, Essex
SQUAD NO: 22
HEIGHT: 5ft 5in
NICKNAME: AB, Mandy
EDUCATION: Shenfield High School,
Brentwood, Essex
TEAMS: England, Durham, Oval Invincibles,
Essex, Sunrisers, Surrey Stars
ROLE: Allrounder
DEBUT: ODI: 2024; T20I: 2019;
List A: 2013; T20: 2013

DURHAM

BEST BATTING: 70 Sunrisers vs Southern Vipers, Southampton, 2023
BEST BOWLING: 4-36 Sunrisers vs Northern Diamonds, Headingley, 2022

FIRST CRICKET CLUB? Bentley CC, Brentford, Essex
BEST PERFORMANCE AS A PRO? Taking 4 for 12 for Oval Invincibles against London Spirit in The Hundred two summers ago
GREATEST PERFORMANCE YOU HAVE WITNESSED? Meg Lanning's unbeaten 133 for Australia in a T20 at Chelmsford during the 2019 Ashes
FAVOURITE FORMAT? The longer formats because we don't get to play much of it
HOBBIES? Watching pottery videos
FAVOURITE TOY AS A KID? I had this football that would attach to my ankle and I would take it everywhere
WHAT WOULD BE YOUR PERFECT BREAKFAST? A big bowl of oats

Batting	Mat	Inns	NO	Runs	HS	Ave	SR	100	50	Ct	St
ODIs	3	3	0	32	14	10.66	103.22	0	0	0	-
T20Is	19	6	3	52	35	17.33	167.74	0	0	9	-
List A	79	73	3	1051	70	15.01	-	0	5	26	-
T20s	141	105	16	1086	55*	12.20	100.83	0	3	43	-

Bowling	Mat	Balls	Mdns	Runs	Wkts	BB	Ave	4wI	5wI	SR	Econ
ODIs	3	90	0	79	3	3-30	26.33	0	0	30.00	5.26
T20Is	19	254	2	282	17	3-10	16.58	0	0	14.94	6.66
List A	79	3269	41	2408	94	4-36	25.61	2	0	34.77	4.41
T20s	141	2093	9	2250	107	4-3	21.02	2	0	19.56	6.45

AMANDA-JADE WELLINGTON · RHB / LB / MVP2

SOMERSET

FULL NAME: Amanda-Jade Wellington
BORN: May 29, 1997, Adelaide, Australia
SQUAD NO: 10
TEAMS: Australia, Somerset, Oval Invincibles, Adelaide Strikers, Barbados Royals, Manchester Originals, Northern Districts, Otago, South Australia, Southern Brave, Southern Vipers, Western Storm
ROLE: Allrounder
DEBUT: Test: 2017; ODI: 2016; T20I: 2017; List A: 2012; T20: 2012

BEST BATTING: 116 South Australia vs Western Australia, Adelaide, 2017
BEST BOWLING: 6-25 South Australia vs Tasmania, Adelaide, 2015

NOTES: Somerset have signed the Australian leg-spinning allrounder for the duration of the season. A star on the world stage, Wellington is no stranger in these parts, having taken 27 wickets and scored over 400 runs for Western Storm last summer. The 27-year-old, who has played for Australia in all three formats, has had plenty of experience in this country, turning out for three different teams in The Hundred and representing Southern Vipers in the Kia Super League. "I really enjoyed my time in the region last year and I can't wait to be a part of Somerset's first-ever professional women's team," Wellington said. "I know a lot of the players and staff from my time with Storm and there is a genuine bond within the group. We have the chance to put down a marker and set the standards for Somerset Women this summer"

Batting	Mat	Inns	NO	Runs	HS	Ave	SR	100	50	Ct	St
Tests	1	1	0	2	2	2.00	16.66	0	0	0	-
ODIs	14	8	2	17	11	2.83	58.62	0	0	3	-
T20Is	8	2	1	9	8	9.00	90.00	0	0	3	-
List A	123	108	26	1620	116	19.75	86.86	1	5	29	-
T20s	266	151	43	1505	55	13.93	123.15	0	1	85	-

Bowling	Mat	Balls	Mdns	Runs	Wkts	BB	Ave	4wI	5wI	SR	Econ
Tests	1	342	9	130	2	1-61	65.00	-	0	171.00	2.28
ODIs	14	672	3	536	18	3-24	29.77	0	0	37.33	4.78
T20Is	8	120	12	112	10	4-16	11.20	1	0	12.00	5.60
List A	123	5910	48	4642	187	6-25	24.82	8	1	31.60	4.71
T20s	266	5128	9	5637	314	5-8	17.95	7	2	16.33	6.59

FRAN WILSON
RHB / OB

FULL NAME: Frances Claire Wilson
BORN: November 7, 1991, Farnham, Surrey
SQUAD NO: 35
HEIGHT: 5ft 4in
EDUCATION: University of Bath;
Loughborough University
TEAMS: England, Somerset, Birmingham
Phoenix, Canterbury, Hobart Hurricanes,
Sunrisers, Sydney Thunder, Trent Rockets,
Wellington, Western Storm
ROLE: Batter
DEBUT: Test: 2017; ODI: 2010; T20I: 2010;
List A: 2006; T20: 2010

BEST BATTING: 110 Middlesex vs Warwickshire, Birmingham, 2015
BEST BOWLING: 1-21 Somerset vs Nottinghamshire, Nettleworth, 2009

FIRST CRICKET CLUB? Bath CC, Somerset
EARLIEST CRICKETING MEMORY? Playing in the back garden
WHAT WILL YOU MISS ABOUT REGIONAL CRICKET? Representing a region
WHAT EXCITES YOU ABOUT THE NEW COUNTY STRUCTURE? Having a home
OPPONENT YOU MOST LOOK FORWARD TO PLAYING AGAINST? Sophia Smale (for the send-offs!)
SPECIALITY SUBJECT IN A PUB QUIZ (EXCLUDING SPORT)? Bad reality TV
ONE THING YOU WANT TO DO BEFORE YOU DIE: Indulge in a silent retreat
HOBBY YOU WOULD LIKE TO LEARN: Woodcraft
WHICH PUBLIC FIGURE INSPIRES YOU (EXCLUDING SPORTSPEOPLE)? David Attenborough
FILM YOU CAN WATCH OVER AND OVER: Mean Girls

Batting	Mat	Inns	NO	Runs	HS	Ave	SR	100	50	Ct	St
Tests	1	1	0	13	13	13.00	24.52	0	0	0	-
ODIs	33	23	2	468	85*	22.28	87.96	0	2	14	-
T20Is	30	26	10	356	43*	22.25	99.16	0	0	7	-
List A	193	171	16	4869	110	31.41	-	2	32	71	-
T20s	194	176	40	3220	99	23.67	-	0	17	49	-

Bowling	Mat	Balls	Mdns	Runs	Wkts	BB	Ave	4wl	5wl	SR	Econ
Tests	1	-	-	-	-	-	-	-	-	-	-
ODIs	33	-	-	-	-	-	-	-	-	-	-
T20Is	30	-	-	-	-	-	-	-	-	-	-
List A	193	138	0	153	4	1-21	38.25	0	0	34.50	6.65
T20s	194	-	-	-	-	-	-	-	-	-	-

EMILY WINDSOR   RHB / RM

DURHAM

FULL NAME: Emily Lauren Windsor
BORN: September 14, 1997, Portsmouth
SQUAD NO: 4
HEIGHT: 5ft 4in
NICKNAME: Winnie
EDUCATION: Springfield School, Portsmouth; Havant College, Hampshire; University of Portsmouth; Sheffield Hallam University
TEAMS: Durham, Hampshire, Lightning, Oval Invincibles, Southern Vipers, Trent Rockets, Welsh Fire
ROLE: Allrounder
DEBUT: List A: 2013; T20: 2013

BEST BATTING: 99 Hampshire vs Northamptonshire, Northampton, 2015
BEST BOWLING: 6-23 Hampshire vs Northamptonshire, Northampton, 2015

FIRST CRICKET CLUB? Havant CC, Hampshire
EARLIEST CRICKETING MEMORY? Alleyway cricket with my brother, dad, grandpa and grandad
WHAT WILL YOU MISS ABOUT REGIONAL CRICKET? Showcasing the game across all regions of the country
WHAT EXCITES YOU ABOUT THE NEW COUNTY STRUCTURE? Being aligned with the men
FAVOURITE WARM-UP SONG? Lollipop by Mika
HOW MANY HOURS DO YOU SPEND ON YOUR PHONE A DAY? Two hours
SPECIALITY SUBJECT IN A PUB QUIZ (EXCLUDING SPORT)? Children's TV programmes
ONE THING YOU WANT TO DO BEFORE YOU DIE: Run the London marathon
HOBBY YOU WOULD LIKE TO LEARN: Play the ukulele
WHICH PUBLIC FIGURE INSPIRES YOU (EXCLUDING SPORTSPEOPLE)? Amy Dowden
FILM YOU CAN WATCH OVER AND OVER: Frozen

Batting	Mat	Inns	NO	Runs	HS	Ave	SR	100	50	Ct	St
List A	91	80	11	1751	99	25.37	-	0	9	12	-
T20s	95	76	27	1023	85	20.87	-	0	4	27	-

Bowling	Mat	Balls	Mdns	Runs	Wkts	BB	Ave	4wI	5wI	SR	Econ
List A	91	653	5	454	27	6-23	16.81	1	1	24.18	4.17
T20s	95	252	1	262	17	2-9	15.41	0	0	14.82	6.23

ISSY WONG

RHB / RFM

FULL NAME: Isabelle Eleanor Chih Ming Wong
BORN: May 15, 2002, Chelsea, London
SQUAD NO: 95
HEIGHT: 5ft 7in
EDUCATION: Shrewsbury School
TEAMS: England, Birmingham Bears, Birmingham Phoenix, Central Sparks, Mumbai Indians, Southern Vipers, Sydney Thunder, Warwickshire, Western Storm
ROLE: Bowler
DEBUT: Test: 2022; ODI: 2022; T20I: 2022; List A: 2018; T20: 2018

BIRMINGHAM BEARS

BEST BATTING: 50 Central Sparks vs South East Stars, Guildford, 2023
BEST BOWLING: 5-49 Central Sparks vs Northern Diamonds, Headingley, 2021

FIRST CRICKET CLUB? Knowle & Dorridge CC, Solihull, Warwickshire
EARLIEST CRICKETING MEMORY? Playing in the playground at primary school
WHAT EXCITES YOU ABOUT THE NEW COUNTY STRUCTURE? Having a consistent home and being aligned with the men's team
FAVOURITE WARM-UP SONG? Life is a Highway by Rascal Flatts
HOW MANY HOURS DO YOU SPEND ON YOUR PHONE A DAY? Three hours
SPECIALITY SUBJECT IN A PUB QUIZ (EXCLUDING SPORT)? Star Wars
FILM YOU CAN WATCH OVER AND OVER: The Prestige

Batting	Mat	Inns	NO	Runs	HS	Ave	SR	100	50	Ct	St
Tests	1	0	-	-	-	-	-	-	-	1	-
ODIs	4	1	0	15	15	15.00	187.50	0	0	2	-
T20Is	12	4	1	22	13	7.33	110.00	0	0	2	-
List A	45	35	8	324	50	12.00	76.05	0	1	12	-
T20s	113	77	13	693	53	10.82	124.86	0	1	25	-

Bowling	Mat	Balls	Mdns	Runs	Wkts	BB	Ave	4wI	5wI	SR	Econ
Tests	1	163	4	100	3	2-46	33.33	-	0	54.33	3.68
ODIs	4	114	0	121	4	3-36	30.25	0	0	28.50	6.36
T20Is	12	221	4	241	9	2-10	26.77	0	0	24.55	6.54
List A	45	1687	27	1396	54	5-49	25.85	3	1	31.24	4.96
T20s	113	1791	8	2126	87	4-15	24.72	1	0	20.82	7.12

NAT WRAITH

RHB / WK / MVP41

BIRMINGHAM BEARS

FULL NAME: Natasha Agnes Jessica Wraith
BORN: October 3, 2001, Bristol
SQUAD NO: 73
HEIGHT: 5ft 6in
NICKNAME: Aggy
EDUCATION: SGS College, Gloucestershire; Cardiff Metropolitan University
TEAMS: Birmingham Bears, Trent Rockets, London Spirit, Gloucestershire, Somerset, Welsh Fire, Western Storm
ROLE: Wicketkeeper
DEBUT: List A: 2016; T20: 2016

BEST BATTING: 73 Western Storm vs The Blaze, Trent Bridge, 2024

FIRST CRICKET CLUB? Frenchay CC, Bristol
EARLIEST CRICKETING MEMORY? Primary school
WHAT WILL YOU MISS ABOUT REGIONAL CRICKET? Playing at Bristol
WHAT EXCITES YOU ABOUT THE NEW COUNTY STRUCTURE? The feeling of being part of a club
FAVOURITE WARM-UP SONG? Just by Bicep
HOW MANY HOURS DO YOU SPEND ON YOUR PHONE A DAY? Three
SPECIALITY SUBJECT IN A PUB QUIZ (EXCLUDING SPORT)? National flags
ONE THING YOU WANT TO DO BEFORE YOU DIE: Have a well-behaved dog
HOBBY YOU WOULD LIKE TO LEARN: Padel tennis
WHICH PUBLIC FIGURE INSPIRES YOU (EXCLUDING SPORTSPEOPLE)? Daisy May Cooper
SURPRISING FACT ABOUT YOU: My grandad is from Bangladesh
FILM YOU CAN WATCH OVER AND OVER: American Sniper

Batting	Mat	Inns	NO	Runs	HS	Ave	SR	100	50	Ct	St
List A	63	56	5	1193	73	23.39	-	0	5	40	17
T20s	79	69	14	812	74*	14.76	104.77	0	1	20	34

Bowling	Mat	Balls	Mdns	Runs	Wkts	BB	Ave	4wI	5wI	SR	Econ
List A	63	-	-	-	-	-	-	-	-	-	-
T20s	79	-	-	-	-	-	-	-	-	-	-

DANNI WYATT-HODGE

RHB / OB

FULL NAME: Danielle Nicole Wyatt-Hodge
BORN: April 22, 1991, Stoke-on-Trent, Staffs
SQUAD NO: TBC
HEIGHT: 5ft 4in
EDUCATION: Stoke-On-Trent Sixth Form College
TEAMS: England, Surrey, Southern Brave, Brisbane Heat, Hobart Hurricanes, Notts, RCB, Southern Vipers, Staffordshire, Sussex, UP Warriorz, Victoria
ROLE: Batter
DEBUT: Test: 2023; ODI: 2010; T20I: 2010; List A: 2005; T20: 2006

BEST BATTING: 129 England vs South Africa, Christchurch, 2022
BEST BOWLING: 7-41 Staffordshire vs Wales, Bloxwich, 2010

FIRST CRICKET CLUB: Whitmore CC, Staffordshire
WHICH TEAMMATE HAS HAD THE BIGGEST IMPACT ON YOUR GAME? Charlotte Edwards – when I first got into the England team, she backed me and made me feel comfortable in the team environment straight away
DESCRIBE YOUR CAREER IN THREE WORDS: Strange, fearless, funny
WHICH PART OF THE SEASON DO YOU MOST ENJOY? July/August – it's hot and there's The Hundred
IF YOU COULD PINCH A PLAYER FROM ANOTHER TEAM, WHO WOULD IT BE? Kirstie Gordon
WHO IS THE TOUGHEST BOWLER TO FACE IN DOMESTIC CRICKET? Naomi Dattani
CHOOSE A FANTASY SLIP CORDON TO SPEND A DAY IN THE FIELD WITH: David Beckham (wk), Margot Robbie, Robbie Williams

Batting	Mat	Inns	NO	Runs	HS	Ave	SR	100	50	Ct	St
Tests	4	8	0	188	54	23.50	68.61	0	1	1	-
ODIs	118	101	14	2038	129	23.42	88.68	2	5	29	-
T20Is	170	149	14	3190	124	23.62	128.99	2	19	42	-
List A	244	223	29	5645	129	29.09	-	9	23	74	-
T20s	394	365	35	9000	124	27.27	-	6	52	102	-

Bowling	Mat	Balls	Mdns	Runs	Wkts	BB	Ave	4wI	5wI	SR	Econ
Tests	4	-	-	-	-	-	-	-	-	-	-
ODIs	118	918	3	770	27	3-7	28.51	0	0	34.00	5.03
T20Is	170	759	3	715	46	4-11	15.54	1	0	16.50	5.65
List A	244	5245	112	3109	152	7-41	20.45	3	2	34.50	3.55
T20s	394	2455	7	2501	118	4-11	21.19	2	0	20.80	6.11

Roll of
Honour

Division One

	Team	Matches	Won	Lost	Drawn	Bat (Bonus)	Bowl (Bonus)	Points
1	Surrey	14	8	2	4	34	37	231
2	Hampshire	14	6	1	7	31	33	214
3	Somerset	14	5	3	6	28	40	196
4	Essex	14	6	3	5	34	36	194
5	Durham	14	4	4	6	30	30	171
6	Worcestershire	14	3	4	7	21	37	162
7	Warwickshire	14	1	4	9	33	38	159
8	Nottinghamshire	14	2	4	8	25	35	155
9	Lancashire	14	3	6	5	15	34	134
10	Kent	14	1	8	5	12	32	99

Division Two

	Team	Matches	Won	Lost	Drawn	Bat (Bonus)	Bowl (Bonus)	Points
1	Sussex	14	8	2	4	40	40	237
2	Yorkshire	14	5	2	7	41	40	217
3	Middlesex	14	5	2	7	28	32	196
4	Northamptonshire	14	2	3	9	22	35	161
5	Leicestershire	14	1	3	10	28	31	155
6	Glamorgan	14	2	4	7	22	30	146
7	Gloucestershire	14	2	5	6	27	29	142
8	Derbyshire	14	1	6	7	20	31	122

Surrey, county champions in 2024
photographed by Ben Hoskins

Surrey fast bowler Dan Worrall
photographed by Ben Hoskins

ROLL OF HONOUR

Group A

	Team	Matches	Won	Lost	Tied	N/R	NRR	Points
1	Somerset	8	6	2	0	0	1.217	12
2	Worcestershire	8	5	3	0	0	0.564	10
3	Hampshire	8	5	3	0	0	0.191	10
4	Derbyshire	8	5	3	0	0	0.048	10
5	Durham	8	4	3	0	1	-0.048	9
6	Middlesex	8	3	4	0	1	-0.764	7
7	Kent	8	3	5	0	0	-0.619	6
8	Northamptonshire	8	2	6	0	0	0.231	4
9	Lancashire	8	2	6	0	0	-0.841	4

Group B

	Team	Matches	Won	Lost	Tied	N/R	NRR	Points
1	Glamorgan	8	6	1	0	1	+1.024	13
2	Leicestershire	8	6	2	0	0	-0.416	12
3	Warwickshire	8	5	2	0	1	+0.629	11
4	Nottinghamshire	8	4	4	0	0	+0.454	8
5	Gloucestershire	8	4	4	0	0	+0.244	8
6	Yorkshire	8	4	4	0	0	-0.232	8
7	Essex	8	3	5	0	0	-0.098	6
8	Surrey	8	2	6	0	0	-0.760	4
9	Sussex	8	1	7	0	0	-0.690	2

QUARTER-FINALS

Warwickshire v Worcestershire at Edgbaston
August 16 – Warwickshire won by 4 wickets
Worcestershire 286-9 (50/50 ov); Warwickshire
288-6 (49/50 ov)

Leicestershire v Hampshire at Leicester
August 16 – Leicestershire won by 3 wickets
Hampshire 290-8 (50/50 ov); Leicestershire 291-7
(49.5/50 ov)

*Note: the two group winners progressed straight
into the semi-finals; the second- and third-placed
teams played two 'quarter-finals'*

SEMI-FINALS

Somerset v Leicestershire at Taunton
August 18 – Somerset won by 23 runs
Somerset 334-4 (50/50 ov); Leicestershire 311-9
(50/50 ov)

Glamorgan v Warwickshire at Cardiff
August 18 – Glamorgan won by 39 runs
Glamorgan 247-9 (50/50 ov); Warwickshire 208
(46.1/50 ov)

FINAL

Glamorgan v Somerset at Trent Bridge
September 22-23 – Glamorgan won by 15 runs
Glamorgan 186-7 (20/20 ov); Somerset 171-6
(20/20 ov)

Glamorgan captain Kiran Carlson celebrates during his side's victory against Somerset in the One-Day Cup final
photographed by Harry Trump

ROLL OF HONOUR

	Team	Matches	Won	Lost	Tied	N/R	Net RR	Pts
	North Group							
1	Birmingham Bears	14	10	4	0	0	1.308	20
2	Northamptonshire	14	8	4	1	1	-0.151	18
3	Lancashire	14	7	4	0	3	1.109	17
4	Durham	14	7	6	0	1	-0.325	15
5	Leicestershire	14	6	6	1	1	-0.119	14
6	Derbyshire	14	6	7	0	1	0.112	13
7	Yorkshire	14	6	7	0	1	-0.035	13
8	Worcestershire	14	4	10	0	0	-0.192	8
9	Nottinghamshire	14	3	9	0	2	-1.699	8

	Team	Matches	Won	Lost	Tied	N/R	Net RR	Pts
	South Group							
1	Surrey	14	9	3	1	1	+0.777	20
2	Sussex	14	9	5	0	0	+0.607	18
3	Somerset	14	8	5	0	1	+0.497	17
4	Gloucestershire	14	7	6	1	0	+0.503	15
5	Essex	14	7	6	0	1	+0.201	15
6	Glamorgan	14	6	7	0	1	-0.592	13
7	Hampshire	14	4	7	0	3	-0.556	11
8	Middlesex	14	3	8	0	3	-1.487	9
9	Kent	14	4	10	0	0	-0.486	8

QUARTER-FINALS

Surrey v Durham at The Oval
September 3 – Surrey won by 5 wickets
Durham 162-8 (20/20 ov); Surrey 164-5 (18/20 ov)

Sussex v Lancashire at Hove
September 4 – Sussex won by 8 wickets
Lancashire 114 (15.3/20 ov); Sussex 118-2 (14.1/20 ov)

Northamptonshire v Somerset at Northampton
September 5 – Somerset won by 17 runs
Somerset 215-3 (20/20 ov); Northamptonshire
198-5 (20/20 ov)

Birmingham Bears v Gloucestershire at Edgbaston
September 6 – Gloucestershire won by 14 runs
Gloucestershire 138 (19.2/20 ov); Birmingham
Bears 124-9 (20/20 ov)

SEMI-FINALS

Surrey v Somerset at Edgbaston
September 14 – Somerset won by 6 wickets
Surrey 153-9 (20/20 ov); Somerset 159-4 (18.4/20 ov)

Sussex v Gloucestershire at Edgbaston
September 14 – Gloucestershire won by 8 wickets
Sussex 106 (18.1/20 ov); Gloucestershire 109-2
(13.4/20 ov)

FINAL

Somerset v Gloucestershire at Edgbaston
September 14 – Gloucestershire won by 8 wickets
Somerset 124 (19.4/20 ov); Gloucestershire 129-2
(15/20 ov)

Table

	Team	Matches	Won	Lost	Tied	N/R	Net RR	Pts
1	Northern Diamonds	14	9	4	0	1	0.097	41
2	South East Stars	14	9	5	0	0	0.246	40
3	Southern Vipers	14	7	6	0	1	0.534	34
4	Sunrisers	14	7	6	0	1	-0.122	34
5	The Blaze	14	7	6	0	1	-0.176	31
6	Lancashire Thunder	14	5	8	0	1	-0.013	25
7	Central Sparks	14	5	8	0	1	-0.299	25
8	Western Storm	14	4	10	0	0	-0.211	18

SEMI-FINALS

Northern Diamonds v Sunrisers at Headingley
September 14 – Sunrisers won by 7 wickets
Northern Diamonds 232-8 (50/50 ov); Sunrisers
234-3 (43.4/50 ov)

South East Stars v Southern Vipers at Beckenham
September 14 – South East Stars won by 3 wickets
Southern Vipers 220-9 (50/50 ov); South East
Stars 221-7 (48.5/50 ov)

FINAL

South East Stars v Sunrisers at Leicester
September 21 – Sunrisers won by 27 runs (DLS)
South East Stars 212 (46.2/50 ov); Sunrisers 121-3
(25/25 ov)

Winning captain Grace Scrivens
photographed by Matthew Lewis

Cordelia Griffith strikes out during her match-winning innings for Sunrisers in the final at Leicester
photographed by Matthew Lewis

Table

	Team	Matches	Won	Lost	Tied	N/R	Net RR	Pts
1	The Blaze	10	9	1	0	0	0.606	39
2	South East Stars	10	7	2	0	1	0.309	34
3	Southern Vipers	10	6	4	0	0	1.001	26
4	Central Sparks	10	6	4	0	0	0.402	26
5	Lancashire Thunder	10	3	6	0	1	-0.727	15
6	Northern Diamonds	10	3	7	0	0	-0.067	13
7	Western Storm	10	2	6	0	2	-0.659	13
8	Sunrisers	10	2	8	0	0	-1.073	8

SEMI-FINALS

Central Sparks v The Blaze at Derby
June 22 – The Blaze won by 5 wickets
Central Sparks 140-9 (20/20 ov); The Blaze 142-5 (18/20 ov)

South East Stars v Southern Vipers at Derby
June 22 – South East Stars won by 5 runs
South East Stars 162-5 (20/20 ov); Southern Vipers 157-9 (20/20 ov)

FINAL

South East Stars v The Blaze at Derby
June 22 – The Blaze won by 7 wickets
South East Stars 141-9 (20/20 ov); The Blaze 144-3 (18.4/20 ov)

The Blaze, T20 champions in 2024
photographed by Nathan Stirk

Leg-spinner Josie Groves in action
for The Blaze during the T20 final
photographed by Gareth Copley

ROLL OF HONOUR

Name	Mat	Inns	NO	Runs	HS	Ave	BF	SR	100	50	0	4s	6s
Colin Ingram	11	18	3	1351	257*	90.06	2102	64.27	5	6	0	182	11
David Bedingham	11	18	1	1331	279	78.29	1705	78.06	6	3	0	147	25
Adam Lyth	14	22	1	1215	147	57.85	1897	64.04	5	5	0	177	8
John Simpson	14	20	4	1197	205*	74.81	2067	57.91	5	4	2	132	13
Dean Elgar	14	21	1	1144	182	57.20	2014	56.80	4	5	1	144	1
Ryan Higgins	13	18	2	1133	221	70.81	1654	68.50	5	2	1	130	18
Alex Davies	14	23	1	1115	256	50.68	1799	61.97	4	3	2	141	10
Haseeb Hameed	14	26	5	1091	247*	51.95	2050	53.21	3	4	2	134	0
James Bracey	13	21	3	1089	207*	60.50	1550	70.25	4	3	2	138	12
Rory Burns	14	22	2	1073	227	53.65	1967	54.55	3	5	2	116	8
Will Rhodes	14	23	2	1020	201	48.57	1881	54.22	3	3	1	137	2
Keaton Jennings	14	23	1	1006	187*	45.72	1815	55.42	4	3	2	136	7
Wayne Madsen	13	23	3	1005	138	50.25	1809	55.55	3	5	3	122	7
Sam Northeast	14	26	6	1004	335*	50.20	1725	58.20	3	2	6	112	6
James Vince	13	22	2	986	211	49.30	1507	65.42	2	5	1	126	5
Max Holden	14	21	1	981	211*	49.05	2034	48.23	2	5	0	106	3
Liam Dawson	13	20	4	956	120	59.75	1426	67.04	3	5	0	87	19
Leus du Plooy	14	21	2	955	196*	50.26	1523	62.70	2	5	0	104	8
Ben Slater	14	26	5	949	168*	45.19	1841	51.54	2	5	1	131	4
Tom Lammonby	14	25	1	941	100	39.20	1714	54.90	1	5	2	125	2
Alex Lees	13	21	1	924	145	46.20	1710	54.03	4	2	1	108	1
Luke Procter	14	22	3	923	116*	48.57	2122	43.49	1	7	3	100	4
Kiran Carlson	14	25	2	923	148	40.13	1523	60.60	1	8	2	108	6
Emilio Gay	10	17	1	919	261	57.43	1340	68.58	2	4	1	117	2
Jordan Cox	11	15	1	918	207	65.57	1300	70.61	4	2	1	105	17
Joe Clarke	14	21	3	917	213*	50.94	1662	55.17	4	4	3	113	9
Nick Gubbins	12	18	2	895	201*	55.93	1936	46.22	3	3	1	108	1
Peter Handscomb	10	14	2	894	139*	74.50	1576	56.72	3	6	0	113	1
Tom Banton	12	19	1	891	133	49.50	1305	68.27	2	5	1	104	14
Sam Robson	11	16	1	872	162	58.13	1389	62.77	4	4	3	112	2
Ollie Robinson (Durham)	13	20	2	871	198	48.38	1040	83.75	2	5	1	105	19
Miles Hammond	13	21	0	868	121	41.33	1407	61.69	2	4	0	108	13
Daniel Bell-Drummond	13	26	2	853	135	35.54	1570	54.33	2	5	1	109	2
Ed Barnard	14	22	1	840	165	40.00	1467	57.25	2	5	3	97	5
James Wharton	9	14	1	833	285	64.07	1209	68.89	2	2	0	99	23
Ben Compton	13	26	0	833	165	32.03	2030	41.03	1	5	3	106	1
Cameron Bancroft	11	18	1	832	184	48.94	1539	54.06	3	2	1	90	2
Dom Sibley	14	22	3	832	150	43.78	1758	47.32	3	3	0	113	3
Tom Haines	14	20	0	819	133	40.95	1190	68.82	3	2	2	117	1
Josh Bohannon	14	23	0	803	205	34.91	1529	52.51	1	3	3	100	7
Tom Westley	13	20	1	801	135	42.15	1716	46.67	2	4	0	103	1
Tom Alsop	14	20	2	799	86*	44.38	1874	42.63	-	8	1	86	5
Kashif Ali	12	20	2	767	133	42.61	1180	65.00	2	5	1	100	9
Joey Evison	13	23	3	753	85	37.65	1500	50.20	-	6	0	83	10
Finlay Bean	14	22	0	746	173	33.90	1238	60.25	2	2	3	95	14
Michael Burgess	14	19	2	745	147	43.82	1202	61.98	2	3	0	75	12
Colin Ackermann	11	18	2	743	186	46.43	1466	50.68	2	2	2	73	2
Rob Yates	13	21	1	738	191	36.90	1116	66.12	1	5	1	101	7

Colin Ingram of Glamorgan
photographed by David Rogers

ROLL OF HONOUR

Name	Mat	Inns	Balls	Overs	Mdns	Runs	Wkts	BBI	Ave	Econ	SR	4	5
Ben Coad	12	20	2007	334.3	79	885	56	6/30	15.80	2.64	35.83	4	3
Jamie Porter	14	26	2172	362	88	1078	56	6/36	19.25	2.97	38.78	1	4
Kyle Abbott	13	22	2294	382.2	85	1120	55	5/25	20.36	2.92	41.70	3	5
Liam Dawson	13	22	3057	509.3	90	1358	54	5/47	25.14	2.66	56.61	3	5
Dan Worrall	11	21	1987	331.1	77	840	52	6/22	16.15	2.53	38.21	4	2
Toby Roland-Jones	12	20	2118	353	74	1173	52	6/58	22.55	3.32	40.73	1	7
Oliver Hannon-Dalby	14	24	2283	380.3	89	1114	50	6/43	22.28	2.92	45.66	0	3
Jack Carson	14	22	2113	352.1	73	1123	50	6/67	22.46	3.18	42.26	2	3
Jack Leach	9	16	2372	395.2	102	1025	45	7/50	22.77	2.59	52.71	1	5
Simon Harmer	14	22	2957	492.5	103	1492	45	4/16	33.15	3.02	65.71	5	0
Sam Cook	11	19	1615	269.1	66	744	43	6/14	17.30	2.76	37.55	2	2
Shane Snater	14	26	1632	272	55	907	41	5/13	22.12	3.33	39.80	2	1
Ben Sanderson	12	20	2247	374.3	87	1096	41	6/64	26.73	2.92	54.80	1	3
Ollie Robinson (Sussex)	12	22	2060	343.2	97	996	39	4/42	25.53	2.90	52.82	2	0
Jordan Clark	13	24	1974	329	56	987	38	5/65	25.97	3.00	51.94	2	1
Mohammad Abbas	11	19	2113	352.1	102	873	36	4/27	24.25	2.47	58.69	2	0
George Balderson	14	22	1852	308.4	54	1080	36	4/50	30.00	3.49	51.44	3	0
Matt Parkinson	13	16	2481	413.3	25	1708	36	6/109	47.44	4.13	68.91	0	2
Matt Critchley	14	19	1628	271.2	23	1043	34	5/88	30.67	3.84	47.88	2	3
Matthew Potts	8	14	1541	256.5	45	838	33	9/68	25.39	3.26	46.69	2	1
Ben Raine	11	20	1948	324.4	74	951	32	5/44	29.71	2.92	60.87	0	1
Jordan Thompson	12	21	1589	264.5	46	985	32	5/80	30.78	3.71	49.65	1	1
Craig Overton	11	21	2125	354.1	77	1067	32	4/32	33.34	3.01	66.40	3	0
Dillon Pennington	8	11	1347	224.3	47	738	31	5/96	23.80	3.28	43.45	1	1
Lewis Gregory	11	17	1227	204.3	38	771	31	4/50	24.87	3.77	39.58	2	0
Zak Chappell	12	17	1567	261.1	54	943	31	6/47	30.41	3.61	50.54	0	2
Timm van der Gugten	7	11	1371	228.3	50	659	30	5/59	21.96	2.88	45.70	1	2
Marchant de Lange	6	12	1296	216	37	808	30	6/49	26.93	3.74	43.20	0	2
Ryan Higgins	13	20	1645	274.1	63	858	30	4/31	28.60	3.12	54.83	2	0
Ethan Bamber	12	20	2095	349.1	68	1111	30	4/68	37.03	3.18	69.83	1	0
James Harris	11	16	1859	309.5	57	1139	30	5/73	37.96	3.67	61.96	2	1
Callum Parkinson	12	18	2893	482.1	71	1598	30	5/131	53.26	3.31	96.43	2	1
Scott Currie	11	16	1491	248.3	38	904	29	5/64	31.17	3.63	51.41	0	1
Mason Crane	11	17	1826	304.2	28	1287	29	5/99	44.37	4.22	62.96	1	2
Nathan Smith	7	12	1071	178.3	36	571	27	4/29	21.14	3.19	39.66	3	0
Tom Taylor	6	10	966	161	20	580	27	6/28	21.48	3.60	35.77	3	1
Matthew Fisher	7	12	1107	184.3	50	601	27	4/55	22.25	3.25	41.00	2	0
George Hill	13	21	1312	218.4	57	631	27	6/59	23.37	2.88	48.59	1	1
Joe Leach	11	19	1744	290.4	61	903	27	6/52	33.44	3.10	64.59	0	1
Tom Bailey	12	20	1893	315.3	53	923	27	4/36	34.18	2.92	70.11	1	0
Lyndon James	14	18	1401	233.3	33	933	27	4/61	34.55	3.99	51.88	1	0
Nathan Lyon	8	14	1849	308.1	53	790	26	4/59	30.38	2.56	71.11	1	0
Ben Mike	9	12	1203	200.3	25	910	26	5/22	35.00	4.53	46.26	1	1
Ed Barnard	14	19	1534	255.4	39	910	25	5/54	36.40	3.55	61.36	0	1
Luke Wells	14	17	880	146.4	15	545	24	4/36	22.70	3.71	36.66	3	0
Andy Gorvin	7	12	1113	185.3	46	575	24	5/40	23.95	3.09	46.37	1	1
Jayden Seales	6	11	1012	168.4	30	582	24	5/29	24.25	3.45	42.16	2	2
Kasey Aldridge	10	18	1201	200.1	19	851	24	5/64	35.45	4.25	50.04	0	2

Ben Coad of Yorkshire
photographed by Nathan Stirk

ROLL OF HONOUR

Name	Matches	Inns	Dis	Ct	St	Max Dis Inns	Dis/Inn
James Bracey	13	22	59	54	5	7 (7ct 0st)	2.68
Ben Foakes	12	21	52	49	3	5 (5ct 0st)	2.48
Gareth Roderick	14	24	46	46	0	4 (4ct 0st)	1.92
Ollie Robinson (Durham)	13	23	45	45	0	4 (4ct 0st)	1.96
James Rew	14	26	45	43	2	4 (4ct 0st)	1.73
John Simpson	14	26	44	42	2	5 (5ct 0st)	1.69
Matty Hurst	14	23	42	41	1	5 (5ct 0st)	1.83
Lewis McManus	13	21	40	33	7	4 (4ct 0st)	1.90
Michael Burgess	14	24	40	37	3	5 (5ct 0st)	1.67
Chris Cooke	14	22	39	36	3	5 (5ct 0st)	1.77
Ben Brown	13	22	36	35	1	4 (4ct 0st)	1.64
Michael Pepper	10	19	33	32	1	5 (4ct 1st)	1.74
Brooke Guest	13	19	30	26	4	4 (4ct 0st)	1.58
Harry Finch	14	21	29	24	5	4 (4ct 0st)	1.38
Jonathan Tattersall	14	18	26	25	1	3 (3ct 0st)	1.44
Jack Davies	14	24	25	25	0	3 (3ct 0st)	1.04
Ben Cox	12	17	19	19	0	3 (3ct 0st)	1.12
Joe Clarke	14	11	17	17	0	4 (4ct 0st)	1.55
Jonny Bairstow	5	8	10	10	0	4 (4ct 0st)	1.25
Tom Moores	4	2	7	7	0	4 (4ct 0st)	3.50
Dane Schadendorf	1	2	6	6	0	3 (3ct 0st)	3.00
Kyle Verreynne	3	4	6	5	1	3 (3ct 0st)	1.50
Peter Handscomb	10	2	5	4	1	3 (2ct 1st)	2.50

'Inns' refers to innings in which the player was the designated wicketkeeper

James Bracey of Gloucestershire
photographed by Michael Steele

Name	Matches	Inns	Ct	Max	Ct/Inn
Rob Yates	13	22	28	3	1.27
Simon Harmer	14	26	25	4	0.96
Finlay Bean	14	26	22	4	0.85
Adam Lyth	14	26	21	2	0.81
James Vince	13	22	20	3	0.91
Calvin Harrison	10	13	19	4	1.46
Keaton Jennings	14	23	18	3	0.78
Rob Jones	13	22	17	4	0.77
Cameron Bancroft	11	20	16	3	0.80
George Bell	12	21	16	2	0.76
Ryan Higgins	13	22	16	2	0.73
Leus du Plooy	14	24	16	3	0.67
Tom Haines	14	26	16	3	0.62
Tom Alsop	14	26	15	3	0.58
James Coles	14	26	15	3	0.58
Aneurin Donald	13	19	14	3	0.74
Wayne Madsen	13	19	14	3	0.74
Jack Leaning	11	17	13	3	0.76
Emilio Gay	10	17	13	3	0.76
Lewis Gregory	11	20	13	3	0.65
Craig Overton	11	21	13	4	0.62
George Hill	13	24	13	2	0.54
Dom Sibley	14	25	13	2	0.52

ROLL OF HONOUR

Rob Yates of Warwickshire
photographed by Gareth Copley

ROLL OF HONOUR

#	Name	County	Batting	Bowling	Field	Total	Mat	Win	Capt.	MVP	Avg.
1	Liam Dawson	Hampshire	271.71	316.51	32.00	635.22	34	10.00	0.00	5.00	18.68
2	James Vince	Hampshire	390.67	-0.40	79.00	489.27	35	9.00	9.00	2.00	13.98
3	Ed Barnard	Warwickshire	246.06	190.79	22.00	480.85	29	12.00	6.00	4.00	16.58
4	Lewis Gregory	Somerset	141.20	241.52	54.00	467.72	34	14.00	14.00	3.00	13.76
5	Keaton Jennings	Lancashire	393.51	0.00	46.00	461.51	31	9.00	9.00	4.00	14.89
6	Alex Davies	Warwickshire	366.41	0.00	70.00	458.41	38	10.00	10.00	2.00	12.06
7	Luke Wells	Lancashire	253.25	135.40	38.00	439.65	34	10.00	0.00	3.00	12.93
8	Craig Overton	Somerset	92.27	269.95	57.00	433.22	30	13.00	1.00	0.00	14.44
9	Michael Pepper	Essex	332.39	0.00	75.00	423.39	31	12.00	0.00	4.00	13.66
10	Tom Banton	Somerset	358.72	-0.58	43.00	418.14	34	14.00	0.00	3.00	12.30
11	Matt Critchley	Essex	148.55	205.08	32.00	399.63	33	13.00	0.00	1.00	12.11
12	Kiran Carlson	Glamorgan	303.30	34.45	28.80	397.95	37	15.60	14.00	1.80	10.76
13	James Bracey	Gloucestershire	261.73	0.00	116.60	397.73	38	15.60	1.00	2.80	10.47
14	Miles Hammond	Gloucestershire	313.43	-0.64	58.40	388.99	38	15.60	0.00	2.00	10.24
15	Rob Yates	Warwickshire	229.84	50.88	94.00	387.72	28	10.00	0.00	3.00	13.85
16	David Bedingham	Durham	369.89	-0.20	6.00	387.69	18	8.00	0.00	5.00	21.54
17	Jordan Cox	Essex	352.66	0.00	24.00	387.66	26	9.00	0.00	2.00	14.91
18	Colin Ingram	Glamorgan	333.51	3.13	32.00	384.83	31	13.60	0.00	2.60	12.41
19	John Simpson	Sussex	251.74	5.34	98.20	381.68	35	17.40	7.40	1.60	10.91
20	Shane Snater	Essex	87.01	257.63	21.00	379.64	28	13.00	0.00	1.00	13.56
21	Jack Leach	Somerset	26.82	308.32	27.00	378.14	24	14.00	0.00	2.00	15.76
22	Dan Mousley	Warwickshire	203.02	123.42	38.00	377.44	35	10.00	0.00	3.00	10.78
23	Cameron Bancroft	Gloucestershire	298.64	0.00	59.60	375.64	36	15.60	0.00	1.80	10.43
24	Dan Worrall	Surrey	17.72	330.89	4.00	365.61	24	12.00	0.00	2.00	15.23
25	Lewis Goldsworthy	Leicestershire	187.20	114.63	45.80	364.43	28	14.80	0.00	2.00	13.02
26	Joe Clarke	Nottinghamshire	322.91	0.00	31.00	363.91	35	5.00	3.00	2.00	10.40
27	Adam Lyth	Yorkshire	288.74	18.44	45.60	363.58	30	9.00	0.00	1.80	12.12
28	Ryan Higgins	Middlesex	190.05	122.07	42.60	362.52	27	6.20	0.00	4.00	13.43
29	Will Rhodes	Warwickshire	265.16	48.27	38.00	362.43	24	7.00	0.00	4.00	15.10
30	Dean Elgar	Essex	307.20	0.00	32.00	355.20	27	13.00	0.00	3.00	13.16
31	Jacob Bethell	Warwickshire	235.47	51.79	54.00	354.26	35	11.00	0.00	2.00	10.12
32	James Coles	Sussex	172.81	121.69	41.00	353.50	38	16.40	0.00	0.80	9.30
33	Gareth Roderick	Worcestershire	235.90	0.00	103.00	351.90	37	12.00	0.00	1.00	9.51
34	Jack Carson	Sussex	103.67	202.64	28.00	350.51	29	15.40	0.00	0.80	12.09
35	Dom Sibley	Surrey	280.44	0.00	42.00	341.44	33	17.00	1.00	2.00	10.35
36	James Rew	Somerset	233.43	-0.10	95.00	341.33	26	13.00	0.00	0.00	13.13
37	Colin Ackermann	Durham	233.84	54.93	40.00	339.77	27	10.00	0.00	2.00	12.58
38	Dan Lawrence	Surrey	187.84	105.90	32.00	339.74	29	13.00	0.00	2.00	11.72
39	Ben Raine	Durham	95.20	224.72	7.00	338.92	28	12.00	0.00	1.00	12.10
40	Daniel Bell-Drummond	Kent	304.15	0.00	25.00	337.15	29	5.00	1.00	0.00	11.63
41	Jordan Clark	Surrey	96.01	206.86	17.00	336.87	32	18.00	0.00	0.00	10.53
42	Kyle Abbott	Hampshire	39.31	269.94	16.00	336.25	21	9.00	0.00	2.00	16.01
43	Saif Zaib	Northamptonshire	176.06	126.19	17.60	333.45	30	11.60	0.00	2.00	11.12
44	Tom Alsop	Sussex	269.70	-0.88	45.20	333.22	34	17.40	0.00	1.80	9.80
45	David Payne	Gloucestershire	19.58	277.23	19.00	330.81	25	10.00	0.00	5.00	13.23
46	Peter Handscomb	Leicestershire	268.59	0.00	40.40	329.99	32	13.00	6.00	2.00	10.31
47	Haseeb Hameed	Nottinghamshire	282.01	-0.30	38.00	327.71	22	6.00	6.00	2.00	14.90
48	Scott Currie	Leicestershire	71.87	194.45	48.20	323.12	31	6.80	0.00	1.80	10.42
49	Ethan Brookes	Worcestershire	160.39	116.67	33.00	322.07	30	12.00	0.00	2.00	10.74
50	Ollie Price	Gloucestershire	183.89	82.76	38.20	320.45	33	13.60	0.00	2.00	9.71

ROLL OF HONOUR

#	Name	County	Batting	Bowling	Field	Total	Mat	Win	Capt.	MVP	Avg.
1	Kathryn Bryce	The Blaze	270.63	81.72	21.00	394.36	28	16.00	0.00	5.00	14.08
2	Amanda-Jade Wellington	Western Storm	131.39	184.29	19.00	344.69	31	6.00	0.00	4.00	11.12
3	Kirstie Gordon	The Blaze	64.44	174.16	41.00	321.60	33	18.00	18.00	6.00	9.75
4	Georgia Adams	Southern Vipers	153.56	101.47	30.00	313.03	31	13.00	13.00	2.00	10.10
5	Grace Scrivens	Sunrisers	242.90	15.50	20.00	303.40	34	11.00	11.00	3.00	8.92
6	Alice Davidson-Richards	South East Stars	234.46	22.81	22.00	297.26	31	15.00	0.00	3.00	9.59
7	Hollie Armitage	Northern Diamonds	206.15	15.97	41.00	289.12	29	11.00	11.00	4.00	9.97
8	Charli Knott	Southern Vipers	121.50	107.24	28.00	272.74	23	13.00	0.00	3.00	11.86
9	Paige Scholfield	South East Stars	218.86	0.00	24.00	257.86	29	13.00	0.00	2.00	8.89
10	Sophia Dunkley	South East Stars	215.71	7.67	16.00	252.38	22	11.00	0.00	2.00	11.47
11	Fi Morris	Lancashire Thunder	95.00	107.05	34.00	247.05	30	8.00	0.00	3.00	8.23
12	Bryony Smith	South East Stars	168.12	30.77	15.00	244.89	32	14.00	14.00	3.00	7.65
13	Eve Jones	Central Sparks	190.39	0.00	30.00	239.39	32	9.00	8.00	2.00	7.48
14	Jodi Grewcock	Sunrisers	97.36	109.32	17.00	236.68	26	11.00	0.00	2.00	9.10
15	Sarah Bryce	The Blaze	143.62	0.00	72.00	232.62	28	16.00	0.00	1.00	8.31
16	Ryana MacDonald-Gay	South East Stars	32.81	141.86	36.00	225.68	30	14.00	0.00	1.00	7.52
17	Erin Burns	Northern Diamonds	74.20	109.21	26.00	223.41	25	12.00	0.00	2.00	8.94
18	Georgia Elwiss	Southern Vipers	148.20	39.88	18.00	220.08	30	11.00	0.00	3.00	7.34
19	Heather Knight	Western Storm	202.10	0.00	14.00	216.10	14	1.00	0.00	3.00	15.44
20	Linsey Smith	Southern Vipers	7.26	169.64	28.00	215.90	25	11.00	0.00	1.00	8.64
21	Katie George	Central Sparks	90.52	70.33	41.00	213.85	32	10.00	0.00	2.00	6.68
22	Sterre Kalis	Northern Diamonds	177.12	0.00	18.00	207.12	30	11.00	0.00	1.00	6.90
23	Lauren Winfield-Hill	Northern Diamonds	134.90	0.00	56.00	204.90	30	10.00	1.00	3.00	6.83
24	Abbey Freeborn	Central Sparks	147.72	0.00	42.00	203.72	30	11.00	1.00	2.00	6.79
25	Heather Graham	The Blaze	57.67	129.17	7.00	202.83	19	8.00	0.00	1.00	10.68
26	Sophia Smale	Western Storm	49.92	106.26	32.00	195.17	32	6.00	0.00	1.00	6.10
27	Mady Villiers	Sunrisers	34.77	116.90	30.00	193.67	32	9.00	0.00	3.00	6.05
28	Emily Arlott	Central Sparks	59.87	112.42	19.00	191.30	28	9.00	0.00	0.00	6.83
29	Freya Davies	Southern Vipers	3.05	157.84	14.00	184.89	30	10.00	0.00	0.00	6.16
30	Charlie Dean	Southern Vipers	62.69	89.25	24.00	183.94	19	7.00	0.00	1.00	9.68
31	Sophie Luff	Western Storm	157.21	0.93	12.00	183.14	23	6.00	6.00	1.00	7.96
32	Seren Smale	Lancashire Thunder	154.94	0.00	14.00	178.94	30	8.00	0.00	2.00	5.96
33	Lucy Higham	The Blaze	74.71	54.86	25.00	171.58	30	17.00	0.00	0.00	5.72
34	Davina Perrin	Central Sparks	126.35	0.13	30.00	167.48	27	10.00	0.00	1.00	6.20
35	Katie Levick	Northern Diamonds	23.34	117.86	12.00	165.20	33	12.00	0.00	0.00	5.01
36	Tara Norris	Lancashire Thunder	50.47	83.38	22.00	161.85	29	6.00	0.00	0.00	5.58
37	Kate Cross	Lancashire Thunder	33.37	101.50	20.00	160.88	19	5.00	0.00	1.00	8.47
38	Phoebe Franklin	South East Stars	44.68	44.46	53.00	160.14	34	18.00	0.00	0.00	4.71
39	Eva Gray	Sunrisers	51.12	86.76	15.00	159.88	30	7.00	0.00	1.00	5.33
40	Jo Gardner	Sunrisers	105.57	8.14	35.00	159.72	35	11.00	0.00	0.00	4.56
41	Nat Wraith	Western Storm	114.50	0.00	36.00	156.50	31	6.00	0.00	0.00	5.05
42	Annabel Sutherland	Northern Superchargers	89.40	62.62	4.00	156.02	7	0.00	0.00	0.00	22.29
43	Tammy Beaumont	The Blaze	129.84	0.00	12.00	152.84	22	11.00	0.00	0.00	6.95
44	Bess Heath	Northern Diamonds	101.07	0.00	39.00	151.07	24	9.00	0.00	2.00	6.29
45	Alexa Stonehouse	South East Stars	22.12	109.68	10.00	150.80	23	9.00	0.00	0.00	6.56
46	Marizanne Kapp	Oval Invincibles	76.11	69.42	2.00	147.53	9	0.00	0.00	0.00	16.39
47	Nat Sciver-Brunt	Trent Rockets	113.96	24.62	7.00	145.57	8	0.00	0.00	0.00	18.20
48	Tilly Corteen-Coleman	South East Stars	0.41	119.82	11.00	145.23	27	13.00	0.00	0.00	5.38
49	Marie Kelly	The Blaze	70.27	3.00	50.00	142.27	29	18.00	0.00	1.00	4.91
50	Grace Ballinger	The Blaze	25.30	88.31	9.00	141.61	33	18.00	0.00	1.00	4.29